Praise for Walter R. Borneman's

THE ADMIRALS

"The first book to deal with the four admirals together, focusing on their intertwined lives, friendships, and rivalries....A very well-crafted book." —John Lehman, *Washington Post*

"In his superbly reported new book, historian Walter R. Borneman tackles the essential question of military leadership: What makes some men, but not others, able to motivate a fighting force into battle?" —Tony Perry, *Los Angeles Times*

"Engagingly written and deeply researched....Mr. Borneman makes it easy to understand the complex series of maneuvers and counter-maneuvers at Leyte Gulf...which is not always the case with accounts of the battle." —Andrew Roberts, *Wall Street Journal*

"A brilliant, intriguing, and important book....In *The Admirals* Borneman not only presents balanced mini-biographies of his four principal subjects but also gives an overview of the evolution of the navy from the late nineteenth to mid-twentieth centuries and provides fascinating details about the naval, political, and diplomatic aspects of World War II." —Timothy J. Lockhart, *Virginian-Pilot*

"Borneman demonstrates comprehensive command of published and unpublished sources, fingertip understanding of the period, and a polished writing style in this unique collective biography of the four men who 'with a combination of nimble counsel, exasperating ego, studied patience, and street-fighter tactics' shaped the modern U.S. Navy to win World War II at sea." —*Publishers Weekly*

"Borneman deftly manipulates multiple narrative strands and a wealth of detail. He vividly fleshes out the numerous vain, ambitious men vying for power at the top and examines their important decisions and lasting ramifications. An accomplished, readable history lesson." —*Kirkus Reviews*

"They were completely different in temperament and personality, but the U.S. Navy's four five-star admirals in World War II shared a sense of vision, devotion, and courage. Walter Borneman has written a rousing tale of victory at sea."

—Evan Thomas, author of *The War Lovers*

"*The Admirals* is a masterpiece of research and storytelling, narrative history at its absolute finest. A vivid, action-packed portrait of four remarkable American giants."

—William Doyle, author of *A Soldier's Dream,*
Inside the Oval Office, An American
Insurrection, and *A Mission from God*

"Walter Borneman's *The Admirals* is an epic group portrait of Nimitz, Halsey, Leahy, and King. Not since the heyday of Samuel Eliot Morison has a historian painted such a fine portrait of the five-star admirals who helped America beat Japan during the Second World War. Highly recommended!"

—Douglas Brinkley, Professor of History at Rice
University and author of *The Wilderness Warrior*

"This is Walter Borneman at his best. The portrait of the forgotten admiral, Leahy, is worth the whole book. But there's scarcely a page where a reader won't learn something unexpected, and occasionally shocking." —Thomas Fleming, author of *Time and Tide*

THE
ADMIRALS

Also by Walter R. Borneman

Rival Rails: The Race to Build America's Greatest
Transcontinental Railroad

Polk: The Man Who Transformed the Presidency and America

The French and Indian War: Deciding the Fate of North America

14,000 Feet: A Celebration of Colorado's Highest Mountains
(with Todd Caudle)

1812: The War That Forged a Nation

Alaska: Saga of a Bold Land

A Climbing Guide to Colorado's Fourteeners
(with Lyndon J. Lampert)

THE
ADMIRALS

NIMITZ, HALSEY,
LEAHY, and KING —
The Five-Star Admirals
Who Won the War at Sea

WALTER R. BORNEMAN

BACK BAY BOOKS
Little, Brown and Company
New York   Boston   London

Back Bay Books / Little, Brown and Company
Hachette Book Group
1290 Avenue of the Americas, New York, NY 10104
littlebrown.com

Originally published in hardcover by Little, Brown and Company, May 2012
First Back Bay paperback edition, May 2013

Back Bay Books is an imprint of Little, Brown and Company, a division of Hachette Book Group. The Back Bay Books name and logo are trademarks of Hachette Book Group, Inc.

Maps by David Lambert

The publisher is not responsible for websites (or their content) that are not owned by the publisher.

The Hachette Speakers Bureau provides a wide range of authors for speaking events. To find out more, go to hachettespeakersbureau.com or call (866) 376-6591.

Library of Congress Cataloging-in-Publication Data
Borneman, Walter R.
　The admirals : Nimitz, Halsey, Leahy, and King—the five-star admirals who won the war at sea / Walter R. Borneman.—1st ed.
　　p. cm.
　Includes bibliographical references and index.
　ISBN 978-0-316-09784-0 (HC) / 978-0-316-09783-3 (PB)
　1. Nimitz, Chester W. (Chester William), 1885–1966.　2. Halsey, William Frederick, 1882–1959.　3. Leahy, William D.　4. King, Ernest Joseph, 1878–1956.　5. Admirals—United States—Biography.
6. United States. Navy—Biography.　7. Naval art and science—History—20th century.　8. United States. Navy—History—20th century.
9. World War, 1939–1945—Naval operations, American.　10. World War, 1939–1945—Biography.　I. Title.
　E746.B59 2012
　359.0092—dc23
　[B]　　　　　　　　　　　　　　　　　　　　　　　　　　2011032394

10 9 8 7

RRD-C

Printed in the United States of America

For all who have served our country

Contents

Part Three: Admirals, 1941–1945

List of Maps

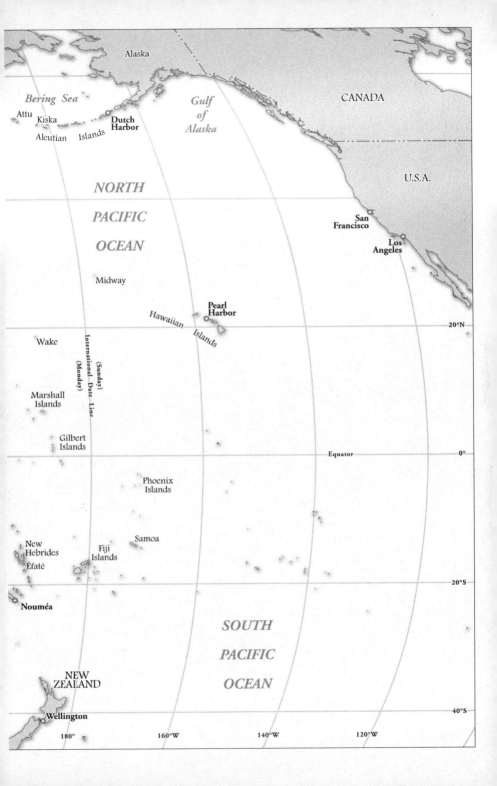

THE
ADMIRALS

The Banks of the Severn

It is graduation day at Annapolis — the United States Naval Academy. The year is not important. The date might be in the past, today, or one of many to come. The speaker's words reverberate across the field, but something more resonates here.

Nearby, the broad estuary of the Severn River meets the waters of Chesapeake Bay. The warm breeze carries with it the scent of tidewater and the squawks of gulls, but there is more here, too, than salty smells and aerial cacophony.

The academy's motto is simple and direct: Ex Scientia Tridens — "From Knowledge, Sea Power." From this place has come that and much more.

The tree-lined pathways, the grassy parade grounds, and even the small boats tugging gently at their moorings are heavy with it. The names of the buildings that rise above the banks of the Severn shout it: history and tradition, duty and honor, vision and courage, abound here.

The granite walls of Leahy Hall are the first stop for aspiring midshipmen. King Hall serves thousands of meals daily with a proficiency its no-nonsense namesake would demand. Nimitz

Library overlooks College Creek, beyond which the academy cemetery holds the bones of many whose history fills its books. Halsey Field House is a testing ground, the focal point of hard-fought athletic competition.

An office building, a mess hall, a library, and a field house—as varied as the men whose names they bear. Consummate diplomat, opinionated strategist, calculating master of detail, pugnacious fighter—all began their naval careers here within a period of eight years near the opening of the twentieth century.

They are the only four men in American history to hold the five-star rank of fleet admiral. None of them envisioned as they walked these grounds the extent to which their diverse personalities and methods would transform Theodore Roosevelt's Great White Fleet of their youth into his cousin Franklin's ultimate weapon of global supremacy.

With a combination of nimble counsel, exasperating ego, studied patience, and street-fighter tactics, William D. Leahy, Ernest J. King, Chester W. Nimitz, and William F. Halsey, Jr., built the modern United States Navy and won World War II on the seas. Each is forever a part of the United States Naval Academy; Annapolis was forever a part of them.

On the graduation field this day, the brigade stands at attention. Another class is about to follow these men, to march into history.

Saturday, December 6, 1941

Vichy, France

Europe has been at war for more than two years. Amid the mineral spas of Vichy, the American embassy occupies what was previously a doctor's office. While its accoutrements are sufficient, the tone and fabric of the entire town mirror the sad conditions that have befallen France. Quick to oppose Hitler's invasion of Poland, France was forced by the German blitzkrieg to accept a humiliating surrender.

The surrender terms—the armistice, the Vichy French prefer to call them—left a provisional government to administer the unoc-cupied southern third of the country, as well as France's colonies around the world. The wild card remains what will become of the French fleet, arguably still among the most powerful in the world.

The U.S. ambassador, retired admiral William D. Leahy, appre-ciates this more than most. He is first and foremost a sailor, but over a forty-year naval career, he has also witnessed the diplomatic side of international power. Admiral Leahy wouldn't be here if President Franklin D. Roosevelt did not trust his ability to wring every last drop of pro-American support from Vichy's shadow government.

But Leahy is discouraged. He is used to serving his chief with fidelity, but the last few months have been frustrating. Vichy France is a nation subservient to the Third Reich in all but name. Leahy goes to bed hoping for a recall to Washington—either to impress the French with the seriousness of Roosevelt's displeasure or simply to allow for his own retirement. Because of the time difference, dawn the next morning will fall upon Vichy twelve hours before it reaches the Central Pacific.

Narragansett Bay

The heavy cruiser USS *Augusta* is already a storied ship. Four months before, the flagship of the Atlantic Fleet carried President Roosevelt to a secret rendezvous with British prime minister Win-ston Churchill off the southeast toe of Newfoundland. After a conference that included a Sunday church service featuring the hymn "Onward, Christian Soldiers," America was not yet at war, but Roosevelt and Churchill were newfound friends.

This particular morning, *Augusta* steams into the sheltered waters of Narragansett Bay and moors at its buoy off Newport, Rhode Island, the fleet headquarters. From its mast flies the four-star flag of Admi-ral Ernest J. King, commander in chief of the Atlantic Fleet. There is neither war nor peace. American ships are being lost in the North Atlantic, but King's response is limited by political considerations.

As *Augusta* rides gently at its buoy, King spends the morning writing a batch of letters. Some are official navy business. Others go to friends in his hometown and Annapolis classmates. His family is another story.

That afternoon, the admiral's barge ferries him into Newport, where he walks up Church Street past the spire of Trinity Church. As is his custom when in port, he drops by the Newport Reading Room, the town's most venerable private club, for a glass of sherry. He is still in a pensive mood when he returns to the *Augusta* and hears its bugler signal the lowering of the colors at sunset. King has always appreciated a sense of history, and in his cabin aboard the darkened ship, he selects a title from his collection of biographies and histories and reads himself to sleep.

Washington, D.C.

The barren limbs on numerous maple, elm, and oak trees along the avenues bespeak the obvious: it is late fall in the nation's capital. The cherry trees—a 1912 gift from the people of Japan—surrounding the Tidal Basin and the nearly completed Jefferson Memorial are also stark and black in the low-angled December sun. Washington itself is in a state of denial as to its increasing role at the center of a rapidly expanding federal government.

As is usual on a Saturday, Rear Admiral Chester W. Nimitz is in his office at the Navy Department Building, a massive structure that sprawls almost four blocks along the north side of the Mall. It is the admiral's turn for a tour of shore duty, and since 1939 he has been chief of the Bureau of Navigation.

Evening brings a respite that Nimitz always embraces—dinner at home with his family. He lives with his wife, Catherine; youngest daughter, Mary; daughter-in-law, Joan; and an eighteen-month-old granddaughter. They occupy an apartment at 2222 Q Street, a block from Rock Creek Park in one direction and the embassies of Massachusetts Avenue in the other. Part of the admiral's daily ritual is to take Freckles, the family's cocker spaniel, for his evening walk along a route that takes them past the Japanese embassy.

The two older Nimitz girls, Kate and Nancy, live across the hall. The only member of the family not present is the admiral's son. A 1936 graduate of the U.S. Naval Academy, young Chet is halfway around the world, assigned to the submarine *Sturgeon* operating out of the Philippines.

At Sea, Two Hundred Miles West of Pearl Harbor

The weather is not cooperating. Task Force 8, comprising the air-craft carrier *Enterprise,* three heavy cruisers, and nine destroyers, pounds eastward into heavy seas. On the bridge of the carrier, Vice Admiral William F. Halsey, Jr., is surprised that the weather is the only thing he is fighting. Halsey has issued orders that *Enterprise* and its escorts operate under war conditions.

Nine days earlier, his ships left Pearl Harbor for a destination known only to the admiral and his closest aides. Once at sea, *Enterprise* welcomed its own air squadrons but also took aboard twelve Grumman F4F Wildcat fighters belonging to Marine Fighting Squadron 211. Its commander told his pilots to expect two days of maneuvers, and no one threw more than a shaving kit and a change of Skivvies into his cockpit.

The marine pilots took off from *Enterprise* for their secret desti-nation in the early dawn of December 4 without incident. Delivery accomplished, Task Force 8 headed back toward Pearl Harbor, not knowing that hundreds of miles to the north a huge Japanese carrier force was roughly paralleling its eastward course.

Halsey planned to dock in Pearl Harbor today, but buffeting winds and waves crack a seam in one of his destroyers and slow refueling operations. The admiral takes it in stride, but his crews are less understanding. A Saturday arrival in Hawaii would salvage a portion of their weekend ashore. Now those off-duty on *Enter-prise* will have to be content to gather on the hangar deck and watch Gary Cooper in *Sergeant York*. Task Force 8 is rescheduled to enter Pearl Harbor about noon on Sunday, December 7.

PART I

SAILORS

1897–1918

In time of war, would we be content like the turtle to withdraw into our own shell and see an enemy supersede us in every outlying part, usurp our commerce, and destroy our influence as a nation throughout the world?
—FRANKLIN D. ROOSEVELT,
Assistant Secretary of the Navy, 1913

Proud of the navy "N" on his sweater—even if he missed a button putting it on—William F. Halsey, Jr., commanded the destroyer *Shaw* (DD-68) off Ireland in the summer of 1918. (F. E. Sellman photo, courtesy of Gary Fabian)

CHAPTER ONE

Leahy

"The Judge"
—Annapolis, Class of 1897

The glistening white bow of the American battleship *Oregon* drove through wave after towering wave as the big ship clawed its way south through heavy seas. Its jack staff at the bow routinely disappeared as fully fifteen feet of blue water broke on the forward turret and threw white spray nearly the length of the ship. It was April 1898, and as the *Oregon* thundered toward the fabled Strait of Magellan, the air hung thick with rumors of war with Spain. In fact, in this era before radio communications, there was no way for the captain to know if war had already begun.

By the standards of any contemporary navy, the *Oregon* was a major strategic weapon. The Union Iron Works of San Francisco had laid down its keel late in 1891 as the third in a line of *Indiana*-class battleships. At 348 feet in length, with a beam of 69 feet and a displacement of 10,288 tons, the ship was a beefy platform for a dazzling array of firepower, including two 13-inch guns each in the main fore and after turrets.

Oregon and its older sisters, *Indiana* and *Massachusetts,* owed their existence to a belated post–Civil War awakening that the

United States, having largely completed its expansion from sea to sea, should now be prepared not only to defend its interests but also to seek other territory well beyond its borders. Not everyone, however, supported this creeping American imperialism. Many avowed isolationists in Congress wanted only coastal defenses and opposed offensive, long-range battleships. The futurists in the U.S. Navy managed to paper over such disputes by calling this new generation of vessels "seagoing coastline battleships."

In addition to its armaments, the *Oregon* relied on a belt of eighteen-inch-thick armor plating around its sides and thinner armor for its gun turrets and decking. The ship also had two other distinct advantages: it was fast for the time—twin screws delivered better than fifteen knots—and its spacious coal bunkers provided a range of more than six thousand miles. Heavily armed, well protected, speedy, and long-range, *Oregon* and its class were clearly the advent of a new generation of naval warfare. They could boast of being the first modern-era battleships of the U.S. Navy.

Among *Oregon*'s complement of 32 officers and 441 enlisted men were 6 green naval cadets. They were 1897 graduates of the U.S. Naval Academy at Annapolis, but not yet full-fledged ensigns because the navy required two years of sea duty before awarding commissions. Service aboard a first-class ship such as the *Oregon* was a plum assignment, even if some of the old hands tended to view the flocking cadets more as nuisance gnats than budding officers.

The pulses of old salts and young greenhorns alike had quickened on March 19, 1898, as the battleship departed San Francisco and passed through the Golden Gate, its destination known only to its captain. After 4,700 miles and the traditional "crossing the equator" ceremony, *Oregon* steamed into Callao, Peru. But ship and crew paused there only long enough to fill the coal bunkers to the brim and secure an extra two hundred tons of coal in sacks on the decks.

Rumors were rife that they might be headed for Honolulu or even the Philippines, but as *Oregon* cleared the harbor, it turned south toward the stormy seas around Cape Horn at the tip of South America. By the time another three thousand miles had fallen astern, the Strait of Magellan beckoned, and an icy southerly gale whipped the battering waves ever higher. "Under the onslaught of these gigantic seas," recalled naval cadet William D. Leahy, "the ship dove, trembled, shook them off, and dove again." According to Leahy, "We said she smelled the Spanish Fleet."[1]

Cadet Leahy's Irish grandparents, Daniel and Mary Egan Leahy, immigrated to the United States in 1836 and settled in Massachusetts. A son, Michael Arthur, was born two years later, shortly before the family moved to New Hampshire. There a second son, John Egan, joined the family. But it was in a tiny village in Dodge County, Wisconsin, just west of Milwaukee, that the Leahys put down roots.

Like so many of their generation, brothers Michael and John Leahy saw military service during the Civil War—not necessarily by choice, but out of a sense of duty. When the Thirty-fifth Wisconsin Volunteer Infantry Regiment was mustered at Milwaukee early in 1864, twenty-five-year-old Michael Leahy became captain of Company D and brother John a first lieutenant in Company C.

Wisconsin certainly had no shortage of famous units. Perhaps best known were those Wisconsin regiments that made up part of the Army of the Potomac's stalwart Iron Brigade. No less storied was the Twenty-fourth Wisconsin. On a raw November day in 1863, the Twenty-fourth Wisconsin formed beneath Missionary Ridge outside Chattanooga, Tennessee. Union troops were trying to lift the siege of the town, but Confederate defenders were proving stubborn. Quite suddenly, without orders, Union regiments in the center of the line began to move forward up the ridge. When their wild advance was over, among the battle flags atop the crest was the standard of the Twenty-fourth Wisconsin, carried there by its eighteen-year-old "boy colonel," Arthur MacArthur, whose son, Douglas, would spend most of his own military career trying to emulate his father's charge.

The Thirty-fifth Wisconsin was not destined for such glory. Its service was mostly garrison duty around New Orleans and Mobile, Alabama, far from the major campaigns of the war. But such duty was not without risk. The regiment suffered only two casualties from battle, but lost 3 officers and 271 enlisted men to disease. The Leahy brothers returned from the war proud of their service, and for the rest of his life, Michael regularly attended meetings of veterans' groups and marched in Fourth of July parades.

After his discharge, Michael studied law at the University of Michigan and earned his degree in 1868. Briefly forsaking Wisconsin, he began to practice law in the small town of Hampton, Iowa, where a Wisconsin girl thirteen years his junior, Rose Mary Hamilton, caught his eye. They married and were still living in Hampton when William Daniel Leahy, the first of their eight children, was born on May 6, 1875.

Michael and Rose were eager to return to Wisconsin, and they soon joined Michael's brother, John, upstate in Wausau. By the time young William—he was "Bill" to just about everyone—was ready for high school, the family moved even farther north to Ashland, on the southern shore of Lake Superior.

As Bill approached his high school graduation in 1892, Michael Leahy encouraged his son to pursue a law degree at the University of Wisconsin and join him in his legal practice. Bill certainly appeared to have an aptitude for law, including an almost stoic, deliberative thought process and attention to detail, but there was something about his father's military service—brief and unsung though it was—that intrigued him. Bill decided instead to seek an appointment to the U.S. Military Academy at West Point.

Congressman Thomas Lynch was impressed with the young man, but Lynch had no West Point appointments that year. He did, however, have an opening the following year at the U.S. Naval Academy at Annapolis. Was Leahy interested in the navy? Despite living near the wind-tossed waters of Lake Superior, Leahy, like most of the country at the time, had not given the navy much thought. During his years growing up, he and the country had focused on the U.S. Army's exploits in the West, such as chasing the Apache leader Geronimo. But at least the Naval Academy was the military and, after all, a free education. Leahy accepted and spent the next year preparing for the entrance exams, particularly a newly added algebra requirement.[2]

Geographically, there is nothing particularly remarkable about Maryland's Severn River to set it apart from dozens of similar rivers, creeks, and runs that pour their waters via broad estuaries into Chesapeake Bay. Exiles from Virginia founded a settlement on the northern banks of the Severn in 1649 but soon moved to a better-protected harbor on the south shore. For a time, this was called Anne Arundel's Towne, after the wife of Lord Baltimore, but in 1694 it became the capital of the colony of Maryland and was renamed Annapolis — not to honor Anne Arundel, but rather Princess Anne, soon to be queen of England.

Annapolis prospered as a trading center until overtaken by growing Baltimore, and then it became quite content as a political and cultural center. Its recently completed statehouse served as the temporary capitol of the fledgling United States during 1783–1784, and it was there that General George Washington tendered his resignation as commander in chief of the Continental Army.

In 1808, Fort Severn — complete with a circular rampart for about a dozen cannons to protect the town — was built on Windmill Point. War with Great Britain was on the horizon, and in September 1814 the British indeed came into the upper Chesapeake Bay in force but bypassed Annapolis in favor of the grander prize of Baltimore — only to be repulsed by the defenders of Fort McHenry.

Despite its successes during the War of 1812, the U.S. Navy languished in the postwar period. The education of a naval officer came by doing on board ship and was frequently a rather hit-or-miss affair. The senior ranks were filled with officers owing their positions more to seniority than command abilities. This changed with the presidential election of 1844. James K. Polk appointed one of the architects of his victory, fellow Democrat George Bancroft of Massachusetts, as his secretary of the navy.

Always a dapper dresser, Bancroft would become best known as a historian, but he energetically set about establishing a formal education for aspiring naval officers — something the army had begun at West Point in 1802. But where to do this was problematic. Bancroft faced general criticism — "You could no more educate sailors in a shore college than you could teach ducks to swim in a garret" — and specific assertions that attempting to convert the existing Philadelphia Naval Asylum School would be defeated by "the temptations and distractions that necessarily connect with a large and populous city."[3]

So Bancroft chose Fort Severn at relatively staid and quiet Annapolis. On October 19, 1845, he arranged for a transfer of the post from the army to the navy and skirted the issue of a congressional appropriation by finding funds within his budget to make the facility operational. It was hardly very grand, but fifty naval cadets and seven professors arrived on the banks of the Severn and planted the seeds of a long and noble tradition. By 1850, the school's official name was the United States Naval Academy, but it would often be called simply "Annapolis."[4]

When William D. Leahy arrived on the banks of the Severn River in late May 1893, Annapolis was definitely the weaker of the two service academies, a weakness mirrored by the country's low regard for its navy. A total of 243 naval cadets—they would not be called midshipmen until several years later—were enrolled in the four-year program. The 1893 enrollment of West Point was 318.

But the navy was determined to lose no time in separating closet landlubbers from true sailors. By the first week of June, Leahy and a third of his incoming class of seventy-seven were aboard the venerable War of 1812–era frigate *Constellation,* sailing eastward across the Atlantic. Leahy was assigned to the fore-topgallant yard, working the uppermost sails atop the foremast. If he had any lingering thoughts of the green fields of West Point, he put them aside and took to this new lifestyle—allowing of course for some major adjustments. When the class of 1897 reflected on its first few weeks at sea in the academy's first yearbook, the adjustments were clear: "Pell mell, slipping, sliding on the slanting deck, our faces distorted with the keenest anguish, we hurried to it, to give our tribute to old Ocean, and then to lie down and feel that death and dry land were the two finest things in the world."[5]

Constellation was scheduled to take the green-gilled cadets all the way to Europe, but stormy seas in the mid-Atlantic diverted the ship first to the Azores and then to the Madeira Islands for repairs. By the time the work was done, *Constellation* stood westward to return to Annapolis for the start of the academic year. Among the officers aboard supervising this new class of cadets was Lieutenant William F. Halsey, whose not-quite-teenage son, William Jr., was determined to enter Annapolis himself one day.

Once ashore, the cadets began classroom work that was grueling and heavily focused on the sciences. Courses ranged from physics, chemistry, and a full range of mathematics to navigation, seamanship, and steam engineering. Daily recitations were the usual order. There were also classes in history, international law, and each cadet's choice of language. Leahy and most of his classmates wisely chose French, then the international language of diplomacy and commerce. The only major drawback in the curriculum, Leahy later observed, was a lack of instruction in writing and speaking proper English. His preparation in that regard was limited to some spelling and the memorization of a few poems he quickly forgot.[6]

His physical looks became rugged but hardly dashing as he grew to five feet ten inches in height. His gray eyes, under brownish hair that quickly began to recede above his brow, were more evaluating than sparkling. Those who didn't know him well would later claim, "There was something sinister about his owlish profile and his always solemn manner. He usually looked in his photographs as if he were forever smelling bad fish."[7]

As a student and an athlete at Annapolis, Leahy was solid but never stellar. He was content to play tackle on the B squad in football, and he sometimes seemed to float his way through classes. One classmate and lifelong friend, future admiral Thomas C. Hart, even recalled Leahy being "not good, a little lazy" as a student. But Hart readily acknowledged that when the chips were down or a sticky problem presented itself, someone would inevitably say, "Let's go and ask Bill Leahy. He's got better sense than all the rest of us put together."[8] That common sense seemed to radiate from Leahy's otherwise reserved and even dour personality throughout his life, and among his classmates it earned him the nickname "the Judge."

On June 4, 1897, William D. Leahy graduated a respectable fourteenth among the remaining forty-seven members of the class of 1897. While this relatively small number of new naval officers reflected the size of the U.S. Navy, no one should underestimate the academy's influence on the navy's future. Twelve of these graduates would reach flag rank and be accorded admiral's stars. But for now, they all faced two years of sea duty and a final round of examinations before being commissioned as ensigns.[9]

When Leahy and five of his classmates were ordered to report to the battleship *Oregon,* they joined the ship in Victoria, British Columbia, where it had steamed to attend festivities celebrating Queen Victoria's Diamond Jubilee. For the sixty years of her reign, "Rule, Britannia" had been the undisputed order of the seas. But now the aging queen and her empire were facing ever-increasing competition. Germany, in particular, was busy launching a new line of steel battleships. Russia, France, and Japan were also adding warships to their fleets, and even Spain seemed determined to use its navy to hang on to the vestiges of what before the rise of Great Britain had been its global empire. *Oregon* itself was proof that the United States had also entered the race.

At the head of the charge for increased American naval power was the thirty-eight-year-old assistant secretary of the navy, who had cut his big teeth on sea power by writing a history of the U.S. Navy's glories during the War of 1812. With excruciating detail of broadside weight and occasional hyperbole, Theodore Roosevelt's bestselling *The Naval War of 1812* — first published in 1882 — had nonetheless become so important to a reinvigoration of the American navy that at least one copy was required to be aboard every navy vessel. Roosevelt's subsequent writing had included a well-received chronicle of American expansion across the continent, and now he seemed determined to win the United States an expanded role around the globe.

Beyond the nautical knowledge he had acquired as a historian, there was not a great deal in Roosevelt's background to recommend him to the post of assistant secretary of the navy. But the position was a political appointment, and Roosevelt was one of many Republicans who had canvassed the country in William McKinley's stead during the 1896 election.

After McKinley won, Roosevelt supporters shamelessly lobbied in his behalf, but McKinley was skeptical. "I hope [Roosevelt] has no preconceived plans which he would wish to drive through the moment he got in," the president-elect fretted to Roosevelt's good friend Henry Cabot Lodge. Of course not, replied Lodge with a straight face. To another Roosevelt supporter, the peaceful McKinley admitted that he knew Roosevelt only slightly but was afraid that the New Yorker might prove "too pugnacious."

McKinley was right to be leery on both counts, but he surrendered to the onslaught of Roosevelt lobbyists, and Roosevelt became assistant secretary of the navy in 1897. Just one week after being sworn in, he presented McKinley with a requested memorandum on fleet preparedness. For all its straightforward detail and balanced analysis, it also contained four separate warnings of possible "trouble with Cuba."[10]

Trouble with Cuba really meant trouble with Spain, which had ruled the island, despite frequent uprisings and occasional interruptions, since the days of Christopher Columbus. The United States had expressed interest in the island for at least half a century, and now there was once again a popular uprising under way that in some minds argued for American intervention.

Later that summer, as Leahy was graduating from Annapolis, Roosevelt told a gathering at the Naval War College, "To be prepared for war is the most effectual means to promote peace." About the same time, Roosevelt struck up a friendship with a navy commodore named George Dewey.

As a young lieutenant under Admiral David Farragut during the Civil War, Dewey had watched in awe as Farragut's wooden ships ran past Confederate forts to capture New Orleans. Later, he missed Farragut's famous utterance, "Damn the torpedoes; full speed ahead!" as the admiral steamed into Mobile Bay, but Dewey always hoped that a similar situation might present itself in his own career, and Roosevelt wanted to make it possible.[11]

To Theodore Roosevelt, the best part of his job was when the secretary of the navy, the mild and grandfatherly John D. Long, took one of his leisurely vacations. Then Roosevelt became acting secretary. The day before Long's return to Washington in late September 1897, Acting Secretary Roosevelt discovered to his horror that another commodore had been recommended to command the Asiatic Squadron instead of Dewey. Roosevelt swung into action, arranging for a senator to speak to McKinley on Dewey's behalf, and had a presidential memorandum requesting Dewey's appointment on Long's desk by the time he arrived back in his office the next morning. Long read it and fumed, as he personally favored the other commodore, but he could hardly argue with the president. Commodore George Dewey soon departed for Hong Kong to become Theodore Roosevelt's man in the Far East.[12]

With the Philippines in Dewey's crosshairs, Roosevelt turned his attention to Cuba. Ironically, it was Secretary Long who suggested that the battleship *Maine* be dispatched from Key West to Havana as a friendly act of diplomatic courtesy. The Spanish in Cuba could hardly refuse, but tensions were such that the *Maine*'s captain refused to permit his crew shore leave upon the ship's arrival.

On the evening of February 15, 1898, as the *Maine* rode at anchor in Havana harbor, a gigantic explosion rocked the ship, almost obliterating the forward third of the vessel. *Maine* sank quickly, taking 266 men with it. Whether this explosion came from a mine or other device external to the ship or from an undetected fire in one of its own coal bunkers adjacent to a powder magazine continues to be hotly debated. At the time, especially to those anxious for war with Spain, the only acceptable explanation was sabotage.[13]

On the afternoon of February 25, with Secretary Long conveniently out of the office, Roosevelt cabled Commodore Dewey in Hong Kong to keep his squadron full of coal and, in the event of a declaration of war with Spain, take offensive operations against the Spanish fleet in the Philippines. When Long returned the next morning, he reported that "Roosevelt, in his precipitate way, has come very near causing more of an explosion than happened to the *Maine*." Significantly, however, Long did not countermand Roosevelt's orders, and as the momentum toward war swept beyond his control a few weeks later, he ordered the *Oregon* to hurry from the West Coast to join the main Atlantic fleet.[14]

The rush to war also overtook the president. On Monday, April 11, 1898, bolstered by public opinion, William McKinley sent a war message to Capitol Hill. Enough isolationists remained there that it took a week's debate before Congress declared war on Spain on April 19—exactly one year to the day since Theodore Roosevelt had joined the Navy Department.

William D. Leahy and his crewmates on the *Oregon* heard the news from the harbormaster in Rio de Janeiro on April 30. Having weathered the Pacific gales and safely transited the Strait of Magellan, *Oregon* was making its way north along the Atlantic coast of South America. Rumors were rife that four Spanish cruisers and three torpedo-boat destroyers were lurking ahead. *Oregon*'s white paint was hastily covered with dull gray and its decks cleared for action. By the time the ship called at Bahia (now Salvador), Brazil, shore gossip was that the Spanish fleet had eluded the U.S. North Atlantic Squadron and captured Philadelphia and Boston.[15]

The truth was even more astounding, and it came from the other side of the world. The nation that had rushed so gaily to war was stunned by the speed and totality of its first victory. Commodore Dewey's Asiatic Squadron of two heavy cruisers—*Olympia* and *Baltimore,* each carrying four 8-inch guns—three light cruisers, and a gunboat had boldly sailed into Manila Bay. Five times, the squadron paraded past the anchored Spanish fleet with guns blazing. "At 7:35 a.m.," reported Dewey, "I ceased firing and withdrew the squadron for breakfast." By the time he returned to the attack, "the Spanish flagship and almost all the Spanish fleet were in flames." Remarkably, no one on the American side was killed, and only seven were wounded.[16]

George Dewey was immediately promoted to rear admiral, and his name quickly became a household word throughout the United States. Dewey had found his long-sought glory, but he also knew full well that Theodore Roosevelt had given him the opportunity. Another in Roosevelt's inner circle, naval strategist Alfred Thayer Mahan, called the Battle of Manila Bay "a grand victory" and predicted that it "would go down into history as the greatest naval battle on record."

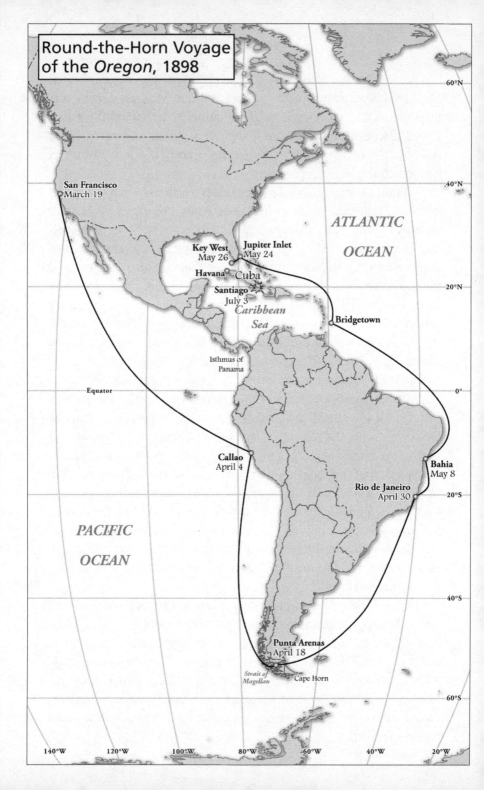

Round-the-Horn Voyage of the *Oregon*, 1898

San Francisco
March 19

Key West
May 26

Jupiter Inlet
May 24

Havana

Cuba

Santiago
July 3

Caribbean Sea

Bridgetown

Isthmus of Panama

Equator

ATLANTIC OCEAN

Callao
April 4

Bahia
May 8

Rio de Janeiro
April 30

PACIFIC OCEAN

Punta Arenas
April 18

Strait of Magellan

Cape Horn

60°N

40°N

20°N

0°

20°S

40°S

60°S

140°W 120°W 100°W 80°W 60°W 40°W 20°W

It was hardly that. But Mahan was becoming quite a cult figure when it came to projecting naval power. Many a junior officer would eagerly devour his assessment that "the result of this engagement plainly indicates that a cool-headed commander who gets into the fight first and proceeds to business has the best of the battle from the start."[17]

Things would not be quite so easy when the *Oregon* encountered the Spanish fleet off Cuba. Four cruisers and three torpedo-boat destroyers had indeed sailed from Spain and were now anchored in the harbor at Santiago, on the island's southeastern shore. *Oregon* joined the battleships of the North Atlantic Squadron at Key West on May 26, having steamed more than fourteen thousand miles in sixty-nine days since leaving San Francisco.

To some, transferring a battleship from one coast to the other in that short of a time was a remarkable achievement. To others, the *Oregon*'s circuitous race *around* South America was taken as strong evidence for the need to build the Panama Canal. To no one's surprise, Theodore Roosevelt was among those standing in the forefront arguing for the canal's construction and its firm military control by the United States. Determined to get into the fray personally, he had just resigned as assistant secretary of the navy in order to recruit a regiment of volunteers and join the war.[18]

After taking on coal at Key West, the *Oregon* proceeded with the principal ships of the North Atlantic Squadron, as well as those of the roving Flying Squadron, and took up blockade positions off Santiago. Leahy's post was in the fore 13-inch gun turret. Acting Rear Admiral William T. Sampson was in overall command, with Commodore Winfield Scott Schley in command of the Flying Squadron. Neither was destined to be much remembered, let alone accorded undisputed fame. On the navy side of the war, George Dewey seems to have had a monopoly on that. And this would not be Manila Bay. Admiral Don Pascual Cervera y Topete knew that he was badly outnumbered and outgunned, but when ordered to do so, he would fight. His four cruisers displaced about seven thousand tons each and had 11- and 10-inch guns. One-on-one, they were no match for the *Oregon* or its sister *Indiana,* but Cervera hoped that in the confusion of battle, at least a couple of his ships might escape.

On the morning of July 3, 1898, with the Caribbean weather looking bright and fair, Admiral Sampson was momentarily absent, having taken his flagship, the battleship *New York,* to confer with army forces that had been landing on the island. Aboard the remaining ships, a month's boredom had set in. It was a quiet Sunday morning. Leahy and most of the junior officers on the *Oregon* were in their quarters getting their badly laundered white uniforms ready for inspection. Suddenly the battle gong rang, much to everyone's surprise and displeasure "at the idea of a battle stations drill on Sunday." One of Leahy's fellow officers declared that "he would not move an inch until the idiot who set off the alarm had the recall sounded." But then came the rattle of drums beating to quarters, and one of Leahy's messmates ran down the quarterdeck shouting, "We have them now for sure, the fleet is coming out."[19]

Cervera's flagship, the black-hulled *Infanta Maria Teresa,* led the way with his admiral's pennant flying. Leahy later claimed that the *Oregon* fired the first shot at the flagship as it cleared the harbor and made a run to the west, followed by the rest of the Spanish fleet. The American ships steamed toward the coast to pin the Spaniards against the shore. *Oregon* was instrumental in forcing *Maria Teresa* to run aground as it began to burn. *Texas* and *Iowa* took hits from the remaining Spanish ships but successfully fought off the Spanish torpedo-boat destroyers. Meanwhile, the *Cristóbal Colón,* arguably the fastest ship on either side, spied an opening to escape west and surged past *Oregon* as Leahy's ship finished off the *Maria Teresa.*

Oregon and Commodore Schley's cruiser, *Brooklyn,* quickly gave chase, and with thick black smoke pouring from their stacks, the three ships churned westward. After several hours and some sixty miles, two shells from Leahy's forward turret neatly straddled the *Cristóbal Colón.* Its captain turned toward shore, ran his ship aground, and struck his flag. By the time Admiral Sampson arrived off Santiago in the *New York,* the battle was over. The Spanish fleet had been destroyed with only two American casualties, one man killed and one wounded. At least six hundred Spanish sailors perished.[20]

In his typical fashion, Leahy described the Battle of Santiago in his journal in crisp, factual language—almost as though he had been a detached observer. Others painted a far different picture of Leahy "standing by his turret, jumping up and down, slapping his leg with his cap, and yelling his head off."[21] Quiet, reserved Bill Leahy was human after all. What's more, even though he would spend the next forty years championing the might of battleships, he had just fought his one and only naval battle.

CHAPTER TWO

King

"Rey"
—Annapolis, Class of 1901

Shortly before midnight on the evening of February 8, 1904, ten sleek Japanese destroyers slipped quietly into the Russian naval base at Port Arthur (now Lüshun), China. Relying on recently developed Whitehead torpedoes, they unleashed a devastating attack on seven battleships and seven cruisers of the Imperial Russian Fleet. It was a stunning Japanese victory. It was also the result of a surprise attack. Diplomatic relations between the two countries were strained and in the process of being terminated, but no state of war yet existed.

To Japan's displeasure, Russia had begun flexing its muscles in this part of the world during the 1890s. As Japan jousted with China over Manchuria and the Korean peninsula, Russia used the disputes as a cover to seize Port Arthur. Its protected harbor sat at the tip of a small peninsula jutting out from the Chinese coast just west of Korea, strategically near the sea-lanes linking Korea, China, and Japan. When Russia demanded a formal lease from China that included the right to connect Port Arthur to the Trans-Siberian Railway, Japan's displeasure deepened. Tsar Nicholas II already had his port on the Pacific at Vladivostok, some twelve hundred miles to the north, and Japan viewed Russia's presence at Port Arthur as an unacceptable intrusion into its sphere of influence.

The destroyers that attacked Port Arthur showed Japan's resolve to do something about it. All had been built in England between 1899 and 1902. Japan, as yet, had no major shipyards of its own capable of building steel warships, and Admiral Heihachiro Togo justified the surprise attack by citing the need to conserve limited naval resources. Head-to-head combat or a lengthy blockade would quickly sap his strength.

The Russians suffered a terrible setback—three of the tsar's biggest ships were badly damaged. The battleship *Retvizan* had a gaping hole in its side. The cruiser *Pallada* glowed red from fires in its coal bunkers. And the battleship *Tsarevitch,* arguably the most powerful in the Russian fleet, sat ignominiously in the mud at the entrance to the inner harbor, its bulkheads shattered and steering compartment flooded. Perhaps most important, the tsar's swagger in the Far East had been seriously humbled.[1]

Fifteen hundred miles to the south at Cavite in the Philippines— now an American naval base thanks to Admiral Dewey—the U.S. cruiser *Cincinnati* was effectively a neutral, but hardly a disinterested, party to what had just happened. *Cincinnati* was only ten years old, but at 306 feet in length and with a displacement of 3,200 tons, it was already inferior to the newer cruisers coming down the ways. Nonetheless, the ship was immediately ordered to run north to Shanghai and then cross the Yellow Sea to the Korean port of Chemulpo (now Inchon) to assess the situation.

Entering the harbor at Chemulpo, the *Cincinnati* found ample evidence that the Japanese had also attacked Russian ships at anchor there. A Japanese torpedo boat menacingly watched the *Cincinnati*'s arrival, but the American cruiser anchored among the warships of other neutral nations without incident. Standing his watch on the *Cincinnati*'s bridge was a recently commissioned ensign named Ernest J. King. For a young officer determined to make his mark, this was a ringside seat to the start of the Russo-Japanese War.[2]

*   *   *

Ernest Joseph King came from a line of builders. His father, James Clydesdale King, was born in Scotland in 1848. James's father died when he was nine, and his mother, a destitute widow with five sons and a daughter, immigrated to the United States to join her brother in Cleveland. James grew up on the shores of Lake Erie. He worked the schooners that plied the Great Lakes, but such employment was seasonal due to the icebound winters and he soon switched to bridge building as a more stable occupation.

Joseph Keam was a master woodworker for the Royal Navy on the docks of Plymouth, England, before iron-hulled steamships cut into his livelihood. He, too, sought brighter prospects in America and took his wife and four eligible daughters to Cleveland in 1872. There he found refinery work with the Standard Oil Company. Their daughter Elizabeth, "Bessie" as she was known, married James King in Cleveland in 1876. The newlyweds traveled by rail to the Centennial Exposition in Philadelphia for their honeymoon.

For several years James followed bridge construction wherever it was available, but such itinerant work made Bessie uneasy. After their first son died in infancy, Bessie urged James to find permanent work closer to home. He took a job in a railroad repair shop in Lorain, Ohio, about twenty miles west of Cleveland. There, in a small cottage near Lake Erie, Ernest Joseph King was born on November 23, 1878. The family moved about some, but Lorain would always be home.

There was never any doubt that young Ernest was his father's son. The boy grew up surrounded by the greasy smells and clanging iron of his father's workplace. Engineers would boost the lad into their cabs as they shuttled locomotives around the yards, and rough-cut workers gladly shared the intricacies of pistons, gears, and steam-driven machinery with him. Whatever inborn qualities of forthrightness and obstinacy Ernest may have inherited from his father and grandfather Keam, they were no doubt accentuated by exposure to this straightforward, no-nonsense group of workingmen.

Diplomacy, tact, and forbearance were not words to be associated with Ernest King, even at a young age. When his mother once scolded him for expressing his dislike of a neighbor's pumpkin pie in front of the hostess, seven-year-old Ernest held his ground. "It's true," he insisted, "I don't like it." Absolute candor, no matter how rude or insulting, became his trademark. "If I didn't agree," King later reminisced, "I said so."

His father could be just as stubborn. When Ernest grandly announced that he was quitting school after eighth grade to get a job, James King relented, but with the stipulation that the boy work at least a year without changing his mind. Ernest found work in a shop making typesetting equipment, but when fall came and his friends trudged back to school, he had second thoughts. His father held firm. They had an agreement and Ernest would complete his year of employment. By the following autumn, Ernest was all too glad to enroll in high school in Lorain.

During his sophomore year, Ernest almost died of typhoid fever. His mother was ill herself and had taken her younger children to live with a sister in Cleveland. An elderly German woman nursed Ernest back to health—calling him "Yonny"—and he would visit her in later years when he returned to Lorain. His mother died the following spring, but by then Ernest was content living alone with his father and he seems to have taken her passing with little pause.

Instead, he began to focus on a career beyond the machine shop. From a local Civil War veteran, King borrowed book after book about the men and battles of that relatively recent conflict. It was exciting reading and it added to his interest in the military, which had been piqued by a magazine article about the U.S. Naval Academy at Annapolis. At some point—never mind that he had once been horribly seasick on Lake Erie—Ernest confided to his father his ambition to attend.

James King talked with his congressman, Winfield Scott Kerr of Ohio's 14th District, when Kerr came to Lorain to campaign for reelection in the summer of 1896. Each congressman handled his academy appointments differently, some handing them out to sons of favored supporters, others insisting on a strict competitive process. Since James King certainly had no political clout, father and son were pleased when Kerr invited Ernest to take competitive exams the following year.

Ernest spent his senior year preparing for the exams, and after delivering the valedictory address to his Lorain graduating class of thirteen, he embarked on the first journey of his life away from home—fifty miles to Congressman Kerr's hometown of Mansfield, Ohio—to vie for the appointment to Annapolis. By now six feet one-half inches tall and a lean 135 pounds, King passed the physical evaluation with no trouble, and when the results of the academic tests were announced, he stood first among the thirty applicants. Ernest J. King was headed for Annapolis.

If young King had reservations, he could hardly let them show among the Lorain townspeople, to whom he had become somewhat of a hero simply by applying for such a far-off adventure. (There was also a girl, Leona Doane, and they parted with an understanding.) James King, however, was not so certain of the outcome. He bought his son a round-trip ticket to Annapolis—just in case.[3]

Ernest J. King arrived at the Naval Academy on August 15, 1897— ten weeks after William D. Leahy had graduated and departed to serve on the *Oregon*. He took the usual entrance exams to validate his appointment and joined eighty-seven classmates in the class of 1901.

As he would always do, King established his personal goals for Annapolis early. When an overbearing upperclassman accused him of bragging that he would be first in his class, King denied it. Another member of King's class, future admiral Adolphus Andrews, overheard this and promptly asserted that *he* intended to be first. The upperclassman then proceeded to berate Andrews for his presumptuousness and the incident gave King pause. If he graduated first in his class, King reasoned, he might become too visible for comfort during his career. Superiors' expectations might be too high. But if he graduated third or fourth, he would still have the prestige without as much of the scrutiny. It was a typical King rationalization, and he would take similar positions in similar situations throughout his career.

There were no Christmas leaves that first year. King's first two roommates "bilged" and dropped out. Then came the war with Spain. First classmen were graduated immediately with no more ceremony than the usual dinner formation and dispatched to ships throughout the fleet. The junior class was ordered to sea after completing annual exams. But the third and fourth classmen were judged to be still in the nuisance category and were ordered home on leave until fall.

King initially took this in stride, but while en route to Lorain, he stopped off with a classmate at his home in Bethesda, Maryland. Quite by accident, the two cadets learned that somehow one of their other classmates had wrangled orders to go to sea. Sea duty in wartime for a fourth-class cadet? If that was true, King certainly was not going to be left out. He and his friend put on their dress uniforms and presented themselves in downtown Washington at the Navy Department, then occupying a building adjacent to the White House.

War creates confusion, and out of it King and four classmates were assigned to the cruiser *San Francisco,* then serving as flagship of the Northern Patrol Squadron. (One might well thank Theodore Roosevelt for conferring this opportunity on young men determined to get into the war, but Roosevelt himself had already resigned as assistant secretary.) The *San Francisco* proved a heady learning experience for all concerned, especially when unknowing cadets were ordered to perform seemingly routine naval maneuvers. It didn't help that cadets like King were quickly certain that they knew all there was to know about seamanship.

At anchor off Provincetown, Massachusetts, King was sent ashore in a small oar-driven boat to fetch foodstuffs. Returning, he was ordered to stop at the cruiser *Dixie.* In typical King fashion, he decided that he could save time if he came alongside the *Dixie* bow to stern rather than turning about and coming alongside bow to bow as was established procedure. The coxswain in the boat with him expressed his disapproval, but King was certain that he knew best. Naturally, when King climbed the ladder to board *Dixie,* the executive officer, Lieutenant Hugo Osterhaus, greeted him with a sharp rebuke: "Don't you know how to come alongside a ship?" King replied that he didn't want to turn around twice in getting to the *San Francisco,* but Osterhaus wasn't persuaded. One way or the other, he would remember this brash cadet. To King's credit, there were other occasions when he gratefully deferred to experienced seamen for advice.[4]

Initially, the *San Francisco* and its squadron were assigned the task of guarding New England against attacks by a rumored Spanish fleet. When it became clear that this threat was illusory, *San Francisco* and its consorts sailed south for Key West. By the time they were ready for action off Cuba, the main Atlantic fleet had won its smashing victory at Santiago, and there was little to do but blockade the island's northern coast, including Havana.

On August 12, King was the junior officer of the deck when the *San Francisco* was ordered close to the entrance of Havana harbor in anticipation of ships attempting to escape the blockade. The cruiser came under fire from Spanish shore batteries and replied in kind. Thoughts of another Santiago quickly evaporated as no ships appeared, but King had seen his first action. By nightfall, an armistice was in place and the short little war was over.

Back in Key West, the *San Francisco*'s naval cadets were suddenly deadweight. They were granted immediate leave before reporting back to Annapolis to start their second year. King hurried home to Lorain and found himself even more of a local hero. Lorain's own Company A of the Fifth Ohio Regiment had made it only as far as Tampa before the war ended, but Ernest King had been in the "action off Havana." He and his shipmates were given the same medal as the victors at Santiago. King returned to Annapolis that fall with two other mementos of the experience — an anchor tattooed on his left arm and a small dagger on his right.[5]

After such an adventure, the ensuing academic year and the practice cruise of the following summer were rather mundane, even if the latter took him across the Atlantic to Plymouth, England, on the sailing ship *Monongahela*. While there, King visited cousins from his mother's family and was still raving years later about high tea with strawberries and Devonshire cream.

Monongahela was becalmed en route back to Annapolis and arrived barely in time for the start of the academic year. It hardly mattered to King, as his encyclopedic mind was well suited to the heavily rote teaching methods. As for the engineering courses, he easily absorbed them after his apprentice-like experiences in the Ohio railroad shops.

Not much of an athlete, King nonetheless played B-squad football for four years (the team was called the "Hustlers") and delighted in ice-skating on his own when the river froze. He gained thirty pounds, and by the end of his third year, he had set his sights on his final objective, to wear the four stripes of a cadet lieutenant commander and command the battalion. To accomplish it, King needed to win the respect and confidence of both his subordinates and his superiors. Such leadership is sometimes a fine line, but King demonstrated it and became the top cadet commander in his class.

But that is not to say that King was without vices. Chasing women and smoking cigarettes almost did him in. His "understanding" with Leona Doane from Lorain was terminated sometime during his third year when Leona wrote that she intended to marry another man. King replied with the utmost grace and good thoughts toward her and may have been secretly relieved. By that time, there was another young woman who had caught his eye.

Mattie Egerton was described as "the most beautiful, the most sought-after young woman at Annapolis," and King determined to be first among the seekers. They both loved to dance and delighted in each other's physical presence. They soon made plans to marry once King completed his two years of sea duty and won his commission.

His smoking violations were another matter. Smoking was strictly forbidden at the academy, although many sneaked habitual cigarettes — a practice that in time would fill the wardrooms of navy ships throughout the world with a blue haze. On report twice for smoking, King was in danger of being expelled — battalion commander though he might be — when an academy officer caught him smoking a third time in an Annapolis café. The officer settled for a sharp dressing-down, and King, who once again showed little regard for sound advice, would spend a lifetime being photographed with a cigarette in his hand.

In addition to his final-year responsibilities as battalion commander, King was one of the editors of the *Lucky Bag* yearbook.

How much input King had into the quote chosen for his own biography is debatable, but it fit: "A man so various that he seems to be,/ Not one, but all mankind's epitome." Even more telling were the assertions "Hops, — well, yes!" and "Temper? — don't fool with nitroglycerin."

Then there were the nicknames. It was a well-established tradition at the Naval Academy that every midshipman had to have at least one and in some cases several. These nicknames frequently stuck with an officer throughout his career, although those privileged to use them were usually limited to his classmates. King was "Dolly" for his handsome good looks and cherubic red cheeks — a name he despised and that rarely surfaced post-Annapolis — and "Rey," Spanish for "king," which he found much more to his liking.[6]

On Graduation Day 1901, sixty-seven cadets of the class of 1901 marched to receive their provisional diplomas. True to his plan, King was fourth in his class. He still had the unused return railroad ticket his father had bought him four years before. His father made the trip from Lorain to see the event and listen to Theodore Roosevelt, now vice president of the United States, give the commencement address.

Three short months in Cuba and a few hours on San Juan Hill had propelled Roosevelt to the governorship of New York. Two years later, William McKinley, who had initially balked at Roosevelt's appointment as assistant secretary of the navy, agreed to take him on as vice president and get him out of New York politics. Within three months of King's graduation, an assassin's bullet would make Roosevelt president.

As King departed Annapolis for his first assignment, there was one other thing he may have noticed. Annapolis was changing. The dismal cadet quarters left over from the Civil War were being replaced by modern Bancroft Hall. Streets in town were being paved and trolleys beginning to appear. Each incoming class brought an increased number of cadets. Annapolis was changing because America was changing and had come to realize, on the waters of Manila Bay and off Santiago, that its presence in the world depended on a modern, well-led, and well-equipped navy.

*   *   *

From Annapolis, King began his required two years of sea duty before being commissioned with assignments aboard the training frigate *Constellation* and survey ship *Eagle.* In the spring of 1902, he was ordered to the newly commissioned battleship *Illinois,* which was bound for Europe as the U.S. flagship in European waters. Among the highlights King experienced was a grand review of naval might representing sixteen nations that assembled off Spithead, England, for the coronation of Edward VII. The *Illinois* moored alongside the German battleship *Kaiser Friedrich III,* and King had plenty of opportunities to inspect the competition.

By the time the *Illinois* made its way around Europe and to the Caribbean for the winter 1902–1903 fleet maneuvers, King faced the sort of political quandary that he seems to have routinely imposed on himself in an effort to advance his career. He was still six months away from taking final exams to be commissioned an ensign, and no less than the captain of *Illinois* advised him to remain aboard. Initially, King agreed, but then he became aware of a vacancy on the cruiser *Cincinnati.* He seized on it because the smaller complement would permit him to command a ship's division and serve as a watch officer before he was commissioned an ensign. *Illinois*'s captain was not pleased, but King went on his way.

King's forty-man division on *Cincinnati* gave him his first direct command and put to the test whether or not he could be stern yet just. By the time his ship reached its station with the Asiatic Squadron in the Far East, King had passed both his commissioning exams as an ensign and his unofficial leadership review by his men. When the enlisted sailors of his division gathered for a group portrait in Shanghai, they insisted that King join them—an unusual compliment that he savored. He had indeed managed to be strict but fair.

Yet King encountered one demon that almost ruined his career. Liquor was then legal aboard ship and unlimited on liberties ashore. Drinking was a fairly common ritual to relieve the boredom, but not everyone could handle it. Returning late from liberty in Shanghai, King staggered aboard the *Cincinnati* clearly drunk and disorderly. When the captain recorded the offense in King's record, King took his usual approach of splitting hairs and debated whether he had been "a few" or "several" hours late.

Two months later, he was late again for a special duty, but by this time the *Cincinnati* had a new captain. This was Commander Hugo Osterhaus, who well remembered Mr. King from the coming-alongside-in-the-opposing-direction incident off Provincetown some years before. This time he would show no mercy. "Ensign King is a young and promising officer," Osterhaus wrote in King's next fitness report, "and it would be unjust to him to overlook an offense of this nature." Thereafter, King was never late for an assignment, no matter how much carousing he had done the night before.

While on station in the Far East, *Cincinnati* made the rounds of port calls from Hong Kong to Shanghai to Yokohama, as well as Chefoo (now Yantai, China), some seventy-five miles south of the Russian base at Port Arthur. Western powers routinely called at Chinese and Japanese ports in those days, and at 37° north latitude Chefoo was a favorite summer rendezvous and training ground where the Asiatic Squadron could escape the heat of the tropics.

Early in December 1903, three battleships and four cruisers of the squadron, including the *Cincinnati,* were suddenly ordered to steam for Hawaii at top speed. Seasonal gales in the Central Pacific lashed the ships, but they made the run in record time. Even their commander did not learn the reason for the sprint until some years later. President Theodore Roosevelt wished to see just how quickly the squadron might come east should trouble develop with Latin American countries over his interest in controlling the route of the proposed Panama Canal. Six weeks later, King and the *Cincinnati* were back in the Philippines when Japanese destroyers struck the Russian fleet at Port Arthur.[7]

Following Japan's surprise attack at Port Arthur, the Russo-Japanese war did not go well for Russia. Its surviving capital ships fought minimal sea engagements in the neighboring waters with only limited success. Japan invaded Korea and laid siege to Port Arthur. As Russia struggled to stay in the conflict, a major problem was supplying its ships and armies by rail across the expanse of Siberia. By

Battle of Tsushima, 1905

Siberia

Sea of Okhotsk

RUSSIA

Sakhalin (Russia)

1905 Treaty Line — 50°N

Sakhalin (Japan)

Manchuria

Trans-Siberian Railway (Original Alignment)

CHINA

Vladivostok

Mukden (Shenyang)

Hokkaido

Sea of Japan — 40°N

Tientsin (Tianjin)

KOREA (Japan)

Port Arthur (Lüshun)

Chemulpo (Inchon)

Honshu

Chefoo (Yantai)

Yellow Sea

Japanese Fleet

Tokyo

JAPAN

Masan

Tsushima Strait

Shikoku

Shanghai

Russian Fleet

Kyushu

— 30°N

East China Sea

0   300 Miles

Formosa

120°E   130°E   140°E

January 1905, Port Arthur, along with the remaining ships of Russia's First Pacific Squadron, fell to the Japanese. A horrific land battle followed at Mukden (now Shenyang), China, with upwards of 35,000 killed and 100,000 wounded on both sides. Another 20,000 Russian troops were captured as the Russian army abandoned the field and made a disorganized retreat northward.

Meanwhile, in October 1904, Tsar Nicholas II dispatched his prized Baltic Fleet—now renamed the Second Pacific Squadron—halfway around the world to reenforce Port Arthur. Rear Admiral Zinovi Rozhdestvenski was in port on Madagascar when word reached him that the outpost had fallen to the Japanese. Rozhdestvenski faced a crucial decision. Should he turn around, with his only loss being pride, and return to the Baltic, or should he continue on to Vladivostok?

Rozhdestvenski chose to continue and in doing so elected to take the most direct route. This led through the South China and East China Seas and the narrow Tsushima Strait between Korea and Japan. These were hardly friendly waters. Before dawn on May 27, 1905, a heavy fog parted long enough for the Japanese to detect the Russian fleet nearing the southern entrance to the strait. Crude wireless flashed the news to Admiral Togo aboard his flagship *Mikasa*. His fleet was waiting at a secret anchorage at Masan Bay, Korea, just to the west.

Next came the tactics that every American naval officer would subsequently study at either Annapolis or the Naval War College. Choosing to fight one grand battle that he hoped would settle the conflict and establish complete naval superiority, Togo assembled a major force. In line astern of the *Mikasa,* his twelve capital ships steamed south to meet the approaching Russian fleet.

Rozhdestvenski had his ships deployed in two parallel lines, with eight lesser battleships and cruisers in the port column and his four principal battleships, including his flagship, *Kniaz Suvarov,* to their starboard. Togo might well have chosen simply to pass the Russian fleet on its weaker port side while going in the opposite direction and duke it out with broadsides right down the line. This may have caused some damage—quite probably to both sides—but it would have left the Japanese headed south and the Russians escaping north to Vladivostok.

Instead, Togo chose to cross the T, not once but twice. In this maneuver, the Japanese line first turned to starboard and passed across the bows of the advancing Russian columns mostly beyond gun range—the first crossing. Then Togo executed a hard U-turn to port back to the east—not in unison, which would have put his flagship in the rear instead of the van, but one ship at a time. For just a moment, the Russians thought that Fortune was smiling on them. As the *Mikasa* led the turn, it appeared momentarily stationary, and the *Suvarov* opened fire. Each of the following Japanese ships would also be sitting ducks as they made the turn.

But coming out of the turn, Togo increased speed and led his fleet back across the head of the Russian columns to cross the T again, this time at much closer range and with a withering effect on the oncoming Russian ships. In so doing, the Japanese ships could bring all of their guns to bear to starboard on the Russian lines, while the Russian ships, coming on at a right angle, could bring only their forward batteries to bear. Rozhdestvenski attempted to get his four main battleships into a line ahead of his weaker ships to protect them, but by then the damage had been done.

Of the twelve capital ships in the Russian battle line, eight were sunk and four captured. While several Japanese ships sustained major damage, Togo's only losses were three torpedo boats and 110 sailors killed. The Russians lost nearly 12,000 men, 4,830 killed and almost 7,000 taken prisoner. The end result of the Battle of Tsushima Strait was that Tsar Nicholas II had little choice but to accept Theodore Roosevelt's offer to broker a peace. The Japanese rejoiced in their newfound naval might, and Admiral Togo became a godlike hero.[8]

King was impressed with Japan's naval performance, but he also noted the empire's proficiency in putting out a steady stream of propaganda claiming victory at every turn. Despite the bitter end for the Russians, the Japanese had also suffered some setbacks over the course of the eighteen-month conflict, including the loss of two battleships to mines. It was a lesson in tactics and politics that King would remember.

Once more back in the Philippines, King had been away from the United States for three years, two and a half aboard *Cincinnati*. He was anxious to return stateside, particularly when he found officers a year his junior being rotated home. His request was granted, and in June 1905 he headed home. He had certainly crisscrossed that part of the globe, but despite his later involvement with events there, Ernest J. King would never again have permanent duty in the Far East.[9]

CHAPTER THREE

Halsey

"Pudge"
—Annapolis, Class of 1904

Hampton Roads, Virginia, had rarely seen such a display of naval power. After fourteen months at sea, sixteen U.S. Navy battleships were returning from a round-the-world cruise meant to demonstrate America's military might and global reach. The architect of this endeavor, President Theodore Roosevelt, was as giddy as a schoolboy as he stood on the deck of the presidential yacht, *Mayflower,* and watched his Great White Fleet pass in review to the booming of twenty-one-gun salutes.

It was February 22, 1909, and the date was no coincidence— Washington's Birthday. But more important, in less than two weeks Roosevelt would be leaving office, and he was not about to miss this exclamation point on his foreign policy. The goals for the navy that he had laid out as assistant secretary even before the dash of the *Oregon* were now triumphant before him.

Connecticut led the line, just as the battleship had when departing Hampton Roads in December 1907. There followed the other ships of the first division, *Kansas, Minnesota,* and *Vermont.* And then, like a grand roll call of states, the rest of the battle fleet:

Georgia, Nebraska, New Jersey, Rhode Island, Louisiana, Virginia, Missouri, Ohio, Wisconsin, Illinois, Kentucky, and the lone nonstate name, *Kearsarge.* All were post–Spanish-American War battleships that displaced at least twice the tonnage of the sunken *Maine*—proof positive of Roosevelt's rush to naval power.

The only slight frustration about this thundering parade was that the weather was not cooperating with the moment. A wintry gray sky shed incessant drizzle as Roosevelt in top hat and dark overcoat clambered aboard the *Connecticut* to extend personal congratulations to the flagship's officers and crew. They assembled on the foredeck below the forward 12-inch gun turret, but as the president started to climb onto the base of the turret to address them, he slipped on the rain-slick surface. Sailors caught him and boosted him up to the makeshift platform as cowboys might push a dude up on a horse. Unfazed as usual, Roosevelt launched into a rousing round of congratulations and assured the assembled sailors, "Those who perform the feat again can but follow in your footsteps."[1]

Out of hearing range on the nearby *Kansas,* Ensign William F. Halsey, Jr., stood at attention. He was delighted to be home. The world cruise had been an eye-opener, but Bill, as his friends called him, had a girl waiting. He had "bombarded her with souvenirs and ardent letters from every port," but since there was plenty of stateside competition for her hand, he was anxious to affirm where he stood.

Still, Halsey had not spent the cruise pining away. He and his shipmates had been the toast of every port of call from Rio de Janeiro to Yokohama, and they had taken full advantage of it. Always one to embrace the social scene, Halsey later confessed, "We needed the stretches at sea to rest from the hospitality ashore."[2]

Standing at attention on neighboring battleships were some of Halsey's Annapolis contemporaries. Lieutenant Harold R. Stark, class of 1903, and Passed Midshipman Raymond A. Spruance, class of 1907, stood on the *Minnesota.* Ensign Husband E. Kimmel, Halsey's close friend and a classmate from 1904, watched from the *Georgia.* By the time another such gathering of naval power occurred, Halsey would command the fleet, and two of those officers would be disgraced. The third would be his rival.

*   *   *

Bill Halsey came from a line sprinkled with sailors and at least one pirate. He described these forebears as "big, violent men, impatient of the law, and prone to strong drink and strong language." One of them, John Halsey, was granted a privateer's commission by the colonial governor of Massachusetts during Queen Anne's War (1702–1713). Among his escapades was a ferocious attack on four ships at once, capturing two in the process. Captain John indiscriminately continued such activity long after his privateer's commission expired, thus becoming a pirate.

A century later, another Halsey, Eliphalet, captained the first Long Island whaler to round Cape Horn and make for the South Pacific whaling grounds. Other Halseys followed Eliphalet to sea, but Charles Henry Halsey chose to remain securely on land as first a lawyer and then an Episcopal clergyman. He married well—Eliza Gracie King was the granddaughter of the Federalist politician Rufus King—but Charles died young when he fell out of a window while inspecting the construction of a rectory. Eliza was left with a brood of six or seven children (the record is not clear), including two-year-old William Frederick Halsey.

Eliza settled in Elizabeth, New Jersey, to raise her fatherless children, but it was a tough lot. Friends repeatedly tried to help, and when Charles's former law partner, George M. Robeson, was appointed secretary of the navy in 1869, William, by now about fifteen, announced that he would like to go to the U.S. Naval Academy. Robeson made the necessary arrangements, giving William a vacant slot from Louisiana, and he proceeded to graduate from Annapolis in the class of 1873.

After William Halsey advanced to lieutenant in 1880, he married Anne Masters Brewster, a childhood friend who traced her roots back to the Brewsters of Plymouth Colony. Shortly after the wedding, the bridegroom reported for a lengthy sea tour, but not before Anne was pregnant. On October 30, 1882, in her father's house in Elizabeth, Anne gave birth to William Frederick Halsey, Jr. By the time the child's father returned from sea, the boy was two and his head was ringed with long golden curls. Much to Anne's chagrin,

Lieutenant Halsey promptly marched his namesake to the barbershop.

The usual naval assignments, with resulting moves about the country, followed, but the Halseys' happiest times may have been when William Sr. was stationed at the Naval Academy as an instructor in physics and chemistry. Certainly, it was during those years of living in close proximity to Annapolis and savoring its daily rituals that young William—still called "Willie"—expressed his desire to attend on his own. Characteristically, he took matters into his own hands when he was fourteen and wrote a rather rambling letter directly to president-elect William McKinley requesting a presidential appointment. Addressing McKinley by his Civil War rank of "Major," young Halsey confessed, "I ... have always wanted to enter the Navy."

Both a strict disciplinarian and a keen academic, William Frederick Halsey, Sr., set a high standard for his son. He had enrolled Willie in a boarding school, Swarthmore Grammar outside Philadelphia, in hopes of readying him for the academy. When the letter to McKinley showed no promise, William Sr. nonetheless ratcheted up the preparation and sent his son to a special prep school in the Annapolis area. Grandly known as Buck Wilmer University, it was run by a retired naval officer—Buck Wilmer himself—for the express purpose of preparing prospective appointees for the rigorous entrance exams.

But there were two problems. First, there was no word from President McKinley despite more letters, and the Annapolis slot from the Halseys' Elizabeth, New Jersey, congressional district was filled. Willie even wrote to the congressman who represented the district in Louisiana from which his father had been appointed, but those had been special circumstances. Second, despite all his studies, it was becoming quite clear that young Halsey wasn't one to excel academically.

By the fall of 1899, with no hope of Annapolis in sight, the Halseys chose another tack for their son. They enrolled Willie in the University of Virginia's medical school at Charlottesville on the theory that he might still enter the navy as a medical officer. The academic result was predictable. Anatomy classes, formaldehyde odors, and cadavers just weren't his thing. Instead, Willie took on the more mature name of "Bill" and plunged headlong into the university's social life, including the Delta Psi fraternity. Then, too, there was his growing interest in football. "I didn't learn much," Bill Halsey later confessed of his year at Virginia, "but I...had a wonderful time."

His father was horrified by Bill's first-semester grades, and his mother redoubled her efforts to win him an appointment to Annapolis. Congressional authorization for five additional presidential appointments in the wake of the navy's Spanish-American War buildup helped. While Halsey later recalled that his mother "camped in McKinley's office until he promised her one for me," the political influence of former New Jersey governor and current U.S. attorney general John W. Griggs may have greased the ways.

When his appointment finally came through, Halsey gave a backward glance at Charlottesville and hurried to Annapolis to take the entrance exams. He crammed with all his energy to make up for past deficiencies and on July 7, 1900, was sworn into the class of 1904, the last incoming academy class of fewer than one hundred cadets.[3]

William F. Halsey, Jr., wasn't destined for academic stardom at the Naval Academy, but he applied himself just enough to make respectable marks without adversely affecting his preferred social and athletic pursuits. Once, when Halsey came dangerously close to failing theoretical mechanics, his father strongly advised him to drop football. That, of course, was out of the question.

Instead, Bill recruited the scholars in the class to tutor him and a few others similarly challenged. When the exam was over, Bill went to his father's quarters for lunch and was immediately asked if the results had been posted. "Yes, sir," Bill answered, and then reported that he had made 3.98 out of 4.0. His father stared at him for a full minute and then finally asked incredulously, "Sir, have you been drinking?"

Football was one of Halsey's passions. Although he played the game aggressively, he never claimed to be any good at it. In fact, Halsey later boasted that he was the worst fullback ever to play for Annapolis. He appeared consigned to the junior varsity, but when an injury sidelined the varsity fullback, Halsey started at that position his third and fourth years, surviving a 40–5 drubbing by Army in 1903.

Aside from football and partying, Halsey took great delight in the summer training cruises, claiming, among other things, never to have been seasick. His father was now head of the Department of Seamanship at the academy, and from sail work on the square-rigger *Chesapeake* to steam indoctrination on the old battleship *Indiana,* the son was determined to show the father that he was becoming an all-around sailor. Young Bill learned a lot, but he was brought back to reality by the academy's chief master-at-arms, who told him, "I wish you all the luck in the world, Mr. Halsey, but you'll never be as good a naval officer as your father!"

Halsey's summer cruise aboard the *Indiana* during his third-class year left him with a souvenir tattoo. His father, who sported no less than four, advised him with the voice of experience against such permanent foolishness. "But as usual," recalled Halsey, "I was too headstrong to listen." The finished work showed a blue anchor with its chain forming "04" and a red "USNA" on its crown.[4]

When Halsey marched to an early graduation in February 1904, the *Lucky Bag,* for which he was an associate editor, called him "a real old salt" and "everybody's friend." And while he might strive to live up to his father's seamanship standards, young Bill — short and stocky though he was — had nonetheless taken on the rugged good looks of a solidly built sailor. He looked, the *Lucky Bag* proclaimed, "like a figurehead of Neptune."

His nicknames were "Willie" and "Pudge" and he seems to have set some sort of informal record for "the number of offices he has held" — even serving on the Christmas Card Committee his plebe year and the Class German Committee as a senior. But his heart belonged to athletics. Halsey's performance on the football field — however lacking by intercollegiate standards — won him a navy "N," one of only four accorded seniors on the team. But the honor he held dearest was the Thompson Trophy. First handed out in 1901 by Cadet Battalion Commander Ernest J. King, it was awarded annually to the first classman who had done the most during the year to promote athletics.

Considering Halsey's shunning of advice over the years, the Dickens quote the *Lucky Bag* chose for him was most appropriate: "It's my opinion there's nothing 'e don't know." But what counted most in Halsey's mind was that while he stood only forty-third out of the sixty-two survivors of his incoming class of ninety-three, he was now Passed Midshipman Halsey and headed out to sea.[5]

In fact, sea duty came almost too quickly. To secure choice service on the battleship *Missouri,* Bill and five classmates forfeited their graduation leave and rushed to Hampton Roads to join the ship before it sailed for Guantánamo Bay, Cuba, and winter training exercises. The irony of this first assignment for Halsey would not become clear for more than forty years.

The *Missouri* was affectionately called the *"Mizzy."* At 388 feet long, and with four 12-inch main guns and a displacement of 12,500 tons, it cruised at a maximum speed of 18 knots. By the time Halsey stood on the deck of the next battleship to be christened *Missouri,* the "Mighty Mo" was of a generation of battleships that boasted nine 16-inch guns, displaced 45,000 tons, stretched 887 feet, and cut through the seas at 32.5 knots. Halsey's progression from one *Missouri* to the other is a graphic example of the evolution of American naval might.

But Halsey served aboard the *"Mizzy"* first, and his cruise was not to be without incident. On Wednesday, April 13, 1904, he was a junior officer on the bridge as the battleship took its turn at the fleet's annual target practice off Pensacola, Florida. Suddenly a heavy blast aft rocked the ship, and a column of flame shot several hundred feet into the air from the top hatch of the 12-inch after turret. A second, sharper blast followed. Powder bags in the turret had caught fire and spread to a dozen more. Thirty-one officers and men perished, and the carnage made a profound and lasting impression on Halsey. Almost fifty years later, he still found the disaster looming "monstrous in my memory" and making him dread the thirteenth of every month, particularly if it fell on the double hex of a Friday.[6]

This accident cast a pall over Halsey's two years on the *Missouri* and the start of his career, but he got a break by being assigned to temporary duty at the Naval Academy during the 1904 and 1905 football seasons. The likable Halsey was detailed as assistant backfield coach despite his less-than-stellar gridiron record. Clearly, it was his bulldog determination that the academy wanted, and in 1905 Navy fought Army to a tie.

After the 1905 football season, Halsey, now two years out of Annapolis, received his commission as an ensign. He was detached from *Missouri* to *Don Juan de Austria,* a former Spanish gunboat that had been salvaged out of Manila Bay. The *Don Juan* bored Halsey terribly as it chugged around the Caribbean on customs duty and at one point anchored for six months in the Bay of Samaná, on the north coast of the Dominican Republic. The only excitement was the weekly mail steamer from the United States.

But a reprieve was in sight. In March 1907, Halsey reported for duty aboard the *Kansas,* the navy's newest battleship, so new that it would not sail for its shakedown cruise until the following August. By then, it was clear that something major was afoot, and when *Kansas* got things squared away, it joined fifteen other battleships—all painted a peaceful white—in the roadstead at Hampton Roads, Virginia. On December 16, 1907, the battleships weighed anchor and steamed in review past the presidential yacht, *Mayflower,* and its nervous occupant.[7]

In the wake of the Russo-Japanese War, the peace that Theodore Roosevelt had brokered was not sitting well in Japan. Admiral Togo may have destroyed the Russian fleet at Tsushima, but the final treaty did not accord Japan any financial indemnity for its losses. The truth of the matter was that both Russia and Japan were broke.

In Japan, this triggered a rush of emigration to the United States, particularly California. When the ensuing backlash against this influx included an attempt to segregate schools in San Francisco for Asian immigrants, Japan strongly protested. It cited the failure of an indemnity and this unequal treatment as evidence that the United States considered Japan a second-rate power and the Japanese a second-class people. Some politicians in both countries engaged in saber rattling.

Roosevelt considered the crisis grave and in response determined that this was one of those cases of speaking softly but carrying a big stick. While assuring Japan of America's friendship, he would use the Great White Fleet as a symbol of American power. Should Great Britain and Germany take a lesson from it as well, so much the better.

Roosevelt wanted it understood "that the Pacific was as much our home waters as the Atlantic, and that our fleet could and would at will pass from one to the other of the two great oceans." At the time, the British and German navies—arguably the first and second most powerful in the world—were skeptical of such a movement. If TR and his navy left a string of disabled battleships at ports around the world, he would be an international laughingstock—thus his nervousness as the fleet departed Hampton Roads.

The sixteen battleships cleared Cape Henry at the entrance to Chesapeake Bay and steered south toward the Caribbean. Christmas 1907 found the fleet in Port of Spain, Trinidad. Then it was on to Rio de Janeiro; Punta Arenas, Chile; and through the Strait of Magellan to Callao, Peru. The fleet was almost retracing the dash of

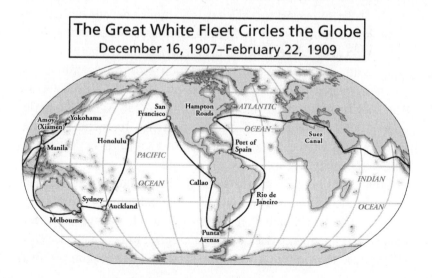

The Great White Fleet Circles the Globe
December 16, 1907–February 22, 1909

the *Oregon* in reverse, which may well have been what Roosevelt was thinking when he conceived the idea. Later, Roosevelt would call the voyage of the Great White Fleet and the construction of the Panama Canal "the two American achievements that really impressed foreign peoples during the first dozen years" of the twentieth century.[8]

As the fleet cruised onward, Ensign Halsey had time to savor the various cultures, but as a junior officer, he also put in his share of time supervising the shore patrol. Getting a load of older and frequently inebriated enlisted men back on board ship was trying for a young officer, but Halsey proved himself up to the task, particularly during a lengthy port call at San Francisco. The gruff ensign made something of a name for himself among the madams of the city by posting shore patrolmen outside their houses of ill-repute and forbidding enlisted men to enter.

Publicly, San Francisco was to have been the fleet's farthest westward advance, but Roosevelt almost certainly had much more in mind from the beginning. To move the American battle fleet from the Atlantic to the Pacific was one thing, but to have it then circumnavigate the globe was a show of real power. Leaving San Francisco in July 1908, the Great White Fleet steamed first to Honolulu, then Auckland, Sydney, Melbourne, and Manila, anchoring in Manila Bay near the site of Admiral Dewey's triumph a decade earlier.

To the chagrin of sailors and Manila businesspeople alike, shore leave was canceled because of a cholera outbreak. There was also the pressing matter of a special invitation. Not to be outdone, the Japanese emperor had extended an invitation to Roosevelt for the fleet to visit Japan. Both the president and Rear Admiral Charles Sperry, commander of the fleet, were cautious. To decline the invitation would be the ultimate insult, but to anchor in Yokohama harbor was risky.

Sperry and his senior officers well remembered what had happened to the *Maine* in Havana harbor—coal bunker explosion or not—and to the Russian fleet at Port Arthur. The Japanese had also made a similar sneak attack on Chinese naval forces in 1894. While Halsey was far too junior to be involved in these councils, he was firmly of the opinion that the invitation was a deceitful Japanese charade.

But the first enemy lurking on the voyage to Yokohama was a typhoon. It struck the fleet in the East China Sea and scattered the ships, causing some minor damage and sweeping two men overboard. It proved the only major disruption of the fourteen-month cruise. It was also Halsey's first encounter with a typhoon; it would not be his last. Meanwhile, the Japanese fleet of ten battleships and twenty-nine armored cruisers was said to be at sea "on maneuvers." Tensely, the American fleet regrouped and steamed into Tokyo Bay two days late on October 18, 1908.

The Japanese proved to be a model of courtesy and decorum. They had not given up their interest in Manchuria, but they were not ready for a war with the United States. Halsey was in the party that was hosted aboard Admiral Togo's flagship, *Mikasa*. Unlike another junior officer named Chester Nimitz, who had visited Japan and met Togo three years before in the aftermath of the Battle of Tsushima, Halsey was impressed by neither the admiral nor his massive ship.

What the Japanese managed to do, however, was force an apparent U.S. snub of China. The emperor's invitation had been on the grounds that the *entire* American fleet call at Yokohama but not China. Thus, when Admiral Sperry dispatched only half of his battleships—not to Shanghai but to the smaller port of Amoy (now Xiamen)—and then returned to Manila with the remainder, China accused the United States of the only diplomatic snub of the voyage.

Once the two groups of battleships reassembled, they steamed into the Indian Ocean and through the Suez Canal to the Mediterranean Sea. The fleet divided up to make port calls, and Halsey got a choice assignment when *Kansas* anchored in a sparkling cove on the French Riviera and was treated to French hospitality for almost two weeks. He and the other younger officers definitely appreciated the sleeveless, stockingless, and low-cut French bathing fashions that had yet to reach the United States.

Finally, it was time for the combined fleet to rendezvous at

Gibraltar early in February 1909 and make the crossing of the Atlantic. Winter storms churned its waters so much that even Halsey confessed to a rare bout of seasickness. On February 21, the sixteen battleships dropped anchor off Cape Henry and spruced themselves up for one final review. The next day, after Theodore Roosevelt finished speaking on the foredeck of the *Connecticut,* Ensign Halsey hurried ashore to meet his girl.[9]

CHAPTER FOUR

Nimitz

"Nim-i-tiz"
— Annapolis, Class of 1905

The 250-foot destroyer *Decatur* was being tossed about like a matchstick. With a narrow beam of not quite twenty-four feet, the slender ship was locked in the vise grip of a Pacific typhoon. Lashed by ferocious winds, it continually rolled 50 degrees to either side. On the bridge, twenty-three-year-old Ensign Chester W. Nimitz fought for his sea legs and was certain that his ship would break in two atop the monster waves. Yet young Nimitz could look to no one else for reassurance. Unusual as it was for someone of his age and rank, he was the captain of the *Decatur,* responsible for its safety and that of its seventy-two-man crew.

It was the spring of 1908, and the *Decatur* was in the South China Sea en route from French-controlled Saigon — then known as "the Paris of the East" — to Manila. For three very uncomfortable days, the typhoon held the *Decatur* in its grip. Nimitz later told his grandfather that it was his first "real live typhoon" and he hoped it would be his last. Remarkably, the *Decatur* made port in Manila only a few hours behind schedule. Several months later, the young captain and his ship would not be so lucky.

On the evening of July 7, the *Decatur* was entering Batangas harbor, south of Manila Bay. Ensign Nimitz was on the bridge as usual. Charts for the area were suspect, and standard procedure was to take position bearings from the surrounding landmarks. Nimitz chose to estimate his position instead of taking bearings, and he may also have failed to consider whether the tide was running in or out. Nonetheless, the *Decatur* proceeded into the harbor without incident until the leadsman charged with taking soundings in the bow suddenly sang out, "We're not moving, sir!" Ensign Nimitz had just committed an unpardonable navy sin and run his ship aground.[1]

The Nimitzes traced their heritage back to a long line of Germanic warriors. Some fought for the "Swedish Meteor," King Gustavus Adolphus, as he blazed his way across northern Europe in the early 1600s. Their fortunes rose and fell with the times. By the early 1800s, they had branched out as dealers in cloth, and the family mantle passed to Karl Heinrich Nimitz, who promptly squandered their wealth. His youngest son, Karl Heinrich, Jr., went to sea in the merchant marine at the age of fourteen to earn his way.

In 1844, after only a few years aboard ships, young Karl joined his parents and some siblings who had immigrated to Charleston, South Carolina. Two years later, the Nimitz clan and other recent German arrivals banded together to purchase a block of land in the new state of Texas. In the sand hills along the Pedernales River west of still tiny Austin, the company founded Fredericksburg, so named in honor of Prince Friedrich of Prussia. Many of the younger settlers promptly anglicized their given names. Thus, Karl Heinrich, Jr., became Charles Henry.

These German Texans were a close-knit group, and German customs and language continued to prevail in the Hill Country for decades. One of the stories that later circulated concerned a young man who left town to go to college. He wrote home saying he was required to take a foreign language, and he asked his parents what he should study. Supposedly they talked it over and then replied, "Take English, son."

In April 1848, Charles Henry Nimitz married Sophia Dorothea

Mueller, the daughter of a fellow settler. Together, they would have twelve children. Charles served briefly in the Texas Rangers, but in 1852 he started the Nimitz Hotel on the east end of Fredericksburg's Main Street. Sophia, despite an almost continual state of pregnancy, did most of the cooking.

As West Texas grew, the hotel prospered. As it expanded, Charles adopted a nautical theme, shaping the marquee like the bow of a ship and adding a balconied upper story that was topped by rooms resembling a pilothouse. Some travelers even called it "the Steamboat Hotel." Given Charles's penchant for storytelling, it was easy for him to embellish his few years at sea and take on the persona of a successful seafarer.

One of Charles and Sophia's many offspring was Chester Bernard Nimitz, a weak lad with a frail constitution. Doctors advised him never to marry, but when he was twenty-nine, he fell in love with the butcher's daughter, Anna Henke. She, too, came from a family of twelve children. Chester and Anna were married in March 1884, but within a year Anna went from bride to wife to widow and mother. Chester Bernard died five months after the wedding, and Chester William Nimitz was born on February 24, 1885. Grandfather Charles thought the birth coincided with Washington's Birthday— February 22—but his mother, Anna, would always associate it with Valentine's Day.

Young Chester revered his grandfather. With an eager audience at his knee, "Captain Charles" became even more of a teller of tall tales. With a flowing beard that went from blond to white as he aged, and twinkling blue eyes, "Opa" Charles indeed looked the role he had assumed. Later, Anna Nimitz remarried his youngest son, William, making William both young Chester's uncle and stepfather. But it was Opa Charles and Anna who would always be the dominant forces in his early life.

Another dominant force was the Texas hill country itself. Chester grew up hunting and fishing on countless camping trips with his grandfather. He mixed it up with the other boys in town, sometimes resorting to fists—probably at his grandfather's urging—to defend himself. And he spent time on his maternal grandfather's cattle ranch, where Henry Henke raised beef for his butcher shops. Whether killing rattlesnakes and scaring girls with the rattles or running across the wide-open prairie, Chester was a part of Texas, and Texas was a part of him.

After William and Anna married, they moved with Chester to nearby Kerrville to manage the St. Charles Hotel. William was not exactly a model of hard work, and Anna ended up doing the lion's share of running the hotel, besides having two more children. But Chester was clearly her favorite, and she was determined that he grow up without the frailties that had killed his father. Chester in return helped all he could, whether at the hotel before or after school or as a delivery boy for the Henke meat market. Unlike his fragile father or increasingly portly stepfather, Chester grew up strong and lean and seemed utterly determined to remain physically fit.

At the age of fifteen, Chester entered Tivy High School, so named for nearby Tivy Mountain. That summer of 1900, two shave-tail lieutenants fresh from West Point stopped at the St. Charles Hotel. Given all the military posts in West Texas, army officers were nothing new to Chester. Many had been frequent guests there and at his grandfather's hotel. But Chester was suddenly struck by how close these two soldiers were to his own age. When he compared his world of hotel work and butcher shops to their spit-and-polish ways and worldly sophistication, he found the prospects for his future decidedly lacking. Then and there, he resolved to take the entrance exams for West Point.

Congressman James L. Slayden was willing to consider Chester, but he offered no encouragement about his prospects. All the congressman's West Point slots were filled, and given the large number of army posts in his district, the waiting list of career officers wanting their sons to go there was long. Chester's dread of a lifetime in the hotel or meat market business again loomed large. Then Congressman Slayden offered another option. Given the increase in enrollment following the Spanish-American War, he had an opening at the U.S. Naval Academy in 1901. Would young Nimitz be interested?

That was only a year away, and Chester would not even be able to finish high school. But taking the plunge, he said yes and embarked on a frenzied year of tutoring, particularly in mathematics. He never graduated from high school, but this preparation allowed him to place first in Slayden's examinations the following spring. That August, Chester W. Nimitz passed the Naval Academy's entrance exams, and on September 7, 1901, he was sworn in as a naval cadet. With wavy blond hair, steely blue eyes, and a ruggedly square jaw, he looked every bit the Germanic warrior of his heritage.[2]

At Annapolis, Chester Nimitz found the changes that Ernest King had seen occurring as he'd graduated the previous June. Massive Bancroft Hall was under construction as a dormitory, and new granite-and-gray-brick academic buildings were replacing crumbling Civil War–era structures. There were 131 cadets in Nimitz's incoming class of 1905, and while that was still small by later standards, it was almost double the number in Bill Leahy's class just eight years before. The naval resurgence inspired by Theodore Roosevelt's foresight and the Spanish-American War was indeed in full swing.

Nimitz was determined that his lack of a high school diploma would not hamper his advancement, so he continued his West Texas habit of rising early—before reveille—to get in extra study time. His first roommate, Albert Thomas Church of Idaho, was a similarly serious student. Together, they engaged in a friendly competition, but more important, they supported each other's studying. Nimitz and Church became such an academic duo that classmates insisted they split up after their first year in an effort to tutor lesser achievers. Their subsequent roommates may have regretted the change when Nimitz and Church got them up for their usual pre-reveille studying.[3]

By all accounts, Nimitz was a hardworking and even-tempered cadet who got along easily with subordinates, peers, and superiors alike. The *Lucky Bag* struck at the core of his personality by observing that he "possesses that calm and steady going Dutch way that gets at the bottom of things." His identifying quote his senior year was from Wordsworth: "A man he seems of cheerful yesterdays and confident tomorrows."

Part of his appeal was that Nimitz had inherited his grandfather's storytelling ability. He passed on some of Grandfather Charles's tall tales and began to spread a few of his own. Nimitz was on the small side for football, but he played a solid set of tennis and made the varsity rowing crew his third year. He was the eighth man, the stroke. This was the rower closest to the coxswain in the stern and the one charged with setting the crew's rate and rhythm. Nimitz was well suited to the position, and it earned him a coveted navy "N." The role of managing tempo was one that he would play many times throughout his career.[4]

Nimitz diligently continued his personal regimen of exercise — running and swimming — when he was not playing team sports. And despite not playing football himself, he enjoyed the game and struck up a friendship with the academy's star promoter of athletics, a cadet one class his senior named Bill Halsey.

Aside from several bouts of pneumonia, Nimitz, his mother's wavy-haired golden boy, took good care of himself. His only serious injury occurred on a summer cruise aboard a destroyer. He developed an abscess in one ear. With no doctor on the ship, the captain ordered an oil syringe from the engine room and squirted boric acid into the affected ear. The light antiseptic seemed to work, even if the cleanliness of the delivery vehicle was suspect. Nimitz experienced a slight deafness for the rest of his life, perhaps the result of the abscess, but more likely an effect of the make-do syringe. In any event, Nimitz adopted his usual positive attitude and learned to compensate by becoming an inconspicuous lip-reader.[5]

There were two other incidents during his Annapolis years that seem to have left a lasting impression on Chester Nimitz's professional development. One commanded national attention; the other was a minor episode that nonetheless underscored a valuable element of Nimitz's leadership style.

Nationally, there was a continuing public debate over the roles Rear Admiral William T. Sampson and Commodore Winfield Scott Schley had played in the Battle of Santiago. Schley had been aboard the cruiser *Brooklyn* on the scene and Sampson momentarily away on his flagship, *New York,* visiting the army. Who, the public debated, deserved to be credited with the victory? (This was one reason why Dewey became the unanimously adored hero of Manila Bay—he had acted alone and without controversy.)

Hot oil was poured on this issue during Nimitz's plebe year at the academy when the third volume of Edgar S. Maclay's *History of the United States Navy* was published and adopted as an academy textbook. Maclay was scathing in his criticism of Schley for "deliberately turning tail and running away" before the *Brooklyn* subsequently turned and engaged the Spanish fleet. The *Brooklyn* had indeed made what other observers considered a deft circular maneuver to check the emerging Spanish fleet; certainly there was no question that the ship joined the *Oregon* in the chase of the *Cristóbal Colón*.[6]

As the partisans of each officer took sides, Schley demanded that the Naval Academy cease using Maclay's book as a text, which it did. But the damage had been done to what otherwise was largely a growing and glowing postwar reputation of the navy. Instead of merely celebrating three heroes—Dewey, Sampson, *and* Schley—the navy was put on public display when Schley demanded a court of inquiry to clear his name. Admiral Dewey had the unwelcome task of presiding over forty days and two thousand pages of testimony. The even greater embarrassment came when the court split in its findings and the entire charade seemed destined to continue. Angered that "his" navy was being made a public spectacle, President Theodore Roosevelt finally slammed his fist and ordered all sides to stand down.

For Nimitz and his classmates, the case provided plenty of fodder for discussion, and there were supporters of both Sampson and Schley. But the lesson Chester Nimitz seems to have taken from this event was that "washing of the Navy's dirty linen in public" was deplorable and should be avoided at all costs.[7] When another war presented other choices of heroes and other courts of inquiry, Nimitz may well have remembered this early lesson.

The other lesson in leadership he learned came from a much more lighthearted event. Nimitz was well known as a "mixer of famous punches"—usually nonalcoholic—and he had no qualms about joining an occasional beer party—quite forbidden, of course.

After his class occupied the newly completed first wing of Bancroft Hall at the start of his senior year, Nimitz and his classmates quickly discovered that its expansive roof offered the perfect, well-concealed beer garden. Procuring such refreshments bordered on child's play, because seniors were granted a "free gate" to make unsupervised treks into downtown Annapolis to visit tailors preparing their post-graduation uniforms.

Lots were routinely drawn for the task of going into Annapolis proper with an empty suitcase and returning with a dozen bottles of cold beer. One Saturday afternoon, despite the fact that he was a "three-striper" company commander with the gold stars of academic excellence on his collar, Nimitz drew the assignment.

He made the trip in uniform—otherwise he would not have been permitted out the gate—and visited his tailor, who was friendly to the cadets' plight and also provided a clandestine beverage service. On this particular occasion, there was another customer, an older, dark-haired gentleman in civilian clothes, in the store. Nimitz paid him no heed, placed his order, and soon returned to his room in Bancroft Hall, "having re-entered the Gate with no more trouble than I had experienced in leaving." The beer party that night was "a great success."

Nimitz gave no further thought to his errand until the following Monday morning, when he marched into his new chemistry class and found his instructor to be the dark-haired stranger—now in uniform as a lieutenant commander newly assigned to the academy. Nimitz squirmed uneasily for a time and assumed he would be summoned before the officer. The summons never came. Even though Nimitz was certain that the officer recognized him, the officer showed no sign of it. "This escapade taught me a lesson," Nimitz later recalled, "to look with lenient and tolerant eye on first offenders when in later years they appeared before me as a Commanding Officer holding Mast."[8]

The beer-garden parties atop Bancroft Hall came to an abrupt end when, due to the urgent need for young officers in Theodore Roosevelt's growing navy, the Annapolis class of 1905 graduated at the end of January instead of in the traditional first week in June.

The term "midshipman" had come to replace "cadet" during Nimitz's tenure, but the navy still required two years of sea duty before awarding the commission of ensign. Thus, Nimitz's class of 114 graduates — of which he stood seventh — went to their first shipboard assignments as "passed midshipmen."

Unlike many of his classmates, Nimitz left behind the assortment of nicknames he had acquired in the course of four years: "Natchew," "Nonnie," "Nim-i-tiz," and, by some accounts, "Natty." What he didn't leave behind was a lifelong camaraderie with his own classmates and those several years ahead or behind him. Sixteen midshipmen in Nimitz's class of 1905 achieved the rank of rear admiral or higher. Other Nimitz contemporaries at Annapolis who would achieve prominence, as well as certain ridicule years later, included Frank Jack Fletcher, John S. McCain, and Raymond A. Spruance.[9]

Because of his class standing, Chester Nimitz was accorded a choice assignment on board the new battleship *Ohio*. Commissioned in San Francisco only the prior October, the *Ohio* was an example of the United States' post–Spanish-American War increase in battleship might. The ship displaced almost thirteen thousand tons and carried main armaments of four 12-inch guns, eight 6-inch guns, and two submerged torpedo tubes. With Nimitz aboard, the *Ohio* departed San Francisco on April 1, 1905, for its assignment as flagship of the Asiatic Squadron. The big battleship's first cruise took it across the Pacific to Manila, where it was soon charged with a semisecret diplomatic assignment.

Late in May came the news that the Japanese had dealt the Russians a deathblow at the Battle of Tsushima. Theodore Roosevelt, who had previously held the Japanese in high regard, was suddenly wary of what the island empire's next move would be. Any nation that could humiliate the Russian bear on both land and sea might well prove capable of challenging U.S. interests in the Philippines or even Hawaii.

The president dispatched the unlikely duo of his mercurial daughter Alice and Secretary of War William Howard Taft to Tokyo. They sailed first to Manila and then embarked on the *Ohio* for the journey north to Japan. While Alice provided the fireworks and held the attention of the press, Taft quietly met with Japanese prime minister Taro Katsura. They discreetly agreed to certain limits of Japan's newfound power vis-à-vis the United States, even as Roosevelt was preparing to act as a neutral mediator between Japan and Russia. Japan, Taft and Katsura agreed, was to have a free hand in Korea—which had been at the heart of the Russo-Japanese War in the first place—but in return, Japan provided Taft with a gentleman's agreement that it would not menace American interests in the Philippines and Hawaii.[10]

Alice Roosevelt was twenty-one at the time, a year older than Nimitz, but it is doubtful that she exchanged so much as a glance with him. She was completely enamored with Congressman Nicholas Longworth, fifteen years her senior and a member of the American delegation. Instead, Nimitz's brush with fame came in Tokyo when officers of the *Ohio* attended a garden party at the imperial palace complete with Russian champagne captured at Port Arthur.

When a table of junior officers saw the victor of Tsushima, Admiral Togo, coming near, it was Nimitz who was pushed forward to invite the admiral to join them. Perhaps with a wry smile, Togo, who spoke fluent English after seven years in England, accepted the invitation and shook hands all around. Nimitz was as impressed by this act of modesty as he was by the admiral's tactical brilliance at Tsushima. He would remember both.[11]

After a year in the Western Pacific, *Ohio* returned to the United States without Nimitz. He stayed in Manila and was briefly assigned to the cruiser *Baltimore,* an aging relic of Admiral Dewey's squadron, while he passed the examinations to receive his commission as an ensign. In January 1907, with commission in hand, Ensign Nimitz was given command of the ninety-two-foot, ex-Spanish gunboat *Panay* and dispatched to cruise the Sulu Archipelago off Mindanao, mostly to show the American flag. His second-in-command, from the Annapolis class just behind him, was John Sidney "Slew" McCain.

In the aftermath of the Spanish-American War, the Philippines officially had become U.S. territory, but among its lesser islands, any semblance of American control was fleeting. Still, Nimitz was proud to command the *Panay* and the tiny naval station of Polloc (now Cotabato) on Mindanao, complete with twenty-two U.S. marines. In fact, Nimitz delighted in honing his seamanship aboard the tiny gunboat. "I can practice piloting and navigation and so forth as well as on a small ship," he wrote his grandfather, "and besides it should teach me a certain amount of self-reliance and confidence."

That self-reliance and confidence were summoned to the forefront on a sultry day in the summer of 1907 when the *Panay* docked at the main U.S. naval base in Cavite, outside Manila. Ensign Nimitz dressed in his whites, buckled on his sword, and reported to the base commander, Rear Admiral Uriah Harris. There were wild rumors of war with Japan, and Harris, a rather stiff, by-the-book individual who never cracked a smile on duty, was taking no chances. He ordered Nimitz to take immediate command of the destroyer *Decatur* and run it to a dry dock in Olongapo, some sixty miles away around the Bataan Peninsula. When Nimitz started to return to the *Panay* for his gear, Harris stopped him mid-stride and sent him directly to the *Decatur* with a gruff, "Your clothes will catch up to you."

So, in sparkling whites, Ensign Nimitz arrived on the run-down destroyer. Nothing was in order and even the engine telegraphs were hooked in reverse so that the first time Nimitz signaled quarter speed astern and tried to back away from the buoy, the ship lunged forward instead. But Nimitz got the job done and made a mark for himself as a doer. Two weeks later, the *Decatur* was out of dry dock and ready for sea. Stuffy Admiral Harris must have been pleased, because he kept Nimitz in command.

Six months later, after weathering the typhoon, the *Decatur* was hard aground on a mudflat at the entrance to Batangas harbor. Nimitz peered over the side into the dark water and ordered full astern. The destroyer shuddered but gave no sign of moving. Turning the helm slowly to port and then to starboard brought no movement either. Finally, Nimitz ordered all stop and pondered his fate. This was definitely a situation that could easily sink a young officer's career.

Then Nimitz, being Nimitz, posted the usual watches and did the only thing that made sense to him. "On that black night somewhere in the Philippines," he later recalled, "the advice of my grandfather returned to me: 'Don't worry about things over which you have no control.' So I set up a cot on deck and went to sleep."[12]

Shortly after dawn the next morning, a passing steamer threw the *Decatur* a line and pulled the ship off the mudflat. That might have been the end of the matter, but regulations dictated that Nimitz report the grounding, which he dutifully did. This set in motion an investigation that relieved him of command of the *Decatur* and required him to face a court-martial for "culpable inefficiency in the performance of duty."

Fortunately for the young ensign, his prior record and performance reviews spoke strongly in his defense. Given those and the inadequacies of the charts for the Batangas area, the charge was reduced to "neglect of duty." Nimitz was found guilty and sentenced to a public reprimand. But even then, the commander of U.S. naval forces in the Philippines concluded that the mere record of the proceedings was enough evidence of a public reprimand and took no further action.

About the only scar on Nimitz's career was the embarrassment of being relieved of command and having to go through the court-martial process. In fact, after three years of continuous service in the Far East, Nimitz was delighted that the end result was that he was ordered home to take a new assignment.

Ironically, he sailed in a derelict gunboat with three others from the Annapolis class of 1905. Their three-month cruise westward across the Indian Ocean, through the Suez Canal, and across the Atlantic to Boston, with numerous ports of call, resembled more of a postgraduation road trip than any prejudicial recall. The only problem, one of the young ensigns later complained, was they "made the trip in half the time we would like to have taken."

But Nimitz was not pleased when he learned of his new assignment. He had requested more duty on battleships. They were the queens of the fleet, and his command experience on the *Panay* and *Decatur* would have put him in good stead for higher responsibility. Instead, the ensign who had just run his ship aground was given duty in submarines, although there is no firm evidence that he was thus assigned as any fallout from the *Decatur* incident.

Submarines were definitely very low on the navy's list of duties, and navy brass would have laughed loudly if someone in 1908 had suggested that they would become a major strategic weapon. The positive side of the posting was that on these much smaller vessels, Nimitz was far more likely to gain another command. So Chester Nimitz maintained his usual positive outlook and took the assignment in stride, even though he would later claim that in those days submarines were "a cross between a Jules Verne fantasy and a humpbacked whale."[13]

CHAPTER FIVE

First Commands

In 1909 as the U.S. Navy basked in the glories of the Great White Fleet, William D. Leahy reported for duty aboard the armored cruiser *California*. Since his baptism of fire at the Battle of Santiago eleven years before, Leahy's career had been typical of promising young officers. He received his commission as an ensign on schedule in 1899 and rotated through duties aboard cruisers and gunboats, achieving his first command on the derelict gunboat *Mariveles* in the Philippines. Next came a year on the supply ship *Glacier,* hauling beef from Australia to American troops occupying that archipelago.

In 1902, Leahy was promoted to lieutenant junior grade (j.g.), and the following year he was assigned to duty on the training ship *Pensacola* in San Francisco. That year, Leahy later wrote, was "the most pleasant and possibly the most eventful year of my life—interesting from every point of view as San Francisco always is to a sailor—and eventful in that I managed during the year to be married to Louise Tennent Harrington."

Louise lived comfortably with her recently widowed mother on the corner of California and Buchanan streets just west of Nob Hill.

Her sister, Mary, was engaged to future admiral Albert P. Niblack, an 1882 graduate of Annapolis and one of Leahy's former officers. Bill was twenty-eight and Louise a few days shy of it when they exchanged vows on February 3, 1904. By then, Leahy had advanced another grade to lieutenant and helped commission the brand-new cruiser *Tacoma*. Six months later, when *Tacoma* was ordered to join the Atlantic Fleet, Leahy swapped assignments with an officer on the cruiser *Boston* in order to remain on the Pacific Coast near Louise, who was expecting.[1]

The next two years took Leahy back and forth between San Francisco and Panama on the *Boston*. Theodore Roosevelt's vision of the Panama Canal was becoming a reality and the president unabashedly stationed capital ships off both coasts of the isthmus to ensure local political stability and overall American control. Lieutenant Leahy missed the birth of his son in October 1904 but happened to be in the Harrington house in San Francisco when the great earthquake of 1906 struck.

The twin themes of his irregular diary entries during these years were the need for better training and the growing threat of Japan. Frequently, they were entwined, as when he speculated that Russia's weakness at Tsushima was a result of poorly trained men. "An untrained man on board a ship in action is of much less value than the space he occupies," Leahy wrote, "and in view of the growing power of Japan in the Orient where our interests must conflict, it would seem wise to look to the training of our men."[2]

In February 1907, Leahy had the opportunity to confront the issue head-on, reporting to Annapolis for duty as an instructor in science. He got a close look at the crop of prospective junior officers under cultivation, but he seems to have been only too glad to rotate out of the academy staff and continue his own naval education. Aboard the *California* late in 1909, he would receive a graduate course in command from Captain Henry T. Mayo, one of the emerging navy's most influential leaders.

Mayo was a combination of old-school manners and twentieth-century vision. Born in Burlington, Vermont, on the shores of Lake Champlain in 1856, he graduated from Annapolis in 1876, a member of one of those meager post–Civil War classes. Mayo took part in the headline search for the Arctic explorer Adolphus Greely and later supervised the first hydrographic survey of Pearl Harbor, but he missed the glories of the brief Spanish-American War while commanding a gunboat on the West Coast. The officers of Roosevelt's increased navy recognized Mayo's potential, however, and after duty aboard the cruiser *Albany* off Central America, he was promoted to captain and given command of the *California*.

Captain Mayo took Leahy back to his early assignment in the forward turret on the *Oregon* and made him *California*'s ordnance officer, setting him firmly on course to become one of the navy's top gunnery experts. Leahy found it a "not altogether agreeable change from navigating officer but a wise one both in view of the experience to be obtained and the insistence of the Captain."[3]

Their first port of call together was Tokyo and the by-now perfunctory audience with Admiral Togo. Unlike Chester Nimitz, who had been impressed with the Japanese admiral, Leahy's impressions more closely mirrored Bill Halsey's. Both thought Japanese hospitality had plenty of show but little genuine warmth. Togo, Leahy recorded in his diary, was "a very ordinary looking Jap with all his gold lace and decorations," but he added that most of the Japanese officers at a large dinner given by the Navy Club "spoke English that one could understand."[4]

Leahy recalled these cruises with Mayo as "perhaps the most valuable and certainly the most agreeable sea duty that I have had." He saw in Mayo qualities that he would emulate in his own commands. In Mayo, he found "a splendid seaman who was also a considerate gentleman and a very capable Naval officer."[5]

By 1910, Leahy was a lieutenant commander and the gunnery officer for the entire Pacific Squadron aboard its flagship, *California*. He proved a strong taskmaster but also a realist. "I have so far been unable to correct apparent faults," the perfectionist Leahy grumbled. "Much could be done by changing some officers that I have neither the rank or influence to reach."[6]

But Leahy was slowly becoming exposed to those who did have rank and influence. Mayo was one, but Leahy had also been introduced to William Howard Taft during Taft's tenure as governor of the Philippines. By the fall of 1911, Taft was well into his only term as president, and Leahy drew the assignment of serving as his temporary naval aide during a four-day visit to San Francisco. With his typical low-key reaction, Leahy confessed, "While it was interesting and instructive to be attached to the President's personal staff, I do not think a permanent assignment to such duty could be either agreeable or valuable."[7] But when Leahy declined another teaching tour at the Naval Academy and instead jumped at the chance to go to Washington as assistant director of target practice and engineering competitions, little did he know how close this assignment would bring him to a future president.

Like Bill Leahy, Ernest J. King was also still enamored with battleships. After leaving the cruiser *Cincinnati* in the Far East, King was almost assigned to a lowly gunboat, but he quickly asked to see the chief of the Bureau of Navigation — essentially the navy's personnel department — in hopes of getting a better assignment. The chief turned out to be King's old commanding officer from the battleship *Illinois,* whose advice about staying aboard King had failed to heed when he sought duty on the *Cincinnati.*

"Admiral," said the aide ushering King into the office, "this is Mr. King, who used to be in the *Illinois.*"

"Yes, I remember him."

"Mr. King wants to go to sea in a battleship," the aide continued.

"That is what I advised him to do some years ago," replied the admiral with a tweak. He held no grudge, however, and King left the interview with an assignment on the battleship *Alabama.*[8]

But before reporting for duty, there was a matter left over from his days at the Naval Academy. Ensign King was still smitten with Martha Rankin Egerton, and she with him. They were married on October 10, 1905, in the chapel at West Point. West Point? Yes, West Point. Mattie was living there with her sister, Florrie, who was married to army lieutenant Walter D. Smith.

The newlyweds' rapture knew no bounds but was short-lived. Mattie, who had been the toast of Annapolis, proved singularly focused on routine family matters and intellectually challenged when it came to other topics. "Dull" was one thing that King never was. His conversations and interests were far-ranging, and his interactions with intelligent and lively people—even if he considered himself more intelligent and lively than anyone else—held sway.

When the infatuation phase passed and Mattie failed to measure up intellectually, King quickly got bored. This didn't stop him from fathering six daughters and one son with her, but his physical and intellectual lust quickly began to scan other harbors. Mattie in turn established a home port in Annapolis near her family and friends and continued to raise their brood there while King sailed all over the world.

There was, however, one aspect of King's interaction with his new brother-in-law that was to color his future views of the army. King struck up a strong friendship with Smith, who eventually became a brigadier general. Together they read books about Napoleon and his marshals, engaged in long discussions about military tactics, and toured Civil War battlefields. The result was that King, who already was fairly convinced that he knew more about the navy than anyone else, now also became convinced that he was an expert on land warfare and generals as well.[9]

One result of King's growing operational confidence was that when he was assigned to staff duty at the Naval Academy after a year on the *Alabama,* he didn't hesitate to put into writing some of his views on shipboard organization—essentially giving division officers more direct command over their men. His contribution to the *United States Naval Institute Proceedings* won the 1909 prize for best essay and got him noticed as a budding authority on naval management. Recognizing the inherent conservatism of the navy, King nevertheless took the command structure to task for "clinging to things that are old because they are old."[10]

After three years on staff at Annapolis, it was time for King to go to sea again. Seeking a command of his own—even if on smaller ships, as Nimitz had done—he applied for destroyers. But Hugo Osterhaus, whose attention King had first attracted by coming alongside the wrong way as a naval cadet, was now a rear admiral.

Recognizing the strong points of King's sometimes overbearing personality, Osterhaus asked him to serve as his flag secretary, essentially the military equivalent of an executive assistant.

Some would have jumped at the chance, but characteristically, King carefully reviewed the political ramifications. First, putting in for sea duty always looked good on one's record. Second, in the still relatively small officer corps, those admirals who were deadwood and a subsequent dead end for their junior officers were readily known. King had already turned down two similar offers because he felt they "would not lead anywhere." But Osterhaus was clearly different, and admirals who were rising stars usually lifted staff officers with them. King deferred his desire for an independent command and said yes to Osterhaus.

King spent a year with Osterhaus, who flew his flag from *Minnesota* as commander of the Third Division of battleships stationed in the Atlantic. When Osterhaus subsequently went to command the Mare Island Naval Shipyard in California, King was assigned to the *New Hampshire* as its engineering officer. But after a year of that, King proved that he had picked his admirals correctly when Osterhaus was appointed commander in chief, Atlantic Fleet, and asked for King to serve again as his flag secretary. Now, as the gatekeeper of all fleet business flowing in and out of the admiral's cabin, King would have growing influence and come to know many senior officers.

Osterhaus came to rely on King's discretion in handling routine correspondence, and this authority only reinforced King's self-important ways. There were limits however. Once, when King found himself without a ride back to the flagship, he ordered the admiral's barge to pick him up across Portsmouth harbor despite the fact that the barge was waiting dockside for Osterhaus. With King aboard, it failed to return on time for the admiral, and King found Osterhaus pacing the dock in a huff. Anyone else would probably have been sent packing, but Osterhaus seems to have genuinely liked *most* of the arrogance that King brought with him and was content simply to admonish him, "Young man, don't you dare to change my orders to my own barge!"[11]

After this second tour with Osterhaus, King went to the U.S. Naval Engineering Experiment Station at Annapolis as its executive officer in the summer of 1912. For the mechanically minded King, it was almost like being back in the railroad shops in Lorain. He delighted in tinkering with everything from boiler corrosion to the integrity of propeller shafts. He even came in contact with the very beginnings of naval aviation. With a congressional appropriation of $25,000, the navy had ordered two land-based airplanes—a Curtiss and a Wright—and one Curtiss amphibian. Three naval officers were dispatched directly to the factories to learn how to fly them.

These planes were based at a modest naval aviation camp adjacent to the station, and King watched their performance with fascination. One of the naval aviators was Lieutenant John H. Towers. King captained a torpedo boat to rescue Towers after a mishap in Chesapeake Bay one afternoon and later made his first flight with him. Despite this friendly beginning, these two egotists would be at odds with each other through most of their careers.

The high-pitched buzzing of these early canvas-covered bird-cages seemed quite remote from the thunderous broadsides of 12-inch guns, but a 1912 report of aviation efforts managed to convey both a deference to the past and a bold prediction for the future. "Those who are engaged in the development of aviation for war purposes do not pretend that it is going to revolutionize warfare," the report reassured the old guard before rushing on to assert, "but it has been fully demonstrated that of two opposing forces, the one which possesses superiority in aerial equipment and skill will surely hold a very great advantage."[12]

In July 1913, after seven years as a lieutenant, King was promoted to lieutenant commander. By the following spring, it looked as if there might be a war with Mexico, and King went to Washington to once again press his request for an independent command. The only vessel available was the relatively new oil-burning destroyer *Terry,* then being held in reserve. King jumped at the chance and joined the ship in Galveston, Texas. Not much came of the Mexican situation as far as the *Terry* was concerned, but King got his first real taste of command sailing back to Charleston, South Carolina, with the entire Reserve Destroyer Flotilla.

The commander of the Second Division was F. T. "Kid" Evans, the son of Admiral Robley "Fighting Bob" Evans of Spanish-American War fame. As the destroyers departed Key West, a strong northeaster made for difficult seas, and the *Terry* struggled to maintain its second position in the column. Evans ordered King to close up, even though the standard distance was three hundred yards. King kept estimating the distance, but Evans finally signaled him to close alongside his leading ship, the *Monaghan*.

Terry surged forward to take up that station, and Evans bellowed at King through a megaphone to hold it there. The only appropriate answer—even for the sharp-tongued King—was a prompt "Aye aye, sir!" and it gave him a crash course in destroyer handling. King "told the officer of the watch to keep so close to *Monaghan* that he would be able to spit from the forecastle to the poop." It worked, and in about an hour, Evans signaled his approval: "*Terry,* well done."[13]

The girl that Ensign William F. Halsey, Jr., had been so anxious to see after the Great White Fleet dropped anchor in Hampton Roads was Frances Cooke Grandy, a belle of Norfolk, Virginia, whose family called her "Fanny." To Bill Halsey, she quickly became just "Fan." Despite the fact that three of Fan's first cousins were among Halsey's friends from his pre-Annapolis year at the University of Virginia, the Grandys were initially skeptical of this Yankee from New Jersey. In part, this was because one of Fan's uncles had been chief engineer on the Confederate ironclad *Merrimac* and at least part of her family was still fighting the Civil War.

Bill and Fan apparently had an understanding before he embarked on his round-the-world voyage. He indeed found her waiting on his return, but not necessarily rushing toward the altar, especially with a lowly ensign. But Halsey soon had an advantage when he passed the examination for lieutenant j.g. and then, because of vacancies in the expanding upper ranks, was immediately jumped another grade, sworn in as a full lieutenant, and given command of the gunboat *Du Pont.*

"Do you realize," Bill lobbied Fan, "you are being offered the heart and hand of a skipper in the United States fleet? How can you afford to delay?"

"Well, now that you make it sound so attractive," Fan said, laughing. "I suppose I would be foolish to procrastinate any longer."

They were married on December 1, 1909, at Christ Church in Norfolk. Among Halsey's ushers were Annapolis grads Thomas C. Hart and Husband E. Kimmel. Thirty-plus years later, after the deadly attack on Pearl Harbor had many calling for Kimmel's neck, Halsey would be among his friend's most vehement supporters. Ten months after the wedding, on October 10, 1910, Bill and Fan welcomed Margaret Bradford Halsey to the family.[14]

Such family bliss saw Bill Halsey flirt with the idea of leaving the navy for a warmer, drier, less uncertain future ashore. But he stayed on, and from 1910, when he reported as executive officer of the destroyer *Lamson,* until June 1932 — except for one year as executive officer of the battleship *Wyoming* — all of Halsey's sea duty was on destroyers.

Like Chester Nimitz's experiences, the best thing about these assignments was that at a very young age, Halsey learned the responsibilities and intricacies of command. As captain of his first ship, the destroyer *Flusser,* he also got a taste of politics.

Flusser was ordered to Campobello Island, off the coast of Maine, to take the new assistant secretary of the navy on a tour of nearby naval installations. Upon returning to the island, the gentleman, who reportedly had some experience in small boats, asked Halsey to transit the strait between Campobello and the mainland and offered to act as pilot himself. Halsey was skeptical and in a bit of a bind. He could hardly say no to his superior, but he was also well aware that "the fact that a white-flanneled yachtsman can sail a catboat out to a buoy and back is no guarantee that he can handle a high-speed destroyer in narrow waters."

Standing close by, Halsey reluctantly relinquished the helm and watched as the assistant secretary began his first turn. The pivot point on the *Flusser* was near the bridge superstructure, and that meant that with roughly two-thirds of the ship's length aft of the pivot, its stern would swing twice the arc of the bow. Clearly, there was much more to this than simply pointing the destroyer's bow down the center of the channel.

Halfway into the turn, the assistant secretary looked aft and checked the swing of the stern just as any seasoned skipper would do. Halsey was relieved and from then on figured that this man knew his business. His name was Franklin D. Roosevelt.[15]

There seems little doubt that Franklin D. Roosevelt intended from an early age to follow his cousin Theodore's footsteps into the White House. What better way to start the journey than by serving as assistant secretary of the navy? When the three-way presidential race of 1912 put Democrat Woodrow Wilson in the White House — defeating Theodore's Bull Moose comeback try — Franklin called in his political markers in New York State and received the appointment. Like his cousin before him, Franklin was nominally subservient to a secretary of the navy who seemed an unlikely fit.

Josephus Daniels was a newspaper publisher from North Carolina who owed his cabinet post to his strong political support of Wilson. With no prior naval experience, he had, however, very decided opinions about how the Navy Department should be managed and its role in U.S. foreign policy. Some labeled Daniels a pacifist, and there is little argument that he was at least a hard-core isolationist. He intended to concentrate on coastal defenses and dramatically retract Theodore Roosevelt's global reach.

As assistant secretary, however, Franklin Roosevelt showed that he was prepared to equal if not surpass cousin Teddy's fervor for a global American navy. Heretofore, no one, not even Theodore, had spoken of challenging Great Britain's long-established naval supremacy. But Franklin was only too willing to stake out such an extreme position in the hope of making a name for himself — shades of his cousin.

Arguing that dreadnought battleships "are what we need," Franklin exhorted, "The policy of our Congress ought to be to buy and build dreadnoughts until our Navy is comparable to any other in the world." His goal was equality at a minimum, not merely ascendancy.

And as for Daniels's coastal defense scheme, Roosevelt thought "our national defense must extend all over the western hemisphere, must go out a thousand miles into the sea, must embrace the Philippines and over the seas wherever our commerce may be."[16]

So it helped the navy tremendously that it was Franklin Roosevelt, far more than his boss, who was inclined to spend time with the fleet. Roosevelt had served no time in the military, never captained a merchantman, and indeed, as Halsey initially suspected, counted his nautical experience at the helms of family yachts, but the sea was in his blood and FDR considered himself a sailor. With the possible exception of Warm Springs, Georgia, he would always find his greatest relaxation upon its restless waves.

Two years later, it was Bill Leahy's turn to captain FDR around. After briefly looking after target practice and engineering competitions, Leahy was recruited as an assistant by his mentor, Henry T. Mayo, now a rear admiral and aide for personnel to Secretary Daniels. This gave Leahy frequent access to both Daniels and Roosevelt, as well as the host of officers lobbying for one assignment or the other.

When his tour was finished, Leahy did his own lobbying and requested command of the new destroyer tender *Melville*. Roosevelt was agreeable to the station, but Daniels overruled him and instead put Leahy in command of the *Dolphin*, the secretary's personal dispatch boat. The downside was that this was something of a beck-and-call messenger service, but the positive aspect was that the Navy Department official doing most of the calling was Assistant Secretary Roosevelt, not Daniels.

This gave Roosevelt and Leahy plenty of occasions to sail together along the East Coast and as far as Campobello during the summers of 1915 and 1916. Doubtless they had at least some conversations about the future of the navy. During an outbreak of polio that summer, Franklin and his wife, Eleanor, kept their children secluded at Campobello longer than usual and then Roosevelt dispatched Leahy and the *Dolphin* to pick them up and take them directly up the Hudson to his home in Hyde Park, New York—a one-way voyage of some six hundred miles with dubious governmental purpose.

It's important to get a mental picture of FDR at the time of his early sails with Bill Leahy. Roosevelt was an energetic and athletic thirty-three-year-old, easily motoring around on his own two legs. About the only similarity between this man who strode purposefully aboard the *Dolphin* and almost demanded his turn at the helm and the wheelchair-bound leader of the Allies three decades later was the pince-nez eyeglasses that perched on the bridge of his nose. The fact that Roosevelt was seven years Leahy's junior didn't stop him from calling the lieutenant commander "Bill." Naval etiquette, as well as Leahy's firm separation of familiarity from duty, demanded that Leahy call FDR either "Mr. Secretary" or "Mr. Roosevelt." But the two hit it off.

Leahy's entries in his diary in those years are sporadic, as well as almost painfully discreet, and he made no mention of Roosevelt, writing only that the *Dolphin* "operated in the Atlantic visiting the Coast of Maine, New York, Norfolk, and Savannah." Years later, however, Leahy acknowledged his "close contact" with Roosevelt on these cruises and wrote that he held "an appreciation of [FDR's] ability, his understanding of history, and his broad approach to foreign problems" and that "there developed between us a deep personal affection that endured unchanged until his untimely death."[17]

As for Secretary Daniels, he may be best remembered for his General Order No. 99. Issued on June 1, 1914, it prohibited alcoholic beverages on board any naval vessel or within any navy yard or station and held commanding officers directly responsible for any violations. With the Prohibition movement sweeping the country and alcohol on navy vessels already limited to officers' messes, this was not, however, quite as radical a measure in practice as it was in the headlines.[18]

The navy's grog ration had gone out before the Civil War, and by 1914 liquor was served only in officers' wardrooms, and then only if an officer wished to purchase it. These "wine messes" were akin to private clubs, where chits were signed and the bill paid monthly. Daniels promised to abolish the messes because they discriminated against enlisted men, who were granted no such access, and because there was some evidence that freedom of drink might corrupt some younger officers — Ernest J. King among them.

Doubtless there were a few impromptu parties on June 30, 1914, the night before the regulation went into effect, and among those mourning were probably Halsey and FDR, the latter of whom was never one to let Prohibition or any other order interfere with his ritual happy hour. King, who had a few run-ins with demon rum early in his career, became one of those who could take it with zest and no morning-after hangover or leave it alone completely— something he did for long periods of time.

But by the end of the summer of 1914, the navy had more on its mind than a mealtime drink. An escalating entanglement of alliances suddenly found Europe at war, despite the fact that the royal leaders of three of the belligerents were related. What role, if any, the United States might play was still murky, but every naval officer knew that the North Atlantic was no longer the barrier it had once been.

CHAPTER SIX

Dress Rehearsal

After grounding the *Decatur* in the Philippines in the summer of 1908, Chester Nimitz reluctantly reported for submarine duty. His characterization of these vessels as "a cross between a Jules Verne fantasy and a humpbacked whale" was slow to change. During his first-class year at Annapolis, Nimitz and his classmates had taken training runs on the Severn River aboard the navy's first commissioned submarine, *Holland*—all fifty-four feet of it—and Nimitz had not been impressed. The only good thing about duty aboard these small "boats"—submarines were never called "ships"—was that they offered plenty of command experience.

Submarines themselves were not particularly new, but neither had they progressed very far in sophistication. The egg-shaped, one-man, hand-driven *Turtle* tried to sink HMS *Eagle,* a sixty-four-gun ship of the line anchored off the tip of Manhattan during the American Revolution. Almost a century later, the Confederate submarine *H. L. Hunley* did in fact sink the Union sloop *Housatonic* in Charleston harbor after ramming it with a torpedo-tipped, harpoon-like device. The resulting concussion waves sank the *Hunley,* too, and its crew was lost.

For the entire nineteenth century, the navies of the world seemed to eschew submarine development out of some foreboding that doing so might disrupt the established dominance of capital surface ships. No one put this matter more succinctly early on than John Jervis, Great Britain's first lord of the Admiralty during the Napoleonic wars. Hearing of Prime Minister William Pitt's infatuation with an early submarine design, Jervis exclaimed, "Pitt is the greatest fool that ever existed to encourage a mode of war which those who command the sea do not want and which, if successful, will deprive them of it."[1]

While upper echelons resisted submarine development, by the late 1890s Assistant Secretary of the Navy Theodore Roosevelt was among those urging the navy to take a closer look. Later, as president, Roosevelt was finally able to do something about it. On August 25, 1905, while he idled at his home, Sagamore Hill, and waited for emissaries to come to terms and end the Russo-Japanese War, Roosevelt embarked on a little diversion. Despite gray skies and choppy seas on Long Island Sound, he descended beneath the waves aboard *Plunger,* the U.S. Navy's second commissioned submarine.

The experience left Roosevelt ecstatic. "Never in my life have I had...so much enjoyment in so few hours," he wrote to his secretary of the navy three days later. But there was much more. "I have become greatly interested in submarine boats," Roosevelt continued. "They should be developed." As for the old guard "at Washington who absolutely decline to recognize this fact and who hamper the development of the submarine boat in every way," the president was quick to order changes. "Worse than absurd" was his discovery that sailors risking their lives on these early craft were not accorded the usual extra pay for sea duty. The president decreed otherwise.[2]

So when Ensign Chester Nimitz reported for duty with the First Submarine Flotilla early in 1909, his assignment at least showed on his record as "sea duty." He assumed command of the *Plunger* and came to grips with one of its basic flaws. *Plunger* and its sisters were powered by gasoline engines on the surface and batteries when submerged. But gasoline proved too volatile a fuel. Not only could it cause disastrous explosions, but also a boat could fill with crippling fumes even when submerged and running on batteries.

Reluctant submariner though he initially was, Nimitz was also always one to embrace the positive in any assignment and put his full energy into it. Characteristically, he assumed the role of problem solver and began a campaign to replace gasoline engines with diesels. The brainchild of the German engineer Rudolf Diesel, diesel engines, too, were in their infancy, but they relied on the heat of compression to ignite the fuel rather than an incendiary spark. (Ironically, the German navy would lag in incorporating this improvement into its own submarine fleet.)

The other recurring theme in submarine development was torpedoes. When Admiral David Farragut damned them and steamed into Mobile Bay during the Civil War, he was only ignoring free-floating and moored mines. No explosive projectiles came speeding toward him. But just after the Civil War, Englishman Robert Whitehead designed the prototype of a self-propelled torpedo powered by compressed air that could be launched underwater.

Fourteen feet long, fourteen inches in diameter, and weighing three hundred pounds, it delivered an eighteen-pound dynamite charge up to seven hundred yards at a speed of six knots. With improvements in directional control, range, speed, and explosive power, Whitehead torpedoes quickly became an offensive staple for navies around the world, albeit still fired from surface ships as the Japanese did at Port Arthur.

The same basic torpedo design was soon put aboard the early *Holland*-class submarines, although the *Plunger* and its six sisters mounted only one torpedo tube each. Bigger boats with more tubes followed, and by 1910 the American navy had commissioned eleven additional submarines of ever-increasing size, still all gasoline powered. Of these, Nimitz commanded the 105-foot *Snapper*, with two torpedo tubes, and the 135-foot *Narwhal*, which mounted four tubes. By then, Whitehead's successors were mixing pure alcohol and water with compressed air to produce a high-pressure steam that turned a turbine connected to the propeller shaft. This improved weapon still left a telltale wake of air bubbles, but it could carry a heavier explosive payload over a much greater distance.[3]

By the fall of 1911, the twenty-six-year-old Nimitz, now a full lieutenant, returned from sea duty aboard the *Narwhal* and was ordered to the shipyard at Quincy, Massachusetts, to oversee the installation of diesel engines in *Skipjack,* the navy's first diesel-powered submarine. Nimitz was to assume command after its commissioning, and he took some satisfaction in knowing that the navy had come around to his way of thinking about the older gasoline-powered boats.

But before taking *Skipjack* to sea, Nimitz was introduced over a bridge game to Catherine Freeman, the daughter of a ship broker. It was not necessarily love at first sight—Catherine's older sister, Elizabeth, was the star attraction for young naval officers—but Catherine was intrigued by "the handsomest person I had ever seen in my life." She described the young submarine captain as having "curly, blond hair, which definitely was a little bit too long because he had just come in from weeks at sea and had not had a chance to have it cut." She "kept thinking what a really lovely person this was,"[4] and by the time *Skipjack* was ready for sea the following spring, Chester and Catherine had begun a lifelong ritual of writing each other daily letters whenever they were apart.

On March 20, 1912, *Skipjack* was conducting normal surface operations in Hampton Roads, when W. J. Walsh, a fireman second class, lost his footing and slipped overboard. It quickly became apparent from Walsh's thrashing that he was not a swimmer and was in immediate danger. Nimitz saw the situation and without hesitation jumped into the water. He reached the sailor with a few strong strokes, but between Walsh's panic and the tide, Nimitz could not fight their way back to the *Skipjack.* Instead, it suddenly looked as if they both might be swept out to sea. With grim determination, Nimitz kept Walsh afloat until a boat from the nearby battleship *North Dakota* finally picked up both of them.

It was an act of personal courage typical of Nimitz, but it also set the naval base at Hampton Roads buzzing with the story of an officer who had risked his life for an enlisted man. Nimitz, however, was never one to draw such distinctions. The Treasury Department later awarded him its Silver Lifesaving Medal, but with his usual modesty Nimitz simply reported to Catherine the next day, "I had to go swimming yesterday, and it was awfully, awfully cold."[5]

That same spring, Nimitz was invited to address the Naval War College in Newport, Rhode Island, on the subject of defensive and offensive tactics of submarines. It was a highly unusual honor for a twenty-seven-year-old lieutenant, but it showed again that his willingness to work hard in whatever assignment he drew had its rewards. The lecture was classified, but Nimitz became a published author when an expanded, nonclassified version appeared in the *United States Naval Institute Proceedings* the following December.

In keeping with generally accepted naval thinking, Nimitz did not presage any great strategic role for submarines, but he certainly recognized their growing offensive importance. "The steady development of the torpedo," he wrote, "together with the gradual improvement in the size, motive power, and speed of submarine craft of the near future will result in a most dangerous offensive weapon, and one which will have a large part in deciding fleet actions."

In addition to those smaller submarines slated for harbor and coastal defenses, Nimitz foresaw the development of what would become the "fleet type" submarine, capable of "the same cruising radius as a modern battleship" and easily able to "accompany a sea-keeping fleet of battleships." He also showed his tactical creativity by suggesting a "ruse" whereby escorts might "drop numerous poles, properly weighted to float upright in the water, and painted to look like a submarine's periscope." Nimitz speculated that these decoys might divert an enemy fleet into other waters where submarines were lurking to make an offensive strike.

Interestingly enough, in this era of early radio communications, Nimitz described an elaborate, thirty-foot-tall radio mast that transmitted and received up to fifty miles and could be "taken down ready for submergence in five (5) minutes," a far cry from the crash dives of thirty years later.[6]

Service in the *Skipjack* and later the *Sturgeon* also made Nimitz by necessity something of an expert in diesel engines. In fact, when the navy decided to experiment with diesel engines in larger surface ships as the transition from coal-fired steam to oil-fired steam was being completed, he was judged the navy's leading diesel expert, and the year before the outbreak of war in Europe, he was dispatched to Germany to inspect Rudolf Diesel's operations.

Upon his return to the United States, Nimitz was assigned to the Brooklyn Navy Yard to supervise the installation of two 2,600-horsepower diesel engines in the new oil tanker *Maumee*. He and Catherine were married by then, and their first child, daughter Catherine Vance, was born on his birthday in 1914. A year later, he was still working on the *Maumee* when his son, Chester Jr., was born.

Like Bill Halsey, Chester Nimitz now flirted with leaving the navy. He had a devoted wife and a wonderful, growing family. What's more, his diesel expertise made him highly sought after by private industry. His navy pay of $240 per month, plus a $48 quarters allowance, paled alongside the $25,000-a-year, five-year contract he was reportedly offered by the Busch-Sulzer Brothers Diesel Engine Company of St. Louis. In fact, had Nimitz played the negotiation game, he might have commanded much more. Instead, after scarcely thinking it over, the quiet, self-effacing Nimitz merely said, "No, I don't want to leave the navy."[7]

With this diesel work on the *Maumee,* Nimitz was a hands-on officer just as he always was. It wasn't unusual to find him in overalls and with dirty hands working next to his men. Once, when a scaffold collapsed, he was knocked unconscious and buried under a pile of lumber. But that wasn't the most serious injury he sustained.

One day, Lieutenant Nimitz had dressed in his whites to give a tour to a group of visiting engineers from all over the country. To keep his hands clean, he put on a pair of heavy, canvas gloves. When one of the engineers asked a question about the exhaust system, Nimitz pointed to the spot in question, as he had done many times. But on this occasion a fingertip of his thick gloves caught between two gears and pulled his finger in after it. The only thing that saved his hand from being chewed to pieces was his Annapolis class ring, which caught in the gears and gave him an instant to jerk his hand away. As it was, he lost two sections of the ring finger on his left hand and was a bloody mess by the time he arrived at the hospital. Characteristically, he wanted to return to finish his tour after being stitched up, but the doctor convinced him otherwise.[8]

By the time the *Maumee* was finally commissioned, the war in Europe had been raging for more than two years. At the outset, submarines seemed to be the least of anyone's concerns. The world's navies combined could muster only about four hundred boats, and most of these were aging gasoline-powered relics unsafe for combat or just about anything else. France led the way, but in numbers only. Its 123 boats were hardly fit to operate beyond sight of its coast. Great Britain floated 72 subs, but only 17 were newer diesel boats. Russia ranked third in numbers but could barely match France in effectiveness. The United States stood fourth with 34, one-third of them diesel powered, thanks in part to Nimitz's influence. Finally, there was Germany. Admiral Alfred von Tirpitz had long been skeptical of the *Unterseeboot* (undersea boat), or U-boat, and half of the Imperial German Navy's 26 vessels were aging smoke-belchers run on kerosene, while the other half were largely untried diesels, many still undergoing shakedown cruises.

At the outset of the war, as befit its role as mistress of the seas, Great Britain used its naval might to impose a blockade against Germany. It was all quite civilized and chivalrous. Under centuries-old international law, British warships had the right to stop any German merchant ship attempting to run the blockade, conduct its crew and passengers to safety, and then either sink or capture the vessel. Neutral vessels were subject to "stop and search" to ascertain that they were not carrying war materials or were not German ships flying a neutral flag as a disguise.

In response, Germany sortied ten of its older submarines to punch a hole in the British blockade. On this first concerted submarine attack in naval history, two U-boats were lost to the elements, and the remainder limped home without recording any damage. Von Tirpitz may well have sniffed and said, "I told you so."

But a month later, *U-9,* another older boat, happened upon three aging British cruisers steaming on a straight course at 10 knots. The U-boat fired two torpedoes at the lead cruiser and scored two hits. The cruiser rolled over and sank in less than thirty minutes. But then the *U-9*'s captain watched in amazement as the other two cruisers, supposing their companion had hit a mine, stopped dead in the water to lower boats and rescue survivors. *U-9* fired two more torpedoes into each of the remaining cruisers, and they quickly settled under the waves. In less than an hour, the British navy had lost three cruisers and fourteen hundred men. Now the fledgling U-boat flotilla had von Tirpitz's attention.

U-boat proponents on the German Imperial Admiralty Staff proposed that Germany ring the British blockade with a wider U-boat blockade of its own. But there were problems with that approach. For starters, Germany's twenty-four remaining U-boats were hardly enough, and stopping suspected neutrals might well expose the U-boats to aggressive countermeasures, not to mention the issue of how to dispose of the numerous passengers. But such chivalry was about to go out the window. It was about to become a different kind of war.

On February 4, 1915, Germany announced a "war zone" around the British Isles and warned that all British ships within it would be sunk. While Germany declared that it would not specifically target neutrals, it also warned that it might be hard to tell the difference from a periscope and that neutrals entering the zone would do so at their own risk. The unlimited scope and concomitant audacity of this new type of warfare was brought home a few months later when the British passenger liner *Lusitania* was torpedoed off the coast of Ireland. It sank quickly, with a loss of nearly 1,200 men, women, and children, including 126 Americans.

Swayed by international condemnation over the *Lusitania*, Germany temporarily backed off its U-boat campaign. When it renewed its efforts early in 1916 to try to force a victory in France, another civilian vessel, the French cross-Channel packet *Sussex,* was hit by a torpedo, with the loss of fifty lives. Once again, the world cried foul and Germany again reduced its U-boat operations, even as newer and faster boats were rolling down the ways of its shipyards.

By early 1917, the European war was well into its third year of stalemate in the trenches of France. Try as it might, and despite the massive Battle of Jutland, the German navy had been unable to defeat the British Grand Fleet decisively in the North Sea. Germany had to do something to break the British blockade, and it chose to unleash an unrestricted campaign of submarine warfare.

On February 1, fifty-seven U-boats put to sea, and for the remainder of the war, an average of thirty-five to forty boats were on station at all times. The initial result was a shock to Allied morale, as well as to shipping tonnage. One thousand Allied merchant ships totaling almost two million tons were sunk during the next three months. U.S. ambassador to Great Britain Walter H. Page intoned the obvious: "The submarine is the most formidable thing the war has produced — by far." It threatened an "absolute and irremediable disaster."

But this unrestricted submarine warfare by the Germans against *all* shipping also brought the United States into the war and united all but America's most extreme isolationists in a way that the attack on Pearl Harbor would do a generation later. On April 6, 1917, at the peak of the U-boat offensive, President Woodrow Wilson tossed aside his slogan of "He kept us out of war" and asked Congress to declare war on Germany in response to numerous attacks on American ships.

Congress readily obliged, and the U.S. Navy dusted off its contingency plan for war with Germany, code-named Plan Black. Plan Black called for assembling American battleship might in the Atlantic and destroying the advancing German fleet in one grand battle à la Togo at Tsushima. But Germany was not Russia, and the bulk of its battleship fleet, far from crossing the Atlantic, was cautiously hidden away in German harbors. After the Battle of Jutland, Kaiser Wilhelm was willing to challenge the Royal Navy only sparingly in the North Sea, let alone sail his fleet across an unruly ocean to fight the United States.

Recognizing that most nations prepare to fight the latest war and are inevitably forced to adapt when the next one comes, Rear Admiral William S. Sims, the U.S. Navy's highest-ranking officer in the

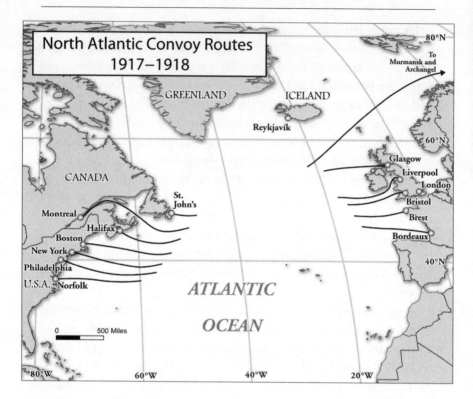

British Isles, put it rather bluntly. Sims urged the rapid deployment of as many destroyers as possible to the seas around Britain for anti-submarine warfare and the institution of a convoy system to better protect merchant ships on the Atlantic crossing.

Ambassador Page told President Wilson much the same thing. "If the present rate of destruction of shipping goes on," Page wrote, "the war will end before a victory is won.... The place where it will be won is in the waters of the approach to this Kingdom [Great Britain]—not anywhere else."

At first, the American naval hierarchy was incredulous, certain that Sims was way off base and had duped Page in the process. Thinking this was the Spanish-American War all over again, the admirals in Washington clung to the idea of one pitched battleship encounter. But as shipping losses continued at a deadly pace, something had to change. U.S. destroyers were finally rushed across the

Atlantic, and the British, who had dragged their feet in implementing the convoy system in part out of fear of massing potential targets for German surface raiders, first instituted the convoy system on a Gibraltar-to-London run on May 20, 1917. By September, convoys were in general use on both sides of the Atlantic.[9]

By then, Nimitz was deep in the middle of the North Atlantic as executive officer and chief engineer on the *Maumee*. Diesel engines for surface ships was an idea that never got very far, but under Nimitz's watch the *Maumee* performed admirably and led the way with a far more important innovation—refueling at sea.

Heretofore, while on duty in the Gulf of Mexico, the *Maumee* had simply stayed at anchor while its customers came alongside to refuel. But now, given the vastness of the North Atlantic and thirsty destroyers both shepherding convoys and chasing after real and suspected U-boats, the fueling station had to come to them. As with his push for diesels in submarines, Nimitz was an early proponent of underway refueling and he worked with the crew of the *Maumee* to craft equipment for a full range of procedures.

Maumee was on station in the North Atlantic to refuel the first six American destroyers dispatched to Great Britain. It was tricky and dangerous work. "Spring and early summer in this area is no time for a vacation," Nimitz later wrote. "Icebergs are numerous and there is much drifting ice. Strong and bitter-cold winds prevail, and there are few days of smooth seas."[10]

But in this storm-tossed environment, *Maumee* was up to the challenge, and by July had refueled all thirty-four of the American destroyers ordered to Queenstown (now Cobh), Ireland, for antisubmarine duty. Such underway replenishing would become indispensable twenty-five years later when the U.S. Navy was flung across the wide Pacific, and Nimitz could say that he had been involved from the very start of such operations.

One destroyer skipper who was not yet in the North Atlantic but who was champing at the bit to sail was Lieutenant Commander William F. Halsey, Jr. After cruising around Campobello Island with Franklin Roosevelt, Halsey had taken command of the destroyer *Jarvis* and refined his tactics and techniques under William S. Sims, then commander of the Atlantic Fleet Destroyer Flotilla.

When the war started in Europe, *Jarvis* was assigned patrol duty off New York harbor. During these days, Halsey's seamanship was never in question. By his own account, he was once running through thick fog when "a hunch too strong to be ignored" caused him suddenly to order, "Full speed astern!" When the *Jarvis* settled to a stop, Halsey hailed a nearby fisherman and asked his position. "If you keep going for half a mile," came the reply, "you'll be right in the middle of the Fire Island Life Saving Station!"

"What caused me to back my engines," Halsey recalled years later, "was probably a feeling of drag from the shoaling water, or the sudden appearance of large swells off the stern; but something told me I had to act and act fast." And that innate sense of the sea, as well as his commanding presence, was more than enough to make his crew follow him willingly anywhere his can-do demeanor and confident swagger led.

But before the United States entered the war, Halsey was assigned to shore duty as the disciplinary officer at the Naval Academy. Bill Halsey had not pushed the disciplinary limits during his own academy days as much as Ernie King had, but neither was Halsey one to take any great delight in enforcing what would later be called "Mickey Mouse" regulations. He found the shore duty less than challenging.

The highlight of his tour at Annapolis may have been the birth of his son, William Frederick Halsey III, on September 8, 1915. It was a great family time with Fan, four-year-old Margaret, and young Bill, but by the following year, Halsey was clearly bored "nursing midshipmen" and desperately yearned to get back to sea. By the time the United States officially entered the war in April 1917, Halsey's yearning had turned to an obsession. For nine months, he sat with his gear laid out and waited for orders. Finally, he learned that Sims, his old commander, was leading the destroyer deployment to Europe and that he had Halsey on a short list of officers he wanted assigned to his command. So, Bill Halsey celebrated Christmas with Fan and their children and then shipped off to Queenstown, Ireland, arriving there on January 18, 1918.

Halsey spent what was called a "makee-learn" month as an executive officer on a destroyer pulling convoy duty. There was the occasional rescue or submarine hunt, but mostly the destroyer sailed west with an outbound convoy to the usual limit of U-boat activity—about five hundred miles west of Ireland—and then picked up an inbound convoy to escort back east. The normal routine was five days at sea and then three days in Queenstown to enjoy the liquid hospitality of the Royal Cork Yacht Club.

After this quick apprenticeship, Halsey was given command of the destroyer *Benham* and then the *Shaw*. Convoy duty continued, along with chases of suspected U-boats. Although Halsey later admitted that he never actually saw a U-boat, his ships dropped their share of depth charges. "First egg I have laid," he recorded in his diary. Later, when his seniority put him in command of two U.S. destroyers and two British sloops, he confessed that he "had the time of my life bossing them around." It was Halsey's first experience in multiple command in a war zone, and he was "proud as a dog with two tails."[11]

The member of the foursome who would sit atop the American naval hierarchy twenty-five years later, and who gained the most insight into fleet operations during World War I, was Ernest J. King. After his baptism piloting the *Terry* back from the Gulf of Mexico, King considered himself a destroyer man and got command of the new one-thousand-ton *Cassin,* which was assigned to the Atlantic Fleet Destroyer Flotilla. In short order, he became the commander of a four-ship division. The war had begun in Europe, but the United States was still a declared neutral.

In 1915, King got a summons, much as William D. Leahy had earlier received, from Henry T. Mayo, who by now was a vice admiral and commander, Battleship Force, Atlantic Fleet. Once again, King mulled over the politics: Should he stay with destroyers and hope to get into the fight, or accept a staff appointment with Mayo? This decision was easy, however, as Mayo was definitely considered an up-and-comer and the probable commander in chief, Atlantic Fleet, by the following summer.

King reported to Mayo's staff in December 1915 as staff engineer, but he was by then far more interested in operational planning than mechanics. When the admiral's staff produced a fleet plan dictating each destroyer's course and speed, King boldly challenged it as unnecessary supervision. Surely, King argued, destroyer captains were capable of devising their individual operations within the broader fleet directives. The next morning, King was hauled before a peeved Admiral Mayo, who might well have told him to mind his own duties or pack his seabag. Instead, the admiral heard King out and agreed to test his captains with more discretion as to their own ships.

In King's mind, he was taking a page from his hero, Napoleon, who instructed his marshals in the grand strategy but permitted them certain discretion in its implementation on their particular piece of the battlefield. To King's credit—and perhaps relief—the destroyer captains performed admirably on their own initiative, and King's standing with Admiral Mayo increased as a result.

Thus, when the United States finally entered the war and Mayo had indeed become commander in chief, Atlantic Fleet, King was right at his side, supervising the required buildup of men and ships and completing the transition from coal- to oil-fired propulsion plants. But King's most valuable experience may have come when he and Mayo sailed for Europe in August 1917 and confronted the issue of how the Americans might best work together with their new British allies.

Admiral Sims was already in Great Britain rushing destroyers into service and implementing the convoy system. For a time, Sims feared that Mayo might assume direct tactical command in Europe and push him aside. But instead Mayo, with King in tow, embarked on a round of diplomatic visits both in Great Britain and on the continent. During these visits, King formed his first impressions of the British general staff and its rather ponderous, ritualistic way of doing business over elaborate lunches and dinners—both floated with ample spirits. The no-nonsense King was not particularly impressed, and this early exposure would color his later reactions when he was a key participant at Allied planning conferences during World War II.

Mayo and King, who by now was a commander and serving as Mayo's deputy chief of staff, also spent their share of time as guests of the Royal Navy. Its battleships and cruisers were still impressive, but they hadn't seen action against the German navy since the Battle of Jutland in 1916, when neither side had been willing to risk the all-out, Nelson-like tactics that may have been the price of complete victory. Despite some 250 ships on both sides, the direct dreadnought-to-dreadnought clash to the death never occurred. The survivors in the German fleet were quickly spirited away to safe ports for the duration, and Great Britain, while it lost more ships and sailors, retained control of the North Sea and the integrity of its German blockade. But there were many critics on the British side who were certain that the Admiralty had parried here and there during the action and lost the chance to annihilate the Germans in another Tsushima.[12]

So the Royal Navy now paraded its battle fleet in routine North Sea maneuvers while Mayo and King had plenty of time to ponder the lost opportunity of Jutland and the future of such fleet-to-fleet encounters. With submarines a threat, and on one occasion King came under enemy fire from aircraft, it was clear that naval warfare was changing. King was a willing pupil under Mayo's tutelage, and he continued to advocate the ongoing study of strategy and evolving tactics for *all* naval officers so that they would be prepared for these changes.

As always, King could be brash, arrogant, argumentative, and even hostile to juniors *and* superiors who failed to measure up to his way of thinking. His volcanic temper with his own subordinates became legendary, and King also bristled and frequently argued with any criticisms that came his way from senior officers.

Admiral Mayo seems to have been one of the few officers in the entire navy whom King truly respected and admired. By King's own admission, Mayo's influence on his career "was more decisive than that of any other officer that he had encountered." This may well have been because Mayo came to refine and espouse the management principles that King himself had proposed some years before in his prizewinning essay on shipboard management.

According to King, the lesson he learned from Mayo that most influenced his later career was "a proper realization of 'decentralization of authority' and the 'initiative of the subordinate.'" To Mayo, this meant "passing down the chain of command the handling of all details to the lowest link in the chain which could properly handle them," while keeping in hand matters of policy and strategic importance.

Reminiscing about Mayo on the admiral's eightieth birthday some twenty years later, King, by then himself an admiral, recalled that Mayo "had an exceptionally open mind, he was always willing to hear all sides of a situation and to discuss any matter of moment." But while Mayo trusted his subordinates, he also required of them "due performance of their proper responsibilities."

There was never any doubt, King continued, that Mayo was always the commander in chief. He alone was in charge. King may well have been describing the goals to which he aspired in his own commands, but only time would tell whether he was truly able to emulate his mentor or simply pick and choose from among his attributes.[13]

By and large, World War I for the U.S. Navy proved a very focused and linear affair. The line ran across the North Atlantic between the East Coast and Great Britain and became a conduit of men, materiel, and provisions to both Britain and France, as well as to Russia. Thus, the navy's role became primarily one of convoy duty and antisubmarine warfare, just as Admiral Sims had urged. The proud U.S. battleships steamed about and one division was temporarily assigned to assist the British fleet, but there was no great clash for the American fleet reminiscent of Dewey at Manila Bay or Togo at Tsushima.

The Americans, however, also decided to dispatch a submarine flotilla to Great Britain. Consequently, the order went out in August 1917 to Chester Nimitz, now a lieutenant commander, to report as engineering aide to Captain Samuel S. Robison, the commander of Submarine Force, Atlantic Fleet. Robison appreciated Nimitz's mechanical abilities, but this staff assignment also exposed Nimitz to a wider view of the navy's command structure. It got him out of the engineering room and started up the ladder of command.

The deployment of U.S. submarines to Europe during World War I was of little military importance, but it gave Robison and Nimitz a close-up opportunity to study the tactics and engineering of both British and German boats. Interestingly enough, in this early period of submarine warfare, the countermeasure that had the highest percentage of effective kills against enemy submarines was opposing submarines. Three hundred Allied destroyers and sub chasers deployed exclusively to hunt U-boats sank forty-one, but an average force at sea of thirty-five Allied subs accounted for eighteen German sinkings.

There is no question that both sides in World War I learned the growing importance of the submarine. Certainly, the Germans saw how close they had come to choking off Great Britain. The Allies belatedly embraced countermeasures and convoy tactics that would be ready at the outbreak of the next conflict. In the final analysis, of course, the greatest naval lesson of the war may have been to prove once again Alfred Thayer Mahan's thesis of the importance of sea power—however evolving—on history. It would be even more essential to the defense or conquest of nations in future struggles.[14]

Some would call the recent conflict "the war to end all wars," but for the American navy, World War I was only a dress rehearsal for a much deadlier and far-reaching conflict two decades later. When that conflict came, the submarines and aircraft that had come of age during World War I would become strategic weapons far outclassing the heftiest of battleships. And the four sailors who traced their bonds to their years at the U.S. Naval Academy would be catapulted into positions of leadership and responsibility the likes of which they could not have imagined during their days at Annapolis.

PART II

SHIPS

1918–1941

It is, in my opinion, time now to get the Fleet ready for sea, to make an agreement with the British Navy for joint action, and to inform the Japanese that we expect to protect our Nationals.

—ADMIRAL WILLIAM D. LEAHY,
Chief of Naval Operations, 1937

Two Vought O2U-2 Corsair biplanes of Marine Scouting Squadron 14 fly by the *Saratoga* (CV-3) while preparing to land, circa 1930. (Naval History and Heritage Command, NH94899)

CHAPTER SEVEN

Battleships

The race to build bigger, faster, and more powerful battleships — particularly between Great Britain and Germany — had fueled the competition that had erupted into global war. Now, in its aftermath, battleships were still the queens of the seas, but their supremacy, which Theodore Roosevelt had trumpeted with the Great White Fleet, had been called into question.

Of the foursome who would sit atop the U.S. Navy twenty years later, it was the senior member, William D. Leahy, who clung to the power of battleships the longest. In part, this was because Leahy was the oldest of the quartet and his Naval Academy indoctrination in these ships had been honed by the *Oregon*'s rush around Cape Horn and subsequent Spanish-American War victories. It may also have been that of the four, Leahy saw the least direct action during World War I — not for lack of trying — and hence had less exposure to the emerging power of submarines and aircraft.

In 1916, Leahy was ordered to take the *Dolphin* to the Caribbean. For a year, he shuttled among its islands, monitoring a revolution in Haiti, assisting in the U.S. acquisition of the Virgin Islands from

Denmark, and keeping tabs on suspected German raiders. By the time he was recalled and assigned to the *Nevada* as its executive officer, the battleship was bound not for the wartime North Atlantic, but for an extended overhaul in dry dock.

Leahy pleaded with his superiors to get him into the action, and he was finally allowed to make one crossing of the Atlantic as captain of the transport *Princess Matoika*—a former German liner. He returned to Great Britain and France a second time in July 1918 to observe naval gunnery before reporting to Washington as director of gunnery and engineering exercises. Leahy's gunnery expertise—now extending over a twenty-year career—was well recognized, and it reinforced his views as a proponent of battleships. And battleships, despite the growing awareness of submarines and airpower, were still very much on the minds of the U.S. naval command, especially when it came to the question of what would happen to defeated Germany's fleet.[1]

In the armistice terms ending hostilities, the Allies demanded the immediate surrender of a sizable portion of the German fleet. Ten battleships, six battle cruisers, and six light cruisers that Germany had dared not risk after the Battle of Jutland were unceremoniously steamed to the sprawling British naval base at Scapa Flow on the northern tip of Scotland. There they dropped anchor and waited. Germany also turned over fifty destroyers and all its submarines to the British.

The Germans considered these ships temporary hostages to ensure their good behavior until a peace treaty could be negotiated. In fact, Great Britain and France had no intention of ever releasing the ships, a point brought home when the subsequent Treaty of Versailles mandated that the German navy also deliver an additional eight battleships, eight light cruisers, forty-two destroyers, and a bevy of torpedo boats. Henceforth, according to the Versailles terms, Germany was to float no more than six aging predreadnoughts, six light cruisers, and a dozen each of destroyers and torpedo boats. For all practical purposes, the German navy would cease to exist.

This rankled Germany to its core, but nowhere did the terms fall more heavily than on the captains of the German ships anchored in Scapa Flow. Had this outcome been foreseen, they might well have chosen initially to fight their way into Scapa Flow with all guns blazing. Now their only real recourse was to deprive the Allies of their ships.

At 11:15 a.m. on June 21, 1919, while the majority of the British fleet was out of the harbor on maneuvers, a prearranged signal fluttered up the mast of the light cruiser *Emden*. "Paragraph eleven, confirm," it read innocuously, but every captain in the impounded German fleet knew that this was the order to open all sea cocks and scuttle their ships. Before the remaining British ships on station could intervene, the German vessels settled into the deep waters of Scapa Flow and, save for a grim collection of masts, vanished from sight. Four hundred thousand tons of naval might went down without a fight.

At first, there was a good deal of Allied outrage at this clandestine maneuver. They had clearly been deprived of the spoils of war. But on closer examination, some in Allied councils held that the Germans had actually done them a favor. Dividing the captured vessels among the victors would likely have led to considerable bickering, and even if the United States and Great Britain had gotten the lion's share, assimilating four or five additional battleships with different armaments and machinery into their fleets would have been problematic and promised nothing but continuing headaches.

On the other hand, the Germans could not be allowed to retain such a potent force — the country may well have been defeated, but the largely unscathed navy certainly had not been. Sinking the German fleet solved both these problems, and the fact that the Germans had done it themselves made it all the more palatable.[2]

With the disposition of the German fleet a nonissue, the remaining naval powers pondered what would happen next. For a short time, it appeared that the United States might lead a naval rearmament race for which neither Great Britain nor Japan had much appetite — the former because it was financially exhausted by the just-ended war and the latter because it wanted nothing more at this point than to consolidate its control over former German mandates in the Marianas, Caroline, and Marshall Islands. As a nominal member of the Allied powers, Japan had acquired these islands, minus Guam (in the Marianas), under the Treaty of Versailles.

But instead, when Republican Warren Harding's isolationist administration came to power in 1920, it engineered an almost complete turnaround in foreign policy. These Republicans blocked Woodrow Wilson's dream of a League of Nations, but not without having very decided views of their own as to how the postwar world should look.

Harding's secretary of state, Charles Evans Hughes, soon issued a call for a disarmament conference among the World War I victors: the United States, Great Britain, Japan, France, and Italy. (The sixth power that had been considered a World War I ally was Russia, but it was deep in the throes of civil war, and its navy had yet to recover from Tsushima.)

Of these, Japan proved the most reluctant participant. It was no secret that there had been friction between Japan and the United States even before the Russo-Japanese War. But Japan could neither afford an arms race with the United States nor risk losing its hard-won status as a first-rate power should it decline to attend. Consequently, representatives of these five countries met in Washington on November 12, 1921, to craft a new world order based on limited naval might.

Laying the entire American disarmament proposal on the table at the start, Hughes suggested limiting future capital ship construction and scrapping certain existing vessels, to result in a 5:5:3 ratio among the United States, Great Britain, and Japan. The eventual aim was to stabilize the world's navies at a total tonnage of 500,000 tons each for the United States and Great Britain; 300,000 tons for Japan; and 175,000 tons each for France and Italy. Among the key provisions, all signatories would honor a ten-year moratorium on building capital ships; total aircraft carrier tonnages would be limited by similar ratios; and no capital ships would exceed 35,000 tons or carry armaments larger than 16-inch guns.

When the treaty was completed, its fine print provided a number of exceptions. The British were allowed to complete the 45,000-ton battleship *Hood*, which for nearly two decades was the largest warship afloat. Japan could complete the 43,000-ton *Mutsu*, in return. The principal U.S. exception allowed for the completion of the 33,000-ton aircraft carriers *Lexington* and *Saratoga*, even though they were over the prescribed 27,000-ton carrier limit.

Significantly, an American proposal to extend the 5:5:3 ratio from battleships down to cruisers and lesser vessels failed because both Great Britain and Japan were well ahead of the United States in existing cruisers. Likewise, Great Britain's distaste for the horrors wrought by German submarines prompted it to attempt to limit their use against merchant ships, but France refused to ratify the provision.

That left the nonfortification clause of the proposed treaty, which was aimed squarely at the broad reaches of the Pacific. Beyond what Japan might do in its home islands and the United States in Hawaii, the signatories agreed not to fortify bases on their island possessions, including such American linchpins as Wake, Guam, and, most important of all, the Philippines.

The U.S. Navy high command was furious about this decision. Just because the United States had not done much to fortify these territories in the quarter century since their acquisition in the Spanish-American War, it did not mean that the navy was willing to abrogate all pretense of their defense. Hughes and his supporters in Congress assumed that it was worth the risk, however, if it kept Japan from fortifying its newly acquired islands. A few years later, of course, Japan would do exactly that without regard for the Washington treaty.

So the Five-Power Naval Limitation Treaty was signed, and pacifists around the world hailed it as the start of a millennium of peace. But a closer look showed its disquieting downside. Although Great Britain, after two centuries of maritime supremacy, finally agreed to naval parity with the United States, future friction between these two countries seemed unlikely. The far bigger concern was how Japan's actions might affect both British and American interests from Hong Kong to Manila, not to mention Australia and even India.

These concerns were well known and freely discussed. As early as 1917, Frederick McCormick published *The Menace of Japan*, and the same year as the Washington Conference, Walter B. Pitkin's book asked, *Must We Fight Japan?* Ironically, Franklin D. Roosevelt was one of those voicing optimism about future relations with Japan. "Shall We Trust Japan?" Roosevelt asked rhetorically in a magazine article. Citing Japan's willingness to join the Washington Conference and noting that there was "enough commercial room" in the Pacific "for both Japan and us well into the indefinite future," Roosevelt answered his question in the affirmative.[3]

But with the benefit of hindsight, it can be argued that what the Washington Conference really did was tie the hands of the U.S. Navy for more than a decade and provide Japan with a closer ratio to American might than it would have enjoyed had the Americans embarked on a major naval buildup or, at the very least, not limited new ship construction. That was not, however, the domestic sentiment of the times, and Theodore Roosevelt no doubt rolled over in his grave at these limits on "his" navy.

Bill Leahy's posting to Washington in 1918 as director of gunnery and engineering exercises prompted him and Louise to buy a house there. Young Bill was well into his teens and hoping to follow his father to the Naval Academy. Barely six months into the job, Leahy was asked to serve as chief of staff to the commander of the Pacific Fleet. It was the sort of operational experience Ernest King routinely coveted, but Leahy was personally relieved when the chief of naval operations vetoed the request and kept him in Washington. Even in the navy, one could take only so much moving about, and Leahy didn't want to disrupt his family again so soon.[4]

Instead, Leahy, now a captain, made frequent trips to sea from his Washington base to observe target competitions and review the efficiency of gunnery departments. This put him squarely in the confrontation as Brigadier General Billy Mitchell of the Army Air Service stepped up claims that airpower was making battleships obsolete. The first field test of this assertion occurred in November 1920 when the navy preemptively decided to conduct its own tests with the aging, pre–Spanish-American War battleship *Indiana*. To its regret, it invited General Mitchell to witness the exercise.

Navy planes dropped dummy bombs from the air while relatively small six-hundred-pound bombs were remotely detonated at key points on and near the ship. Just what the correlation was between the simulated aerial attack and these static explosions was open to question. Certainly, Mitchell criticized the entire demonstration as a charade. But in a post-action report, Leahy defensively declared that the operation had demonstrated "the improbability of a modern battleship being either destroyed completely or put out of action by aerial bombs."

The navy brass bristled further when General Mitchell disclosed these "confidential" tests to the House of Representatives Appropriations Committee and repeated both his criticisms and his boasts. Secretary of the Navy Josephus Daniels, who was on his way out with the rest of the Wilson administration, struck back and was quoted in the *New York Times* as saying that he "knew of no development of the World War or experiment since that would justify any conclusion that battleships were practically rendered useless by aircraft development."[5]

Mitchell continued his attacks until the navy finally permitted him to plan a simulated search-and-destroy mission with dummy bombs against the obsolete battleship *Iowa* (BB-4), which was equipped as a radio-controlled target, as well as a live-fire exercise against the captured German battleship *Ostfriesland*. Mitchell declined to undertake the offered exercise against *Iowa*—the navy insisted it was because he was afraid his planes wouldn't even be able to locate the moving ship—but he rushed to drop six 2,000-pound blockbusters in quick succession on the stationary *Ostfriesland*.

The battleship sank in just twenty-one minutes, and the navy cried foul, citing its agreement with Mitchell to conduct the attack slowly so that crews could assess the damage between strikes. The end result was that the navy claimed the sinking was inconclusive because the *Ostfriesland* was not under way and fighting back. Mitchell retorted that the result would have been even more spectacular if the battleship had been operational and carrying its normal complement of magazines and fuel. The interservice rivalry continued, but what stuck in the public's mind was that no matter how he had done it, "Mitchell had sunk a battleship, as he claimed he could."[6]

Bill Leahy stuck to his guns, both literally and figuratively, but some of his postwar assignments broadened his perspectives well beyond battleships. In addition to his gunnery and big ship expertise, his talents as a diligent and efficient staff officer were being recognized, as well as certain skills as a diplomat. He got his first direct taste of melding military might with diplomacy in the spring of 1921, when he was sent to Constantinople to take command of the cruiser *St. Louis.* The ship was an aging veteran whose chief purpose in the Turkish capital was diplomatic rather than militaristic.

Turkey was at war with Greece, and the harbor at Constantinople (soon to become Istanbul) was crowded with warships sent to observe the action, as well as to monitor any Russian ships or expatriates flowing out of the Black Sea. This Greco-Turkish war was largely a result of Greece, a nominal member of the Allied powers, trying to grab territory as the Ottoman Empire, a member of the defeated Central powers, was being dismembered—giving rise to the new republic of Turkey.

This was Leahy's first post in which his diplomatic skills were at least as important as his naval ones. His overriding concern was to safeguard American interests—always a subjective standard—while remaining carefully neutral. The post also showed him the social side of diplomacy, something he would come to know intimately. "I find it a necessary part of my efforts to acquire information to attend many dinner dances and receptions at the residences of the diplomatic and military officials," Leahy wrote. "These social affairs are invariably interesting because of the different antagonistic and friendly nationalities represented and because of the exchange of gossip and misinformation that can best be accomplished in a gathering that apparently has no official status."[7]

Perhaps Leahy's most lasting indoctrination into the delicate balance of diplomacy came one night when the watch on the U.S. destroyer *Sturdevant* picked up a teenage boy swimming toward the ship. He was Greek and obviously in a panic, having just escaped Turkish-held territory. If Leahy ordered him returned, the boy would almost certainly be shot as a spy. But keeping him risked a potentially explosive breach of neutrality. Leahy's decision was to bring the lad aboard the *St. Louis,* dress him in sailor's clothes, give him his first decent food in months, and then allow him to pose as a member of the crew. All hands embraced the ruse, and when a nervous Leahy later confessed his actions to his superior, the admiral advised him to forget all about it. Humanity, it seemed, had a role in diplomacy.[8]

When Leahy returned to the United States at the end of 1921, he should have been in line for a year at the Naval War College. It was an important step if he desired to attain flag rank, but instead he was ordered back to sea as the commanding officer of the minelayer *Shawmut.* He was also given additional duty as the commanding officer of Mine Squadron One. The positive aspect was that Leahy got his first experience commanding multiple ships. On the negative side, the command had him shuttling about the East Coast and the Caribbean on a host of minor assignments.

One particular duty in 1923, however, gave him another experience with naval aviation. His ships were detailed as lifeguard stations between Hampton Roads and the Canal Zone as a squadron of eighteen torpedo planes made a practice deployment. Every plane had some trouble en route, two turned back, and one was lost at sea. Leahy's ships then shepherded a deployment of scout planes from Key West to the canal with similar results. Plane after plane experienced mechanical problems before limping into its destination.

Once in Panama, these aircraft joined in fleet maneuvers and were reported to have an operational radius of eight hundred miles. Leahy, in particular, found that to be a bad joke. He had seen naval aviation in operation and rescued a part of it from the waters of the Atlantic. If this was the best airpower could do, battleships did not have much to fear, despite Billy Mitchell's theatrics.

As part of these exercises, the old battleship *Iowa,* still equipped with a radio-controlled device, was placed in Leahy's charge as a target drone for live-fire exercises. The ship proved tougher than expected and outlasted the first day's fire, taking 5-inch shells and three 14-inch shells in stride. The second day was different. The *Mississippi* opened up at fifteen thousand yards with armor-piercing shells. Its second salvo proved fatal, and the *Iowa* sank in fifty fathoms of water. Apparently, the lesson to some in the navy was that it still took a battleship to sink another battleship, although Leahy bemoaned, "There was something very sad about seeing the old veteran destroyed by the guns of its friends."[9]

Shortly after these 1923 maneuvers, Leahy was assigned to the Bureau of Navigation as a detail officer, a post he would hold for three years. This meant that while the chief of the bureau made the major decisions on personnel assignments, Leahy was tasked with making sure that each ship had the proper complement of officers and that the officers themselves had the required mix of sea and shore duty, as well as school and practical experience. It was a time of reduced military spending and low nationwide military priorities. As one admiral put it, the navy was "laboring under economy run wild."[10]

The assignment put the Leahys back in Washington and they took regular advantage of its cultural activities, particularly the theater and symphony. In both, Leahy preferred the classics and eschewed some of the wilder social exuberance and excesses of the by now Roaring Twenties. If the officer corps of the navy was itself rather conservative, Bill Leahy was decidedly more so.

Early the following year, by coincidence on the Leahys' twentieth wedding anniversary, Woodrow Wilson died. He had become a broken and pitiful old man, but Leahy's words in his diary were not charitable: "Thus ends the career of a man who had the greatest opportunity that has ever been presented in the cause of world peace, and who failed completely to take advantage of it."[11] Unbeknownst to him, the next time a man had a similar opportunity, Leahy would be at his side as one of his most trusted advisers.

Bill Leahy may have been a battleship man, but there was no question that Bill Halsey, now a commander, had become well established as a destroyer man. Like him, destroyers were small but tough, nimble yet hard-hitting. They had proved their worth in antisubmarine and convoy operations during the war, but their mobility and beefed-up arsenal of torpedoes also put them in the category of offensive weapons, particularly against slower and more ponderous battleships.

In the closing days of World War I, Halsey had returned to the United States to assume command of the newly commissioned destroyer *Yarnall*. One of the *Wickes*-class destroyers, with their distinctive four smokestacks, *Yarnall* was 314 feet long with a narrow beam of 31 feet that could slice through the waves at a top speed of 35 knots. The ship's complement of 122 officers and crew manned batteries of four 4-inch and two 3-inch guns, but the offensive punch came from twelve torpedo tubes.

Halsey thought that taking his new ship to Europe as an escort for President Wilson's voyage to the Paris Peace Conference would be the perfect shakedown cruise, and he volunteered *Yarnall* for the duty. The outbound leg went smoothly enough, but as Wilson preached and his counterparts procrastinated, the conference dragged on for months. Much to Halsey's chagrin, *Yarnall* was reduced to ferry service in the English Channel and North Sea, shuttling servicemen between the continent and Britain.

When the destroyer finally returned to the United States in the summer of 1919, it was assigned to the newly formed Pacific Fleet. The destroyers were to be based at San Diego, and in addition to the *Yarnall,* Halsey was given command of a division of six destroyers. The overall commander, Destroyers, Pacific Fleet, was to be Rear Admiral Henry A. Wiley, one of Admiral Sims's disciples, and Wiley was determined that his ships be models of efficiency and smartness no matter how relaxed the rest of the postwar navy was becoming. Wiley did the job so well that by the end of the admiral's tour, Halsey claimed, "You could tell a destroyer man by the way he cocked his cap and walked down the street."[12]

Wiley's successor, Captain William V. Pratt, took this spit and polish to the next level. Pratt relentlessly drilled Admiral Sims's mantra of teamwork and coordinated attacks into his skippers. As one naval veteran put it, "Devout destroyermen beamed with approval (and sometimes envy) upon the division of graceful destroyers:

bones in their teeth, rooster tails churning astern, pirouetting in union with signal flags snapping in the breeze, plunging into steep seas and shaking green water from their forecastles—six commanding officers understanding one another perfectly, a brotherhood of proud and confident fighters and seamen."[13]

Halsey's squadron commander was the same F. T. Evans who had pushed Ernest King to close up formation in the *Terry*. Evans took Pratt's tactics to the extreme and devised various attack formations that were executed not by fluttering signal flags but by whistle blasts. As Halsey recalled, "When a squadron of nineteen destroyers maneuvers by whistles—at night, blacked out, at 25 knots—it's no place for ribbon clerks."[14]

Halsey thrived on this sort of action, as did another destroyer skipper in Evans's division, Lieutenant Commander Raymond A. Spruance. Four years Halsey's junior in age and a 1907 graduate of Annapolis, Spruance was the opposite of Halsey in just about every way except for his love of destroyers. Halsey was boisterous and outgoing; Spruance was quiet and shy. Halsey piloted ships and later airplanes by the seat of his pants; Spruance was meticulous and calculating in every plan and every action. Halsey thrived on the public's attention and courted it; Spruance shunned the spotlight and kept a very low profile. Halsey was the crashing wave, the rushing stream; Spruance was the epitome of the expression "Still waters run deep."

Yet in these wild days of racing destroyers around the Pacific, these two men bonded and became best friends. Their wives and families did the same ashore. Fan Halsey and Margaret Spruance took to each other, and six-year-old William F. Halsey III found a playmate in six-year-old Edward Spruance. But here, too, they were opposites. The Halseys roared through life ashore with endless rounds of "boozy picnics, boisterous beach parties, and evening revels" that frequently left the Spruances awed and more often than not on the sidelines with studied self-restraint.[15]

In the spring of 1921, Halsey's squadron of nineteen destroyers, including Spruance in command of the *Aaron Ward,* was ordered on war games that included a simulated torpedo attack on four battleships sortieing from Long Beach. *Texas, Mississippi, New Mexico,* and *Idaho* were on station there as concrete evidence that the United States would brook no Pacific interference from Japan. As the senior division commander, Halsey took charge of the "attacking" destroyers and found himself in control of the largest fleet of his career thus far.

Once the destroyers reached the starting point of the exercise, Halsey was free to operate as he saw fit. Accordingly, he split his command into two parallel columns about one thousand yards apart and led them toward the battleships at twenty-five knots, signaling as he did so for his ships to make smoke.

Captain Pratt was on the bridge next to Halsey as an observer. Pratt raised an eyebrow and asked, "What do you intend to do?"

"What's the limit?" Halsey responded.

"The sky," Pratt replied, evidently not fully appreciating Halsey's competitive nature.

The two columns of destroyers rushed onward and intercepted the advancing line of battleships from both sides. As the destroyers fired their dummy torpedoes, they quickly turned away and ducked into the obscurity of the smoke screen. The battleships had hardly anticipated this close-in attack — and from both sides! But the problem in this simulation was that while the torpedoes indeed contained only dummy warheads, their compressed air–fuel mixture was itself subject to a lesser explosion if they struck their intended targets too early in their run. By the time Halsey's trailing ships launched their torpedoes, the length of this run was down to only seven hundred yards.

One torpedo rammed *Texas,* and the resulting concussion from the compressed air explosion jarred the battleship's engine room and blew out the circuit breakers for most of its electrical gear. Two or more torpedoes exploded close to the *Mississippi*'s propellers and mangled them. A similar hit on the *New Mexico* ruptured some plating and flooded the ship's paint locker. Only *Idaho* stood unscathed. "In a minute and a half Halsey's destroyers had done a million and a half dollars' worth of damage" in a mock attack that should have been a rude wake-up call to the battleship admirals.

Instead, Pratt and Halsey were summoned aboard the flagship *New Mexico* and firmly told that in the next round, there would be no more close-in attacks. The destroyers must fire their dummy torpedoes from no less than five thousand yards. Thus handicapped, Halsey's ships achieved only a few hits on the second day and the battleships were able to declare victory. Nonetheless, on returning to shore, the destroyers were greeted with a newspaper headline that blared, "Destroyers Decisively Defeat Battleships."[16]

But once again, a generation of senior admirals, whose careers had been largely won and honed aboard battleships, ignored the prophetic results. Coming at it from two very different perspectives, Billy Mitchell and Bill Halsey had both demonstrated serious threats to battleship might. In the future, torpedoes stealthily fired from over and under the waves, and airborne assaults from carrier-based planes were to pose far more of a threat than an opponent's 16-inch guns.

CHAPTER EIGHT

Submarines

After inspecting submarine operations throughout Europe, Chester Nimitz spent the winter of 1918–1919 in Washington on special duty in the office of the chief of naval operations as the resident expert on submarine design. The best part may have been that he was able to have his growing family—Catherine, young Catherine, and Chester junior—with him for a short time. A second daughter, Anna, who would be nicknamed "Nancy," was born later in 1919.

In the wake of World War I, the submarine service to which Nimitz had reluctantly reported in 1909 was enjoying an increased visibility and popularity. In the immediate postwar period, before pacifist budget cuts could take hold, forty-three O- and R-class boats were in commission, and fifty-one of the newer, larger S-class boats were coming down the ways. These S-boats were the first small step toward taking the American submarine beyond its initial role as a coastal defense and turning it into a long-range offensive weapon. The sheer number of these boats in commission gave many junior officers their first commands, just as Nimitz had realized a decade before.

And while Nimitz focused on submarine design and engineering, those with a strategic sense for the future could not help but tally up wartime losses and find that for every U-boat lost by Germany, thirty-two Allied ships had gone to the bottom. The exact numbers showed that Germany had lost 178 U-boats, while sinking 5,708 Allied vessels, totaling 11 million tons. These astounding numbers, and the close margin by which destroyers and convoys had held these undersea predators at bay, were not lost on the victors, and they certainly would be remembered by the vanquished Germans in the years ahead.[1]

By now, Nimitz was quite content to stick with submarines, but his command track required that he spend a year aboard the battleship *South Carolina* as its executive officer. The ship made two round-trips to Europe bringing home American troops and then settled in at Norfolk. Unfortunately, Nimitz was unable to find suitable quarters for Catherine and their children to join him. "It wouldn't be so bad if I were at sea," he lamented to his mother. "Then separations are to be expected."[2]

As his year on the *South Carolina* wound down, Nimitz thought that he might work again with his mentor, Admiral Samuel S. Robison. The up-and-coming admiral was the newly appointed commandant of the Boston Navy Yard, and he offered Nimitz a position as his industrial aide. But the command track that Robison had pushed Nimitz toward during the war won out when the Bureau of Navigation decreed instead that Nimitz report to Pearl Harbor. There Nimitz would get plenty of command experience, as well as a chance to employ his engineering skills. His orders were to build a Pacific submarine base from scratch out of World War I salvage materials.

Pearl Harbor in the early 1920s was a far cry from the mammoth installation it would become just two decades later. Despite spacious, multipronged lochs, its entrance was historically quite shallow, so much so that early visitors keyed in on Honolulu harbor, a few miles to the east. Nonetheless, by 1845, while on an extensive survey of the Pacific, Commodore Charles Wilkes of the U.S. Navy offered the opinion that should its mouth be deepened, Pearl Harbor "would afford the best and most capacious harbor in the Pacific."

In 1887, with American interest in the Pacific increasing, the

United States renegotiated a commercial treaty with King Kala-kaua's Hawaiian government for the exclusive right to establish a coaling and repair station in Pearl Harbor and improve the entrance as it saw fit. In one of the darker chapters of American imperialism, the country's reach to the Philippines soon swept aside any respect for Hawaiian sovereignty and the United States simply annexed the islands in 1898.

When the U.S. Navy finally built its first facilities there within months of annexation, they were at Honolulu, not Pearl Harbor. The issue remained the difficulty of channel access. Not until 1908 did Congress authorize dredging the Pearl Harbor entrance and the lochs to accommodate the navy's largest ships. Construction of a dry dock and accompanying shops and supply buildings also began. This took time, and the harbor facilities—Naval Station Pearl Harbor—were not officially dedicated until August 1919. The acquisition that same year of Ford Island, in the harbor's center, by the army and navy as shared—albeit begrudgingly—airfield facilities and Chester Nimitz's arrival to build a submarine base were evidence that construction here was only the beginning.[3]

As a thirty-five-year-old lieutenant commander, Nimitz had his work cut out for him. Materials for everything from a machine shop to a foundry had to be scrounged from East Coast shipyards and sent west via the Panama Canal. Despite his orders, Nimitz was accorded only marginal cooperation from commanders who didn't know what they were going to do with rusting war surplus but didn't want anyone else to have it, just in case. Here Nimitz's rapport with hard-nosed chief petty officers paid off. He was always quick to acknowledge their skills and, being quite willing to do anything and everything for Commander Nimitz in return, the chiefs con-ducted more than their fair share of "moonlight requisitioning."

Up and down the East Coast, Nimitz's marauding chiefs begged, stole, and borrowed materiel likely never to be missed—or used—while their commander did his own arm-twisting to persuade reluc-tant officers to part with other equipment. Even Nimitz was surprised, however, when their salvage was off-loaded at Pearl Harbor and the chiefs presented him with a staff car they had somehow acquired along the way. Years later, Nimitz liked to joke that the Pearl Harbor submarine base was built mostly from stolen materials, although it was really only a case of transferring them from one government pocket to another.

The aging cruiser *Chicago* was to be Nimitz's temporary headquarters while land overgrown with cacti and palms was cleared on a peninsula that jutted into the southeast loch east of Ford Island. Once, the cruiser had been the command of Alfred Thayer Mahan, but now, with its engines inoperable and its propellers removed, it had seen better days. The ship served as bachelor quarters for unmarried officers, while enlisted personnel were assigned to wartime barracks recently dismantled and shipped from Europe.

The majority of the work was accomplished in about a year. Nimitz was promoted to commander and stayed on for another year to command both the base and Submarine Division Fourteen. His new office looked out across the harbor, past his submarine charges, and westward to Ford Island. On this first tour of duty at Pearl Harbor, Nimitz could hardly have imagined that twenty years later, he would be back in this very same office, surveying a maze of destruction in the harbor below as the newly appointed commander in chief, Pacific Fleet.

These two years in Hawaii were a grand time for the Nimitz family—certainly among their happiest memories. The world was at peace, and Chester was involved with a challenging project, yet he could come home at night and enjoy Catherine's company and that of their children. Young Catherine and Chester junior were in elementary school. And with a true family home—they rented a large house—Chester and Catherine were able to continue their tradition from their days in Brooklyn working on the *Maumee* and entertain a host of younger submarine officers with their simple yet gracious hospitality.[4]

One of those young submariners was Lieutenant j.g. Stuart S. Murray, newly assigned as the commanding officer of *R-17*. Murray was all of twenty-one, and *R-17* was his first command. The R-class boats had a tendency to fishtail at slow speeds, and it was relatively easy to bump the propellers or dent the nose of one's boat into the propeller guards on an adjacent sub as one pulled into or away from the tightly packed moorings. The result of such a miscalculation was at best a loud, grinding noise that Nimitz could hear on shore in his office, or at worst a badly mangled prop that put the sub out of commission for several days.

Murray had just such an encounter one day and reluctantly trudged up to Nimitz's office to report that *R-17* would be out of commission while the boat had a propeller changed. Nimitz heard Murray out without comment. Ernie King would no doubt have ripped the young lieutenant up one side and down the other. Nimitz, perhaps remembering that day in 1908 when *Decatur* had sat aground off Batangas harbor, reacted differently. "Murray," said Nimitz patiently, "every submarine commander has a starting credit: one tail and one nose [of the submarine], or two tails, or two noses. When he's used up that credit, then he's going to be in trouble sometime. You're only half gone. You've only used one tail. Now, go on back and try not to take the rest of your credit."[5]

After two years at Pearl Harbor, Nimitz was ordered to the Naval War College in Newport, Rhode Island. Once again, the assignment allowed him to have his family with him, but it was also an important step up in his career. The ongoing education of naval officers was receiving greater emphasis and no one had been sounding that theme more loudly than Ernest J. King.

After following Admiral Mayo around Europe, King was more than ready for a tour ashore. The fact that it was to be as the new head of the Naval Postgraduate School at Annapolis was all the better. This would give King an opportunity to put into practice the ideas he had been honing about naval officers continuing their education right up through the ranks. It also put him back home with Mattie and their growing brood.

Just as the Nimitz family enjoyed its time at Pearl Harbor, the Kings would also fondly remember these years at Annapolis. Their older daughters were starting to attract the attention of nervous midshipmen, and Ernest and Mattie would finally have a son. A favorite King family story tells of a woman asking King how many children he had, to which he replied, "Six daughters and a son." When the woman asked his son's name, proud King puffed up and replied, "Ernest Joseph King, Junior." Well, huffed the woman, "it should have been 'Ernest Endeavor.' "[6]

King continued to exhibit his trademark of unstoppable nervous energy and maintained his reed-thin appearance — he tried to quit smoking a few times, but never succeeded. But around the house, Mattie, despite her failure to connect with her husband on intellectual topics, ran the roost. King, who was so quick to press juniors as well as superiors with his sharp-tongued, sea-lawyer tactics, rather meekly submitted to Mattie's rule. In part, this may have been because King's intellectual energies were more than challenged by his work at the postgraduate school.

This was a period of great transition for the U.S. Navy. Its ranks had undergone a sharp increase from the days of Theodore Roosevelt, growing from 22,492 officers and enlisted men at the beginning of the Spanish-American War in 1898 to a total of 530,338 at the end of World War I in 1918. But now the challenges of peace and demobilization included figuring out how to maintain and train an officer corps that would stand ready to confront the new types of warfare so recently brought into focus — not the least of which were the submarine and the airplane.

Working with two other officers, Dudley Knox and William S. Pye, with whom King had a great rapport — the exception, it appears — King produced a report that outlined a four-phase approach to naval education: the Naval Academy, preparing midshipmen for division officer assignments; the General Line School, preparing lieutenants for department head assignments; the Junior War College, preparing lieutenant commanders for independent command and staff assignments; and the Senior War College, preparing captains for flag rank.

King's report also recommended that line officers acquire a subspecialty in an area of naval management, from ordnance categories (torpedoes, mounted guns, etc.) to navigation or personnel management, so that the navy would have its own in-house experts in each field. Finally, perhaps remembering his numerous visits to the Bureau of Navigation to plead for assignments that fit his career aspirations, King suggested a standardized system of assignment from ensign to admiral, so that an officer might be able to chart his career path without the helter-skelter that seemed to accompany many assignments.

In typical King fashion, he crafted the final report in little more than a day, putting it into simple and clear language. There was no padding, no unnecessary posturing. And just so his efforts wouldn't disappear into the navy's vortex of young officers' suggestions never to be heard again, he published the report in the *United States Naval Institute Proceedings.* This gave his work wide circulation and further boosted his image as an organizational guru of some standing. In time, most of his recommendations were adopted. Most important to World War II was the establishment of Junior War College (1923) and General Line School (1927) courses.[7]

King's pleasure in his duty at the Naval Postgraduate School came to an abrupt end in the spring of 1921 when he learned that Rear Admiral Henry B. Wilson was to become the new superintendent of the Naval Academy. King was both stunned and angry. According to King, Wilson was the antithesis of everything that King had been preaching about continuing education for naval officers. Wilson had even gone so far as to advise certain officers not to waste a year of their careers attending the postgraduate school.

It didn't help matters, of course, that both men disliked each other. In King's case, that dislike may have resulted from some tiff before or after Wilson succeeded Admiral Mayo as commander in chief, Atlantic Fleet. For his part, Wilson, a gentleman of the old-school navy, quite likely was just one of the many senior officers who bristled in King's frequently abrasive presence.

Determined to bargain his way out of an unpleasant encounter with Wilson, King went to the Bureau of Navigation at Washington to apply for sea duty. "What's the rush?" asked the detail officer. "You rate a third year at Annapolis."

"You know damn well why I want to go to sea," King growled in return.

The Bureau of Navigation may have been sympathetic, but it was not very helpful. King was simply too junior for any captain's command on a battleship or cruiser and too senior to command a division of destroyers. Given the postwar cutbacks, there was nothing else available. But persistent King continued to lobby. Finally, the detail officer threw up his hands and offered King the *Bridge,* a plodding refrigerator ship that was commonly known around the fleet it serviced as a "beef boat." It was hardly a glamour job or even one to get King further notice, but command of the *Bridge* did get him out of Annapolis and back at sea.

For the better part of a year, King and the *Bridge* steamed about the Atlantic as a floating commissary. It may have been the most boring year of King's life, but he stuck it out and then once more presented himself at the Bureau of Navigation. Now what?

The Bureau's answer was much the same as before. In the reduced navy, there wasn't any command available that fit King's qualifications, neither in big ships nor as commander of a smaller flotilla. Once again, King prepared to camp out in front of the detail officer's desk until offered another opportunity. This time, the Bureau of Navigation came up with the idea of submarines. Spend three or four months at the New London, Connecticut, submarine school, King was told, and he could have command of a submarine division of four boats. Pleased at any cost to be off the beef boat, King said yes. For once, he would be following in Chester Nimitz's footsteps.[8]

King entered the submarine school at New London as somewhat of a curiosity, "a captain among some fifty very junior officers." Ostensibly, he was there as a student to learn, but "as usual," he later wrote, "I had ideas of my own." Established doctrine—even after the scare put into Allied shipping by the U-boats—still taught that submarines were to be used for limited defensive purposes. King disagreed and not only advocated long-range offensive uses but also argued that submarines should work in units much like surface ships and coordinate their attacks. To accomplish this, the crews had to get off their cozy tenders or out of their port housing and live aboard their boats, taking them to sea for extended periods rather than merely conducting a few hours of training cruises per day.

When he completed his training, true to the Bureau of Navigation's word, King was given command of a four-boat division, and he made most of his ideas stick. His crews lived on their boats, and he was soon leading his division to sea to sail all the way from New London to the Caribbean for the fleet's annual winter maneuvers.

The sea voyage proved to be a disaster. King's boat, *S-20,* broke down, and he ordered the remainder of his division onward. Similar mechanical breakdowns soon befell the others and it was only with great difficulty that they regrouped at St. Thomas, in the Virgin Islands.

The ensuing fleet exercises were no less dysfunctional. Doing things his own way as usual, King ordered his division to get under way without asking routine permission to do so from the senior officer. "Why are you underway without my permission," came the query from the flagship. "I am underway in accordance with your operation order," King signaled back. *S-20* then proceeded to lead the other three division boats to sea, with the flagship still blinking furiously astern. Like so many other encounters, King took it all as a game of wills and thereafter spent many months writing letters back and forth with the commanding admiral debating the finer points of the regulations, until King was at last ordered to cease and desist.[9]

For some reason, King was never accorded the highly sought-after dolphin insignia that certified that he was a qualified submariner. (Chester Nimitz wore his throughout his career.) Such qualification usually required about a year aboard a sub and a demonstration of full knowledge of its operations. Whether King avoided taking the qualifying exams out of fear of failure so late in his career or whether he simply considered them an unnecessary hurdle is debatable. But not receiving the dolphin insignia did not keep him from always fondly embracing the undersea brotherhood, nor did it keep him from his next assignment.

Despite his disruptive academic opinions and his less-than-stellar operational performance, King was given command of the submarine base at New London in September 1923. Suddenly, he was in charge of the largest sub base in the country and the center of all training functions for the entire submarine service.

King lost no time in assuming all the trappings of the role and moved Mattie and the children into a veritable mansion, complete with four servants and a car and chauffeur. Naturally, his gig stood crewed and ready whenever he wanted to go anywhere by water. Unabashedly, King took on the role of the navy's ambassador in the entire state of Connecticut. When a junior officer involved in a civilian motor vehicle accident boldly suggested to King that his interest in the matter was both unnecessary and outside his jurisdiction, King drew himself up to his full ramrod height. "Young man," he barked, "when anything happens that reflects on the Navy, it *is* my business."[10]

Similarly, when the *Waterbury Herald* ran a story about a "sub base man" being fined for certain lewd behavior, King was quick to write the editor and protest that the offender belonged to a Coast Guard vessel and not to the submarine base. "Our own personnel come in for their share of notoriety," King concluded, "without receiving that which is not due them."[11]

In the early summer of 1925, after almost two years in command at New London, King received a letter from Admiral Charles F. Hughes, soon to become chief of naval operations, which jolted his smug little fiefdom. Looking to King's future, Hughes was quite candid. Phrased as "a friendly hint" that King could take or leave, "but ask no questions," Hughes suggested that King's entire naval reputation was in some jeopardy. The backroom talk among flag officers was that King had been too picky in his choice of assignments and had rarely put his career on the line.

"You are sure to be compared with others that have taken the hard knocks of the service and have come through with credit," Hughes lectured; "you would be surprised how your record of service is looked upon." Then Hughes offered some pointed advice that no doubt echoed around the halls of King's comfortable quarters: "Get a job at sea where you can do some of the drudgery of the service."

For one of the very few times in his calculating career, King was genuinely taken aback and momentarily cowed. He had indeed mapped out his career long ago; he had indeed done his share of plotting for the best assignments; but he had, after all, also done his time on the navy's requisite rungs of command, not the least of which was his recent, inglorious year on the beef boat.

In King fashion, he replied to Hughes thoroughly, but without the sharp arrogance of his usual writing. Admitting that he had always looked to his future, King told the admiral that he had nonetheless "never, in any degree, knowingly avoided or shirked any duty of any kind." If his staff assignments with Admirals Osterhaus and Mayo had been plums, it was because they had selected him. Defensively, he reviewed the remainder of his assignments and pronounced himself "not unfitting for future usefulness." Nevertheless, in a show of rare humility, he "promised to heed Hughes's friendly warning."[12]

This exchange with Admiral Hughes may well have been weighing on King's mind a few months later when, in late September, he and Mattie took a week's leave and drove through New England to view the fall colors. Out of touch with his office and the daily papers, King was greeted on his return by his daughters, one of whom immediately exclaimed, "Daddy, wasn't it just awful about the loss of the *S-51*?"

Several days before, on the morning of September 25, 1925, *S-51* had put to sea for engineering trials in Block Island Sound, southeast of New London. *S-51* was running on the surface under diesel power late that evening when the lights of the steamer *City of Rome* came into view well astern. By all reports, the bridge officers on the steamer also saw the white navigation light atop the sub's conning tower, although there was some controversy over whether or not the sub's red and green running lights were visible.

Nevertheless, in one of those freak "how in the world could this happen?" accidents, the *City of Rome* plowed onward, the *S-51* and the steamer both altered course very late in the process — turning toward each other rather than away — and the *City of Rome* rammed the sub and tore a thirty-foot gash in its port side. The boat quickly filled with water and sank with thirty-four officers and crew. Only three men managed to escape the nightmare.

Recriminations flew from both sides. The steamship company

charged that "rookies" were in command of the sub at the time of the collision; the navy wondered how the captain of the *City of Rome* could have failed to radio a report of the collision for almost two and a half hours, conduct only a cursory search for survivors, and then steam nonchalantly on his way.

In an unofficial note to an Annapolis classmate then at the Naval War College, King was particularly blunt. "All hands here [in New London] are deeply resentful," King reported, "over the performances of this 'road hog of the sea' [*City of Rome*], whose criminal stupidity and incompetence have caused the utterly needless waste of valuable lives."

As commandant of the submarine school, King was not in the direct chain of command for the *S-51,* but he was certainly part of the close fraternity. When asked if it was possible that some of the crew might still be alive, King was quoted in the *New York Times* as saying, "Men cling to life under incredible conditions."[13]

There were to be no other survivors, but King was ordered to get involved directly as the officer in charge of the salvage operations. Never mind that King had no particular salvage experience. The navy was determined to blunt public criticism of the incident and prove to skeptical civilian salvage operators that the submarine could indeed be raised from a depth of 130 feet. The operation would be dicey, and it would be watched carefully. The navy's prestige—and suddenly King's, too—was on the line.

According to one source, "It was the first time in his career that he had received orders without negotiating in advance and without weighing how they would affect his career." [14] Perhaps Admiral Hughes had been right after all. King hesitated at first when the telephone call came, but then quickly avowed that he would be glad to lead the operation. It would not be easy.

King assembled a fleet of salvage vessels, including the minesweeper *Falcon,* and a willing group of very brave navy divers. They were led by Edward Ellsberg, who would go on to a distinguished career in salvage operations and write many volumes on the subject. But no part of the operation was yet established textbook procedure. *Falcon* moored directly over the sunken sub but took repeated poundings in the open waters east of Block Island. Divers previously limited to about 90 feet of water pushed their own limits and that of their equipment and probed the 130-foot depths. The plan was to pump compressed air into the sub's watertight compartments, attach eight giant pontoons to its hull, and then lift.

But winter was not far away. The Navy Department kept pressing King to complete the job as soon as possible, but by mid-December, gale-force winds, choppy seas, and freezing temperatures conspired to force a delay until spring. King spent the next few months in limbo, wondering what he had gotten himself into. He was scheduled to return to sea duty in the summer of 1926 regardless of the *S-51* operations. Bill Leahy, nearing the end of his three-year tour at the Bureau of Navigation as a detail officer, wrote King in mid-February proposing command of the transport *Henderson*. It was hardly the cruiser command King sought, but it wasn't exactly a beef boat.

King replied to Leahy with an abundance of caution. "It seems to me that I am in a dilemma," King confessed, "chiefly on account of the job of raising the *S-51*." He didn't consider himself indispensable to completing the task—at least he didn't say so to Leahy—but King did stress that the job was "about halfway to completion" and that he was "thoroughly familiar with all the problems involved, and feel that I should finish it, both as a matter of professional pride and for the good of my service reputation, in the spirit of *finishing* what you have begun."[15] Admiral Hughes's criticism may well have continued to ring in his ears.

King had gotten himself into a "damned if he did, damned if he didn't" situation. He could leave the *S-51* salvage operations early and risk being called a quitter, or he could see them through, gamble on their outcome, and take whatever assignment might be available when they were finished.

Leahy confirmed that King was unlikely to get a desired command after salvaging *S-51,* but King chose to stick with it, and he returned with his salvage flotilla to the unruly waters of Block Island Sound in mid-April 1926. It was slow work, particularly learning how to operate the eight pontoons as a team rather than independently breaching whales. Finally, on June 21, with plenty of newspaper reporters circling the scene to report on their efforts, the salvage team was ready to attempt to lift the sub the following morning.

But then a bitter summer storm swept in from sea. King decided to postpone the operations only to have *S-51* take on a mind of its own and bob to the surface, tangling lines and bouncing off pontoons in the process. As the storm gained strength, King decided that the only solution was to sink the sub again to prevent it from breaking apart. As towering waves battered the sub and surrounding salvage ships, navy divers—whom King would later praise far beyond his normal regard for subordinates—braved the waters to open the vents on the pontoons and send the entire mess back to the bottom.

By the time the storm had blown through and the waters calmed, King was ready to try again, but the diving supervisor suddenly lost his nerve. There was no turning back now, of course, and King sent the man ashore and pressed on with others willing to take the risks. At last, on the afternoon of July 5, *S-51* bobbed to the surface of the Atlantic and stayed there. What remained was a long tow, still supported by the pontoons, to the Brooklyn Navy Yard.

The appearance of the raised sub and King's accompanying flotilla caused something of a sensation along the East River as it made its final port. It also unleashed a media frenzy that had been held in abeyance while the outcome of the operation was in doubt. The navy had gotten the job done, and King and his men in turn got the lion's share of the praise. King, Ellsberg, and the commander of the *Falcon* received the Distinguished Service Medal (the navy's second-highest decoration), and the principal divers were awarded the Navy Cross. King had gambled and won. He received national publicity, and his reputation within the navy suddenly skyrocketed. He was now a permanent captain, and clearly head and shoulders above many of his contemporaries. The sky was the limit.[16]

CHAPTER NINE

Aircraft Carriers

The first airplane had barely made it into the air when visionaries started talking about shipboard takeoffs and landings. Shortly after the Wright brothers' 1903 flight, a French inventor named Clément Ader made some rather startling predictions. Ader's early aircraft models had done little more than bounce along the ground, but that didn't stop him from espousing the concept of aircraft carriers in a 1909 book promoting military aviation.

"An airplane-carrying vessel is indispensable...[and] will be constructed on a plan very different from what is currently used," Ader prophesied. "First of all, the deck will be cleared of all obstacles. It will be flat, as wide as possible without jeopardizing the nautical lines of the hull, and it will look like a landing field....The speed of these ships should at least be that of cruisers and even exceed it in order to escape them."[1]

The first step toward this realization occurred on November 14, 1910. Aircraft pioneer Glenn Curtiss and his civilian test pilot, Eugene Ely, hoisted a Curtiss pusher-type biplane onto a wooden platform constructed over the bow of the cruiser *Birmingham*. The platform was 83 feet long and 22 feet wide, and it canted down toward the bow at a 5-degree angle. Originally, the plan was for the *Birmingham* to steam across Hampton Roads and provide a little wind streaming over the wings to help with lift, but low, overcast skies forced a postponement, and the ship dropped anchor to await better weather.

Shortly after three that afternoon, the skies hinted at a brief respite, and Ely climbed into the pilot's seat. Scarcely had the *Birmingham*'s anchor chains begun to rumble and clang as a signal that the ship was getting under way, when another bank of clouds started to descend. Ely decided that under way or not, he would wait no longer, and he gunned the plane down the short ramp. Off the bow it went, but as Ely fought for any measure of altitude, the spindly craft dropped farther and farther until it hit the flat surface of the water with a smack.

Ely got a lucky bounce back into the air and kept going, but the impact cracked his twin propellers, which caused the airplane to vibrate violently. Still, it was enough. Eugene Ely was airborne and had just made history with the first takeoff from a ship. Taking no more chances, he turned toward Willoughy Spit and gently set the plane down in the sand. Less than two months later, it was time to attempt to reverse the process.

Curtiss and Ely took their aircraft to the Mare Island Naval Shipyard, near San Francisco, where the cruiser *Pennsylvania* (recommissioned in 1912 as *Pittsburgh* to free the state name for a new battleship) had been outfitted with a wooden platform over its afterdeck. This one was a little longer and wider than *Birmingham*'s— 120 feet by 30 feet—because Ely was going to attempt a landing. Ropes weighted by sandbags on each end were strung across the makeshift flight deck. Ely's landing gear was outfitted with hooks to snag the ropes and slow the plane. A final "crash barrier" of canvas was stretched across the end of the platform to stop pilot and plane just in case the hooks didn't catch the ropes. In its most rudimentary form, this is the same basic system that is still used to land carrier-based aircraft a century later.

And it worked. Shortly before noon on January 18, 1911, while the *Pennsylvania* sat at anchor in San Francisco Bay, Ely came buzzing toward its stern despite a ten-knot tailwind. He caught the lines and slowed to a stop. "Oh boy!" exclaimed his wife, Mabel, who was on board. "I knew you could do it."

While the *Pennsylvania*'s captain took them below for lunch, the platform was cleared of its arresting gear and the Curtiss turned around in preparation for takeoff. After lunch, Ely did just that, completing the first successful landing and takeoff from a ship. The navy was intrigued enough to detail Lieutenant Theodore Gordon "Spuds" Ellyson to Curtiss's aviation camp at North Island, San Diego, to learn to fly and become Naval Aviator No. 1.[2]

It would be a while, however, before the United States Navy embraced the new technology that Ely had pioneered. Because of the demands of World War I, it was Great Britain that modified a number of existing ships to carry airplanes. Britain also laid down the keel of HMS *Hermes,* the first aircraft carrier built specifically for that purpose. But the vessel was not launched until the fall of 1919, and, given postwar economies as well policy debates such as the Washington Disarmament Conference, the ship, with its bow-to-stern flight deck and an offset, "island" superstructure, was not commissioned until 1923. "To an officer used to destroyers," recalled Bill Halsey after he first laid eyes on the *Hermes* at Malta, "she was an off-center, ungainly bucket, something a child had started to build and had left unfinished."[3]

By then, the U.S. Navy had commissioned a converted carrier of its own. The *Jupiter* was originally launched in 1912 as a collier and saw most of its initial service tending to the Atlantic Fleet. The ship hauled coal to Europe to facilitate the postwar rush of returning doughboys and then reported to the navy yard at Norfolk for a complete makeover. A flat flight deck was built over its 542-foot length from bow to stern, but with no island or superstructure above it, giving quick rise to the nickname "the Covered Wagon."

Recommissioned in 1922 as *Langley* — to honor the deceased astronomer and aviation pioneer Samuel P. Langley — the ship had two obvious problems: it was neither very large nor very fast. Its flight deck was cramped, and the old collier's engines maxed out at 15 knots even with its lighter load of planes instead of coal. But the *Langley* was to serve one undeniable purpose. As the next generation of aircraft carriers slid down the ways, they would be manned by pilots and crews who more often than not had learned their basic operational skills aboard it.[4]

Pioneer though the *Langley* was, the converted collier was only a stopgap as an aircraft carrier. Once the treaty limiting battleship tonnages was signed, the U.S. Navy looked to its shipyards and found two hulls that had originally been laid down as battleships. Battle Cruiser CC-1 was under construction at the Fore River Shipyard in Quincy, Massachusetts, and Battle Cruiser CC-3 was taking shape at the New York Shipbuilding Corporation in Camden, New Jersey. Under the treaty, these couldn't be launched as battleships. So on July 1, 1922, the order was given to complete both ships as aircraft carriers. They were launched in 1925 and commissioned within weeks of each other late in 1927. (A ship has three dates of significance in its construction: the date it is "laid down"—construction starts on its keel; the date of its launching and christening—it slides down the ways and floats; and the date it is commissioned—considered operational and entered on the U.S. Navy rolls as an active-duty ship.)

CC-1 became the carrier *Lexington* (CV-2), and CC-3 was christened *Saratoga* (CV-3). *Lexington* displaced a beefy 41,000 tons and was 888 feet long with a 105.5-foot beam. *Saratoga* had less armor plating and weighed a respectable 33,000 tons, with the same dimensions. Both carriers could more than double the speed of the *Langley,* churning along at 34 knots when required, and carried a complement of eighty-one aircraft.[5]

From the hands-on command experience of building a submarine base, Chester Nimitz was ordered to report to the Naval War College in Newport, Rhode Island. His record there proved that his high standing at Annapolis was no fluke. As much of a doer as he was a mechanic, Nimitz was also well suited to devouring a full range of books and papers on tactics, strategy, and military history. He found academic life stimulating and later termed his year in Newport "one of the truly important assignments of my career."

To be sure, there were war games on a huge plotting board—almost invariably with Japan as the aggressor in the Pacific—but there was also keen scrutiny of the fleet tactics employed in the Battle of Jutland. Whatever else could be said about the movements of the British and German fleets there, it was well acknowledged that both formations had been extraordinarily cumbersome and complex. The cruising formation of the British fleet, for example, deployed twenty-four battleships in six columns abeam, with screens of destroyers and cruisers extending over twenty miles. Turning such a multilegged formation in unison, let alone deploying it into battle lines, was problematic at best.

The president of the Naval War College overseeing these discussions in 1922 was none other than Admiral William S. Sims, who had already influenced Ernie King's and Bill Halsey's development of destroyer techniques, not to mention the convoy system. When Sims spread his war games fleet across the plotting board, he introduced aircraft carriers to the mix—even though *Lexington* and *Saratoga* were still months away from commissioning—and he argued that the aircraft carrier would replace the battleship as the navy's capital ship. The reason was that carriers presented a 360-degree range of firepower via their aircraft that far outdistanced the radius of a battleship's guns. The battleship sailors scoffed in disbelief, much as they had done at Sims's initial World War I arguments for antisubmarine warfare and convoys, but that did not stop Sims from envisioning future battles between surface fleets hundreds of miles apart that would attack only with carrier-based planes.

Sims's fixation with a widening circle of projected power may have influenced Nimitz's fellow classmate—both at Annapolis and now at the Naval War College—Commander Roscoe C. MacFall when he took his own turn at the plotting board. Rather than placing ships in long lines, MacFall arrayed his fleet in concentric circles around his capital ships—admittedly still battleships. The tactical advantage was that with a common pivot point in the center of the circle, all ships could turn together and remain in formation.

The circle formation also had the advantage of concentrating anti-aircraft fire around the capital ships.

As it turned out, it was Chester Nimitz who would supervise the integration of these two developments — MacFall's concentric-circle formations and Sims's concept of the aircraft carrier as capital ship — into fleet operations at sea. After his tour at the Naval War College, Nimitz was picked by his old mentor from his World War I submarine days, Admiral Samuel S. Robison, to become Robison's assistant chief of staff when he became commander in chief, Battle Fleet, the second-highest operational command in the navy. Nimitz reported aboard Robison's flagship, the battleship *California,* and during the fleet's first round of maneuvers, he convinced both the admiral and his senior captains to try the circle formation. When they did, it worked surprisingly well.

Aligning off the flagship, the entire fleet could pivot together as all the ships kept a constant bearing and distance from the flagship. When the fleet was deploying into battle formation, a battleship led the way out of the circle, and the trailing ships followed accordingly. (Maintaining formation at night became more problematic, but these difficulties lessened when ships were finally equipped with radar.)

As this tactic was refined over a succession of maneuvers, however, there was one obvious exception to the circular formation. Flight operations require aircraft carriers to turn into the wind so that aircraft can take off and land with the benefit of the wind just as they do on land. A carrier with its bow pointed into a twenty-knot wind and steaming ahead at fifteen knots provides a pilot with the advantage of thirty-five knots of wind moving over his plane's wings even before he shoves the throttle full. Similarly, turning into the wind to land aircraft allows for slower landing speeds. For example, an aircraft with a normal landing speed of sixty-five knots has an effective deck speed of only thirty knots when landing on a carrier surging at fifteen knots into a twenty-knot wind.

When the *Langley* was required to launch or recover its planes, the carrier left the circular formation and sailed into the wind accompanied by only two destroyers. The ship was easy prey for submarines and frequently ended up some distance from the main force.

To Nimitz, the solution was obvious. Admiral Sims was right: the carrier, not the battleship, was the chief capital ship, and the concentric-circle formation should have the carrier at its center. That way, when the carrier was required to turn into the wind for flight operations, the entire fleet turned with it. Under pressure from Nimitz, Admiral Robison sought permission from the Navy Department to combine *Langley* with his battle force for maneuvers. The result was that the carrier always had the protection of the surrounding screen of ships, and those ships always had the protection of the carrier's planes. It was only 1924, but Nimitz later regarded those pioneering maneuvers with carrier-centered, circular task-force formations "as laying the groundwork for the cruising formations that we used in World War II in the carrier air groups and practically every kind of task force that went out."[6]

While Ernest J. King was still uncertain about the outcome of the *S-51* salvage operation, his conversation with William D. Leahy in the Bureau of Navigation had not offered King much hope for a plum sea-duty assignment. In his anxiety, King went to see Rear Admiral William A. Moffett, the chief of the navy's Bureau of Aeronautics. A native of South Carolina and an 1890 graduate of Annapolis, Moffett had cut his teeth on cruisers and battleships before accepting the appointment as the first chief of aeronautics in 1921. He had become devoted to aviation, and while some—including King—would question his fascination with lighter-than-air craft, Moffett was strongly committed to naval aviation as an integral part of fleet operations and not as a separate service. "Hell, we won't secede from the Navy," Moffett admonished his junior officers. "If we are half as good as we think we are, we'll take it over."[7]

Moffett sympathized with King's plight about a future command and offered an intriguing alternative. Congress was tinkering with navy regulations so that aviation commands would require qualification as naval aviators or at least observers. The problem was that most qualified aviators were far too junior to assume command of a naval air base or one of the two carriers nearing completion. King was almost fifty, but if he was willing to qualify to fly, Moffett promised him command of an aircraft carrier.

An aircraft carrier? That thought got King's blood racing. Much like the previous promise of a flotilla command if King went to submarine school, Moffett's offer seemed to be King's ticket up to the next rung of the career ladder. The offer of command of a capital ship did not come lightly. But typical of King, he pondered the decision for several months while he finished raising *S-51* and still hoped that a cruiser command might open up. "I suppose that Bill Leahy has told you of my strenuous desires to get command of one of the scouts [light cruisers]," King wrote Captain Thomas R. Kurtz, an Annapolis classmate now in the Bureau of Navigation. "I hope that you will keep me in mind for that duty."[8]

But then King got itchy. "It seemed to me," King later said, "that aviation was the coming thing in the Navy." A month before *S-51* was raised, he accepted Moffett's offer and expected to report for flight training at Pensacola after the salvage operation was complete. But Moffett suddenly had a more pressing need, and with *S-51* barely in dry dock, King was ordered to take command of the seaplane tender *Wright*.

Wright's job was to shuttle seaplanes around and serve as a mobile support base. It had a reputation as "an easy ship," but that changed immediately when King marched up its gangplank. His bite equaled his bark, and within weeks the *Wright* was smartening up while its new captain was taking his first flights in the open-air rear cockpit of a two-man seaplane.

King wasn't a natural, but he learned enough over the next few months that he pressured Moffett to designate him a student aviator. It was King's usual response: he got a brief introduction, and suddenly he was an expert. Moffett demurred and instead ordered King to report to Pensacola early in 1927 for the complete course in flight training.

The naval air base at Pensacola was a rather down-and-out operation in those days. Funds were tight, the whole idea of naval aviation still had plenty of skeptics, and a batch of newly minted ensigns fresh out of the academy were being lumped together with old fuddy-duddies like King. This all made for an experience where the only rank that really mattered was how well one did in the pilot's seat.

As he had always done when studying was a means to an end, King threw himself into his course work and spent as much time in the air as permitted. This became one of those times in his life when he abstained from alcohol, preached abstinence to his fellow students, and "badgered the base commander to enforce the prohibition laws."

Then one Saturday afternoon, King strolled into the officers' quarters and found a drinking party under way. Knowing well his previous rants, one of the instigators thrust a drink into King's hands and waited for his reaction. King looked from the glass in his hand to the assembled crowd and back again and then took a sip. That was all he needed. From then on, whether it was drinking or poker, Captain King became "the damnedest party man in the place." As usual, once he embraced something, he did it full bore.

And none of this reveling, of course, had any negative impact on his flying. Thanks to his lessons aboard the *Wright,* King soloed soon after arriving in Pensacola, He was very mechanical in his approach, did everything by the book, and seemed to relish flying, but he never became totally comfortable serving as pilot in command. He simply didn't have the innate seat-of-the-pants mentality that characterized so many pilots of that era. King earned his wings because he was required to do so for advancement, but after they were pinned on his chest on May 26, 1927, he never again flew alone. He delighted in taking the controls on flights, but he also wanted the safety net of another pilot on board (and in fact the navy later mandated this policy for senior officers over fifty).[9]

His pilot's license requirement fulfilled and certified as Naval Aviator No. 3368, King was summoned by Admiral Moffett to report back to command of the *Wright.* After a ten-day leave with Mattie and his family in Annapolis, King did so and then watched expectantly as *Lexington* and *Saratoga* were commissioned late in 1927. Patience, Admiral Moffett counseled, but then a call from the chief of naval operations interrupted both of their plans. Another submarine, *S-4,* was down off Cape Cod after colliding with a Coast Guard cutter. This time, there really might be survivors, and King was ordered to take command of the rescue operations.

In weather too stormy for flying, King raced to New York by train and then sped from Penn Station to the Brooklyn Navy Yard in a police motorcade. There he hopped into a seaplane from the battleship *New York,* gave the pilot thumbs-up, and endured two frigid hours of flying to Provincetown, Massachusetts.

Arriving on the scene, King found the reliable *Falcon* over the crash site and tapping coming from the submerged hull. But the weather was worsening, and attempts to blow the sub's ballast tanks full of air and force it to the surface failed. Similar attempts to rig an air hose and pump fresh air into the boat to sustain the crew also failed. The press corps flocked about Provincetown with its own litany of second-guessing. Finally, the commander of the Atlantic Fleet submarines ordered the *Falcon* and its support ships into the harbor at Provincetown to ride out a furious gale. It lasted for days, and on Christmas Eve 1927, the navy was forced to announce that everyone aboard *S-4* was presumed dead.

Now King faced another difficult salvage operation — one that was once again exacerbated by wintry weather. Then came the letter from Admiral Moffett that he had been expecting. He was offered command of the *Langley.* It wasn't the *Lexington* or *Saratoga,* but it was an aircraft carrier. And King hesitated. Just as he was during the operations to recover *S-51,* he was torn between seeing the present operation through to completion and taking the command. Then too, just as he had continued to covet a cruiser command before flight training, he not so secretly still hoped that Fortune might see him on *Lexington* or *Saratoga.*

"I hardly know how to reply at this time," King responded to Moffett. But in the end, he determined to stay with the *S-4* salvage operations and take his chances because "developments regarding the Lexington and Saratoga commands, may, in June or thereabouts, be of interest and importance to me."

As it turned out, King was rewarded on all counts. In mid-March

1928, *S-4* bobbed to the surface after the deployment of a series of pontoons similar to those used on *S-51*. He reported back to the *Wright* in May with his second Distinguished Service Medal (the peacetime navy was a little more generous with this honor in those days). Then Moffett made good on his pledge and King received his orders to take command not of the proffered "Covered Wagon" *Langley,* but of the shiny new *Lexington*. King was walking on air — for about three weeks.[10]

Quite suddenly, on July 28, 1928, the Bureau of Navigation canceled his coveted orders to the *Lexington,* and — apparently at Moffett's request — he was assigned instead to the Bureau of Aeronautics in Washington as Moffett's assistant. He reported promptly but was less than pleased. It seems unlikely that Moffett purposely employed a bait and switch but that he instead belatedly caved in to pressure from a recently qualified aviator five years senior to King who desperately wanted the *Lexington* command. Writing his memoirs twenty years later, King still could not bear to cite the *Lexington* by name: "He learned to his disgust that he was presently to be shifted from his highly congenial new command at sea." To him, the whole affair of changed orders was an "annoying period."[11]

King was assured that he would "love the job" of Moffett's assistant. But Moffett was clearly the well-established heavyweight in the bureau, the man who had fought for its creation and nurtured its growth. He was energetic, resourceful, and not afraid to be combative in pursuit of his goals. These were exactly the words that might just as well have been used to describe King, and his sudden proximity to Moffett produced predictable friction.

It wasn't that Moffett and King didn't like each other, but rather that each was used to having his own way. King played no favorites — his or anyone else's — and Moffett was content to coddle certain naval aviators who were bringing in good press, the polar explorer Commander Richard E. Byrd among them. King fretted, too, over Moffett's direct control of aviation assignments outside the normal channels of the Bureau of Navigation. Without such control, King might well have been strutting the bridge of the *Lexington* and not haggling with Moffett.

Finally, after King had been on the job about nine months, the friction rose to the boiling point, and Moffett sputtered, "It seems to me you want to be chief of the Bureau." That was probably true, but King merely replied, "Admiral, I request a change of duty so you can have a different assistant."

Moffett readily obliged, but far from exiling King to some outpost, he gave him command of the naval air station at Norfolk, then, as now, among the major naval aviation facilities. They might not have gotten along, but Moffett clearly respected King's talents. And within a year, Moffett promised King that in the summer of 1930 he would at long last have command of a carrier, the *Saratoga*.

Most captains with an eye toward the stars of a rear admiral would have been ecstatic, but King proved his usual, particular self. Because *Saratoga* was the flagship of the carrier force, its captain had an admiral on board inevitably looking over his shoulder. King wanted the *Lexington* and a good measure of freedom. He told Moffett so in no uncertain terms. Moffett might well have put King in his place, but he didn't. He gave King the *Lexington* as requested. It had taken twenty-nine years since his Annapolis graduation, but Captain Ernest J. King was at last the master of what he and many others thought was "the finest ship command in the world!"[12]

Lexington had been commissioned for only two and a half years when King stepped aboard the carrier in June 1930. Much was still being learned about these floating behemoths. *Lexington*'s crew of around 2,100 officers and enlisted men was twice that aboard the largest battleship of the era. The sheer number of men and the numerous departments tended to decentralize the chain of command. And the air squadrons that rotated duty aboard the vessel presented their own set of problems. Some pilots treated the carrier as a cruise ship and expected to do little duty beyond flying. Others looked to their squadron commander, not the carrier captain, as the ultimate authority. None of this sat very well with Ernest J. King.

First and foremost, King reminded everyone—including the pilots from the air squadrons—that there was only one code of conduct and that was the Navy Regulations. Departmental idiosyncrasies fell by the wayside as "King made it his business to know everything that was happening on the ship."[13] As for the pilots, King ordered them to conduct thorough inspections of their aircraft before *and* after each flight and to put in their time on watch as naval officers. This was the U.S. Navy, gentlemen, not a barnstorming circus or brunch at the Hotel del Coronado.

King's approach worked. *Lexington* went from being a "loose" ship to being a taut one ruled by King's iron hand. "If a man knew his business," recalled future admiral J. J. "Jocko" Clark, then the commander of one of *Lexington*'s air squadrons, "it was easy enough to get along with Ernie King. But God help him if he were wrong; King would crucify him."[14] Along the way King's penchant for experimentation brought much-needed innovation to the operations and tactics of America's new carrier fleet.

King's first chance to show off the *Lexington*'s snappiness, as well as his own command abilities aboard it, took place during fleet maneuvers off Panama early in 1931. After initially being sent on what he considered a wild-goose chase, King ordered *Lexington* to come about and race at full speed back into the area where he suspected *Langley* was posing as an "enemy" carrier. As *Lexington* closed to within the maximum range of its aircraft, established protocol dictated launching scouts to locate the target, to be followed by bombers and torpedo planes.

But King was impatient to score a "kill" before darkness fell, and he launched his bombers and torpedo planes thirty minutes after the scouts. Navigation by aircraft at sea was then still rudimentary at best. Once one's home carrier receded from view, pilots relied on dead reckoning with a compass and estimates of wind and speed to get back to where the carrier was supposed to be.

An hour or so later, with evening approaching, the scouts returned on schedule to the *Lexington* and reported no sign of either the "enemy" or the trailing bombers and torpedo planes. King paced the bridge and watched the darkening skies for any sign of the planes. Fleet regulations required all aircraft to be recovered by sunset, for the very good reason that night landings had yet to be attempted.

Lexington's radio sent out a flurry of dots and dashes, black smoke poured from its stack, and searchlights frantically probed the descending darkness. If ever King doubted himself, now, on the verge of losing thirty-one aircraft on his first major operation, might have been one of those times.

Twilight in the tropics is fleeting, and just before it vanished, the missing aircraft lumbered into view, having found and "attacked" the *Langley*. The pilots began to make what became for all but the first few aircraft their first night carrier landing. When all were aboard safely, the flight commander hurried to the *Lexington*'s bridge.

Characteristically, King greeted him with a gruff, "Where the hell have you been?" When the flight commander protested that *Lexington* was not where he had been briefed it would be, King dressed him down for misunderstanding the briefing. Whatever the fault, it certainly was not King's. As one of the aviators later recalled, "Everyone was out of step but him!"

And King put the best possible spin on the entire matter, immediately recognizing the potential of night operations. Among his other innovations during these maneuvers, he implemented combat air patrols (CAPs) circling overhead to protect his ship from enemy attacks. Competitive and hard-driving, he pushed his ship and men to their fullest and himself always one notch above that.

Recollections of junior officers are replete with tales of King making mistakes or merely compounding problems with his thundering. Once he stormed to the flight deck to rearrange parked aircraft because he wanted more room for takeoffs and no one could do it to his satisfaction; by the time he was done, he had lost ten feet of space.

Quite a few officers simply withered under King's sharp demeanor. He was a force few could withstand, but those who did usually earned King's begrudging respect. When a torpedo plane missed the flight deck and landed in the starboard gun gallery one afternoon, its pilot faced the inevitable summons to the bridge. His squadron commander, John J. Ballentine, made it there first.

"Ballentine," King barked, "what is wrong with your pilots?"

"Nothing," Ballentine replied. "Your ship is not into the wind, and until it is, I will not let any more of my pilots land."

After Ballentine stormed off the bridge, King adjusted

Lexington's course directly into the wind, and the recovery operations continued. But King remembered Ballentine. Later, when King returned to sea duty wearing admiral's stars, he specifically requested that Ballentine become his operations officer.

"Under King," wrote his principal biographer, "the fit survived and developed into some of the Navy's finest captains and admirals. The unfit were eliminated." Still, there was another side of King, and the line he walked between them could sometimes be quite narrow. Aboard ship, King was sharp, demanding, and generally intolerant of anyone who didn't follow regulations or anticipate his every command. Onshore, however, it was a different story.

King never did anything halfway, and that included his partying. Scarcely had the *Lexington* docked after the Panama war games than King—despite days without sleep and the Prohibition laws—was ashore and in the back of a bar nursing a private bottle of bootleg Scotch. He was soon surrounded by a group of junior officers, and such events became an established norm. King called it "play time," but such fraternization created potential problems. Aboard ship, King was the lord and master; ashore at parties, he was "Uncle Ernie." His advice was, "You ought to be very suspicious of anyone who won't take a drink or doesn't like women."[15]

Fleet maneuvers the following year, 1932, were held in the warm waters around Hawaii. The general premise was a carrier-based air strike against Pearl Harbor and other installations on Oahu. The weather was atrocious, with high waves. Aircraft were slow to take off and equally slow to land on the pitching decks. Still, the "attack" was successful, and it set some minds to thinking.

Lexington was ordered eastward shortly afterward to engage a threat from an "enemy" force that had transited the Panama Canal. King honed his tactics and chose to "attack" the opposing carrier near dusk when most of its planes had just returned from sorties and were on deck, unarmed and without fuel. The mission was judged a success, but the complete destruction of the "enemy" fleet was made possible by an aggressive torpedo attack led by destroyers under the command of William F. Halsey, Jr.

Halsey had looked up to King ever since their days at Annapolis, when King had been the four-striper in command of the battalion and Halsey a lowly plebe. Their paths hadn't crossed much in the intervening years—save for their days driving destroyers in the North Atlantic under Admiral Sims—as Halsey had stuck with destroyers while King had tried his hand first at submarines and then at carriers. But this close association during the 1932 fleet maneuvers seems to have brought Halsey to King's attention as a man who got things done.[16]

Prior to that, in between Halsey's sea duty aboard destroyers, he had spent a year in Washington at the Navy Department's Office of Naval Intelligence commanding, as Halsey told the story, an LSD—"a Large Steel Desk." Writing about this year in his memoirs, Halsey made an interesting observation that some would say he should have remembered when a typhoon was bearing down on his fleet in the Philippine Sea. Saying that the function of Naval Intelligence was to "collect, coordinate, interpret, and disseminate," Halsey professed that the most difficult step was the last. "It isn't enough to get the right information to the right man at the right time," he wrote; "you have to make sure he doesn't let it molder in his 'in' basket."[17]

From Washington in September 1922, Halsey had been posted to the American embassy in Berlin as the naval attaché. It is difficult to imagine Bill Halsey in any sort of a diplomatic role, and a sense of his unease even emanates from photographs of him during this tenure, a sailor far more at home on the bridge of a warship than at a diplomatic reception. Finding conditions in postwar Germany physically spartan and socially resentful, Fan managed to endure the conditions with young Bill, but the Halseys soon sent daughter Margaret to boarding school in Switzerland.

After leaving Berlin in July 1924, Halsey was back aboard destroyers for a year, showing the flag around Europe and the Mediterranean. Fan and young Bill joined Margaret in Switzerland for the duration. Then, in the fall of 1925, all the Halseys returned to the States, and Fan and the children settled in Asheville, North Carolina, while Bill reported for his lone nondestroyer sea duty during this period. In preparation for promotion to the rank of captain, he served as executive officer of the battleship *Wyoming*. Meanwhile, Fan put her own spin on all the moves navy wives endured by flatly asserting that she spent her time "buying and abandoning garbage cans all over the world."

After Bill's promotion to captain in February 1927, there was yet another move—this one to Annapolis, where he was given command of the receiving ship at the Naval Academy, an aging salvage from the Spanish-American War named the *Reina Mercedes*. From this flagship, Halsey was responsible for every vessel in the academy's fleet. The *Reina Mercedes* served as his living quarters, as well as barracks for enlisted men.

Fan took one look at the dismal captain's quarters and ordered an immediate overhaul. When she was finished, their "porch" on the afterdeck, with views down the Severn River to Chesapeake Bay, became one of the best entertaining spots on the base. The Halseys launched into their usual rounds of partying and young midshipmen added to the merriment by calling on seventeen-year-old Margaret. Life was good. The next three and a half years at Annapolis passed pleasantly and remained "one of the most delightful tours" in Halsey's career.

But those years also gave Halsey occasion to flirt with flying. In addition to commanding the academy's ships, Halsey was in charge of its small aviation detail. When he expressed some reservations about being responsible for something he knew nothing about, the lieutenant commanding the detail had a quick response. "Fine! Let's go flying!" They did, and Halsey loved it.

Right then and there, Bill Halsey became a loud proponent of naval aviation. So loud, in fact, that after this tour at Annapolis was over, the Bureau of Navigation asked if he would like to take flight training at Pensacola. "I jumped at the chance," he recalled, but then, to his chagrin, he failed the eye examination. Instead, he was ordered to command DESRON-14, a destroyer squadron of nineteen ships then attached to the Atlantic Fleet. Like it or not, he was still wedded to destroyers. And his commanding officer, the commander of Destroyers, Scouting Force, was to be Bill Leahy.[18]

CHAPTER TEN

First Stars

By the spring of 1926, Captain William D. Leahy had put in three years with the Bureau of Navigation, and it was time for him to rotate to sea duty. Given his contacts in the bureau, Leahy should have had an inside track on his next assignment, but he was at one of the defining crossroads that all career officers face.

The next year would mark the thirtieth since his graduation from Annapolis. If fifty-one-year-old Leahy drew command of a minor vessel, he was almost assured that he would soon be on the retirement list as a captain. But if he was posted to command a capital ship, the odds were strongly in his favor that he was destined for flag rank. If that happened and he was accorded admirals' stars, Leahy would join a line that might someday lead to the office of chief of naval operations or commander in chief, U.S. Fleet.

When Leahy's orders finally came through, they were for the battleship *New Mexico*. His future with the navy was secure. Commissioned in the closing days of World War I, *New Mexico* (BB-40) displaced 32,000 tons in its 624-foot length and mounted twelve 14-inch guns among four turrets. Despite being eight years old, the ship was largely state-of-the-art for battleships then on the navy's rolls. In fact, because of the limitations imposed by the Washington Conference treaty—and obligingly followed by the United States—the grim truth from Leahy's perspective was that the United States commissioned no new battleships between *West Virginia* (BB-48) in 1923 and *North Carolina* (BB-55) in 1941.

Captain Leahy had grave misgivings about what this lull in construction meant for the navy's future, particularly as tensions of one sort or another with Japan had been afloat almost his entire career, but he was delighted to move aboard *New Mexico* and take command. The battleship was the flagship for the commander of Battleship Division Four, but unlike Ernie King, Leahy didn't seem to mind an admiral's presence in the flag quarters. During part of Leahy's tour, his executive officer was Commander John S. McCain. Together, they ran a taut ship, and *New Mexico* garnered fleet awards in gunnery, engineering, and overall efficiency.

On one occasion, *New Mexico* was slated to conduct a full-power speed trial, both to test the efficiency of a recent overhaul and as part of fleet competitions. For the first twenty-two hours of the twenty-four-hour run, *New Mexico* surged smoothly through the seas at better than twenty-one knots. Then, with two hours to go, a heavy vibration shook the ship, indicating a bent or broken propeller.

Just because Bill Leahy was usually reserved and quiet does not mean that he lacked a competitive instinct—far from it. A lesser captain might have slowed his ship and given up. Recognizing, however, that *New Mexico* "had an excellent chance to win... if the full-speed trial should be successful and no chance if the trial failed," Leahy decided to maintain full speed. The shaking became so severe that the crew feared that a main mast might snap, but *New Mexico* charged through the final two hours and won the engineering trophy.[1]

As Bill Leahy's year aboard the *New Mexico* came to a close, he got the silver stars he sought and a top job to go with them. Promoted to rear admiral, he was assigned to be chief of the Bureau of Ordnance. The man with the long history of battleships and firepower was now the head of the navy's department of big guns. One navy publication called him "a shark on gunnery."[2]

Leahy would be among the last of the big-gun battleship admirals to rise to the top. Those officers destined to keep pace and follow him were more attuned to the emerging roles of submarines and aircraft carriers, but for Leahy, his advancement to flag rank marked a steady rise up the rungs of the old navy hierarchy, from his duty aboard the *Oregon* to his coveted new membership in the elite club of admirals.

And it was, particularly during the lean defense-spending years of the late 1920s and early 1930s, definitely an elite club. As cosmopolitan as a naval officer's experiences might be—frequently taking him (and in those days it was only a masculine pronoun) to all corners of the globe—his personal friendships and those of his family were usually restricted to the United States Navy. It was a small, tight-knit circle, where there were strong bonds of camaraderie and loyalty, as well as inevitable competition and conflict. And the connecting thread was usually the United States Naval Academy. Assignments ashore and on ship came and went, but one's academy classmates were forever. From Manila to Panama or Honolulu to Guantánamo Bay, the fraternity gathered just as if its members were still on the banks of the Severn.

Prohibition was still in effect, and while Leahy had no qualms about taking a quiet nip in the privacy of his home, he certainly avoided the carousing crowds of which Ernie King and Bill Halsey were usually at the center. There was an oft-repeated, tongue-in-cheek admonishment that claimed "a naval officer never drinks. If he drinks, he doesn't get drunk. If he gets drunk, he doesn't stagger. If he staggers, he doesn't fall. If he falls, he falls flat on his face with his arms under him so no one can see his stripes."[3]

In 1927, there were 8,944 officers in the United States Navy. When one reached the rank of commander, as Leahy, King, Nimitz, and Halsey had all done by 1918—albeit for Nimitz and Halsey, these were wartime ranks not made permanent until later—he was usually assured of remaining in the service until retirement after thirty years. The promising commanders were promoted to captain—something the foursome had all achieved by 1927—and then the captains were carefully evaluated for elevation to flag rank, as Leahy had just been, or put on the retirement list.

When Leahy was accorded the stars of a rear admiral, he joined an elite group of active-duty admirals—every one a graduate of the Naval Academy. The academy certainly wasn't an absolute requirement for flag rank, but between the Spanish-American War, when Annapolis increased its enrollment, and World War II, no nongraduate attained flag rank. Leahy realized that he was "the first of my Naval Academy date to reach flag rank, which is either something to have accomplished or extraordinarily good luck." He was now assured of employment until he reached the mandatory retirement age of sixty-four, and quite possibly by then, he would reach the office of chief of naval operations (CNO).[4]

In 1927, the CNO's position was one of stature and prestige, but it was certainly not the powerful position it would become. Secretary Josephus Daniels's pre–World War I reorganization of the navy's hierarchy was still in place. There were eight largely independent bureaus with their bureaucratic abbreviations—Construction and Repair (BuC&R), Engineering (BuEng), Medicine and Surgery (BuMed), Navigation (BuNav), Ordnance (BuOrd), Yards and Docks (BuYard), Supplies and Accounts (BuSandA), and the new kid on the block, Aeronautics (BuAer). Each of the bureau chiefs was a chieftain within his own realm—fighting with his fellow chiefs for budget and other priorities—and the chief of naval operations was merely the *primus inter pares,* or "first among equals."

Within Leahy's Bureau of Ordnance, the battleship was still king. But the continuing adherence of the United States to the restrictions of the Washington treaty meant that no new battleships were coming down the ways. What's more, some isolationists and antimilitary types claimed that the limits of the treaty were only caps not to be surpassed and that it was just fine if naval strength fell well below those levels. In fact, opposition to the military in general during the late 1920s was so strong that senior officers in both the navy and army were ordered to wear civilian suits instead of uniforms if they were on duty in Washington. Too much braid showing was judged to be a bad thing.

Attempting to increase fleet strength, the navy's General Board—essentially an advisory group of senior admirals who were putting in time until retirement—battled the Coolidge and Hoover administrations' political opposition to all but a minimum of defense spending. Efforts came to a head at events surrounding the London Naval Conference of 1930. Admiral Leahy had to step adroitly to avoid being caught in the crossfire. If battleships had been the focus of the Washington Conference of 1921, cruisers were in the forefront in London.

Aside from dickering with Great Britain and Japan on overall ratios, the American delegation found itself divided on whether heavy or light cruisers best served its purposes. While the British sought a larger number of 5,000- to 6,000-ton "light" cruisers mounting 6-inch guns, most American representatives favored the 10,000-ton "heavy" cruisers mounting 8-inch guns, which would be more self-reliant in the vast distances of the Pacific and equally useful should the need arise in the Atlantic.

While the preponderance of navy brass supported heavy cruisers, President Herbert Hoover tapped Admiral William V. Pratt, then commander in chief, U.S. Fleet, to be his administration's chief spokesman. Pratt—who had earlier taught destroyer tactics to Bill Halsey—sought compromise with the British by recommending eighteen heavy cruisers—instead of the twenty-three championed by the General Board—and allocating the remaining tonnage to light cruisers, on the theory that they were not necessarily unsuited to Pacific operations.

This theory was not unreasonable, but when the U.S. Senate ratified the results of the London Conference in July 1930, the General Board cried foul and asserted that Admiral Pratt had sold out the U.S. Navy to appease the British. Chief of Naval Operations Charles F. Hughes, a Leahy mentor as well as the admiral who had once advised King to take more risks in his career, was particularly incensed. Leahy mirrored Hughes's thinking that the treaty granted

Japan and Great Britain "advantages that they had not previously possessed...[and] was not advantageous to our National defense."[5]

Although the treaty gave Japan parity with the United States in submarines, it also showed how idealistic negotiators were in thinking that they could put the offensive power of the submarine back in the box and outlaw unrestricted submarine warfare. It decreed that "except in the case of persistent refusal to stop on being duly summoned, or of active resistance to visit or search, a warship, whether surface vessel or submarine, may not sink or render incapable of navigation a merchant vessel without having first placed passengers, crew and ship's papers in a place of safety." For these purposes, the ship's boats were "not regarded as a place of safety unless the safety of the passengers and crew is assured, in the existing sea and weather conditions, by proximity of land, or the presence of another vessel which is in a position to take them on board."[6]

Such naïveté! Submarine skippers had seen enough antisubmarine efforts during World War I to know that the last thing they would do in another war would be to surface and politely hail a likely target. But it was the cruiser debate that rankled Admiral Hughes the most, and he spoke his mind about it, including to Admiral Pratt. As evidence of how little power the CNO held in those days, Pratt, far from being cowed by CNO Hughes, went to President Hoover and requested that he be named as Hughes's replacement. This threatened to split the navy's admirals into pro-Hughes and pro-Pratt camps. Leahy might have kept quiet and attached his future to Pratt, who appeared to be the rising star, but he loyally supported Hughes and the heavy cruisers instead.

But Pratt was a force not to be stopped, and when Hoover proposed extensive budget cuts that Hughes had no desire to implement, he took early retirement, and Hoover hastened to appoint Pratt to his position. This left Leahy in the uncomfortable role of a bureau chief who had opposed the new CNO.

Leahy decided rather quickly that staying in Washington in close proximity to Pratt was likely to lead to a clash of wills that might spell doom for his own plans to occupy the CNO's office. So he was delighted to be asked by a pro-Hughes admiral, Jehu V. Chase, who had replaced Pratt as commander of the U.S. Fleet, to go to sea as his chief of staff. But Pratt quickly flexed the muscles that Leahy was wary about and soon replaced Chase with a choice of his own. Leahy scrambled to find another position and settled on commander, Destroyers, Scouting Force, where one of his division commanders was to be Captain William F. Halsey, Jr.[7]

Bill Leahy returned to sea duty in the spring of 1931 with a great sense of relief. But while he was able to escape the political infighting of Washington, he was unable to avoid either the gathering clouds of international unrest or the economic downturn of the Great Depression. That September, Japan invaded the Chinese province of Manchuria—arguably the opening round of World War II. But the rest of the world was strangely disconnected from events in Asia. Only one week before the invasion, Great Britain's representative to the League of Nations had declared, "There has scarcely been a period in the world's history when war seems less likely than it does at present."[8] Now China furtively appealed to the League for assistance.

On the home front, the excesses of the Roaring Twenties had finally run their course, and as the country fell headlong into an economic black hole, money for military personnel and operations was squeezed to a trickle. Men like Bill Halsey pleaded to take their destroyers to sea for training exercises, but fuel oil for their engines was just one of many requirements in tight supply.

In one rare case of extravagance, the navy participated in the 150th-anniversary commemoration of the Battle of Yorktown and the French naval victory over the British at the Battle of the Capes. The principal French participant attending the celebration was Marshal Henri-Philippe Pétain, still hailed as the victor of the catastrophic bloodbath at Verdun during World War I. Pétain, who exuded the supreme, if somewhat misplaced, confidence of France between the two world wars, was met by a host of American military officers, including Leahy, who would have occasion to meet Pétain again a decade later under far different circumstances in Vichy, France.

The festivities included daily luncheons attended by the foreign guests and all flag officers of the American fleet. One day there was a ceremony at the College of William and Mary, in Williamsburg, Virginia, dedicating a plaque to French soldiers who had died there in an improvised field hospital a century and a half before. The requisite luncheon with ample liquid refreshment followed at nearby Carter Hall, a recently restored colonial mansion. "At Carter Hall," Leahy wryly noted, "the 18th Amendment [Prohibition] did not apply."

President Hoover came down from Washington to review the ships assembled for the Yorktown occasion and delivered a speech that Leahy, perhaps still smarting over Hoover's support of Admiral Pratt, found "very mediocre." When a gust of wind scattered pages of the president's prepared remarks from the lectern, aides scurried to retrieve them while Hoover "stood mute and apparently uninterested." That seemed to be the attitude of his audience as well. "A more vigorous wind," Leahy recorded, "would not have annoyed the spectators."[9]

It may have been the perspective of his advancing years and new rank, or some combination of the current unrest in Manchuria and the historical retrospective of Yorktown, but Leahy's diary at about this time began to contain more of his thoughts on policy and strategy for the United States, rather than merely recounting the people and places he had seen. During these years, Leahy was rather unabashedly an isolationist who eschewed foreign entanglements for America, but he nonetheless firmly believed that the United States had to maintain a strong defense to protect that isolation.

The possibility of war with Japan was openly discussed, just as it had been since Leahy's early days in the navy. Leahy didn't like the prospect. "A war with Japan at the present time," he wrote, "would be of sufficient length to almost certainly destroy the existing social order in America and it would seem that some strong character must appear in our political organization to bring us back to the fundamental principle of 'No entangling alliances.'"[10]

"Some strong character" was indeed rushing in from the wings. Having persevered over the confining indignities of polio, Franklin D. Roosevelt was again on the national stage. Elected governor of

New York in 1928, Roosevelt was physically but a shadow of the man who had sailed with Leahy on the *Dolphin* to Campobello. But if anything, Roosevelt's mind now worked overtime to make up for his physical limitations. Witty, infectiously cheerful, and a master of small talk to obscure anything of substance he wished to keep to himself, Roosevelt promised to be a strong tonic to the aloofness of Herbert Hoover.

"Franklin Roosevelt is a gentleman by all standards of comparison...," Leahy wrote in his diary. "In any event he would start with the advantage of facing a situation and an executive organization where any change will be an improvement."[11]

But such change would not necessarily be painless. As the Depression deepened and unemployment soared, the good news for military personnel was that at least they had steady, albeit low-paying, jobs. But then, in the fall of 1932, just as the presidential election was in full swing, the Navy Department ordered all officers to take one month's leave without pay each year and instituted a 10 percent reduction in their allowances for quarters and subsistence. "This is a hardship on officers," Leahy grumbled, "because they did not during prosperous times receive any increase of compensation and now in times of distress they are required to contribute to the country's deficit."[12]

These cutbacks meant that Leahy's destroyers and the rest of the fleet spent most of the summer of 1932 in port in San Diego. Bill Halsey was among those chafing at the confinement, although he and Fan at least had more riotous social distractions than Bill and Louise Leahy allowed themselves.

If nothing else, this downtime gave Leahy an opportunity to put more of his growing concerns for the future into writing. Among his prescient predictions were that Germany would refuse to pay its war reparations under the Treaty of Versailles and demand military parity with the rest of Europe, the League of Nations would prove impotent in maintaining friendly relations in Europe or forestalling Japanese aggression in Manchuria, and another war in Europe was "inevitable."[13]

While there is no record of his doing so, Leahy, if he voted at all, almost certainly voted for Franklin Roosevelt in the 1932 election and contributed to FDR's eighteen-point margin of victory. Roosevelt's election was particularly pleasing to Leahy because he believed "from personal knowledge of the man that he will use his office more directly for the benefit of the United States.... The Country and the Navy undoubtedly face a bad period, but I believe their policies will now be directed by a man whose point of view is wholly American."[14]

But the pain was indeed coming. The following January, Leahy received notice that the Colusa County Bank had closed its doors and glumly noted, "This probably destroys the remainder of my life-time savings."[15]

A few weeks later, Leahy listened along with "everybody" to Roosevelt's "stirring inaugural address." He found it "a definite promise of leadership, and perhaps this Roosevelt is the American that we have been wishing for."

But Roosevelt was barely inaugurated when the pay of all government workers, including the military, was cut by 15 percent. This action, and the fact that the number of men authorized for the navy was also cut, weighed heavily on Leahy as he came ashore in the spring of 1933 to take his second bureau chief position at the Bureau of Navigation. "We believe that our personnel is at least as good as that of any other nation and hope it is better," Leahy wrote just before his final round of maneuvers with the Pacific Fleet. "Knowing that through pacifist activities our ships have been allowed to fall below those of other powers, and with a certain belief that they will be called upon for war service in the not distant future I wish I knew that our personnel is in a better state of training than that of any possible enemy."[16]

But if anything, the politics that Leahy had sought to escape two years before were still rampant. Admiral Pratt was nearing the end of his term as chief of naval operations. Despite his heavy-handed tactics against Admiral Hughes, Pratt had been generally content to operate as first among equals with the bureau chiefs; however, his successor, William H. Standley, wanted a stronger command authority over the chiefs and considered them his subordinates.

All that the Navy Regulations said about the relationship was that the CNO "should so coordinate all repairs and alterations to vessels and the supply of personnel thereto as to insure at all times the maximum readiness of the Fleet for war." But to do so without any direct supervisory authority meant that the CNO had to work with the eight independent bureau chiefs and accomplish the same by exerting his powers of persuasion rather than issuing direct orders. Admiral Pratt had been content to do so; Admiral Standley was not.

Interestingly enough, the two bureau chiefs who most adamantly opposed the CNO exerting more authority were Bill Leahy and Ernest King, the latter recently appointed chief of the Bureau of Aeronautics. Both felt that the bureaus should be directly responsible to the secretary of the navy and not the CNO. Admiral Standley protested so loudly that the entire matter was referred to President Roosevelt for a decision. FDR opted to keep the status quo — muddy though it was — and continued to charge the CNO with responsibility for operational readiness even though he had to achieve it by reaching consensus with the bureau chiefs.

Leahy's and King's opposition to greater CNO authority may have served them well in their current positions, but given the fact that neither had ever been shy about voicing his own aspirations to be CNO someday, one wonders whether they were truly thinking long-term. For his part, Admiral Standley never forgave them for their opposition.[17]

Two years later, when Leahy was ready to move back to sea duty after his term as chief of the Bureau of Navigation, the feud was still raw. Admiral Joseph M. Reeves, the commander in chief, U.S. Fleet, recommended that Leahy become commander of Battleships, Battle Force, with the rank of vice admiral. Standley tried his best to stop it.

"Admiral Standley is now persistently and vigorously opposing this nomination with the purpose of eliminating me from any prospect of promotion in the Fleet or of succession to his office when he retires," Leahy wrote in his diary. "Secretary [of the Navy] Swanson wants me to succeed Admiral Standley which is undoubtedly the cause of the latter's attitude."[18]

CNO Standley chafed even more when his "first among equals" position prevented him from ordering otherwise. But Leahy was also lucky that he enjoyed good relations with the White House; Carl Vinson, the chairman of the House Committee on Naval Affairs; and Secretary of the Navy Claude A. Swanson. When Vinson wrote Swanson to give high praise to Leahy upon his appointment to the fleet, Swanson's response was unequivocal. "I concur in everything you say regarding Admiral Leahy," Swanson told Vinson. "Admiral Leahy enjoys to the fullest extent the esteem and confidence of his fellow officers"—Admiral Standley apparently notwithstanding.[19]

There were others who also seemed to hold Bill Leahy in high regard. The 1935 "Propaganda Book" for the Japanese navy recognized him as a rising star. "He is a thoroughgoing advocate of the big-ship–big-gun doctrine and is known as a tactician of the highest authority on their use in a decisive battle. In other words, he is a student of the strategy of a powerful navy forcing a weak enemy into decisive action." The Japanese report went on to describe Leahy as "a proponent of decisive battles with big ships and the leading advocate of big guns," but it also gave him credit for understanding that "the forerunner of the big-gun battle is control of the air by a powerful air force."[20]

Leahy and the navy had certainly not forgotten the rising force of airpower, and in the meantime Ernie King had pushed Bill Halsey to embrace it full bore.

After Bill Halsey's tour commanding destroyers in the Pacific for Leahy, his shore duty took him to the Naval War College in 1933 for the junior course. Newport proved an unexpected reunion of sorts. Steady Raymond Spruance was on the faculty, and Captain Ernest King was there that year taking the senior course. And living nearby part-time and giving an occasional guest lecture was a mentor to all three, retired admiral William S. Sims, who had, if anything, grown more vocal in his criticism of a navy he felt was not adequately in step with the future.

Bill Leahy had never been particularly enamored with Admiral

Sims, because he felt that Sims's "arbitrary employment of publicity for his own ends alienated most of his following." Leahy had, in fact, carried oral instructions to Sims during World War I to stop his "publicity agents." Leahy thought, "For those of us who are familiar with his service history Admiral Sims provides a splendid example of what not to do."[21] Given his usual low profile, Leahy clearly believed these words; King and Halsey certainly did not.

As it turned out, King's year in Newport was cut short in April 1933 when the airship *Akron* crashed in a storm off the coast of New Jersey. Among the seventy-three dead was Rear Admiral William A. Moffett, King's friendly nemesis as chief of the Bureau of Aeronautics. King rushed to Washington for Moffett's burial in Arlington National Cemetery and more important, to lobby for Moffett's job. King was due his first stars that year, and as a new rear admiral, an immediate posting as a bureau chief would be a sign that he was still seen as an up-and-comer. Moffett, who had a love-hate relationship with King, would likely have preferred Captain John H. Towers, who had given King his first airplane ride on the Severn two decades before. Towers lobbied for it, too, but King had five years' seniority and got the job.

Meanwhile, Bill Halsey completed his year at the Naval War College and then had the good fortune to spend another year as part of an exchange program for select officers at the Army War College in Washington. Two of his classmates were Lieutenant Colonel Jonathan Wainwright and Major Omar Bradley.

By then, Rear Admiral King, as chief of the Bureau of Aeronautics, made Halsey a proposal much like the one Admiral Moffett had once made him. King smiled on Halsey and offered him command of the *Saratoga* if he would take the aviation observers' course at Pensacola. It was hard to tell which excited Halsey more — the chance to get into the air again or the opportunity to command a vaunted carrier.

But Halsey didn't rush to accept on either count. He talked it over with Fan, who said that she would consent to such craziness only if the chief of the Bureau of Navigation, then still Bill Leahy, agreed that it was a good idea. Bill and Fan "both had enormous respect" for Leahy's judgment, and when he not only agreed, but also did so without reservation, Halsey was off for Pensacola.

Only when he was on the road by himself did he have his own belated reservations. "Bill," Halsey said to himself, "you're fifty-one years old and a grandfather, and tomorrow morning you'll begin competing with youngsters less than half your age!" With that thought in mind, he later claimed, he swore off liquor for one whole year.[22]

Halsey reported to Pensacola on July 1, 1934. Shortly after his first flights, he appears to have changed his designation from student observer to student pilot. Just how he managed it with his poor eyesight is a matter of some speculation, but his original orders to Pensacola were so modified. After twelve hours of dual instruction, Halsey took his first solo. As the last of his class to do so, he was in line for a toss in the harbor. When his ensign and lieutenant j.g. classmates hesitated to lay hands on the grandfatherly captain, Halsey egged them on, and into the harbor he went. He was always determined to be one of the boys.

But there was one superior he hesitated to tell about his new student-pilot status. When he finally broke the news to Fan, she waved his letter in their daughter Margaret's face and practically screamed, "What do you think the old fool is doing now? He's learning to fly!"[23]

To Bill Halsey's credit, he crammed every last bit of required training into a course necessarily condensed in time because of his impending assignment to the *Saratoga* and fully earned his wings as a naval aviator. And true to his word, Rear Admiral King gave him command of the big carrier. Although Halsey would command other famous flagships, he always considered the *"Sara"* his queen and kept a special place in his heart for the ship. "First, I loved her as a home," he later reminisced. "I commanded her for two years and flew my rear admiral's flag on her for two more, which means that I lived on board her longer than I ever lived anywhere else. Second, I loved her as a ship; she helped me make my debut in the carrier Navy, and she initiated me into the marvels of fleet aviation."[24]

But to Halsey, who was used to maneuvering destroyers as if they were 16-foot powerboats, ship handling was ship handling. It really didn't matter the size, as long as one understood the technique. That rationale may have been called into question one day when Halsey brought the 880-foot *Saratoga* into Coronado Roads at San Diego. He later claimed that it was an emergency, but he dropped the anchors while the *Sara* was still making 9 knots, backed full, and had the ship dead in the water by the time 75 fathoms of chain had paid out.[25]

Halsey was truly grateful for his command of the *Saratoga,* and he and King forged something of a mutual admiration society that had its roots in Halsey's destroyer proficiency during the 1932 fleet maneuvers. Halsey was a guy who got things done and King definitely liked and respected that quality.

As much as King had a reputation for being cold, aloof, and impossibly demanding on many occasions, he also had a soft side. King's papers are filled with letters to and from subordinates long since posted elsewhere or retired who admired him, and he always reciprocated with genuine warmth. When King was appointed chief of the Bureau of Aeronautics and accorded his first stars, one of those sending congratulations was a chief petty officer who had served under King years before. Writing from his current station at Guantánamo Bay, Cuba, John N. LaChance told King that he had not been surprised to read of King's promotion because "I think of you often as a great naval officer." King responded in kind, telling LaChance, "I expect you, as I've told you before, to come to see me whenever you are in my vicinity. I have strong and pleasant recollections of our service together—and still feel that you are one of the best *real* Chief Petty Officers that I've ever known."[26]

King also could be appreciative of those who helped his career. "I owe much, if not all, to my good friends, like yourself, who turned to and lent a hand," King wrote Edward E. Spafford. The occasion was King's appointment as aeronautics chief, and Spafford, a New Yorker and past national commander of the American Legion, was glad to have been of help but dubious about King's career path in aviation. King reassured him, "Please do not think I am in a 'blind alley' — that is not my view."[27]

*   *   *

King definitely had a long-range career plan, and his three years as chief of the Bureau of Aeronautics was a key part of it. But in the depths of the Great Depression, and with naval appropriations of any sort tight, it didn't help matters that working with Congress and testifying before its ponderous committees were not among King's talents. He was the lone wolf, sure that he was right and totally bored by such bureaucratic rituals.

The navy's guardian angel in the House, Naval Affairs Committee Chairman Carl Vinson, tried to help King along, but even Vinson couldn't always save him from himself. After King testified one day about the importance of retaining flight pay for aviators, Vinson lobbed the admiral a softball question about what effect a pay cut would have on aviation morale. "I do not wish to be thought facetious, Mr. Chairman," King replied, "but to be perfectly straightforward, as I wish to be, we are becoming so accustomed to these matters that I really think we could muster up another grin and bear it."[28] Less is usually more in such situations, but King never understood the need to corral his tongue.

Yet he did work well with Bill Leahy, then his counterpart at the Bureau of Navigation. Together they established the Naval Aviation Cadet Program, which recruited college graduates to take aviation training and then become aviators in the Naval Reserve. It was another unheralded step toward preparation for a global war. Together, too, Leahy and King continued to joust with Chief of Naval Operations Standley over the independence of the bureaus.

Where they differed was that Leahy seems to have enjoyed more frequent access to President Roosevelt, largely because of discussions of personnel. The lack of presidential association may have hurt King when it was time to rotate out of his bureau chief's job and back to an operational command in 1936. There were only two seagoing jobs for an aviation flag officer, commander, Aircraft, Battle Force, a vice admiral who commanded the navy's four carriers (*Ranger* had joined the fleet in 1934) and their aircraft squadrons; and commander, Aircraft, Base Force, a rear admiral who commanded the navy's seaplane patrol squadrons, centered largely on the West Coast and in Hawaii.

As the only qualified aviator—never mind that he never flew solo—King should have had precedence over flag officers who were merely aviation observers. With characteristic force of personality, he lobbied for the Battle Force assignment and the three stars of a vice admiral, but he ran into opposition from both Admiral Standley and King's Annapolis classmate Rear Admiral Adolphus Andrews, who had succeeded Leahy as chief of the Bureau of Navigation. Andrews "had no intention of allowing King to get three stars before he did," and King lacked the presidential clout to do anything about it. The result was that King ended up still a rear admiral in command of the Base Force of seaplanes.[29]

But one thing was certain. Out of the economic chaos of the Great Depression, the growing uneasiness of the world order in both Europe and the Far East foreshadowed ominous events. Bill Leahy and Ernest King had gotten their first stars, and now they, and the entire United States Navy, would be increasingly pushed into positions of projecting power.

CHAPTER ELEVEN

Projecting Power

After his years at the Naval War College and at sea with Admiral Robison gaining experience in fleet formations built around aircraft carriers, Commander Chester W. Nimitz was again detailed to an academic setting, but this time he was the teacher. Despite the overriding sentiment in the 1920s against the military, Congress bowed to the wishes of the Navy Department and in 1925 created the Naval Reserve Officers Training Corps (NROTC). Bill Leahy was assigned to the Bureau of Navigation at the time and strongly supported the move. While the program's initial funding was sparse, the NROTC quickly provided the navy with a nucleus for the expanded manpower and expertise that would be sorely needed a few years later.

Nimitz was one of six officers ordered to command sixty-man NROTC units at Harvard, Yale, Northwestern, the University of Washington, Georgia Tech, and the University of California at Berkeley. Nimitz drew the assignment at Berkeley and found that among his first duties was recruiting interested prospects to fill the sixty slots. In addition to their regular college courses, enrolled midshipmen took seamanship, navigation, engineering, and related courses and were eligible upon graduation for a commission in the Naval Reserve.

At first, Nimitz was leery that such a shore assignment might derail his chances for higher command, but with Admiral Robison as his mentor and others, including Bill Leahy in the Bureau of Navigation, becoming increasingly aware of his abilities, Nimitz need not have worried. In fact, the three years that the Nimitz family spent in Berkeley were among the happiest of their lives — even more so than those in Hawaii because the children were older.

Son Chet, who wanted to follow in his father's footsteps at Annapolis, and young Catherine, increasingly called Kate to distinguish her from her mother, were into their teens, and Nancy wasn't far behind. Not only did Nimitz find the cultural interaction with a university community stimulating — one of the rare occasions he was outside the close-knit navy fraternity — but he also had plenty of time for family activities, including vacations and camping trips into the nearby Sierras. His children would always remember him as very involved and hands-on, just as he was in his professional activities.

And if Bill Leahy had once grumbled that the navy had not adequately prepared him to write articulately, Nimitz made sure in grading his midshipmen's papers that he corrected spelling and grammar as well as facts. As for his own advancement, he forged a bond with the university community, and Cal Berkeley in particular, that lasted all his life. He was promoted to the permanent rank of captain in 1927, and when his tour at Berkeley ended in 1929, his exemplary service and the high regard in which he was held — by civilian academics and fellow officers alike — left no question that Chester Nimitz was slated for continued advancement.[1]

Nimitz went next to San Diego as commander, Submarine Division Twenty. He was forty-four and almost a quarter of a century out of Annapolis. When asked for a sketch of his career to date for a twenty-fifth-anniversary yearbook, he replied that he had enjoyed all his assignments because, he believed, "of my making it a point to become as deeply immersed and as interested in each activity as it was possible for me to become." Indeed, he confessed to knowing "no other profession for which I would forsake my present one."[2]

But in the early 1930s, the navy, as Bill Leahy had learned, was sailing choppy political seas. Captain Nimitz was next assigned to command the *Rigel,* a tender charged with watching over a fleet of about thirty-five out-of-commission destroyers in San Diego. The sight of these ships sitting idle rankled Nimitz, but the good news was that once again, he was able to have his family with him for an extended period. A third daughter, Mary, was born in 1931.

Chester and Catherine made it a point of parenting junior officers as well, just as they had done with NROTC midshipmen in Berkeley and young officers from the Brooklyn Navy Yard years before. This San Diego assignment also gave Nimitz occasion to indulge his passion for playing tennis and taking long hikes, occasionally in the company of Captain Raymond Spruance, then chief of staff to the commander, Destroyers, Scouting Force.[3]

But the payoff was coming. On October 16, 1933, Captain Nimitz assumed command of the heavy cruiser *Augusta* and sailed the ship to the Far East Station for duty as flagship of the Asiatic Fleet. Six hundred feet in length, with a beam of sixty-six feet and a displacement of nine thousand tons, *Augusta* and its sisters in the *Northampton* class, including the *Houston,* were capable of knifing through the water at better than 32 knots. Augusta, Maine, would try to claim the ship, but the cruiser had been sponsored by Evelyn McDaniel of Augusta, Georgia, and named for that southern city.

Commissioned only in 1931, the cruiser was the result of a building program that had proceeded while battleship construction was stymied by the limits of the Washington treaty. But after a hurried overhaul at the Bremerton Navy Yard in Washington State, and with most of the 735-man crew new to the ship, Nimitz the teacher had his work cut out for him. His manner was not to bark orders and intimidate with ultimatums, as Ernie King might have done, but rather to convey his expectations quietly yet firmly from top to bottom. Nimitz himself set the example of hard work, competence, and pride in oneself that he expected his subordinates to follow.

Nimitz's teaching style was sometimes so understated as to be powerfully profound. The captain was keen on giving every officer and enlisted man "as much responsibility as he could handle" and never shied away from providing young ensigns experience at the conn. One day, coming into an anchorage, a young ensign named Odale D. "Muddy" Waters approached with far too much speed and "had to back the ship full power and lay out 90 fathoms of chain [540 feet] before he got her stopped, then had to heave back to 60 fathoms." Captain Nimitz watched the entire procedure without a comment and then asked, "Waters, you know what you did wrong, don't you?"

"Yes, sir, I certainly do," replied Waters. "I came in too fast."

Nimitz nodded in agreement—end of lesson. Waters later became a rear admiral.

But Nimitz was also never afraid to teach from his own experiences. Coming alongside the anchored oiler *Pecos* in exceptionally blustery winds, Nimitz himself took the conn. It seemed like a perfect landing until a freak gust sent the *Augusta*'s bow into the lifeboat davits of the *Pecos* and snagged an anchor just as the lines were being made secure. A quick strain on the number 3 line and a fortuitous shift of wind untangled the mess, but Nimitz quickly sent for the lieutenant who had been supervising the lines.

"Thompson," Nimitz snapped without his usual calm, "what did I do wrong?"

E. M. "Tommy" Thompson gulped and then replied, "Well, sir, you were overconfident and misjudged the effect the wind would have on a ship riding lightly on the water."

"That's right," Nimitz affirmed. "Now, Thompson, what should I have done?"

"Probably the safe thing to have done, sir, would have been to have gone ahead, drop the starboard anchor, and to have backed down on it."

"That's right," Nimitz said with a scowl, "and, Thompson, *don't you ever forget it!*" It was no coincidence that Thompson, too, became a rear admiral. He had a great teacher.[4]

The Asiatic Fleet was hardly a powerhouse—aside from the *Augusta,* it consisted of a squadron of destroyers, a squadron of submarines, and a collection of gunboats and auxiliary ships—and the chief duty of its admiral was to show the flag up and down the Chinese coast and from Manila to Yokohama. Per long-established procedures, these exercises moved north and south following the temperate climate. It was not entirely risk-free, because Japan continued its control of Manchuria and eyed more Chinese territory farther south, but social calls were the order of the day when in port.

The occasion Nimitz remembered most was a port call in Tokyo Bay in 1934 that coincided with the funeral of Admiral Togo, whom Nimitz had met on his 1905 visit to Japan as a passed midshipman. Foreign ships boomed salutes, flags flew at half-mast, and a delegation of the *Augusta*'s sailors and marines marched in the funeral procession. The following day, Nimitz was among those invited to the service at Togo's modest cottage in the forest outside Tokyo. His opinion of the admiral continued to be one of high respect, and he never wavered in that view.

By the following spring, it was time for Nimitz to give up the *Augusta* and return to shore duty in Washington as assistant chief of the Bureau of Navigation. It was hard to say who was sadder at the parting, the crew or its captain. Nimitz's eyes glistened as he said farewell and his junior officers accorded him the unusual honor of rowing him in a whaleboat to the liner that would carry him home.

"I think one can safely say," recalled one of those officers, yet another of Nimitz's protégés who would wear admiral's stars, "that the *Augusta* had reached an absolutely unheard-of level of high moral, high pride, and competence at every level down to the lowliest mess cook."[5]

Upon Nimitz's arrival back in the United States, Chet, who by now was a midshipman at the Naval Academy, asked his father where he expected to get in the navy and how he was going to do it. His father unabashedly replied that he intended to follow the route he had always taken and do his very best at whatever he was assigned. He was confident that if he did so, his own road would someday lead to the office he said he would like to have—chief of naval operations.[6]

When Captain Nimitz reported to Washington and the Bureau of Navigation, Bill Leahy was heading to sea as a vice admiral and commander, Battleships, Battle Force. A year later, on March 30, 1936, Leahy was accorded the four stars of a full admiral and made commander, Battle Force, essentially the backbone of the U.S. Fleet. Under his command were fourteen battleships, nine cruisers, forty-three destroyers, eight minelaying destroyers, and the navy's four aircraft carriers, the aging *Langley, Saratoga* (still under Bill Halsey's command), *Lexington,* and *Ranger.* In all, Leahy was responsible for 78 ships; 2,762 officers; and 30,370 enlisted men.[7]

But Leahy's time at sea, flying his four-star flag, was to be short-lived. Admiral Standley's objections to the contrary, Franklin Roosevelt wanted Leahy to replace Standley as chief of naval operations, effective January 2, 1937. Leahy took the news in typical stride, with hints of both humility and nostalgia. He certainly recognized the honor of the post and that it signified his climb to the top of the navy pyramid. But his pleasure at the selection was also "tempered by a realization," he acknowledged, "that it brings to an end a service at sea that commenced on board the frigate *Constellation* in June 1893 and that has in the forty-three intervening years provided splendid opportunities for service and adventure in peace and war in many parts of the world."[8]

An article in *Newsweek* after Roosevelt announced his appointment called Leahy "gruff in voice, a strict disciplinarian, he drives himself and everybody else." The reporter was particularly impressed by the sixty-one-year-old Leahy's endurance during the recent fleet maneuvers, when the need for the men to remain constantly on duty wore down some of his junior officers. It was said that "Old Bill can stick on the bridge for six weeks without sleep." But the article also showed Leahy's well-liked other side: "Off duty he is kindly, friendly, and as comfortable as an old shoe."[9]

Leahy's appointment as CNO depended, of course, on FDR's reelection in November 1936, but that matter was never really in doubt. It was a Roosevelt landslide, and "in view of friendly personal relations of long standing with Frankyn [*sic*] Roosevelt, and a complete belief in his exalted ideals of service to the Nation," Leahy wrote, "his election by an overwhelming majority of the electorate is particularly pleasing to me." Still, Leahy's innate conservatism could not help but show through. "Roosevelt at the present time," Leahy confided to his diary, "is definitely a Liberal, and it is the hope of many of his friends that he can detach himself from radical members of his present entourage and incline his efforts more toward conservatism."[10]

That was not going to happen, but there is no doubt that Leahy's flag-rank rise and his increasing measure of influence derived in large part from FDR's support. Roosevelt was most comfortable when working within a "good old boy network" of those he had known for a long time. That doesn't mean that Roosevelt didn't reach out to recommended new talent, but if he knew someone personally, as he did Leahy and Halsey, or was aware of someone's accomplishments, such as King's salvaging of the *S-51*, Roosevelt was more apt to pick that person over an unknown no matter how highly recommended.

Popular perception has long suggested that FDR favored the navy over the army, but when it came to budgets, deployments, and promotions, he was evenhanded as commander in chief. On an emotional level, however, Roosevelt's combination inspection-fishing-vacation trips—such as he enjoyed aboard the cruiser *Houston*—were among his favorite occasions. And his long-standing relationships with the navy's admirals, particularly the duty-minded Leahy, made him more comfortable having them around. This contrast is underscored by remembering that the army chief of staff from 1930 to 1935 was Douglas MacArthur. The general was still trying to emulate his father's advance up Missionary Ridge during the Civil War, and his visits to the White House often took on the aura of a state visit. FDR was not intimidated by MacArthur—or anyone else—but neither was he terribly comfortable with him. When MacArthur left Washington for the Philippines and Malin Craig, whom Roosevelt did not know well, became army chief of staff, it was only natural that Roosevelt gravitated toward the loyal and understated Leahy as his chief military adviser.

With a still sluggish economy, an increasingly unstable world community, and a navy only slowly embarking on a capital ship construction program to keep pace with the other powers, Roosevelt and Leahy had their work cut out for them. "It is hoped," Leahy wrote as he began his term as CNO, "that the fleet's war efficiency can be maintained and that America with an efficient and adequate sea defense can avoid being drawn into any foreign wars."[11]

Three weeks later, Admiral Leahy stood in the rain on a reviewing platform behind FDR for two hours as the president's second inaugural parade trooped by on Pennsylvania Avenue. Nominally, the president's first-rank naval adviser was the secretary of the navy, but Claude A. Swanson was in failing health. A seventy-four-year-old Virginian, Swanson had served his state since 1893 as congressman, governor, and United States senator and had been appointed secretary of the navy by Roosevelt in 1933. When Swanson was unable to attend cabinet meetings and other occasions because of his health, it was Leahy who frequently represented the Navy Department as acting secretary. This gave him even greater access to the president's inner circle.[12]

While the alliance of a reinvigorated Germany and Italy held attention in Europe, the third member of the growing Axis alliance was causing a stir in the Pacific. Japan's aggression against China erupted into total war early in July 1937, and with Japanese forces advancing on Shanghai, Roosevelt became concerned that American commercial and military interests were at risk of being caught in the crossfire.

That same month, Amelia Earhart disappeared on her attempted globe-circling flight. After navy search efforts failed to find her, Leahy pressed to occupy other islands near her intended target of Howland Island, while American naval forces were in the vicinity. But Roosevelt remained focused on Shanghai. "How many Marines do we have in Shanghai?" the president asked Leahy at a cabinet meeting. When Leahy gave an answer of 1,050, FDR said that he wished they were not there. Leahy recalled the rationale that they were protecting about four thousand Americans in Shanghai, but Roosevelt quickly countered that "there were about twenty-five thousand Americans in Paris and not a single American Marine."[13]

Roosevelt and Leahy were certainly opposed to any action that might provoke a clash involving the marines, but FDR protested that some Americans were going to get hurt nonetheless. When part of the International Settlement at Shanghai evacuated, the rest dug in, remaining an uncomfortable sliver of neutrality both for its occupants and the invading Japanese, who found the continuing foreign presence annoying. Even before Chinese forces completely abandoned Shanghai and the Japanese directed their attack toward Nanking, Japan announced that it would conduct an extensive bombing attack on Nanking and warned all foreigners to leave the city.

"This threat by Japan," Leahy bristled, "to conduct a bombing raid against the civil population of the Capital of China is another evidence, and a conclusive one, that the old accepted rules of warfare are no longer in effect. It establishes another precedent that will be seriously destructive of the rights and privileges of neutrals and noncombatants. . . . There is today an urgent need for a restatement of the international rules governing the conduct of war. . . . Someday Japan must be called to account for its abuse of power in this instance."[14]

But doing this would be difficult, if not impossible. Despite Roosevelt's pro-Chinese sympathies, he recognized that a large portion of his countrymen remained decidedly isolationist in temperament. The United States was still mired in the Great Depression — folks had their own problems at home. Leahy, and undoubtedly Roosevelt too, understood that Japan would only grow stronger if China was subjugated, but in Leahy's words, "From all indications the present splendid opportunity [to check Japan] will be lost through lack of decision on the part of the major world powers."[15]

Early in October, Roosevelt spoke in Chicago and gave what came to be called his Quarantine speech. Citing a rise in world lawlessness, he suggested at a minimum an economic embargo of those nations promoting the same. But the speech landed with a thud amid American isolationism. And on the world stage, the future Allied powers were certainly not acting in unison or with any degree of resolve in countering the growing aggressiveness of Adolf Hitler. For most, Asia too remained a remote sideshow. Then came an incident that might have meant war.

*   *   *

December 12, 1937, was a Sunday, but it was far from a quiet one near the Yangtze River port of Nanking. Shanghai, 170 miles downstream, was in fact in Japanese hands after a bitter siege, and the Japanese were advancing on Nanking, which had been serving as the capital of the Chinese Nationalists. As such, the city was home to embassies and international diplomats, as well as a host of newspaper reporters.

In the wide and muddy Yangtze, patrol boats from several neutral nations attempted to look after their nationals. These included the American gunboat *Panay,* not to be confused with the Spanish-American War derelict of the same name that Chester Nimitz and "Slew" McCain had once motored around the Philippines. This *Panay* was one of five shallow-draft, 190-foot river gunboats built in the late 1920s specifically for patrolling the Yangtze River. Their assignment initially was to protect American commercial interests during the Chinese civil war—lately put on hold to counter the Japanese threat.

On board the *Panay,* in addition to its crew of fifty-five officers and men, were the last personnel from the abandoned U.S. embassy and American, as well as two Italian, newspaper reporters who had all sought refuge there the day before. The *Panay* and three small Standard Oil tankers had then moved upriver some distance to escape the dueling Japanese and Chinese artillery barrages. Japanese aircraft also crisscrossed the skies, but with a large American flag flying from its stern and another stretched out horizontally atop the pilothouse, there did not appear to be much chance that the Japanese would mistake the *Panay* for a belligerent. Indeed, the *Panay*'s two 3-inch deck guns, its principal armament along with ten .30-caliber antiaircraft machine guns, were covered.

But Sunday lunch was barely over when three Japanese navy planes quite suddenly made directly for the *Panay* and dropped a total of eighteen bombs. The ship's machine guns were unlimbered in self-defense, but the initial attack wrecked the forward 3-inch gun and the pilothouse and wounded the captain, Lieutenant Commander J. J. Hughes, and several others. Had it truly been a case of mistaken identity, the attack might have then stopped, but instead twelve more dive-bombers and nine fighters appeared and made run after run at the ship, as well as at the nearby Standard Oil tankers.

Within thirty minutes, all power and propulsion were lost and the *Panay* was settling fast into sixty feet of water. Captain Hughes gave the order to abandon ship, but Japanese fighters continued to strafe some of the lifeboats as they made their way to shore. Two crew members and one of the Italian reporters were killed, and a total of eleven officers and men were seriously wounded. Almost everyone aboard had some measure of injuries from flying shrapnel and wood splinters.

When the American ambassador to Japan, Joseph C. Grew, heard of the attack, all he could think of was the bombing almost forty years earlier of the *Maine*. Grew told the press, "I had been working for five years to build up Japanese-American friendship and this incident seemed to me to risk shattering the whole structure." Indeed, Grew "began to plan the details of hurried packing in case we had to leave—precisely as we began to pack in Berlin after the sinking of the *Lusitania* in 1915."[16]

Bill Leahy heard the news via a telephone call that interrupted a dinner party being given by Secretary of War Harry H. Woodring. Later that evening, Leahy was summoned to a conference with Secretary of State Cordell Hull that lasted past midnight. "It is, in my opinion," Leahy said, "time now to get the Fleet ready for sea, to make an agreement with the British Navy for joint action, and to inform the Japanese that we expect to protect our Nationals."[17]

Leahy proposed a blockade of Japan that would deprive the island nation of the rubber, petroleum, and other raw materials from the East Indies that were fueling its war aims. Two days after the attack, he met with the president and urged him to send the "ships of the Fleet to Navy Yards without delay to obtain fuel, clean bottoms, and take on sea stores preparatory to a cruise at sea." Years later, with the benefit of history, Leahy felt even more strongly that had "we then blockaded Japan, we could check the Tokyo bandits' ideas of conquest, possibly even without a war."[18]

Franklin Roosevelt certainly didn't discount the growing

Japanese threat, but he knew the sentiment of his countrymen. While American public opinion might generally support China over Japan, 70 percent of American voters interviewed in a Gallup poll in January 1938 "favored a policy of complete withdrawal from China— Asiatic Fleet, Marines, missionaries, medical missions, and all."[19]

And this public sentiment aside, Roosevelt himself was just then under considerable attack from isolationists in Congress who were backing a constitutional amendment introduced by Democrat Louis Ludlow of Indiana. It required a national referendum before any congressional declaration of war was effective except in blatant circumstances of a direct attack on the United States or its possessions. If passed, it would turn presidential war powers back more than a century. The January 1938 vote of 209–188 in the House of Representatives to return the matter to the Judiciary Committee showed just how closely contested the matter was.

In the end, Japan's official inquiry into the *Panay* attack called it all a terrible mistake, but that still failed to explain how American flags could be mistaken for Chinese at such close range. The United States Naval Court of Inquiry reached the opposite conclusion and called the sinking deliberate, but Roosevelt's willingness to accept profuse apologies and a $2.2 million indemnity put the matter to rest. As it turned out, Neville Chamberlain, then prime minister of Great Britain and heavily focused on events in Europe, would likely have been no more inclined to support Leahy's plea for a joint blockade or take any firmer action against Japan than he had against Nazi Germany.

One result of the *Panay* sinking, however, was that American press coverage of the event was heavily anti-Japanese and underscored that Japan was a shameless aggressor. One of those aboard the *Panay* was Universal News cameraman Norman Alley. He captured dramatic 16 mm movie footage of the evacuation and subsequent attack and sinking. When Leahy and his staff saw this film at the Navy Department on December 31, it confirmed without doubt that the *Panay* had been "subjected to a very severe, long continued bombardment."

The film was initially without audio, but when Universal Pictures released it into theaters, the scenes of the wounded and the sinking ship, set against dramatic background music and a narrator calling the Japanese "war-crazed culprits," made an impression that would slowly bring the country around to Leahy's way of thinking.[20]

The end of a tumultuous year also brought Leahy a "Dear Bill" note from FDR, thanking him for "the nicest Christmas present I have had." It was a model of the new battleship *North Carolina,* the first to be laid down since the limits of the Washington Conference treaty, but not due to be launched until 1940. Speed up the construction, the president kidded, so that he could take a cruise on the ship. Then he added, "The good old Navy is coming strong."[21]

Franklin Roosevelt's assertion of an up-and-coming navy was part cheerleading, but one reason for his optimism was the work that Ernest King had been doing with naval aviation. King had been disappointed when he was denied the chance to break out a three-star vice admiral's flag as commander, Aircraft, Battle Force. The result was that he remained a rear admiral and was put in command of the Aircraft, Base Force, of seaplanes, centered largely on the West Coast and in Hawaii. But in retrospect, this put him in charge of two very important and related developments in naval aviation.

The first was the initial deployment of the venerable PBY flying boat, nicknamed the "Catalina." Powered by two Pratt & Whitney engines and carrying a crew of about eight depending on the model, this high-wing aircraft had a range of about 2,500 miles. Some four thousand PBYs would be built and see service in World War II for patrol and reconnaissance, antisubmarine duty, convoy escorts, and search-and-rescue operations. Nowhere, of course, would they become more valuable than in the wide watery expanses of the Pacific. King pushed his PBY pilots to their limits, just as he did everyone else, requiring them to train under wartime conditions.

The second important contribution King made was to sail his flagship, the tender *Wright,* which he had once commanded, all over the Central Pacific and as far north as the Gulf of Alaska scouting suitable seaplane bases. He didn't need much for a base, usually just a lagoon sheltered by a coral reef or a protected fjord along Alaska's coast. These locations greatly improved the navy's operational reach in the Pacific, and more often than not, the PBY proved to be the lifeline between far-flung outposts.

Writing a less-than-friendly Admiral Standley shortly before Leahy succeeded him as CNO, King admitted that he was "disappointed at having to come to sea in this billet," but in "some three months" he had become both an expert on and a champion for these flying boats. "The advent of the 60 new PBY airplanes (now beginning)," King assured Standley, "will provide the means of demonstrating the capabilities of 'airboats' in what should be a convincing way."[22]

King went out of his way to tell another officer who had recently completed his flight training at an advanced age much the same thing. Fifty-two-year-old Captain John S. McCain, Annapolis class of 1906, had been hoping to command the new aircraft carrier *Yorktown,* but he was given the air base at Coco Solo in the Canal Zone under King's command instead. King, too, seemed to expect that McCain would get a carrier, but *Yorktown* was behind schedule, and with a philosophical navy version of *que sera, sera*—"different ships—different long splices"—King assured McCain that he was glad to have him "joining this command, in which you will gain first-hand knowledge of that important (and little-known) adjunct of the Fleet—the flying boats."[23]

King, of course, planned to be in the seaplane assignment only for one year, but when he next made the trek to Washington in January 1937, not much had changed as far as his own advancement. Bill Leahy was now chief of naval operations, but both Leahy and King had spoken out loudly against any increase in power for that office. Consequently, Leahy was not in much of a position to help King when Adolphus Andrews, as chief of the Bureau of Navigation, still insisted that King's "services were needed to continue with the expansion, organization and development of patrol squadrons."[24]

King grumbled but went back to the Pacific for another year, including another summer cruise to Alaskan waters. Sometimes the navy changed command designations to confuse matters, but in this case, King's deployment of PBYs and other aircraft all over the Pacific prompted the designation of his command to be changed from "Aircraft, Base Force" to "Aircraft, Scouting Force." It might seem a subtle distinction, but King had put seaplanes on the move along with the rest of the navy.

And, not surprisingly, King came up with a plan during his second year in the Pacific to put himself on the move as well. When the commander, Aircraft, Battle Force, retired in November 1937, even Andrews found it impossible to deny his classmate the vice admiral post. Far from sending Andrews his thanks, however, King sent him a reminder of his own ultimate goals. "I have always assumed that you would wish to know the views and desires of flag officers as to their own personal preferences where their professional prospects are concerned," King wrote Andrews, without pausing to think that the answer was probably no. Discounting any appearance of "a tinge of 'ambition' or even of 'selfishness,'" King nonetheless reminded Andrews that he had frankly discussed his personal objectives with Andrews when he had come into BuNav and "They are now some six months 'behind schedule' — and 'age 64' looms just that much nearer!"[25]

King's solution was to combine his carrier command with the light cruisers, destroyers, and patrol planes of the Scouting Force. Operationally, this would have removed the speedy 33-knot carriers from working with the slower 21-knot battleships and made for "fast-moving and far-ranging independent operations" — exactly King's preferred modus operandi. Command-wise, the move would have merged two vice admiral commands into one. King, of course, unabashedly proposed that he be given the combined command.

Andrews declined. The tactical worth of what King proposed would prove itself in a few short years when Bill Halsey was leading fast-strike carrier raids all around the Pacific. But in 1937, the battleship had not yet been demoted from its perch atop the navy's strategic arsenal. There may, however, have been another motive in Andrews's thinking. A few weeks later, it was his turn to leave the Bureau of Navigation and head for sea duty. Andrews took the Scouting Force command himself, and with it the three stars of a vice admiral.[26]

King flew his own three-star flag from the *Saratoga* and immediately began to put his squadrons through his usual intense training, particularly night operations in preparation for the 1938 fleet maneuvers. Experience and techniques had progressed quite a bit since Fleet Problem XII in 1931, when King had almost lost his airplanes after dark. But nighttime carrier operations were still very dicey. Many squadrons thought that night flying meant taking off at sunset and coming back in an hour. King thought differently.

On one foggy, misty night, King ordered the air groups from the *Lexington* and *Saratoga* to launch simultaneously well after sunset. The chaos was predictable but, in King's mind, instructional. A number of pilots simply headed for shore-based airfields; some of those vowed to quit if King continued such drills. But the pilots whom King came to value returned to their correct ships and landed without mishap.

As always, King was the ultimate authority, the one and only arbiter. One night when the communications watch officer groped his way across the darkened flag bridge, he bumped into an unrecognized figure. "Sir, are you on duty?" he queried. "Young man," came the response, "this is the Admiral. I am always on duty."[27]

As an admiral overseeing his fleet of carriers, including the one serving as his flagship, King later professed that "he subscribed heartily to Admiral Mayo's view that flag officers must never interfere in the management of their flagships." But in 1938, that was not yet the case. King simply couldn't let go of any measure of control. He would formally advise the captain of his appointed flagship that he was to act as if King were not aboard, but in practice, King could not help interfering.[28]

Late in 1938, King transferred his flag to *Lexington*. His flag bridge was one level above the ship's bridge, and whenever the *Lexington*'s captain, John H. Hoover, "handled the flagship in a manner that did not please King, the admiral would lean over the flag bridge railing and loudly berate the skipper before the two bridge crews." To his credit, Hoover, himself later a vice admiral, would merely wave a hand in acknowledgment and go on with his job, not at all rattled by King's tirade.[29]

*   *   *

Another subordinate who was not rattled by King was Bill Halsey. He had spent two years in command of the *Saratoga* and then rotated ashore for a year as commandant of the Pensacola Naval Air Station. In March 1938, Halsey was promoted to rear admiral and two months later ordered back to sea as commander of Carrier Division Two, the new carriers *Yorktown* and *Enterprise.*

These were the next generation of American aircraft carriers. Bigger, faster carriers with roomier flight decks to accommodate more aircraft and more rapid launching and recovery operations were needed; *Yorktown* and *Enterprise* were just the first step in that direction. Displacing almost 20,000 tons each, 809 feet in length, and capable of making almost 33 knots when pressed, these sisters carried between eighty-one and eighty-five aircraft. Both were built at Newport News, Virginia, with *Yorktown* (CV-5) commissioned on September 30, 1937, and *Enterprise* (CV-6) on May 12, 1938.

The operational backbone of all carriers was the flight deck, but the hangar deck, one level below, was a close second. Efficiently shuttling the right type of aircraft between decks via the carrier's elevators was essential to smooth flight operations. Early carriers, including *Yorktown* and *Enterprise,* had elevators built into the middle of their flight decks. Not only did these in-line elevators create potential confusion for flight operations, but they also made the hangar deck more vulnerable to attacking aircraft when the elevators were lowered or when a mechanical problem or battle damage stalled an elevator in the down position and left a gaping hole in the flight deck.

Halsey's task during the latter half of 1938 was to get both *Yorktown* and *Enterprise* fully operational and to work out the kinks. King, as Halsey's immediate superior, was looking over his shoulder and wanting *Yorktown* and *Enterprise* ready for Fleet Problem XX maneuvers in the Caribbean early in 1939. "As you can readily understand," Halsey wrote King in mid-November, "it is going to be a scrap right up to the last minute to get these ships clear from the material bureaus and Navy Yard by 3 January. However, every time an objection is raised, we listen and say, 'Fine, the ships will leave on 3 January.' I hope it works."[30]

King was hardly one to rely on hope from a subordinate, but he seems to have been convinced that Halsey was doing his best and showing great effort in the process. While *Enterprise* received last-minute adjustments in the Norfolk Navy Yard, Halsey arranged to have fuel and fresh provisions loaded directly onto the ship while it was there — no small matter considering that 350 tons of food had to be transported by barge or refrigerated cars. King congratulated Halsey on his "enterprise and initiative in arranging for the fueling and provisioning" in order that both carriers "may make a prompt get-away early in January."[31]

The carriers made it, and Carrier Division Two with Bill Halsey flying his flag as its commander, COMCARDIV2, rendezvoused with King and the carriers *Lexington* and *Ranger*. *Saratoga*, Halsey's favorite, was absent because of an impending overhaul at the Bremerton Navy Yard, and *Ranger* was now under the command of Captain John S. McCain, who had finally gotten his carrier.

But Vice Admiral King was in an unusually foul mood. Somehow, during a dark night en route to transiting the Panama Canal from the Pacific, he had slammed into a deck grating outside his cabin on the *Lexington,* badly bruising one of his legs. He was ordered to rest in bed for at least several days, but he wanted these 1939 maneuvers to be the capstone to his career at sea, as well as the impetus to propel him to the CNO's job when Bill Leahy retired later that year. King refused to rest and snarled his way around the flag bridge of the *Lexington.*

Enterprise in particular was still very green when Halsey joined up with King for the maneuvers. The pilots of its recently formed air squadrons were a little green, too. Predictably, King became upset at a delay in *Enterprise* launching planes. He sent one of his usual accusatory signals and demanded to know the name of the officer responsible for the delay. Not one to shirk his own responsibility as a commanding officer or to blame a junior, Halsey signaled back "COMCARDIV2," meaning himself.[32]

In the end, the fleet exercises went well enough. The crews of

Enterprise and *Yorktown* gained confidence and King gave the battleship admirals, as well as President Roosevelt, who watched the final round from the cruiser *Houston,* a lesson in what naval aviation could do. Afterward, the flag officers met FDR at a reception aboard *Houston,* and each in his own way may have done some not-so-subtle lobbying to succeed Leahy. King always claimed that he refrained because "he had never 'greased' anyone during his forty-two years of service and did not propose to begin, particularly at a moment when many of the admirals were trying so hard to please Mr. Roosevelt that it was obvious."[33]

King's claim to never having been a self-promoter was disingenuous at best, but the truth of the matter seems to be that Leahy's successor had already been agreed upon. It would not be King. Perhaps he had stepped on too many toes, ruffled too many egos. Some said that his reputation for drinking — even if he seemed to be able to turn it on and off at will — was a problem. Others undoubtedly questioned his trademark "lone wolf" approach.

But in a navy that still had only three admirals who could be considered naval aviators — King, Halsey, and Charles A. Blakely — it was hardly surprising that Leahy's replacement would come from the remaining seventy-one preponderantly battleship admirals. So King was forced to swallow both pride and disappointment and cheerily congratulate Rear Admiral Harold R. Stark on his pending appointment. How long Stark might last was another matter.

"Rey," Stark reportedly told King, "you are the man that should have had that job." When King replied, "Other people don't think that," Stark graciously responded, "Well, I do myself."

Another fellow admiral agreed with Stark but scolded, "Why Rey, you should have gotten that job. But why the hell didn't you start getting along in the Gun Club [the battleship admirals]?" King characteristically responded, "They had their chance...and they didn't take it, so to hell with them."[34]

Some years before, King had readily acknowledged that he "had a proper ambition to get to the top, either Commander in Chief of the United States Fleet or even to become Chief of Naval Operations."[35] But now that seemed forever out of reach. He was to be assigned to the General Board to put in his last three years until mandatory retirement.

King was terribly down and glum about his future, certain he had none. The U.S. Navy simply had not yet come to understand the full power of naval aviation as King had worked to develop it. Despite his frequently raucous, theatrical, and antagonistic ways, he had pushed naval aviation to a point where it could assume a very lonely and almost impossible burden two and a half short years hence.

"Dear Ernie," wrote an admirer in a handwritten note, "It has been an education, and a very pleasant one, to serve under you this past winter. May I thank you for your patience of me personally and for the professional lessons you have given me—I should be proud to serve under you any time—anywhere, & under any conditions. The best of luck always—may your new job be to your liking—and here's hoping for more stars afloat. Always sincerely yours, Bill Halsey."[36]

Halsey now raised his flag on the refitted *Saratoga* and assumed King's old job as commander, Aircraft, Battle Force. By the strange twist of the navy's temporary rank system, as King was detailed to the General Board to await the end of his naval service, he reverted to his permanent rank of rear admiral. When Halsey relieved King, Halsey became a temporary vice admiral and as such outranked King.[37]

Meanwhile, Bill Leahy was also apparently nearing the end of his naval service. Leahy turned sixty-four on May 6, 1939, and six days later, President Roosevelt announced at a press conference that he would nominate the admiral to be governor of Puerto Rico. The Washington rumor mill was rife with speculation that Leahy might be appointed secretary of the navy—the ailing Swanson would finally die in July—and FDR appears to have considered that option. The governorship of the territory of Puerto Rico was of some importance to the overall defense and stability of American interests in the Caribbean. It was hardly on a par with the navy post, but at the time Roosevelt's thinking may have been inclined toward emphasizing civilian control of the Navy Department while he slowly pulled the country away from isolationism.[38]

Leahy wasn't entirely sure what he was getting into in Puerto Rico, as the island was divided by numerous internal political factions, but he took the assignment with good grace, as he had always done. "Some of the recent visitors to the Spanish Main," Leahy wrote to Admiral Claude "Claudius" Bloch, "assure me that the Office is sufficiently full of grief to keep even an old sailor moving rapidly. However, as you and I know so well, old sailors will try anything once, and we will endeavor to survive, if not to enjoy, such incidents as may come to us." [39]

The *Washington Post* predicted that Leahy's tenure in Puerto Rico would be "anything but quiet and restful" but badly missed the mark when it attempted a comparison. Had Leahy been chosen to become governor of Hawaii instead, the paper speculated, "he could look forward to a pleasant term of service in an important but not too strenuous position." [40]

Leahy's retirement was set for August 1, in part to allow him to participate in the June state visit of Great Britain's King George VI and Queen Elizabeth to the United States. Leahy was also honored to give the commencement address at the Naval Academy. Mincing no words, the retiring chief of naval operations told the 578 graduating midshipmen of the class of 1939 that "a grave emergency comes once in every generation and that they must be prepared to meet one before their retirement." [41]

On July 28, Leahy was in the Oval Office conferring with FDR on Puerto Rican matters when the president surprised him by having an entourage of photographers and navy brass enter the room just before presenting him with the Distinguished Service Medal. Praising Leahy's role in the navy's greatest peacetime expansion, the citation concluded, "The extraordinary qualities of leadership and administrative ability that have marked his tenure as the highest ranking officer in the Navy have been exemplified throughout his entire Naval career." [42]

Three hundred officers of the Navy Department feted Leahy at a formal dinner in his honor at the Mayflower Hotel that evening as a testament to his high standing. But the accolades that mattered most for Leahy's future came the next day in a letter from FDR.

Emphasizing Leahy's "conspicuous administrative ability," Roosevelt voiced his "sincere hope that after retirement from the Navy your valuable experience will be given for a long time to the public service and that you will enjoy many years of health and happiness." Then, across the bottom of the page in his own hand, the president scrawled, "Dear Bill, I just *hate* to have you leave. FDR." [43]

Below his typed diary entry for August 1, 1939, Leahy wrote in longhand, "This brings to an end forty-six years of active service in the Navy of the United States." Privately, the president assured the retiring admiral, "Bill, if we ever have a war, you're going to be right back here, helping me to run it." [44]

CHAPTER TWELVE

At War All but in Name

William D. Leahy's tenure as governor of Puerto Rico was a temporary assignment. To be sure, the island was central to the defense of the Caribbean in the event of war, and it was doubly certain that the defense of the Panama Canal would be of great importance. But Franklin Roosevelt seems to have had a broader plan for Leahy even as Bill and Louise sailed to the island in early September 1939.

The war of which FDR had spoken had come to pass much more quickly than expected, even if the United States was not yet in it. On September 1, having already used ominous threats to gobble up Austria and Czechoslovakia, Adolf Hitler unleashed his airplanes and tanks against Poland. Great Britain and France responded by declaring war on Germany. A week later, Roosevelt proclaimed a limited national emergency in the United States and authorized a call-up of reserves.

The burden of preparing for an ever-increasing global role fell particularly hard on the navy's Bureau of Navigation and its new chief, Rear Admiral Chester W. Nimitz. After his term as assistant chief ended in 1938, Nimitz received his first stars and went to sea in command of a cruiser division. But he had barely reported when a hernia repair caused him to lose a month ashore. Nimitz—never one to be inactive—fretted that he would lose his cruiser command because of it. He did, but when he reported back for duty, he was appointed commander of a battleship division instead.

Nimitz thought he was in his element aboard his flagship, the *Arizona*. The last battleship to be commissioned prior to the American entry into World War I, *Arizona* mounted twelve 14-inch guns in two turrets fore and two turrets aft. At 31,400 tons, the 608-foot-long ship was capable of 21 knots—like most battleships of that era, a beefy platform for armaments but not a speedy one. Nimitz threw himself into the task of commanding his division and followed his usual practice of being interested in how well men did their jobs, whether a captain or a mess steward.

As it turned out, Nimitz's real element was not in the giant ships he loved so much, but in managing men. Through his NROTC classes, his commands at sea, and his tour as assistant chief at BuNav, Nimitz had come to know so many so well and, understanding the needs of the fleet as he did, he had an uncanny ability to put the right man in the right job. Thus, while he professed disappointment at having his sea cruise as commander, Battleship Division One, cut short, few were surprised when Nimitz was called ashore to become chief of the Bureau of Navigation in the spring of 1939.

Admiral Claude Bloch, commander in chief of the U.S. Fleet, regretted to see him leave. "While the Navy Department gains in this transaction," Bloch told Nimitz, "I feel that the fleet loses heavily and in as much as my activities are centered in the fleet I am very sorry to see you go.... You have a big job on your hands in the Bureau of Navigation. Those who are dissatisfied by reason of not having been promoted are growing in numbers and strength and it is my conviction that your ingenuity and cleverness both are going to be taxed to the utmost."[1]

As he disembarked from the *Arizona*, Nimitz received another unexpected note of remembrance and prophesy. Miller Reese Hutchison, a member of Thomas Edison's team of inventors and himself the principal inventor of the first electrical hearing aid, sent Nimitz his congratulations on his new post and remembered two visits Nimitz had made as a young officer to the Edison lab in 1914. "Hutch" now recalled Thomas Edison saying, "Lieutenant Nimitz possesses more brains and is more practical, in my estimation, than any of the young Officers who have visited us. I predict he will, some day, be filling Admiral Dewey's shoes. There is no foolishness about him. He wants to know and is successful in getting all the facts." Hutchison closed his letter by saying, "Mr. Edison's prediction is, I believe, very close to fruition."[2]

Among Nimitz's early responsibilities at BuNav was telling Admiral Bloch that when his tour with the fleet was completed in January 1940, he would be assigned to his final post as commandant of the Fourteenth Naval District. The United States and its territories and possessions were divided into fifteen such districts, and their command involved all-inclusive supervision of shore installations, coastlines, and sea-lanes. "Whether this is important duty or not," Bloch responded to Nimitz, "hinges on circumstances; it may turn out to be very important or, on the other hand, it may turn out to be quite different."[3] The headquarters of the Fourteenth Naval District was in Honolulu, Hawaii.

Bloch's replacement as commander in chief, U.S. Fleet, was to be James O. Richardson, Annapolis class of 1902, a year behind King and known by his academy nickname of "J.O." or "JO." Born in Paris, Texas, in the extreme northeast corner of the state, Richardson was a big-gun admiral who had served on destroyers, been the first captain of the cruiser *Augusta,* and commanded the Battle Force. While in Washington, he had gotten plenty of staff exposure as assistant to the chief of BuOrd, assistant CNO, and Nimitz's immediate predecessor at BuNav. Richardson's most important task as commander in chief was to deploy the fleet to Hawaii for its 1940 maneuvers. To his surprise and displeasure, he would be ordered to keep it there.

Nimitz's other duties were numerous and time-consuming. Roosevelt's declaration of a limited national emergency included a call-up of reserves on a voluntary basis, but that was only the beginning.

The universities offering NROTC had increased from six when Nimitz first went to Cal Berkeley to twenty-seven. Congress increased the enrollment at Annapolis by giving five appointments to each congressman and senator instead of four, and the academy's course was temporarily reduced from four years to three. The naval training stations at San Diego, Norfolk, Newport, and the Great Lakes were enlarged, and the basic training course for recruits was shortened from eight weeks to six. There was a rush about everything, and everything required more manpower.

By then, Chester and Catherine Nimitz had found an apartment at 2222 Q Street, where their two older daughters, Kate and Nancy, were also living. Nancy, at age twenty, was flaunting the intellectual and political freedom that was long her trademark, and her father patiently gave her plenty of rope. But one afternoon while the Nimitz family were guests of the secretary of the navy aboard the yacht *Sequoia,* the presidential yacht, *Potomac,* with presidential flag flying, came chugging from the opposite direction. All aboard the *Sequoia* hurried on deck to render respects, but Nancy groaned, "I don't know whether I want to salute Roosevelt." That was enough for her father. "Whether you salute Roosevelt or not is your own business," Nimitz told his daughter, "but you are going to salute the President." [4]

Predictably, Ernest J. King's posting to the General Board had caused him particular anguish, and it only got worse. Suddenly, the world was going to war, and from all appearances, King was going into retirement. Some days, King was flat-out depressed, calling himself a "has-been." Yet on other occasions, he bristled with his usual confidence and asserted to junior officers, "They're not done with me yet." In between these extremes, King refused to fall into the reflective ease embraced by many of his fellow admirals on the General Board. Instead, he embarked on another round of intense study on naval deployments and the world situation almost as if he were cramming for a final exam. [5]

In March 1940, King was suddenly assigned to accompany Acting Secretary of the Navy Charles Edison (the inventor's son) on a tour of the Pacific Fleet. No one, including King, seemed to know just why he was delegated to accompany Edison, but since the suggestion apparently came from the president himself, it was not questioned. Admiral Richardson, in charge of the Pacific Fleet, "wondered what the hell I was doing there," King recalled, "[but] I went along for the ride."[6]

The benefit of the trip to King proved to be that Edison was impressed by his knowledge and talents and gave him free rein upon their return to Washington to oversee a thorough overhaul of antiaircraft batteries throughout the fleet. King cut through bureaucratic red tape with his usual lack of finesse and got the job done in record time. It was just the sort of jolt that Edison thought the entire navy needed to break out of a "peace-time psychology" and "throw off a routine state of mind." Edison told Roosevelt that King had the leadership skills to force this needed transformation, and he urged King's future appointment as commander in chief, U.S. Fleet, to replace Richardson.[7]

For his part, Roosevelt, despite having detailed King to Edison's side for the Pacific trip, was mum. The inside scuttlebutt was that Roosevelt—he of the ritual afternoon happy hour—was among those who thought King drank too much. Instead, in September 1940 King was summoned to the office of the CNO, Admiral Harold R. Stark, to hear the offer of command of the Atlantic Squadron (subsequently briefly called the Patrol Force), then a rather inferior group of aging battleships and cruisers, since the bulk of the navy's aircraft carriers and newer firepower was in the Pacific. Rear Admiral Chester Nimitz, as chief of the Bureau of Navigation, was on hand to deliver the bad news that if King took the appointment, he would have only his rear admiral rank, not the three stars of a vice admiral he had enjoyed when last at sea. King waved Nimitz aside. It didn't matter, he said. He very much "wanted to go to sea," and he readily accepted Stark's offer.[8]

A number of King's colleagues were stunned by the assignment. King of the carriers, King of the vaunting ambition, was taking what many considered a junior command—certainly a step down from his deferential, if less-than-useful position on the General

Board. Nonetheless King prepared for the assignment with his usual gusto. Then a routine physical revealed that he, too, had a hernia that needed to be repaired before he was ready for sea. The month's recuperation gave him plenty of time to think. Recognizing how well his tour with Acting Secretary Edison had gone, King volunteered to accompany Frank Knox, the newly appointed secretary of the navy, on an inspection tour of Caribbean bases and Atlantic Squadron maneuvers slated for just before King was to assume command.

Knox's appointment as secretary of the navy was part of Franklin Roosevelt's 1940 presidential election strategy to stifle Republican isolationism and win bipartisan support for the looming global conflict. Knox was a newspaper publisher from Chicago who had been the Republican vice presidential candidate on the ill-fated Alf Landon ticket of 1936. One might question his specific navy credentials, but Knox's role model was Theodore Roosevelt, under whom he had served as a Rough Rider during the Spanish-American War. That in and of itself harbored well for the navy. Not only would the Caribbean trip give King a chance to win points with Knox — much as he had done with Edison — but King also could evaluate his new command from the sidelines before hoisting his flag.

King immediately assumed the role of tour guide and squired Knox on a whirlwind itinerary that used aircraft to cover a lot of ground from Washington to the Canal Zone and back. Some reports had King drinking too much — or at least too much for his fellow revelers. His personal specialty was "The King's Peg," a potent concoction of champagne poured over brandy in flutes or tall glasses with little or no ice. "Admiral King embarrassed all of us with his intoxicated behavior," reported the commander at Key West, but if the report was true, Knox seemed not to notice or mind. By the end of the two-week tour, Knox shared Edison's evaluation of King as a man who could get things done.[9]

Meanwhile, Bill Leahy's tenure as governor of Puerto Rico was subject to world tensions as well as internal political friction on the island. Germany launched its blitzkrieg against France in May

1940, and Italy soon joined Germany in declaring war against Great Britain and France. After British troops evacuated the continent at Dunkirk, France pleaded for an armistice, which Adolf Hitler gleefully accepted in the same railcar used for Germany's 1918 surrender. Governor Leahy was particularly glum about what this meant for the United States. "With only England offering effective resistance to the Nazis," Leahy wrote, "and with China fighting alone and almost helplessly against Japan, I could see little or no prospect of our not being attacked on one side or the other sooner or later."

Despite his Puerto Rican duties, Leahy spent much of May and June 1940 in Washington and conferred with FDR on numerous occasions about global issues. Roosevelt continued to lean heavily on Leahy for advice and perspective, even if by now Leahy was outwardly resigned that American involvement in the war was all but inevitable. FDR may have privately agreed with Leahy's pessimism, but in a presidential election year, he had to remain publicly optimistic that the United States could somehow avoid sending another generation of young Americans into battle. Leahy termed this their "friendly disagreement," but it certainly did not stop the president from once again affirming that in the event of U.S. involvement in the war, Leahy would be recalled to Washington.[10]

In Puerto Rico, Leahy was strict but fair as he tried to keep local elections free from the partisan violence that was usually sparked by claims for Puerto Rican independence. There also may have been an anti-German sentiment in the back of his mind. If the second-hand gossip Secretary of the Interior Harold Ickes recorded is to be believed, Leahy told columnist Drew Pearson that if the broader European war should involve the United States, several hundred Germans in Puerto Rico "simply would disappear [and] no one would ever hear of them again."

Ickes admitted that "this streak in an American naval officer who has come out of the soil of Iowa does startle me a little," and it seems out of character for Leahy to have spoken candidly with Pearson in the first place. But Leahy was definitely a hard-core conservative as opposed to the liberal Ickes. "Leahy thinks that there may be an attempt on his own life," Ickes observed later that fall, "but he seems to be prepared for it, and I don't believe that he would hesitate to shoot down anyone who might attack him."[11]

No doubt this was the advice that Leahy continued to give FDR when he returned to the United States again for consultations in October, just before the 1940 election. Leahy had lunch with the president and listened as Admiral James O. Richardson, who for a time had been assistant CNO under Leahy, objected to the Pacific Fleet's continued presence at Pearl Harbor. It was bad for navy morale, Richardson argued, because the facilities there simply could not support a prolonged deployment. In Richardson's mind, it wasn't a matter of foreign policy — that the fleet was either a provocation or a deterrent to Japan in the Pacific. Rather, Richardson's argument for a withdrawal was a logistical one — Pearl Harbor was simply too far away to support adequately.

Then Leahy watched as Richardson practically threw himself off a cliff and professed to FDR, "The senior officers of the Navy do not have the trust and confidence in the civilian leadership of this country that is essential for the successful prosecution of a war in the Pacific."[12]

One can almost hear Franklin D. Roosevelt grinding his teeth on his usually jaunty cigarette holder. FDR appreciated military men who spoke their minds about military issues in private counsels with him — that's why he valued Leahy and would come to value George C. Marshall. But Richardson had made the unpardonable error in Roosevelt's mind of crossing the line between military and political matters. FDR mumbled something in reply about the limits of what could be done in an election year, but Richardson had shown his hand too well. It was only the pending election that kept FDR from terminating him right then and there.

Leahy returned to Puerto Rico, and Roosevelt won a third term handily enough, but on November 17, as the president reviewed the challenges ahead, he sent Leahy a blunt telegram. The French armistice with the Germans had left a shadow government in Vichy led by World War I hero Marshal Henri-Philippe Pétain and nominally in control of the southern third of the country, as well as the French fleet. Roosevelt told Leahy that the situation was "increasingly serious" because there was some "possibility that France may actually engage in the war against Great Britain and in particular that the French fleet may be utilized under the control of Germany."

Leahy was "the best man available for this mission" as ambassador to Vichy France, FDR said, because he could "talk to Marshal Pétain in language which he would understand and the position which you have held in our own navy would undoubtedly give you great influence with the higher officers of the French Navy who are openly hostile to Great Britain." Roosevelt hoped that Leahy would "accept the mission to France and be prepared to leave at the earliest possible date." Leahy, of course, was far too much of a sailor to take FDR's "hope" for anything less than an order. He replied immediately, "I can leave Puerto Rico in a week."[13]

Several weeks later, Rear Admiral Ernest J. King boarded his new flagship, the aging, pre–World War I battleship *Texas,* and led his Atlantic Squadron of largely secondhand ships back to the Caribbean for amphibious training exercises with army and marine units. For all King's talk of glorying in Napoleon's ability to envision the grand strategy and then empower his subordinates to execute it, King had always had his hand in everything, and even as recently as the 1939 carrier maneuvers with Bill Halsey, he had not refrained from interfering with details best left to subordinates.

Yes, in the last war King had convinced Admiral Henry T. Mayo of the importance of delegating and then trusting his destroyer captains; he had preached the importance of individual training and career advancement so as to be fully capable of executing such instructions; but when push came to shove, King had always had a terrible time biting his own sharp tongue and trusting that his orders would be carried out.

If there was to be an epiphany, perhaps it occurred one dark night in January 1941 during the Caribbean maneuvers. King was up to his usual behavior. He ordered his ships darkened and then sent a radio message to prepare to alter course. Before all the ships had acknowledged, King gave the command to execute the turn. In the bedlam that followed, it was a miracle there were no collisions, as

King ordered turn after turn and his ships struggled to keep up. Finally, he ordered a cruising formation and left the bridge, to the relief of all hands.

But a few hours later, when the watch officer ordered a routine course change and matter-of-factly reported it to the admiral, King stormed back to the bridge and cussed a blue streak, demanding to know who had signaled the course change. The watch officer, Francis S. Low, whose nickname was "Frog," unabashedly replied, "I did, sir." How dare he assume King's authority, the admiral thundered.

Finally, after the tirade subsided, King approached Low, who had retreated to a dark corner of the bridge, and patted him on the shoulder with a proffered semi-apology. "Admiral," sputtered Low as he wheeled around, "aside from asking for my immediate detachment, there is not one goddamn thing you can do to me that I can't take."[14]

Low's outburst may or may not have gotten King to thinking, but over the next several months, he issued a series of orders on the exercise of command, essentially mandating less detailed orders on "how" to execute a mission and more initiative in executing the "what" of the mission. "We are preparing for—and are now close to," King told his Atlantic Squadron on January 21, "those active operations (commonly called war) which require the exercise and the utilization of the full powers and capabilities of every officer in command status." Not assuming any personal blame for his own self-centric and controlling persona, King nonetheless urged that the "initiative of the subordinate" in "how to do it" should be supported after ordering "what to do" unless the particular circumstances demanded otherwise.[15]

"Sometimes I got a kind of obsession of interfering with admirals who had to do the job," King later wrote with some understatement, but even when he "sometimes believed I could have done a better job myself," he got himself "in hand enough not to interfere unless it seemed that it really had to be done."[16]

For King, this change in attitude, admittedly a long time coming, could not have occurred a moment too soon. Bossing carriers or small task forces was one thing, but King was about to command a much larger operation in which delegation, trusting subordinates' initiative, and picking the right ones in the first place was the only way things were going to get done efficiently and effectively.

Barely had King arrived in the Caribbean for these January 1941 maneuvers, when he received a message from Secretary of the Navy Knox that President Roosevelt had reorganized the U.S. Fleet and, in recognition of a two-ocean threat, had divided it into three separate fleets. Henceforth, there would be the Atlantic, Pacific, and Asiatic Fleets, and King's Atlantic Squadron would form the nucleus of the Atlantic force.

The details came in a communication from Nimitz at BuNav. King's stars were on the way. His interim appointment to vice admiral was effective immediately, and he would receive the four stars of a full admiral befitting his fleet command posthaste. Roosevelt used the same flurry of changes to relieve James O. Richardson with Husband E. Kimmel and designate Kimmel as commander in chief, Pacific Fleet. There would be no more talk about the fleet leaving Pearl Harbor.

Kimmel had been one of Bill Halsey's groomsmen at his wedding and remained one of Halsey's closest friends. Up to a point, their careers had been similar. Kimmel had cut his teeth on commanding destroyers and then destroyer divisions, but while Halsey went into aviation, Kimmel remained with the big-gun surface ships, eventually commanding the battleship *New York* and the Cruisers, Battle Force.

"Needless to say," Kimmel wrote Nimitz after learning of his appointment, "I am much flattered and pleased with the assignment, but my satisfaction is mixed with anxiety as to whether or not I shall measure up to the job. However, no efforts on my part shall be spared."[17]

But for whatever shortcomings Kimmel thought he faced, at least he had a modest supply of ships. For King in the Atlantic, it was a different story. There was still too much "business as usual," King wrote Knox shortly after assuming command. Things had to change. Knox heartily concurred and told King in return that he was "not at all surprised, but... gratified to know that the Commander-in-Chief of the Atlantic Fleet recognizes the existence of an emergency and is taking proper measures to meet it. I knew you would!"[18]

One of King's first steps was to hasten most of his ships into port for long-overdue overhauls and modifications to improve their combat readiness. Depth charges for antisubmarine warfare and anti-aircraft batteries were high on the list. The result was the Atlantic Fleet was "temporarily immobilized in the shipyards," but it emerged far better prepared to fight a long war.

Recognizing that the navy, indeed the entire American armed forces, was short of men, ships, and materiel, King assured Nimitz at BuNav that he would work with what he was given and then issued his "Making the Best of What We Have" order. Shortages would be no excuse for poor performance. "I expect the officers of the Atlantic Fleet to be the leaders in what may be called the 'pioneering spirit,'" King ordered. "We must all do all we can with what we have."[19]

But for all of King's newfound assertions about the "initiative of the subordinate" in "how to do" something, he found himself in somewhat of a quandary as to just "what to do" himself. President Roosevelt had just provided Great Britain with fifty Lend-Lease destroyers in exchange for Caribbean and Canadian bases, but beyond a general support for British shipping, the rules of engagement were rather sketchy.

There was also the matter of his base of operations. King had ships protecting the North Atlantic sea approaches to the eastern United States and the soft underbelly of the Caribbean, including the vital Panama Canal. He also had a patrol squadron of four largely obsolete cruisers and five destroyers covering the South Atlantic between Brazil and Africa. King himself had to be close to Washington, as Roosevelt, Knox, and CNO Stark all came to call on him more and more, but he also wanted to be near the action at sea. So King chose Newport, Rhode Island, and the waters of Narragansett Bay, within sight of the Naval War College, as his home port.

Never one to run at half speed, he found the uncertainty over rules of engagement in the Atlantic as draining as the regular commutes he made to Washington for staff conferences. "Well," King would grumble, "I've got to go down to Washington again to straighten out those dumb bastards once more."[20]

On April 18, 1941, while King was in Washington on one of his visits, he received a call from the White House asking him to meet the president at Hyde Park at three o'clock the following afternoon. The summons itself was somewhat unusual, but it was the "come alone" part of the message that most aroused King's curiosity. He flew to a small airfield near Poughkeepsie, New York, was met by a car, and then was driven to Hyde Park. There, from behind the wheel of his 1936 Ford Phaeton, specially outfitted with hand levers, FDR motioned King into the passenger seat and drove up the hill to his secluded stone cottage. This would indeed be a very private talk.

Despite all that Roosevelt had been doing to aid Great Britain, the situation there was grim, and the president was determined to meet face-to-face with Prime Minister Winston Churchill as soon as practical. The meeting had to be conducted with the utmost secrecy, a condition that argued against Washington, D.C., or any other point of easy access. So Roosevelt spread out his charts of the Canadian Maritime Provinces and proposed to meet Churchill at one of the U.S. Navy's new Lend-Lease bases on the southeastern toe of Newfoundland—if Admiral King could get him there.

One might imagine that FDR would have felt more comfortable with either Leahy or Halsey in this role. He had, after all, sailed with both of them. But Leahy was in Vichy France and Halsey far off in the Pacific. King, with at least FDR's acquiescence, was the commander in chief of the Atlantic Fleet that would have to orchestrate the ruse.

The first plan was for Roosevelt to slip east from Ottawa by rail to Gaspé, at the mouth of the St. Lawrence, after attending a conference with Canadian prime minister Mackenzie King. From Gaspé, one of Admiral King's cruisers would take FDR to Argentia, on Placentia Bay. King left Hyde Park that day sworn to secrecy, but there were potential problems. The rail segment was long and apt to attract attention, and the mid-May date that Roosevelt proposed might find the Gulf of St. Lawrence still clogged with river ice. FDR decided to postpone the trip, and King heard nothing more from him until late July.[21]

In the meantime, King shifted his flag from the venerable *Texas* to the much newer and sleeker cruiser *Augusta*. This ship had been Chester Nimitz's prized command, and it was destined to be on the scene of all the great Atlantic Theater campaigns of World War II. After eight years in the Pacific, *Augusta* had returned to Mare Island Naval Shipyard for a complete overhaul in November 1940. After King urged that the work be expedited, the ship came through the Panama Canal and arrived at King's disposal in late April 1941.

Within a few weeks of moving aboard, King's attention was fixed on Great Britain's desperate sea chase after the German battleship *Bismarck*. After exiting the Denmark Strait between Greenland and Iceland, *Bismarck* and the heavy cruiser *Prinz Eugen* sank the pride of the British fleet, the gigantic battleship *Hood,* and badly damaged the accompanying battleship *Prince of Wales*. Churchill warned Roosevelt that these wolves were loose in the North Atlantic and intended a formidable raid against merchant shipping. "Give us the news" of their whereabouts, Churchill pleaded, "and we will finish the job."[22]

King alerted his ships and dispatched long-range patrol planes from Newfoundland to probe the fog-enshrouded seas. Many of their pilots were still fairly green, and there were many close calls with the weather and navigation. None encountered *Bismarck,* but some aircraft were forced to land at alternate points. One PBY put down before King's very eyes in Narragansett Bay, despite his order that the planes avoid public scrutiny by not flying over more populated areas.

"Admiral," stammered his nervous air officer, "there must be a Narragansett Bay in Newfoundland."

"There had better be," King growled.[23]

Swordfish torpedo planes flying off the British aircraft carrier *Ark Royal* ultimately crippled *Bismarck*'s steering mechanism to the point that its subsequent wobbly course to a safe port in occupied France was intercepted by other elements of the Royal Navy. The giant battleship was finally sunk after a concerted attack by battleships, carrier-based planes, and torpedo-firing cruisers and destroyers. By now, neither King nor anyone else in the U.S. Navy with any foresight doubted the power of carrier-based aircraft. Still, at the British Admiralty's request, King put several older American battleships on station in the western Atlantic to guard against a similar outbreak.

On the day that *Bismarck* went down, May 27, 1941, President Roosevelt proclaimed an "unlimited national emergency." The difference between this and FDR's "limited national emergency," in place since September 1939, was largely a matter of semantics. The president was slowly bringing the American public around to Bill Leahy's pessimistic outlook. Certainly, the events that King was charged with orchestrating that summer bespoke an inevitable escalation toward war.

American forces had already assumed the defense of Greenland. In June, U.S. troops relieved the British garrison in Iceland, freeing up British troops for duties elsewhere and, even more important, providing King's ships with another port from which to shepherd convoys. While Roosevelt was still reluctant to protect British ships, King was ordered to conduct convoys of American and Icelandic ships from the United States to Iceland and include any ships from friendly neutrals that chose to sail along. Then, on July 25, 1941, King was again summoned to Hyde Park. This time, Roosevelt intended to use the cover of an August vacation aboard the presidential yacht, *Potomac,* to board the *Augusta* in secrecy and sail to Argentia to meet Churchill. Barely a week later, on Sunday, August 3, *Augusta* anchored off City Island at the western end of Long Island Sound. King had not even told its captain the purpose of the trip, but the hurried construction of several ramps that could accommodate a wheelchair offered a strong clue.

That afternoon, a destroyer came alongside and transferred Chief of Naval Operations Harold Stark and Army Chief of Staff George C. Marshall to the *Augusta*. It was the first time King had more than a passing encounter with Marshall. Major General Henry H. Arnold, chief of the Army Air Corps, and other senior aides from both the army and navy went aboard the nearby cruiser *Tuscaloosa* at the same time. *Tuscaloosa* was to accompany *Augusta* to Newfoundland and serve as a backup in case any calamity befell King's flagship. Then, the two cruisers, screened by a division of destroyers, got under way and steamed slowly eastward along the northern shore of Long Island to Smithtown Bay, where they anchored for the night.

Sixty-some miles to the northeast across the waters of Long Island Sound, President Roosevelt departed the submarine base at New London, Connecticut, that same afternoon aboard the *Potomac,* with all the trappings of a weeklong fishing trip. *Potomac* leisurely sailed eastward with the Coast Guard cutter *Calypso* as escort and anchored for the night at Port Judith, Rhode Island. On Monday morning, Roosevelt even managed to put a touch of royalty on his charade at a port call just south of New Bedford, Massachusetts, when he entertained Princess Martha of Norway, who was a regular guest at the White House after Germany's invasion of Norway.

By nightfall, the *Potomac* had made its way to Menemsha Bight, near the western tip of Martha's Vineyard. There the *Augusta* and its escorts were waiting, having passed across the waters of Block Island Sound that King knew so well. In the morning, the president, his personal physician, and two military aides came on board. King lost no time in getting under way, while the *Potomac,* with the presidential flag still flying, carried on its deception. The yacht even transited the Cape Cod Canal with a crew member seated on deck wearing a floppy FDR fishing hat and tossing an occasional wave.

There was no apparent rush, as Churchill was not due in Argentia until August 9, but King ordered the *Augusta* and its consorts to 21 and then 22 knots. Radar had recently been installed on the cruisers, and King apparently placed great reliance on it. Despite dense fog off Cape Breton Island and the crowded shipping lanes then hurrying support from the mouth of the St. Lawrence to Great Britain, King maintained his speed. No doubt he meant to show the president a bit of dash, both personally and for the navy as a whole, but one wonders what might have happened had the *Augusta* encountered a stray merchantman or fishing trawler in the gloom. Early radar was certainly not foolproof.

The skies were clear, however, on the morning of August 7, when Cape St. Mary loomed above the entrance to Placentia Bay. The destroyers busied themselves with patrol duty, while *Augusta* and *Tuscaloosa* anchored in their assigned locations off Ship Harbour. For two days, the Americans waited as the sunny weather gave way to the more typical Newfoundland fog.

Winston Churchill couldn't have scripted it better had he tried. For out of the mist, on the morning of August 9, still bearing the scars from its encounter with the *Bismarck,* the battleship *Prince of Wales* glided into the harbor, with its crew lining the rails, its band playing, and Churchill standing unmistakably on a wing of the bridge. Those susceptible to historical hyperbole might even claim that it was the moment when the Allies won World War II.

But in truth, it was only the beginning. *Prince of Wales* anchored astern of *Augusta,* and Churchill and his military retinue came aboard to pay their respects. While Roosevelt and Churchill dined privately for lunch, King hosted a luncheon for the assembled staffs. This was an event of some importance because it was the first meeting—however relaxed for the moment—of what would be called the Combined Chiefs of Staff. King was not yet at their level—Admiral Stark still represented the U.S. Navy—but King's presence at this conference gave him an introduction to his British counterparts, as well as a proximity to Roosevelt, Churchill, and Marshall that would serve him well in wartime conferences to come. Although there would be rancorous debates between the American and British chiefs, First Sea Lord Sir Dudley Pound admitted a few weeks after Argentia that he had "formed a very good opinion of Admiral King."

The next day was Sunday, and FDR accepted Churchill's invitation to attend church services on the quarterdeck of the *Prince of Wales.* The American destroyer *McDougal* ferried the president and his party from the *Augusta* to the British man-of-war, coming alongside in bow-to-stern fashion to better accommodate the president's transfer via a narrow gangway. King, who had once been called to task for bringing his dinghy alongside a ship in just such a manner, made no comment on this occasion.

Churchill chose the hymns, which included "Onward, Christian Soldiers" and "O God, Our Help in Ages Past." This seemed to seal the emotional bonds, and before they parted, Roosevelt and Churchill crafted what came to be called the Atlantic Charter. It enumerated eight common goals, essentially war aims. Given the United States' official status as a neutral, they had to be couched, in Roosevelt's words, as "certain common principles in the national policies of their respective countries on which they base their hopes for a better future for the world." Among them were self-determination for all peoples, "the final destruction of the Nazi tyranny," and the time-honored freedom of the seas.[24]

That freedom of the seas was soon to be tested. During the frenzied hunt for the *Bismarck* the preceding May, a German submarine, *U-69*, had torpedoed the five-thousand-ton American merchantman *Robin Moor* in the Atlantic between Brazil and Sierra Leone. The commander of *U-69* gave proper warning and permitted the thirty-eight crew members and eight passengers to evacuate into lifeboats before sending the ship to the bottom. But the lifeboats drifted with sparse food and water for five days before serendipitously being rescued.

The delay in learning of the sinking and the *Bismarck* story pushed the *Robin Moor* off the front pages, but Roosevelt was determined that it not set a precedent. Characterizing the sinking as "a warning that the United States may use the high seas of the world only with Nazi consent," FDR told Congress, "We are not yielding and we do not propose to yield."[25]

Then came the *Greer* incident. The *Greer* was a *Wickes*-class destroyer of World War I vintage assigned to the North Atlantic convoy routes. On September 4, 1941, a British patrol plane signaled the ship that a German U-boat was lurking ten miles ahead. The *Greer*'s sonar picked up a contact, and the plane dropped four depth charges before departing the scene because of low fuel. But the destroyer kept up a pursuit until the U-boat fired a near-miss torpedo, after which the *Greer* unleashed a flurry of depth charges. Another torpedo and more depth charges were exchanged before *Greer* discontinued the engagement.

Critics thought that the *Greer*'s captain, Commander George W. Johnson, had been too aggressive, perhaps even provoking the U-boat. But King stood behind him one hundred percent. Don't worry, King assured Johnson, "As long as I command the Atlantic Fleet, no one is going to nail your tail to the mast because you defended yourself."[26]

In fact, Roosevelt used the encounter to adopt a "shoot on sight" policy against both U-boats and German surface ships in the North Atlantic, but the result was predictable. In October, a torpedo struck the U.S. destroyer *Kearny,* with the loss of eleven men. Then the oiler *Salinas* and the destroyer *Reuben James* were hit. The latter sank, with the loss of many of its crew members, prompting Woody Guthrie to pen a song about the dead sailors asking, "Tell me what were their names."[27]

Part of Guthrie's angst stemmed from the American public not yet comprehending the full sacrifices that King's men, and all those in the armed forces, were beginning to make. In typical bureaucratic fashion, the Navy Department hoped that it might compensate and boost morale by awarding medals and commendations. King wasn't convinced.

"I suggest that we 'go slow' in this matter of making 'heroes' out of those people who have, after all, done the jobs they are trained to do," King told Admiral Stark. "The earlier incidents [*Salinas* and *Kearny*] loom large by contrast with peacetime conditions — but can be expected to become commonplace incidents as we get further along."

"Personally," King reiterated to Nimitz, "I do not favor such awards unless the incidents indicate clearly deeds which are 'above and beyond the call of duty.'" Perhaps forgetting that he himself had been the recipient of the Navy Cross largely for transiting the Atlantic during World War I, King hoped "there will be no repetition of certain awards made during the last war where people were, in effect, decorated when they lost their ships." King, being King, could not help but conclude by volunteering, "I do not consider my opinion as being 'hard-boiled' — naturally! — merely 'realistic.'"[28]

That same November, King noted his sixty-third birthday. But despite appearing in a feature article in *Life* magazine as "King of the Atlantic," the admiral was in no mood to celebrate. He now had but one year until retirement, and it looked as though his career would end in this uncomfortable and uncertain time.[29]

Meanwhile, the man who was soon to be on a seat as hot as Admiral King's was Vice Admiral William F. Halsey, Jr. Since the summer of 1940, Halsey had been commander, Aircraft, Battle Force, in charge of the navy's aircraft carriers in the Pacific. His mission of keeping his carriers battle ready meant that at least one was usually undergoing an overhaul at any time. Perhaps the most significant change that occurred was the installation of radar. Halsey was intrigued by its possibilities and awestruck the first time the *Yorktown* used its antenna array to locate an opposing war games force "out of sight over the horizon." With each subsequent improvement in equipment, radar ranges increased farther and farther and vastly expanded the eyes of the fleet.

By the summer of 1941, *Yorktown, Ranger,* and the recently commissioned carrier *Wasp* were deployed with King's forces in the Atlantic. That left Halsey operating out of Pearl Harbor with *Saratoga, Lexington,* and *Enterprise.* Halsey and Admiral Kimmel organized task forces of cruisers and destroyers around the three carriers and made it a general rule that only one task force would be in port at Pearl Harbor at any one time, to better protect the fleet from attack or sabotage.[30]

Kimmel and Halsey had good reason to be concerned, but they were hardly alone. War with Germany, if not with Japan as well, had taken on an air of inevitability. Newspapers and magazines of this period were filled with stories of a buildup in American military forces and FDR's slow but steady gearing up of what later would be called the military-industrial complex.

Roosevelt had really started the buildup in 1933, when he had diverted a slice of a Depression-era public works bill to the navy for the construction of warships, including *Enterprise* and *Yorktown.* In 1934, in part in response to Japan flexing its muscles in China, the Vinson-Trammell Act authorized naval strength to be increased to the maximum limits of existing treaties. By FDR's 1938 Naval Expansion Act, across-the-board increases of 20 percent boosted tonnages that much further. Finally, the Naval Expansion Acts of June 14 and July 19, 1940 — the latter called the Two-Ocean Navy Act — authorized the construction of 7 new battleships, 18 aircraft carriers, 29 cruisers, 115 destroyers, and 42 submarines.

Weapons, tanks, and aircraft, such as the new B-17 bomber and the P-40 fighter, were also coming off assembly lines in increasing numbers. Ads encouraged young men to join their favorite branch of the armed forces, and if patriotism itself wasn't enough of an inducement, FDR signed the Selective Training and Service Act into law and required registration for a "peacetime" draft. America was girding for war on the home front as well as at its far-flung Pacific outposts and on the stormy seas of the North Atlantic.

In the summer of 1941, Roosevelt froze Japanese assets in the United States and instituted an embargo of American oil, steel, and other strategic exports to Japan in an attempt to slow its war-making capabilities — exactly the action Leahy had urged four years before in the wake of the *Panay* attack. Now, this had the effect of increasing the urgency Japan felt to strike southward, beyond its continuing involvement in China, and control the rubber, oil, and other natural resources of Southeast Asia — threatening to envelop China and consume British interests in Malaya and Burma in the process.

There was a long-standing sentiment in the American military that *something* was about to happen, but there was no strong consensus as to what, when, or certainly where. "The three ring circus simply enlarges every day," CNO Stark wrote Admiral Bloch at the Fourteenth Naval District in Honolulu in July. Stark had just told Kimmel that he had ordered the Asiatic Fleet in the Philippines to lay mines and stretch antisubmarine nets. "This perhaps will tell you better than anything else," Stark told Bloch, "my feeling that most anything may happen in the Far East at any time."[31]

Bloch turned around and pleaded with Nimitz that "practically every district has been supplied with officers of greater experience and ability than the Fourteenth Naval District has." With personnel stretched thin and forced to rotate officers and men of even marginal experience around the fleet, Nimitz was hearing much the same thing from every other district and command. "It looks to me as though any day we may be in the wrangle," Bloch stressed, before wishing Nimitz himself back with the fleet. "I think it would be an excellent idea," Bloch concluded, "to have one, Chester Nimitz, out here in command of one of the important task groups."[32]

By November 1941, events were moving forward with almost alarming speed. "Wake Island is making splendid progress and if you can hold off unpleasantness until after April or May, I believe that we will have enough harbor completed to get a thirty-foot ship into a protected anchorage," Bloch reported to Stark.[33]

But there would be no holding off. On November 27, based on intercepts of Japanese messages, the War and Navy departments sent what came to be called their "war warning" to all commands: "Negotiations with Japan looking toward stabilization of conditions in the Pacific have ceased and an aggressive move by Japan is expected within the next few days." The American bases in the Philippines—the legacy of Admiral Dewey—would likely be in the way of any Japanese thrust southward, but there was no telling how far east the Japanese navy might move to protect its eastern flank.

That same day at Pearl Harbor, Kimmel and Halsey held a long strategy session with Army Lieutenant General Walter C. Short, commanding land forces in Hawaii, and members of their respective staffs. At issue was the ordered reinforcement of aircraft to Wake and Midway islands. Short wanted to send the best available, the army's new P-40s, but Halsey was quick to point out that army pilots were forbidden to fly more than fifteen miles from shore. What good would they be in protecting an island? Halsey grumbled. "We need pilots who can navigate over water."

It was decided that Halsey would sail immediately with *Enterprise* and deliver Major Paul A. Putnam's Marine Fighting Squadron 211 of F4F Wildcats to the more distant and potentially dangerous destination of Wake. Later that afternoon, Halsey sat alone with Kimmel talking about possible outcomes. There was a strong likelihood that Halsey would encounter elements of the Japanese navy—even if only to spot a snooping periscope or to be overflown by reconnaissance planes. Knowing that any overt act might precipitate just the sort of undeclared war that King was fighting in the Atlantic, or worse, Halsey asked Kimmel bluntly, "How far do you want me to go?" Kimmel looked at his good friend and snapped, "Goddammit, use your common sense!" [34]

So it was that it came to be December 6, 1941. In Vichy, Admiral Leahy pondered the collapse of the last remnants of a free France. Aboard the *Augusta* in Narragansett Bay, Admiral King stewed about fighting an undeclared war with one arm tied behind his back. In Washington, Admiral Nimitz took a break from manpower shortages and walked his dog past the Japanese embassy. And somewhere west of Pearl Harbor, Admiral Halsey nervously scanned the empty skies for an attack he felt certain would come. Tomorrow would be Sunday, December 7, 1941.

PART III

ADMIRALS

1941–1945

*No fighter ever won his fight by covering up — by merely fending off the
other fellow's blows. The winner hits and keeps on hitting even though
he has to take some stiff blows in order to be able to keep on hitting.*

—ADMIRAL ERNEST J. KING,
Commander in Chief, U.S. Fleet, 1942

Nimitz, King, and Spruance on board Spruance's Fifth Fleet flagship, the cruiser
Indianapolis (CA-35), in the Marianas, July 18, 1944. (National Archives,
80-G-287121)

CHAPTER THIRTEEN

Searching for Scapegoats and Heroes

Several hundred miles north of the Hawaiian island of Oahu, the big aircraft carrier slowly turned into the wind and began to launch its planes. In the predawn light, they climbed into squadron formations and streaked south to attack Wheeler and Hickam army airfields and the naval base at Pearl Harbor. The result was complete surprise. Actual damage, however, was limited to the wounded pride of the defenders. This was the morning of March 29, 1938, and the planes were from the American carrier *Saratoga,* operating under the command of Vice Admiral Ernest J. King as part of Fleet Problem XIX maneuvers. Almost four years later, the tactics would be largely the same, but the parties and results quite different.[1]

The Japanese attack on Pearl Harbor on Sunday, December 7, 1941, became one of those indelible generational markers. Everyone of age to understand would always remember where he or she was when the news crackled out of a radio or sprawled across the front page of a newspaper. The magnitude of the attack was sobering, but it was the long-planned, secretive manner in which it was executed — without a declaration of war and even as tenuous diplomatic relations still existed—that truly enraged the American people. Franklin D. Roosevelt had been slowly chipping away at American isolationism for years, but in two hours on a Sunday morning, Japan finished his task. America stood incensed and united in purpose as never before. It was inevitable, however, that in the chaos that followed, there would be a search for scapegoats as well as heroes.

Vice Admiral Bill Halsey was having a second cup of coffee in his flag quarters aboard the *Enterprise* as the carrier neared Oahu after its delivery of marine fighter planes to Wake Island. Earlier that morning, *Enterprise* had launched eighteen of its own planes to fly ahead to Pearl Harbor and land at the naval air station on Ford Island. The phone from the bridge rang, and Halsey's flag secretary, Lieutenant H. Douglass Moulton, answered it. "Admiral," Moulton exclaimed, "the staff duty officer says he has a message that there's an air raid on Pearl!"

Halsey leaped from his chair. "My God, they're shooting at my own boys! Tell Kimmel!"

For reasons of radio silence, *Enterprise* had not notified Pearl Harbor of the inbound planes, and Halsey assumed a dreadful mistake in identification had occurred. It was actually much worse. Just then, Halsey's communications officer burst into his cabin and handed him a dispatch from Kimmel to all ships: "Air raid on Pearl Harbor X This is no drill." *Enterprise* went to general quarters.[2]

It was early afternoon Washington, D.C., time and Rear Admiral Chester Nimitz was at home enjoying a radio broadcast of the New York Philharmonic. Suddenly, a flash bulletin interrupted the program announcing that the Japanese had bombed Pearl Harbor. Nimitz barely had time to grab his overcoat when his aide, Captain John F. Shafroth, Jr., telephoned to say that he was on his way to the Navy Department and would pick up the admiral en route. Chester kissed Catherine good-bye and went out the door telling her, "I won't be back till God knows when."[3]

Aboard the cruiser *Augusta* in Narragansett Bay, a marine orderly delivered a priority message with the news to Admiral Ernest J. King's chief of staff. It was immediately passed on to the admiral, who read it without comment. The political constraints under which his fleet had been operating in the North Atlantic for the past six months were about to be removed. The remainder of the day off Newport was eerily calm as King waited for the summons he knew would come.

Nimitz telephoned early the next day and passed on verbal orders to King to report to Washington immediately. King and his aide, Lieutenant Commander Harry Sanders, left the *Augusta* dressed in civilian clothes to appear as inconspicuous as possible and boarded the afternoon express train from Boston to Washington. Civilian attire or not, the tall, ramrod-straight King was a hard man to miss. A navy enlisted man stared at him across the Pullman car for a long time before finally getting up his courage to ask, "Aren't you Admiral King?" The admiral obliged the sailor with a requested autograph.[4]

Several hours earlier, President Franklin D. Roosevelt had gone before a joint session of Congress and labeled the events of December 7 a day of "infamy." He asked for a declaration of war against Japan. In Vichy, France, where a light snow had been falling, Ambassador William D. Leahy listened to FDR's speech on the BBC. The president's voice boomed over the radio waves and gave Leahy "a dramatic picture of the most powerful nation of the world embarking on an all out war to destroy the bandit nation of the Orient." Leahy professed no doubt that the result would be "the destruction of Japan as a first class sea power regardless of how much time and treasure are required to accomplish that end."[5]

In the beginning, however, Washington was in complete disarray. With Roosevelt's remarks still reverberating over the airwaves, Secretary of the Navy Frank Knox left on a hurried inspection trip to Pearl Harbor. Part politician and part newspaperman, Knox sensed that some immediate showing of the administration's flag on the scene was essential to public morale and confidence going forward. Knox declined to stay with Admiral Kimmel, saying that such contact might appear to prejudice his findings.

Arriving at the Navy Department on the same day Secretary Knox departed for the Pacific, King roamed its corridors, attended meetings there and at the White House, and saw to the immediate needs of his Atlantic Fleet. But some suspected much more was afoot, and there occurred one of those apocryphal King stories. The admiral was making his way along a corridor on the third floor of the Navy Department when he encountered Captain John L. McCrea, soon to be FDR's naval aide. McCrea was well known to King, having once skippered an accompanying destroyer when King had command of the *Lexington*.

"Admiral," asked McCrea, "is this story true that I hear about you?"

"Well, John, I don't know," replied King, deadpan. "Which story is it?"

"They tell me," McCrea went on, "you were heard to say recently, 'Yes, damn it, when they get in trouble they send for the sons of bitches.'"

King couldn't help but smile. "No, John," he replied, "I didn't say it. But I will say this: If I had thought of it, I would have said it."[6]

King remained in Washington for just four days, during which time Germany declared war on the United States and Congress reciprocated. King returned to Newport before being ordered back to Washington on December 16. Secretary Knox was already back from Pearl Harbor after a whirlwind six days, a flying visit that made his jaunt around the Caribbean with King the year before look like a pleasure cruise. Knox wasted no time reporting to the White House and telling FDR what had to be done.

First, Knox was convinced that Admiral Kimmel and his army counterpart, Lieutenant General Walter C. Short, had to be relieved; there was simply no way that either officer could command confidence from either superiors or subordinates. Second, with a wounded, two-ocean navy now facing an unlimited two-ocean war, there needed to be one operational boss in charge of all fleets; henceforth, a commander in chief, U.S. Fleet, must supervise the three admirals in command of the Atlantic, Pacific, and Asiatic fleets (the latter admittedly quickly disintegrating). Finally, there had to be an immediate board of inquiry to determine the failures of the Pearl Harbor defenses and, undoubtedly, find the requisite parties to blame.

Roosevelt agreed with all points and immediately turned to who should have supreme command of the fleets. The president seems not to have considered recalling Leahy from France to take the post, at least in part because his mission there was critical. CNO Stark was himself not free from the Pearl Harbor fallout. Who else was there? Knox was ready with what to him was the only answer. There was only one man, in Knox's opinion, who had demonstrated on the front lines of the North Atlantic that he got things done and who had been totally out of the Pearl Harbor chain of command. Eighteen months before, he had been consigned to the General Board and reluctantly counting the months until his retirement. Now Admiral Ernest J. King was about to be appointed commander in chief of the U.S. Fleet.

Roosevelt and Knox left the question of Kimmel's replacement until a second conversation the following morning, but that too became obvious. They needed a man who was well versed in both ships and men and who was also untainted by the recent disaster. "Tell Nimitz," commanded Roosevelt, "to get the hell out to Pearl and stay there till the war is won."[7]

No one seems to have asked why Nimitz instead of Halsey. Roosevelt and Knox knew both men, and they were themselves good judges of men. Halsey, with three stars on his collar and arguably the navy's top carrier commander save perhaps King, would seem to have been a logical choice. Halsey was, in fact, senior to Nimitz by a year at the academy, and his permanent flag rank predated Nimitz's by almost four months.

At a minimum, Knox may have swayed FDR toward Nimitz because he knew Nimitz better from his stint at the Bureau of Navigation, during which time Halsey was sailing around the Pacific. But in a far broader sense, both FDR and Knox may have looked at the situation in the Pacific and decided that although there would be plenty of brawling for a man like Halsey, wringing victory from the shards of defeat would require something more.

King reported to the White House later that day and conferred with Roosevelt and Knox, as well as CNO Stark. Never one to softpedal an opinion, King voiced a number of concerns. In a two-ocean global war, the commander in chief must command from a shore headquarters in Washington, not some seagoing battleship, no matter what tradition dictated. It was also critical that a clear delineation be made between the new commander in chief position and Stark's continuing responsibilities as CNO.

Then there was the matter of perception. King had always focused on perception—if he looked and sounded like an admiral, junior officers would tremble in his presence. Consequently, the perception of the established acronym for commander in chief, U.S. Fleet—CINCUS—just wouldn't do. Its pronunciation, "sink us," was hardly appropriate after what had just occurred at Pearl Harbor. Thus, King wanted the acronym to be COMINCH.

The biggest change was that King, who had long opposed the command authority of the CNO over the bureaus, particularly when he was chief of the Bureau of Aeronautics, now insisted just the opposite—that COMINCH have full authority over the long-independent bureaus. Roosevelt hesitated only on this final point. That would require a change in federal law, the president told King, but in the interim he assured King that he would replace any bureau chief who did not cooperate with him.[8]

Two days later, Roosevelt signed Executive Order 8984, "Prescribing the Duties of the Commander in Chief of the United States Fleet and the Co-operative Duties of the Chief of Naval Operations." It was sweeping in its scope and gave King powers that heretofore had been spread across the secretary of the navy, the bureaus, fleets at sea, and naval forces ashore. There was now no question that King held "supreme command of the operating forces comprising the several fleets of the United States Navy and the operating forces of the naval coastal frontier commands [the naval districts]." And as such, he would be "directly responsible, under the general direction of the Secretary of the Navy, to the President of the United States."[9]

The CNO's role remained technically unchanged, and for the moment left Stark to jolly the bureaus into getting the required logistics in place for action and to prepare long-range war plans. How well this dual leadership would work remained to be seen, and King's memoirs gives his own pointed view by calling it "joint consulship."[10]

King later claimed—somewhat disingenuously, one suspects—that he had told Knox earlier that morning that Stark was the logical choice to command the fleets and that King would gladly serve under him. "Dolly" King and "Betty" Stark were on friendly enough terms, Stark having been two years junior to King at Annapolis. But this was to be not only the role of a lifetime but also the role for which King had spent his lifetime preparing.

While most of official Washington evidenced some measure of shell shock in the days immediately after Pearl Harbor, such fog had rarely afflicted King, particularly when it came to major decisions. It is difficult to imagine him deferring to Stark, beyond some small measure of perfunctory graciousness. Far more in keeping with King's personality was the letter he wrote Stark several days later, in which he asked Stark to enumerate the duties the CNO's office would transfer to King as the new COMINCH.[11]

When Knox returned to his office in the Navy Department, he sent for his chief of the Bureau of Navigation, who had been existing on three to four hours sleep a night as he shuttled manpower into the fight. Knox asked Nimitz how soon he could be ready to travel, and the admiral replied with the standard, "Where and for how long?" Knox delivered the news that he was to be commander in chief, Pacific Fleet (CINCPAC). That evening, Nimitz made it home early to tell Catherine.

"You always wanted to command the Pacific Fleet," Catherine responded brightly. "You always thought that would be the height of glory."

"Darling," replied Chester, "the fleet's at the bottom of the sea. Nobody must know that here, but I've got to tell you."[12]

That night, Nimitz also faced his daughters, although they guessed that he was headed for Pearl Harbor even before he could get out the news. Afterward, anticipating that he would have to make some statement to the press, Nimitz took a tablet and wrote in his neat hand, "It is a great responsibility, and I will do my utmost to meet it."

He passed the pad around the dining room table for comment, and when it reached Kate, she tore off the page and pocketed it, claiming that she was sure it was history and her father could simply make another copy. He did, but this time it was Chet's wife, Joan, who snapped it up. Finally, on his third try, he was able to keep his brief but direct statement. Soon it would be Nimitz's turn to take a train trip.[13]

He spent two hectic days turning the Bureau of Navigation over to his successor. On Friday morning, December 19, he paused for a quiet hour with Catherine to attend daughter Mary's school Christmas pageant. A family lunch followed, and then his flag lieutenant H. Arthur Lamar, arrived with a car and driver to take them to the Navy Department for brief good-byes to Stark and Knox and then to Washington's Union Station. Knox had offered a plane, but Nimitz pled exhaustion and asked for several relatively calm days on a transcontinental train to study reports and gather his thoughts before descending into the Pearl Harbor cauldron. So the Baltimore and Ohio's Capitol Limited carried Nimitz and Lamar westward to Chicago later that afternoon.

Lamar was under strict instructions from all concerned that his primary job was to get the admiral to relax, and he brought along two bottles of Scotch to help with the process. They each had two healthy highballs and ate dinner, and then Nimitz, exhausted, fell into his first good sleep in two weeks.

Shortly after breakfast the next morning, the Capitol Limited pulled into Chicago, and Lamar hailed a taxi for a quick trip to the Navy Pier so that Nimitz could get an overdue haircut. Afterward, the admiral checked the progress of the Naval Reserve Midshipmen's School, then renting space in Abbott Hall on Northwestern's campus. The navy would now need every one of the men. Then Nimitz and Lamar rode to Dearborn Station; boarded the vaunted Chief of the Atchison, Topeka and Santa Fe Railway; and settled into adjoining compartments as the train started its journey westward across the heartland, bound for Los Angeles.

Lamar poured an afternoon libation, and the admiral began to read the ten pounds of reports on the Pearl Harbor attack. They had been entrusted to Lamar with instructions to show them to Nimitz only west of Chicago, after he had had a day of rest. It was grim business. Perhaps most heartbreaking to Nimitz personally was the photograph of the *Arizona,* his flagship as commander, Battleship Division One, now resting broken in the mud. Gone were more than a thousand of its crew, including Nimitz's friend since Annapolis, Rear Admiral Isaac C. Kidd, who had rushed from his flag quarters to the battleship's signal bridge at the first sounds of the attack.

Eight battleships, 3 light cruisers, 3 destroyers, and 4 auxiliary craft lay either sunk, capsized, or heavily damaged. Naval aviation had lost 92 planes, including 46 patrol bombers and 5 of Halsey's incoming planes from the *Enterprise* mistakenly shot down. (That evening, four of the *Enterprise*'s F4F Wildcats, returning from searching for the Japanese fleet, were also shot down by friendly fire.) Army air losses were equally staggering: 77 planes destroyed and 128 heavily damaged. Then there was the human toll: 2,403 navy, marine, army, and civilian personnel killed and 1,178 wounded.

And there was continuing angst all across the Pacific. Japanese aircraft sank the British battleships *Prince of Wales* and *Repulse* off Malaya; bombs rained down on Hong Kong, Singapore, and Manila; and Japanese soldiers invaded the Philippines. Guam fell on December 10 (December 9, Washington, D.C., time), but Wake Island fifteen hundred miles closer to Hawaii still held out. A relief force centered on the carrier *Saratoga,* newly arrived from the West Coast and commanded by Rear Admiral Frank Jack Fletcher, was en route to Wake, while Halsey and the *Enterprise* sailed off Midway in support and as a deterrent to another Japanese attack on Hawaii. The third Pacific carrier, *Lexington,* was momentarily making a feint toward Jaluit, in the Marshall Islands.

By the time the Chief thundered over the big bridge across the Mississippi, Nimitz paused to write his daily letter to Catherine, which was his ritual whenever and for however long they were apart. Having made an analysis of the reports, he told her, "my conscience will now permit me to relax," although he admitted that he found "it difficult to keep on the cheerful side." He was "convinced that there will be more action in the Pacific than elsewhere for many a day to come" and that "by the time I reach Pearl Harbor, I will be able to meet the requirements of the situation."

Four days later, after high winds foiled one takeoff attempt and cost him a day, Nimitz was airborne from San Diego in a Consolidated PB2Y Coronado four-engine flying boat en route across the wide Pacific. It was Christmas Eve, and showing his typical concern for those serving under him, the admiral told Catherine that he greatly regretted taking its pilots and crew away from their families just before Christmas, but he had "no choice on my part."[14]

Leahy heard the news of King's and Nimitz's appointments via the BBC in Vichy. "These three admirals all of whom I know intimately," Leahy wrote in his diary of King, Nimitz, and Thomas C. Hart, who was to remain in command of the dwindling Asiatic Fleet, "are in my opinion the best qualified by experience, talent and temperament of all the flag officers known to me for high sea command in war."[15]

Leahy told FDR much the same thing in a letter the next day. "Given a free choice," Leahy said, he would have selected exactly those three "as the best." Of them, he considered "Hart the most reliable, the least likely to make a mistake, [but] as being physically doubtful because of his age." Leahy may have leaned toward the older Hart, an Annapolis classmate, because of the time-honored academy pecking order, but he was not above admitting to an earlier mistake. "One error of judgment in regard to the selection of a CinC which I made in the past," Leahy confessed to FDR in reference to his support of Admiral Richardson, "should make me doubtful but one can feel pretty sure of Hart, King and Nimitz."[16]

By then, King had already received his official orders from both Knox and Roosevelt, the latter addressing him on White House stationery: "Sir...you are hereby designated as Commander in Chief, United States Fleet, and will continue the rank of admiral." Having returned to Newport to wind up matters there, King departed the *Augusta* permanently for Washington the same day.[17]

As previously constituted, CINCUS, now COMINCH, had been a seagoing command. King's most immediate task was to assemble a fleet staff, land based in Washington, to become his headquarters and support his operational directives as well as his future global travels. Rooms were hastily arranged on the third floor of the Navy Department Building on Constitution Avenue, but subordinates answering the summons to King's staff found barren offices, void of all but the most basic furniture and an ample collection of dirt.

Captain Francis S. "Frog" Low, who had first earned King's respect by standing his ground under the admiral's berating on the bridge of the *Texas,* was called from the Atlantic Fleet. Rear Admiral Russell Willson, then superintendent of the Naval Academy and a shipmate of King's from their days on Hugo Osterhaus's staff, reluctantly reported to become King's chief of staff and swallowed his disappointment that he wasn't given a seagoing command. Summoned as deputy chief of staff was Rear Admiral Richard S. Edwards, lately in command of the submarine base at New London, Connecticut, and another key member of King's North Atlantic team.

Edwards arrived in Washington on December 29 and found King "enthroned in the most disreputable office I have ever seen." King and Willson were sharing a beat-up desk with a couple of chairs. Edwards and Low "borrowed a broken down table from a friend who was out to lunch and set up shop in a corner of the Admiral's office.... As the headquarters of the greatest navy in the world it fell somewhat short of being impressive."[18]

But while King was assembling a staff, his attention was also required at the White House. Winston Churchill swept into town three days before Christmas, encamped on the second floor of the White House, and showed no inclination to leave until he and his new ally had come to grips with basic strategy. This first of Roosevelt and Churchill's wartime conferences — counting their Atlantic Charter meeting as occurring while America was technically neutral — also marked the first time King directly participated in strategy sessions at the chiefs-of-staff level. Admiral Stark was also present as chief of naval operations, and there was still some uncertainty over who was the senior American naval officer. This run of meetings between American and British military leaders — officially the First Washington Conference — lasted into January and was code-named Arcadia.

Churchill was thrilled by the United States' entry into the war, but he was also concerned lest Japan's onslaught in the Pacific distract America's attention from the war against Germany that Great Britain had been fighting for nearly two and a half soul-draining years. The results of Arcadia reassured Churchill that the United States was indeed committed to a strategy of "Germany First" and that Germany's defeat was the ultimate key to victory over Italy and Japan. What this strategic concept of Germany First meant in tactics in the field was another matter. Figuring that out would occupy a considerable part of King's attention over the next three years, as well as nag at his responsibilities to float a two-ocean navy and prosecute a global war in the Pacific at the same time.

Meanwhile, for all the orders from Roosevelt and Knox, King still had not assumed formal command as COMINCH. There is at least anecdotal evidence that he wanted to delay his formal assumption of command until January 1, 1942, "hoping that history would disassociate him with the disastrous events of December 1941." Certainly, this is just the sort of politically savvy decision making King frequently practiced throughout his forty-year career. As a voracious and opinionated reader of history and biography, King may well have been thinking of history's verdict, although the exigencies of the moment would seem to have influenced him otherwise.

King may simply have wanted to get better organized before he hoisted his flag. This was his excuse when Knox repeatedly urged him to set a date late in December. Finally, an exasperated Knox asked King, "Well, what are you waiting for?" and King took command as COMINCH on December 30, 1941.[19]

King's orders to Nimitz were more readily acted upon. Nimitz flew into Pearl Harbor at 7:00 a.m. on Christmas Day 1941. Gunners were still very jumpy, and the admiral's PB2Y Coronado was met over Molokai by a fighter escort and shepherded into a watery landing near the submarine base east of Battleship Row. Still wearing a civilian suit, Nimitz climbed into a whaleboat for the short trip to the dock and realized that he didn't dare sit down. The tiny craft was fouled with debris and covered by a thick oily residue inside and out. It was a microcosm of what Nimitz saw when he looked about him. The air wreaked of black oil and burned wood. The usually bright waters of the East Loch were littered with the sources of the smells. Behind him, the capsized hull of the *Oklahoma* protruded above the water.

As horrific as the scene was, Nimitz had a pressing question on his mind. "What news of the relief of Wake?" he asked the three officers who met him. It was grim. Under Japanese attack from air and sea, Wake's defenders had radioed, "Issue in doubt." Admiral William S. Pye, Kimmel's temporary replacement, overruled a counterattack and ordered all forces eastward. Rumor had it that when Halsey, aboard *Enterprise,* heard the news, he cussed a blue streak for half an hour.

Nimitz remained silent. "When you get back to your office," he quietly told Kimmel's chief of staff, "call Washington and report my arrival." Then, perhaps to himself, he muttered, "This is a terrible sight, seeing all these ships down." That evening, Nimitz was only too glad to have Christmas dinner with Kimmel and Admiral and Mrs. Pye. Later, he wrote Catherine that the country "must be very, very patient because we are confronted with a most difficult period."[20]

At 10:00 a.m. on Wednesday, December 31, 1941, Nimitz stood on the deck of the submarine *Grayling* and read his orders assuming command of the Pacific Fleet. Later, Nimitz liked to joke that the *Grayling*'s deck was the only one in the fleet undamaged and free of debris, but given his years in submarines, it was a fitting choice.

King's operational orders to Nimitz were as simple and concise as the geography of the Pacific made executing them overwhelming and complex: first, Nimitz was to secure and hold the communication and supply lines between Midway, Hawaii, and the West Coast; second, he must maintain a similar lifeline between the West Coast and Australia via Samoa, the Fiji Islands, and New Caledonia. Most Americans had never heard of these places, but if the Japanese were allowed a toehold on any of them, they would push a bulge of military influence well eastward into the South Pacific and detour any support for Australia southward around New Zealand — a wildly circuitous route.

In undertaking these tasks, Nimitz quickly came to the same

conclusion as King. This was to be a different kind of war. The days of Commodore Dewey standing on the bridge of his flagship, leading his fleet into battle, and uttering some pithy remark were over. The numbers of men and ships flung across the sprawling Pacific demanded that Nimitz maintain his headquarters at Pearl Harbor, where some measure of central command and control afforded him half a chance of keeping the big picture in mind.

In looking out across Pearl Harbor from his new CINCPAC offices at the submarine base, Nimitz quickly came to realize that production plants, shipyards, dry docks, support ships, and a host of operations behind the scenes would factor as heavily into winning the war as a night carrier launch or a torpedo fired down the throat at an onrushing destroyer. Other men would get to command the spear point; Nimitz would calmly and diligently manage the arm that held the spear.

And in examining how he might go about it, he came to a second, prophetic conclusion. Nothing could ever replace the treasure of America's men and women killed or forever maimed by Japan's attack, but Nimitz looked around Pearl Harbor and decided that it could have been much worse. On the list of physical casualties, there were three glaring omissions that would prove to be major strategic blunders on the part of the Japanese.

The American aircraft carriers — albeit a lonely three in number in the Pacific — had escaped unscathed. Equally important, the American submarine base, whose construction Nimitz had supervised twenty years before, was largely untouched. No American submarines were sunk or heavily damaged in the attack. In the opening six months of the war, while America tried to establish a defensive perimeter and searched for both scapegoats and heroes, these carriers and submarines would aggressively counterpunch.

Nimitz recognized one other oversight by the attacking Japanese. The dry docks, maintenance facilities, and oil storage tanks were generally unscathed. The battleship *Pennsylvania* had taken some hits as it sat in one of the dry docks, but it was back afloat and headed for the West Coast for repairs by the time Nimitz took command. The maintenance shops hummed with round-the-clock activity repairing damaged ships. But perhaps the greatest asset was the surviving oil tanks. Had 4.5 million barrels of fuel oil been blown up, what was left of the Pacific Fleet would have been forced to limp back to the West Coast and have its operations in the Pacific severely curtailed. That action, not Japan's sinking of a few aging battleships, would have given Japan the free rein it sought in the South Pacific.

Japan's intent had been to cripple the American battleship might that could rapidly disrupt its drive south toward the natural resources it needed in the Netherlands East Indies and Southeast Asia. In that, the Japanese succeeded. But within a year, all but two of those battleships would be refloated and heading west to seek revenge, even as the very nature of Japan's attack had proven that their days as strategic weapons were fading.

The other man who recognized these failings in the Pearl Harbor attack as readily as Chester Nimitz was Admiral Isoroku Yamamoto, Japan's architect of the attack. His country was flush with victory and his pilots even more so, but Yamamoto understood the industrial might of the United States and feared for Japan's future. He felt strongly that Admiral Chuichi Nagumo, the leader of the Japanese attack force, should have delivered a final knockout blow. Yamamoto would never forgive Nagumo for following his orders only to the point where King would have demanded that "the initiative of the subordinate" take over.

In Japan, there would be a continuing controversy about whether Nagumo should have ordered a third attack wave to hit the dry docks, fuel tanks, submarine base, and more—not just striking a blow against the American fleet, but crippling its refuge. No formal actions against him were ever taken, of course, because on the face of it, Japan had won a great victory.[21]

On the American side, it was a different story. Frank Knox's whirlwind tour was just the beginning. The Roberts Commission, chaired by Supreme Court justice Owen J. Roberts and composed of two navy and two army officers, arrived in Honolulu even before Admiral Nimitz. The panel took testimony from 127 witnesses and pored over stacks of documents. Not surprisingly, the most damning words in the commission's final report were aimed squarely at Kimmel and Short. In view of prior warnings to be on the alert for possible attacks in the Pacific, including the "war warning" of November 27 that Kimmel discussed with Halsey just prior to Halsey's departure for Wake, the report concluded that it had been a "dereliction of duty" for both Kimmel and Short not to have consulted with each other about the warnings and better coordinated the appropriate defense measures each was undertaking.

"Dereliction of duty" was not an offense subject to court-martial, but it might just as well have been. Under considerable pressure to do so, both Kimmel and Short applied for retirement and were granted the same at their permanent grade ranks of rear admiral and major general, respectively.[22]

Among Kimmel's staunchest and most vocal supporters was Bill Halsey, Kimmel's friend since Annapolis and in whose wedding Kimmel had been a groomsman. Halsey stood by Kimmel from the time *Enterprise* steamed into Pearl Harbor on December 8 until the day Halsey drew his last breath, feeling that no one had worked harder than Kimmel to prepare the fleet for war and that the success of the attack had been due to a lack of patrol planes. Halsey boldly told the Roberts Commission that he himself had been prepared for a Japanese attack while en route to Wake "because of one man: Admiral Kimmel." Years after the war, Halsey was still telling Kimmel that he believed "you and Short were the greatest military martyrs this country has ever produced."[23]

Ernie King was also initially sympathetic. "I wish to express in writing — what I feel you already know — that you have my sincere regrets over what has occurred," he told Kimmel in a "Dear Kim" note as he was preparing to assume his COMINCH command; "it is something that might well have happened to any of us!" Two months later, on the eve of Kimmel's retirement, King bemoaned the omissions of the Roberts Commission and claimed that the result of the attack would have been the same no matter who had been in command. "*No one*," King concluded with his own emphasis, "thought the Japs would strike — or even that they were ready to strike!"[24]

King's comforting words reflected a view that was then quite rampant: America had suffered a grave defeat; it could have come about only as the result of a sneak attack. Indeed, much would be written about the "surprise" attack on Pearl Harbor and the extent of U.S. culpability, but the fact remains that increasingly throughout the fall of 1941, the American military hierarchy, from President Roosevelt on down, expected the Japanese to attack somewhere in the Pacific. The pure audacity of a strike against Pearl Harbor seems to have escaped the attention of most, and even when that possibility was discussed, enemy submarines coming into the harbor and sabotage from Japanese residents on the island were the suspected vehicles, not a carrier-borne air wave — even though King himself had simulated just such an attack in war games three years earlier.

By 1944, when a Navy-led court of inquiry concluded "that no offenses have been committed nor serious blame incurred on the part of any person in the naval service," King, as chief of naval operations, disagreed. He didn't go so far as to repeat the "dereliction of duty" charge, but he did find both Kimmel and King's own predecessor, Admiral Stark, "lack[ing] of the superior judgment necessary for exercising command commensurate with their rank and assigned duties."[25]

After the war, with the world and King himself much more mellow, King swung back to a defense of Kimmel in notes prepared for his autobiography but not published. King believed that Kimmel and Short had been " 'sold down the river' as a political expedient!" Remembering that the army had had long-standing responsibility for the defense of the islands, King felt that it, including Short, had been particularly circumspect when it came to providing information or offering insight. "They very carefully said nothing about this during the investigation," King maintained, "something for which *I* [emphasis in original] will never forgive them, for they could at least have taken part of the blame."[26]

General Short died in 1949, having remained largely quiet about the entire affair through no less than nine different investigations. Kimmel died in 1968, having spent almost thirty years after the attack attempting to wipe away the charge of dereliction of duty. It was a campaign that his surviving sons carried into the twenty-first century. The ultimate test of any military commander, however, is that he rises or falls with whatever glories or misfortunes befall his command. Sometimes he is responsible, sometimes he is not, but as the commander he is always accountable nonetheless. Had even one of thirty-six patrol planes been in the air—instead of on the ground—that morning and spotted the Japanese carrier force or the waves of inbound aircraft in time to allow fighters to scramble and every antiaircraft gun on ship and shore to be trained skyward as the first wave of Japanese planes swept over the island, Kimmel and Short—no matter what else their shortcomings in hindsight—would have gotten the credit. Having been caught flat-footed, they got the blame.

Ever the considerate superior, no matter how difficult the situation, Nimitz no doubt supported a letter that his successor at BuNav, Rear Admiral Randall Jacobs, appears to have written to a bewildered Kimmel on January 15, 1942. Jacobs advised Kimmel that with his appearance before the Roberts Commission complete, he was being assigned to the Twelfth Naval District in San Francisco. Both men knew that this would be only temporary, but Jacobs omitted the word "temporary" from Kimmel's orders so that his family might travel to San Francisco at government expense.

"Naturally," Jacobs concluded, "none of us here know all the facts connected with the Pearl Harbor incident, and I am doubtful, personally, whether all the facts ever will be known. Needless to say, I feel deeply for you."[27]

One other responsible party to the overall events of December 7 appeared beyond reproach. Regardless of what Douglas MacArthur had been doing in the Philippines for the past six years as a military adviser to the Philippine government, the general had been recalled to active duty by President Roosevelt in July 1941 and given command of U.S. Armed Forces Far East (USAFFE). As such, MacArthur had received a host of alert admonishments throughout the fall, including Marshall's "war warning" message of November 27.

In the wee hours of Monday, December 8, Manila time, MacArthur's bedside telephone rang in his penthouse. "Pearl Harbor!" the general exclaimed when he heard the news. "It should be our strongest point." A few minutes later, at 3:40 a.m., as MacArthur hurriedly dressed, a second call came from Brigadier General Leonard T. Gerow in the army's War Plans Division in Washington. Gerow confirmed the news and told MacArthur that he "wouldn't be surprised if you get an attack there in the near future."

Nine hours later, after other Japanese air attacks against northern Luzon were reported, several hundred Mitsubishi bombers and Zero fighters roared over Clark Field outside Manila and destroyed the bulk of American airpower in the Philippines — MacArthur's air force — as it sat on the ground. Even after years of increasingly hostile Japanese intentions and fair evidence that something was building to a head in the Far East, some might be tempted to forgive MacArthur for being the victim of a surprise attack. But how could he still have his airplanes lined up wingtip to wingtip nine hours after being notified of the attack on Pearl Harbor? Two days later, with Philippine skies generally void of defending planes, another Japanese air attack destroyed the American naval base at Cavite.[28]

MacArthur "might have made a better showing at the beaches and passes, and certainly he should have saved his planes on December 8," a newly appointed brigadier general who had long served as the general's aide confided to his diary. "But," wrote Dwight D. Eisenhower, "he's still the hero."[29]

The man was clearly fallible, but the legend was not. In the dark days of early 1942, when rallying cries and heroes were in short supply, the legend had to be preserved at all costs. FDR knew it. Leahy appears to have blindly affirmed it. King, Nimitz, and Halsey would all come to grips with it in their own ways. But for now, America desperately needed a hero, and Douglas MacArthur was the man of the hour. In short order, the United States Navy would provide a few heroes of its own.

CHAPTER FOURTEEN

Spread Thin

After Admiral Chester W. Nimitz read his orders assuming command of the Pacific Fleet on the deck of the *Grayling*, he summoned various staff officers to an afternoon conference. Some were longtime members of Admiral Kimmel's staff and as such had been as intimately involved in pre–December 7 preparations and precautions as the admiral himself. Others were from Admiral Pye's staff and had seen their attempt at a relief effort evaporate well short of Wake Island. All gathered with a decided air of apprehension and uncertainty. Were they losers, just unlucky, or both?

The new CINCPAC made his feelings clear on all counts. Nimitz promptly declared that he had complete confidence in all present and that he would need each and every one of them in the task ahead. What's more, as the former chief of the Bureau of Navigation, Nimitz had likely been the one who had sent them to the Pacific Fleet in the first place, and they wouldn't be there if they weren't fully competent and qualified in their positions. Those who absolutely wanted to leave could, Nimitz told them, but "certain key members of the staff I insist I want to keep."[1]

Among those were Captain Charles H. "Soc" McMorris and Lieutenant Commander Edwin T. Layton, who had been Kimmel's war plans and intelligence officers, respectively. McMorris had been among those concluding that an attack on Pearl Harbor was unlikely, while Layton had warned that something major was about to happen somewhere in the Pacific. Such evenhanded, across-the-board determination not to assign blame for the past but to treat everyone the same going forward proved a much-needed tonic for morale. It quickly spread throughout the entire Pacific Fleet. There was a new admiral in charge, they had his confidence, and he would lead them to victory.

Nimitz's quiet but firm action in immediately addressing his command was as significant a decision as any he made in those early days. Reaching out to all concerned and assuring them of their worth worked wonders to shore up morale, put as much of the Pearl Harbor disaster behind them as possible, and get his command looking forward instead of backward. Still, in the months ahead, they were all going to be spread thin.

Even as Roosevelt and Churchill were affirming a Germany First strategy at the Arcadia Conference, the immediacy of military events focused eyes on the South Pacific. The Japanese onslaught continued unabated. Within weeks, the oil, rubber, and other natural resources of the Netherlands East Indies would be theirs, and the last bastion of British influence in the area, Singapore, despite Churchill's adamant assurances to the contrary, would fall on February 15. MacArthur continued to hold portions of the Philippines by a dubious strategy of massing his forces on the dead-end peninsula of Bataan, but the Americans and their allies desperately needed a counterpunch.

Having returned to Pearl Harbor from the stillborn Wake Island relief expedition a few hours after Nimitz assumed CINCPAC command, Bill Halsey reported to his new commander. If Halsey had any regrets that their roles were not reversed, he certainly did not show them. Instead, despite his continuing loyalty to Kimmel, Halsey seems to have readily embraced Nimitz in his new role.

It helped, of course, that they were old friends from their days at Annapolis, when Halsey was a football player and Nimitz an interested observer. Although they had never served together and their families had never socialized, as had the Halseys and Spruances, they were at ease with each other and usually began their conversations by swapping a story or two—trademarks of both men.

At this first encounter, they discussed the task ahead, and then Halsey departed Pearl Harbor to escort an approaching convoy from the West Coast the remaining miles to Oahu. After his return, Nimitz sent for him on January 9 and got right down to business without the usual exchange of stories.

The Japanese had seized the British mandate of the Gilbert Islands within three days of Pearl Harbor. Their growing sphere of influence in the South Pacific pointed directly at Samoa and threatened the West Coast–Australia lifeline that King had directed Nimitz to preserve at all costs.

The marine garrison on Samoa was being reinforced with troops from San Diego in a task force led by Rear Admiral Frank Jack Fletcher aboard *Yorktown,* which King had hastily dispatched to the Pacific from the North Atlantic. Nimitz wanted Halsey to take *Enterprise* directly to Samoa, link up with Fletcher after his delivery, and then sail northwest to raid Japanese forces in the Gilberts and the nearby Marshall Islands, hopefully disrupting any plans for their advance against Samoa. "How does that sound?" Nimitz asked Halsey. "It's a rare opportunity."

Halsey furrowed his bushy eyebrows. He wasn't so sure. The Marshalls had been Japanese since the 1919 Treaty of Versailles, and it was a good bet that they had been heavily fortified despite agreements to the contrary. Little was known about them, and this dearth of information had even sparked theories that Amelia Earhart's globe-circling flight was in fact a spy mission to overfly and photograph Japanese military installations there. (Leahy, it will be recalled, had unsuccessfully urged the American occupation of islands in this general area during the search for Earhart.)

Unsure what he was up against, Halsey was also nagged by the results of a game-board exercise conducted a few months before

Pearl Harbor. Then, an American raid against the Marshalls and their main base at Kwajalein had had the advantage of protection on its flank from amphibious planes based on Wake — no longer under American control. Still, Halsey could hardly be anything less than game. Just two days later, with *Enterprise* loaded down with planes, armaments, and supplies, Nimitz came down to see Halsey off and said, "All sorts of good luck to you, Bill!"[2]

But good luck at first seemed to be in short supply. That same day, *Saratoga* was torpedoed while patrolling off Hawaii and went limping back to Pearl Harbor, and later the West Coast, for repairs. This cut the American carrier strength in the Pacific back to three — *Enterprise, Lexington,* and the arriving *Yorktown.* Then Halsey's outbound cruise became a comedy of errors. A pilot carelessly broke radio silence to report engine trouble, a destroyer lost a man overboard, a turret explosion killed a seaman on the heavy cruiser *Salt Lake City,* a scout plane crashed on *Enterprise,* and one of the carrier's torpedo planes went missing.

As Halsey's task force neared its rendezvous with Fletcher's command, the bad luck continued. Another scout plane was lost; a torpedo plane scored a direct hit on a Japanese sub, but the bomb failed to detonate; and recognition problems with allies caused friendly-fire attacks against a British schooner and an Australian patrol plane.

Then, lurking American submarines reported that the Marshalls might not be so heavily defended after all, and rather than just hitting the eastern edge at Wotje and Maloelap, Miles Browning, Halsey's mercurial chief of staff, urged the admiral to strike straight into the island group and attack Kwajalein itself. "It was one of those plans," Halsey admitted, "which are called 'brilliant' if they succeed and 'foolhardy' if they fail," but it was also just the sort of audacity that appealed to him. Nimitz concurred and directed Halsey to expand the assault.[3]

While Fletcher and *Yorktown* attacked the Gilberts and southern Marshalls, Halsey took *Enterprise* straight west almost within rifle shot of Wotje. It was dicey work because the Japanese closure in recent decades meant that any charts were old and suspect. Two hours before a dawn carrier strike was to be launched, the staff duty officer burst into Halsey's flag plot from the bridge and exclaimed, "Sir, sand has just blown in my face!"

Check it out, ordered the admiral, hurrying the officer back outside, even as he pondered his aircraft carrier piling up on some beach while making 25 knots. The officer soon returned with a sheepish grin. He had wet his fingers, touched the "sand" that had fallen on the deck, tentatively tasted it, and, spying one of the bridge crew stirring a cup of coffee, concluded that the "sand" was an errant helping of sugar.

The laughter that followed calmed more than a few precombat jitters, and it also broke the bad-luck run of the outbound cruise. Nine torpedo bombers and thirty-seven dive-bombers took off for Kwajalein an hour later. While they surprised planes and ships in the harbor there, Halsey's accompanying cruisers under the command of Raymond Spruance bombarded coastal defenses on Wotje. All through the day on February 1, 1942, *Enterprise* launched and retrieved planes that flew strike after strike, pausing only long enough to be refueled and rearmed, while their pilots gulped a hasty cup of coffee and some food.

Finally, about three in the afternoon, after *Enterprise* had been jockeying in and out of the wind in a very confined area, the commander of one of the bombing squadrons returned from his third mission and, reporting to the bridge, asked, "Admiral, don't you think it's about time we got the hell out of here?"

"My boy," Halsey responded, "I've been thinking the same thing myself!" Halsey later claimed that the exchange was the beginning of the phrase "Haul Out with Halsey," less delicately termed "Haul Ass with Halsey."[4]

But before they could make their escape, a flight of five twin-engine Mitsubishi G3M "Nell" bombers attacked the carrier, dropping fifteen bombs that fell close enough to cause minor damage and start a small fire. After forty-two years in the navy, it was Halsey's first time to come under direct enemy fire. One Nell, with both engines smoking, turned back toward the carrier and bore down on the planes assembled on its flight deck.

A young aviation mechanic named Bruno Gaido bravely jumped into the rear seat of an American SBD Dauntless dive-bomber and opened up with its machine gun. Despite a hail of fire, the Nell staggered onward. At the last possible moment, *Enterprise*'s skipper threw its helm over in a hard turn to starboard. The attacking bomber sliced the tail off Gaido's plane, but then bounced off the port edge of the flight deck—according to Halsey, the first kamikaze of the war.

When *Enterprise* and its cruiser consorts returned to Pearl Harbor on February 5, the place went wild with cheers and sirens. The Marshall affair would later be termed a mere "nuisance raid" in the grand strategy of things, but knowing that their efforts would not be unopposed gave the Japanese pause. More important, it gave Americans another huge boost in morale and ignited an offensive spirit. Perhaps most important of all, Halsey had shown that far from hiding carriers behind battleships, putting them at the core of a small, nimble task force capable of moving at 30 knots yielded an offensive capability that could strike surprise tactical blows almost anywhere.

The first person to come aboard *Enterprise* that day did so via a bosun's chair even before the carrier's gangway was in place. To no one's surprise, it was Nimitz. He climbed out with a grin and pumped Halsey's hand with a hearty "Nice going!" Rear Admiral Robert Theobald, soon to be commander of Pacific destroyers, came next but was more pointed. Shaking a finger in Halsey's face, Theobald, who had opposed the raid as too risky, exclaimed, "Damn you, Bill, you've got no business getting home from that one! No business at all!"[5]

But the business had been so successful that Nimitz soon had a similar mission for Halsey. This time, the destination was recently captured Wake Island. But when Soc McMorris, Nimitz's war plans officer, delivered the operational orders, Halsey, his number thirteen phobia firmly in place from that day aboard the old *"Mizzy"* as a young officer, was astounded that not only was his command now designated Task Force 13, but he was being ordered to sortie on February 13, a Friday! That was simply too much for him. McMorris agreed, quickly changing the designation to Task Force 16 and the departure date to February 14.

The Wake mission went off without a hitch, although it too was largely in the category of a nuisance raid. It was notable, however, because it was the first time aerial-photography reconnaissance was used prior to an attack. But before Halsey could retire eastward, Nimitz flashed him another directive: "Desirable to strike Marcus if you think it feasible."

Marcus Island (aka Minami Tori Shima) was eight hundred miles beyond Wake on a direct line with Japan and only about thirteen hundred miles from Tokyo. It was a tiny, barren spot with little more than an airstrip, but it was almost in Japan's backyard. Halsey turned Task Force 16 westward but then was forced to make a detour south to find better weather for refueling his ships. "Fueling is not a foul-weather operation," he later recorded in his memoirs, something with which he would become eminently familiar a few years later in the Philippine Sea.

Refueling was finally completed by March 1, but with seas still choppy, Halsey ordered his destroyers to stay with the oilers while he struck toward Marcus Island with *Enterprise* and the cruisers *Northampton* and *Salt Lake City*. The surprise was complete, and while the attack held no strategic value, it may well have been a factor in a plan that Nimitz presented to Halsey a few days after his return to Pearl Harbor.

Nimitz was blunt. "Do you believe it would work, Bill?" he asked Halsey after giving him the overview.

"They'll need a lot of luck," Halsey replied.

"Are you willing to take them out there?"

When Halsey replied that he certainly was, Nimitz made it official. Good, he told Halsey; the operation is "all yours!"[6]

Meanwhile, Ernest J. King had wasted no time asserting himself as COMINCH. Predictably, the "joint consulship" with CNO Stark quickly dissolved. Roosevelt and Knox clearly lost confidence in Stark after Pearl Harbor, but broader political considerations kept them from immediately replacing him as they had Kimmel. Too much of a shake-up in America's military might signal panic.

With King gathering power as COMINCH, Roosevelt and Knox may well have decided from the very beginning that Stark's days as CNO were numbered. Indeed, when King once insisted to Roosevelt and Knox that the command relationship between the two offices be further clarified, FDR supposedly replied, "Don't worry. We'll take care of that." Still, the action they took in March 1942 was unprecedented. Stark was relieved of his CNO duties and dispatched to London to oversee American naval forces in Europe and become the senior U.S. Navy representative to the British government. King was assigned additional duties as CNO.[7]

Executive Order 9096, which FDR signed on March 12, 1942, made it official: "The duties of the Commander in Chief, United States Fleet, and the duties of the Chief of Naval Operations, may be combined and devolve upon one officer who shall have the title 'Commander in Chief, United States Fleet, and Chief of Naval Operations,' and who shall be the principal naval adviser to the President on the conduct of the War." It further made clear that while King had been promised the *cooperation* of the bureaus as COMINCH, they were now ordered to be under both "the coordination *and direction*" [emphasis added] of the CNO.[8]

After years of withholding power from the CNO as an independent bureau chief, King had achieved just the opposite. His combined offices of COMINCH and CNO gave him the most sweeping accumulation of American naval power in the hands of one man since the days when the navy had floated only one ship under the command of John Paul Jones.

There was some remaining uncertainty as to where Secretary Knox stood in the hierarchy. King was still charged with operating under his "general direction." But words in the same sentence also made King "directly responsible" to the president for all naval forces, and in practice he enjoyed full access to the White House with or without Knox. On the military side, there was no longer any doubt that King was America's top sailor and that when he spoke, he did so as the unqualified supreme commander of all naval forces.

The best evidence that FDR was firmly behind this new arrangement may have come to King via a letter written by the president's right-hand man and alter ego, Harry Hopkins. "I think it is perfectly grand," Hopkins told King, "and I have a feeling it is going to be one of the most important things the President has done during the war."[9]

National newsmagazines also embraced King's dual appointment as a very positive step in the war effort. "Combining the two top Navy jobs," reported *Life,* "cleaned away a long accumulation of bureaucratic trash." *Time* called King "boot-tough" and noted that the "shake-up in the top drawer put an airman alone at the top." The man now unquestionably in charge was termed one of "the Navy's toughest 'sundowners' [Navy slang for a strict disciplinarian] and... most offensive-minded officers."[10]

As he had done when assuming command of the Atlantic Fleet two years before, King wasted no time in reiterating his general philosophy in a press release circulated on March 26. Saying that he had little to add to what he had been saying as COMINCH over the past three months, King nonetheless noted, "Since repetition is a form of emphasis, it may not be amiss to repeat that this will be a long and a hard war." But, admonished King, "it is high time to stop talking defense — and above all to stop thinking defense....We must strike the enemy when and where we can — and keep on striking him heavier and heavier blows as mounting production puts into our hands more and more tools of war. Our days of victory are in the making."[11]

But not all battles were to be on the seas or distant shores. Cooperation between the army and navy had never been anything to cheer about, and nothing had brought to light the deficiencies in interservice teamwork more than the recent disaster at Pearl Harbor. Ultimately, such cooperation and mutual respect had to start at the top of each service.

King's well-established counterpart as chief of staff of the army was General George C. Marshall. In an army as dominated by West Point graduates as the navy was by Annapolis alumni, Marshall was somewhat of an anomaly. He had not attended West Point but had graduated instead from the Virginia Military Institute, attaining his commission as a second lieutenant in 1901, the same year King graduated from Annapolis. Marshall served in infantry assignments and then caught the eye of commanding general John J. Pershing, who became a mentor and made Marshall a member of his staff after World War I.

Marshall spent the interwar years with training commands, War College assignments, and general staff work, receiving promotion to brigadier general in 1936. In November of that same year, while in command of Vancouver Barracks in Washington State, Marshall met King for the first time at the Northwest Air Meeting in Portland, Oregon. Three years later, Roosevelt promoted Marshall over the heads of thirty-four senior officers to become army chief of staff. At age fifty-eight, he inauspiciously assumed the duties on September 1, 1939, the same day Germany invaded Poland.

Usually outwardly reserved and gracious, Marshall next met King in Washington, D.C., early in 1941. As King recalled the encounter, Marshall was, "although polite, distinctly cool in his manner." This may have been due merely to Marshall's general demeanor, or he may have been smarting over a run-in several of his staff officers had recently had with King while observing amphibious landings in the Caribbean shortly after King assumed the Atlantic Fleet command. King was certain that his marines were providing accompanying army troops a topflight example of how it was done, while the army officers busily critiqued the marines.[12]

Their next encounter was on the *Augusta* en route to and from the Atlantic Charter Conference. They appear to have gotten along splendidly. The very first thing Marshall did upon returning to Washington was to write King a letter of thanks and express his "deep appreciation of the consideration shown me while I was aboard the *Augusta*." By Marshall's standards, the letter was downright syrupy. Marshall told King that he hoped very much to have "another opportunity to travel under your protection and guidance" and offered full cooperation for "anything I can ever show you or do for you in the Army," concluding, "I am yours to command."[13]

But by early 1942, tensions were high all around. One army officer who did not hesitate to make his impressions of Admiral King quite clear, if only to his private diary, was Marshall's up-and-coming protégé, newly appointed brigadier general Dwight D. Eisenhower. Arriving in Washington in December 1941, Eisenhower found "lots of amateur strategists on the job, and prima donnas everywhere."[14]

Eisenhower formed a definite opinion of Admiral King and described him as "an arbitrary, stubborn type, with not too much brains and a tendency toward bullying his juniors." Ike was wrong on the brains part, of course, but hardly alone in his description of King's other characteristics. "But," Eisenhower continued, "I think he wants to fight, which is vastly encouraging. In a war such as this, when high command invariably involves a president, a prime minister, six chiefs of staff, and a horde of lesser 'planners,' there has got to be a lot of patience—no one person can be a Napoleon or a Caesar."[15]

But it seems that Eisenhower thought that King was trying to be either or both. "One thing that might help win this war," Eisenhower snarled on March 10, "is to get someone to shoot King. He's the antithesis of cooperation, a deliberately rude person, which means he's a mental bully...who is going to cause a blow-up sooner or later."

Eisenhower wrote this entry in his diary the very day he learned that his revered father had died and that there was nothing he could do "but send a wire." He may have been venting his emotions at King's expense. After he became supreme commander and was far removed from the relative freedom of expression of a junior brigadier, Ike admitted, "In glancing back over old notes I see that Admiral King annoyed me. In justice I should say that all through the war, whenever I called on him for assistance, he supported me fully and instantly."[16]

At the time, four days after his "shoot King" comment, Eisenhower was still steaming. "Lest I look at this book sometime and find that I've expressed a distaste for some person, and have put down no reason for my aversion, I record this one story of Admiral King." Supposedly, General Henry H. Arnold's office sent King an important note that was inadvertently addressed to "Rear Admiral King," two stars below his current rank. The letter came back unopened with an arrow pointing to the word "Rear." If "that's the size of man the navy has at its head," Ike recorded, "he ought to be a big help winning this war." Much later, Eisenhower recanted these harsh words, too.[17]

What appears to have changed Eisenhower's mind—other than perhaps a maturing awareness that interservice cooperation had to be attained and preserved at any cost—was a face-to-face encounter he had with King shortly after this. According to Eisenhower, what broke the ice and changed his opinion of King occurred when Marshall had dispatched him to King's office with a request. King was "performing true to form," Ike later recalled. He scarcely looked up from his desk and in response to Eisenhower's question barked a one-word answer: "No!" But as others who had earned King's respect had done, Eisenhower stood his ground and replied that such an attitude "could not do much to assure co-operation between the two services."

At that, King looked up. In fact, he stood up, and just when the "blow-up" Eisenhower had predicted seemed imminent, King's entire demeanor changed and he motioned to a couch and said, "Sit down, Eisenhower." Explaining that sometimes he got a little too wrapped up in his navy way of thinking, he asked Eisenhower to restate his request. Ike did so, and King replied, "Why, I think we can do it, surely." From then on, recalled Eisenhower, "I had a friend in the Navy." In fact, when it came time to pick a commander for the Allied invasion of North Africa, it was supposedly King who said, "Why not put it under Eisenhower."[18]

Eisenhower's boss had a similar encounter with King. Shortly after King became CNO, and as such Marshall's equal at the Joint Chiefs of Staff level, as well as commander of the navy's combatant forces, King called on Marshall at his office in the Munitions Building. When he arrived, Marshall was in the midst of a very heated exchange with an Australian diplomat who was well known as a loose cannon. It took Marshall some minutes to defuse the matter at hand, and in the meantime, King, who was not used to waiting for anyone, stalked out in a fit of pique.

Having resolved one crisis, Marshall turned to a potentially serious one with King and hurried over to the admiral's office. Marshall explained that far from being discourteous, he simply had not been willing to turn the Australian loose without calming him down. As for their own relationship, he and King had to work together for the good of the country. They simply "couldn't afford to fight, so we ought to find a way to get along together." King listened carefully, thought for a moment or two, and then thanked Marshall for coming over to see him. "We will see if we can get along," King said, "and I think we can." The two would never be warm friends, but henceforth they would be courteous allies.[19]

There was, of course, one other prima donna determined to have center stage, with whom Marshall and Eisenhower were well acquainted and King soon would be. From Roosevelt on down the question was debated at length: what were they going to do with Douglas MacArthur?

The general once described Eisenhower as "the best clerk I ever had," and after serving MacArthur as an aide in both Washington and the Philippines, Eisenhower was well versed in his theatrical ways. "In many ways MacArthur is as big a baby as ever," Eisenhower noted. "But we've got to keep him fighting."[20]

Few in official Washington disagreed with either of those points. MacArthur, whom FDR had once called "one of the two most dangerous men in the country," the other being Huey Long,[21] required constant reassurance for his ego. Always his own favorite general, MacArthur was not above putting out press releases making him sound as if he was the only American totally engaged in the war effort and able to keep Japanese troops from riding San Francisco cable cars. Indeed, in the first three months of 1942, *Time* magazine alone made mention of King seven times and Nimitz twice, while news of MacArthur's exploits appeared thirty-two times. But Roosevelt and Marshall realized that with the Allies in full retreat across all of Southeast Asia, MacArthur's very verboseness made him the logical rallying point.

MacArthur's position in the Philippines, however, was tenuous at best. A lack of airpower in this new kind of war was at the crux of it. The general had lulled Roosevelt and Marshall with overly optimistic predictions of the power of his air force and then failed either to use it or protect it. As for the subsequent deterioration of conditions there, Marshall reiterated a common theme: "It's all clear to me now except one thing. I just don't know how MacArthur happened to let his planes get caught on the ground."[22]

Having declared Manila an open city and eschewed any form of the guerrilla resistance that had characterized Filipino opposition to foreign invasions dating back two centuries, MacArthur ordered his combined forces of about 15,000 Americans and 65,000 Filipinos to mass on Bataan. He himself hunkered down on the nearby island of Corregidor. Admittedly, this concentration on Bataan had long been part of the Americans' Plan Orange against Japan, which presupposed a quick relief thrust through the Central Pacific after fighting the requisite major sea battle à la Dewey en route. But like so many prewar assumptions, this, too, quickly changed and MacArthur failed to adapt.

Clearly not understanding the dead end into which MacArthur had led American and Filipino troops on Bataan, Bill Leahy in far-off Vichy inexplicably joined those waving MacArthur's banner. "MacArthur is the only army commander on the Allied side who has been successful up to the present time and he can be depended upon to use his available forces efficiently." This is one of Leahy's more startling comments. Unlike the verve of Eisenhower's diary, Leahy's diary was usually bland and not very enlightening as to his true feelings. One wonders why he was inclined to make such a bald statement in MacArthur's defense, particularly given Halsey's successful exploits against Kwajalein and around Wake Island.[23]

Eisenhower had another take on the matter. "Bataan is made to order for him," Ike wrote of MacArthur's situation. "It's in the public eye; it has made him a public hero; it has all the essentials of drama; and he is the acknowledged king on the spot."[24]

The debate over what to do with MacArthur consumed much of January and February 1942. Some in Congress wanted him evacuated and appointed supreme commander over *all* American armed forces—everything, everywhere. That was enough to make Roosevelt, Marshall, and King gag. But the consensus was that MacArthur had to be saved. The Japanese simply could not be allowed the psychological victory of killing him or, worse, parading him through some propaganda spectacle. Recognizing that MacArthur might or might not follow the orders of someone he had once said had "no superior among Infantry colonels," Marshall made it clear to him that whatever his orders, they would come directly from the president himself, a manner quite befitting the general's ego and his genuine regrets about leaving his troops.[25]

And, finally, late on Sunday afternoon, February 22, Roosevelt summoned Marshall, King, and Harry Hopkins to confer on MacArthur's fate. When the meeting concluded, FDR told Marshall to draft a presidential directive ordering MacArthur to Australia. Three weeks later, after a harrowing PT boat ride and a B-17 flight from Mindanao, MacArthur, his family, and a close cadre of staff touched down at an emergency airfield near Darwin. "MacArthur is out of Philippine Islands," Eisenhower wrote in his diary. "The newspapers acclaim the move—the public has built itself a hero out of its own imagination."[26]

Meanwhile, Bill Halsey was about to execute Chester Nimitz's latest order. Captain Francis S. "Frog" Low, Admiral King's operations officer, had come up with a daring plan designed "to strike an offensive blow against the Japanese homeland which would encourage and cheer up 'all hands' during those particularly dark days." What's more, such an offensive strike might prompt Japan to tighten air defenses around its home islands at the expense of campaigns in the South Pacific.

Low's idea was as simple in concept as it would be complicated in execution: bomb Tokyo. Navy planes did not have sufficient range for the job, and army planes with the range lacked either proximate

Ernest J. King, Annapolis class of 1901. (Naval History and Heritage Command, NH50033)

Chester W. Nimitz, Annapolis class of 1905, with his proud grandfather, February 1905. (Courtesy of the National Museum of the Pacific War, Nimitz Education and Research Center, FPA 63, nerc_000246)

Nimitz as a young ensign, circa 1907, made it a point during his career "to become as deeply immersed and as interested in each activity as it was possible." (Naval History and Heritage Command, NH49740)

William D. Leahy served as a temporary naval aide to President William Howard Taft during his visit to San Francisco in October 1911 but did not think "a permanent assignment to such duty could be either agreeable or valuable." (Naval History and Heritage Command, NH49834)

Even after World War I, there were many admirals in the U.S. Navy who thought that a line of battleships was the solution to any crisis. (National Archives, 80-G-695093)

Captain King and his team raised the sunken *S-4*, March 1928. (Naval History and Heritage Command, NH784)

Vice Admiral Leahy on board his flagship, the battleship *West Virginia* (BB-48), in September 1935, when he was commander, Battleships, Battle Force, U.S. Fleet. (Naval History and Heritage Command, NH49862)

Rear Admiral King, newly appointed as commander, Aircraft, Base Force, arrives on board the carrier *Lexington* (CV-2) on June 2, 1936. His personal Curtiss SOC-1 Seagull was painted a shiny "flag" blue. (National Archives, 80-G-457421)

Suits were the usual dress for high-ranking military officers serving in Washington, D.C., during the 1930s, as an ailing Secretary of the Navy Claude A. Swanson congratulates Leahy on becoming chief of Naval Operations, December 31, 1936; at left is outgoing CNO William H. Standley. (Courtesy of the Library of Congress, LC-H22-D-453)

On February 28, 1939, FDR met with flag officers on board the *Houston* (CA-30) off Culebra Island, Puerto Rico, at the conclusion of Fleet Problem XX. The contenders for Leahy's CNO job were present, as were many to become prominent during World War II. Seated, left to right: Rear Admiral H. E. Kimmel, Rear Admiral A. E. Watson, Admiral W. D. Leahy, Roosevelt, Admiral C. C. Bloch, Vice Admiral J. W. Greenslade, Rear Admiral W. C. Watts, Rear Admiral A. W. Johnson; standing, left to right: Rear Admiral W. L. Calhoun, Rear Admiral W. H. Halsey, Rear Admiral G. J. Rowcliff, Rear Admiral H. R. Stark, Rear Admiral W. S. Anderson, Vice Admiral A. Andrews, Admiral E. C. Kalbus, Vice Admiral E. J. King, Rear Admiral F. A. Todd, Rear Admiral C. A. Blakely, Brigadier General R. P. Williams, Rear Admiral J. D. Wainwright, Rear Admiral W. S. Pye, Rear Admiral J. M. Smeallie, Rear Admiral C. S. Freeman. (Courtesy of the Library of Congress, William D. Leahy Papers, Box 16, FF CNO, August 1938 to February 1939)

Roosevelt and Churchill chat on board the HMS *Prince of Wales* at the Atlantic Charter Conference in August 1941, as U.S. Army Chief of Staff George C. Marshall looks on; King and Chief of Naval Operations Harold Stark stand behind them. (Courtesy of the George C. Marshall Foundation, Lexington, Virginia)

Vice Admiral Halsey, circa 1941, while he was serving as commander, Aircraft, Battle Force. (Naval History and Heritage Command, NH95552)

Admiral King found an influential benefactor in Secretary of the Navy Frank Knox, here together on the cruiser *Augusta* (CA-31) during the secretary's September 1941 visit to Bermuda while King was commander in chief, Atlantic Fleet. (Naval History and Heritage Command, NH56978)

Admiral Nimitz (center), the old submariner, assumes command of the U.S. Pacific Fleet on board the submarine *Grayling* (SS-209) on December 31, 1941, at Pearl Harbor. (Courtesy of the National Museum of the Pacific War, Nimitz Education and Research Center, FPA 52, nerc_002519)

As a fleet oiler tags along, a TBD-1 torpedo plane has just taken off from the *Yorktown* (CV-5) somewhere in the Coral Sea, April 1942. This photograph was retouched to obscure the radar antennas atop the foremast for national security reasons. (National Archives, 80-G-640553)

A handful of American carriers made the difference in the Pacific during 1942, and some paid the price, such as the *Lexington* (CV-2), abandoned and sinking after the battle of the Coral Sea. (Naval History and Heritage Command, NH51382)

A TBM Avenger torpedo plane has just landed on the *Enterprise* (CV-6) while another flies overhead, as the carrier supports landings in the Gilbert Islands, November 22, 1943. (National Archives, 80-G-333207)

Through posters, photographs, and a steady stream of press reports trumpeting naval successes, Halsey's became one of the most recognizable faces of the American war effort. (Naval History and Heritage Command, NH76342)

Late in the pivotal year of 1942, Nimitz inscribed his photograph, "11 Nov 42, Vice Admiral Frank Jack Fletcher, a fine fighting admiral and a splendid shipmate, with much affection, C. W. Nimitz." (Frank Jack Fletcher Collection, Box 2, Folder 41, American Heritage Center, University of Wyoming)

Polar opposites in personality and leadership styles, King (left) and Marshall nonetheless came to work together on behalf of the American war effort. They are pictured here before a meeting of the Joint Chiefs of Staff, October 31, 1942. (Courtesy of the George C. Marshall Foundation, Lexington, Virginia)

A proud father shakes hands with Lieutenant Commander Chester W. Nimitz, Jr., who has just received the Silver Star for his performance as skipper of the submarine *Haddo* (SS-255). (Courtesy of the National Museum of the Pacific War, Nimitz Education and Research Center, FPA 48, nerc_002517)

The Joint Chiefs of Staff, minus Leahy, tour the beachhead at Normandy, June 12, 1944. Left to right, in the foreground: General Henry H. Arnold, General Dwight D. Eisenhower, General George C. Marshall, Lieutenant General Omar N. Bradley (pointing), and Admiral Ernest J. King. (Courtesy of the George C. Marshall Foundation, Lexington, Virginia)

The weekly luncheons of the Joint Chiefs of Staff fostered an air of civility and camaraderie for Arnold and Leahy (left) and King and Marshall. Note Leahy's ashtray and the buzzer, to summon staff, at Marshall's side. (National Archives, 80-G-K-14010)

Nimitz, King, and Halsey stand outside Nimitz's CINCPAC headquarters at Pearl Harbor on September 28, 1943. Nimitz and Halsey are in traditional khakis. King was a uniform "tinkerer" who introduced a much-despised gray uniform with plain cap. Some said it made him look like a bus driver. Others simply mistook him for a petty officer, as did the reporter who once brushed him aside with a curt "Get out of the way, chief. I want to get a picture of Admiral Nimitz." (Courtesy of the National Museum of the Pacific War, Nimitz Education and Research Center, FPA 37, nerc_000388)

Leahy was conspicuous by his absence from the Casablanca Conference, January 1943, only in retrospect. He was sidelined by bronchitis in Trinidad and not yet indispensable. Seated (left to right): Marshall, Roosevelt, King; standing (left to right): Harry Hopkins, General Henry H. Arnold, Lieutenant General Brehon Somervell, and Averell Harriman. (Courtesy of the George C. Marshall Foundation, Lexington, Virginia)

Seated (left to right): Stalin, Roosevelt, and Churchill at the Teheran Conference in November 1943. Leahy stands behind Churchill, while King is hidden two hats behind Stalin. Contrast the faces of the three world leaders here with their photograph at Yalta fifteen months later. (Courtesy of the Library of Congress, LC-USZ62-91957)

Roosevelt, Churchill, and the Combined Chiefs of Staff at the Second Quebec Conference in September 1944. Seated (left to right): Marshall, Leahy, Roosevelt, Churchill, Field Marshal Sir Alan Brooke, and Field Marshal Sir John Dill; standing (left to right): Brigadier Leslie Hollis, Lieutenant General Sir Hastings Ismay, King, Air Chief Marshal Sir Charles Portal, Arnold, and Admiral Sir Andrew Cunningham. (Courtesy of the George C. Marshall Foundation, Lexington, Virginia)

Churchill, Roosevelt, and Stalin at Yalta, February 1945. Leahy stands immediately behind Roosevelt with Marshall behind him. King and Field Marshal Brooke are on the step to the left. (National Archives, 111-SC-260486)

Halsey's flagship, the battleship *New Jersey* (BB-62), plows through a wave on November 8, 1944, after Leyte Gulf but six weeks before the big typhoon. The carrier *Intrepid* (CV11) steams in the distance. (National Archives, 80-G-291047)

Halsey shares a belated Thanksgiving dinner with his crew on his Third Fleet flagship, November 30, 1944. (National Archives, 80-G-291498)

Halsey on his flag bridge on the *New Jersey* shortly before the December typhoon. (National Archives, 80-G-471108)

Whether it was pitching horseshoes with enlisted men or shooting a pistol on the firing range, Nimitz made a habit of taking a moment or two to relax. (Courtesy of the National Museum of the Pacific War, Nimitz Education and Research Center, FPA 13, nerc_000355)

King in the COMINCH conference room, showing his usual command presence. (National Archives, 80-G-416886)

But, yes, he could laugh. King at a reunion of his Annapolis class in 1944. (National Archives, 80-G-45387)

General Douglas MacArthur in his leather jacket with Roosevelt and Nimitz on the deck of the cruiser *Baltimore* (CA-68) at Pearl Harbor, July 26, 1944. Leahy (second from left), another naval officer, and the president's Secret Service men stand in the background. (National Archives, 80-G-241479)

Vice Admiral John S. "Slew" McCain (left) confers with Halsey in Halsey's cabin on the *New Jersey* (BB-62). The big question: was this just before or after the December typhoon? (National Archives, 80-G-470859)

Leahy stands behind Harry S. Truman as Truman takes the oath of office upon Roosevelt's death, April 12, 1945. (National Park Service, Abbie Rowe, Courtesy of Harry S. Truman Library)

Chief of Naval Operations Nimitz, presidential Chief of Staff Leahy, President Truman, and Admiral Marc Mitscher on the bridge of Mitscher's flagship, the carrier *Franklin D. Roosevelt* (CV-42), April 22 or 23, 1946. Truman was not above tweaking his chief of staff for his dour manner. On the back of Leahy's copy of this photograph, Truman scrawled, "Admiral: You do not seem to approve! HST." (U.S. Navy, courtesy of the Harry S. Truman Library)

land bases or the ability to return to aircraft carriers — assuming, of course, that they could lift off the length of a carrier's deck in the first place. Low suggested launching army B-25 twin-engine medium bombers from a carrier quickly deployed close to Japan. After dropping their payloads, the bombers would continue flying west to friendly bases in China. King, who had been ranting about pushing the offensive, seized on Low's idea and had his air operations officer, Captain Donald B. Duncan, sell it to General Henry H. "Hap" Arnold, chief of staff of the Army Air Corps.[27]

Arnold had just the man for the job, and within days the pilots of sixteen B-25s under the command of Lieutenant Colonel James H. Doolittle were wondering why they were practicing so many short-field takeoffs. The answer slowly dawned on them and their four-man crews after Doolittle led his squadron to Naval Air Station Alameda on San Francisco Bay and they watched their bombers loaded aboard the *Hornet* (CV-8), the most recent addition to the American carrier fleet.

When Nimitz handed Halsey the task of getting Doolittle as close to Japan as possible, Halsey insisted that he meet Doolittle in person to size him up and stress the hazards of the mission. Halsey and his chief of staff, Miles Browning, secretly flew from Pearl Harbor to San Francisco to confer with Doolittle and the *Hornet*'s commanding officer, Captain Marc Mitscher. Halsey pulled no punches. Doolittle had to understand that if Halsey's ships came under attack before Doolittle's planes could be launched, Halsey would push the bombers over the side in order to launch his own protective aircraft. Doolittle nodded. They seemed to be kindred spirits and they had a deal.

In the company of the cruisers *Vincennes* and *Nashville,* four destroyers, and an oiler, *Hornet* put to sea as TF (Task Force) 18. It headed for a rendezvous north of Oahu with a supporting force Halsey would lead from Pearl Harbor. But Halsey almost missed the trip. Strong westerly winds delayed his and Browning's return flight to Pearl Harbor, and then the admiral came down with a bout of what he thought was the flu. By the time Halsey finally landed and went aboard *Enterprise,* the entire operation was a day behind schedule. A drugged sleep in the PB2Y en route seemed to cure some of his symptoms, but he kept scratching at an annoying rash.

Enterprise, the cruisers *Northampton* and *Salt Lake City,* four destroyers, and an oiler cleared the antisubmarine nets at the mouth of Pearl Harbor and headed for the rendezvous with *Hornet*'s group. Only when he was some distance from Oahu did Halsey dare to announce, "This force is bound for Tokyo." *Enterprise* erupted with the loudest cheer Halsey had ever heard, stoked in part by frustrations over the fall of Bataan just four days earlier.

The two task forces joined up at 6:00 a.m. on April 13, blessedly not a Friday for Halsey's phobia, and a day later crossed the international date line, thereby jumping to April 15. Things went almost too smoothly as *Enterprise* and *Hornet,* and their cruiser consorts, refueled and, leaving the destroyers and oilers astern, started the final high-speed run toward Japan. Then, early on the morning of April 18, after dodging one radar contact, the combined force was sighted by a Japanese picket ship. Six hundred fifty miles from Tokyo, instead of the planned four hundred, Halsey had no choice but to order *Hornet* to launch Doolittle's planes and then turn for Pearl Harbor at 25 knots.

Colonel Doolittle and his pilots and crews flew on into legend, although the increased flight distance meant that none of the planes reached the haven of airfields in China. Most crews bailed out over China and made their way into friendly hands. Remarkably, out of eighty men only three fliers were killed outright, and the Japanese executed another three, an event that outraged Halsey. In typical fashion, he vowed, "We'll make the bastards pay!"[28]

The Doolittle Raid may have been one of the best-kept secrets of the war. King later claimed that just seven people knew the complete plan — King, Nimitz, Halsey, Arnold, Duncan, Low, and Doolittle — and that King himself went to the White House to tell Roosevelt only after the carriers were almost to their launching point. And the entire operation remained quite mysterious. The navy was not interested in signaling to the enemy how far-ranging its carriers had been, and the army hoped to make the Japanese paranoid about the range of its bombers and the threat of future raids from, well, who knew where. When asked at a press conference where the planes had come from, FDR told one of his folksy stories that had them flying "from our new secret base at Shangri-La!"[29]

Halsey's ships returned from the Doolittle Raid and sailed into Pearl Harbor on April 25. This time, Nimitz was not on hand to greet him. For Nimitz, April 1942 was one of the defining watersheds in his career. As Japanese advances in the South Pacific continued unchecked, and with Admiral King still giving many orders from Washington, CINCPAC had flown east to San Francisco to consult with COMINCH. It was the first of sixteen face-to-face wartime conferences between King and Nimitz in San Francisco, Pearl Harbor, or Washington.

During the first few months of 1942, one staff officer characterized Nimitz as "scared and cautious," while a foreign observer later recalled him as "an old man, slow and perhaps slightly deaf." The last was indeed true, due to his ear injury years before as a midshipman, but the other impressions were, in fact, only those of a calm and steady hand getting his sea legs as a theater commander in a tenuous environment.[30]

The Japanese were marshaling forces at Truk and Rabaul. It appeared to Nimitz that they would attempt a major, concerted attack — either to capture Port Moresby, on the southeastern toe of New Guinea, as a base from which to threaten Australia or to drive eastward to threaten New Caledonia, Fiji, and Samoa astride the critical West Coast–Australia lifeline. To do either — or both, as Nimitz feared — would require control of the Coral Sea. *Lexington* and *Yorktown* were on station there under Rear Admiral Frank Jack Fletcher's command.

Basing his actions in part on Japanese intelligence reports gathered in the wake of the Doolittle Raid, Nimitz determined to commit the full strength of his Pacific carriers — *Lexington* and *Yorktown,* as well as the returning *Enterprise* and *Hornet* — not only to repulse these threats but also to seize the initiative for offensive operations that King had begun to formulate. But King was initially reluctant to commit the carriers en masse, seeking instead to keep them dispersed for supposedly safer hit-and-run raids, as had been the strategy to date. COMINCH further complicated matters by fixating on the South Pacific deployment of older, slower battleships that Nimitz understood to be a millstone, preventing nimble operations. King, of course, also knew that from his experiences throughout the 1930s, but it took Nimitz's forceful lobbying at their San Francisco conference to persuade him that now was the time to concentrate the four carriers—sans battleships—into one powerful strategic force.

This was a major shift in the way the U.S. Navy viewed its carriers, and it marked Nimitz as exerting aggressive leadership as a theater commander. In retrospect, it may also have marked him as more aggressive than King had previously thought—always a good thing with King. Even then, King did not agree to such action until the day after the conference had adjourned and Nimitz was back in Pearl Harbor.[31]

Thus, on April 30, after only five days' rest following the Doolittle Raid, Halsey sortied as Task Force 16 with *Enterprise* and *Hornet* and their cruiser, destroyer, and oiler escorts, the latter ships once again commanded by Halsey's polar opposite and good friend, Rear Admiral Raymond Spruance. Once joined with Fletcher's forces, Halsey would assume overall tactical command.

On May 4, planes from Fletcher's *Yorktown* struck a new Japanese naval anchorage at Tulagi, just north of Guadalcanal. In the smoke and confusion of their first pitched strike, Fletcher's pilots returned to *Yorktown* with wildly inflated claims of destruction, including two destroyers sunk and a badly mangled seaplane tender and large cruiser. Fletcher flashed the news to Nimitz, who professed wary congratulations and then cautioned, "Hope you can exploit your success with augmented force," meaning *Lexington,* which was refueling to the south.[32]

As it turned out, Nimitz's caution was well founded. Actual damage from the Tulagi strike proved to be only one destroyer and some minor small craft. Then, as *Yorktown* stood south to rendezvous with *Lexington,* a Japanese carrier force circled into the Coral Sea around the eastern end of the Solomons. Confusion was rampant on

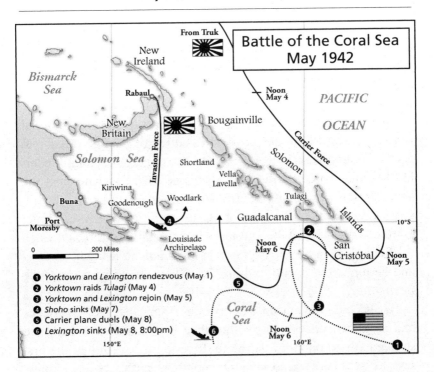

Battle of the Coral Sea
May 1942

❶ *Yorktown* and *Lexington* rendezvous (May 1)
❷ *Yorktown* raids *Tulagi* (May 4)
❸ *Yorktown* and *Lexington* rejoin (May 5)
❹ *Shoho* sinks (May 7)
❺ Carrier plane duels (May 8)
❻ *Lexington* sinks (May 8, 8:00pm)

May 7 on both sides as Japanese planes from the carriers *Shokaku* and *Zuikaku* streaked south, not in pursuit of the American carriers, but to attack the destroyer *Sims* and oiler *Neosho,* which had been erroneously reported to be an American carrier and cruiser.

Meanwhile, B-17s flying from Australia spotted the Port Moresby invasion fleet, including the light carrier *Shoho,* steaming into the Coral Sea between New Guinea and the Solomons. As the two big Japanese carriers focused on *Sims* and *Neosho,* Fletcher's two carriers moved west to engage them, but wound up attacking the invasion force instead. American planes sank the *Shoho,* to the excited cry of one of the *Lexington*'s dive-bomber leaders: "Scratch one flattop!"[33]

But by that evening, the two principal carriers on each side still had not directly engaged one another. That changed the next morning when planes from the opposing carriers found their targets, leaving *Lexington* the most heavily damaged of the four after taking two torpedoes and two direct bomb hits. With *Yorktown* also damaged from a bomb amidships, Fletcher chose to retire southward as expeditiously as *Lexington* could manage. The Japanese carriers, with *Shokaku* heavily damaged as well, likewise retired north of New Guinea with the repulsed Port Moresby invasion fleet.

Late in the afternoon on May 8, gasoline vapors from ruptured fuel lines deep within the *Lexington*'s hull ignited and spiraled into a series of gut-wrenching explosions. The carrier's captain, Frederick Sherman, ordered the ship abandoned, and Fletcher had the grim duty of assigning a destroyer to sink the flaming wreck with torpedoes to avoid any chance of its salvage by the Japanese. Nimitz got the news by sporadic and long-delayed radio traffic, and when the final blow came, the engineer in him couldn't help but surface, and he muttered, if only to himself, "They should have saved the *Lexington*."[34]

But it could have been much worse. Tactically, the Americans had sustained heavier losses, but they had nonetheless managed strategically to blunt the Japanese drive toward Australia, the first setback to Japan's unchecked, five-month, post–Pearl Harbor romp. The Battle of the Coral Sea also sealed the fate of the battleship— though none were present—by proving that carrier aircraft might well fight major battles without surface ships ever coming into direct contact with one another.

And there was a third result. The battle left COMINCH King, though ten thousand miles away, with a strong apprehension that Frank Jack Fletcher was not the man to command an aggressive campaign. If Halsey had been at Coral Sea, King mused, things might have been different. Still, it was hard for most other observers to criticize Fletcher for the outcome. Five months after Pearl Harbor, he had taken on a slightly superior force and at worst emerged with a draw. At best, he had saved Australia.

Recognizing that part of his role was as cheerleader and morale booster, and before he had learned of the loss of the *Lexington,* Nimitz sent Fletcher a warm note of praise, no doubt thinking strategically: "Congratulations on your glorious accomplishments of the last two days. Your aggressive actions have the admiration of the entire Pacific Fleet. Well done to you, your officers, and men. You have filled our hearts with pride and have maintained the highest traditions of the Navy."[35]

Nimitz recommended to King that Fletcher be promoted to vice admiral and be awarded the Distinguished Service Medal. King balked. In King's mind, losing a carrier, particularly the *Lexington,* which he had once commanded, was hardly reason to bestow stars or medals or both. Nimitz should have remembered King's words from the North Atlantic late in 1941, when he strongly opposed medals for commanders who lost ships — even if they did win battles.

The question now became what to tell Halsey and *Enterprise* and *Hornet* as they finally neared the Coral Sea. Halsey, who had been itching for a fight, was now scratching like crazy at his infuriating dermatitis and getting less and less sleep. King — smarting over the loss of *Lexington* — momentarily reverted to his pre–Coral Sea caution and signaled Nimitz that it would be "inadvisable" for Halsey's force "to operate beyond the coverage of our shore-based air or within range of enemy shore-based air." This had the effect of greatly restricting Halsey's operations and left him "mad as the devil."[36]

In appraising the overall Pacific situation, King and Nimitz were both heavily relying on intelligence garnered from the sleuth work of three groups of code breakers in Australia, Washington, and Hawaii, the latter led by Commander Joseph J. Rochefort, a number-crunching nerd who combined a computer-like mind with unabashed intuitive insight. How the two admirals now chose to apply that intelligence, however, differed greatly.

King still thought the Japanese would attempt a drive, perhaps as far as Fiji and Samoa, to restrict or sever the West Coast–Australia lifeline. With *Yorktown* en route to Pearl Harbor for repairs, King and Nimitz had initially agreed that *Enterprise* and *Hornet* would remain in the South Pacific. But now Nimitz wasn't so sure. He read Rochefort's latest reports as suggesting a change in direction of the main Japanese attack from the South Pacific to the Central Pacific, at least as far as Midway.

The week before the Coral Sea engagement, as he was massing

his carriers in the South Pacific, Nimitz had taken two precious days and flown eleven hundred miles to inspect Midway's defenses, in part to reassure King that things were under control on that front. Midway wasn't much of a place. Two tiny islands, crisscrossed by airstrips, totaled barely fifteen hundred acres on the edge of a lagoon circled by a jagged reef. But in May 1942, Midway may have been the most heavily defended acreage in the Pacific. Certainly, the outpost was a thorn in the side of any Japanese operations passing within range of its aircraft. Nimitz crawled into gun pits, squirmed through underground command posts, and kicked the dirt with the island's defenders in the earthy, teamwork-inspiring manner that he exhibited so strongly. When it was time to return to Pearl Harbor, he left with a sense that the island could be held.[37]

For several weeks after the Battle of the Coral Sea, Halsey remained in limbo. King wanted him to stay in the south, Nimitz wanted him in the north, and wherever he was, King's air umbrella directive threatened his flexibility. As the officer in tactical command, however, Halsey felt compelled to push, if not outright ignore, King's momentary caution, which in itself was decidedly counter to all that King had taught Halsey about carrier operations in the first place. King didn't scrutinize Halsey's actions, but he procrastinated when Nimitz pressed him to order Halsey back north to counter the growing threat against Midway. What, Nimitz wondered, was King waiting for?

Finally, Nimitz received enough intelligence from Rochefort to convince him that the next big push was indeed coming in the Central Pacific. Japanese radio intercepts increasingly pointed away from Port Moresby and the South Pacific in general. To Nimitz, this meant that Japan's carriers were elsewhere—most likely the Central Pacific—and he could wait for King no longer. As CINCPAC, Nimitz ordered Halsey north.

Nimitz told King and Halsey that while he was convinced that Japan was planning "three separate and possibly simultaneous enemy offensives"—against the Aleutians to cover their northern flank, another try for Port Moresby, and a carrier-intensive strike along the "Midway–Oahu line"—the latter was to be the most serious. If King, who was still focused on the South Pacific leg of this triple threat, felt strongly enough, he could countermand Nimitz's order or even relieve Nimitz. In the meantime, Nimitz had made a firm decision. Not only did he hurry Halsey north with *Hornet* and *Enterprise,* but he also directed Fletcher to expedite his return to Hawaiian waters and repair the damaged *Yorktown* at Pearl Harbor.

Still, having once again taken bold steps to mass his carriers, Nimitz wanted some sign from King that he concurred. Finally, on May 17, it came. King acknowledged having "somewhat revised my estimate and now generally agree with you," although he tried unsuccessfully to convince Nimitz to order *Yorktown* to the West Coast for its repairs, an action in keeping with his cautious carrier dispersal rather than Nimitz's aggressive concentration.[38]

This period of uncertainty between the Battle of the Coral Sea and the looming confrontation at Midway established the modus operandi between the two commanders that would last for the duration of the war. King might well have ordered Nimitz to do this or that, or countermanded his move of Halsey. Instead, King finally embraced Admiral Henry T. Mayo's manner of trusting one's subordinates closer to the action. For years, King had preached the doctrine of the "initiative of the subordinate," and now he seemed finally able to practice it, even though he remained dubious of the risks of fighting one pitched battle for Midway.

It helped, of course, that King had his hands full with global strategy, including negotiating with his American and Allied chiefs of staff and implementing the North Atlantic campaigns. But in the case of Nimitz—despite having some ongoing reservations about him being too lenient on his subordinates—King adopted a "command by consensus" approach. He offered advice; he wanted to know what Nimitz was doing; but he generally avoided direct orders. Nimitz for his part reciprocated by respecting King's judgment, keeping him adequately informed, and not unnecessarily opposing his views just for the sake of opposition.

Still, just before the Battle of Midway, chafing over the loss of *Lexington,* King could not refrain from ordering Nimitz to be sure "to employ strong attrition tactics and not repeat *not* allow our forces to accept such decisive action as would be likely to incur heavy losses in our carriers and cruisers."[39]

When *Enterprise* docked at Pearl Harbor on May 26, Halsey made the trip to the CINCPAC office at the sub base. Nimitz couldn't believe his eyes. His star carrier commander had lost twenty pounds, looked like he hadn't slept in two weeks — which was almost true — and had the most hideous rash Nimitz had ever seen. No matter what the cause of his skin eruption, fifty-nine-year-old Bill Halsey had just spent an almost uninterrupted six months on the bridge of the *Enterprise* since sailing for Wake Island at the end of November 1941. He was exhausted.

Still, Halsey protested the inevitable order to report to the hospital. The doctor proved as adamant as he was in return. "Sir," he told Halsey, "where your health is concerned, I am the one who gives the orders."[40]

But Halsey had one last request of Nimitz. When Nimitz asked him for recommendations as to who should now command Task Force 16 as it rushed back to sea, Halsey did not hesitate and offered only one name: Raymond Spruance. Nimitz gave no indication of his thoughts, but King was about to appoint Spruance Nimitz's chief of staff. Clearly, steady Spruance was highly thought of.

So Task Force 16, with Spruance in command aboard *Enterprise* and accompanied by *Hornet,* departed Pearl Harbor on May 28. Nimitz sent Spruance off with instructions that what King called "calculated risk" govern his movements. Nimitz told Spruance that he was to interpret that to mean "the avoidance of exposure of your force to attack by superior enemy forces without good prospect of inflicting, as a result of such exposure, greater damage to the enemy."[41]

Two days later, after a frenzied three-day effort to make the carrier as battle ready as possible, *Yorktown* and its Task Force 17 followed, still flying Frank Jack Fletcher's flag. Fletcher would assume overall tactical command when the two forces joined up at a point Nimitz had optimistically named Point Luck.

King still had his doubts about Fletcher, but Nimitz had spent a couple of hours with him after *Yorktown*'s arrival from the Coral

Sea and come away convinced of both his competence and his courage. "Dear King," Nimitz wrote as Fletcher sailed, "What appeared to be a lack of aggressiveness" on Fletcher's part has been "cleared up to my entire satisfaction...[and] I hope...you will agree with me that Fletcher did a fine job and exercised superior judgment in his recent cruise to the Coral Sea." [42]

As the American carriers moved to rendezvous northeast of Midway, the Japanese fleet was indeed intent on capturing the island as a likely jumping-off point for a planned invasion of Hawaii later that year. In its sights, too, were islands in Alaska's Aleutian chain, as a means of pushing its outer defensive line forward as far as possible. But paramount in Admiral Yamamoto's mind was to finish the task that had eluded Nagumo at Pearl Harbor: he had to sink the bulk of the American fleet in one grand battle and encourage peace negotiations before American shipyards could send new carriers to the Pacific. To that end, Yamamoto sailed personally in the 863-foot, 73,000-ton mammoth battleship *Yamato* with a battle force that trailed the four carriers of the strike force.

In all, Yamamoto deployed 162 ships of the Imperial Japanese Navy, practically its entire fighting force, in support of the Midway operation. (No wonder Rochefort reported things suddenly quiet around Port Moresby.) But an exceedingly complicated battle array, and perhaps a measure of overconfidence, may have gotten the better of him. There was the strike force of the veteran Pearl Harbor carriers—*Akagi, Kaga, Soryu,* and *Hiryu*—once again led by Admiral Nagumo. There was a Midway occupation force of five thousand men in twelve transports protected by battleships and cruisers. There was Yamamoto's main force of battleships and cruisers. And finally, there was a northern force of two light carriers, cruisers, and transports, sailing toward Alaska to bomb Dutch Harbor and occupy Adak, Attu, and Kiska. (If there is any doubt about Fletcher's contribution at Coral Sea, that battle cost the Imperial Japanese Navy the potential use of three more carriers at Midway—the damaged *Shokaku* and *Zuikaku* and the sunken *Shoho*.)

Yamamoto initially planned to attack Dutch Harbor and Midway simultaneously on June 3 in a double-fisted punch designed to lure the American fleet into one pitched battle and annihilate it whether it steamed north to rescue the Aleutians or west to support Midway. But as *Enterprise, Hornet,* and *Yorktown* lurked patiently near Point Luck, Nimitz refused to respond to the attack on the Aleutians on June 3 and instead remained focused on Midway after the Japanese attack on that island had fallen behind a day. The next morning, his patience was rewarded.[43]

When the sun set in the Central Pacific on June 4, 1942, *Yorktown* was crippled for good, but the 4 Japanese carriers that had celebrated the attack on Pearl Harbor just six months before, 257 of their planes, and 121 of Japan's most skilled combat pilots, along with thousands of men, were sunk or sinking.[44] Stunned at having lost four carriers and his air superiority, Yamamoto turned his main battle force around and sailed for Japan, with no more territory to show for the operation than the occupation of two mostly uninhabited islands in the Aleutians. Midway would remain in American hands. Spruance grumbled that *Hornet*'s planes should have put *Hiryu* out of action before it launched the crippling blow against *Yorktown,* but ultimately the Japanese offensive momentum that had been blunted at Coral Sea had been stopped at Midway.

The Battle of Midway was, as historian Walter Lord characterized it, an "incredible victory" for the United States. Captain Hideo Hiraide, chief of the naval press section at Imperial Japanese Headquarters, put a different spin on the entire outcome. "The enormous success in the Aleutians," he reported to the Japanese people, "had been made possible by the diversion at Midway."[45]

"The Battle of Midway," King later wrote, "was the first decisive defeat suffered by the Japanese Navy in 350 years. Furthermore, it put an end to the long period of Japanese offensive action, and restored the balance of naval power in the Pacific."[46] Nimitz, at the time, remained focused on the long-term goal: "Vengeance," he said on June 6, 1942, "will not be complete until Japanese sea power is reduced to impotence." But he couldn't help injecting a little pun. "Perhaps," he added, "we will be forgiven if we claim that we are about midway to that objective."[47]

Fletcher and Spruance had proved to be a good team. Patient, even tempered, and both willing to trust Nimitz's intelligence reports, they managed to be in the right place at the right time. "Your courage to accept the intelligence that led up to that operation," Spruance readily acknowledged to Nimitz, "and your prompt decision and action to throw all available forces [*Enterprise, Hornet,* and *Yorktown*] into it were all that prevented a serious disaster for us."[48]

Spruance, whom Fletcher released to operate independently with Task Force 16 after *Yorktown*'s condition worsened, was equally laudatory of Fletcher's role and the flag staff on the *Enterprise* that Spruance had inherited from Halsey. "This letter has been much longer than I had expected it to be," Spruance wrote in his after-action report to Nimitz, "but I cannot close it without expressing my admiration for the part that Fletcher in the YORKTOWN played in this campaign." He and Fletcher had had "a fine and smoothly working co-ordination between the two Task Forces," Spruance reported, and "Halsey's splendid staff have made my job easy."[49]

Subsequent naval historians would downplay, or even overlook completely, Frank Jack Fletcher's role at Midway. This may have been the result of Spruance's later prominence and success in the Central Pacific, but it also clearly had something to do with King's propensity "for writing off a subordinate at the first suspicion of irresolution or timidity." Deserved or not, King thought Fletcher guilty of both prior to and during the Battle of the Coral Sea and never forgave him.

Raymond Spruance, Fletcher's clear subordinate at Midway until Fletcher turned him loose, thought differently. "It was tough luck that the *Yorktown* had to stand those two attacks," Spruance wrote Fletcher within a week of the battle. "If it had not been for what you did and took with the *Yorktown,*" Spruance continued, "I am firmly convinced that we would have been badly defeated and the Japs would be holding Midway today." No matter their future destinies and appraisals, Spruance retained his appreciation for Fletcher's role and bristled at histories that denied Fletcher proper credit.[50]

This begs the question of what might have happened had Bill Halsey been in tactical command at Midway instead of itching in a hospital bed. Would he have been as patient? Would he have driven west after sinking the Japanese carriers and encountered Yamamoto's main force, likely in a night surface battle, instead of safely retiring eastward as Spruance had done? Might he have achieved the exact success of Spruance and Fletcher?

Others would debate these points, but the one man who would replay Halsey's failure to be at Midway the most was Halsey himself. He had arrived too late at Coral Sea and been sidelined at Midway. Missing these two key battles would have a strong influence on his actions two and a half years hence off the Philippines. Midway was, in Halsey's words, "the crucial carrier duel of the war," and not being a part of it was "the most grievous disappointment in my career."[51]

CHAPTER FIFTEEN

Deciding the Course

While Bill Halsey sat out a round and fought severe dermatitis, other battles were raging over the conduct of the war. How was command of a global war effort to be divided up on land and sea? Should President Roosevelt appoint one supreme military chief? And despite the commitment to Germany First with America's British and Russian allies, how would this play out in practice against the pressing needs in the Pacific?

Admiral King had laid out his preferred strategy in a memo to General Marshall several weeks before King became CNO and COMINCH. He had remained adamant at every turn about his initial charge to Nimitz to maintain the Hawaii/West Coast–Australia sea-lanes at all costs. Just how, Marshall now asked, did King propose to accomplish this?

In but one example of the communications between army and navy this early in the war, Marshall's request took a week to travel from his office, then in the Munitions Building, to King's office in the adjacent Navy Department Building less than two blocks away. It finally arrived just one day before the Joint Chiefs of Staff

(JCS)—still only Marshall, King, and Arnold—was to hold only its third meeting since the Arcadia Conference six weeks before. But in characteristic fashion, King did not hesitate or plead for more time. Instead, he dictated a reply, approved a final draft, and had copies distributed at the JCS meeting the next day.

"The general scheme or concept of operations," King wrote, "is not only to protect the lines of communications with Australia but, in so doing, to set up 'strong points' from which a step-by-step general advance can be made through the New Hebrides, Solomons, and the Bismarck Archipelago." Marshall immediately seized on the words "general advance." The Japanese were rushing toward Australia, Churchill was bemoaning the fall of Singapore as akin to the end of Western civilization, and both Roosevelt and Churchill had just agreed to a Germany First strategy. How could King even consider a "general advance" in the Pacific?

But King was emphatic about how he could and would accomplish it. Using marines as the spear point, King intended to seize and occupy strategic positions along the all-important Hawaii–Australia lifeline, not only securing the route to Australia but also establishing staging points from which to strike generally northwest from that line. The army would follow to garrison the acquired strongholds.[1]

Three days later, King repeated his plan for Roosevelt, who was trying to find some way to bolster Churchill's momentary gloom. King reminded FDR that the United States was, almost by default and with British acquiescence, assuming chief responsibility for Pacific operations, the British having been generally driven west of the Malay Peninsula, save Australia and New Zealand. King strongly concurred with Roosevelt's previously expressed view that with limited resources and an almost unlimited geography over which to fight, the United States should determine "a *very few* lines of military endeavor and concentrate our efforts on these lines." Those lines might well change in the future, King said, but they "should be kept at a *very few*." (Emphasis in original in both cases.)

The most important line of the "very few" to be allocated to the Pacific was support for "Australasia"—the continent and its northern approaches—by keeping Samoa, Fiji, and New Caledonia as strongpoints along the Hawaii–Australia lifeline, securing the New Hebrides (now Vanuatu) and Ellice Islands (now Tuvalu) as additional strongpoints, and then driving northwest from there into the Solomons, including an island called Guadalcanal.

"Such a line of operations will be offensive rather than passive," King maintained, "and will draw Japanese forces there to oppose it, thus relieving pressure elsewhere, whether in Hawaii, ABDA area [the Southwest Pacific], Alaska, or even India." This became "an integrated, general plan of operations" that King summarized like this: "Hold Hawaii, Support Australasia, Drive northwestward from New Hebrides."[2]

Roosevelt seized on King's plan and passed it on to Churchill as a way to encourage him to think that, Singapore aside, all was not lost in the Pacific. Churchill fretted that *any* American offensive in the Pacific would come at a cost to operations against Germany, but Roosevelt reassured him of the overall commitment to Germany First, even if some resources, particularly American contributions to air operations against Germany during 1942, would inevitably be diverted to the Pacific.

King's general operational strategy for offensive operations in the Pacific—as opposed to mere defensive containment—was thus adopted, even though Roosevelt would vacillate on it depending on his audience. "Although it was not at once apparent (perhaps not even to King)," King's principal biographer wrote with some hyperbole, "King had embarked upon the most important contribution he would make to victory in the Second World War."[3]

King and Marshall's next task was to divide the vast Pacific into operational areas with some measure of unified command between the army and navy. Since both men were initially much more inclined to send each other memos rather than walk next door and knock, this was easier said than done. And it complicated matters further that one of those watching how big a piece of the pie he would get was Douglas MacArthur.

Roosevelt's recall of MacArthur from the Philippines had been premised in part on the need to put him in a larger role—at least that was the perception trumpeted in both the American and Australian press. The general's "I shall return" remark upon reaching Australia fit the situation, as well as his persona, perfectly. Marshall further supported this image by arranging for MacArthur to be given the one military award the general truly coveted, the Medal of Honor, so that he might emulate his father, who had won it for his reckless dash up Missionary Ridge almost eighty years before.

Marshall, of course, had a more practical motive than merely massaging the general's ego. "I submit the recommendation to you," Marshall wrote Secretary of War Henry L. Stimson, "not only because I am certain that General MacArthur is deserving of the honor, but also because I am certain that this action will meet with popular approval, both within and without the armed forces, and will have a constructive morale value." Having played a large role in both rescuing and elevating MacArthur, Marshall remained convinced that MacArthur's "dominating character is needed down there to make the Navy keep up their job in spite of rows which we shall have between them."[4]

But Marshall had also by now had enough exposure to King to know that he had no intention of turning over command of navy ships in the Pacific to MacArthur or anyone else. Nimitz was CINCPAC, and that was that. In fact, far from merely keeping up their job, King had just outlined how the navy would take the lead.

Yet when Marshall's war plans chief, Brigadier General Dwight Eisenhower, drew up the army's Pacific overview, he tentatively assigned the entire Pacific, from the Philippines to Samoa and west of 170° west longitude (decidedly *east* of New Zealand), to MacArthur. This left the navy idling around Hawaii and the West Coast and implied that MacArthur would command the navy and marine forces that King proposed to deploy in support of his pronounced offensive strategy. King strongly opposed Eisenhower's division, and Marshall agreed to revisit the map of the Pacific.

What's more, King advocated unity of command at the tactical level in each theater of operations, but wanted strategic decisions to be made only at the Joint Chiefs level and then transmitted from

Marshall and King to their respective commands. When adopted, this structure had the effect of making the Joint Chiefs the supreme military authority and Marshall and King the undisputed heads of their services subject only to the president.

So the three chiefs of staff—Marshall, King, and Arnold, the latter subservient to Marshall—with Roosevelt's ultimate blessing set about carving the Pacific into four areas of tactical command. In the Southwest Pacific Area, which included Australia, New Guinea, and the Netherlands East Indies, MacArthur was designated commander in chief, Southwest Pacific (COMSOWESPAC), over all army and navy forces of the Allied powers in that theater, principally the United States, Great Britain, Canada, Australia, New Zealand, and the Netherlands, effective April 18, 1942. As CINCPAC, Nimitz retained command over all units of the principal American fleet should it sail into the Southwest Pacific Area (as it had at Coral Sea), as well as being the commander in chief of all Allied army and navy forces in the remaining Pacific Ocean Area (CINCPOA).

As the final lines were drawn, Marshall wanted one seemingly minor change: to push MacArthur's area northward from the East Indies to include the Philippines, doing so, he said, for "psychological reasons." At this point in the war, it seemed a relatively innocuous move, and King agreed to the concession. What it did, of course, was inadvertently sanction MacArthur's determination to return to the Philippines whether or not such action was in the best interests of wider strategic concerns.

Nimitz's Pacific Ocean Area was further divided into the North Pacific Area, north of 42° north latitude; the South Pacific Area, south of the equator and east of 160° east longitude; and the remaining swath of the core Central Pacific Area. One problem that would soon arise was that the dividing line between the Southwest Pacific (MacArthur) and the South Pacific (Nimitz) areas along 160° east longitude ran right through Guadalcanal. The broader issues of independent areas of command and "MacArthur's Navy," as well as that of the Philippines, would reverberate throughout the war.[5]

Prior to his first wartime conference with Nimitz in San Francisco just before the Battle of the Coral Sea, King had selected an

King's Pacific Strategy and Division of Comma

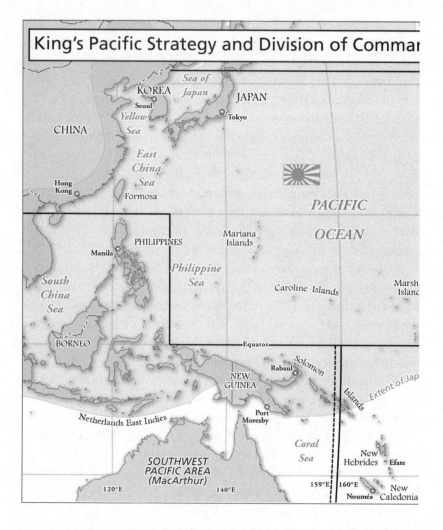

KOREA
Seoul
Yellow
Sea
CHINA
East
China
Sea
Hong
Kong
Formosa
Sea of
Japan
JAPAN
Tokyo
PACIFIC
OCEAN
PHILIPPINES
Manila
South
China
Sea
Philippine
Sea
Mariana
Islands
Caroline Islands
Marsh
Island
BORNEO
Equator
Solomon
Rabaul
NEW
GUINEA
Islands
Extent of Jap
Netherlands East Indies
Port
Moresby
Coral
Sea
New
Hebrides
Efate
SOUTHWEST
PACIFIC AREA
(MacArthur)
120°E
140°E
159°E
160°E
Nouméa
New
Caledonia

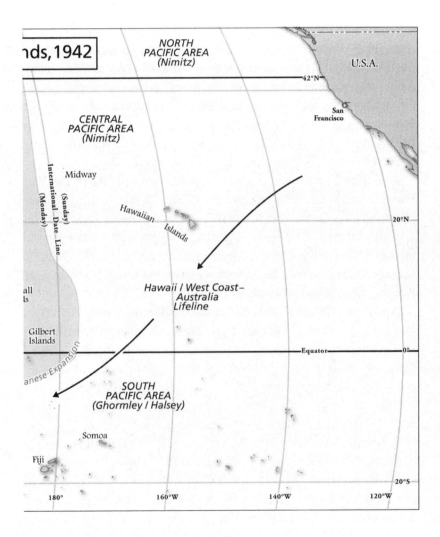

ds, 1942

NORTH
PACIFIC AREA
(Nimitz)

U.S.A.

42°N

CENTRAL
PACIFIC AREA
(Nimitz)

San
Francisco

Midway

International Date Line
(Sunday)
(Monday)

Hawaiian Islands

20°N

Hawaii / West Coast–
Australia
Lifeline

all
s

Gilbert
Islands

anese Expansion

Equator

0°

SOUTH
PACIFIC AREA
(Ghormley / Halsey)

Somoa

Fiji

20°S

180°   160°W   140°W   120°W

area commander for the South Pacific. This was not to be his most enlightened personnel decision. The man he chose as commander in chief, South Pacific (COMSOPAC) was Vice Admiral Robert L. Ghormley. A 1906 graduate of Annapolis, one year behind Nimitz, Ghormley had a well-deserved reputation as a skilled planner and thoughtful strategist. While his sea duty included tours in cruisers and battleships, his record was heavy with staff work in Washington, including a stint as assistant chief of naval operations. Since August 1940, Ghormley had been in Great Britain as a special naval observer. But the very fact that Ghormley was still in London when replaced by banished ex-CNO Harold Stark in the spring of 1942 and knew little about the South Pacific should have been a warning flag.

And there were others. Ghormley had been director of the War Plans Division when Bill Leahy was CNO. Despite Leahy's strong efforts to plan for the threat of a two-ocean war, Ghormley had disappointed the chief by pessimistically reporting that the navy could not wage "an offensive naval war simultaneously in the Atlantic and the Pacific." Now, faced with exactly that task, it was unclear whether Ghormley's outlook had changed.[6]

Apparently, Nimitz's first choice for the South Pacific assignment had been Admiral William S. Pye, Kimmel's temporary relief and still in command of Pacific battleships. To naval aviator King, Pye's battleship affinity was a problem, and having no fondness for another possible candidate, Frank Jack Fletcher, King insisted on Ghormley. This was somewhat unusual in that King — rarely one to forgive past transgressions, particularly against himself personally — had been haughtily denied access by Ghormley to key British-American agreements upon assuming command of the Atlantic Fleet.[7]

While King and Nimitz would ultimately work well together in pursuit of the final objective of victory, the Ghormley appointment was representative of the fact that they brought two very different styles to the table. King seized on Nimitz's years with the Bureau of Navigation and thought him somewhat of a "fixer" because of it — ready to smooth things out rather than make waves as was King's style. King "respected Nimitz's judgment and solicited his advice" on personnel matters, but when Nimitz was content to give an officer the benefit of the doubt, King thought Nimitz was much too lenient. A common Nimitz expression was "That fellow is doing all right," but to King that was damning with faint praise.[8]

By contrast, the general public perception of King was that he demanded "nothing less than perfection of performance from his subordinates" and habitually reserved his infrequent pats on the back for officers who solved problems by attacking.[9] King "could never understand why people in command were so touchy about kicking people out."[10]

Nimitz told King in their first conference that he wanted BuNav to take the lead in the assignment of Pacific Fleet officers, but behind the scenes and in between their subsequent conferences, Nimitz had frequent discussions about personnel options with BuNav chief Randall Jacobs, a longtime Nimitz friend.[11] Publicly, Nimitz was frequently content to let BuNav and/or King make any controversial assignments and then blame either for any required dismissals. In Ghormley's case, however, even the congenial Nimitz would give him very little rope.

As much as King was doing to shape overall strategy, there was another admiral who was about to reenter the inner councils of American military policy. It is remarkable that out of the military names readily associated with World War II, two of the men who did the most to advance grand strategy are largely unknown to the general public—King and William D. Leahy. Nimitz and Halsey would come to overshadow them in the public's eye because they held more glamorous, media-rich battlefield commands. But Leahy and King participated in the major strategic decisions that ultimately directed Nimitz and Halsey's tactical roles.

Leahy's primary task as ambassador to Vichy France had sounded as simple as it was complex: make friends with Pétain and keep him and the few Frenchmen still loyal to him from completely selling out to the Germans. Despite the bleak global picture at the beginning of 1942, Leahy had been optimistic. The Allied forces were indeed spread thin, but the ambassador found that the prospects "for free people" were "much better at the beginning of this year than they were twelve months ago." America and its allies, Leahy wrote, were "leagued together in a common interest" to defeat those nations engaged "in a barbarous war...imposing their will on inoffensive peoples."[12]

But Leahy was becoming increasingly frustrated with his role of coddling the mercurial French. "The barometric French opinion," Leahy advised Roosevelt soon after Pearl Harbor, "has reacted to [America's entry into the war] with a leaning over toward our side of the question but with reservations and with preparations to jump back on a moment's notice."[13]

In mid-February 1942, Leahy delivered to Pétain what amounted to an ultimatum from Roosevelt. Vichy France must give official assurance to the United States that no military aid would be given to Germany or Italy and that French ships would not be used to move Axis troops and supplies between the continent and North Africa. Otherwise, Leahy would be recalled "for consultation," diplomatic jargon that a change in relations was likely.

When British bombers struck Renault and Ford automobile plants outside occupied Paris a few weeks later, Admiral Jean-Louis Darlan, the commander of the French fleet, reacted in a rage of Anglophobia. Appealing to Leahy's membership in the shared naval fraternity, Darlan expressed outrage at Roosevelt's demands and Great Britain's attacks on what were now, in fact, German-controlled factories. Noting that his defeated country had been placed in "a painful situation," Darlan did not refrain from attempting to bully Leahy. "I did not believe," Darlan lectured the ambassador, "that the Government of a nation which owes its independence in great part to [France] would take advantage of this fact to treat it with scorn."[14]

Leahy responded immediately without consulting Roosevelt. Yes, they were brothers of the sea, Leahy told Darlan, but the United States was now "involved in a total war in defense of its existence as a free nation." His government would prosecute that war aggressively "in order to secure a complete victory." Under those circumstances, it was unreasonable to expect it "to look with complaisance upon the provision by a friendly nation of any assistance whatever to the military efforts of the enemy powers." In other words, Leahy was telling Darlan, use the French fleet to aid Germany at your peril.[15] When Roosevelt learned of Leahy's reply, the president heartily concurred, calling it "absolutely perfect." Still, he was not yet prepared to recall Leahy in the face of ever closer cooperation between Vichy France and Germany.[16]

Roosevelt, while sympathetic to Leahy's increasingly tenuous position, was swayed by the advice of the Joint Chiefs. Militarily, Marshall, King, and Arnold saw Vichy France and its North African colonies as the Allies' "last bridgehead to Europe," and they urged the president to "postpone as long as possible any evidence of change in our relations with France." As for Leahy, who perhaps was thinking that he might be more useful in a direct military role, the chiefs recommended that he stay in France. FDR concurred, writing to Leahy, "To hold the fort as far as you are concerned is as important a military task as any other in these days."[17]

Leahy's continued presence in Vichy was to have one terrible personal consequence. Bill and Louise remained very close. Theirs was a continuing love affair and Louise's only rival for Bill's attention was their granddaughter, little Louise, upon whom Bill doted. As a navy wife and hostess, Louise graciously and effectively supported Bill's career and garnered much admiration and respect for her performance of the social roles required of diplomats' wives. Fluent in French, she was particularly well received during this trying year in Vichy.

On April 6, 1942, the day after Easter, Bill and Louise went for a two-hour drive in a wooded area outside Vichy and found the countryside "bursting into its spring activity." White anemones were so thick that they carpeted the forest floor and Leahy hastened to pick a large bouquet for his wife. The next evening, Louise entered the local clinic for a hysterectomy that French doctors advised could not be postponed until her pending return to the United States. The procedure seemed to go well.

Then, on April 16, upon hearing that the pro-German Pierre Laval was to become the new head of the Vichy government, Roosevelt cabled Leahy his recall and said he could return to the United

States as soon as Louise was fit to travel. But things unraveled. On April 21, two days after the Laval government was officially announced, sixty-six-year-old Louise Harrington Leahy suffered an embolism while still recovering in the hospital. She died quite suddenly, with her husband at her bedside.

Bill Leahy's personal reserve was legendary. His penchant for avoiding in his diary all but the rarest glimmer of emotion would prove a frustration to his later biographers. But upon Louise's death, his words of tribute to her and the expression of the despair he felt were as human and emotionally vulnerable as Leahy ever allowed himself to appear in print.

"Louise was a great lady," he wrote, "a remarkably successful Ambassadrice [*sic*], and an outstanding representative of America in Europe. She was accepted with enthusiasm and admired by all classes from members of the Royal family to the peasants who . . . all admired her understanding sympathy and innate goodness." As for his own loss, her death "has left me not only crushed with sorrow, but permanently less than half efficient for any work the future may have in store for me and completely uninterested in the remaining future."[18]

"Dear Bill," cabled FDR, "My heart goes out to you in the overwhelming loss which has come to you in a difficult and distant post of duty so far away from the legion of friends who loved Mrs. Leahy dearly." But even these heartfelt wishes from a man Leahy had known almost thirty years and who was now president of the United States could not lift the deep gloom that hung over him.[19]

Leahy came home, haggard and worn, to the house at 2168 Florida Avenue, N.W., in Washington that he and Louise had bought in 1927 upon his promotion to rear admiral. Living there alone this soon was out of the question, and he briefly settled on 19th Street, at the home of his daughter-in-law, Elizabeth Leahy, and her father, Dr. Robert S. Beale. Leahy's son, William Harrington Leahy, by now a lieutenant commander, was in London as an assistant naval attaché to the American ambassador, and his and Elizabeth's children, thirteen-year-old Louise and five-year-old Robert Beale Leahy, provided pleasant distractions.

On June 3, Louise was buried in Arlington National Cemetery following an overflow service at St. Thomas Episcopal Church, where they had been members for many years. Leahy met with FDR two days later and was told to take a rest. Instead, he spent several miserable weeks in a dismal office at the State Department completing reports on the situation in Vichy. Then on Monday, July 6, Leahy answered the telephone in his office and heard a familiar voice asking him to come to the White House for a noontime conference.

Upon Leahy's arrival, Roosevelt told him that he would be recalled to active duty and appointed the president's senior military adviser. FDR did not take the decision lightly, nor had he arrived at it quickly. For six months, America's war machinery had haltingly labored to transition from small numbers and an almost country club pace — witness the Marshall-to-King memo regarding Pacific strategy — to the constant urgency of increasingly massive and complex global operations. Roosevelt was reluctant to relinquish or in any way diminish any of his powers as commander in chief, but it was increasingly clear that the information he received and the orders he gave had to pass through a common gatekeeper on whom he could rely.

Heretofore, Marshall, King, and Arnold had jockeyed for time with the president as they needed decisions, but as the war pace picked up, they sought more frequent contact. Conversely, any military advice that the president desired required one or more chiefs to appear at the White House at all hours of the day. At that July 6 meeting with Leahy and at lunch the following day, Roosevelt outlined a position that would have daily contact with the three chiefs of staff and summarize reports flowing from them to the president. He would be the president's personal representative on the Joint Chiefs of Staff. What was less clear at this point was how much command authority Leahy would carry, with presidential directives flowing in the opposite direction. "He did most of the talking," Leahy recalled of FDR in these two sessions, adding perceptively, "He always did."[20]

Among those strongly supporting Leahy's new role was George

Marshall. The army chief of staff had been encouraging Roosevelt to appoint a chief of staff over all military services since the JCS first met formally in February 1942. Marshall had promoted this as a necessary step to focus unity of command and coordinate the three branches. In Marshall's mind, it was definitely a military position.

When Roosevelt had countered that he as president and commander in chief was in fact his own chief of staff, Marshall patiently explained to him "in great frankness that it was impossible to conceive of one man with all of his duties as president being also, in effect, the chief of staff of all the military services." The presidency "was a superman job," Marshall admitted, but he "didn't think that even the exaggeration of the power of Superman would quite go far enough for this."[21]

Leahy visited with Marshall shortly after his return from France and heard him voice the same need for such a coordinating position. Not that Leahy lacked support from Roosevelt, but Marshall's strong recommendation of him for the role may have encouraged Roosevelt to make the appointment. In fact, it was Marshall who talked with Leahy about what his exact title should be, deciding on "Chief of Staff to the Commander-in-Chief of the United States Army and Navy." But by the time FDR met with Leahy on July 18 and officially gave him the post, it was clear that Leahy was to be the president's personal representative on the JCS first and foremost and, second, a neutral chairman arbitrating service rivalries and focusing military efforts.

Secretary of War Stimson thought that Marshall's proposal of Leahy as JCS chairman, rather than Marshall himself, was done with "great magnanimity and self-effacement," but shrewd Marshall undoubtedly realized that King would resist his elevation. Naval officer Leahy, as a fourth member of the JCS and its chairman, would counter any and all claims King might have about the navy's underrepresentation. "I thought," Marshall correctly surmised, "the Navy couldn't resist [Leahy], and from what I had learned I was willing to trust Leahy to be a neutral chairman."[22]

Leahy's next stop was with King. The admiral had indeed been "holding out against the idea of a White House military adviser" primarily because he assumed it would be an army man and as such "detrimental to the interests of the Navy." But when Marshall initially suggested Leahy to King, it put the matter in an entirely different light. "If he will take it," King told Marshall, "it will be all right with me." King now told Leahy the same thing and pledged his support. Years later, King told his biographer that he had "always liked Leahy" because he had taken such a firm stand against the Japanese after they sank the *Panay*.[23]

Roosevelt announced Leahy's recall to active duty and his appointment as chief of staff to the commander in chief at a press conference late on the afternoon of July 21. Leahy did not attend. If FDR meant to downplay the move, the press would have nothing of it. "Mr. President, can you tell us what the scope of Admiral Leahy's position will be?" asked a reporter. The president repeated the title he had already announced. "Will he have the staff of the Army, Navy and Air also under him?" fired another. In jaunty FDR fashion, the president replied that he didn't have "the foggiest idea," and besides, the question had "nothing to do with the 'price of eggs.'"

Far more substantively, Roosevelt then denied rumors that Leahy's return to Washington was somehow connected to the usual speculation about British and American plans for a second front against Germany—the first being the Soviet Union's lone stand in the east. The president then answered a question about rubber shortages at home, but other reporters would not let go of the Leahy appointment. Roosevelt was asked if it would mean that the president would "take a more active part in the strategic conduct of the war." FDR laughed and said that would "be almost impossible."

Almost casually, Roosevelt said that he spent an "awful lot of time" scrutinizing war strategy, and having a chief of staff to summarize reports, gather information for him, and maintain direct contact with various agencies—not just the military—would save him valuable time. Then, using a term that the assembled reporters knew well but that was not necessarily a compliment, the president said that Leahy would help do his "leg-work."[24]

"The President was cagey, as he always was in dealing with the newsmen," Leahy noted afterward, "and did not tell them very much."[25] If anything, this lack of information fueled rumors as to the scope of Leahy's assignment. The *New York Herald Tribune* tried to have the last word the next day: "All of Washington was speculating as to just how much power had thus been conferred on the sixty-seven-year-old diplomat and Navy officer and whether, in fact, it meant that he was to be America's war lord of the second front."[26] *Time* got closer to the truth. If "Generalissimo Leahy was a legman, the editor was still Franklin Delano Roosevelt."[27]

As usual, Roosevelt also had a political motive behind this military move. Public outcry for a reorganization of the nation's military had not abated, and while Roosevelt denied that Leahy was to be "a supreme commander of all the American forces," there was definitely some truth to a British report that Leahy's appointment managed "to take some of the wind out of the sails" of the movement to name MacArthur supreme commander of armed forces.[28]

MacArthur had his hands full in the South Pacific, and favorable reactions to Leahy's appointment seemed to accomplish FDR's secondary purpose. Emphasizing Leahy's sterling reputation in Washington circles, George Fielding Eliot, military affairs correspondent for the *New York Herald Tribune,* confessed that while "it is true that his duties are but vaguely defined at present...the personality of the man is a sufficient guaranty that he will find a means of discharging his duties...to the immense benefit of the country he has served so well."[29] Further singing Leahy's praises, Walter Lippmann of the *Washington Post* pronounced him clearly the most qualified candidate, "so much so that many have begrudged the time he spent in Vichy when he was so obviously needed in Washington."[30]

Whatever Leahy's evolving role, Roosevelt desperately needed a steadying hand between his geopolitical considerations and the military's implementation of overall strategy. Despite his professed enthusiasm for King's Pacific offensive earlier in the spring, Roosevelt wanted to commit American troops to Europe in 1942 in part because of continued lobbying from Churchill but also because he clearly saw the need to support the Soviet Union.

Western perspectives, particularly when subsequently colored by Cold War tensions, frequently understate the Soviet Union's critical role in defeating Nazi Germany. Roosevelt, however, recognized it immediately. On June 26, 1941, just four days after Hitler invaded his gargantuan neighbor, FDR wrote Leahy, still in France. "Now comes this Russian diversion," Roosevelt characterized the move. "If it is more than just that it will mean the liberation of Europe."[31]

A year later, 4.5 million German troops that might engage the Allies elsewhere were far from defeated but increasingly mired in Russia's expanse. Roosevelt and Churchill wanted them to stay there and the Soviet Union to remain an active Allied combatant. King's March 5, 1942, memo on Pacific strategy also recognized that America's "chief contribution" to Russia would "continue to be munitions in general," although that would not keep him from occasionally bristling when aircraft and ships were diverted to the effort.[32]

Thus, in late June 1942, Marshall dispatched Dwight Eisenhower, who in just sixteen months had jumped from colonel to lieutenant general as Marshall's right-hand man, to London to confer with their British counterparts and implement Roosevelt's goal of American troops in combat in Europe before the end of the year. Roosevelt strongly preferred Operation Sledgehammer, a small-scale, cross-Channel invasion of Europe. It was meant to establish a British-American bridgehead for future operations on the continent, but more important, it would distract Germany from a victory on the Eastern Front that might take the Soviet Union out of the war.

Eisenhower, however, found nothing but chaos in London. The buildup of American forces there (code-named Bolero) was only beginning, and the British evidenced a lack of both planning and desire to prepare a cross-Channel invasion of any sort. The British instead trotted out Operation Gymnast, a previously discussed invasion of Morocco on the north coast of Africa. Neither Marshall nor Eisenhower supported such a circuitous route into Europe, and they looked around for yet another alternative. King was all too happy to provide one by pushing for additional forces in the Pacific.

Leahy was not quite a member of the Joint Chiefs, but Marshall and King had been working well together in implementing King's proposed Pacific strategy. Now they momentarily became the ultimate teammates by jointly advising Roosevelt that if the British prevailed and the United States undertook any operation except the buildup of troops in Great Britain in anticipation of Sledgehammer or some other direct European attack, "we are definitely of the opinion that we should turn to the Pacific and strike decisively against Japan; in other words, assume a defensive attitude against Germany, except for air operations; and use all available means in the Pacific." Marshall may well have been bluffing the British, or even Roosevelt, but King was dead serious.[33]

Not so fast, said FDR. If at least one of his military chiefs was bluffing, the president decided to call it. From the quiet of Hyde Park on Sunday morning, July 12, Roosevelt ordered an immediate, same-day estimate of the men and materiel necessary to implement this all-out Pacific alternative and the impact the same would have on operations in the Atlantic. Marshall scurried to Washington from his country home in Leesburg, Virginia, to join King in gathering what, given the time constraints, was only a cursory overview.

Just two days after reading it, having known full well in advance that his opinion would not be changed, Roosevelt hand-wrote a draft in response. "My first impression," FDR scrawled, "is that it is exactly what Germany hoped the United States would do following Pearl Harbor. It does not in fact provide use of American troops in fighting except in a lot of islands whose occupation will not affect the world situation this year or next.... It does not help Russia or the Near East. Therefore it is disapproved."[34]

Two days later, Roosevelt ordered Marshall and King to depart for London immediately, along with presidential confidant Harry Hopkins. They were to seek Eisenhower's advice as the man on the scene and then get the British to commit to a definite plan. "Sledgehammer is of such grave importance," Roosevelt wrote the trio in his instructions, "that every reason calls for accomplishment of it." But if the British position remained immovable and an invasion of the European mainland was "finally and definitely out of the picture," the president directed his chieftains to determine another place for U.S. troops to fight in 1942. Among Roosevelt's suggestions was the Middle East, which Marshall and King found even more appalling than Gymnast as a potential quagmire and lacking in strategic merit.[35]

"It will be a queer party," chief of the British Imperial General Staff Sir Alan Brooke predicted beforehand, "as Harry Hopkins is for operating in Africa, Marshall wants to operate in Europe, and King is determined to stick to the Pacific!" Brooke would side with Hopkins, who appears to have taken his cue from Churchill. That did not, however, keep Hopkins from assuring Roosevelt, "Marshall and King pushed very hard for Sledgehammer, I wanted you to know."[36]

But in the end, the British could not be moved, and Gymnast, a thrust into North Africa, prevailed. Eisenhower characterized the abandonment of Sledgehammer as "the blackest day in history." He was no less pleased that North Africa would be the alternative, fearing that it could only lead to a "further dispersal of the Allied forces." But within a month, Eisenhower had his orders to become supreme commander of the combined Allied landings in North Africa, now renamed Torch.[37]

But Marshall and King were not quite finished lobbying FDR. When they returned to Washington, they stressed to Roosevelt that embarking on Torch necessarily canceled Sledgehammer, as well as Operation Roundup, a planned full-scale invasion of Europe in the spring of 1943. The president remained adamant about Torch but characteristically failed to accept that it was a trade-off for the others. On July 30, the American Joint Chiefs met with their British counterparts in the first session of the Combined Chiefs of Staff that Leahy chaired. Marshall and King still thought there was room to negotiate on Torch, in part because the outcome of the summer battles raging on the Eastern Front was still in doubt and there had been no formal abandonment of Sledgehammer or postponement of Roundup.

But now there was another player in the room. Far more than simply mediating disputes between the American services, Admiral William D. Leahy, Chief of Staff to the Commander in Chief, soon made it abundantly clear that he was indeed the president's man on the spot. Leahy told the Combined Chiefs that Roosevelt and Churchill considered the agreement on Torch in the late fall of 1942 — less than four months away — to be final. When Marshall and King protested that no irrevocable decision had been made despite the discussions in London, Leahy assumed his role and assured them he would discuss the matter with the president.

That same evening, Leahy delivered Roosevelt's answer to Marshall and King. "Very definitely," the JCS minutes recorded Leahy reporting, Roosevelt, "as Commander-in-Chief, had made the decision that Torch would be undertaken at the earliest possible date." The president considered it "our principal objective," and assembling the means to carry it out would "take precedence over other operations," including delaying the American buildup in Great Britain (Bolero) and hampering King's operations in the Pacific.[38]

Meanwhile, King and the U.S. Navy had certainly not forgotten about the North Atlantic. King knew firsthand, both from his World War I days and more recently from the tensions of 1941, that German U-boats sinking Allied merchantmen were as much or more of a threat to the war effort than a clash of giant battleships. The number of Allied ships lost to U-boats reached an all-time high in July 1942, and during the first six months of the year American merchant losses alone to enemy action exceeded the total losses during World War I. The Germans indeed remembered how close they had come to winning the war at sea, and they were determined to do so this time. Churchill called the Battle of the Atlantic "the dominating factor" of the war. "Never for one moment could we forget," he wrote in retrospect, "that everything happening elsewhere, at sea, or in the air, depended ultimately on its outcome."[39]

King readily agreed with Churchill about the desperateness of the situation, particularly along the Atlantic Coast of the United States. Flaming ships sinking within sight of East Coast cities were not only a major blow to the flow of war supplies, but such events also had the dismal secondary effect of torpedoing American morale. King and the navy in general came under criticism for not organizing convoys for all shipping.

Even Roosevelt lectured King by memo, saying, "Frankly, I think it has taken unconscionable time to get things going." King politely agreed but pointed out that while their mutual goal was "to get every ship under escort," that result would require upwards of one thousand seagoing escort vessels, essentially destroyer escorts, or corvettes. It was simply going to take time for American industry to produce those ships, and in the meantime—still doing the best with what he had—King concentrated convoys in the most dangerous areas, including the dreaded Murmansk and Archangel runs to support Russia. These Arctic convoys were principally Great Britain's responsibility, but British ship commitments and heavy losses there worked to pull U.S. resources from the North Atlantic and stretch King's forces that much thinner.[40]

And they were made thinner still when King begrudgingly agreed to spare enough ships to protect the troop convoys that were soon assembled in Virginia and sent across the Atlantic for the much-debated invasion of North Africa. Torch was, in fact, a series of landings from French Morocco, on the Atlantic coast, eastward into the Mediterranean to Oran and Algiers in French-controlled Algeria. "This African adventure," as Leahy termed it privately, "had long been under consideration by President Roosevelt" and went off surprisingly well.[41]

French admiral Darlan, who despite his earlier outburst at Leahy was no friend of the pro-German Laval, had managed to keep the French fleet out of Axis hands. As the Torch invasion force bore down on the North African coast, Darlan was in Algiers visiting a son who was very sick with polio. After the Allied landings met with initial Vichy French opposition, Darlan ordered opposition to cease. This caused considerable confusion throughout Vichy. For several days, conflicting orders to fight or surrender were given before Germany quickly occupied the remainder of France. The end result was that the French fleet was scuttled at Toulon before it could fall into German hands, and the Allies—with Free French forces a part of the effort—established a front in North Africa from which to relieve pressure on British forces in Egypt by attacking the rear of Erwin Rommel's vaunted Afrika Korps.

As Roosevelt told Eisenhower, who led the assault, "Our

occupation of North Africa has caused a wave of reassurance throughout the Nation not only because of the skill and dash with which the first phase of an extremely difficult operation has been executed, but even more because of the evident perfection of the cooperation between the British and American forces."[42]

Upon sailing for Africa, Eisenhower had already expressed to Admiral King his own "very real and deep appreciation for the magnificent support that has been given to me by you personally and by all elements of the United States Navy with which I have come in contact." Considering King's other commitments, especially the battles then raging in the South Pacific, Eisenhower was "particularly appreciative of your action in standing by original commitments."[43]

It was hardly that harmonious, but Torch provided the United States with a valuable testing ground for men and machinery, and it lent a particularly American feel to the conflict. Leahy would later say that Roosevelt "never made a single military decision with any thought of his own personal political fortunes," but that public recollection seems entirely in keeping with Leahy's "loyal soldier" persona and not with Roosevelt's always-calculating political agenda.[44]

Torch was originally scheduled for October 30, 1942, a few days before the midterm elections. With far more candor, Marshall recalled briefing FDR on preparations for Torch and the president holding up his hands in an attitude of prayer and remarking, "Please make it before Election Day." When the landings were later postponed until November 8, a week after the election, Roosevelt did not complain, however, and "never said a word."[45]

With typical understatement, Leahy showed in hindsight that he perfectly understood his role with FDR: "It has been said that Roosevelt ordered 'Operation Torch' in the face of opposition from his senior advisers. I never opposed the North African invasion. I told the President of the possibilities of trouble, but it looked to me like a feasible undertaking."[46] Certainly, Torch was the first test of the wartime partnership of Roosevelt and Leahy and only the beginning of their work together on deciding the course, one that would include dealing with avowed enemies as well as difficult allies.

CHAPTER SIXTEEN

Fighting the Japanese — and MacArthur

General Douglas MacArthur was the most brilliant, most important, and most valuable military leader in American history — at least that's what Douglas MacArthur thought. When asked by a proper British gentlewoman if he had ever met the famous general, Dwight D. Eisenhower — himself about to march into history — supposedly replied, "Not only have I met him, ma'am; I studied dramatics under him for five years in Washington and four years in the Philippines."[1]

MacArthur owed his escape from the Philippines to navy PT boats, but that did not stop the general from questioning the veracity of the navy in coming to his aid or from placing the blame for the eventual fall of the islands at the navy's door. "The Navy, being unable to maintain our supply lines," MacArthur wrote in his memoirs, "deprived us of the maintenance, the munitions, the bombs and fuel and other necessities to operate our air arm."

Conveniently overlooking the fact that his planes were caught sitting on the ground nine hours after the Pearl Harbor attack, MacArthur went on to assert, "The stroke at Pearl Harbor not only damaged our Pacific Fleet, but destroyed any possibility of future Philippine air power." Still, MacArthur jabbed, "a serious naval effort might well have saved the Philippines, and stopped the Japanese drive to the south and east."[2]

At his new headquarters in Melbourne, Australia, MacArthur granted *Time* correspondent Theodore H. White an interview and "managed to denounce all at once, and with equal gusto and abandon," Franklin Roosevelt, George Marshall, Harry Luce (*Time*'s publisher), and the U.S. Navy. "White," MacArthur lectured, "the best navy in the world is the Japanese navy. A first-class navy. Then comes the British Navy. The U.S. Navy is a fourth-class navy, not even as good as the Italian navy."[3]

With such personalities at play, it was no surprise that sometimes the navy thought it was fighting MacArthur as much as the Japanese. Ernest J. King, himself of no small ego, questioned MacArthur's views from the start, and while Admiral King enjoyed a momentary sigh of relief after the Battle of Midway, he was still livid at comments General MacArthur had made on the eve of the Battle of the Coral Sea one month before. MacArthur had warned newspapers that a major Japanese invasion fleet was bearing down on Port Moresby and possibly even Australia. Let them come, scolded King, but under no circumstances let the Japanese know we know they're coming! To do so raised a huge flag that the Americans had succeeded in breaking the Japanese naval code.

The entire issue of American intelligence being able to read the Japanese naval code with increasing precision was a heavily guarded secret. This effort had been under way prior to Pearl Harbor, and later the intelligence had greatly aided Nimitz in making fleet deployments at Coral Sea and in particular at Midway. King strongly preferred to say as little as possible about the outcomes of these battles — positive though they were — and even less about the navy's ability to prepare for them by reading coded intercepts.

But on the morning of Sunday, June 7, 1942 — when few details of the Midway battle were known publicly — the *Washington Times-Herald* ran an article asserting that the Americans had known in advance that the Japanese were targeting Midway, as well as Dutch Harbor in the Aleutians. King was furious, but General Marshall was even more so. Marshall had already encouraged King to "treat the operation as a normal rather than an extraordinary effort" and to downplay for the press any spectacular intelligence success. After Marshall saw the *Times-Herald* on Sunday morning, he fired off a two-page memo to King, urging, "the way to handle this thing is for you to have an immediate press conference" and then practically scripting King's remarks at the same. "I am strongly of the opinion that this should be done today," Marshall admonished. King clearly agreed and called an unusual 5:00 p.m. Sunday press conference in his office to deal with the matter largely along the lines that Marshall had suggested.[4]

Recognizing the goal of news outlets "to acquaint the public in detail with news of action with the enemy at the earliest practicable date," King nonetheless professed his very firm feeling "that military considerations outweigh the satisfying of a very natural and proper curiosity." Then, taking Marshall's advice and downplaying the existence of any specific intelligence pipeline, the admiral launched into a folksy description worthy of FDR, saying that military intelligence was like the piecing together of a jigsaw puzzle and that after Coral Sea, the pieces just fell into place. "Looking at the map," King opined, "anybody could see that among our various important outposts, Dutch Harbor and Midway offered [the Japanese] the best chance of an action... with some hope of success." Thus, U.S. naval forces were providentially placed off Midway to counter the strike.

But then King went off the record and zeroed in on the *Washington Times-Herald*. By publishing "an item which purported to be a 'chapter and verse' recital of the composition and functions of Japanese forces advancing toward Midway," King lectured, the *Times-Herald* had compromised "a vital and secret source of information, which will henceforth be closed to us. The military consequences are so obvious that I do not need to dwell on them—nor to request you to be on your guard against, even inadvertently, being a party to any disclosure which will give 'aid and comfort' to the enemy." The room was silent.

King then opened the press conference to questions, acknowledging to nervous chuckles that he didn't guarantee he would answer them. A number dealt with the Japanese thrust against Alaska, bombing Dutch Harbor and invading the islands of Kiska and Attu. King again tried to downplay what was in fact the first direct invasion of American territory in North America since the War of 1812. Not wanting to be diverted from the South Pacific, King assured the reporters that "even the seizure and occupation of Dutch Harbor [which did not happen] is not a determining factor in the conduct of the war... [and that] until they have got to Kodiak I feel they have done nothing momentous. Our pride will be hurt, yes, but we have enough to go around."

Then King repeated the doctrine of taking calculated risks with concentrated forces that Nimitz had just employed at Coral Sea and Midway. "Don't forget the proposition," the admiral told the reporters, "that the minute you try to be strong everywhere, you have only the men available — it means you will be weak everywhere." Asked in conclusion if the admiral intended to hold regular press conferences, King replied, "No, indeed."[5]

What King did intend to do — even as Roosevelt sent him to Great Britain with Marshall to hammer out the broader Allied strategy — was to take one of those calculated risks in the South Pacific and jab back at the Japanese. On one level, this was in keeping with King's announced policy of going on the offensive as rapidly as possible, but on another, the Allies were left with little choice if they were to preserve the West Coast–Australia lifeline that King had proclaimed as sacrosanct.

The problem was that despite their setback at Coral Sea, the Japanese were consolidating their hold on the Solomon Islands. If they succeeded in establishing strong airfields there, this airpower would threaten the heart of the West Coast–Australia sea-lanes running past the New Hebrides and Ellice Islands and New Caledonia. Once fortified in the Solomons, the Japanese might well attack these outposts or even New Caledonia itself and disrupt if not sever the link. When the Japanese began to construct a seaplane base on the tiny island of Tulagi, just north of Guadalcanal, in May 1942, King knew that such action required an immediate Allied response.

General MacArthur's solution right after the Midway victory was to boast that if given the First Marine Division and two carriers with appropriate escorts, he would add three army divisions under his command and attack the main Japanese base at Rabaul in the Bismarck Archipelago, about a thousand miles west of Guadalcanal. King and Nimitz looked at the map and were appalled — not so much by MacArthur's audacity, but by his total lack of regard for what might happen to the navy's precious few carriers. They would be put into the center of poorly charted, reef-strewn waters that were surrounded by a complex of Japanese bases, from which would come waves upon waves of land-based aircraft.

A strike at Rabaul was clearly premature, and King advocated approaching the stronghold through a series of island conquests starting in the Solomons. Not only would this begin an advance on Rabaul and launch King's cherished offensive strategy, but most important to the immediate situation, it would stop the Japanese sweep through the Solomons and safeguard the lifeline to Australia.

King argued that the new seaplane base at Tulagi had to be captured in a matter of weeks. But General Marshall and the army didn't concur and wanted to postpone any invasion of the Solomons three to four months, "when we would be in a better situation." King snorted and supposedly replied, "If we were to wait until that time, every exact button of their gaiters would be buttoned up."[6]

So as soon as the Midway outcome became clear, King pushed ahead with his plan, asking Marshall, "When will the time be ripe since we have just defeated a major part of the 'enemy's' fleet?" Nimitz, who was always the loyal subordinate whenever King issued a direct order, professed eagerness to get on with it. By contrast, Vice Admiral Robert L. Ghormley, who had immediate command of the South Pacific Area, pleaded for "more time and more ships, planes, and troops and also supplies and munitions, etc. just as the J.C.S. had," which, King recalled, "I didn't like."[7]

Part of Marshall's reluctance was that unlike King with Nimitz, Marshall did not have a willing subordinate in that part of the world.

George Marshall had been only a long-term colonel when Douglas MacArthur had served as army chief of staff during the 1930s. Thanks to MacArthur's own press releases, the public sang his praises and Marshall more often than not cajoled MacArthur in the desired direction rather than issued him direct orders. Now MacArthur stormed to Marshall that the navy was making every effort to subordinate the army's role in the Pacific. Never mind Rabaul; if there was to be an invasion of the Solomons, he, Douglas MacArthur, must be in command of it.

One can almost hear the hawklike Ernie King laugh in reply. There was no way, short of the eternal fires, that King was going to turn over command of major naval vessels and marines to MacArthur — or any other soldier — particularly in the first major offensive of the war. Marshall and MacArthur further complicated matters by evidencing in memos their shortcomings in understanding command and control for ship deployments and amphibious operations.

King had agreed to the wisdom of an army officer having supreme command ("unity of command" was the catchphrase) of theater operations in Europe, where most of the fighting was to be on land. After some heated discussions, Marshall was forced to acknowledge that there was little he could do but acquiesce to the reverse in the South Pacific, where so many of the operations were to be on or near water. King later described these discussions as having "to 'educate' the Army people."[8]

When MacArthur squinted at the line along 160° east longitude dividing MacArthur's Southwest Pacific Area from Ghormley's South Pacific Area and found it bisecting Guadalcanal, he still insisted on command of any operation there. King and Marshall solved that problem by simply moving the dividing line west 1 degree of longitude (about seventy miles near the equator) and left Guadalcanal entirely in Ghormley's theater of operations. (MacArthur would soon have his hands full, as contemporaneous with their move to secure Guadalcanal, the Japanese also launched an overland attack on Port Moresby from Buna, across the rugged Owen Stanley Range.)

* * *

With the row over Guadalcanal settled, King hurried to San Francisco to meet with Nimitz to review the details of the planned operation. Nimitz almost didn't get there. Leaving Pearl Harbor with his immediate aides, he flew east on a four-engine flying boat. This airplane was a one-of-a-kind prototype built by Sikorsky in 1935 to win a navy contract that eventually went to Consolidated Aircraft for the PB2Y Coronado. The Sikorsky XPBS-1 could accommodate forty passengers on short hops, but it was outfitted with sixteen bunks for the 2,500-mile, 15-hour trip—at about 160 miles per hour—between Honolulu and Naval Air Station Alameda, just north of San Francisco.

As the plane made its approach into Alameda, Nimitz and Captain Lynde D. McCormick were ready in their blues for the reception, but busy playing a last game of cribbage. Commander Preston V. Mercer, the admiral's flag secretary, sat by the window cradling an all-important briefcase containing the after-action report from the Battle of Midway for King. Others in the cabin were relief pilots, crew members, and an officer bumming a ride to a new stateside assignment. As the plane neared its splashdown, Mercer suddenly mumbled, "Oh-oh!"

The big flying boat hit the water a little down in the nose, but the cause of Mercer's concern was debris floating in the landing area. The plane immediately struck a piling the size of a telegraph pole. Its bow shot skyward, the plane flipped over onto its back, and the fuselage cracked in half. As passengers scrambled out a freight hatch onto what moments before had been the underside of a wing, Mercer anxiously asked Nimitz his condition. "I'm all right," muttered the admiral, "but for God's sake save that briefcase."

McCormick and the other passengers weren't as lucky. McCormick suffered head lacerations and two cracked vertebrae. Everyone else had at least one broken bone, and the copilot, twenty-nine-year-old Lieutenant Thomas M. Roscoe of Oakland, California, was killed. As crash boats and navy corpsmen arrived, Nimitz, despite his share of bumps and bruises, insisted on remaining on the sinking wing while there were still men inside the plane. Each time a corpsman draped a blanket around the admiral's shoulders, he promptly removed it and wrapped it around an injured man.

Concerned for those around him, Nimitz kept avoiding the hands that attempted to steer him off the wing and into a crash boat. Finally, an eighteen-year-old seaman second class lost patience with the white-haired gentleman, and knowing neither his identity nor his rank, he shouted out, "Commander, if you would only get the hell out of the way, maybe we could get something done around here." Nimitz merely nodded and finally clambered into the waiting boat.

Draped with a blanket that this time stayed around his shoulders, Nimitz stood up to survey the scene as the boat backed away from the wreckage. "Sit down, you!" yelled the angry coxswain. Nimitz again obeyed, and in doing so caused the blanket to fall, revealing his uniform sleeve. Seeing the rows of gold braid, the coxswain tried to stammer an apology, but Nimitz cut him short. "Stick to your guns, sailor," the four-star admiral replied. "You were quite right."[9]

Reportedly, a strong tailwind had sped the airplane along to arrive well ahead of schedule, and the naval air station crew had been lax in monitoring the landing zone. Nimitz took the accident in stride and even got to spend a couple of days recuperating with Catherine, who was living in temporary quarters—as were so many military wives—at the Hotel Durant in Berkeley.

King, who had almost lost his valued commander in chief, Pacific, took a different view. He circulated a memo to all commands, demanding more vigilance in the "Policing of Seaplane Landing and Take-off Areas." King included paragraphs from the official report and concluded that the extracts, "representing as they do a case of 'it did happen here' are forwarded as being illustrative of what may be expected when those duties are neglected."[10]

Finally, after King's delays with Marshall and Nimitz's near-disaster landing, the two admirals met at the St. Francis hotel for their second face-to-face meeting of the war. There was much to discuss about the Solomons operation, but King was his usual expansive self in looking far ahead. He sketched out the long-range, next phase of operations against Japan by outlining an advance directly west across the Central Pacific via Truk, Guam, and Saipan once the initial drive through the Solomons and New Guinea had secured the southern flank. Later, MacArthur would have plenty to say about this strategy.

But meanwhile, King and Nimitz had received intelligence reports that Japanese construction battalions had landed on Guadalcanal and were busy constructing an airfield. King now ordered that *both* Tulagi and Guadalcanal had to be captured *before* any Japanese airfield became operational on the latter — quite possibly within the month.

The clock was ticking, and King picked an assault date of no later than August 1, 1942. Everything was in short supply. There was a frantic rush of men and materiel, coordination between ship and shore commands was still in its infancy, and even the veteran First Marine Division had yet to make an amphibious landing under enemy fire. But in all instances, it was a situation where the best training might well come by doing the real thing.

Ostensibly, Vice Admiral Ghormley was in overall command of the operation as commander in chief, South Pacific. With Bill Halsey still in Virginia recuperating from dermatitis, Frank Jack Fletcher, newly promoted to vice admiral, would command three carrier task forces centered around *Enterprise,* indefatigable as always; *Wasp,* newly arrived from the Atlantic; and *Saratoga,* back in action after torpedo damage the previous January. Nimitz had finally succeeded in getting Fletcher his third star despite King's continued ambivalence.

Rear Admiral Richmond Kelly Turner, an attendee at the King-Nimitz conference and recently King's chief of the War Plans Division, was to command the amphibious forces. Turner had a tough-as-nails reputation and in temperament usually deserved his nickname "Terrible." Marine Major General Alexander Archer "Archie" Vandegrift led the reinforced First Marine Division and would assume command of the ground forces.

A week after the King-Nimitz conference, Ghormley flew from his temporary headquarters in Auckland, New Zealand, to confer with General MacArthur in Australia and coordinate MacArthur's operations in defense of Port Moresby with the attack on the Solomons. Not much came of the meeting except for Ghormley to get a case of "the slows" from MacArthur. MacArthur had talked brashly about attacking the stronghold of Rabaul, but now he wanted to delay the Guadalcanal and Tulagi landings — code-named Watchtower — until greater Allied strength could be marshaled.

When King heard this, his opinion of MacArthur sank lower, taking Ghormley's down a notch with it. Only two weeks earlier, MacArthur had been all for charging into Rabaul, King raved to Marshall, but now, when "confronted with the concrete aspects of the task, he...feels he not only cannot undertake this extended operation [Rabaul] but not even the Tulagi operation." King's only concession was begrudgingly to grant Ghormley a one-week reprieve and move D-day back one week to August 7.[11]

So, on this new schedule, the first of sixteen thousand marines splashed ashore to moderate resistance on Tulagi and initial light resistance on Guadalcanal, succeeding in capturing the uncompleted airfield, soon renamed Henderson Field, on D-day plus one. Fletcher's three carrier groups paraded south of the island, providing air cover. But by late afternoon of that same day, August 8, Fletcher asked Ghormley for permission to withdraw his carriers farther southward, citing a need to refuel and concerns about a presumed Japanese counterattack. Ghormley replied in the affirmative very early on the morning of August 9, and at 4:30 a.m., Fletcher led his carriers southward toward a refueling rendezvous.

Turner, Vandegrift, and many sailors and marines left on or near the Guadalcanal beachhead would later claim that Fletcher deserted them. In fact, Fletcher had told Turner and Ghormley while planning the operation that he intended to remain on station off Guadalcanal with his carriers only two to three days after the landings. Nimitz, too, in the initial planning of the invasion after his early July meeting with King, had envisioned only "about three days" of close-in carrier support off Guadalcanal.[12]

A large part of the angst at Guadalcanal came from an unexpected and ferocious battle between cruisers and destroyers that occurred in the wee hours of August 9 around Savo Island, at the

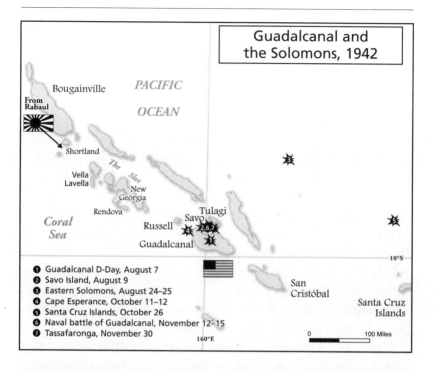

Guadalcanal and the Solomons, 1942

Bougainville

PACIFIC

From Rabaul

OCEAN

Shortland

Vella Lavella

The Slot

New Georgia

Rendova

Russell

Tulagi

Savo

Coral Sea

Guadalcanal

San Cristóbal

10°S

❶ Guadalcanal D-Day, August 7
❷ Savo Island, August 9
❸ Eastern Solomons, August 24–25
❹ Cape Esperance, October 11–12
❺ Santa Cruz Islands, October 26
❻ Naval battle of Guadalcanal, November 12–15
❼ Tassafaronga, November 30

Santa Cruz Islands

160°E

0   100 Miles

western entrance to the sound between Tulagi and Guadalcanal. A substantial force of one Australian and four American heavy cruisers and four destroyers had been positioned to plug the approaches to what became known as Ironbottom Sound in order to protect the transports and cargo ships unloading at the beachheads.

The feared attack came, but the Allied ships reacted slowly and suffered great losses against a lightning assault by five Japanese heavy cruisers and two light cruisers. The Australian *Canberra* and three American cruisers — *Astoria, Vincennes,* and *Quincy* — sank with considerable loss of life, while the *Chicago* took a torpedo in the bow and two destroyers also were damaged. It was "the severest defeat in battle ever suffered by the U.S. Navy."[13]

The only good news was that the Japanese cruisers had circled Savo Island and returned westward rather than pushing east and attacking the undefended transports off the beachheads. But the naval losses were so great — six ships and upwards of a thousand men — that King's duty officer woke him in the middle of the night when the news finally reached Washington. King read the dispatch several times before asking that it be decoded again in hopes that there was an error. But the news was correct, and King called it "the blackest day of the war," not to mention a clear setback for his policy of attack, attack, attack.[14]

Characteristically, Nimitz's first reaction was calmly to rally his subordinates. Radio communications with Ghormley were wretched and were equally so among Ghormley's commands. Adding to Nimitz's confusion was the fact that the Japanese had changed their naval code. He was getting little information from his forces, little insight from Japanese code intercepts, and a steady stream of queries from King as to what was happening. As late as August 19, with Turner's amphibious ships back in New Caledonia and sixteen thousand marines temporarily isolated on Guadalcanal and Tulagi, Nimitz could send King little more information than "our losses were heavy and there is still no explanation of why. The enemy seems to have suffered little or no damage."[15]

Meanwhile, Japanese destroyers had landed nine hundred troops near the American beachhead on Guadalcanal. Turner desperately directed reinforcements of his own to the island, particularly marine fighters to the hurriedly completed airstrip at Henderson Field. Fletcher maneuvered his carriers out of range of Japanese land-based aircraft, but close enough to counter any assault by a major Japanese carrier force that was rumored to be forming at Truk, fifteen hundred miles to the north-northwest. The most nagging question was, when might an attack come?

Through this uncertainty, Fletcher began to rotate his three carrier groups one at a time to the south to refuel as conditions permitted. When aerial reconnaissance and radio intercepts seemed to indicate no immediate Japanese threat from Truk, Fletcher dispatched the *Wasp* group south to refuel, only to learn that a major Japanese force with the repaired Coral Sea carriers *Shokaku* and *Zuikaku,* the light carrier *Ryujo,* and substantial surface ships was bearing down on the eastern end of the Solomons.

Enterprise and *Saratoga* steamed to engage, and their planes sank the *Ryujo* before a counterstrike from the main Japanese carriers severely damaged *Enterprise*. The *"Big E"* made for Pearl Harbor under its own steam, but a week later, a Japanese submarine torpedoed Fletcher's flagship, *Saratoga,* and this carrier, too, was forced to limp to Pearl Harbor for repairs. That left *Wasp* and *Hornet,* the latter already en route south before the *Enterprise* was damaged, as the only two American carriers operational in the entire Pacific. Fletcher returned to Pearl Harbor with *Saratoga,* while Rear Admiral Leigh Noyes assumed Fletcher's carrier command.

Once again, the Japanese had been beaten back, though with tough American losses. Some, particularly in hindsight, seized on Fletcher's untimely refueling of the *Wasp* task force as evidence of his incompetence. If three American carriers had been on station and the right intelligence had been received, Fletcher's fleet would have outnumbered the Japanese and perhaps won another battle of the proportions of Midway.

At the very least, King was again certain that Fletcher should have used his destroyers to make a surface attack against the Japanese, even as Fletcher withdrew his own carriers. Though a strong proponent of airpower, King was also always urging more aggressive surface actions. Barely had the *Saratoga* recovered its planes when Fletcher collapsed into a chair on its flag bridge and remarked to his staff, "Boys, I'm going to get two dispatches tonight, one from Admiral Nimitz telling me what a wonderful job we did, and one from King saying, 'Why in hell didn't you use your destroyers and make torpedo attacks?' and by God, they'll both be right."[16]

When *Saratoga* reached Pearl Harbor, Nimitz promptly gave Fletcher, who had been slightly hurt in the carrier's torpedoing, a much-needed leave. Nimitz continued to feel that Fletcher had acquitted himself well and quite likely would have kept him in the heat of the Pacific action. King continued to feel quite differently. He had never forgiven Fletcher for the loss of *Lexington* at Coral Sea or *Yorktown* at Midway, and now there was the appearance — warranted or not — of Fletcher's having abandoned the Guadalcanal beachhead and misjudged his carrier deployments at what came to be known as the Battle of the Eastern Solomons.

Frank Jack Fletcher would subsequently be portrayed by a long

list of military historians as somewhat bumbling and inept, preoccupied with refueling operations, and reluctant to risk his carriers
for a knockout punch. Nimitz stood by Fletcher, particularly after
Coral Sea, but King seems to have lacked confidence in him from
the start. But whatever his perceived shortcomings and less-than-
generous press, Fletcher was at the center of the three great naval
battles that stopped the Japanese advance in 1942 and turned the
tide of the war in the Pacific. Yes, he lost King's beloved *Lexington*
and the *Yorktown,* but in exchange he sent six Japanese carriers to
the bottom. Fletcher, because of the gentleman sailor he was, would
serve without complaint or any subsequent attempt at vindication.

Fletcher was exiled to command the Thirteenth Naval District
(Pacific Northwest) and the Northwest Sea Frontier, the coastal
waters of Oregon, Washington, and Alaska. He would be eclipsed
by the operations of Bill Halsey and Raymond Spruance, but they
both owed much to his steady, tactical competence throughout the
pivotal year of 1942, and, so too, did Nimitz and King.

Nimitz later gave Fletcher a photo of himself autographed "11 Nov.
42, Vice Admiral Frank Jack Fletcher, A fine fighting admiral and a
splendid shipmate, with much affection, C. W. Nimitz." Their letters
throughout the war and afterward were frequently addressed "Dear
Chester" and "Dear Frank Jack." Nimitz even once sent Fletcher "a
fine safety razor with accompanying brushless cream," for which
Fletcher was "very grateful to be remembered by you." King, for his
part, made only passing reference in his memoirs to Fletcher being at
Coral Sea, a circumstance repeated by King's principal biographer.[17]

In early September, King headed west to confer once again with
Nimitz in San Francisco. But this time he brought a surprise with
him. Bill Halsey was rested and well and itching only to get back
into the fight. Just the week before, Halsey had told a packed audito-
rium of midshipmen at Annapolis, "Missing the Battle of Midway,
has been the greatest disappointment of my life, but I am going back
to the Pacific where I intend personally to have a crack at those yel-
low-bellied sons of bitches and their carriers."[18]

At their three-day conference, King and Nimitz spent considerable time dissecting the disastrous cruiser defeat at Savo Island, and, with Halsey's return, it was only natural that they would start with Ghormley and review the entire command structure in the Pacific. Halsey was to have his old job back as commander of the *Enterprise* task force and assume Fletcher's role as senior tactical commander whenever the dwindling carrier forces acted in concert. If King had been suspicious of Fletcher's command abilities, he had quickly grown equally so of Ghormley's, even though both he and Nimitz had initially agreed on Ghormley's appointment as COMSOPAC.

Nimitz promised to check out Ghormley in his usual low-key fashion and invited Halsey to accompany him on an inspection tour of the *Enterprise* after they both returned to Pearl Harbor. The *"Big E"* was in port being repaired after the damage it had suffered during the Battle of the Eastern Solomons. Nimitz had medals to present, including the Medal of Honor to Chief Petty Officer John William Finn for his inspired machine-gun defense of PBYs at Kaneohe Bay on December 7, and an announcement to make.

Halsey's bulldog-like face was not yet well known, but his name was already well recognized throughout the navy as a fighting admiral, both for his early raid in the Marshall Islands and his daring delivery of the Doolittle Raiders. Looking lean and fit, he received little attention as he marched aboard the carrier behind Nimitz. But then Nimitz stepped to the microphone and motioned Halsey forward. "Boys," Nimitz told the assembled sailors, "I've got a surprise for you. Bill Halsey's back!" A roar went up along the flight deck. There was no hint of defeatism among this ship's company. They were only too willing to embrace a fighter, and Halsey's eyes brimmed with tears at the tribute.[19]

But there was a strong sense of defeatism in the South Pacific, and Nimitz's next task was to ferret it out. The day before Nimitz hailed Halsey on board *Enterprise,* the *Wasp* had been sunk by three torpedoes fired from the Japanese submarine *I-19* while the carrier was escorting the Seventh Marine Regiment to Guadalcanal as reinforcements, and *Hornet* was now the only operational American carrier remaining in the Pacific.

On September 24, Nimitz and his staff, including the faithful Hal

Lamar, who was once again serving as his flag lieutenant, left Pearl Harbor in a PB2Y Coronado and flew south. After an unexpected overnight on the island of Canton because a bearing in one of the Coronado's engines burned out, Nimitz arrived at Ghormley's sweltering headquarters on the aging transport *Argonne* in the port of Nouméa, New Caledonia. Ghormley had not even managed to convince the French, who nominally controlled the island, to provide suitable headquarters space ashore. There was indeed defeatism in the air, but it certainly didn't come from the marines dug in on Guadalcanal. In almost two months since its invasion, Ghormley had never visited Guadalcanal.

Having flown almost four thousand miles from Pearl Harbor, Nimitz invited MacArthur to join him in Nouméa for a joint planning session. MacArthur, only a thousand miles away in Brisbane, Australia, declined. Nimitz was welcome in Brisbane, MacArthur said, but the general was simply too busy to make the trip to Nouméa. Instead, MacArthur dispatched his chief of staff, Major General Richard K. Sutherland, and Lieutenant General George Kenney, the chief of his air forces, to meet with Nimitz.

CINCPAC had plenty of questions for all concerned. Why were Japanese reinforcements flowing through MacArthur's territory to Guadalcanal with such impunity that the beleaguered marines there called the convoys "the Tokyo Express"? And if the situation on Guadalcanal was so desperate, why weren't army troops arriving in New Caledonia being immediately sent to bolster them? Perhaps most disconcerting, twice during the conference at Ghormley's headquarters a SOPAC staff officer delivered high-priority radio dispatches to Ghormley, only to have him mutter, "My God, what are we going to do about this?"[20]

Nimitz decided to see for himself — a courageous decision given the situation there. After flying north in the Coronado to Espíritu Santo in the New Hebrides, the admiral, joined by Commander Ralph Ofstie and Lieutenant Lamar, took off for Guadalcanal in a four-engine B-17 bomber because there was no suitable seaplane landing zone on the island. The pilot was young and a little green — as were so many men in those early days of the war — and he finally admitted to being lost, in part because there were no adequate charts of the Solomons. Lamar solved the problem by producing a National Geographic map of the South Pacific from his bag, and in the pouring rain, the big bomber touched down on the matted runway of Henderson Field.

The marines' Archie Vandegrift was on hand to greet the admiral and tell him "hell, yes," they could hold, but since Henderson Field was the key to Guadalcanal and Guadalcanal the key to that end of the Solomons, the airfield had to be made a strongpoint at all costs. There could be no more talk—as had come from both MacArthur and Ghormley—about pulling out.

And there was one more thing. Over a quiet, private drink later that night, Vandegrift bluntly told Nimitz that there were too many navy commanders in the theater acting timid and shying away from a fight because they were afraid of losing their ships. What was needed, Vandegrift said, were commanders who weren't going to be taken to task by desk admirals just because they lost a ship by fighting it hard—a lesson that appeared to have been lacking around Savo Island.

Nimitz nodded. He could relate. He remembered that day long ago in the Philippines when as a young ensign with a destroyer entrusted to his command, he had run it aground and might well have sunk his career save for understanding superiors who looked beyond that one incident to see his total worth.

The next morning, Nimitz handed out medals and engaged in his usual folksy banter with the marines. Then it was time to go. In the laid-back, hard-pressed South Pacific, a barefoot Army Air Corps major with a black beard and grungy coveralls stepped forward to pilot the admiral's return B-17. Two thousand feet of the Henderson runway was covered with metal matting; the other thousand feet, extended to accommodate B-17s, was dirt turned into mud by the rain. The departing bomber would need every foot to get airborne.

Looking over plane and pilot, Nimitz asked how he intended to take off. "Admiral," drawled the pilot, "I thought I'd start at this end, even though it's downwind. I can get up to flying speed easy here on the metal matting. I'll probably be up to flying speed before I reach the dirt section."

Several in Nimitz's group eased into the background and made toward a second B-17, but Nimitz merely said, "All right," and climbed right into the bombardier's area in the Plexiglas nose of the plane. Those who were going with him got aboard as well, and the pilot gunned the B-17 down the matted runway. The jungle on either side rolled by, but when the plane hit the last thousand feet of dirt, the pilot decided that he couldn't get airborne and aborted the take-off. The bomber lugged into the mud, skidded toward the end of the runway, and finally ground-looped to a stop at the very end, with its tail at the edge of a steep ravine.

The pilot nonetheless restarted his engines and taxied back through the quagmire to the rest of Nimitz's party. The admiral, as usual, was nonplussed. Climbing down from his nose perch, he simply suggested they adjourn to Vandegrift's quarters for lunch before trying again.

By the second try, the rain had let up, and the wind freshened from the matted end of the runway. This time, Lamar saw to it that Nimitz was in a more secure seat in the fuselage. The pilot in his coveralls taxied the bomber down to the dirt end of the strip, turned into the wind, and roared down the meager runway. This time, the plane climbed into the sky, and Nimitz was on his way back to Espíritu Santo. There had been a couple of dicey moments, but Nimitz's show of concern on Guadalcanal was a huge boost to marine morale, as well as indicative of his own style of leadership. When he returned to Pearl Harbor, he realized that he had to infuse more of the same in the South Pacific.[21]

By then, Bill Halsey had been growing anxious waiting around Pearl Harbor while repairs to *Enterprise* were completed. Finally, Nimitz ordered him south on October 15 to review the situation before *Enterprise* arrived on station. After stopping at Canton Island as Nimitz had just done, Halsey's PB2Y Coronado continued on to Nouméa and had barely landed and shut down its engines when a navy whaleboat came alongside, and Admiral Ghormley's flag lieutenant passed Halsey a sealed envelope. Inside was another sealed envelope marked SECRET.

With King's hearty concurrence, Nimitz advised Halsey, "You

will take command of the South Pacific Area and South Pacific forces immediately." Halsey read the dispatch twice and then handed it to an aide, exclaiming, "Jesus Christ and General Jackson! This is the hottest potato they ever handed me!"[22]

Nimitz had become convinced that Ghormley "was on the verge of a nervous breakdown" and that the "panicky and desperate tone" of his dispatches left no doubt that he needed to be replaced immediately. If the situation was as bad as Ghormley indicated, Nimitz "needed the very best man we had to hold down that critical area."[23]

In more diplomatic terms, Nimitz advised Ghormley, "After carefully weighing all factors, have decided that talents and previous experience of Halsey can best be applied to the situation by having him take over duties of ComSoPac as soon as practicable after his arrival Noumea [October] 18th your date."[24] Nimitz went on to voice his appreciation for Ghormley's "loyal and devoted efforts," but in a private letter to Catherine, he expressed his "hours of anguished consideration." It was a "sore mental struggle," but "Ghormley was too immersed in detail and not sufficiently bold and aggressive at the right times." With the decision made, he confessed to his wife, "I feel better now that it has been done."[25]

The South Pacific Area would soon feel better, too. It was certainly not all Admiral Ghormley's fault, but the navy needed a leader who understood that "you can't make an omelet without breaking the eggs." Bill Halsey fit the bill. *Time* magazine described him as looking "saltier than sodium chloride" and "known throughout the Navy as a tough, aggressive, restless man."[26]

Those who knew Halsey at all or had heard of him were quick to embrace the change. "I'll never forget it!" exclaimed one muddy and exhausted air combat intelligence officer on Guadalcanal. "One minute we were too limp with malaria to crawl out of our foxholes; the next we were running around whooping like kids."[27]

But in the beginning, Halsey would not have an easy time. In fact, his first month on the SOPAC job — late October to early November 1942 — was one disaster after another. Halsey prepared to build a new airfield on Ndeni, in the Santa Cruz Islands, but

Japanese pressure on Guadalcanal forced him to reconsider. General Vandegrift flew south to Nouméa to confer with Halsey and hear him ask the pointed question face-to-face: "Are we going to evacuate or hold?" Never one to equivocate, Vandegrift, whom Halsey later called "my other self," growled back, "I can hold, but I've got to have more active support than I've been getting." Promising Vandegrift everything he had, Halsey immediately canceled the Ndeni operation and poured all of his available resources into reinforcing the marines on Guadalcanal.[28]

Scarcely had this decision been made when a major Japanese force of carriers, battleships, and cruisers attempted another end run around the eastern Solomons, similar to the one that Fletcher's carriers had met and repulsed two months before. Patched-up *Enterprise,* back on station in the South Pacific, moved with *Hornet* to intercept. Rear Admiral Thomas C. Kinkaid was in command of the combined *Enterprise* and *Hornet* task forces, and Halsey exhorted him, "Strike — Repeat — Strike."

A PBY Catalina from Espíritu Santo found the Japanese fleet just before dawn, but a mix-up in radio communications delayed the news at Kinkaid's carriers for a full two hours, giving the Japanese a head start in attacking the Americans. *Enterprise* came away damaged, but *Hornet* took the brunt of the blows, and Kinkaid was forced to order the ship sunk. Halsey never forgave him — neither did a host of naval aviators.

The general feeling was that in directing control of both *Hornet* and *Enterprise,* Kinkaid, a battleship admiral, had allowed the combat air patrol (CAP) being flown by *Enterprise* for both carriers to drift away from *Hornet.* Halsey simply thought that Kinkaid had not been aggressive enough in launching preemptive attacks. But Halsey also came under subsequent criticism for having pushed his carriers too far north, near the limit of Allied land-based air support, instead of keeping them south of Guadalcanal and focusing on its defense. In any event, this action was part of the growing pains of multiple-carrier operations. It was the last time a non-aviator commanded a carrier task force, but equally important, it put Halsey and Kinkaid on less-than-friendly terms.[29]

Tactically, the Battle of the Santa Cruz Islands was a Japanese victory, but improved American antiaircraft batteries and fighter pilots took such a heavy toll on Japanese carrier-based planes that all three Japanese carriers, among them the heavily damaged light carrier *Zuiho,* were forced to return to Japan for more planes and pilots. Japan could not match the ever-increasing supply of both warplanes and pilots beginning to flow from the United States.

The fight for Guadalcanal was far from over, but at least Japanese carriers would no longer play a role. After being on the SOPAC job two weeks, Halsey sent an eight-page, single-spaced "Dear Chester" letter to Nimitz. It was full of information and analysis, but short on complaining — exactly as Nimitz had hoped. "I have been fairly well occupied," Halsey told Nimitz, and "as a consequence, this is one of the first opportunities I have had to write.

"As you may well imagine," Halsey continued, "I was completely taken aback when I received your orders on my arrival here. I took over a strange job with a strange staff and I had to begin throwing punches almost immediately." First, there was the issue of a proper headquarters ashore. "The so-called Fighting French," as Halsey called them, were still playing "a Ring around the Rosey," but he intended to have all headquarters elements of the various commands moved into one building ashore within the week, because "as you must have seen, while here, it is perfectly impossible, to carry on efficiently on this ship [the *Argonne*]."

Nor did Halsey intend to waste precious time sending ships back to Pearl Harbor for repairs. "It will be my utmost endeavor," Halsey assured Nimitz, "to patch up what we have and go with them.... This may mean operating the *Enterprise* with a slightly reduced complement of planes and under difficulties, but under the present circumstances, a half a loaf is better than none."

And "Fighting Bill," as at least one newspaper report had already labeled him, was determined to keep that half loaf intact. Maintaining battleships and carriers continuously at sea in submarine-infested waters was a mistake — a deadly mistake, Halsey might have said, remembering *Wasp* caught sailing the same support area. "On every occasion so far our intelligence has given us two or more days notice of impending attack. At present it is my intention to hold heavy ships out of the area and to depend on these reports for bringing them in when the necessity arises." In pencil in the margin of Halsey's letter, Nimitz wrote, "I agree," and initialed the comment "CWN."

But how was this son of a sailor getting on with the army? The army, Halsey wrote, was "the biggest and best thing....They have made available to us various mechanics, electricians and welders, and I would like to see it widely advertised that the Army is helping us here. I have never seen anything like the spirit there is in this neck of the woods." This time, Nimitz's initialed margin note called for a letter to King quoting the appropriate text.

Wrapping up with a paragraph that would have done an FDR fireside chat proud, Halsey assured Nimitz that while "we are in need of everything we can get," such a reminder was "not offered in complaint or as an excuse but just to keep the pot boiling." The men around him were "superb," Halsey concluded, and "not in the least downhearted or upset by our difficulties, but obsessed with one idea only, to kill the yellow bastards and we shall do it." Alongside which Nimitz scrawled in the margin, "This is the spirit desired."[30]

And it would take more of that spirit, because despite having turned their carriers around after the Battle of the Santa Cruz Islands, the Japanese were still making a major effort to capture Guadalcanal. Halsey learned of their latest thrust on November 10 and sent Kinkaid hurrying north with Task Force 16 — two battleships, one heavy cruiser, one light cruiser, and eight destroyers grouped around the partially repaired *Enterprise*.

But before Kinkaid could get within range, Admiral Richmond Kelly Turner ordered Rear Admiral Daniel J. Callaghan and Rear Admiral Norman Scott to lead five cruisers and eight destroyers against the advancing Japanese in order once again to save the beachhead and Henderson Field. Callaghan and Scott paid for the effort with their lives, but by November 14–15, Kinkaid's battleships and planes flying from both Henderson Field and *Enterprise* had inflicted heavy losses among the Japanese convoy and its escorts.[31]

Although American cruisers would take one more beating, again at the western end of Ironbottom Sound from Japanese torpedoes at the Battle of Tassafaronga at the end of November, this marked the end of Japanese attempts to capture Guadalcanal. King's strategy of taking the offensive to protect the West Coast–Australia sea-lanes and build a stronghold from which to start the drive toward Japan had worked after a frightful cost—twelve hundred American marines lay dead on Guadalcanal, and upwards of four thousand American sailors rested beneath the surrounding seas.[32] But the tide had been turned. In recognition of his "can-do" leadership and the mounting forces under his command, Bill Halsey was promoted to the four stars of full admiral, joining Leahy, King, Nimitz, Stark, and the Atlantic Fleet's Royal Ingersoll in that rank.

The promotion and his success in the Solomons put Halsey on the cover of *Time,* although the magazine was quick to point out that the painting depicting Halsey with only three stars had been commissioned before his promotion. This was the American public's first really good look at Bill Halsey, who had a "pugnacious" nose, "aggressive" eyes, and eyebrows "as impressive and busy-looking as a couple of task forces." It is important to note that no one had as yet called him "Bull." Instead, the article reiterated Halsey's mantra: "Hit Hard, Hit Fast, Hit Often."

Nimitz's own comments in the cover article did much to cement Halsey's image with *Time*'s readers. "Halsey's conduct of his present command leaves nothing to be desired," *Time* quoted Nimitz. "He is professionally competent and militarily aggressive without being reckless or foolhardy [and] he has that rare combination of intellectual capacity and military audacity and can calculate to a cat's whisker the risk involved...." His nomination to admiral by the president, Nimitz concluded, was a reward "he richly deserves."[33]

Four-star insignia were nonexistent in the supply-short South Pacific, but two rear admiral two-star insignia were quickly welded together. Halsey removed his vice admiral's stars, handed them to an aide, and reportedly said, "Send one of these to Mrs. Scott and the other to Mrs. Callaghan. Tell them it was their husbands' bravery that got me my new ones."[34]

In a lengthy letter to Nimitz that same month, Halsey stressed "a crying need for boats of all kinds," including "some of the laid up boats in Pearl." Nimitz's margin note was again to the point: "Send them," he ordered. A tank farm was under construction on Guadalcanal, and once it was completed, Halsey expected "to be able to blast hell out of the Japs in the Shortland [western Solomons] area and later on at Rabaul." Signing himself, "As ever, cheerfully yours, Bill H.," Halsey reiterated that his command was "not in the least downhearted" and "as you may rightly interpret, my growls and grouches are the privileges of an old sailorman."[35]

But Halsey had more requirements to wage war than just men and ships. In the same letter to Nimitz, Halsey wrote, "Please tell Raymond [Spruance] to discontinue personal shipments to me. We have made other arrangements here. In the meantime, I am deeply appreciative for what he has done."

And just what was that? In addition to now serving as Nimitz's chief of staff and housemate, Spruance had also had the job of keeping Halsey supplied with alcoholic refreshment in the first weeks after he was dispatched to the South Pacific. Henceforth, another Halsey buddy, Rear Admiral C. W. Crosse, in the Service Force of the Pacific Fleet, would handle that task. "A little preliminary dope so that you won't get nervous," Crosse told Halsey in a "Dear Bill" letter. "I have your verbal directive (threat) via Mason, namely ten cases of scotch and five cases of bourbon monthly. Can do."

The shipments, charged to Halsey's personal account, were to be "marked with the usual shipping indicators for Nouméa but will also have three stars stenciled on the cases to indicate the consignee as old Killer Bill." By the time this letter reached Halsey, Crosse was one star short and someone, perhaps Halsey himself, penciled "4 stars" in the margin of the letter. Crosse went on to propose a code for future correspondence, including a promised radio message whereby a reference to "URSER TEN DASH FIVE" would mean ten cases of Scotch and five cases of bourbon. War or not, someone, it seemed, had time on his hands. In a postscript, Crosse noted, "Your crowd at Nouméa were sadly lacking in any recreational equipment," and he promised to send along baseball gear to distribute "among the boys and let 'em go to it."[36]

A week later, Crosse wrote Halsey the "latest dope on '10-5,'" advising, "Ten cases of Black & White are loaded in the S. S. JOHN BABCOCK, scheduled to leave here the 28th and ETA EPIC [Nouméa] is December 20th." Crosse gave Halsey the name of the chief mate who had signed for the special cargo and told him, "In case you are thirsty and can hardly wait, it is stowed in a locker on the boat deck, starboard side, aft."[37]

Alcohol was a cherished commodity in all commands and all theaters throughout the war and a much-sought-after form of unwinding after the stress of battle, whether in the cockpit of an F4F Wildcat or a sweltering office nervously awaiting radiograms describing the action. Ironically, one of the few top commanders who usually eschewed hard liquor—save maybe a rum punch—was Raymond Spruance, Halsey's early supplier.

Later, when it became easier logistically to supply all commands with a liquor ration, many commanders, Halsey included, continued to get their own personal shipments. As a COMSOPAC directive pointed out some months later, these shipments to Halsey were outside the scope of the regular shipments to Nouméa because "such stores [Halsey's personal supply] are maintained largely for the purposes and needs of official and semi-official entertaining." Weekly consumption was estimated "to be approximately limited to one bottle per regular mess member, which is, however, exclusive of entertainment requirements."[38]

And so, as 1942 drew to a close, Allied troops around the globe paused to celebrate another wartime Christmas. It had been a year in which the issue had been in doubt more times than not. But in hindsight, despite ferocious losses of men, ships, and planes, it was remarkable what the entire Allied effort had accomplished in just one year's time, since the attack on Pearl Harbor.

In the South Pacific, Guadalcanal was secure. MacArthur's forces had saved Port Moresby and pushed the Japanese back across the Owen Stanley Range. The British had won a decisive victory in Egypt at El Alamein and were pursuing Rommel's Afrika Korps across North Africa toward the Allied forces landed under Operation

Torch. In Russia, the expanse of that country and the determined resistance of its soldiers had worn down the German onslaught, and the Russians had entrapped a portion of the German forces at Stalingrad.

There would be many more moments of high drama and uncertainty, but on all fronts, November 1942 had been a watershed that forecast a hint of victory. It was far from the beginning of the end, but it was, as Winston Churchill opined, "perhaps, the end of the beginning."[39]

Ernest King's portrait appeared on the cover of *Time* the week after Halsey's. The cover date was December 7, 1942. "I'd say they started something at Pearl Harbor that they are not going to finish," remarked the admiral. "We are going to win this war." Indicative of the general measure of increasing confidence, King talked more freely than usual with the press about the year's successes as well as its losses. Perhaps most important, he repeated what he had said at the beginning of the year: "Our days of victory are in the making."[40]

When Chester Nimitz was asked which moment during the war had scared him the most, he replied, "The whole first six months."[41] But now to all of his fighting men in the Pacific, he sent this Christmas greeting: "To all fighting men in the Pacific X On this holiest of days I extend my greetings with admiration of your brave deeds of the past year X The victories you have won, the sacrifices you have made, the ordeals you now endure, are an inspiration to the Christian world X As you meet the Jap along this vast battle line from the Aleutians to the Solomons, remember, liberty is in every blow you strike X Nimitz"[42]

There was a momentary lull in the interservice wars in Washington as well. Having begrudgingly come to respect each other, General Marshall and Admiral King exchanged cordial Christmas notes. "Dear King," wrote Marshall, "This is a note of Christmas greetings to you, with my thanks for the manner in which you have cooperated with me to meet our extremely difficult problems of the past year. With assurance of my regard and esteem, and full confidence in the prospects for the New Year, Faithfully yours, George Marshall."

"Dear Marshall," King responded a day later, "I wish to thank you for your kind note of Christmas greetings and to express my hearty reciprocation of your views as to the manner and extent of our cooperation throughout the past year. With the background we have, I am confident that we will go on to even closer cooperation in the conduct of the war. With renewed assurance of my respect and esteem, I am, faithfully yours, E. J. King."[43]

The momentary pause on all fronts even caused a lull in the ongoing feud with MacArthur, although King, for one, would never be taken with him. King always resented MacArthur's sharp criticism of the early efforts of Admiral Thomas Hart's tiny Asiatic Fleet against the Japanese onslaught — something akin to stopping a flood with a paper towel. Then, too, King was used to being his own favorite martinet. Neither he nor MacArthur was accustomed to sharing the stage with anyone.

Halsey would come to seek his own moments in the sun, but he would do so much more as "one of the guys" — the top guy to be sure — but his demeanor was far friendlier and folksier than anything King or MacArthur evidenced. King's cameo roles as "one of the guys" during his prewar partying had long since stopped, and Douglas MacArthur was never one to have really close friends. Ironically, one of those historically closest to him — other than MacArthur's similarly self-important wartime chief of staff, Richard Sutherland — may have been Dwight Eisenhower, because of their long association in Washington and the Philippines.

Halsey, who had yet to meet MacArthur face-to-face, couldn't resist tweaking the general just a little for his rather plush headquarters in Brisbane. "Would not MacArthur enjoy knowing," Halsey asked Nimitz parenthetically in one of his letters, "that we are sending people from the combat zone for rest and recuperation, in sight of his headquarters?"[44]

CHAPTER SEVENTEEN

From Casablanca to Teheran

In congratulating Major General Dwight Eisenhower on the success of the Torch landings, Franklin Roosevelt gave no hint that he might soon be visiting North Africa himself. This was to be Roosevelt's first wartime trip outside the United States, and Leahy, Marshall, and King were all scheduled to accompany him.

In one respect, King counted himself fortunate to be included. The prewar retirement age of sixty-four that King feared had arrived for him on November 23, 1942. One month to the day prior, King wrote Roosevelt with some trepidation: "My dear Mr. President: It appears proper that I should bring to your notice the fact that the record shows that I shall attain the age of 64 years on November 23d next—one month from today. I am, as always, at your service."

"So what, old top," the president scrawled on the letter as he returned it. "I may send you a birthday present!"[1] Just what that was to be was open to question, but Roosevelt, who was himself about to turn sixty-one and already in worse health than King or many of his top commanders, was not about to push any of his fighters into retirement. The retirement age was a handy excuse for those the president wanted retired, but he never enforced it during the war for those he needed. Bill Leahy would turn sixty-eight the following May.

Leahy would remember 1943 as "a year of conferences." Roosevelt and Churchill and their key military advisers met on no less than five major occasions. But for all the dickering over strategy that would dominate these sessions, even the location of this first presidential visit abroad was subject to lengthy negotiation. Churchill had come to the United States twice during 1941 and 1942, but that was politically much different than the president of the United States going to London. FDR wanted to avoid giving his critics ammunition by even the slightest appearance of subservience to Great Britain.

Churchill suggested Iceland in hopes of enticing Stalin to attend, but Stalin's journey there from Murmansk or a similar point would have had its own dangers, and in any event, warm-blooded FDR decreed the location much too cold. Churchill, with his flamboyant love of the historic and adventurous, went to the other extreme and suggested Marrakesh, in Morocco, but that remote location posed transportation and communication problems. Then Stalin declined to leave the Soviet Union for *any* destination while the fate of the German Eastern Front remained so unsettled.

Finally, Casablanca — Morocco, to be sure, but more accessible than Marrakesh — was suggested. It was perfect. By arriving in nearby Fedala (now Mohammedia), where elements of Major General George Patton's Torch forces had landed, Roosevelt could highlight the American effort in North Africa and appear quite independent of his British allies.[2]

Marshall, King, and Arnold left Washington in two C-54 four-engine transports en route to Casablanca on January 9, 1943, planning to arrive a few days before the presidential party to confer with the British chiefs of staff. Roosevelt, Leahy, and a small contingent left the capital late that same evening by rail from a special railway siding hidden under the Bureau of Engraving and Printing near the Tidal Basin. This was the first use by the president of the Ferdinand Magellan, a private Pullman car originally built in 1922 that had just been refurbished with heavy armor, bullet-resistant glass, and special escape hatches. FDR occupied the presidential suite, and the remaining four staterooms were reserved for Leahy; Harry Hopkins; Ross McIntire, the president's physician; and Grace Tully, the president's secretary. Henceforth, whenever FDR traveled by rail and Leahy accompanied him, Leahy was accorded these special accommodations in the closest practical proximity to the president.

Leahy's identification for the trip bore the nomenclature "Register No. 2" and asserted that the bearer—described as 67, 5 feet 10 inches, 162 pounds, gray-brown hair, and gray eyes—was "a member of the party of the President of the United States." If there was any question as to Leahy's status in the party, only FDR himself was designated with a lower number, "Register No. 1."[3]

The presidential train pulled into Jacksonville, Florida, on the evening of the tenth, and Grace Tully left the party. At 5:00 a.m. the next morning, the remainder of the president's retinue departed Jacksonville in two Pan American Airways flying boats bound first for Port of Spain, Trinidad. The president's plane and its consort landed without incident or any of the uproar that accompanied the C-54s carrying Marshall, King, and Arnold when they landed in Puerto Rico. Accounts long afterward by both King and Arnold demonstrated that interservice rivalries could surface in the most trivial of matters.

Marshall and Arnold were in the first plane to leave Washington, and King and various army and navy staff officers flew in the second. Inexplicably, King's plane arrived over Borinquen Field in Puerto Rico first, but was required to circle for about half an hour until Marshall's plane landed, because Marshall's commission at four-star rank was senior to King's. Just who insisted on this adherence to protocol is uncertain, but King was always convinced that "it came from Marshall or Arnold." Supposedly, upon finally landing, King snapped to Marshall, "That performance cost you about a hundred gallons of gas."[4]

Arnold was more diplomatic. In his memoirs, he simply noted, perhaps a tiny bit wryly, that either King's pilot flew a more direct course or his plane was a little faster, but had to circle, "waiting for the senior plane to arrive. A delay in landing, such as that, especially in hot weather, always causes a bit of ill humor, but once we were down and had been assigned to comfortable quarters..., everyone was happy again."[5]

The casualty of FDR's stop in Trinidad, however, proved to be Leahy. The admiral awoke on the morning after the layover with a fever above 101°F and what Dr. McIntire diagnosed as bronchitis. McIntire recommended, and the president decreed, that Leahy remain in Trinidad to rest and rejoin the party on its return. Leahy did so, and FDR flew on to Casablanca without his closest military aide. Had this happened two years hence en route to Yalta, it would have been unthinkable, but Harry Hopkins was still closer to the president overall and FDR quite confident of his own capabilities.

Upon the return of the entire party to Washington, the president briefed Leahy on his meetings with Churchill, and Marshall and King did the same regarding the sessions of the Combined Chiefs of Staff. Perhaps because none of them made Leahy feel that he had missed something really big, he was left with the impression "that little of value toward ending the war" had been accomplished.[6]

In fact, three major decisions came out of the Casablanca Conference. First, it was agreed that offensive operations from the North African front would continue with the July 1943 invasion of Sicily. Second, there would be no cross-Channel invasion during 1943— much to the chagrin of Stalin, who even in absentia kept pushing for a true second front in Europe. Offensive operations against Germany would focus instead on winning the antisubmarine war in the North Atlantic and ratcheting up Arnold's plan for pinpoint, daylight bombing. Finally, the overall Allied strategy of Germany First did not prevent King from insisting upon an increase in resource allocation for the Pacific—for both MacArthur and Nimitz—from about 15 percent to 30 percent of the total war effort. This set the stage for increased operations throughout the Pacific once Halsey prevailed in the Solomons.

Two other issues from the Casablanca Conference were first, an announcement in the final news conference by Roosevelt and Churchill of an Allied policy of unconditional surrender, which Leahy fretted had not been discussed among military channels, and second, Roosevelt's growing recognition that Charles de Gaulle would be a thorn in Anglo-French relations — something Leahy had been saying since his tenure in Vichy. When Roosevelt and Churchill had difficulty getting de Gaulle to attend the conference and accept French general Henri Giraud's leadership role in North Africa, Roosevelt asked Churchill, "Who pays for de Gaulle's food?" Churchill responded, "Well, the British do." To which Roosevelt suggested, "Why don't you stop his food and maybe he will come." Whether or not Churchill did so, de Gaulle finally appeared.[7]

Another conference early in 1943 promised at least as much drama as the one between Roosevelt and Churchill: Bill Halsey was about to meet Douglas MacArthur face-to-face. Halsey's first encounter with MacArthur — albeit only via cables — had gotten their relationship off to a rocky start. MacArthur had his hands full pushing the Japanese back across the Owen Stanley Range from the outskirts of Port Moresby, and the general wanted naval units from Halsey's South Pacific Area to support amphibious landings near Buna, on the north shore. Even MacArthur's own area naval commander, Vice Admiral Arthur S. Carpender, was reluctant to commit his ships to those reef-strewn waters and be subjected to Japanese air attacks from Rabaul.

New on the job and fighting for his life on Guadalcanal, Halsey also declined to do so. "Until the Jap air in New Britain [Rabaul] and northern Solomons has been reduced," he told MacArthur, "risk of valuable naval units in middle and western reaches of Solomon Sea can only be justified by major enemy seaborne movement against south coast of New Guinea or Australia."

MacArthur immediately appealed to Marshall and huffed that "although he had faithfully supported the South Pacific command during its crises," when he was "under acute pressure" and needed assistance, there was none to be had. As usual, MacArthur portrayed his own crisis as the gravest threat, but Carpender, Halsey, Nimitz, and King were "unanimous in opposing the dispatch of fleet units to the Buna area."[8]

MacArthur's turn came a few months later when the Japanese

staged a number of diversionary sea and air attacks in the Solomons to cover their attempts to evacuate Guadalcanal. Halsey appealed to MacArthur for the loan of a few heavy bombers, but the general tersely replied by radio dispatch, "My own operations envisage the maximum use of my air forces."

Then MacArthur launched into one of his strident lectures, suggesting to Halsey that he was "in complete ignorance of what you contemplate." There was a chance, MacArthur pontificated, that he might be able to launch some support missions in the future, but only if Halsey provided him with "some knowledge of your intentions." Requiring a detailed battle plan for the loan of a few planes struck Halsey as meddlesome at best and critical of Halsey's overall competence at worst.

Halsey thought he was being treated akin to a schoolboy asking to use the restroom and forwarded a copy of the general's dispatch to Nimitz. Regardless of what he thought himself, Nimitz counseled calm. Halsey ultimately agreed, telling Nimitz of MacArthur, whom he referred to as "Little Doug," "I refuse to get into a controversy with him or any other self-advertising Son of a Bitch."[9]

But by March 1943, things looked better on both fronts. MacArthur's forces had fought a bloody campaign and captured Buna, reestablishing a toehold on the northern coast of New Guinea. Japanese attempts to reinforce Lae, to the northwest, met with disaster in the Bismarck Sea when American and Australian bombers and fighters repeatedly attacked a convoy en route from Rabaul to Lae, sinking eight transports and four destroyers. Meanwhile, Halsey's SOPAC forces had finally secured Guadalcanal. The question was, Where next?

As Halsey prepared to push west through the Solomons beyond the line of 159° east longitude, dividing his South Pacific Area from MacArthur's Southwest Pacific, the Joint Chiefs determined that Halsey be accountable to MacArthur as the supreme theater commander for broad strategic direction, even though he continued to answer to Nimitz in every other regard. This made for a potentially awkward two-hat situation for Halsey. Consequently, after forces in both areas weathered a furious aerial onslaught meant to check

MacArthur at Buna and Halsey on Guadalcanal — it was organized by Admiral Yamamoto himself — Halsey decided that he must insist on an audience with MacArthur even if he had to camp outside his headquarters in Brisbane to get it. (Only two months before, MacArthur had rather unceremoniously gone out of his way to persuade Nimitz and Secretary of the Navy Knox not to visit him when on an inspection tour of the South Pacific after once again declining Nimitz's invitation to meet in Nouméa.)[10]

Somewhat to Halsey's surprise, when he wrote MacArthur about his plans, the general responded with a glowing invitation to arrive in Brisbane on April 15. MacArthur was rarely lukewarm. He was either hot or cold. Having made the decision to meet Halsey, MacArthur received him like some favored Roman consul returning from far-flung provinces. He was at the wharf in person as Halsey's PB2Y taxied to a stop, and the general readily shook Halsey's hand with undeniable MacArthur charm.

But as the group moved away from the wharf to the waiting cars, one innocuous comment almost ruined the mood. Brigadier General Julian Brown, who had been Halsey's "enforcer" in dealing with the recalcitrant French on New Caledonia, was walking with Commander H. Douglass Moulton, Halsey's longtime flag secretary. "Say, Doug," Brown began with a gesture to Moulton. MacArthur, whose eternally devoted wife, Jean, even addressed him as "General," stopped short, spun on his heel, and fixed an icy stare at Brown, who frantically gestured that he had been speaking to Moulton and not the general himself. MacArthur wheeled back around and continued to engage Halsey in conversation as he led the way to the cars.[11]

"Five minutes after I reported," Halsey later recalled, "I felt as if we were lifelong friends. I have seldom seen a man who makes a quicker, stronger, more favorable impression.... The respect that I conceived for him that afternoon grew steadily during the war and... I can recall no flaw in our relationship." Sure, Halsey admitted, they had their arguments, "but they always ended pleasantly."[12]

At this first face-to-face meeting, MacArthur professed to remember Halsey's efforts on the gridiron against West Point, while

Halsey noted that their fathers had met while on their respective army and navy duties in the Philippines forty years before. And MacArthur may have been a lot like King in immediately sensing and respecting any officer who wasn't afraid to stand his ground before him. Halsey was "blunt, outspoken, dynamic," MacArthur in turn recalled, and "had already proven himself to be a battle commander of the highest order." Halsey was "a strong advocate of unity of command in the Pacific," which sat well with MacArthur, as did what the general called Halsey's willingness "to close with the enemy and fight him to the death." Later, undoubtedly because MacArthur never found so welcome an admirer in King or Nimitz, he would say of Halsey, "No name rates higher in the annals of our country's naval history."[13]

In most respects, then, the MacArthur-Halsey relationship quickly became a mutual admiration society of the highest order, and it led to a quick agreement to push the lines forward. Operating from New Guinea, MacArthur would seize the islands of Kiriwina and Woodlark, while Halsey, having already taken the small, unoccupied Russell Islands just west of Guadalcanal, would invade New Georgia Island in the western Solomons. The effect would be to keep the Japanese from exiting the Solomon Sea and put their key bases at Rabaul and Bougainville within range of land-based bombers and fighters.

By mid-May 1943, one of Nimitz's routine communications with Halsey started with "Dear Bill, I enclose a clipping from this morning's Honolulu Advertiser which you may find of interest. I note that 'General MacArthur and Admiral Halsey are kindred souls.'" Even if Nimitz couldn't resist the poke, he was delighted by the truce, no matter how it had been generated.[14]

"I have just received an enthusiastic letter from Bill Halsey," Nimitz wrote Carpender, MacArthur's naval commander, several days later, "and I am very gratified at the entente cordial that I am convinced exists between the South and Southwest Pacific people." Then, just to be sure the MacArthur camp hadn't gotten too removed from CINCPAC, Nimitz encouraged Carpender with a postscript: "As Admiral Halsey is my agent in all dealings with the Southwest

Pacific Area, I am sending him a copy of this letter and I request that you send him a copy of your reply to me."[15]

Halsey's return to Nouméa from MacArthur's headquarters was postponed a few days while he made a goodwill swing through Canberra, Melbourne, and Sydney. With Nimitz having gotten no closer than Nouméa and King farther away still, Halsey quickly became the face of the American naval upper echelon in Australia and an Aussie favorite, in part for his straight-talking manner. Such talk had gotten him in trouble at the end of 1942 when, in a bout of overexuberant cheerleading, he had boldly predicted the war would be over in a year. Much like General George Patton, Halsey, who played so well to the press, would become—with the encouragement of his staff—a little gun-shy of them.[16]

But this showing of the flag also meant that Halsey was absent from his headquarters when one of the most dramatic plans of the war was carried out. It began on the morning of April 14, when Commander Edwin T. Layton, CINCPAC's chief intelligence officer, was ushered in to see Nimitz. The code-breaking operations that were so sensitive and secret had plotted in intricate detail the whereabouts and travel itinerary of Admiral Yamamoto. Nimitz read over Layton's transcribed dispatch and then studied the map. April 18 in the South Pacific would be the key date and place. Yamamoto's travels would bring him within three hundred miles of P-38 fighters just arrived at Henderson Field on Guadalcanal. Ironically, this date was the one-year anniversary of the Doolittle Raid.

"What do you say?" Nimitz asked Layton. "Do we try to get him?"

Layton was enthusiastic. Of course we do. Yamamoto carried almost hero status with the Imperial Japanese Navy, which still may not have grasped his forebodings after Pearl Harbor. Losing Yamamoto would be a supreme blow to Japanese morale, not only in the military but also across the civilian population. "You know, Admiral Nimitz," continued Layton laconically, "it would be just as if they shot you down. There isn't anybody to replace you."

Nimitz couldn't help but smile. He was far too humble to believe that, but in Yamamoto's case, Layton's observation sealed his decision. "It's down in Halsey's bailiwick," Nimitz replied. "If there's a way, he'll find it."[17]

Halsey (or possibly his deputy) received Nimitz's orders and passed them on to Rear Admiral Marc Mitscher, commander, Air, Solomons. Twin-engine army P-38 Lightnings equipped with long-range drop tanks were assigned the mission. But to preserve the secrecy of Layton's code breakers, Nimitz attributed the source of Yamamoto's itinerary to Australian coast watchers, and Mitscher ordered subsequent long-range patrols so that the key intercept flight would not stand out to the Japanese.

On that Sunday morning, the P-38s shot down two Japanese "Betty" bombers after a perfectly timed rendezvous over Bougainville. Admiral Yamamoto was among the casualties. After the chaos and adrenaline of several frantic minutes of aerial combat, there was no conclusive evidence as to which American pilot of the attacking Lightnings, Thomas G. Lanphier, Jr., or Rex T. Barber, had shot down the bomber carrying Yamamoto. Lanphier made the first boastful claims upon returning to Henderson Field, but circumstantial evidence gradually favored Barber. Then, too, Major John Mitchell, the mission leader, who had flown with the covering fighters, may well have deserved almost as much credit for planning and executing the intercept so perfectly. (It helped, of course, that Yamamoto's punctuality was well known.)

But another issue arose: whether Yamamoto should have been targeted individually in the first place and from how high in the American chain of command the final order had come. Among the ambiguities in the record is whether Halsey had already departed Nouméa for his meeting with MacArthur when Nimitz's orders arrived. If so, Halsey's deputy, Vice Admiral Theodore S. Wilkinson, carried them out in his name. But Halsey, whose wartime comments against the Japanese transcended military enmity and bordered on overt racism, had no qualms whatsoever about targeting Yamamoto.

Nimitz approached the matter more cerebrally and concluded that Yamamoto was an acceptable strategic target. But Nimitz also clearly recognized that this was more than a routine attack and passed the question up the chain of command even as he issued orders to Halsey's command. King does not appear to have been personally involved in this referral, but some accounts suggest that Secretary of the Navy Frank Knox was. Knox was concerned about the implications of targeting an individual and reportedly passed the problem to the White House.

Roosevelt had left Washington by train on April 13 for a tour of military bases en route to Monterrey, Mexico, to boost Mexican-American relations. The White House Map Room reportedly sent dispatches about the proposed intercept to the train, but the record is silent on any response from Roosevelt or Leahy in the president's behalf. When the confirming order went back to Nimitz, it invoked the authority of the president but was signed by Frank Knox.

Considering Leahy's generally conservative leanings and his reported comments before the war about doing away with German sympathizers who might cause trouble in Puerto Rico, it is unlikely that Leahy had any moral questions about the Yamamoto mission. If FDR did, he wanted to keep them private and distance himself from what he hoped would remain a military, rather than a political, decision.[18]

With sweeping characterizations, even Douglas MacArthur managed to convey a sense in his memoirs that somehow he had been involved in the Yamamoto mission and was responsible for its results. But in truth, many of MacArthur's moves during 1943 were made with an eye toward a far greater mission. There would be a presidential election in 1944, and a bevy of conservatives were whistling "Hail to the Chief" in the general's ear—much to the frustration of Leahy, Marshall, and the president himself.

Leahy was far more conservative than Roosevelt, and as early as FDR's second election, in 1936, Leahy had echoed the hope of many of the president's friends that he "incline his efforts more toward conservatism."[19] That hadn't happened, and neither did Leahy's role as FDR's chief of staff stop him from continuing his relationships within Washington's conservative circles. As whispers of MacArthur's presidential desirability increased, it made for some interesting evenings for the admiral.

Leahy claimed that he followed "a fixed policy of not becoming involved in any domestic partisan politics," but that did not keep him from events such as an April 1943 dinner with Democratic senator Peter Gerry of Rhode Island, Democratic senator Harry F. Byrd, Sr., of Virginia, and former Republican senator Frederick Hale of Maine. All three were, in Leahy's words, "leaders in a growing opposition in Congress to the Administration of President Roosevelt," and Byrd's name was being floated as a running mate for General MacArthur.

The conversation that evening proved a far-ranging discussion of the need to change domestic policies—Byrd in particular was a harsh critic of the New Deal—but the senators also asked Leahy many questions about the war and foreign relations. Leahy called them "friends of mine of long standing" and for that reason assumed they "probably felt no hesitation in expressing their thoughts in my presence." But it must have put Leahy on a very fine line. One minute he was chatting with friends of "long standing" about Roosevelt's political shortcomings, and the next he was reporting to the president, sometimes about those very conversations. The fact that Leahy could do this—and that he did not shy away from acknowledging that he had done both—is indicative of his strong sense of fidelity to his superior above all else. It was a Leahy trait Roosevelt recognized early on and came to rely on more and more.

"When possible," Leahy recalled, "I would tell Roosevelt about these and similar conversations I heard from time to time. If there was opportunity, I would tell the President in advance of my acceptance of invitations of this nature to be sure that he had no objection—not from the political angle—but because the conversation might turn to military matters. The President never objected, as he knew I wasn't going to divulge any secrets."[20] That subtle comment may well have been the reason Leahy grew increasingly close to the fulcrum of presidential power while at the same time staying largely out of the public spotlight.

It was about this time that Bill Halsey acquired what was apparently a new nickname. At Annapolis, he had been "Willie" or "Pudge," names he had gladly left behind. But now he began to be called "Bull" by an increasing number of newspaper correspondents.

The first time this occurred is uncertain, and even Halsey's principal biographer does not offer an opinion. Among the earliest occurrences may have been in the *Tucson Daily Citizen* on November 25, 1942, in an article written as Halsey was turning around American fortunes on Guadalcanal. "This Is 'Bull' Halsey, Folks," read the headline on an unsigned piece, likely picked up from the Associated Press. J. Norman Lodge, a senior AP correspondent attached to Halsey's headquarters in Nouméa, was the probable author. Leading with Halsey's mantra of "Kill Japs, kill Japs, kill more Japs" and singing Halsey's praises, the article concluded with, "Glad to 've met you, Admiral 'Bull' Halsey. Be seeing you again, we'll betcha."[21]

Two weeks later, Robert Trumbull, the *New York Times* correspondent who had reported Halsey's return to Pearl Harbor the previous September as "Fighting Bill," wrote a piece attributing the "Bull" nickname to the football field at Annapolis forty-some years before. Trumbull claimed, "His team mates called him 'Bull' Halsey, and to them and others who can call an admiral by a nickname and get away with it he is still 'Bull' Halsey."[22] But if this was indeed true, it seems strange that there are no letters in Halsey's papers in which his Annapolis classmates address him as "Bull," similar to those collegial missives to "Rey" King or "Betty" Stark.

As mentions of "Bull" Halsey increased, Rear Admiral C. W. Crosse, a 1907 Annapolis graduate who overlapped one year with Halsey, wrote him a letter with the salutation "Dear 'Bull' (Where the hell did the papers get that name for you?)." Writing back to "Dear Charlie," who was the source of his private liquor ration, Halsey replied, "I do not know where the name 'Bull' came from. It was invented by the newspapers mayhaps. They decided I talked too much and put in part of the colloquialism."[23]

So, increasingly he became "Bull" Halsey, but his hard and determined streak was definitely pointed at the Japanese, and when it came to promoting interservice cooperation—long before his initially wary visit to MacArthur—Halsey got equally high marks.

Simple as it seems, one of his chief innovations was to decree that no ties would be worn with khaki uniforms in the South Pacific. This eliminated any easy distinction among army, navy, and marine personnel, the latter two of which had been wearing ties, and put the term "unity of command" into rank-and-file practice.

Fastidious though he usually was in his personal appearance, Halsey was also not above playing to reporters by giving interviews shirtless, under a palm tree, with a knife strapped to his belt. Then there was the hat. Senior military commanders like MacArthur seemed to take their own personal style of headgear as a privilege of rank, and Halsey adopted a shabby cap more in line with a retired railroader than a commanding admiral. It was "easy to wash, cheap to buy, and not worth a damn as a hat," he readily admitted to a fellow Annapolis grad, who was now president of the Monsanto Chemical Company, who had criticized it. But "it accomplishes one of my chief aims out here, and that is to make it very difficult to distinguish between the officers of the Army, Navy, and Marines." There was no time, Halsey told him, "for anything but team play and no service rivalry."[24]

"Halsey's visit was most welcome and did a world of good," Arthur Carpender, MacArthur's naval commander, acknowledged to Nimitz after Halsey's Australia visit. "The good effect of his personality and sound common sense can hardly be overestimated."[25]

Even George Marshall was impressed, which wasn't an easy accomplishment. "Halsey seemed to be the easiest [naval commander] to do business with," Marshall recalled. "He was always trying to smooth out things instead of arousing things.... In the single practice of taking the tie off the shirt he made a move to broaden general unanimity."[26]

But as 1943 went forward with its rush of Allied strategy sessions, unanimity was frequently in short supply. In May, the Americans hosted the Third Washington Conference, code-named "Trident," for their British counterparts. On May 12, the day the meetings began, 230,000 German troops surrendered in Tunisia, effectively bringing the North African campaign to a successful conclusion.

That was the good news. The Americans and British had demonstrated that they could conduct a joint operation in a remote location and press it home to victory. But around the conference table, the air remained clouded by an atmosphere of mutual suspicion over strategic goals.

Marshall and his fellow American chiefs had become skeptical about the British commitment to invade Europe directly at *any* time. Chief of the Imperial General Staff Sir Alan Brooke, and his British cohorts begrudged King every PT boat, landing craft, and soldier, sailor, airman, or marine sent to the Pacific. Brooke blamed Pacific operations — a "diversion" in his mind — not only for scuttling any cross-Channel invasion, but also for threatening ongoing Mediterranean operations, including the planned invasions of Sicily and Italy. Brooke further dashed American hopes for a quick victory in Europe by declaring, "No major operations would be possible until 1945 or 1946, since . . . in previous wars there had always been some 80 French divisions available on our side."[27]

For his part, King was still suspicious that Great Britain and its commonwealth might drop out of the war against Japan once Germany was defeated. Others, including General Joseph Stilwell, argued the other side of that coin: if Great Britain aggressively pursued the Pacific war, it was doing so only to reestablish Singapore and its colonies in the Far East. This prospect had its origins in Churchill's own famous statement that he did not intend to be the prime minister who presided over the dismantlement of the British Empire. (Churchill might well have delivered just such a self-inflicted blow himself when he insisted that Brooke, the British chiefs of staff, and a vast cadre of their planners and theater commanders all sail together for Trident aboard the *Queen Mary*. One lucky German U-boat might have altered the course of the war.)[28]

Leahy, too, was suspicious of British designs to push eastward through the Mediterranean. Churchill expounded at length on the merits of taking Italy out of the war and strengthening ties to Turkey. But while Churchill "made no mention of any British desire to control the Mediterranean regardless of how the war may end," Leahy counted himself among those who believed that British access to India via Suez and the eastern Mediterranean was "a cardinal principle of British national policy of long standing."[29] Churchill, meanwhile, appeared in no great rush to set a date for a cross-Channel invasion.

Brooke bemoaned the "hours of argument and hard work trying to convince [the Americans] that Germany must be defeated first," but in reality, American recalcitrance was directed not against a Germany First plan, but against Great Britain's rather circuitous route—North Africa, Sicily, and Italy—to achieve it. King, in particular, thought very little of the strategic value of the British plan to take Italy out of the war. Italy was clearly the weakest member of the Axis and a drain on Germany and Japan that King did not want to assume should it be conquered. As for attacking Germany from there, "Hannibal and Napoleon crossed the Alps," King remarked sarcastically, "but times are different now."[30]

Whenever the British procrastinated on setting a firm date for a cross-Channel invasion, King was not above forcefully reminding them of the "dangers of tying down forces and equipment to await eventualities." In other words, this was King's less-than-subtle threat that if there was to be no rapid deployment of resources in the European Theater, King would divert them to the Pacific.[31]

Having missed the Casablanca Conference with bronchitis, Leahy assumed the chairman's role of the Combined Chiefs of Staff at a summit conference for the first time at Trident. He was quite comfortable in this role and evidenced a moderate temperament and reasoned voice that went about building consensus in the most disarming of ways. "Well George," he would say to Marshall after the army chief of staff had promoted a plan of which Leahy was skeptical, "I'm just a simple old sailor. Would you please back up and start from the beginning and make it simple, just tell me step one, two, and three, and so on."

By the time Marshall or anyone else had made such a careful recitation, the proponent frequently saw flaws in his own plan, which was exactly the result Leahy intended in the first place. This didn't always work, of course, and it was King who sometimes felt able to call his fellow sailor's bluff. Once, during a discussion of

Japanese operations, Leahy questioned King about his uncharacteristic caution. "When I was a boy," said Leahy, "I was brought up with the idea that the U.S. Navy was invincible."

"Admiral," responded King, "when you were a boy, who would have believed that the Japanese would have taken over the Philippines and Southeast Asia?"[32]

But such easy banter did not always work with their British allies. The root of the problem, according to Brooke, "really arises out of King's desire to find every loophole he possibly can to divert troops to the Pacific!"[33]

When discussions, particularly between Brooke and King, remained tense after the first few days of Trident, Marshall loaded up the Combined Chiefs after a Saturday morning session—save Hap Arnold who was in Walter Reed Hospital recovering from a heart attack—and whisked them off to Williamsburg, Virginia, for what might be called a getaway weekend. John D. Rockefeller, Jr., put his recently completed Williamsburg Inn at their disposal, and Rockefeller even dispatched his personal butler from New York to attend to the details.

Scrumptious food, fine wine and liquor, bird-watching (Brooke was a devoted birder), swimming, and even croquet gave one and all a chance to cultivate a more personal relationship with their counterparts. Outdoor activities and sipping brandy by a roaring fire lent a more human side to the stern uniforms who routinely gathered around the conference table, particularly when, in one of the most oft-recounted episodes of the weekend, Air Chief Marshal Sir Charles Portal dove into the swimming pool in a borrowed pair of oversize trunks and came up without them. Roosevelt, meanwhile, took Churchill to Shangri-La (later Camp David).[34]

When the conference resumed in Washington, the differences were still there, but Marshall's low-key way of instilling a sense of camaraderie had taken some of the edge off the discussions. By the time the Trident Conference ended a week later, Roosevelt, Churchill, and their chiefs had agreed to a May 1, 1944, date for a cross-Channel invasion of Europe, soon to be code-named Overlord.

In exchange for the British concession of a firm invasion date, the

Americans agreed to pursue British plans in the Mediterranean, provided definite target dates were met for the buildup of men and materiel in Great Britain in anticipation of Overlord. Leahy, Marshall, and King were all adamant on this point as a way of ensuring that Churchill's lust for the eastern Mediterranean would not irrevocably suck American resources away from a direct thrust against Germany. And, once again, it should be remembered that while Joseph Stalin still had not made an appearance at one of these Allied conferences, the burdens his country was suffering on Germany's Eastern Front were continuing to deplete Germany's overall war-making capacity.

Meanwhile, King had made a sweeping presentation on the importance of the Mariana Islands to the entire Pacific operation. His very mention of the name sent planners scurrying to their maps, and King admitted that it had taken him "three months to educate Marshall" about their importance.

But sitting in the Central Pacific, the Marianas were indeed the hub of a wheel of considerable strategic influence. A supply line ran eastward to Pearl Harbor. To the south, the Caroline Islands and the major Japanese naval base at Truk could be isolated. Westward the path led to the Philippines, Formosa (now Taiwan), or Okinawa via whichever route MacArthur and the Joint Chiefs might choose in order to sever Japan's supply lines from the East Indies. And to the north, beyond the tiny atoll of Iwo Jima, lay Japan itself. Reassured of Germany First and knowing that whatever happened in the Pacific, the Americans would bear the brunt of it, even Brooke admitted, "We dealt with the Pacific and accepted what was put forward."[35] So as Trident adjourned, King hurried west to San Francisco to confer with Nimitz and implement the drive through the Central Pacific.

Nimitz's attention during the spring of 1943 had been focused on the occupied islands of Attu and Kiska in the Aleutians. Japanese forces on American territory posed a threat to morale, but there was also a strategic element involved. Despite bitter weather that made operations on both sides problematic, there was always the risk that the Japanese would attack farther eastward along the chain and even threaten the air routes that were delivering desperately needed warplanes to the Soviet Union across the Bering Strait. King and Nimitz wanted this far-flung right flank of their Central Pacific drive secure, and at this point in the war, there was also some thought that a renewed American presence only two thousand miles from Japan's northern island of Hokkaido might keep Japan guessing about the Allies' next move.

Throughout February and March, two veteran cruisers and four destroyers under Rear Admiral Charles H. McMorris, recently CINCPAC planning officer and about to become chief of staff of the Pacific Fleet, effectively blockaded Attu and Kiska against most resupply efforts. But early on the morning of March 26, McMorris's ships tangled with a Kiska-bound convoy, guarded by four heavy cruisers and four destroyers of Japan's Northern Force, near the Komandorski Islands.

Despite being outgunned two to one in heavy ships, McMorris engaged and fought a fierce surface battle until the cruiser *Salt Lake City* went dead in the water. As a last-ditch effort, McMorris ordered his destroyers to lay smoke and launch a torpedo attack against the oncoming Japanese cruisers. Just then, in one of those quirks of war, *Salt Lake City* ran out of armor-piercing shells and started firing high explosives. Their white phosphor trails looked somewhat like bombs falling from the sky. The Japanese assumed they were under attack by bombers from American bases in the Aleutians and hurriedly broke off the engagement. The Battle of the Komandorski Islands broke the Japanese supply line to Attu and Kiska and cleared the way for their invasion.

Rear Admiral Thomas C. Kinkaid, now North Pacific Area commander, promoted a plan with Nimitz to bypass more heavily defended Kiska and attack Attu first. With foul, foggy skies precluding any air support and wild seas rocking the transports, elements of the Seventh Infantry Division landed at three points on the island to an eerie silence. Twenty-six hundred Japanese troops had retreated into the hills, from which they soon unleashed a fury of fire. On May 29, the nineteenth day of what was supposed to be an easy occupation, eight hundred remaining Japanese stormed the

American lines in a final suicide attack. When Kiska was invaded later in the summer, the Americans found that its garrison had been evacuated without detection amid the Arctic mists.[36]

Meanwhile, King and Nimitz discussed the lessons of Attu at their post-Trident meeting in San Francisco—most important, the concept of bypassing strongly defended points in what would come to be called "island-hopping"—and moved forward with their Central Pacific plans. While Halsey and MacArthur continued their drives in the Solomons and New Guinea, Nimitz would first strike the islands of Tarawa and Makin in the Gilbert Islands, seizing an airfield and a seaplane base, and then assault the key anchorages of Kwajalein and Eniwetok in the Marshall Islands, en route eventually to the Marianas.

What made this surge possible was the addition to the United States Navy during 1943 of seven *Essex*-class aircraft carriers and nine smaller *Independence*-class light aircraft carriers. Contrast these sixteen carriers newly commissioned in one year with the *total* of eight carriers that the American navy had floated on December 7, 1941, five of which were lost during 1942. This was exactly the outpouring of America's industrial might that Admiral Yamamoto had feared if Japan did not win the war in the first year after Pearl Harbor. And many more carriers were on the ways readying to be launched and commissioned during 1944.

The *Essex*-class carriers (CVs) were about 872 feet long, displaced a loaded weight of about 36,000 tons, had a top speed of 33 knots, and carried 90 to 100 planes. The *Independence*-class light carriers (CVLs) were about 619 feet long, displaced a loaded weight of about 16,000 tons, had a top speed of 32 knots, and carried 30 to 40 planes. The CVLs were laid down on *Cleveland*-class cruiser hulls and thus had an easily recognizable thin bow protruding from the forward end of their flight decks. Added to these vessels were another sixteen escort, or "jeep," carriers (CVEs) launched in 1943. They ranged from 492 to 553 feet in length, had top speeds of about 17 knots, and carried a complement of 25 to 30 planes.

While Admiral Yamamoto had feared this onslaught of production, Admiral King had waited, perhaps not too patiently, to receive it. As these carriers became available through 1943, he was particularly anxious to move forward with Central Pacific operations before the Combined Chiefs of Staff met again and backtracked on the Trident agreements.

To that end, King approved Nimitz's recommendations to promote Raymond Spruance to vice admiral and give him command of the Central Pacific Force, soon to be called the Fifth Fleet, and to move Rear Admiral Richmond Kelly Turner north from Halsey's South Pacific Area to command its amphibious component. Within weeks, the marines successfully lobbied King for a fifth division in the Pacific, and Nimitz appointed Major General Holland M. Smith to command all the marines in Turner's force. With "Terrible" Turner and "Howlin' Mad" Smith at Spruance's side, King, who once had conceded that Spruance was the only naval officer smarter than King himself, could be assured of plenty of leadership.[37]

Hardly had King set these wheels in motion with Nimitz when it was time for another Allied conference. This one, code-named Quadrant, took place in Quebec, as Washington was sweltering in the dog days of August 1943. More than a few of the participants thought that such a gathering so soon after Trident was unnecessary, but both sides were determined to solidify the agreements just made there.

Sicily was about to fall to the Allies on August 17, after a thirty-nine-day campaign, although Generals George Patton and Bernard Montgomery had taken American-British rivalries around the conference table to the extreme by racing each other to Messina via circular routes around the island. Landings on the boot of Italy would come next. But the Americans were focused on the Overlord buildup, and Roosevelt was determined to go no farther up the Italian peninsula than Rome, and then only to acquire air bases from which to bomb Germany.

Churchill, however, continued to intersperse place names such as Greece, Rhodes, and the Aegean into his lengthy discourses. While sparked in part by Churchill's great sense of history — sometimes misplaced, as the World War I campaign at Gallipoli had proved —

this continuing discussion of operations in the eastern Mediterranean again threatened to take the Allied focus farther and farther afield despite agreements to the contrary at Trident. To the most skeptical Americans, Churchill's words simply reinforced British priorities for a postwar empire in the Middle East and not the direct annihilation of Germany. Finally, it wasn't volcanic Ernie King but calm, genteel George Marshall who had enough.

When Churchill continued to press Roosevelt a few weeks later for an invasion of Rhodes, in the Aegean, claiming that a short-term diversion of landing craft from the Overlord buildup would not be detrimental, Marshall resorted to rare profanity to make his point. He told Churchill, "God forbid, if I should try to dictate, but not one American soldier is going to die on [that] goddamned beach." Later, Marshall recalled, "I doubt if I did anything better in the war than to keep [Churchill] on the main point. I was furious when he tried to push us further into the Mediterranean."[38]

So the Americans held the line in the Mediterranean, and the British reluctantly restated their commitment to a firm Overlord date. But who was to hold supreme command of this venture was still in doubt. Shortly after Trident, Churchill, acting quite on his own, made the first of three assertions to Brooke that he was to command Overlord. Whether these were, in fact, merely Churchill's "wishes," Brooke took them as a certainty and clearly reveled in the opportunity.

But by the time of the Quadrant Conference in Quebec, it was clear that Churchill had spoken without the consent of his transatlantic partner. With it becoming increasingly clear that American troops would outnumber the British in any cross-Channel invasion, Roosevelt was not about to have them under any but an American supreme commander. Odds favored Marshall at that point, but whoever it was, he would be an American. When Churchill confronted Brooke with the news just before he was to chair a meeting of the Combined Chiefs at Quebec, he was devastated, all the more so because Churchill "offered no sympathy, no regrets at having had to change his mind, and dealt with the matter as if it were one of minor importance!"[39]

If nothing else, the Quadrant Conference was also notable for one oft-told anecdote, the details of which seem to vary with the telling. The acrimony among the Combined Chiefs of Staff was certainly no secret. Thus, when gunshots were heard from inside the meeting room one afternoon, a staff member waiting outside exclaimed, "Good heavens, now they've started shooting each other!"

But the impetus for the shots proved to be even stranger than the most heated of arguments. Lord Louis Mountbatten, soon to be supreme Allied commander of the Southeast Asia Theater, was an inveterate tinkerer. During a break in one session of the Combined Chiefs, Mountbatten asked to demonstrate the qualities of a secret new product, a mixture of ice and wood pulp called Pykrete, after its inventor, the British Geoffrey Pyke. Mountbatten envisioned using the material—buoyant and reputedly nearly indestructible—to build a gigantic, self-propelled, floating airfield, the ultimate aircraft carrier, from which fighters could cover amphibious landings off the coast of France.

"Just look," raved Mountbatten, as he brandished a loaded revolver and proceeded to fire first into a block of ice—it shattered—and then into the pykrete. The harder pykrete failed to absorb the bullet, which went ricocheting around the room, nicking the leg of King's trousers—according to King—with its last gasp. Pykrete never made it into production, and the chiefs of staff all escaped unharmed.[40]

Despite Churchill's propensity for oratory, it was Roosevelt who had the last word. After the final meeting on August 24, Roosevelt and Churchill met with reporters to discuss the results of the conference. As Churchill's remarks escalated into a full-blown speech, FDR leaned over to Leahy and whispered, "He always orates, doesn't he, Bill?"[41]

Time put Soviet marshal Aleksandr Vasilevsky on its July 5, 1943, cover with the caption "Summer for bleeding, winter for victory." What this meant was that Germany's summer offensive, a steamroller of almost two hundred divisions, would fail and that Soviet troops would counterattack from the Black Sea to Leningrad. Victory was far from certain, but winter would once again be a Russian ally.

Joseph Stalin finally felt he could afford to leave his country to meet his fellow Allied leaders, provided he did not have to go very far. Thus, Roosevelt and Churchill agreed to meet him in the Iranian capital of Teheran late in November after reviewing positions between themselves in Cairo en route.

Leahy left the White House at about 9:30 p.m. on November 11 with Roosevelt and his inner circle of Harry Hopkins, naval aide Rear Admiral Wilson Brown, Major General Edwin "Pa" Watson, and presidential physician Rear Admiral Ross McIntire. They motored to Quantico, Virginia; boarded the presidential yacht, *Potomac;* and sailed down the Potomac River to Chesapeake Bay. There, the following morning, the sight of America's newest battleship, *Iowa* (BB-61), greeted them. Commissioned only the previous February, *Iowa* was more than twice as long and fast and three times as heavy as the *Oregon,* the ship that had carried Leahy around the Horn forty-five years before.

Marshall, King, and Arnold, along with their respective staffs, were already on board, and the battleship steamed to Hampton Roads to top off its fuel. Unlike Bill Halsey, Roosevelt and Leahy were not superstitious of the number thirteen, but many sailors, including Roosevelt, considered it unlucky to put to sea on a Friday. Consequently, the *Iowa* loitered in Hampton Roads for a few hours and finally got under way at 12:01 a.m. in the early morning of Saturday, November 13. In the company of three sleek destroyers, the battleship passed through the capes of the Chesapeake and raced eastward.[42]

U-boats were a concern, although King was well along in winning the Battle of the Atlantic. Still, the *Iowa* took precautions to steam at 25 knots and zigzag. On the second day out, Roosevelt and Leahy were sitting on deck just forward of the president's quarters, watching a demonstration of antiaircraft fire, when the loudspeaker blared, "This is *not* a drill — *repeat* — this is *not* a drill." Both men felt the big ship heel to port and surge forward as its rudder was put over and flank speed rung up. Batteries unleashed a furious fusillade at cries of "Torpedo in the water!" and there followed a horrendous explosion astern of the ship.

Admiral King was never far from the bridge of any ship he was on, and he stuck his head inside, close to *Iowa*'s commanding officer, Captain John McCrea, who had once been FDR's naval aide. Quite uncharacteristically he snarled quietly through clenched teeth, "Captain McCrea, what is this interlude?"

Inexplicably, one of the accompanying destroyers, *W. D. Porter,* had taken the occasion to track the *Iowa* as a practice target for a torpedo attack. That was bad enough, but a torpedo had accidentally fired and gone streaking toward the presidential ship. McCrea's quick actions had prevented a catastrophe, and the warhead had been destroyed by gunfire. One may well imagine King's subsequent explosion directed at the captain of the *Porter,* but FDR reportedly told King to forget the entire incident in order to avoid publicity about the president's travels.[43]

That evening, King joined McCrea in the captain's sea cabin and launched into one of his rambling reviews of various naval personnel from Mahan to the present. When he had worked his way to McCrea, King told him that he regarded McCrea as a good officer, but that he had one outstanding weakness. Naturally, McCrea politely inquired what that might be.

"Your big weakness, McCrea," said King, "is that you are not a son of a bitch. And a good naval officer has to be a son of a bitch."

"Admiral," McCrea replied, "you might be right, but you are a good naval officer and I have never heard anyone refer to you as a son of a bitch."

That ended the conversation as King gave McCrea a scowl and stomped out of his cabin, knowing full well that he was lying. Truth be told, of course, King was well aware of his own reputation—and seemingly pleased about it—and it was McCrea who had asked King about referring to himself as a son of a bitch in the corridor of the Navy Department Building just after Pearl Harbor.[44]

The remainder of the Atlantic crossing went without incident. Disembarking from the *Iowa* at Mers el-Kebir, outside Oran, Algeria, the presidential party was met by Dwight Eisenhower and then flown east to Allied headquarters at Tunis. While Leahy was necessarily obliged to accompany FDR for the evening, Eisenhower invited both Marshall and King to spend the night at his "little cot-tage" in nearby Carthage, a respite away from the hurry-scurry of the presidential party that truly seemed to please both men. It was inevitable, however, that the conversation would turn to command of Overlord, now firmly targeted for the late spring of 1944. Char-acteristically, it was King who brought up the matter and gave its history, as he knew it, including the story of Churchill's offer to Brooke and his subsequent reversal.

King opined to Marshall and Eisenhower that FDR had tenta-tively decided to give the Overlord command to Marshall, despite King's strenuous objections. Marshall, King said, simply couldn't be spared from the work of the American Joint Chiefs of Staff and particularly from that of the Combined Chiefs of Staff. King went on to say that the only mitigating circumstance was the fact that Eisenhower was apparently slated to take Marshall's chief of staff position. Clearly, King had become an Eisenhower advocate — in part because Ike had shown the sort of backbone King respected when standing up to him in their early encounters. Still, King said that he firmly "believed it was a mistake to shift the key members of a winning team."

Marshall listened to King's discourse in embarrassed silence. He already knew how King felt, and King was equally certain that "Marshall always wanted that command." But the basic trouble in King's mind was "that Eisenhower had had command in the field and Marshall never had."

King's views certainly should not be taken as being anti-Marshall. King had, in fact, made a similar determination as to the appropri-ateness of his own field command. Throughout 1943, Secretary of the Navy Knox repeatedly urged King to take personal command of the Pacific Fleet and win some glorious naval triumph. King thought that was "the craziest idea," for exactly the same reason he now opposed the switch in roles between Marshall and Eisenhower. "Don't you understand," King told Knox, "you can't shift the fellow who is working up that command? To try to send me over there to take command in the field is absolutely wrong in every way."[45]

The next morning, Roosevelt spoke generally about the Overlord command with Eisenhower, who on the basis of King's remarks the previous evening thought he should be packing his bags for Washington. FDR was as cagey as ever in not tipping his hand, but Ike suddenly realized that the Overlord position was indeed "a point of intense official and public interest back home." Roosevelt noted, however, that he "dreaded the thought of losing Marshall from Washington," before the historian in him added, "You and I know the name of the Chief of Staff in the Civil War, but few Americans outside the profession do."[46]

On then to Cairo, where the Americans and British were supposed to perfect a united front with which to greet Stalin in Teheran. Instead, the Cairo Conference proved to be more unsettling than most. King and Brooke got into a terrible row over the proverbial issue of landing craft—this time, whether they should be diverted to the usual British interests in the Aegean or to the Bay of Bengal, where King was championing an invasion of the Andaman Islands as a step toward retaking Rangoon. Incredibly, Churchill was still talking about Rhodes, despite the fact that in Leahy's words, "the American Chiefs had rejected this idea completely weeks before, but the Prime Minister was not easily discouraged."[47]

Added to the mix was the presence in Cairo of Generalissimo and Madame Chiang Kai-shek. China, like the Soviet Union, was often the forgotten ally in the war. The British seemed less interested in China, but Roosevelt and the American Joint Chiefs recognized that chaotic, disorganized, and barely manageable though it was, China had several million men under arms and was drawing considerable resources away from Japan just as the Soviet Union was draining German resources. And at this point in the war, there was significant support among Leahy, King, and Nimitz for the idea that Japan would ultimately be attacked from land bases in China.

With little resolved at Cairo, the American delegation flew east to Teheran on the morning of November 27, after waiting three hours for a clingy early fog to dissipate. Roosevelt's party had intended to stay at the American Legation in downtown Teheran, but Stalin's delegation reported rumors of an assassination attempt on the president and invited his party to stay at the Soviet compound two miles away instead. Dubious about eavesdropping, Roosevelt nevertheless agreed, and while a formal motorcade distracted attention, Roosevelt, Hopkins, Leahy, and a lone Secret Service driver raced along back roads and arrived at the Soviet compound before the official caravan. The Russian guards were so strict that they stopped *everybody* to examine their passes. The Americans were advised to stop immediately if challenged and only King seems to have been upset by the less-than-normal questioning of just who he might be.

Having failed to resolve their continuing Overlord versus Mediterranean differences, the Americans and British were put in the unusual position of having Stalin essentially make the decision for them. It had to be Overlord, Stalin said. He had been urging a second front in Europe for two years, and he simply did not believe that Italy or any other Mediterranean avenue provided the necessary direct thrust against Germany. Churchill spun a tale of various ventures, including his goal of bringing Turkey into the war on the side of the Allies, but Stalin stood firm, saying that the only proof of an Allied commitment to the Soviet Union would be the long-delayed cross-Channel invasion.

But even Roosevelt was put slightly on the defensive in this regard when Stalin asked him who was to be the supreme commander of that effort. Admitting that he hadn't decided yet wasn't good enough. Stalin insisted that he would not consider Overlord "actually under way" until such an appointment was made. Nonetheless, the key result of the Teheran Conference was a "firm" decision — this time the British really meant it — that Overlord and a coordinated invasion of southern France would take place in the late spring of 1944.[48]

Returning from Teheran, the British and American parties stopped once again in Cairo, this time for a postmortem. Somewhere along the line, Roosevelt made his decision on an Overlord commander, evidently without much counsel. Flying from Cairo back to Tunis on December 7, Roosevelt told Leahy that it would be Eisenhower. "His selection was something of a surprise," Leahy admitted, noting that the Joint Chiefs had never recommended Eisenhower or anyone else and that they had just assumed it would be Marshall.[49]

Upon landing in Tunis, the president had barely been lifted into his automobile when he turned to Eisenhower and remarked conversationally, "Well, Ike, you are going to command Overlord." Roosevelt admitted that he had considered giving the command to Marshall but had decided—with or without Ernie King's input—that Marshall simply could not be spared from Washington. Marshall himself, good soldier that he always was, was said by the president to be in "full concurrence" with the decision. A few days later, typical of his usual graciousness, Marshall sent Eisenhower the original of FDR's scrawled order: "The immediate appointment of General Eisenhower to command of Overlord operation has been decided upon."[50]

Thus, the crescendo of 1943 swelled into what was to be the climactic year of 1944.

CHAPTER EIGHTEEN

Take Care, My Boy

The only thing more difficult than ordering men into harm's way is sending one's own son into battle. It happened throughout World War II, as men in command found themselves making decisions that affected a younger generation that included their own offspring. These sons were grown men of fighting age to be sure, but at some point each of their steely fathers couldn't help but mutter a silent prayer: "Take care, my boy."

Chester Nimitz expressed those concerns in a 1942 Mother's Day message. He was on the cover of *Time* magazine, in a dress uniform, binoculars draped around his neck, and his kind yet determined blue eyes blazing with overstated brilliance. "Who wants to know where the Fleet is?" the caption asked. But amid a report on the Battle of the Coral Sea were excerpts from a radio address Nimitz delivered to "mothers of America."

In a steady, reassuring voice, Nimitz told his own wife, Catherine, and millions of other mothers across the country, "This Mother's Day finds your sons fighting for freedom on worldwide battlefields. There will be long periods of silence when your boys will be active at their stations in far places from which no word can come." And unfortunately, he went on, "there will be losses along the road to victory. If it is God's will that your son or mine be called to make the supreme sacrifice, I know that we will face this stern reality as bravely as they do themselves."[1]

Nimitz's own son, Chester W. Nimitz, Jr., was in submarines. Father and son had been very close while young Chet was growing up, but once Chet entered Annapolis and donned the navy uniform, he couldn't help but view the veteran officer who stood before him with just a bit of reserve — even if it was his own father.

Chet graduated from Annapolis in 1934 and initially went to sea on the cruiser *Indianapolis* before following in his father's footsteps to submarines. It was no small coincidence that many senior naval commanders had sons in the submarine service. Just as it was in Admiral Nimitz's junior days, submarine duty was still an early route to a command of one's own. And when a son who had already continued the family tradition by attending Annapolis was determined to make his old man proud, no one could ever say that he had shirked danger or given less than his best if his duty was in submarines.

At the outbreak of the war, young Nimitz was the third officer on the *Sturgeon* operating out of the Philippines. Within months, he was the boat's executive officer and then the exec of the *Bluefish*. After a second patrol aboard *Bluefish,* Chet got his own command. "Boy oh boy!" the new lieutenant commander of the *Haddo* wrote his admiral father. "I get the delicious trembles when I think of my first patrol as C.O." But Chet's first sortie with *Haddo* in March 1944 proved a frustrating experience when a load of torpedoes with supposedly improved magnetic exploders went off prematurely or not at all.[2]

Still, young Chet's admiration for his father was reflected in his every move, and the letters he posted home from his submarine commands throughout the Pacific were enough to make any father proud, and probably shed a private tear or two. This was especially true on those nights when the father knew so well what the son was facing one hundred, two hundred, or three hundred feet below the surface, listening to the metallic click that signaled another round of depth charges rolling off the fantail of some Japanese destroyer.

Haddo and young Nimitz had better luck on a subsequent patrol off Mindoro, in the South China Sea, when, working with four other subs, they attacked a large convoy. The initial torpedoes brought a furious onslaught of depth charges from the enemy escorts that were so loud and continuous that Nimitz had to shout to be heard in the *Haddo*'s conning tower. But then the convoy turned and presented Nimitz with perfect silhouettes. He fired six bow torpedoes at two large transports and sank both, his first confirmed kills. Later on that patrol, Nimitz fired four torpedoes down the throat at an onrushing destroyer. All missed, but he sank another destroyer instead.

By the time *Haddo* finished that patrol, Nimitz had sunk five ships totaling almost fifteen thousand tons, putting *Haddo*'s cruise on the list of the top twenty-five war patrols by number of ships sunk and ranking its skipper 77th on the list of 465 World War II sub commanders by ships and tonnage sunk. But there was a bitter downside. Nimitz and his crew were safe, but one of the other boats, the *Harder,* along with its seemingly indestructible captain, Sam Dealey, had been lost. Nimitz was the one who reluctantly had to send the message, "I must have to think he is gone."[3]

And there were others lost. Manning Kimmel, 1935 graduate of Annapolis and son of Rear Admiral Husband E. Kimmel, served as a junior officer on the submarine *Drum* even as his father was under scrutiny for the surprise attack on Pearl Harbor. Eleven days afterward, in a letter that would warm any father's heart, Manning wrote, "There is so little to say at a time like this — but...my complete confidence and belief in you has not been shaken a bit and I think you are the grandest Dad in the world."[4]

By April 1942, the *Drum,* under the command of Robert H. Rice, a son-in-law of King's chief of staff, Russell Willson, was in action in the Pacific and sank the nine-thousand-ton seaplane tender *Mizuho,* the largest Japanese combat vessel sunk by submarines up to that time. Manning Kimmel went on to serve as executive officer on the *Drum* and then on the *Raton* before being given command of the *Robalo* in the spring of 1944.

Sent into the South China Sea from the sub base at Fremantle, Australia, Kimmel conducted a "wildly aggressive patrol," firing twenty torpedoes in four attacks but sinking only one tanker, which was not confirmed by postwar records. *Robalo* was subsequently caught on the surface by Japanese bombers, which damaged both periscopes, sprang the conning tower hatch, and knocked out the boat's radar. Despite this, Kimmel kept the *Robalo* on station until the end of its patrol. It was a brave effort, but Kimmel's squadron commander thought it a little foolhardy as well. "Anybody else would have come home long before," grumbled Heber H. "Tex" McLean. "I worried that Kimmel was a little too anxious to put the name of Kimmel high in Navy annals."[5]

Kimmel and *Robalo* were next dispatched to the South China Sea via Balabac Strait, a narrow passage between Borneo and the Philippines that was heavily mined by the Japanese. Returning through the strait after its patrol, *Robalo* apparently hit a mine and sank. Early reports had all hands going down with the boat, but the explosion may have thrown as many as six or seven men, including Kimmel, from the bridge into the water. Other reports had these survivors picked up and imprisoned as POWs. Rumors of their capture trickled out, but any surviving *Robalo* crew members were apparently killed by the Japanese in grisly fashion in retaliation for an Allied air raid.

Regardless of Manning Kimmel's final fate, when Admiral King heard the news that Kimmel's boat had been lost, he ordered Manning's brother, Thomas, to shore duty. Thomas Kinkaid Kimmel, Annapolis class of 1936, had already made five war patrols on the aging *S-40* and briefly served as engineer on the *Balao*. He was hoping for a command of his own despite his brother's fate, but King refused to budge, no doubt thinking that the Kimmel family had already suffered enough because of the war.[6]

The navy, of course, had no monopoly on such situations. Army Chief of Staff George Marshall's first wife was quite sickly and died without having children. When Marshall remarried in 1930, he acquired three stepchildren. He was particularly devoted to the youngest, Allen Brown. In September 1942, Brown, by then married with a young son of his own, enlisted in the army and asked no special treatment from his stepfather, whom he always called "George"—making him one of the few people accorded permission to do so. (Once, when the glad-handing Franklin Roosevelt called Marshall "George" instead of "Marshall" or "General," Marshall noticeably bristled, as if stabbed with a bayonet.)

Brown went through officer training and graduated from the Armored Forces Center at Fort Knox. He deployed first to Africa and then to Italy. On May 29, 1944, as Brown led his tank unit in the drive from the Anzio beachhead toward Rome, he stood up in the turret of his tank to reconnoiter the advance through his field glasses. A German sniper bullet killed him instantly. Marshall learned the news in his office at the Pentagon and immediately went to his quarters at nearby Fort Myer to tell his wife. Inspecting the Italian front some weeks later, Marshall not only visited Brown's grave in the cemetery near Anzio but also insisted upon viewing the site of his last battle from both the air and the ground.[7]

Bill Leahy's son, William Harrington Leahy, was among the luckier ones. He was Bill and Louise Leahy's only child, but being somewhat older—thirty-seven at the war's outbreak—he held more senior positions. Young Bill graduated from Annapolis with the class of 1927 and within weeks married Elizabeth Marbury Beale. Always the supportive father, Leahy nonetheless was "acutely disappointed by the boy's decision to marry at this time"—thinking it would "certainly adversely affect his career as a naval officer."[8]

But the navy between the wars was becoming more accommodating to junior officers, and young Bill and Elizabeth's early years went well as he reported as an ensign to the battleship *California*. Bill and Louise missed the wedding, but only because Bill's own orders sent him hurrying to join the battleship *New Mexico*.

By the time the United States entered World War II, young Leahy was posted to the U.S. embassy in Great Britain as assistant naval attaché. After Louise died during those last few weeks in Vichy, young Bill arranged ten days' leave to meet his father in Lisbon during the ambassador's homeward journey and proved to be a source of comfort to him. After the war, William Harrington Leahy would rise to the rank of rear admiral and command the naval station at Pearl Harbor.

King's son, Ernest Joseph King, Jr., followed his famous father to Annapolis but only with considerable fatherly prodding. "Ernest Endeavor," for whom King had waited patiently through six daughters, entered the academy with the class of 1945. He was described as having been "a meek little boy, thoroughly terrified of his father." If a family story told by Rear Admiral Russell Willson, then academy superintendent, is true, young King, who was going by his middle name, "Joe," attempted to enlist Willson's assistance in persuading Admiral King to permit him to resign during his unhappy first year. Supposedly, Willson refused and told Joe, "Maybe you are ready to sacrifice *your* career but I'm not ready to sacrifice *mine!*" Actually, Willson persuaded young King that he was far better off at the Naval Academy "than as the enlisted draftee he would undoubtedly become if he resigned."[9]

Admiral King may or may not have known about Joe's attempt to leave Annapolis, but Joe persevered and stayed to graduate. He was immediately posted as an ensign to the cruiser *Savannah,* which drew escort duty for FDR's presidential party aboard the cruiser *Quincy* en route to the Yalta Conference in 1945. When the ships called at Malta during the preliminary round of talks before the American and British delegations flew east to meet the Russians, King took his son to the Officers' Club for dinner and proudly introduced him to the gathering of senior officers.

Although young Joe was cut more from his mother's cloth than his father's, he nonetheless made a career in the navy and retired as a commander. It was Ernest Joseph King, Jr., who received the flag from his father's casket at the admiral's funeral, and he lies buried beside the graves of his parents on the tree-covered knoll of the United States Naval Academy Cemetery overlooking the Severn River at Annapolis.[10]

*   *   *

In the navy, war was truly a family affair. William Frederick Halsey III desperately wanted to follow the family tradition and enter Annapolis, but just as less than 20/20 vision had plagued his father's flying, young Bill simply could not meet the visual standards for admission without corrective lenses—then forbidden. Instead, Bill entered Princeton with the class of 1938 and emulated his father's athletic skills on its grounds. He played lacrosse, became the university's 135-pound boxing champion, and served as president of the Intramural Athletic Association.

By the late summer of 1942, Ensign Halsey was in the Naval Reserve, bound for duty in the Pacific as an aviation supply officer. When Admiral Halsey returned to duty in the Pacific en route to the Guadalcanal fight at about the same time, Nimitz surprised both father and son by arranging a reunion as their paths crossed at Pearl Harbor. In typical Nimitz fashion, he invited both for dinner and to spend the night in his personal quarters. Afterward, young Halsey reported for duty aboard his father's favorite ship, the carrier *Saratoga,* then being repaired from torpedo damage sustained early in the Solomons campaign.

Later, with the *Saratoga* operating in and out of Nouméa near Admiral Halsey's headquarters, father and son got to see each other on the occasions when young Bill had shore leave. They were both careful, however, not to seek or accept special privileges. In fact, many of young Halsey's shipmates simply didn't know that he was the admiral's son.

Soon a lieutenant j.g., young Bill was "hard-working and unassuming" and "certainly never traded on his father's reputation." But that didn't mean that he lacked the Halsey brashness. Once, when a group of junior officers were discussing a newspaper quote attributed to Admiral Halsey, one of them opined as to how "the old son of a bitch is full of hot air," not realizing that his son was seated at the table, too. Those in the know quickly looked at Bill, but he was laughing his head off. "What's so funny?" the officer making the remark demanded, only to be told, "The old son of a bitch is Bill's old man." The newcomer stammered an apology, but Bill waved it off, saying that he didn't care and he was sure "his father wouldn't have objected either."

On another occasion, an aviation machinist's mate came on board the *Saratoga* and asked for an ignition harness, adding authoritatively that it was for Admiral Halsey's personal plane. Young Bill didn't divulge his identity and reluctantly let him have one, even though that left only four for the carrier's full complement of planes. A couple of weeks later, the machinist's mate was back, saying that the first harness had broken and he needed another. Again, Bill turned one over without comment.

By the third time this happened, it was a senior officer making the demand over the intercom from another part of the ship, but Lieutenant Halsey decided he had had enough. "I have another three," he replied, "but you can't have one."

There was a vacant pause, followed by the officer saying that his junior had clearly misunderstood. "This harness is for Admiral Halsey's plane."

"Oh, I understand, all right," replied Bill cheerfully. "You can tell Admiral Halsey to shove it in his ear."

When the officer on the line demanded his name, Bill replied, "William Frederick Halsey," and hung up. He heard no more about it and kept his three remaining harnesses for the *Saratoga*'s planes.[11]

On August 7, 1943, the *Saratoga* put into Efate, and young Bill used the occasion to fly down to Nouméa for spare parts, as well as a visit with his father. He spent the night in the admiral's quarters and then started back to the carrier as a passenger in a flight of three torpedo planes. The evening of his son's departure, Admiral Halsey came down with a severe attack of flu that took him out of any coherent action for several days.

When Halsey was finally able to focus, his operations officer came to his cabin and reported, "Admiral, we have had three torpedo planes missing for two days."

Halsey knew at once. "My boy?" he asked.

"Yes, sir."

Halsey told him, "My son is the same as every other son in the combat zone. Look for him just as you'd look for anybody else."

But that brave statement hardly did anything to assuage the worry. Another day passed, and then two, making four days since the planes had been reported missing. Halsey, who had often been asked to hold out hope for missing men, now faced his own cruel realization: "Only a miracle can bring him home."

And it came. Late on August 12, searchers spotted several rubber rafts beached on an island between New Caledonia and Efate. The missing planes had strayed off course and been forced to make water landings, but all ten men aboard, including Lieutenant Halsey, were safe, except for the effects of exposure. The day they were all rescued turned out to be Friday, August 13, long the admiral's dreaded jinx. "From then on — for awhile," wrote the senior Halsey, "I spit in the eye of the jinx that had haunted me on the thirteenth of every month since the *Missouri*'s turret explosion thirty-nine years before."[12]

And there was one other particularly poignant father-son relationship. Rear Admiral "Slew" McCain's son, John Sidney McCain, Jr., Annapolis class of 1931, was in command of the submarine *Gunnel* as it participated in the North Africa landings. The chaos of America's first major amphibious assault was punctuated by mechanical problems with the *Gunnel*'s engines and poor recognition signals that at one point put the *Gunnel* under attack from Allied bombers.

A year later, McCain and *Gunnel* were on patrol in the Yellow Sea, still experiencing engine problems. McCain had the good fortune to sight no less than four enemy carriers during his patrols, but engine problems and faulty torpedoes kept him from sinking any. Tough Slew McCain worried about his boy, but perhaps the only thing tougher was twenty-some years later when John Sidney McCain, Jr., was an admiral in command of all Pacific operations and his own son, John Sidney McCain III, a naval aviator, was shot down over North Vietnam and endured five and a half years of captivity.[13]

It was not, of course, any easier on the wives. Bill Leahy had lost his beloved Louise just before he returned from Vichy in the spring of 1942. It had been his "good luck," he wrote more than a decade after her death, "to be married to a highly talented example of American womanhood who expected her husband to accomplish favorable progress, and who took her full share of the hardships involved."[14]

Few love affairs could surpass the devotion, companionship, and mutual adoration shared by Chester and Catherine Nimitz. They were first and foremost—in the catchphrase of a later generation—"soul mates." They routinely wrote each other almost daily when they were apart, and no matter what the turmoil swirling around them, their letters always managed to convey an intimate, personal touch, as if the other was truly the most important person in the world—which they were. "You are ever in my thoughts," he told her, "and I am happiest when I know you are well and happy."[15]

Ernest King's marriage was another matter. His interactions with Mattie—seven children aside—were frequently as distant and detached as most of his other relationships. King could send a chatty letter to a chief petty officer with whom he had served years before or quietly arrange maternity care for the wife of a junior officer who was himself convalescing in a hospital, but when he went home during his war years in Washington, it was to his quarters on the *Dauntless,* moored at the Washington Navy Yard, and not to Mattie at his official residence at the Naval Observatory.[16]

What affection King showed was reserved for his daughters and a few special wives of younger officers to whom he was frequently a father figure. There were certainly whispers of his infidelity, but investigating them three-quarters of a century removed has yielded little more than the proverbial "everybody knew he was doing it." In any event, Mattie stayed the good sailor to the end and lies by his side at Annapolis.[17]

Bill Halsey's marital story may be the grimmest of all. Bill and Fan were well down the path to emulating Chester and Catherine Nimitz when Fan began to suffer from alternating bouts of mania and depression in the late 1930s. Her illness became worse as the war progressed and made for uncomfortable reunions whenever Bill returned to the States. Eventually, it became clear that they couldn't live together, even though Bill always provided for her care.[18]

* * *

What is certain is that the war and its inherent dangers and uncertainties took its toll on the best of relationships and frequently severed the worst of them. Some of the sons who were rushed into manhood would not return home. Many daughters would do their part in America's industries and in military support roles around the world. There would be, as Chester Nimitz intoned on the first Mother's Day of the war, "losses along the road to victory."[19]

It was gruff Halsey, writing more quickly after the war than Leahy, King, or Nimitz, who summed up the human cost of the inexorable march of events they had witnessed. As Halsey looked over his shoulder from his campaigns across the Pacific, "the old battlefields were already disappearing into the jungle or under neat, new buildings. Where 500 men had lost their lives in a night attack a few months before, eighteen men were now playing baseball. Where a Jap pillbox had crouched, a movie projector stood. Where a hand grenade had wiped out a foxhole, a storekeeper was serving cokes. Only the cemeteries were left."[20]

CHAPTER NINETEEN

Driving It Home

The U.S. military's drive westward through the Central Pacific began in earnest on November 20, 1943, with the invasion of the atolls of Makin and Tarawa in the Gilbert Islands, code-named Operation Galvanic. The campaign provided a steep but necessary learning curve. Nimitz and his planners had expected to overwhelm the Japanese defenders with firepower as well as manpower and complete the assault in a day—the main island, Tarawa, was but two miles long and six hundred yards wide, with a high point of ten feet in elevation.

Instead, a close-in naval barrage fired on a relatively flat trajectory created a scene of apparent wild destruction but failed to penetrate the deeply dug-in fortifications. Coordination between air support, naval bombardment, and the assault waves hitting the beaches left much to be desired. A full thirty minutes elapsed between the end of the shore bombardment and the first assault wave, giving the defenders ample time to emerge from their bunkers and defend the beaches. And while LVTs (landing vehicles, tracked) floated over the surrounding coral reefs without difficulty, other landing craft grounded on them during an unforeseen low tide. They were forced to disgorge their troops into deep water and deadly fire.

Makin fell to the army's Twenty-seventh Infantry Division on November 23 with only light casualties, but dug-in defenders on Tarawa cost the veteran Second Marine Division over three thousand casualties, more than a third of them killed. These delays on the ground also cost the navy. Once the invasion target was confirmed, Japanese planes and submarines keyed on the Gilberts.

Despite the criticism leveled at Admiral Fletcher in moving his carriers off the beachhead at Guadalcanal the previous year, Nimitz instructed Spruance to do just that in the Gilberts after a torpedo plane disabled the light carrier *Independence*. But the deadliest loss came off Makin when a Japanese submarine fired a torpedo into the escort carrier *Liscome Bay*. These half-pint "jeep" carriers were intended to bear the burden of close-in air support and fighter protection for amphibious landings, but they were frequently as vulnerable as floating gasoline cans. The torpedo exploded the *Liscome Bay*'s magazine, quickly sinking the ship and killing nearly 650 officers and crew out of a complement of about 900. Among those missing and presumed dead was enlisted man Doris "Dorie" Miller, to whom Nimitz had awarded the first Navy Cross to an African-American, for his heroism during the Pearl Harbor attack. Clearly, it was deadly to linger around beachheads.

In typical fashion, Nimitz wanted to rush to Tarawa and see the difficulties firsthand in order to better educate his forces for the next go-round. Spruance advised him to wait a day or two, as mopping-up operations were still under way, but Nimitz would have nothing to do with that. On November 25, he flew with selected staff in a PB2Y Coronado from Pearl Harbor to the Ellice Islands and then hopped a Marine Corps DC-3 for the flight to Tarawa. Even then, the plane had to circle while bulldozers worked on the recently captured airstrip.

"I have never seen such a desolate spot as Tarawa," Nimitz wrote Catherine. "Not a coconut tree of thousands was left whole."[1] His men, however, saw him, and just as on his visit to Guadalcanal, word spread quickly through the Second Division: "The old man? Oh yeah, he came by my post last night." The effect on morale was incalculable.

But Tarawa's heavy casualties brought a howl of protest in the United States. Some of it was pointedly personal. "You killed my son on Tarawa," one bereaved mother wrote to Nimitz. To the admiral's credit, he insisted that every piece of mail be answered.[2]

Other criticism came from closer at hand. Amphibious forces commander Marine Corps Major General Holland M. Smith was indeed "howlin' mad" at the casualties, and he vented his frustration on Nimitz when they regrouped back in Pearl Harbor. Smith claimed that Tarawa wasn't worth the price paid and that it should have been left to "wither on the vine" rather than be taken by direct assault.[3]

On an island-by-island basis, Smith's argument might have been made almost anywhere, but in the broader picture of the Central Pacific, the tactical lessons of Tarawa had to be learned someplace. Grieved though he was by the casualties, Nimitz, with King's continuing support, was glad that these lessons were learned early in the Gilberts. But to Smith's point, perhaps the most important lesson of Tarawa was that it reinforced in the minds of all the top commanders the island-hopping strategy that Thomas C. Kinkaid had already pioneered in the Aleutians and Halsey was embracing in the Solomons.

The most immediate effect of the bloody land and sea battles on and around Tarawa was to make Nimitz's chief lieutenants suddenly leery and extremely cautious about their next thrust into the Marshall Islands. That was the scene of Halsey's early 1942 raid with *Enterprise*. Now, instead of just commanding the cruisers in Halsey's task force, Raymond Spruance was in command of the entire Fifth Fleet.

Cerebral Spruance may have initially underestimated Nimitz. Their early encounters had been largely social, and Nimitz's low-key, aw-shucks manner tended to camouflage his razor-sharp thinking. Any skepticism certainly changed to admiration, however, after Spruance relied on Nimitz's general directives at the Battle of

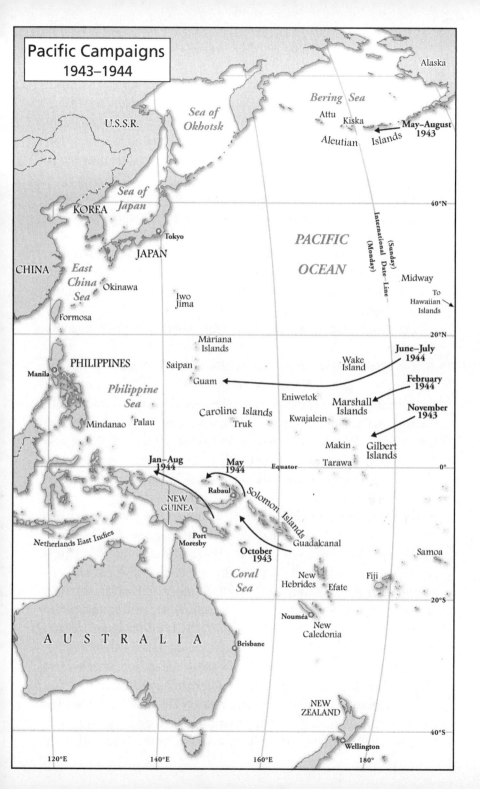

Midway and then spent a year with Nimitz as his chief of staff, housemate, and general confidant. "The better I got to know him," Spruance recalled, "the more I admired his intelligence, his open-mindedness and his approachability for any who had new or different ideas, and, above all, his utter fearlessness and his courage in pushing the war."[4]

Admittedly, Nimitz procrastinated in giving Spruance command of the Fifth Fleet, but not out of any hesitancy about his qualifications. Nimitz simply wasn't sure he could do without Spruance's close counsel, but in the end he determined that Spruance would be an even greater asset with the fleet. Their year together at Pearl Harbor had given each a clear understanding of the other. "The admiral thinks it's all right to send Raymond out now," a CINCPAC staff officer joked. "He's got him to the point where they think and talk just alike."[5]

But when it came to the Marshalls invasion, Spruance was far from ready to mimic Nimitz. In concert with amphibious task force commander Kelly Turner and Holland Smith, who would again command the landing forces, Spruance recommended a two-step approach to Nimitz, first seizing the outer islands of Wotje and Maloelap and then using airfields there to support a second attack on the Japanese headquarters on Kwajalein, in the heart of the islands. After Tarawa, this seemed particularly prudent.

Nimitz weighed the advice of his commanders and also considered new reconnaissance that showed the Japanese to be heavily fortifying Wotje, Maloelap, and the outer islands to provide a protective ring around Kwajalein. Nimitz agreed that it would be difficult to mount a simultaneous assault on multiple islands. But then he shocked Spruance, Turner, and Smith by suggesting that while carrier planes neutralized the enemy airfields on the outer islands, one major thrust would be made directly against Kwajalein instead. The Marshalls could thus be secured in one fell swoop, or at least so said Nimitz in the face of his staff's adamant opposition.

Considerable discussion ensued, and on December 14, with the clock ticking, Nimitz was forced to make a final decision. He asked Spruance, Turner, and Smith in turn where in the Marshalls they should strike, and each said the outer islands. "Well, gentlemen," Nimitz said quietly after a moment of silence, "our next objective will be Kwajalein."

After the conference ended, Turner and Spruance felt so strongly about Nimitz's decision that they stayed behind to argue against it. Turner called the decision to strike directly at Kwajalein "dangerous and reckless," and Spruance agreed. Finally, when their arguments began to wind down, Nimitz, still as calm as ever, leaned back in his chair and said, "This is it. If you don't want to do it, the Department will find someone else to do it. Do you want to do it or not?" That settled the matter. Of course they would do it.[6]

Once this decision was made, both Nimitz and Spruance came under pressure from King to conduct the Marshalls operation— code-named Flintlock—very quickly. King wanted to keep up the offensive momentum and not give the Japanese time to regroup and fortify new forward positions. There was also the issue of the fast carriers. King had directed Nimitz to send them south after the Marshalls were captured, to support Halsey's drive westward from the Solomons. Consequently, King was adamant that the Marshalls operation commence no later than January 16, 1944. Given the increasing distances from Pearl Harbor for ships and supplies, Spruance was equally adamant that it could not begin until February 1. Nimitz served as sort of a mediator between King and Spruance during this time—recognizing both sides—and in the end the main assault on Kwajalein began on February 1.[7]

In the meantime, King and Nimitz had decided that command of the fast carriers had to go to a more aggressive officer than Rear Admiral Charles "Baldy" Pownall. Spruance thought Pownall had performed admirably enough off Tarawa, but subsequent to that, Pownall led a raid on the Marshalls to hinder enemy airfields. When reconnaissance after a first strike at Kwajalein revealed numerous undamaged planes still on the atoll, Pownall turned his carriers away from the threat rather than launching a second strike. These planes eventually found Pownall's force and put a torpedo into the stern of the new *Essex*-class carrier *Lexington* (CV-16) before returning to Kwajalein, where they remained a threat to any invasion force.

Vice Admiral John H. Towers, who had taken Ernie King for his first airplane ride above the Severn River decades before, led the charge to replace Pownall. King had promoted Towers to be Nimitz's deputy CINCPAC and aviation expert in part to get him out of Washington. King disliked him, or at least was jealous of Towers's political connections. Nimitz was not a fan of Towers either, but he accepted him at Pearl Harbor and chose to rely on his aviation expertise. "Towers was a very ambitious man," the usually reserved Spruance noted and then summed up the feelings of many Pacific Fleet officers when he observed, "If you were not an admirer of Towers and did not play on his team, your path was not made smooth if he could help it."[8]

It rankled Spruance even more when King and Nimitz — without directly consulting Spruance — followed Towers's recommendation to give Rear Admiral Marc Mitscher the fast carrier command, designated Task Force 58, under Spruance as the overall fleet commander. Mitscher would soon prove his worth, but Spruance's early apprehension may have stemmed from his own lack of appreciation of the full potential of fast-strike carriers, as well as his personal impression — deserved or not — that Mitscher had not acquitted himself particularly well as captain of the *Hornet* during the Battle of Midway.[9]

In the big picture, these tensions were the inevitable growing pains of transforming aircraft carriers from a tactical support role into a strategic-weapons spearhead. The end compromise was that King and Nimitz agreed that all major commanders, including Spruance, who were non-aviators, had to have an aviator as their chief of staff or deputy, and conversely that all major commanders who were aviators had to have a surface officer in the second position.[10]

So with Mitscher's carriers ready to subdue airfields in the Marshalls and block any reinforcements from Truk or the Marianas, Spruance led his fleet against Kwajalein. He expertly applied the lessons of Tarawa and struck with "violent, overwhelming force, swiftly applied." He also insisted on the "isolation of the objective area." In other words, keep the enemy from reinforcing the objective and provide a sure corridor in for one's own supplies.[11]

The good news was that after a more accurate naval bombardment that didn't end until the first wave was five hundred yards offshore, casualties were much lighter than at Tarawa. Marines from the new Fourth Marine Division overran the islets of Roi and Namur, on the north side of the atoll, and the army's Seventh Division, battle trained in the tough Aleutians campaign, fought its way across the length of Kwajalein in five days. Some 42,000 American troops were engaged, with only 372 killed and about 1,600 wounded.

On February 8, Spruance's flagship, the cruiser *Indianapolis,* anchored along with hundreds of ships of the Fifth Fleet in the relative safety of the Majuro lagoon, twenty-four miles long and five miles wide, on the eastern edge of the Marshalls. There they were protected from high seas and enemy submarines, but most important, the service units of the fleet, from oilers to repair ships and tugs, could establish a secure forward base two thousand miles closer to Japan than Pearl Harbor.

But now it was Spruance's turn to urge King and Nimitz to speed up the timetable. Four hundred miles west of Kwajalein lay the atoll of Eniwetok. Its lagoon, with a circumference of fifty-some miles, easily provided the largest natural harbor in the Pacific. Reconnaissance photos showed Spruance that the atoll was at present lightly defended, but the recent arrival of several thousand Japanese troops suggested that a buildup was under way. If the Japanese were given another two and a half months until the Joint Chiefs' target date of May 1, 1944, for an invasion, they might well turn it into a fortress.

In record time, the Joint Chiefs agreed, and King set a landing on Eniwetok for February 17. In the meantime, Spruance got the news that upon Nimitz's recommendation and King's hearty concurrence, he had been promoted to full admiral. This made Spruance, at fifty-seven, the youngest naval officer to attain that rank and at the time only the seventh admiral to fly four stars, behind Leahy, Stark, King, Nimitz, Royal Ingersoll of the Atlantic Fleet, and Halsey.[12]

Spruance promptly transferred his flag from the more nimble *Indianapolis* to the new *Iowa*-class battleship *New Jersey.* Teaming other fast battleships up with Mitscher's carriers in Task Force 58, Spruance led a raid against Truk in the Carolines. For decades,

Truk had been the principal Japanese naval base in the Central Pacific, and reports of it being the "Gibraltar of the Pacific" had been ingrained into a generation of American naval officers. Spruance wanted to be on board the big *New Jersey* in case the Japanese moved to engage in a major surface action. That didn't happen, but the raid caused considerable damage to the shore facilities around Truk Lagoon, scattered a host of Japanese merchant ships, and sank a cruiser and several destroyers.

The advance through the Gilberts and Marshalls had been impressive, but this blow against the reputedly impregnable Truk had almost as high a morale factor as the Doolittle Raid two years before. A cartoon on the front page of the *Washington Evening Star* on Washington's Birthday, February 22, 1944, said it all. Captioned "The George Washington Influence," it showed a grinning Chester Nimitz dusting off his hands as Prime Minister Tojo sat amid the ruins of Truk in the background. "I cannot tell a lie," said the admiral. "I did it with the fleet he annihilated [at Pearl Harbor]."[13]

Meanwhile, Europe had certainly not been forgotten. With King's battle against the German U-boats largely won, men and munitions flowed eastward across the Atlantic in a steady stream, reinforcing the war effort in Italy and stocking up Great Britain for the long-planned invasion of France. On June 4, Rome finally fell to Allied forces, marking almost a year of dogged fighting on the Italian peninsula after the previous summer's race around Sicily.

President Roosevelt announced the news about Rome in a radio address the next day. FDR coyly gave only a hint of what he knew was even then under way in the skies above Normandy. But close observers focused on something else. Five months in, this was Roosevelt's first fireside chat of 1944, and he had been conspicuously absent from Washington during much of April. Just how was the president's health, and would he run for an unprecedented fourth term?[14]

By the following day — June 6, 1944 — such speculation was momentarily swept aside by the news that Allied soldiers, sailors, and airmen under General Dwight Eisenhower's supreme command had crossed the English Channel and begun the liberation of Europe via Normandy. In what may have been part of an elaborate ruse to throw off German spies, the president's chief of staff was not even in Washington at the time.

Instead, Bill Leahy was visiting his birthplace in tiny Hampton, Iowa, having arrived in the state on June 4 to give the commencement address at Cornell College, in Mount Vernon, and receive an honorary doctor of laws degree. On the morning of June 6, he was having breakfast at the home of a daughter of his father's old law partner when "the radio brought to Iowa news that the invasion of France had begun." Only that evening did Leahy motor to Mason City and board a Milwaukee Road train en route back to Washington.[15]

Leahy's fellow Joint Chiefs had also stayed relatively low-key — at least as low-key as King was capable of being. Calm Marshall apparently did not even rise early to tune in initial radio reports of the attack from his quarters at Fort Myer. In truth, there was little concrete news that early, and even Eisenhower waited impatiently at Portsmouth, England, to get a clearer picture. But within forty-eight hours, Marshall, King, and Arnold were all off for Great Britain to see firsthand the results of their two-year effort.

With Marshall and Arnold in one C-54 transport and King in another, they flew from Washington to Newfoundland and then across the North Atlantic to an attempted landing at Prestwick, Scotland. Heavy fog obscured the field, and the planes were diverted south to Wales. There an aide flagged down the Irish Mail and hastily arranged for an unheated car to be added to the train. With only a tin of strong, scalding tea among them, the three American chiefs sat through a six-hour ride to London, arriving at Euston Station to be greeted by Sir Alan Brooke and his British chiefs of staff at 7:45 p.m. on June 9.

The Americans were quartered at Stanwell Place in Staines, about twenty miles southwest of London, and the next morning the Combined Chiefs of Staff met at the War Cabinet office for a review of all fronts. But their thoughts kept returning to Normandy. Early on Sunday morning, June 11, King and Arnold decided to pay an impromptu visit to Supreme Headquarters Allied Expeditionary Force and get the latest information on the landings firsthand. It was supposed to be only a twenty-minute drive, and Arnold's aide assured the general that he knew the route. Forty-five minutes later, Arnold and King were reduced to asking directions from bobbies, to no avail. Finally finding their way back to Stanwell Place, but without any information, Arnold recorded, "Admiral King was somewhat irked."

But they need not have worried. The boy soldier in Churchill had been itching to get to the Normandy front, and he proposed an excursion that soon took on the feeling of a school field trip. The Combined Chiefs took a special train to Portsmouth, and early on June 12 they were met there by a beaming Dwight Eisenhower. Victory was far from assured, but the initial progress was encouraging. Marshall, King, Arnold, and Eisenhower then boarded the American destroyer *Thompson* and set off for the American beaches of Omaha and Utah, while Churchill and the British chiefs boarded a British destroyer and embarked on a similar inspection of the British sector.

As the *Thompson* surged across the Channel at 30 knots, through a mass of hundreds of ships of all types and sizes, King no doubt took pride in what the U.S. Navy had accomplished. But perhaps there was an even more profound sight overhead. There were four thousand American and British planes in the air that day, but not one German aircraft. Arnold called the harbor at Portsmouth and the mass of ships moving across the Channel "a bomber's paradise," but the Allies had clearly established air superiority. It was as graphic a demonstration as possible of the entwined roles of air and sea power.

This did not mean, however, that all friction between the army and navy had been eliminated. As four P-51s and three Spitfires fell to friendly fire from King's ships, Arnold noted, "Our own Navy [is] far more dangerous than GAF [German Air Force] in spite of [the] fact that they demand overhead cover from our Air Force."

Off Omaha Beach, Eisenhower and the American chiefs transferred first to a smaller sub chaser and then to a DUKW (pronounced "duck"), a six-wheeled amphibious craft built by General Motors and capable of either land or water travel, for the ride to the beach. There was to be no theatrical splashing ashore as Douglas MacArthur would soon stage in the Philippines. Instead, army photographers caught the group climbing somewhat awkwardly over the side of the vehicle and onto French soil. They toured the beach area in jeeps, met U.S. ground commander Lieutenant General Omar Bradley, ate lunch in a field kitchen, and visited wounded soldiers about to be flown back to England.

Late in the afternoon, Arnold opted to return to England by air, while Marshall and King retraced their journey by DUKW to the *Thompson*. Being punctual almost to a fault, both men wanted to be on time for a celebratory dinner Churchill was hosting on his private train upon everyone's return to Portsmouth. Churchill's concept of time was quite different, however, and he had no qualms about detouring his own destroyer to fire a few rounds into the German lines, despite the fact that this made him quite late.

King passed the time in Churchill's well-stocked railcar bar, and as Churchill's arrival got later and later, King drank more and more sherry. When Churchill finally arrived, it was obvious that Churchill, too, had been drinking en route, and the host insisted that it continue. Endless rounds of champagne atop sherry were almost too much for King, but he "managed it." According to Thomas B. Buell, his biographer, "It was the only time we know of that King broke his vow of sobriety during the war." (Marshall seems to have avoided any such condition.)[16]

Meetings of the Combined Chiefs of Staff continued the next day, but even after the apparent success of the Overlord landings—or perhaps because of it—the British were once more questioning the need for a planned second invasion of France from the Mediterranean. The strategic theme that wouldn't die—Churchill's fixation with Italy and the Balkans—reared its head again. King, in particular, stood by earlier arguments in favor of what was then being called Operation Anvil (later Dragoon). He saw a need for a second deepwater port (Cherbourg being the first), liked the idea of a direct sea link from the United States to Marseilles, and thought that an Allied attack on southern France would divert German resources from the Normandy front. In this, King retained Marshall as his ally against the prospect of Churchill plunging eastward from Italy into the Balkans.

From King's viewpoint, there was so much congestion in the

English Channel that the efficiency of movements there was becoming saturated. "There are so many craft involved now," King had told Roosevelt earlier in the year, "that one could almost walk dry-shod from one side of the channel to the other."[17]

Capturing the port at Antwerp, Belgium, was a possible alternative, but Leahy diplomatically noted, "The slowness of the British divisions on our left flank [in that direction] was displeasing." This left the landings in the south of France front and center. Eventually, the British agreed to a second front in France, and Allied troops landed near Marseilles on August 15. No wonder, however, that when the Joint Chiefs returned to Washington and briefed Leahy, he responded that Overlord had been a success, "but I did gather from the conversations of our Chiefs on their return that there was considerably more argument and criticism of the British than has appeared in publicized accounts."[18]

The British were still bulling their way into the Balkans later in the year after German troops withdrew from Greece. Churchill wanted to use American LSTs (landing ship, tank) to land British troops to occupy Athens, even in the face of resistance from Greek Communists. The official American position was that this resistance was an internal matter for the Greek people to address, and King chose, on his own authority, to order a halt in LST support. Churchill immediately got on the transatlantic hotline and pleaded his case to Harry Hopkins, who just as quickly conferred with Leahy.

With the war winding down, the lines between military and political decisions were beginning to blur, and Leahy told King that whatever the merits of his order, he "had intruded into politics and had bypassed the chain of command." It was one of the rare reprimands King received from Leahy, but it underscored that Leahy had no hesitancy in enforcing political directives. True to his methods, however, King quickly devised a face-saving maneuver, arranging to transfer the LSTs to the British as part of larger Lend-Lease operations. King avoided countermanding his orders, Churchill got his support, and the overarching policy of no U.S.-flagged vessels in Greek waters stood.[19]

But it was Leahy who expressed the overriding sentiment in

Europe after the Overlord and Dragoon invasions. "Before 1944 had ended," the admiral wrote, "we had met Hitler's best on a battlefield that favored the defenders, and without any superiority in man power were driving back the Führer's legions with a speed that amazed everyone, particularly our sensitive Russian allies."[20]

What made the Allied success at Normandy all the more impressive was that halfway around the world, King's navy was almost simultaneously conducting another major amphibious operation—not thirty miles across the English Channel from well-stocked bases, but three thousand miles across the wide Pacific from Pearl Harbor. This was the invasion of the Mariana Islands, principally Saipan, Tinian, and Guam, that King had long claimed held the key to victory over Japan.

That the Normandy and Saipan landings occurred within the same month just thirty months after Pearl Harbor was a testament to America's industrial might. It was also a testament to King's global vision. Even with his begrudging support of Germany First, King had still managed to wrangle, plead, beg, and borrow enough resources for the Pacific to get the job done. There had never been any long, defensive holding action in the Pacific, but rather a continuing offensive, just as King had initially insisted on during the grim early months of 1942.

With Eniwetok and the Marshalls secure as a forward base, King and Nimitz were free to push on to the Marianas, completing the encirclement of Truk and arriving within striking distance of the Philippines, Formosa, and Japan itself. But it would not be easy, particularly because their first opponent would be Douglas MacArthur. Throughout early 1944, MacArthur had grown increasingly nervous about an advance on one of his flanks—not from the Japanese, but from Nimitz's forces in the Central Pacific. Taking the Gilberts and the Marshalls had not particularly ruffled MacArthur's plans, but a leap to the Marianas would not only consume massive amounts of men and ships but also pose the possibility that such a thrust might get to mainland Japan before MacArthur's own efforts via the Philippines.

During the cautionary period that gripped most of Nimitz's staff, between bloody Tarawa and the success at Kwajalein, MacArthur promoted a plan to stop the Central Pacific drive at the Marshalls and divert all efforts southward to support his own advance. The Joint Chiefs rejected this notion, but much like Churchill over the Balkans, MacArthur was not one to be denied.

On the eve of the landings at Kwajalein, MacArthur sent his three key staff members—chief of staff Richard Sutherland, air commander George Kenney, and naval commander Thomas Kinkaid— to a strategy conference at Pearl Harbor to plead his case. Even as they did so, MacArthur was sending criticisms of the navy and assurances about his own strategy outside the chain of command to Secretary of War Stimson and, through him, to Roosevelt himself.[21]

The Pearl Harbor conference proved to be a congenial affair, largely because MacArthur's representatives chose to hear what they wanted to hear. Their one-front strategy along the MacArthur-Halsey line was not ruled out, and Nimitz's staff, quite occupied with the pending Marshalls invasion, did not promote any specific plans regarding the Marianas.

Nimitz routinely reported the conference discussions to Admiral King, but MacArthur wrote General Marshall as if a major shift in strategy had occurred. MacArthur brashly assumed that all air, land, and naval forces in the Pacific, including those of the British, were about to be put under his supreme command. Such an outright transfer of forces—even in the unlikely event that King concurred—was unthinkable without causing mass confusion in the command structure then in place. At the very least, it would have placed Nimitz subordinate to MacArthur. King had made clear his opposition two years before, but the general blindly thought the same was about to occur.

MacArthur even wove a web for Halsey. "I'll tell you something you may not know," MacArthur confided to Halsey privately. "They're going to send me a big piece of the fleet—put it absolutely at my disposal." He'd need a ranking admiral, of course. "How about *you*, Bill?" MacArthur asked, before promising, "If you come with me, I'll make you a greater man than Nelson ever dreamed of being!" To Halsey's credit, he didn't take the bait.[22]

King, of course, with the concurrence of the Joint Chiefs, hotly opposed MacArthur's machinations. But King also found fault with Nimitz—"indignant dismay," he termed it—for even *listening* to the MacArthur plan.

"Apparently, neither those who advocated the concentration of effort in the Southwest Pacific [MacArthur's staff], nor those who admitted the possibility of such a procedure [Nimitz and his staff]," King scolded, "gave thought nor undertook to state when and if the Japanese occupation and use of the Marianas and Carolines was to be terminated. I assume that even the Southwest Pacific advocates will admit that sometime or other this thorn in the side ... must be removed." And if there was any doubt as to where King placed MacArthur's overall strategy, the admiral affirmed, "The idea of rolling up the Japanese along the New Guinea coast ... and up through the Philippines to Luzon, as our major strategic concept, to the exclusion of clearing our Central Pacific line of communications to the Philippines, is to me absurd."[23]

But Nimitz also got himself crosswise with King over the issue of invading Truk. After the success of Spruance's raid there and the landings in the Marshalls, Nimitz was optimistic about westward progress. He seems to have at least toyed with invading Truk rather than focusing on King's goal of the Marianas. "I am sorry to say," King wrote Nimitz, "that the impression prevails here—rightly or wrongly—that you seriously contemplate taking Truk by assault." This simply would not do, said King. Truk was a vital Japanese base, but pushing westward to the Marianas would have "the effect of pinching off Truk" and isolating it—the classic island-hopping operation applied on a grand scale. Truk would, in effect, become the hole in an encircling doughnut of American air and naval power.

But King was only getting warmed up. "You may be surprised to know," he lectured Nimitz in a paragraph headed "Another Subject," "how widely you are quoted as the basis for comment and speculation as to what we are going to do next in the Pacific Ocean Area." Nimitz had "said nothing much but what would be obvious to military men," King agreed, "but the use of it has, I fear, verged on 'giving aid and comfort to the enemy.'" King went on to caution Nimitz to "watch your step in dealing with the press, etc." before signing off with the platitude "Remain cheerful—and keep up the splendid work you are doing."[24]

It was a bumpy month or two for Nimitz because, having gotten himself into trouble with King by appearing too accommodating to MacArthur, he now ran into the general's buzz saw as well. MacArthur and Halsey had devised a plan to bypass the Japanese strongholds of Kavieng and Rabaul and jump ahead to Manus in the Admiralty Islands, much as King had long advocated in regard to Truk and the Marianas. Halsey's South Pacific command—still in the dual role of answering to MacArthur for overall strategy but to Nimitz for everything else—took Green Island, east of Rabaul, and then supported MacArthur's efforts to take Los Negros Island and its fine Seeadler Harbour, on the east side of Manus.

All of this went generally according to plan, but then Nimitz, knowing that Halsey had been directly involved in the planning of a major fleet installation in Seeadler Harbour and had the Seabees to undertake the operation, innocently suggested to King, with a copy to MacArthur, that Halsey's South Pacific Area be extended westward to include Manus. MacArthur reacted as if Nimitz had snatched his only child.

He immediately summoned Halsey to Brisbane and went into a tirade in front of Halsey, Kinkaid, and Halsey's chief of staff, Robert B. "Mick" Carney. Not only would he oppose any such efforts by Nimitz—MacArthur insisted on calling him *Neemitz* when peeved—but he also would see to it that the harbor be restricted to ships of Kinkaid's Seventh Fleet and not permit one ship of the Fifth Fleet to anchor there.

After a fifteen-minute lecture, MacArthur, who had once offered to make Halsey grander than Nelson himself, pointed the stem of his ever-present pipe at Halsey and demanded, "Am I not right, Bill?"

"No, sir!" Halsey shot back, and proceeded to tell MacArthur that not only did he disagree entirely, but if the general stood by his order, he would "be hampering the war effort!" MacArthur's courtiers gasped, but Halsey had made his point. Still, it took another two rounds of debate before MacArthur calmed down.[25]

Even so, the general sent a similar message to Marshall, arguing that Nimitz had "proposed to project his own command into the Southwest Pacific by the artificiality of advancing South Pacific Forces into the area" and that somehow this involved MacArthur's "personal honor." MacArthur asked to present his case to the secretary of war and to the president.[26] Marshall assured MacArthur that his honor was not at stake and told him he would arrange for him to see Roosevelt. Privately, Marshall no doubt rolled his eyes and thought, Here we go again. Years afterward, Marshall was still of the opinion, "With Chennault in China and MacArthur in the Southwest Pacific, I sure had a combination of temperament."[27]

With his usual, maddening understatement, Leahy described this latest MacArthur-Nimitz squabble thusly: "It appeared that MacArthur's ideas might conflict with those of Nimitz, and the difference in the personalities of these two able commanders was going to require delicate handling."[28]

Consequently, Nimitz and MacArthur were both summoned to Washington to work out their differences. But by then, in typical fashion, MacArthur pleaded that he simply couldn't be spared from his command and sent Sutherland in his stead. When the conference ended, the Joint Chiefs had categorically made two major Pacific Theater decisions: first, there would be no more talk of taking Truk—Nimitz would bypass it; and second, the timetable for the Marianas invasion would be moved forward from October to mid-June. Additionally, Marshall informed MacArthur—carefully as always—that his visions of grandeur would once again be limited to his continued advance along the coast of New Guinea and that his full cooperation with Nimitz was a given.

Having been thus subdued, only then did MacArthur, who had snubbed Nimitz twice on the latter's visits to nearby Nouméa, do an about-face and cordially invite Nimitz to Brisbane for a personal conference with all the assurances of "a warm welcome" so that "the close coordination of our respective commands would be greatly furthered."[29]

Steady Raymond Spruance sailed westward in the *Indianapolis* to lead his Fifth Fleet against the Marianas. There is no question that

Spruance's command style was diametrically opposed to Halsey's. Spruance always had a detailed operations plan that he followed — occasionally, it will be seen, to subsequent criticism. Halsey, by contrast, was quick to shoot from the hip. "You never knew what you were going to do in the next five minutes or how you were going to do it," George C. Dyer, who commanded the cruiser *Astoria* under both Halsey and Spruance, complained. This was frequently because Halsey himself did not know.

Dyer, who later served King as his intelligence officer, confessed that his feeling "was one of confidence when Spruance was there and one of concern when Halsey was there." Nimitz put it quite differently, recognizing at least part of the difference when he said, "Bill Halsey was a sailor's admiral and Spruance, an admiral's admiral."[30] The one thing both Halsey and Spruance had going for them, however, was that Nimitz trusted them to accomplish their missions.

The Marianas campaign was to be a much more complicated operation than those against the Gilberts and Marshalls. Saipan, Tinian, Guam, and even smaller Rota were much larger islands with sizable civilian populations. They were defended by 60,000 troops entrenched in rugged terrain and supported by tanks and artillery. At his disposal, Spruance had about 127,000 assault troops backed by more than 600 ships.

The Northern Attack Force of the Second and Fourth Marine Divisions, with the Twenty-seventh Infantry Division in reserve, targeted Saipan for a June 15 landing, while the Southern Attack Force of the Third Marine Division and the First Marine Brigade was scheduled to land a few days later on Guam, depending on the success of the Saipan operations. Once again, Mitscher's Task Force 58 was responsible for ensuring that Spruance had an isolated target.[31]

The Japanese, however, had other ideas. The Japanese fleet had not sortied en masse since the Battle of Midway two years before, and Nimitz and Spruance were inclined to think that it would not contest the landings in force. Nonetheless, Spruance prepared for surface action just in case. By now, any misgivings Spruance might have had about Mitscher had vanished, and he put his trust in him as his carrier ace just as Nimitz had done.

Heavy bombardment of the invasion beaches began on D-Day minus 2, but almost at once an American submarine reported a Japanese force of at least four battleships, six cruisers, and six destroyers on the move off the northern tip of Borneo. But where were their carriers? Nimitz's best intelligence estimates put nine battle-ready Japanese carriers somewhere in the southern Philippines. Under the right circumstances, they could still wreak plenty of havoc against Spruance's fifteen opposing carriers.

The landings on Saipan went off on schedule, but that evening Spruance received another report of battleships and carriers exiting San Bernardino Strait, in the Philippines, and steaming eastward into the Philippine Sea. The next morning, yet another submarine sighted a Japanese task force northeast of Mindanao, also heading east. It appeared that the western Philippine Sea was filling with at least two major Japanese forces queuing for a concerted strike against the American landing forces on Saipan, the American fleet, or both.

Spruance postponed the landings on Guam and ordered Task Force 58 and his other forces to concentrate near the Marianas by June 17. When Kelly Turner told Spruance that there was no way he could withdraw transports and supply ships eastward, out of harm's way, without compromising the beachhead, Spruance replied, "Well, get everything that you don't absolutely need out of here to the eastward, and I will join up with Mitscher and Task Force 58 and try to keep the Japs off your neck."[32]

It continues to be debated just how essential those transports were to Turner's efforts. Spruance took Turner at his word that they could not be moved and thus committed his fleet to a largely defensive role within easy range of Saipan. Given well-known Japanese tactics of dividing forces, Spruance was particularly concerned that while one enemy unit engaged his principal carriers, another unit might slip around either of his flanks and strike Turner's transports. Spruance was prepared to engage the Japanese fleet, but his overriding concern became protecting the beachhead and guarding against an end run.

On June 17, as the battle for Saipan continued fierce and deadly,

Task Force 58 searched westward during the day for any sign of the approaching Japanese, but then retired eastward toward evening to be tied to the beachhead. Seaplanes hastily sent to Saipan and carrier scouts failed to locate the Japanese carriers, but Japanese scouting planes seemed to be shadowing the American carriers, attempting either to find a way around them or to coordinate a strike at them from a safe distance. The Japanese weren't steaming straight into a melee off Saipan, but this only caused Spruance additional angst over the possibility of an end run.

The prevailing winds didn't help either. Steady winds from the east meant that every time the Americans conducted flight operations—either to launch or recover planes—the big carriers had to turn into the wind and run east for some distance. This had the effect of increasing the distance between them and the oncoming Japanese, while the Japanese, heading eastward, could conduct air operations while continuing to close the distance.

On the night of June 18, despite submarine reports of the enemy closing, Spruance elected once again to steer eastward in order to be near Saipan, instead of continuing west to position his carriers for a dawn strike against the oncoming Japanese. Mitscher favored the latter but followed Spruance's orders and crafted a defensive battle line of battleships, cruisers, and destroyers out in front of his carriers.

The next morning, the entire American fleet came under a concerted attack from carrier-based planes, as well as from airfields on Guam and Rota. Wave after wave of attacking aircraft became ensnarled with the antiaircraft fire of Mitscher's battle line and then found themselves outmatched by his aviators. In what came to be called the Marianas Turkey Shoot, 383 Japanese planes went down in flames, against only 25 American losses. The American carriers remained untouched, but so did the Japanese carriers—save one crippled by a submarine torpedo—and therein lay the root of the criticism that would soon come Spruance's way.

By the morning of June 20, Spruance had finally become convinced that there would be no end run, and he instructed Mitscher to proceed west to find the Japanese carriers. But by then, staggered by their air losses, the Japanese were withdrawing westward, and the continuing east wind meant that whatever westward pursuit Mitscher mounted would be halting, as he would be forced to turn eastward from time to time for flight operations. The day slipped away, and it was late afternoon before scouts located the Japanese carriers. Mitscher's pilots were game to attack, despite being almost at maximum range and with the late hour almost certainly meaning a night landing—if they made it back at all.

The attacking squadrons finally found the Japanese carriers and, low on fuel, made their runs as quickly as possible and then headed eastward. Mitscher ordered his carriers' lights turned on to receive them, but mass confusion ensued, and more American planes ditched in the ocean than were shot down all day by the Japanese. By the time dawn came on the 21st, the American fleet was in disarray, and the retreating Japanese were well out of range.

Then came the critics. Towers, in particular, blamed Spruance for letting the enemy carriers escape and screamed for his head, much as he had done against Kinkaid after the Battle of the Santa Cruz Islands. Characteristically, Towers suggested himself as Spruance's replacement, but Nimitz would have none of that. Despite lost opportunities, it was hard to argue against overall losses of 476 planes and 445 aviators for the Japanese and 130 planes and 43 pilots for the Americans. The Japanese also lost two of their nine carriers to U.S. submarines and another to the belated evening air attack.

When King and Nimitz visited Saipan a month later, after it had been subdued, King's first words to Spruance as he stepped off their plane were, "Spruance, you did a damn fine job there. No matter what other people tell you, your decision was correct."[33]

But even Spruance had his doubts, although he never backed down from his determined duty to protect Turner's beachhead. "As a matter of tactics," Spruance wrote after the war, "I think that going out after the Japanese and knocking their carriers out would have been much better and more satisfactory than waiting for them to attack us; but we were at the start of a very important and large amphibious operation and we could not afford to gamble and place it in jeopardy."[34]

A week after the battle, *Time* put Spruance on its cover, complete with his four stars of a full admiral. "After the Marianas," the caption read, "The Empire," meaning Japan itself. Doubtless Douglas MacArthur, fearing a route that would bypass the Philippines, was among those not cheering.[35]

By all accounts, the Battle of the Philippine Sea was an American victory. Japanese airpower sustained huge and irreplaceable losses. The beachhead on Saipan was safe, and landings would soon occur on Guam. In Japan, Tojo's government fell as he called the loss of Saipan "an unprecedentedly great national crisis."[36]

But what continued to nag at many American naval commanders were the six Japanese carriers that remained to fight again. On the Japanese side, their planners realized that the Americans would continue to key on any enemy carriers that threatened their amphibious operations. On the American side, the failure to destroy the enemy fleet would weigh heavily on U.S. command decisions the next time such an opportunity presented itself.

CHAPTER TWENTY

The Crippling Blow:
Submarines or Airpower?

If one had asked Chester Nimitz in the opening days of 1944 where the direct offensive against the Axis powers lay, he would have said through the Central Pacific—from the Marshalls, past the Marianas, and on to Japan itself. MacArthur's drive northward from New Guinea was a steadying movement on Nimitz's left flank. If one had asked Douglas MacArthur the same question, he would have said that the direct offensive led north from New Guinea to the absolute must of the Philippines and then on to Japan. Nimitz's drive through the Central Pacific was a steadying movement on MacArthur's *right* flank. George Marshall, of course, would have continued to say that the principal offensive thrust was the cross-Channel invasion of Europe.

But a follow-up question to these answers that presupposed the occupation of enemy territory—be it islands in the Pacific or hedge-rows in France—would have been, What is the ultimate strategic weapon that is bringing the enemy to its knees? "If I had to give credit to the instruments and machines that won us the war in the Pacific," Bill Halsey offered in retrospect, "I would rank them in this order: submarines, first, radar second, planes third, bulldozers fourth."[1]

*   *   *

From the day he assumed command of the Pacific Fleet aboard the submarine *Grayling*, Nimitz looked to the submarine force — almost unscathed by opening hostilities — "to carry the load until our great industrial activity could produce the weapons we so sorely needed to carry the war to the enemy."[2] Submariners readily assumed this burden, but early in the war, their overall effectiveness was hampered by a host of defective torpedoes.

Given his background in engineering and submarines, Nimitz understood the mechanics, as well as the frustrations, better than most. The principal torpedo of World War II, the Mark XIV, was 21 inches in diameter and 20 feet 6 inches long. It weighed 3,200 pounds, about a fifth of which was its explosive warhead. Steam powered by methane gas, it left a telltale wake.

The Mark XIV came equipped with a Mark VI magnetic exploder. In theory, the torpedo would pass under the hull of a target, because the keel was more vulnerable than its more heavily armored sides. A compass needle in the torpedo responded to the magnetic force of the ship and closed an electrical circuit to trigger the warhead. As a backup, the Mark VI also had a relatively simple contact exploder.

When BuOrd finally admitted that Mark XIVs were routinely running about ten feet deeper than set and thus harmlessly passing under their targets, adjustments were made, but some torpedoes still failed to explode or exploded prematurely. Even when skippers fired for direct impact, the contact exploder tended to crumple on impact before it could send an electrical impulse to the trigger mechanism.

All this made for a crapshoot, and in the early years of the war, a proper hit was more the exception than the rule. It was easy for BuOrd to blame rookie skippers for this record, but when experienced captains came home with reports of one dud after another, the deficiencies of the Mark XIV slowly became obvious. "If the Bureau of Ordnance can't provide us with torpedoes that will hit and explode," Charles Lockwood, Nimitz's submarine commander in the Central Pacific, fumed to Admiral King on a visit to Washington, "get Bureau of Ships to design a boat hook with which we can rip the plates off the target's sides!"[3]

In July 1943, a frustrated Nimitz finally ordered his submarine commanders to do what some had already been doing on the sly: disconnect the magnetic component of the Mark VI exploder. That solved the problem of premature explosions, but it took more exasperated skippers and tests against undersea cliffs off Oahu to pinpoint the weakness of the contact exploder crumpling before it could make contact. In response, the support housing was strengthened. "At last," Lockwood later revealed, "almost two years after the beginning of the war—U.S. submarines went to sea with a reliable torpedo."[4]

"Our submarines continue to turn in a fine performance of duty," Nimitz wrote Halsey in the spring of 1943, at the height of the torpedo frustrations. "With a gradual increase in the number of submarines in the Western Pacific, the Japs' ability to keep their far-flung island Empire supplied will gradually wane, and the time will come when they will have to make tough decisions regarding the abandonment of this, that or the other distant island base, simply because it cannot be kept supplied."[5]

Just how increasingly effective submarine operations became is evidenced by their impact on Japanese armed forces in the field and the Japanese war industry at home. Seventeen percent of army supplies shipped from Japan were sunk during 1943; 30 percent during 1944; and 50 percent in 1945. Just as draining on the Japanese navy was a shortage of fleet tankers that deprived their fleet of the mobility and staying power that would become almost routine among the growing American carrier forces. At home, for example, the disruption of Japan's shipping lanes from Southeast Asia had reduced coal and ore imports by two-thirds by 1944. By March 1945, "imports of coal virtually ceased and iron ore was cut off entirely," because the Japanese were forced to use whatever shipping capacity remained to haul much-needed foodstuffs.[6]

Conversely, the Japanese achieved great initial offensive success with submarines, but then inexplicably diverted them to such mundane operations as resupplying distant outposts. In the first full year of the war, before this change, Japanese submarines almost managed to deliver a deathblow to America's carriers. *Saratoga* was crippled and temporaily put out of action by a Japanese torpedo off Hawaii early in 1942. The *I-168* sank the damaged *Yorktown* after the Battle of Midway before it could be towed to safety. *Wasp* was torpedoed off Guadalcanal. Other warship casualties at the hands of Japanese submarines that year included the sinking of the cruiser *Juneau,* with losses that included the five Sullivan brothers, and the crippling of the battleship *North Carolina.*

But rather than push offensive submarine warfare, the Japanese subsequently diverted the vast majority of their boats to nuisance raids, supply missions, and evacuations. Submarines were never used aggressively against Allied merchant shipping—such as the constant flow of ships in the West Coast–Australia lifeline—which suggests that the Japanese simply failed to appreciate the havoc their German allies were causing in the North Atlantic. Japan continued to concentrate on warships instead of merchant vessels, and as warships were generally more protected, Japanese casualties were higher, with less return. Two obvious exceptions were the sinking of the escort carrier *Liscome Bay* during the invasion of the Gilbert Islands and the sinking of the heavy cruiser *Indianapolis* during the last month of the war.

By the end of the war, Japanese naval and merchant shipping losses totaled 3,032 ships displacing 10.6 million tons. Of this total, U.S. forces alone—not counting British, Dutch, Australian, or other allies—sank 2,728 ships totaling 9.7 million tons. American submarines led the way, sinking 1,314 ships of 5.3 million tons, followed by navy-marine carrier-based aircraft, accounting for 520 ships of 2.1 million tons.[7]

These submarine numbers represent 1,113 merchant ships, or 55.5 percent of all merchant tonnage sunk, and 201 naval vessels, or 27.5 percent of all naval tonnage sunk. Of the 288 submarines in commission during the war, 52 were lost by the war's end. By comparison, the six-year Battle of the Atlantic, waged from 1939 to 1945, claimed 3,500 Allied merchant ships sunk, totaling 14.5 million tons.

Submarine warfare had become much more destructive and far more of a strategic weapon than anything Chester Nimitz had imagined when he wrote his pre–World War I treatise that included launching bobbing telephone poles to masquerade as submarine periscopes. But what about airpower?

First and foremost, airpower had become an inseparable component of sea power. After the attack on Pearl Harbor and the sinking of the British battleships *Prince of Wales* and *Repulse* off Singapore, no commander—Japanese, American, or British—dared to launch a major operation without local control of the air. The decisive Battles of the Coral Sea, Midway, and the Philippine Sea were almost singularly carrier air actions. And land-based air continued to show its power, as MacArthur's air force had done against Japanese transports in the Battle of the Bismarck Sea.

As both Nimitz and MacArthur drove closer to Japan, much of the focus in the Central Pacific turned to seizing island bases from which to bomb the Japanese home islands. Halsey worried that such a focus might give him short shrift in the South Pacific, but Nimitz reassured him otherwise. "You may rest assured," Nimitz told Halsey, "that my Staff and I will continue to look out for your interests, although it may appear to some of you occasionally that your Force has been forgotten. We have a good over-all picture of what is happening in the Pacific, and will see that you are not left without tools when the time comes."[8]

Even before massive B-29 bombers began to rain destruction on Japan—first in small numbers from China and then from bases that would be seized in the Marianas during 1944—Nimitz kept a steady eye on all aspects of the Pacific war. He was convinced that his submarines were wreaking havoc on Japan's economy long before the B-29s took flight. And the Japanese appeared to agree. Relying initially on a steady flow of natural resources from Southeast Asia, Japan at first showed tremendous economic performance. But even at its peak, Japanese production reached only about 10 percent of the potential output of the American economy. Japan spent most of 1942 consolidating its new territorial gains and waiting for an American response instead of desperately increasing its own economic output and attempting to deliver a knockout blow.[9]

Meanwhile, America's industrial output was turning out aircraft carriers, planes, and tanks in record numbers. By September 1943, the Japanese general staff began a study of the war's lessons up to that time. Based on air, fleet, and merchant ship losses to date, Japan's declining ability to import essential raw materials, and the looming threat of air attacks on the home islands, the study concluded that Japan could not win the war and should seek a compromise peace. This determination was made after the grand total of U.S. bombers to attack mainland Japan numbered as yet only the sixteen B-25s of the Doolittle Raid. The driving power behind such Japanese pessimism was not American airpower, but American submarines.[10]

Japan fought on, of course, but a postwar American survey of bombing results found that "by August 1945, even without direct air attack on her cities and industries, the over-all level of Japanese war production would have declined below the peak levels by 40 to 50 percent solely as a result of the interdiction of overseas imports."[11] The massive B-29 firestorm raids against the Japanese mainland late in the war destroyed infrastructure, killed hundreds of thousands of people, and generally demoralized the civilian population. The evidence, however, shows that Japan's capacity to wage war had already been severely reduced by offensive submarine operations. The B-29s pulverized Japan's industrial plants, but many of those plants had been idled by a lack of raw materials.

In emphasizing the impact of submarines against Japanese shipping, it should not be overlooked that naval airpower also played an important role in this regard. Witness the number of ships and tonnage sunk by navy and marine carrier-based aircraft, particularly after U.S. carriers struck close to Japan in 1945. There was also a little-known campaign by Army Air Force B-29s to drop mines into Japan's home island sea-lanes and further sink and disrupt inter-island commerce. Some even argue that had this mining effort been implemented sooner than it was, late in 1944, it would have complemented submarine efforts even more and eliminated all measure of Japanese shipping.[12]

What the B-29 raids did do was bring the gloom and inevitable doom of the conflict home to the average Japanese citizen. The destruction was graphic and pervasive. Premier Kantaro Suzuki,

Japan's prime minister in the closing days of the war, told the Allies afterward, "It seemed to me unavoidable that in the long run Japan would be almost destroyed by air attack so that *merely on the basis of the B-29's alone* [emphasis in original] I was convinced that Japan should sue for peace."[13]

But even as late as the summer of 1945, from the perspective of Hap Arnold's Army Air Force, "there [was] no way to escape the conclusion that the B-29 assaults had thus far failed to force a Japanese surrender in spite of the almost indescribable destruction."[14] This left the American submariners in the Pacific the unheralded heroes of the war. As King wrote afterward, "They made it more difficult for the enemy to consolidate his forward positions, to reinforce his threatened areas, and to pile up in Japan an adequate reserve of fuel oil, medical supplies, rubber and other loot from the newly conquered territory. Submarine operations thus hastened our ultimate victory and resulted in the saving of American lives.... Through their efforts the Japanese were much nearer the end in the late spring of 1945 than was generally realized."[15]

In the end, of course, it was a combined effort. Nothing can be taken away from the raw heroism of flying near thirty thousand feet, sucking oxygen in a leather flight jacket, while hammering away at enemy fighters or dodging exploding flak—whether in B-17 Flying Fortresses and B-24 Liberators over Hamburg and Ploesti, or in B-29s high above Yokohama. It took guts. It also took guts to sweat in the narrow confines of a submarine three hundred feet below the surface, with explosions rattling every instrument and fitting in one's boat, or to hunker down beyond a burning German Tiger tank and advance up the road to Berlin.

World War II demonstrated that airpower alone, or sea or land power alone, could not win a war in the twentieth century. It took a combination, and this realization nurtured the unity-of-command refinements that developed during World War II, ultimately resulting in the creation of the Department of Defense.

CHAPTER TWENTY-ONE

Halsey's Luck

No matter their level of competence, most great commanders are blessed with a certain amount of luck. In 1944, one needed to look no further than recent experiences in the current conflict to support that. Commanders make educated decisions based on facts, experience, and gut-level instinct, but at some point, a willingness to roll the dice takes over. Dwight Eisenhower faced such a moment weighing the weather odds before Normandy. Chester Nimitz had a similar moment before Midway, trusting American intelligence and dispatching Fletcher and Spruance to Point Luck. If luck seems too casual a term, if serendipity too flighty, then call it the vagaries of war. Those vagaries were about to descend on Bill Halsey.

Having spent twenty months in command of the South Pacific Area, Halsey was reassigned to command the Third Fleet. This force was essentially Spruance's Fifth Fleet. As the Central Pacific drive gained steam, King and Nimitz devised a command rotation between Spruance and Halsey so that while one admiral and his staff were at sea executing current operations—as Spruance did that summer in the Marianas—the other was at Pearl Harbor planning the next operation. It didn't hurt matters that the use of different fleet numbers for essentially the same forces added a level of confusion for Japanese intelligence. As Halsey put it, "Instead of the stagecoach system of keeping the drivers and changing the horses, we changed drivers and kept the horses."[1]

As Halsey left the South Pacific command on June 15, 1944, he bade his officers and men an emotional farewell. Halsey told them that if a shoulder patch was ever designed for those who had served with him during those lean months, he wanted it to show three things: "a piece of string, a can of beans and a rusty nail."[2] Sending Halsey his own farewell, Douglas MacArthur assured him that it was "with deepest regret we see you and your splendid staff go" and called him "a great sailor, a determined commander, and a loyal comrade."[3]

After an official transmittal of the command change, Halsey replied to MacArthur on a personal level. "You and I have had tough sledding with the enemy," Halsey acknowledged, but "my own personal dealings with you have been so completely satisfactory that I will always feel a personal regard and warmth over and above my professional admiration."[4] A few months later, MacArthur, loyal to a fault, would stand by Halsey when Halsey's luck was sorely tested.

In the interim, the time had finally come for the ruler to summon the pretender. Franklin D. Roosevelt, as commander in chief, ordered MacArthur, who had not seen Roosevelt or been in the United States since 1937, to meet with him in Honolulu. MacArthur had successfully avoided other top-level conferences by sending minions and pleading the impossibility of an absence from his headquarters. But he could not ignore this direct order from the president.

Besides, this might well be MacArthur's best chance to force the issue of Pacific strategy beyond the Marianas. King and Nimitz were promoting a stab directly westward to Formosa and an eventual linkup with mainland China, bypassing the Philippines in the process. MacArthur, who had vowed in 1942 that he would return to the Philippines, was still as determined as ever to do just that—and *not* via Formosa.

On the evening of July 13, 1944, Roosevelt and Leahy left

Washington by train for Hyde Park. As always, their itinerary and final destination were well-kept secrets. The presidential train arrived on the west bank of the Hudson opposite FDR's beloved Springwood in time for breakfast the next morning, followed by an inspection of progress on the adjacent Roosevelt Presidential Library.

"After a pleasant day," the presidential party reboarded the Ferdinand Magellan at 6:30 p.m., bound for California. Along with FDR, Eleanor Roosevelt, Leahy, and "the usual communication and Secret Service personnel" were military aide Pa Watson, naval aide Wilson Brown, the indispensable Grace Tully, and both Rear Admiral Ross McIntire, the president's physician, and Commander Howard G. Bruenn, a young cardiologist who had also been attending the president in recent months.[5]

But there was to be an intermediate stop before reaching California. The presidential special roared west from Albany on New York Central tracks and shortly after noon on July 15 pulled into Chicago, where the party faithful were gathering for the upcoming Democratic National Convention. Only four days before, after what seemed an interminable period of either indifference or shrewdness that had frozen out any serious challengers, Roosevelt had finally acknowledged at a press conference that he would accept his party's nomination for a fourth term.[6]

He would not be denied, of course, and that left open only the question of a vice presidential candidate. The current vice president, Henry Wallace, had fallen out of favor with Roosevelt and the Democratic Party establishment for his increasingly eccentric views. Contenders as replacements included Supreme Court justice William O. Douglas and James F. Byrnes, the former South Carolina congressman and senator who had become FDR's domestic policy guru and, some said, almost an "assistant president" for the home front.

Leahy seems to have heavily favored Byrnes at that time, and in various conversations with Roosevelt, "he frequently slipped in a strong recommendation for his favorable consideration of Byrnes." On the trip from Hyde Park to Chicago there was certainly no shortage of speculation, and the president's party "talked frequently about our preferences for the second highest post—that is, all of us except the President himself."

The stay in Chicago was short, and even before the convention convened the president's special was westbound from Chicago. FDR announced to his fellow travelers the "surprising information that he had recommended Senator Harry Truman" for the vice presidential nomination. Except for Truman's work investigating national defense issues, Leahy confessed he "knew almost nothing about him."[7]

Arriving in San Diego, Roosevelt and his party spent two days watching amphibious landing exercises while the Chicago convention convened and went about the process of renominating him. On July 21, after Truman's nomination for vice president was also in place, Roosevelt boarded the cruiser *Baltimore*. The president settled into the captain's cabin, and Leahy occupied the flag officer's cabin. Then, because it was a Friday, the *Baltimore* "waited after midnight to sail from San Diego."[8]

Five days later, at 3:00 p.m. on July 26, after a voyage Leahy termed "without incident" and accompanied by generally pleasant weather, the *Baltimore* docked alongside a seawall within the confines of Pearl Harbor. Nimitz and the hierarchy of the Pacific Fleet immediately went aboard to pay their respects. But where was Douglas MacArthur?

The general had left Brisbane the day before in his personal B-17, named *Bataan,* and made a twenty-six-hour flight from Brisbane across the Pacific to land at Hickam Field on Oahu about an hour before the *Baltimore* docked. Upcoming strategy session aside, MacArthur spent most of the flight pacing the aisle and grumbling about the "humiliation of forcing me to leave my command to fly to Honolulu for a political picture-taking junket." There was certainly to be some of that, but as usual MacArthur proceeded to top all comers when it came to the theatrical.

Just as Roosevelt, Leahy, Nimitz, and their entourage were disembarking from the *Baltimore* for shore accommodations, the terrific wail of a siren filled the dockside. A long open car with a motorcycle escort swept into view, did a circling lap around the dock, and came to a stop at the foot of the *Baltimore*'s gangplank.

In the car were a chauffeur in khakis and one lone figure in the backseat in a battered cap and leather flying jacket, despite the summer heat of Hawaii. There was no mistaking Douglas MacArthur.

He had taken the opportunity to stop by his guest quarters to take a bath—understandable after a full day in the air—but by lingering there, he had clearly picked the perfect moment of entrance for the maximum attention. MacArthur stepped smartly from the automobile and strode up the gangplank to a thunderous ovation.

Never one to be upstaged, Roosevelt greeted MacArthur warmly. Leahy, whose relationship with MacArthur went back nearly forty years to "when as young officers we had good times together in San Francisco," remarked dryly, "Douglas, why don't you wear the right kind of clothes when you come up here to see us?" Disregarding his time in the bath, MacArthur gestured to the heavens and replied, "Well, you haven't been where I came from, and it's cold up there in the sky."[9]

In the morning, MacArthur's suspicions about a political motive for the trip were confirmed when Roosevelt squeezed the general and Nimitz into the back of the same open car that MacArthur had just used and, with Leahy in front with the chauffeur, set off on a whirlwind tour of Oahu military installations. Nimitz later maintained that there were only two open cars in all of Honolulu: one belonged to a well-known madam and the other was the fire chief's bright red vehicle. The chief's was chosen because riding in the madam's vehicle might have serious repercussions.[10]

MacArthur was long past being a viable presidential candidate—in 1944, at least—but he still held considerable sway in Republican circles, as well as being genuinely popular with the American public at large. Shrewd Roosevelt had weighed the political benefits of either appearing before a partisan crowd at his nominating convention or being seen in the field as commander in chief in the company of two of the most popular military heroes of the day—MacArthur and Nimitz. It was an easy choice.

Political cartoonist Jim Berryman caught the mood when he depicted MacArthur, Nimitz, and a vibrant-looking FDR with "Commander-in-Chief" on his sleeve seated at a table labeled "Pacific War

Council." MacArthur and Nimitz are looking over their shoulders at another FDR leaning jauntily against a palm tree, cigarette holder in hand and lei around his neck, while his hat reads "Democratic Nominee." "Oh, don't mind him, gentlemen," FDR's commander in chief character says. "He just came along to get away from politics!"[11]

As usual, the press paid Leahy little mind during these tours, but Halsey added additional star power when he joined the group for dinner. Only after that did the serious discussions begin, with only Roosevelt, Leahy, MacArthur, and Nimitz in the living room of a Waikiki residence that was bedecked with maps. FDR addressed MacArthur first: "Well, Douglas, where do we go from here?" With pointer in hand, MacArthur jabbed at a huge map of the Pacific and replied, "Mindanao, Mr. President, then Leyte — and then Luzon."[12]

With MacArthur arguing the Philippines alternative, it was left to Nimitz to put forward the case for Formosa. In a session that lasted until midnight and then continued the following morning, Nimitz and MacArthur took turns congenially debating the pros and cons of each plan.

King had long favored an invasion of Formosa as the most effective means of severing the flow of natural resources between the East Indies and Japan. American submarines had certainly choked that supply line, but King wanted it cut completely with a fleet presence in Formosa. Having leaped to the Marianas, Nimitz was convinced that he could make the jump to Formosa, although his lines of communication and supply would be squeezed between Okinawa to the north and Luzon to the south. Somewhere along that line, such a thrust was bound to precipitate a final pitched battle with the Japanese fleet.

King, by the way, had just departed Hawaii after his visit to Saipan with Nimitz, and in fact flew over the *Baltimore* on his way east. He was not invited to attend the conference, nor were the other members of the Joint Chiefs, Marshall and Arnold, who had accompanied the president to all the other important strategy conferences. With the breakout from the Normandy beachhead just under way, it might be said that Marshall, Arnold, and King were busy winning the war, while the president was indeed indulging in political posturing with his two high-profile field commanders.

King's views on the Honolulu conference were summed up by the subtitle of the corresponding section in his autobiography: "President Roosevelt Intervenes in Pacific Strategy." King also recounted that a few weeks before the Pearl Harbor conference, Leahy came into his office and asked that the navy stop using the long-held title "Commander in Chief, Pacific Fleet" (or Atlantic Fleet) and simply say "Commander, Pacific Fleet." King asked if this was an order, and the deft Leahy replied that it was not, nor was it even a request, but he knew the president "would like to have it done." King said he would gladly follow a direct order but otherwise would take it under advisement. He did, and did nothing, but there was at least the inference in the discussion that FDR was determined that any reference to "commander in chief" be only to him.[13]

There is some evidence that the final decision between the Philippines and Formosa was more political than military. Supposedly, MacArthur managed to corner FDR alone for ten minutes and chastise him that bypassing the Philippines, with its millions of friendly inhabitants, under American protection since the Spanish-American War, would foster a "most complete resentment against you at the polls this fall." In any event, Roosevelt went to bed that evening demanding an aspirin and grumbling, "In all my life nobody has ever talked to me the way MacArthur did."[14]

By the time MacArthur departed after the morning conference on the third day, FDR, on the issue of Formosa versus the Philippines, was leaning toward the latter. King later felt that Nimitz let him down in his arguments for Formosa. In reality, Roosevelt may well have already decided to placate MacArthur before Nimitz spoke. In either event, the Joint Chiefs continued to debate the issue for another month before a final decision was made in favor of the Philippines. When it was, Leahy strongly supported that route because he thought it was "of a more conservative nature at a lesser cost of lives" than an attack against Formosa or Kyushu.[15]

As usual, it was Leahy who painted a serene picture of the Honolulu scene: "After so much loose talk in Washington, where the mention of the name of MacArthur seemed to generate more heat than light," Leahy recalled, "it was both pleasant and very informative to have these two men [MacArthur and Nimitz] who had been pictured as antagonists calmly present their differing views to the Commander-in-Chief."[16]

On Saturday, July 29, the day after MacArthur departed, Roosevelt again toured military facilities and then lunched at Nimitz's quarters—hastily revamped to accommodate the president's wheelchair. After lunch, they made a tour of the five-thousand-bed Aiea Naval Hospital and returned to the president's temporary residence so that Roosevelt could hold a late afternoon press conference.

Roosevelt expressed satisfaction at seeing his commanders and noted that whenever and however the invasion of the Philippines came about, General MacArthur would "take a part in it." As for Leahy, he recorded in his diary that evening perhaps an even greater strategy issue than the Formosa versus Philippines debate.

"Their agreement on the fundamental strategy that should be employed in bringing defeat to Japan," wrote Leahy of MacArthur and Nimitz, "and the President's familiarity therewith acquired at this conference, will be of the greatest value to me in preventing an unnecessary invasion of Japan." The planning staffs of the Joint Chiefs and the War Department had been advocating just such a preparation, "regardless of the loss of life," and Leahy was decidedly opposed to a ground invasion.

While Leahy admitted that General MacArthur "seems to be chiefly interested in retaking the Philippines," he was convinced that both MacArthur and Nimitz "are in agreement with me...that Japan can be forced to accept our terms of surrender by the use of sea and air power without an invasion of the Japanese homeland."

With that, the president's party reboarded the *Baltimore* and sailed east. "I look forward to little of value in the remainder of our scheduled cruise on the *Baltimore*," Leahy noted, "but the entire journey has already been fully justified by our conferences with MacArthur and Nimitz in Honolulu." Just where the *Baltimore* was headed was once again a closely guarded secret.[17]

Meanwhile, despite his public pronouncements of support for Spruance after the Battle of the Philippine Sea, Admiral King was personally "disappointed in the results" and reiterated to Nimitz, "If an opportunity arises or can be contrived to destroy a major part of the main Japanese fleet, this becomes the primary objective."[18]

This emphasis on engaging ships was hardly new. In May 1943, Nimitz had bemoaned that a Japanese cruiser had been damaged but left on a reef and permitted to escape despite Nimitz's request to MacArthur for his planes to finish it off. "As you well know," Nimitz told Halsey then, "ships, combatant and merchant type, are still our prime objective for all kinds of strikes."[19]

The Japanese were about to oblige such an opportunity, and making the most of it was certainly Bill Halsey's priority as he sailed west from Pearl Harbor on August 24 in the battleship *New Jersey,* ultimately to cover MacArthur's landings in the Philippines. Two days later, command of the fleet officially passed from Spruance to Halsey.

Halsey's choice of the *New Jersey* as his flagship is interesting, particularly in light of later events. His "first inclination" had been to pick a carrier because, he said, "I had spent so many years in them that I would have felt more at home there than in anything but a destroyer, *which was now too rough for my old age* [emphasis added]." But, Halsey worried, the carriers would be particularly vulnerable to attack, and "we could not afford to risk having flag functions interrupted by battle damage."

That left the new *Iowa*-class battleships, the only big ships that could match the speed of the 32-knot carriers. During the Marianas campaign, Halsey had dispatched observers to Spruance's flag plot on *Indianapolis,* Marc Mitscher's flag carrier, and several battleships, and the result of this review of efficiency was that his staff was able to craft a flag plot on the *New Jersey* that Halsey called "the best in the fleet."[20]

By the time Halsey rendezvoused with Mitscher's fast carrier task force—now numbered Task Force 38, instead of 58, to account for the Fifth Fleet becoming the Third Fleet—Mitscher's planes had been blanketing the Palau Islands and Mindanao in the Philippines. Running out of enemy resistance, Halsey ordered strikes in the central Philippines as well. Over the course of three days in early September, the sixteen carriers of Task Force 38 launched more than 3,000 sorties that shot down 173 Japanese planes, destroyed another 305 on the ground, and caused havoc to shipping—all with minimal losses. This set Halsey to thinking.

MacArthur's invasion of the Philippines via Mindanao was scheduled for November 15, with landings at Leyte in the central Philippines to follow by December 20. In the meantime, Nimitz's Central Pacific forces were to seize the intermediary islands of Peleliu and Angaur in the Palaus on the same day that MacArthur landed on Morotai, halfway between New Guinea and Mindanao. But if these outer defenses were protecting a largely empty shell in the central Philippines, why not strike directly to the heart of the matter and invade Leyte instead of Mindanao, expediting the time-table and bypassing the outlying resistance in the process?

Halsey sat in the corner of the flag bridge of the *New Jersey* chain-smoking cigarettes and mulling it over. Dare he recommend such a move to Nimitz? Finally, the admiral summoned his chief of staff and told him, "I'm going to stick my neck out. Send an urgent dispatch to CINCPAC."[21]

The invasion of Peleliu was only forty-eight hours away and intended to coincide with MacArthur's strike at Morotai. Nimitz agreed with Halsey about striking Leyte directly, but the tightness of the Peleliu invasion was vexing. Eighteen thousand men of the veteran First Marine Division and another eleven thousand from the Eighty-first Infantry Division were on board transports headed for the island. They might have been recalled, but such an action would have clogged the endless supply lines that were by now pouring men and materiel into the Pacific. Nimitz fretted but decided to go ahead with the landings. After Peleliu proved to be heavily fortified with a system of limestone caves, the operation turned into another bloody Tarawa for the First Marines and became one of Nimitz's more con-troversial decisions.

But meanwhile, Nimitz flashed Halsey's suggestion about Leyte to King, who was in Quebec with his fellow Joint Chiefs attending yet another strategy session with Roosevelt and Churchill. General Marshall was reluctant to make such a momentous decision without input from MacArthur, but MacArthur was on board the cruiser

Nashville under radio silence en route to the invasion of Morotai. His alter ego and chief of staff, Richard Sutherland, made the decision in MacArthur's absence and wired a hearty concurrence in MacArthur's name.

This message reached the Joint Chiefs in Quebec while they were attending a formal dinner given by Canadian officers in their honor. When a staff officer interrupted, Leahy, Marshall, King, and Arnold excused themselves and "left the table for a conference." Ninety minutes after the message was received, orders were en route to MacArthur and Nimitz to execute the Leyte operations on October 20. "Having the utmost confidence in General MacArthur, Admiral Nimitz, and Admiral Halsey," Marshall later wrote, "it was not a difficult decision to make."[22]

With the invasion of Leyte moved up, Halsey led the Third Fleet northwest toward Formosa — not for purposes of an invasion, but to neutralize airfields there and prevent reinforcements from reaching the Philippines. The American carrier pilots were becoming so proficient — and Japan was running out of top-line fliers — that the Formosa raid achieved great success. But then Halsey's dreaded Friday the thirteenth jinx struck at sea.

Since young Bill's rescue, Halsey's phobia had been dormant, but on the evening of October 13, as the Third Fleet was retiring eastward from Formosa, the American heavy cruiser *Canberra* (CA-70) was hit by an aerial torpedo and went dead in the water. Halsey faced the decision to abandon the ship and either sink it, or take it under tow. He chose the latter and prepared "to fight our way out" at the agonizingly slow speed of four knots.

This was not all bad, because although the *Canberra* became an easy target for the remaining Japanese aircraft, the combat air patrols from Halsey's carriers shot down many of them. But late on the evening of October 14, another aerial torpedo found its mark in the light cruiser *Houston* (CL-81). Now Halsey had two cripples on his hands. Both of these cruisers were namesakes of other ships sunk earlier in the war, in 1942 — the Australian heavy cruiser HMAS *Canberra* (D-33) in the Battle of Savo Island, and the American heavy cruiser *Houston* (CA-30) near Java.

Halsey was now faced with abandoning two ships or continuing to tow the cruisers eastward. At first, he was inclined "to sink them and run beyond the range of the Japs' shore-based air before a worse disaster struck us." But then his chief of staff and operations officer suggested using the crippled cruisers as bait to lure out a heavier concentration of Japanese ships. If they could do so, it would provide them with an opportunity to destroy "a major portion of the enemy fleet" per their orders.

Halsey dispatched two of his carrier groups to lurk just outside of the range of enemy patrol planes and the other two to pound airfields on Luzon. Meanwhile, the *Canberra* and *Houston* and their escorts were designated "the Bait Division" and told to keep up a steady stream of distress messages.

Japanese planes continued to attack the cruisers with detrimental results because of the combat air patrols, but no major concentration of Japanese warships appeared. By the time the Bait Division was safely out of range and bound for the navy's new forward base at Ulithi, Halsey's attention was focused on MacArthur's landings on Leyte. It would soon become clear that part of the reason the Japanese did not take Halsey's proffered bait was that they were baiting a trap of their own.[23]

After two years of a steady erosion of its position across the Pacific, the Imperial Japanese Navy was desperately seeking another Tsushima-type victory. For a brief time, wildly inflated Japanese propaganda reports suggested they had achieved it by destroying a major portion of Halsey's fleet off Formosa. Save for the damage to *Canberra* and *Houston,* this was largely nonsense. So many Japanese planes had in fact dropped burning into the sea that it was difficult for attacking pilots to realize that the American ships themselves were not afire.

Admiral Soemu Toyoda, commander in chief of the Combined Fleet, was not swayed either way. He had already committed his remaining forces to a do-or-die defense of the Philippines. Toyoda later testified that "questions were beginning to be asked at home as to what the navy was doing after loss of one point after another down south," but the loss of the Philippines—or Formosa, if King had had his way—would cut the Japanese jugular.

If Toyoda's fleet stayed in its home waters, it could not obtain fuel from the East Indies. If it remained south of the Formosa–Philippine choke hold, it could not be resupplied with men and ammunition from Japan. "There would be no sense," Toyoda acknowledged, "in saving the fleet at the expense of the loss of the Philippines."[24] Thus, the Japanese navy's imperative was to repulse MacArthur's landings at Leyte and hope for a Tsushima-like surface engagement with the American fleet.

To do so, Toyoda devised a massive four-pronged offensive that was much more concentrated and complex than any prior thrusts at Pearl Harbor, Coral Sea, or even Midway. It is interesting to speculate what such an assemblage of Japanese naval power might have done toward subjugating the Hawaiian Islands immediately after Pearl Harbor or parading up and down the West Coast of the United States early in 1942. But instead, Japan had stabbed here and there and then been content to wage a holding action. It had not mounted another major operation with its Combined Fleet until the Battle of the Philippine Sea, and even then the confrontation had not resulted in the long-awaited surface duel between battleships that some strategists on both sides still thought must inevitably occur.

On the American side, there would later be many questions about divided command during the Battle of Leyte Gulf, but the Japanese also had their own command and control issues from the start. While Toyoda gave overall strategic direction from southern Formosa, four semi-independent fleets sailed toward Leyte. The Main Force (which the Americans called the Northern Force) assembled in Japan's Inland Sea under Vice Admiral Jisaburo Ozawa. It consisted of one large carrier, three light carriers, two cruisers, and a dozen destroyers.

But far from being the main attack force, Ozawa's command was charged with drawing Halsey and the Third Fleet away from the Leyte beachhead, something Ozawa had been unable to do against Spruance in the Marianas four months before. If successful, this would open the way for an attack on the beachhead but likely cost

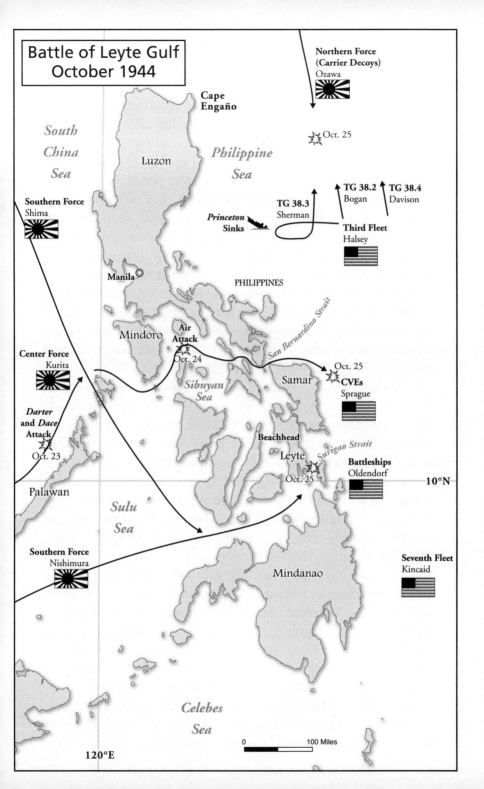

Battle of Leyte Gulf
October 1944

South
China
Sea

Luzon

Cape
Engaño

Philippine
Sea

Northern Force
(Carrier Decoys)
Ozawa

Oct. 25

Southern Force
Shima

TG 38.3
Sherman

Princeton
Sinks

TG 38.2
Bogan

TG 38.4
Davison

Third Fleet
Halsey

Manila

PHILIPPINES

Mindoro

Air
Attack

Oct. 24

San Bernardino Strait

Samar

Oct. 25

CVEs
Sprague

Center Force
Kurita

Sibuyan
Sea

Darter
and Dace
Attack

Oct. 23

Beachhead

Leyte

Surigao Strait

Battleships
Oldendorf

10°N

Palawan

Sulu
Sea

Oct. 25

Southern Force
Nishimura

Mindanao

Seventh Fleet
Kincaid

Celebes
Sea

0   100 Miles

120°E

Japan these carriers. Two years before, such a sacrifice would have been unthinkable, but now the bulk of these carriers' aircraft and pilots had either been lost in the Philippine Sea and off Formosa or sent to land-based fields, from which the less experienced pilots were presumed to stand a better chance of survival.

The First Striking Force (called the Center Force by the Americans) under Vice Admiral Takeo Kurita packed the most punch. Centered on three battleship divisions, the first of which included the 64,000-ton, 18-inch-gunned *Yamato* and *Musashi,* it was supported by eleven heavy cruisers and a bevy of light cruisers and destroyers. Kurita's mission was to sail east from Brunei Bay on Borneo, traverse the Sulu Sea, and snake through the mid-Philippines via the Sibuyan Sea and San Bernardino Strait. Rounding Samar Island on the east, this massive firepower would then pounce on the transports and assorted supply ships off the Leyte beachhead and engage any units that might rush to their assistance.

The Second Striking Force of three cruisers and seven destroyers also assembled in the Inland Sea under Vice Admiral Kiyohide Shima. It was to rendezvous with the Third Section of Kurita's Center Force under Vice Admiral Shoji Nishimura and then transit Surigao Strait, to the south of the Leyte beachhead. Together, they would engage any elements protecting these southern approaches and distract attention from Kurita's operations. Shima and Nishimura were each generally aware of the other's participation, but true coordination was sorely lacking. The Americans would call these combined operations the Southern Force.

But what of the Americans? Halsey's Third Fleet was roaming far and wide, charged with destroying the Japanese fleet if an opportunity to do so presented itself. It was secondarily responsible for suppressing major offensive threats to the beachhead by its far-flung aerial strikes against both land bases on Luzon and any approaching sea targets. What the Third Fleet was not charged with doing, Halsey pointedly maintained, was protecting the Seventh Fleet. This was "MacArthur's Navy," under the command of Vice Admiral Thomas Kinkaid and responsible to MacArthur, whereas Halsey was answerable to Nimitz. Kinkaid's orders were to protect the mass of assembled ships off the Leyte beachhead, which were also under his command, and — via smaller escort carriers — provide both close-in air support for operations ashore and combat air patrols over the ships off the beachhead.

Compared to American forces at Pearl Harbor, both of these fleets were massive. Given its offensive role, the Third Fleet definitely boasted the cream of the crop. Its combatant ships, essentially the fast carriers with battleship and cruiser support, were concentrated in Task Force 38. This was divided into four task groups numbered Task Group 38.1 through Task Group 38.4. In all, there were the veteran carrier *Enterprise,* seven new *Essex*-class carriers, eight light carriers, the new battleships *Iowa* and *New Jersey,* four older battleships, six heavy cruisers, nine light cruisers, and fifty-eight destroyers.

Given its largely defensive and supporting role, the Seventh Fleet was assigned older and slower ships, but that did not mean it lacked firepower. Kinkaid's battle line was under the command of Rear Admiral Jesse Oldendorf and included six battleships (five of them Pearl Harbor survivors), three heavy cruisers, five light cruisers, twenty-six destroyers, and about forty hard-stinging PT boats. Additionally, Kinkaid's forces included three groups of escort carriers (CVEs), totaling sixteen in all, with ten destroyers and eleven destroyer escorts.[25]

On October 20, 1944, MacArthur's forces landed on Leyte, and for a time all operations progressed smoothly. Then, early on October 22, two American submarines patrolling the western approaches to the Philippines, *Darter* and *Dace,* detected elements of Kurita's Center Force and reported the first indications that a massive Japanese naval movement was afoot. The subs lost contact during the day but reestablished it again that night and worked into a firing position. *Dace* was credited with sinking the heavy cruiser *Maya.* *Darter* damaged the heavy cruiser *Takao* and sank the heavy cruiser *Atago,* which by luck happened to be Kurita's flagship. Kurita transferred his flag to the battleship *Yamato* and pushed eastward, well aware that the Americans now knew he was coming and with at least some shock that he had already had one ship blown from beneath him.

Reports of these attacks reached Halsey on the *New Jersey* shortly before dawn on the morning of October 23, and he ordered his task groups to refuel and prepare for extensive air operations against Kurita's force as it entered the Sibuyan Sea in the heart of the Philippine archipelago. Given the hectic pace of the past two months, however, Halsey had begun to rotate his groups eastward to Ulithi for provisioning and rearming, and whatever brief recreation might be had on the atoll. This meant that even as Task Force 38 prepared to engage Kurita, Task Group 38.1, with more than a quarter of the task force's strength, was sailing away from the battle.

Task Group 38.1 was under the command of Vice Admiral John S. "Slew" McCain. While the four task groups were nominally of equal weight, McCain's was certainly the strongest, having five of the sixteen carriers and six of the fifteen assorted cruisers, albeit no battleships. The next day, when the magnitude of the Japanese assault was apparent, Halsey ordered McCain and Task Group 38.1 to come about, refuel at sea, and return to Philippine waters, but such a maneuver would take precious time.

Early on the morning of October 24, carrier planes from the remaining three task groups — Task Group 38.2 under Rear Admiral Gerald Bogan, Task Group 38.3 under Rear Admiral Frederick Sherman, and Task Group 38.4 under Rear Admiral Ralph Davison — searched for Kurita's Center Force. Planes from Bogan's group off San Bernardino Strait sighted it first, along with the immense *Yamato*. Aircraft from Davison's group, operating to the south, also soon located Shima and Nishimura's converging Southern Force.

When Halsey learned of Kurita's whereabouts, he urgently signaled all three task groups, "Strike — Repeat — Strike." He ordered both Sherman's group to the north and Davison's group to the south to converge with Bogan's middle group and hammer away at Kurita. Despite the appearance of the Japanese forces headed for Surigao Strait, Halsey elected, in the words of his battle report, "to shift target to the Center Force on the assumption that SEVENTH fleet forces could take care of the smaller Southern Force."[26]

Without air cover, Kurita's ships were highly vulnerable. One wonders what the Japanese were thinking, what lessons of the new age in naval warfare they had overlooked. This was not Tsushima. Even if the Imperial Japanese Navy's remaining carriers had been dispatched with the Northern Force as decoys, there was no reason why land-based aircraft on Luzon couldn't have performed the covering role—none except for a decided lack of communication between the navy and the army controlling those planes *and* a rather dubious Japanese decision to use their remaining aircraft to target American ships rather than defend their own.

When the day was over, the super-battleship *Musashi* had been sunk, with a loss of eleven hundred men—half its complement—and Kurita, particularly discouraged by the lack of air cover, had reversed course and was reported to be steaming away from Leyte. But Sherman's Task Group 38.3, the northernmost of the three groups on station, had also taken some losses. It had been attacked by land-based planes from Luzon, as well as the remnants of Ozawa's carrier-based planes. Sherman's planes fought off the attackers extremely well, but one lone bomber managed to break through the combat air patrol and hit the light carrier *Princeton,* starting an inferno that soon engulfed the ship.

To Halsey, the loss of the *Princeton* was evidence that the Japanese still packed a punch, but at least he now knew that Ozawa's carriers were close. Prior to hearing that Kurita's force had turned around, Halsey issued a battle plan that four battleships (including his own *New Jersey*), two heavy cruisers, and assorted light cruisers and destroyers would be culled from the three task groups and formed as Task Force 34 to block Kurita's exit from San Bernardino Strait. Kinkaid directed Oldendorf to do much the same thing with his battle line at the exit to Surigao Strait. The difference between Halsey and Kinkaid was that whereas Kinkaid executed his order and Oldendorf steamed into position, Halsey's message was only a plan to be executed upon his command, which was never given. He specifically clarified this two hours later with a follow-up radio message: "If the enemy sorties [through San Bernardino], TF 34 will be formed *when directed by me* [emphasis in original]."[27]

As evening fell on that day of massive air strikes, Halsey faced a command decision that only he could make. To his mind, he had three alternatives. First, he could divide his forces, "leaving TF 34 to block San Bernardino Straits while the carriers with light screens attacked the Northern Force." This option he rejected, largely because he did not know the full complement of the Northern Force and might need his battleships as well as his full carrier strength. (If Task Force 34 was indeed to be formed, it would need several carriers for its own air cover unless it was to suffer Kurita's naked fate. With McCain's Task Group 38.1 out of reach, Halsey feared he might not in fact have overwhelming superiority.)

Second, Halsey could sit off the eastern end of San Bernardino Strait with his combined force and wait for whichever Japanese force might appear — Kurita through San Bernardino Strait should he try again, or Ozawa from the north. This, too, Halsey rejected, as it gave Ozawa far too much initiative to operate "unmolested" and might well mean the eventual escape of the Japanese carriers. Halsey did not even hint at it in his after-action report, but one senses that what he left unsaid was that this alternative smacked too much of Spruance's actions at the Battle of the Philippine Sea. They had proved prudent and — thanks to American pilots — decisive in crippling Japan's air arm, but sitting and waiting to be attacked was hardly Halsey's style.

Finally, there was the option of striking north against Ozawa's carriers with all his combined strength. This would leave San Bernardino Strait unguarded, but at the moment it appeared that Kurita's Center Force was retreating west. Based on pilot reports — perhaps overly optimistic reports, as tended to be made on both sides — Halsey concluded that the fighting power of Kurita's Center Force had been "too seriously impaired to win a decision." In truth, it had been battered, but only the *Musashi* had been sunk by aircraft. Thus, Halsey became convinced that this option "would contribute most to the over-all Philippines campaign even if a temporarily tight situation existed at Leyte."[28]

Halsey turned to Mick Carney, his chief of staff in the flag plot of the *New Jersey*, jabbed a finger at the Northern Force's charted position some three hundred miles away, and made his decision. "Here's where we're going. Mick, start them north." With that, the admiral, who along with most of his flag staff had been fighting a flu bug, went to bed for a few hours of sleep. The record is not entirely clear if he did so before or after a lone search plane flashed the news from high above the Sibuyan Sea that Kurita's Center Force had turned around and was once again bearing down on San Bernardino Strait.[29]

Aboard the carrier *Lexington* in Task Group 38.3, Vice Admiral Marc Mitscher, the Task Force 38 commander, was somewhat surprised that he was not asked for his opinion before Halsey's decision to run north. Mitscher, too, wanted to strike the Japanese carriers, but with a smaller, more nimble force. Done quickly, it might well trounce the carriers and be back off Leyte in time to help pin Kurita's force outside San Bernardino Strait—if it came through, which now again seemed quite plausible.

Mitscher's chief of staff, Captain Arleigh Burke, was concerned that Ozawa's carriers might be decoys, particularly now that he had the information about Kurita's renewed advance. But Mitscher appeared reluctant to press the matter with Halsey. "Admiral Halsey is in command now," Mitscher told his staff with some sign of resignation. Burke pressed the issue with Mitscher but didn't get very far. "I think you're right," Mitscher told Burke, "but I don't know you're right [and] I don't think we ought to bother Admiral Halsey."[30]

Halsey would assume that Kinkaid's air reconnaissance was doing the job, and Kinkaid would assume that the entire battle line of phantom Task Force 34 was in place there. But why Halsey did not leave so much as a picket destroyer or a submarine to monitor the eastern end of the strait—or at least request Kinkaid to do so with one of his units—has never been satisfactorily answered.

Meanwhile, Shima and Nishimura's twin forces were converging on Surigao Strait, and there appeared to be a great reluctance on the part of the two commanders to coordinate their operations. Shima, coming south from Japan, was the ranking officer, but Nishimura was older, had more battle experience, and, as a subordinate of

Kurita's Center Force, may have felt the need to rush ahead to maintain his time schedule as the southern pincer of Kurita's move against Leyte. And that is just what he did. Shima's force of two heavy cruisers, a light cruiser, and four destroyers may not have made much of a difference against Oldendorf's slow but steady battle array, but Nishimura attempted to force the strait alone.

Oldendorf's tactics at the Battle of Surigao Strait were superb. Not only did he succeed in routing the advancing Southern Force, but he did so in a night engagement with classic tactics of the age of battleships, parading his Pearl Harbor survivors back and forth and crossing the enemy's T after his cruisers and destroyers had harried its flanks. The Japanese had sought another Tsushima, but Oldendorf won one for the Americans.

Nishimura went down with his flagship, the battleship *Yamashiro*. The battleship *Fuso* and the cruiser *Mogami* also sank. By the time Shima's force entered the strait and fought its way past American PT boats, the remnants of Nishimura's force were fleeing toward him. Shima turned his force around and sailed west. The threat to the Leyte beachhead from Surigao Strait was over. Jesse Oldendorf's day, however, was not.

At 7:28 on the morning of October 25, Oldendorf received a "well done" dispatch from Kinkaid. But before he could even savor a cup of coffee, he was handed a second dispatch from Kinkaid that bespoke a terrible new urgency. Kurita's force had indeed exited San Bernardino Strait and was firing on the northern group of escort carriers off Samar Island. "With his fuel dangerously low, his torpedoes almost exhausted, and his ammunition near the vanishing point," Oldendorf put his battle line on course for Leyte Gulf to lend what assistance he could.[31]

As the Battle of Surigao Strait was winding down, Kinkaid had gotten nervous about San Bernardino Strait. His operations officer spoke the obvious: "We've never asked Halsey directly if Task Force 34 is guarding the San Bernardino Strait." No, Kinkaid agreed, they hadn't, and he directed that a message be sent asking, "Is TF 34 guarding San Bernardino Strait." The query went out at 4:12 a.m. on

October 25, but given the frequently circuitous radio communications—particularly between fleets—Halsey did not receive it until 6:48 a.m., a full two and a half hours later. Preoccupied with operations up north, Halsey shot back, "Negative. Task Force Thirty Four is with carrier groups now engaging enemy carrier force."[32]

But Kinkaid wasn't the only one wondering about the location of Task Force 34. In Pearl Harbor and in Washington, Nimitz and King had been monitoring radio traffic routinely copied to them for information purposes. Just as Kinkaid had done, Nimitz grew nervous about San Bernardino Strait, but questioning Halsey about it was a dicey matter. Like King, Nimitz didn't question his commanders in the field, and he was reluctant to press Halsey on the matter now. Finally, however, one of Nimitz's aides suggested that Nimitz send the most basic of queries and simply ask, Where is task force 34? Nimitz thought for a moment and concurred.

All such radio traffic was routinely buffered by nonsense phrases inserted by operators and intended to confuse Japanese code breakers. Receiving operators routinely stripped out the same so that command recipients saw only the pertinent information. A double consonant separated the real message from the gibberish that was supposed to have absolutely nothing to do with the former. There could be no chance of confusion. But confusion was about to occur in spades.

The operator encoding Nimitz's query added the buffering gibberish "Turkey trots to water" before the question "Where is Task Force 34?" and then closed with additional gibberish—or at least it was supposed to be such. The message Halsey received on the *New Jersey* read, "Where is Task Force 34? The world wonders."[33]

Inexplicably, the sending operator in Pearl Harbor had added buffering at the end of the message that could be confused with the message itself. And it was. Later, much would be made of the fact that October 25 was the ninetieth anniversary of the Crimean War's Battle of Balaklava, immortalized by Alfred, Lord Tennyson's "Charge of the Light Brigade." Twice the poem critically asserts, "All the world wonder'd" at such a military blunder. The young ensign who encoded the message later claimed that "The world wonders" buffer was "just something that popped into my head."[34] But every man of Halsey's generation knew well the reference, and the damage had been done.

Halsey reread the message in his flag plot on the *New Jersey* and jumped to the immediate conclusion that not only was Nimitz questioning his tactical deployments but also he was mocking the same to the world. By his own recollection, Halsey was "as stunned as if I had been struck in the face." He snatched off his cap, "threw it on the deck and shouted something" he was ashamed to remember. Only Mick Carney's quick intervention seems to have stopped a full-blown tirade.[35]

A good deal of the tension came from the fact that Kinkaid, having discovered the exit from San Bernardino Strait was indeed unguarded and Kurita's main Center Force was steaming through to engage his escort carriers off Samar Island, had just implored Halsey that his situation was critical. Only fast battleships and air strikes, Kinkaid radioed Halsey, could prevent Kurita from destroying the CVEs and entering Leyte Gulf.[36]

Halsey had already radioed McCain in TF 38.1 to expedite his return to the Leyte vicinity and launch air attacks when within range of Kurita's forces. But that might not be enough. For about an hour, Halsey stewed about his own course of action with the remainder of Task Force 38, including the battleships and cruisers that were to have formed the phantom Task Force 34.

To the north of Halsey's onrushing ships, four of Ozawa's carriers and their escorts of the Japanese Northern Force had come under attack from Mitscher's carrier planes, and in less than two hours they would be within range of the 16-inch guns of the *Iowa* and *New Jersey*. It had all the makings of the great sea battle between fleets that both sides had long anticipated. But it was also clear that the main Japanese battleships were with Kurita outside San Bernardino Strait and that if TF 34 had formed a battle line there as Oldendorf had done off Surigao Strait, a similar battleship encounter would have occurred.

At 11:15 a.m. on October 25, Halsey reluctantly gave the order to his selected battleships to form Task Force 34 and join with the carriers of Bogan's TF 38.2 to turn 180 degrees and race south to support the efforts of Kinkaid's escort carriers off Samar Island. Mitscher, with TF 38.3 and 38.4, was to continue north and use his airpower to finish off the Japanese carriers of Ozawa's force—all of them now mostly without aircraft.

Halsey told Kinkaid not to expect his arrival until 8:00 a.m. the next day, but even when Halsey charged ahead with *Iowa* and *New Jersey* at nearly 30 knots and arrived seven hours before that, he was too late. Determined resistance and heroic sacrifice by the American CVEs and their escorts had led to a cautionary withdrawal by Admiral Kurita just when full speed ahead might have been called for. The escort carriers *Gambier Bay* and *St. Lo* were lost, along with the destroyers *Johnston* and *Hoel* and destroyer escort *Samuel B. Roberts,* which made valiant covering torpedo attacks, but the remainder of Kinkaid's Seventh Fleet and the Leyte beachhead were safe.[37]

After the war, Kurita explained that "lack of expected land-based air support and air reconnaissance, fear of further losses from air attack, and worry as to his fuel reserves induced him to withdraw." His American interviewers concluded, "As a result of this decision to retire, the Japanese failed to secure the objective for which catastrophic losses had been risked and suffered by the other two Japanese forces."[38]

The bulk of Kurita's Center Force, including the battleship *Yamato,* slipped back through San Bernardino Strait before Halsey could arrive. The planes of Bogan's TF 38.2 and McCain's oncoming TF 38.1 hounded their westward voyage the next day, but once again there was to be no battleship-against-battleship encounter.

If the Battle of the Philippine Sea had been a major American victory with some controversy, the Battle of Leyte Gulf proved more so on both counts. It was indeed a major American victory, perhaps the greatest ever fought by the United States Navy. From the first torpedo attacks by *Darter* and *Dace* to Mitscher's attacks against the Northern Force carriers—what would be called the Battle of Cape Engaño—and Oldendorf's deft battle line at Surigao Strait, Japanese losses totaled twenty-six combatant ships: three battleships, one large carrier, three light carriers, six heavy cruisers, four light cruisers, and nine destroyers—a staggering 305,710 tons. Against this, the Americans lost one light carrier (*Princeton*), two escort carriers, two destroyers, and one destroyer escort, a total of 36,600 tons.[39]

By any measure, it was a victory that reduced the Japanese navy to home-water operations by survivors such as the *Yamato* and increasingly desperate kamikaze strikes. But could Halsey have accomplished even more? The criticism of Spruance's tentativeness off Saipan was nothing compared to the controversy that now descended on Bill Halsey. Against the steadied calm of Oldendorf at Surigao and the finesse of Mitscher's carrier operations, Halsey was seen to be racing first north and then south without directly engaging the enemy.

Halsey's immediate reaction and his enduring belief were to declare a massive victory and move on. Publicly, Nimitz and King did the same. Roosevelt even rushed the news of the victory to the press before all the details were known—no doubt wanting to announce so sweeping a result *before* the November 7 presidential election, but also because MacArthur, in typical fashion, had jumped ahead with his own premature press release of victory and forced the navy's hand.

Privately, it was a different story. On the evening of October 25, even as he raced back south in the *New Jersey,* Halsey sent Nimitz, MacArthur, Kinkaid, and King a top secret message justifying his actions. When searches by carrier planes located the Northern Force, it completed the picture of all enemy naval forces, Halsey maintained, and "to statically guard San Bernadino Straits until enemy surface and carrier air attacks could be coordinated would have been childish." Halsey stressed his belief that the Center Force "had been so badly damaged" in the Sibuyan Sea that it could no longer be considered a serious menace to the Seventh Fleet. In proof of that, Halsey offered up Oldendorf's victory at Surigao, neatly forgetting that it had been against only the *southern* prong of the triple Japanese attack.[40]

Three days later, Nimitz passed his own thoughts on to King in a letter marked both "Personal" and "Top Secret." He was "greatly pleased" with the fleet operations of the past week, Nimitz told

King, with two exceptions. The first was the use of the cruiser *Birmingham,* instead of a destroyer, to come alongside the burning carrier *Princeton.* A huge explosion aft on the carrier's flight deck had decimated the upper decks of the *Birmingham.* Then there was the matter of Task Force 38. "It never occurred to me," Nimitz told King, "that Halsey, knowing the composition of the ships in the Sibuyan Sea, would leave San Bernardino Strait unguarded, even though the Jap detachments in the Sibuyan Sea had been reported seriously damaged. That Halsey feels that he is in a defensive position is indicated in his top secret dispatch 251317 [quoted above]."[41]

But Nimitz was very careful not to criticize Halsey in any way or to allow even a hint of controversy to enter the official records. He well remembered the uproar during his days at Annapolis over the actions of Sampson and Schley at the Battle of Santiago during the Spanish-American War, and he wasn't about to condone even a whisper of criticism tarnishing such a stunning victory. Such criticism would come, of course, and be fought by Halsey for the rest of his life, but it would come from historians and armchair observers, not from Halsey's direct superiors.

When the initial draft of CINCPAC's battle report sharply questioned Halsey's tactics, Nimitz sent the draft back to its author with this note: "What are you trying to do, [Captain Ralph] Parker, start another Sampson-Schley controversy? Tone this down. I'll leave it to you."[42]

King said very little about the entire Leyte affair in his memoirs, other than to question why Kinkaid had not done a better job on his own of air reconnaissance of the Center Force. By then, he and Halsey were once again exchanging "Dear Bill" and "Dear Ernie" letters, passing on war cartoons of themselves that the other might not have seen.[43]

But when Halsey and King first met after the battle the following January, Halsey's opening words to King were, "I made a mistake in that battle."

King didn't want to hear it. He held up his hand and said, "You don't have to tell me anymore. You've got a green light on everything you did."

In Halsey's mind, however, his mistake was not in leaving San Bernardino Strait unguarded, but in turning Task Force 38 around just before it could engage the Japanese carrier forces in a surface action—"my golden opportunity," Halsey had termed it in his October 25 message.

"No. It wasn't a mistake," concluded King. "You couldn't have done otherwise."[44]

But at the time, King was as anxious as Nimitz to know about Halsey's dispositions off San Bernardino Strait. COMINCH monitored the radio traffic that proposed forming Task Force 34, noted that an "Execute" had never been heard, but assumed that "one had been sent by a means we were not covering and we turned in that night feeling secure about a guard on San Bernardino Strait." When King's staff intercepted Nimitz's "Where is…" query, they were "as amazed as Nimitz the next morning to find this was not so."[45]

So, too, was Douglas MacArthur, who ranted and raved throughout the uncertainty of the CVE battle off Samar that Halsey had failed "to execute his mission of covering the Leyte operations" and "should be relieved" because MacArthur no longer had confidence in him.[46] But in public, with both his Leyte beachhead and a major naval victory secure, MacArthur closed ranks just as the navy had done and heaped praise on Halsey. That did not stop some of MacArthur's staff from criticizing Halsey's actions, until one evening at dinner MacArthur himself pounded his fist on the table. "That's enough," the general commanded. "Leave the Bull alone. He's still a fighting admiral in my book."[47] MacArthur, loyal to a fault, was standing by one who had stood by him.

Nimitz faced his own dinnertime criticism of the Leyte command decisions, and it came from an impertinent source. During a cocktail hour discussion of the battle with his senior staff the day after Halsey's sprint back to San Bernardino Strait, a young lieutenant commander who had been invited as a guest expressed surprise that Nimitz had not queried the location—or even the existence— of Task Force 34 much earlier.

Later, when the discussion turned to Nimitz's operational orders to take every opportunity to engage and destroy the enemy fleet, the same lieutenant commander asserted that Nimitz had practically given Halsey "carte blanche to abandon the beachhead." The room fell silent as Nimitz turned a steely gaze on this outspoken young officer, who went by the name of Chester W. Nimitz, Jr. He told his son, "That's your opinion" — ending the discussion.[48]

In the end, it was King who said of Halsey and his luck, "I should not say it but it is true. Halsey made two mistakes; not the great battle; what I had against him were the two typhoons."[49]

CHAPTER TWENTY-TWO

Two Typhoons and Five Stars

If countries reflexively prepare to fight the last war, can commanders help but be influenced by the latest battle? Bill Halsey's buddy Raymond Spruance had done his strategic duty in defending the amphibious landings on Saipan and in the process had still put his planes in a position to render the bulk of Japanese naval aviation — save for those who would turn to kamikaze attacks — largely impotent. But according to some critics, Spruance had missed a chance to destroy the main Japanese fleet.

The next opportunity for destroying the Japanese fleet — even carriers whose decimated air wings rendered them largely decoys — had proved irresistible to Halsey, a dogged fighter who had missed the earlier clashes at Coral Sea and Midway. Even Halsey's most vehement critics can understand his rationale for his actions at Leyte. Far less understandable are Halsey's actions in not one but two crippling typhoons in the weeks and months that followed.

After the Battle of Leyte Gulf, Halsey's Third Fleet was called upon to provide continuing air support for MacArthur, as his "I have returned" pronouncement for a time appeared a little premature. Leyte land operations bogged down in a sea of mud and miserable monsoon-weather flying conditions. Japanese land-based aircraft on Luzon, lying to the west in a protected rain shadow, took advantage of this and repeatedly challenged American control of the air above the eastern Philippines. A major part of this effort was led by the first concerted kamikaze attacks, which momentarily upset the fighting punch of Halsey's carriers, as well as those transports and supply ships that the Japanese targeted off the beachhead.

Just as the Japanese navy had determined the defense of the Philippines to be a do-or-die effort, the Japanese army made a similar effort. In fact, it had managed to land two thousand reinforcements on Leyte even as the sea battles raged around it. Because many of Kinkaid's CVEs were exhausted and short of aircraft after the Leyte Gulf fight, MacArthur requested Halsey to stay on station around the Philippines with the big carriers of the Third Fleet for another month instead of raiding Tokyo. Nimitz concurred and directed Halsey to do so. Meanwhile, Nimitz's old shipmate from the gunboat *Panay,* "Slew" McCain, replaced Marc Mitscher as the commander of Task Force 38 under Halsey.

Operating in concert around the Philippine archipelago, McCain's carrier planes and submarines took a toll on Japanese transports and shipping to the islands, and by early December a quarter of a million American troops on Leyte had succeeded in getting the upper hand. But kamikaze raids continued to batter Halsey's fleet. One carrier after another sustained heavy battle damage.

McCain had enough aircraft to initiate what came to be called the big blue blanket. It gave air cover to the big blue fleet by monitoring every Japanese airfield within range and attacking the enemy's aircraft as they took off. There were also innovations in recognition signals. Returning American aircraft did a slow flyby of picket destroyers to keep kamikazes from slipping into the landing pattern and then plunging onto a flight deck. Finally, the Third Fleet retired eastward to the anchorage at Ulithi for a well-deserved two-week rest and resupply.

Halsey and his staff used the interval to plan their next set of operations. Their first priority was to return to the Philippines and support MacArthur's planned invasion of Mindoro on December 15. Even as they did so, Halsey was anxious to strike westward and take operations into the South China Sea. On December 17, with commitments to MacArthur to strike Luzon on December 19, 20, and 21, Task Force 38 steamed for a refueling rendezvous some three hundred miles east of the Philippines.

As the refueling of destroyers from the larger ships started while en route, Commander George F. Kosco, Halsey's chief aerologist, fretted over a series of weather warnings that were both vague and at least twelve hours old. Somewhere in their part of the wide Pacific, a tropical storm was gathering strength. That noon, as Halsey joined his staff for lunch aboard the *New Jersey,* he got a close-up glimpse of what lay ahead.

The destroyer *Spence* came alongside the big battleship's starboard side to take on fuel. This was in the lee of the battleship and should have made for easy maneuvering. But a fluky 20- to 30-knot wind was blowing across the running sea, and it proved difficult to hold the destroyer in position. Halsey watched from his flag mess as the *Spence* first dropped astern and then raced ahead, only to drop astern again, all the while pitching and rolling heavily. Suddenly, the *Spence* yawed sharply to starboard and then twisted back to port on a collision course with the *New Jersey.* Halsey reflexively ducked as the destroyer's superstructure came within feet of slamming into his flagship.[1]

Kosco quickly excused himself from lunch and went to the navigation bridge to analyze the latest weather information, while Halsey himself was soon swamped with numerous reports of similar fueling difficulties throughout the fleet. Well versed in at-sea refueling though they were — a far cry from Nimitz's early experiments during World War I aboard the *Maumee* — Halsey's sailors reported hoses snapping like bullwhips and the lighter destroyers bouncing wildly with all the control of fishing bobbers.

Finally, Halsey ordered refueling attempts to cease and set a new rendezvous location with the services group for 6:00 a.m. the next day, one hundred and fifty miles to the northwest. These decisions

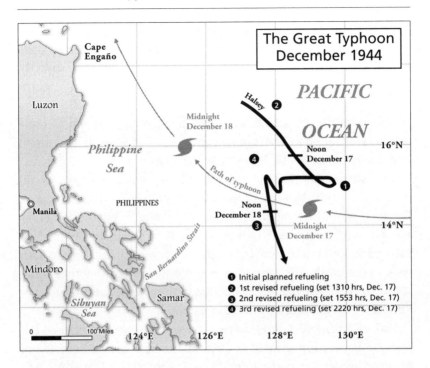

The Great Typhoon
December 1944

PACIFIC

OCEAN

1 Initial planned refueling
2 1st revised refueling (set 1310 hrs, Dec. 17)
3 2nd revised refueling (set 1553 hrs, Dec. 17)
4 3rd revised refueling (set 2220 hrs, Dec. 17)

were made in large part on Kosco's best guess that the storm was 450 miles to the southeast and would track north to northeast and clear the fleet to the east. Actually, it was only about 120 miles from Halsey's position, and far from veering northward, it was doggedly following the fleet northwest on this new course.

Halsey's commanders followed his orders, but not all did so without questioning his sense of the weather. Captain Jasper T. Acuff, commanding the services group of oilers and support ships, conferred with the captains of two escort carriers in his group, and all three concluded that the 6:00 a.m. rendezvous would be smack in the path of what increasingly appeared to be a building typhoon. On board the new *Essex*-class carrier *Lexington,* Rear Admiral Gerald Bogan, commander of Task Group 38.2, was certain, based on his own aerologist's report, that a typhoon was forming and moving in a northwesterly direction with the fleet.[2]

For some reason — probably because these subordinates assumed that Halsey had both sea sense and weather information superior to theirs—these analyses were not passed on to Kosco or the admiral himself. Instead, Halsey conferred with Kosco and, as winds continued to build, picked a second revised refueling location directly to the west. But instead of diverging at a wider angle from a storm track running north or northeast, this course took the fleet on a course generally parallel to the oncoming storm. Bogan finally radioed his frustration to McCain, the task force commander, and urged that the best chance of escape lay to the south.

As it turned out, this second revised rendezvous location would have been better than the third location that Halsey picked late on the evening of December 17. Evidently concerned about his commitments to MacArthur to launch air raids on December 19, Halsey set course for another revised rendezvous at 7:00 a.m. on the 18th back to the north. He apparently ignored Kosco's advice that doing so might bring the fleet right into the path of what Kosco was convinced was becoming a powerful typhoon.[3]

Halsey asked McCain's advice as to the storm's location, but McCain merely replied that he thought the fleet should not attempt to refuel under the current conditions. Aboard the key command ships, everyone seemed to have a different opinion as to where the center of the storm was located. By 5:00 a.m. on December 18, it was in fact about ninety miles east-southeast of the *New Jersey.*

Halsey finally ordered a course change to 180 degrees due south, but the delay running north had kept the fleet in the crosshairs of the advancing storm. By 8:00 a.m., McCain, with Halsey's concurrence, ordered a momentary jog back to the northeast in yet another attempt to refuel the destroyers before turning south again, but this lapse only had the effect of holding the fleet in the storm's path.[4]

By the time McCain changed course to 220 degrees and then finally ordered the ships to steam at will, the battleships and large carriers had been battered, but the smaller destroyers and services ships had suffered a frightful toll. "No one who has not been through a typhoon can conceive its fury," Halsey later recalled. "The 70-foot seas smash you from all sides. At broad noon I couldn't see the bow of my ship, 350 feet from the bridge. What it was like on a destroyer one-twentieth the *New Jersey*'s size, I can only imagine."[5]

But Halsey certainly had a very good idea. He was first and foremost a destroyer man. If he was being tossed about on the mass of the *New Jersey,* he had to know what hellish conditions his destroyers and destroyer escorts were facing, not to mention the pitching decks of his smaller escort carriers. Where was the innate seamanship that Halsey had exhibited so often throughout his career? Where was that intuitiveness that had caused him to bring the destroyer *Jarvis* to a halt in a dense fog off the coast of Long Island in 1914?

If other experienced commanders in his fleet had qualms about the weather, why did Halsey vacillate on a course to clear the storm? Even if he was getting conflicting estimates of its track, the general consensus was that a decided run south on the afternoon of December 17, rather than repeatedly trying to turn back north, would have avoided much of the catastrophe.

The answer seems to be Halsey's determination to keep his commitment to support MacArthur — a commitment he may have been feeling particularly sharply in light of criticism that he had forsaken the Leyte beachhead just six weeks before. "Have been unable to dodge storm which so far has prevented refueling," Halsey signaled MacArthur, as he was unable to strike the intended targets. A few minutes later, Halsey reported to Nimitz, "Baffling storm pursues us."[6] But no matter the reason, there seems in hindsight little rationale to subject a fleet to such a pounding.

Three destroyers, including the *Spence,* capsized, with the loss of most of their crews. The *Independence*-class light carriers *Cowpens* and *San Jacinto* suffered minor damage, but their sister, *Monterey,* was almost lost when loose aircraft on the hangar deck ignited a horrible inferno. A thirty-one-year-old lieutenant from Grand Rapids, Michigan, named Gerald R. Ford was among those who led the charge to save the ship. The total toll for the Third Fleet was 790 officers and men dead and 156 aircraft destroyed.

By midafternoon on the 18th, the typhoon's fury had passed, and a massive search-and-rescue operation was launched. From the *Spence*'s complement of 336 men, only 24 were pulled from the water. Meanwhile, Halsey stubbornly tried to keep his commitment to MacArthur, and on the 20th he steamed westward toward Luzon.

Heavy seas on the 21st and a large measure of damage and confusion prompted a cancellation. The fleet came about and headed back to Ulithi to regroup and repair.

Early on the morning of December 24, Halsey's battered fleet moved into the protected anchorage at Ulithi, and within a few hours a plane carrying Chester Nimitz touched down in the broad lagoon. Nimitz brought along a Christmas tree and holiday greetings to Halsey and his staff, but once the public pleasantries were over, he sat down with Halsey on Christmas Day and ordered a court of inquiry into the loss of the three destroyers and general damage to the fleet. Save for a few encounters such as at Savo Island, it was a far greater calamity than anything that had befallen the American navy since Pearl Harbor. If this court of inquiry so determined, full-blown courts-martial might later be convened against those found wanting in the discharge of their duties—including, quite possibly, Halsey himself.

The court of inquiry called the principal participants, including Halsey, McCain, Bogan, and Kosco. Halsey wasted no time blaming the weather warning system in the Pacific, at one point calling it "nonexistent." But when asked just two questions later on what basis he had testified that the storm was curving to the northeast, Halsey gave a long answer clearly indicating that some weather information had been available. Even so, when asked if he had had a "timely warning" of the storm, he maintained that he had had "no warning." Pacific weather information was indeed somewhat hit-or-miss, but Halsey's effort to cast blame elsewhere flew in the face of testimony from Bogan and others that local conditions certainly indicated an approaching storm and apparent track.[7]

It also flew in the face of Halsey's own testimony. When asked to compare the conditions on December 17, when the *Spence* encountered its refueling problems alongside *New Jersey,* with those on the morning of the 18th, Halsey replied, "On the morning of the 17th I was under the impression that we were on the fringes of a disturbance. On that morning of the 18th there was no doubt in my mind that we were approaching a storm of major proportions and that it was almost too late to do anything."[8]

And he did nothing. For a period of nineteen hours, Halsey failed to issue a fleet-wide advisory that the storm center was much closer than initially plotted. Focusing on this, the court of inquiry found Halsey "at fault in not broadcasting definite danger warnings to all vessels early morning of December 18 in order that preparations might be made as practicable and that inexperienced commanding officers might have sooner realized the seriousness of their situations."[9]

Ultimately, the court held Halsey accountable for "mistakes, errors and faults," but then backpedaled and classified such as "errors in judgment under stress of war operations and not as offenses." The court then went on to recommend impressing on all commanders the adverse weather likely to be found in the Western Pacific and urged the navy to upgrade its weather operations with special weather ships and increased reconnaissance planes staffed by qualified weather observers.[10]

Nimitz approved the court's opinion, but in his endorsement he got Halsey off the hook a bit further. Noting that the court was of the "firm opinion that no question of negligence is involved," Nimitz affirmed that not only were Halsey's errors in judgment "committed under stress of war operations," but also that they stemmed "from a commendable desire to meet military commitments"— supporting MacArthur.[11]

When Nimitz allowed himself some measure of criticism, it was limited to a general indictment of the reliance on new technologies over raw seamanship in a memo titled "Damage of Typhoon, Lessons of," which he sent to the entire Pacific Fleet. Perhaps remembering his own experience with a typhoon aboard the *Decatur* in his early years, Nimitz found general fault with captains and aerologists alike who placed too much reliance on radio reports and other outside sources for warnings of dangerous weather. It might well be necessary, Nimitz lectured the fleet, "for a revival of the age-old habits of self-reliance and caution in regard to the hazard from storms, and for officers in all echelons of command to take their personal responsibilities in this respect more seriously."[12] No one, of course, should have been more aware of that level of innate seamanship than Bill Halsey.

King concurred in Nimitz's opinion but softened its indictment of Halsey even more by adding "resulting from insufficient information" after "errors of judgment" and changing Nimitz's "commendable desire" to "firm determination."[13] It was too late in the war to jettison one of the navy's biggest heroes. Nimitz knew it, King knew it, and doubtless Leahy and FDR knew it. But on a gut level, perhaps Halsey, too, knew that he had been saved. In the end, Halsey, who was so loquacious about so many things, never mentioned the court of inquiry in his memoirs.

While Bill Halsey was battling Pacific typhoons, a whirlwind of a different sort was coming to a climax in Washington. For several years, there had been discussions about creating a five-star rank above that of the four stars of a full general in the army and a full admiral in the navy. King, in particular, was in the vanguard of those urging the new rank, while George Marshall, typically, was far more reticent about the matter.

Some of the reasons for the higher rank were indeed related to ego, but there were also practical issues. In dealing with the British chiefs of staff, the Americans always came up one star short against the five stars of a field marshal, air marshal, or admiral of the fleet. Aside from such tradition-bound circumstances as whose plane should land first or whose flag should be flown during joint exercises, there was the general perception that somehow members of the American military were not quite equal to their British counterparts, a perception that became even more important when a bevy of Russian field marshals was added to the mix.

But it is also true that on the American side, the ranks of general officers were swelling, and four stars was not the apex it had once been. In the navy, for example, there had been only four prewar slots authorized for four-star rank. At the time of Pearl Harbor, the CNO and the commanders in chief of the Pacific, Atlantic, and Asiatic Fleets wore these stars. (The four-star rank of the Asiatic Fleet commander was more a matter of parity with the other fleet commanders — American and otherwise — than a reflection of the size of the fleet.)

When the Asiatic Fleet was disbanded early in 1942, the four slots were filled by King as COMINCH, Nimitz as CINCPAC, Royal Ingersoll as commander in chief of the Atlantic Fleet, and Harold Stark, who managed to keep his rank when sent to London despite no longer being CNO. By that July, Roosevelt had accorded four stars to Leahy upon his return to active duty, and largely through the good graces of Congressman Carl Vinson, Halsey received four stars after his successful efforts in the Solomons. At the same time, Eisenhower was promoted to four-star rank in the army behind only Marshall and MacArthur.

King wasn't opposed to these promotions, but he wanted a formal policy of advancement and a clear path above four-star rank. King's own suggestions of the higher ranks of "Arch-Admiral" and "Arch-General" fell on deaf ears. Secretary of the Navy Knox, usually King's champion, agreed with King on "the idea of an increase of rank for you and Marshall" but thought "Arch-Admiral" sounded "too much like a church designation."[14]

Leahy claimed that Roosevelt first mentioned his promotion to five-star rank early in January 1944 by saying, "Bill, I'm going to promote you to a higher rank." Gracious Leahy expressed surprise and told FDR that "the other members of the Joint Chiefs of Staff who were working for him exactly as I was were entitled to the same reward as he proposed to give me."[15]

Considerable debate in Congress followed over nomenclature and the number of authorized slots. In the end, the British equivalents of "admiral of the fleet" and "field marshal" were also discarded for the more uniquely American "fleet admiral" and "general of the army." When Congress finally passed the legislation on December 14, 1944, it authorized four officers of five-star grade in the active rolls of each service at any one time. And, significantly, the legislation provided that the president's authority to make such appointments and the grades themselves would terminate six months after the cessation of the current hostilities.[16]

When these sets of five stars began to fall, it was no surprise that the first to receive them was Bill Leahy. In a military establishment where date of rank determines seniority within grades, there could be no question that Leahy was both FDR's and the country's ranking officer. His appointment was dated December 15, 1944, and the other recipients followed, one day after another.

With Leahy and the navy taking top billing, there was also no question — in Roosevelt's mind, at least — that George Marshall would become the first five-star general of the army. Whatever glories others had found on far-flung battlefields or nurtured in the public's perception of them, they all owed the organization and the resources that made their efforts possible to Marshall's leadership.

King's promotion to fleet admiral was dated December 17, 1944, making him third on the five-star list. For someone who had once worried about approaching retirement age before achieving his goal of CNO, it was the epitome of his expectations.

The fourth slot belonged to the army. Even though Dwight Eisenhower had skillfully led supreme Allied commands from Torch to Overlord and was arguably the principal implementer of Germany's defeat, there was another that Roosevelt felt compelled to put ahead of him. Douglas MacArthur could hardly argue with the choice of Marshall, but politics and public image dictated that he receive five-star rank ahead of his one-time "clerk." And whatever the realities of MacArthur's role in the Pacific, in the minds of a great many Americans, he personified the Pacific war effort. Chester Nimitz held much the same position on the navy's side and became the third fleet admiral on December 19. Eisenhower got his five stars the next day.

Roosevelt might well have stopped there with six — three fleet admirals and three generals of the army. But parity on the American Joint Chiefs, as well as with the British air marshal on the Combined Chiefs of Staff, encouraged the appointment of Army Air Forces Chief of Staff Henry H. "Hap" Arnold to the seventh set of five stars on December 21. (In 1949, with the department of the Air Force now separate from the army, Arnold would be honored as the only "general of the air force" and the only American to hold five-star rank in two military branches.)

Then FDR did pause. No one on the navy side *had* to be promoted to the fourth fleet admiral slot, but with four five-star generals of the army, the navy was not about to be left out. But who would be accorded the fourth set of five stars as a fleet admiral?

King, who rarely allowed himself to be put in an awkward position, seems to have been forced into just such an uncomfortable spot on this issue. James Forrestal, who had become secretary of the navy following Frank Knox's death, told King to make a recommendation. King was inclined to pick Raymond Spruance, the only officer in the navy who King felt was his intellectual superior and who had been steadfastly reliable from Midway to the Marianas.

But Congressman Carl Vinson, who as chairman of the Naval Affairs Committee in the House of Representatives since 1931 was the veritable godfather of the navy, remained Bill Halsey's champion. To slight Vinson in this regard might spell trouble for King, since he had lost his own protector in Frank Knox and would have a rocky relationship with Forrestal. Then there was Halsey's public persona. He had become "Bull" Halsey, the hard-hitting darling of the press who was seemingly immune from mistakes or too much scrutiny of his military decisions. His reputation had been built on the Marshalls and Wake Island raids of early 1942, when the country desperately needed a hero, and solidified by his gritty talks with war correspondents in the Solomons. Few ever mentioned that when Halsey assumed command of the Third Fleet from Spruance in August 1944, he had not had a sea command in two and a half years — since before Midway — and that the logistics of commanding the Third Fleet could not begin to compare to those of commanding the smaller task forces he had overseen in the earlier hit-and-run raids.

Bill Halsey's most vehement defense of his actions throughout — whether at Leyte Gulf or in the typhoon — was always that only the man on the spot could truly understand what led him to the decisions he made. Seventy years later, that remains a valid point, and the very fact that those seventy years have done little or nothing to dim Halsey's reputation in the popular press or among the general public shows how extraordinarily revered he was. Everyone needs heroes, and for the American people and the United States Navy in

World War II, Bill Halsey was the hero who personified the effort and the ultimate victory.[17]

This says something about men making their reputations on the battle line, even if the contributions of those in staff assignments frequently provide the battlers their opportunities—as Spruance readily acknowledged of Nimitz at Midway. Leahy, and to a lesser extent Nimitz, both eschewed the spotlight. Nimitz got more of it because he was more readily accessible to the press and his subordinates. Leahy is usually present in the photos of the major strategic conferences of World War II, but his role—which fit him perfectly—was to give advice and support to only one man, FDR.

King was never shy about promoting his talents, but despite his role as COMINCH, it was Nimitz and his principal deputies who got more press attention. And while King usually held the respect of even his critics, he was simply too aloof and lacked the likability and follow-you-anywhere personality that radiated from both Nimitz and Halsey. From Nimitz, it came from studied calm; Halsey's resulted more from his volcanic "hit 'em again harder" football mentality.

If Marshall and King had agreed on only one thing, it would have been that each of them had their public heroes to nurture and attempt to control: MacArthur for Marshall and Halsey for King. And in the end, it was this recognition of Halsey's place in the public consciousness that seems to have tipped King from Spruance to Halsey in recommending that fourth set of five stars. Halsey was too much of an institution in the American press to be denied.

Had Spruance been of a similar ilk as Halsey and sought the spotlight rather than shunned it, the result might have been different. As it was, Spruance passed off attempts to be called the hero of Midway by recognizing the staff he had inherited from Halsey and Frank Jack Fletcher's commanding role.

"It was a tough thing to decide who should be the fourth five-star admiral," King wrote to Spruance after the war. He had "hoped that the Congress would make a fifth five-star admiral."[18]

"The fourth five-star promotion went where it belonged when Bill Halsey got it," Spruance replied, "and I never had any illusions about Congress ever creating a fifth vacancy." Then, in a show of the genuine humility and decency that made Raymond Spruance the man he was, he told King, "I have always felt that I was most fortunate in being entrusted with the command of the operations that I had during the war, and their successful outcome was ample reward in itself."[19]

Heat-of-battle decisions at Leyte and the typhoon aside, it is difficult to argue that Bill Halsey didn't deserve the five stars of a fleet admiral, although with King's procrastination, he didn't receive them until December 11, 1945. But there is convincing evidence that of the remaining American admirals of World War II, Raymond A. Spruance was no less deserving of five stars than Halsey. Indeed, with the exception of Spruance, it is difficult to imagine another of their contemporaries on the same level as Leahy, King, Nimitz, and Halsey. In 1950, Congress resolved a similar dilemma in the army when it accorded Omar Bradley a fifth set of army five stars, in part for his postwar role. It could have done Spruance similar justice by making a similar provision for the navy.

As it was, Nimitz tried his best throughout the 1950s to get Carl Vinson to revisit the five-star issue for Spruance. "I appreciate more than I can tell you," Spruance wrote Nimitz in 1957, "what you said to Mr. Vinson about me — not that I have any idea that anything can or will be done in the matter at a time like this, but it is very gratifying to know how you feel. The good opinion of my fellow officers in the Navy means a great deal to me, and you and King are at the top of my list in that respect."[20]

And what of Spruance and Halsey, who had been prewar buddies in California? "So far as Bill Halsey and I are concerned," Spruance wrote Halsey's biographer nine years after Halsey's death, "I was always a great admirer of Bill, as we had served together prewar in destroyers; and I was most happy during World War II to go to sea again under his command."[21]

Before Bill Halsey received his five stars, however, there was to be one more controversy on his record. King was right. There was not one typhoon, but two.

After the court of inquiry into the December typhoon concluded, the Third Fleet sailed from Ulithi to conduct air raids against Formosa and the Ryukyu Islands in an effort to stifle the flow of reinforcements to the Philippines. A few days later, the fleet struck northern Luzon to pave the way for MacArthur's landings at Lingayen Gulf north of Manila. Once again, kamikaze attacks were the principal threat to the fleet until McCain was able to spread the big blue blanket even wider.

On the evening of January 6, 1945, Halsey led Task Force 38, the fighting core of the Third Fleet, through the Luzon Strait between the Philippines and Formosa and into the South China Sea — what had once been considered a veritable Japanese lake. Reports that the battleships *Ise* and *Hyuga,* which had retreated from the Cape Engaño action off Leyte largely intact, were lurking about again got Halsey's combative juices flowing. No battleships appeared to oppose him, but Third Fleet aircraft sank forty-four lesser ships and destroyed large numbers of Japanese aircraft that now would not find their way to reinforce the Philippines.

By January 25, Halsey and his ships were back in the safety of Ulithi Lagoon, and it was time for Halsey and McCain to rotate their commands to Spruance and Mitscher. Gruff guy that he could be, Halsey was also a sentimental sort, and he always had kind and affectionate words for his subordinates upon leaving a command. "I am so proud of you that no words can express my feelings," he told the Third Fleet. "We have driven the enemy off the sea and back to his inner defenses. Superlatively well done!"[22]

So as Halsey and McCain returned stateside for a little rest and relaxation and to plan future operations, the task of invading Okinawa, in the Ryukyus, fell to Spruance and Mitscher. First, there was the campaign against tiny Iwo Jima, a five-week ordeal to capture eight square miles of rock that cost the lives of almost seven thousand Americans. Once the U.S. flag was raised on Mount Suribachi and the rest of the island secured, Iwo Jima was used as an emergency landing base for B-29s bombing Japan and as a staging area for the next step to Okinawa. Those landings began on April 1.

Nimitz had planned to rotate commanders from Spruance and Mitscher back to Halsey and McCain at the end of the Okinawa campaign, but the island proved tough. The American Tenth Army spent six weeks in the spring of 1945 barely moving against Okinawa's devilish array of pillboxes and caves, while supporting navy ships offshore endured furious kamikaze attacks. Nimitz decided to rotate command at the end of May whether or not Okinawa was subdued.

This change occurred between Spruance and Halsey on May 27, 1945, and between Mitscher and McCain the following day. Once again designated Task Force 38, McCain's various task groups continued to pound Okinawa and provide air support over the island.

Then the weather began to sour. Early on the morning of June 4, with McCain aboard the carrier *Shangri-La* in tactical command of the task force, McCain recommended to Halsey on the battleship *Missouri* that due to an approaching storm, air operations should be canceled and the task force should momentarily retire eastward from the Okinawa area. Halsey agreed and ordered a course to the east-southeast at 110 degrees, even though McCain had recommended due east. Part of the problem would become that the oncoming storm had split in half, with one portion trailing away to the west but a greater concentration gathering strength to the south.

By 8:00 p.m., Task Force 38 consisted of Task Group 38.1, which had just completed refueling and was under the command of Rear Admiral J. J. "Jocko" Clark; Task Group 38.4, which had been with McCain and Halsey all along; and Services Squadron 6, the oilers, cargo ships, and escort carriers under the command of Rear Admiral Donald B. Beary. McCain, still in overall tactical command, wanted to keep moving east out of the path of the storm. But he consulted with Halsey, who ordered a U-turn to the northwest and settled on a course of 300 degrees — slightly north of due west.

"What the hell is Halsey doing," McCain asked his staff incredulously, "trying to intercept another typhoon?"[23] Later, with Halsey's concurrence, McCain brought the fleet to due north, but the tightly packed southern half of the storm still had the ships in its sights. Halsey and McCain were in Task Group 38.4 leading the line, with Clark's Task Group 38.1 in the middle, about sixteen miles to the south, and Beary's services group following another eighteen miles south of it.

As the task force ran due north, the typhoon struck with a vengeance. Task Group 38.4 was far enough north that it rode out the fury with little damage. Beary made the mistake of signaling his ships to proceed independently to the northwest—right into the storm center. But it was Task Group 38.1, in the center of the fleet, that took the brunt of the storm's punch.

At 4:00 a.m. on June 5, Clark requested permission to steer clear of the storm center by turning to a course of 120 degrees. Once again, McCain checked with Halsey, who signaled McCain that Clark was to maintain his heading due north. Evidently, both Halsey and McCain felt they were getting into calmer seas at the northern end of the line, and unlike Clark, neither apparently could see the storm center on his radar.

McCain waited to reply to Clark's request to turn to 120 degrees while he mulled over Halsey's insistence on continuing due north. Finally, McCain signaled Clark that he could use his own judgment, but by then, when Clark made a series of course changes in search of calmer seas, the moves left his task group near the eye of the storm.

Clark's group suffered major damage to the fast carriers *Hornet* and *Bennington,* two escort carriers, and three cruisers, including the *Pittsburgh,* which lost its entire bow. Twenty-six other ships reported minor damage, and 146 aircraft aboard the carriers were destroyed or damaged. The only bright spot was that the human toll—six—was much lower than in the December typhoon.

Clark reported aboard the *Shangri-La* the next day to confer with McCain about the damage. When he told McCain that he could have avoided the brunt of the storm had he been permitted to deviate from the base course earlier, McCain was noncommittal. It seemed clear to Clark that McCain was reluctant to criticize Halsey's actions. By the time both McCain and Clark reported to Halsey on the *Missouri,* it seemed equally obvious to Clark that Halsey was fully aware that his own actions were to blame for Clark's losses.[24]

Crippled though it was, Task Force 38 soon regrouped and headed westward for more strikes against Okinawa. Tough Jocko Clark, back on board *Hornet,* ignored its warped flight deck over the bow and steamed full astern at eighteen knots for two days in order to launch and recover planes. By then, the Okinawa campaign was finally showing signs of winding down, and Task Force 38 withdrew to San Pedro harbor in Leyte Gulf, the navy's most recent advance base. There Halsey, McCain, Clark, and Beary were summoned aboard the *New Mexico* to appear before a court of inquiry convened to investigate the second thrashing of an American fleet by a typhoon in just six months.

Halsey led off by once again blaming the weather service, but it was hardly that simple. Clark's counsel presented a chronological record complete with track charts and photographs of the radar images that showed the task force to have been eastward of the storm path when Halsey ordered the course change to 300 degrees. If the fleet had continued eastward, the storm would have passed astern.

In the end, the court of inquiry concluded that Halsey had failed to heed Nimitz's admonishment after the December typhoon to improve the coordination and timeliness of weather reports and that Halsey was to blame for the "remarkable similarity between the [two] situations, actions and results." It further concluded that the proximate cause of the damage to the Third Fleet "was the turning of the Fleet to course 300."[25]

Secondarily, the court blamed McCain for his twenty-minute delay in granting Clark permission to steer eastward to 120 degrees. It might not seem like much of a delay, but in the face of this concentrated typhoon, minutes made all the difference. Clark and Beary also incurred some blame because they had continued on courses and speeds "although their better judgment dictated a course of action which would have taken them fairly clear of the typhoon path."[26] Actually following their better judgment in the face of Halsey's orders to stay the course would, of course, have required a good deal of brass.

The court of inquiry recommended that Halsey and McCain be sent letters of reprimand pointing out their errors and "lack of sound judgment displayed"—lessons, it noted, which might have been learned from the December encounter, but which were "either disregarded or not given proper consideration." The court also recommended that "serious consideration" be given to assigning Halsey and McCain to other duties—that is to say, relieving them of their sea commands.[27]

Halsey's shot at the fourth set of five stars might have vanished on that note, but once again Nimitz and King stepped in to save him. According to Jocko Clark, Nimitz was privately furious with Halsey and "minced no words in charging Halsey with gross stupidity in both typhoons, especially the latter, where Halsey had good weather information."[28] But such an outburst, if indeed Nimitz made it, would never be given a public airing.

"CINCPAC has considered," Nimitz wrote the court in his official response, "not only the events under inquiry, but the outstanding combat records of the officers to whom responsibility has been attached in this case." Halsey had "rendered invaluable service to his country. His skill and determination have been demonstrated time and again in combat with the enemy."

King retraced the court's opinion by noting in his own endorsement, "The gravity of the occurrence is accentuated by the fact that the senior officers concerned were also involved in a similar, and poorly handled situation, during the typhoon of December 1944." King felt that Halsey and McCain could have avoided the worst of this second storm "had they reacted to the situation as it developed with the weather-wise skill to be expected of professional seamen." But that was the end of his lecture. "Notwithstanding the above," King wrote, he recommended "no individual disciplinary measures be taken, for the reason stated by ... Fleet Admiral Nimitz."[29]

Halsey was untouchable, but Slew McCain was not so lucky. He was expendable, and Nimitz quietly prepared to relieve McCain of his task force command notwithstanding King's official pronouncement. It does not seem an exaggeration to say that McCain took the fall for Halsey. McCain had always been a loyal "King man," and this result may have grated on King at least as much as his public posturing in Halsey's defense. Small wonder, then, that King would be inclined to admit, "I should not say it but it is true. Halsey made two mistakes; not the great battle; what I had against him were the two typhoons."[30]

CHAPTER TWENTY-THREE

Interim President

After the politically charged FDR-MacArthur-Nimitz conference at Pearl Harbor in July 1944, the presidential party had put back to sea on the cruiser *Baltimore*. As always, the president's itinerary was a well-kept secret, but this time even Leahy, who of course knew their destination, was skeptical of its worth. "Reaching a sufficient distance from Diamond Head to make observation from shore impossible," Leahy noted, the *Baltimore* swung almost due north and, with an antisubmarine screen of four destroyers, surged forward at 21 knots, bound for Adak in the Aleutian Islands of Alaska.[1]

Roosevelt was playing the role of commander in chief to the hilt, but why Alaska? After the reconquest of Kiska and Attu in 1943, there had been some thought to marshal forces in Alaska and strike a blow from there against Japan's Kuril Islands, or even its northern island of Hokkaido. This potential threat kept the Japanese guessing, but the major drawback to a northern front — in addition to its routinely dismal flying and fighting weather — would be that an attack against Japan from the north would do nothing to disrupt Japan's key arteries of natural resources flowing from the south.

(King certainly understood that as he argued for an attack against Formosa.)

So by mid-1944, the Alaskan frontier had transitioned from potential invasion springboard to somewhat of a backwater. After a round of dismal port calls in heavy fog and damp, chilly weather—the presidential flotilla was unable even to enter Dutch Harbor because of limited visibility—Roosevelt may well have asked himself why, indeed, Alaska. A cruise to warm, southern waters, even a publicity transit of the Panama Canal and a return up the eastern seaboard, might just as well have conveyed to the public the vigor of a hands-on commander in chief. Instead, the Alaskan cruise, including a trip along the beautiful Inside Passage in a cramped and crowded destroyer, left the president haggard and worn. But what happened at the navy yard in Bremerton, Washington, only made matters worse.

The presidential destroyer *Cummings*—according to Leahy, the first destroyer that Roosevelt had traveled any distance on as president—arrived at the Bremerton Navy Yard late on the afternoon of August 12 so that the president could address several thousand workers. The speech was broadcast on radio and meant to be an up-to-the-minute report to the American people on his whirlwind tour of the Pacific. Instead, it proved to be one of his weaker efforts. Everything that could go wrong did.

Without his usual speechwriters and the editing of Grace Tully, who was not on the Pacific trip, Roosevelt dictated the speech to an assistant naval aide. Remarkably, he then chose to deliver it standing upright in his braces from the destroyer's forecastle—despite having not worn his braces in some months and lost considerable weight in the interim. The crowd, having just gotten off work on a Saturday and looking forward to rushing elsewhere, was unresponsive. Roosevelt's delivery was halting, in part because the rough text was rambling and lacked his usual smooth style. A breeze ruffling his papers didn't help the situation. To all who heard him, the president sounded tired, slightly confused, and at times short of breath.

But then, about halfway through the speech, Roosevelt was seized by a chest pain that radiated outward to both shoulders. Only his iron will kept him upright and in some semblance of control. When he finally finished, the president confessed the pain to Howard Bruenn, his cardiologist. Bruenn diagnosed an attack of angina and not a heart attack, but it was nonetheless proof positive for Bruenn of coronary disease in his patient. Clearly, the routine, cheery reports of the president's health from White House physician Ross McIntire were overly optimistic, if not downright false.[2]

Bruenn's medical concerns were kept quiet, but on the basis of Roosevelt's bungled Bremerton speech, there were many — even among his most ardent supporters — who wondered whether FDR was up to the task of another campaign, let alone another four years in the presidency. Did Roosevelt still have his old political magic? How would he respond to the onslaught of Republican attacks?

On September 23, 1944 — blissfully late for the official opening of a presidential campaign even then — Roosevelt addressed the Teamsters Union at the Statler Hotel in Washington, D.C. In the aftermath of his Alaskan cruise, a fiction had spread that somehow Roosevelt's pet Scottish terrier, Fala, had been left behind at one of the Aleutian ports and that the president had dispatched a destroyer to retrieve him. In a speech slated to rank near his "nothing to fear" and day of "infamy" utterances, the old master grandly touched all the bases and then turned Fala loose against the entire Republican establishment.

"These Republican leaders," Roosevelt declared with mock seriousness, "have not been content with attacks on me, or my wife, or on my sons. No, not content with that, they now include my little dog, Fala." He and his family took such attacks as a matter of course, asserted FDR, but Fala resented them. "You know," continued FDR in his folksy way, "Fala is Scotch, and being a Scottie, as soon as he learned that the Republican fiction writers in Congress and out had concocted a story that I had left him behind on the Aleutian Islands and had sent a destroyer back to find him — at a cost to the taxpayers of two or three, or eight or twenty million dollars — his Scotch soul was furious. He has not been the same dog since."[3]

Roosevelt's audience in the hall and those listening on radio across the country howled in delight. The grand old man still had it, but how long would the magic last? Chief of Staff Leahy may well have wondered the same thing more deeply than most, but characteristically, he kept his thoughts on the matter to himself.

On November 7, 1944, Franklin Delano Roosevelt was elected to an unprecedented fourth term as president of the United States. Despite his failing health and the looming postwar challenges, Roosevelt seems to have taken an almost cavalier attitude toward continuing in office. He was comfortable there; the country was comfortable with him being there. Why do anything different? And, perhaps in his mind, why not die there? But all this begs the question, if Roosevelt's famed attention to detail and the parceling out of responsibilities among subordinates so that only he had the full picture diminished with his decreasing faculties, and if he was in fact less than a full-time president, who was running the government?

To be sure, there was great inertia within the country. Since December 7, 1941, the country had been united in purpose, and that purpose — the ultimate defeat of Germany, Italy, and Japan — dominated all decisions. There was no crossroads that called for a major change in policy. The American public might take comfort in FDR's words of hope and determination emanating from their radios, but Roosevelt himself, having set the wheels in motion, could find satisfaction in the knowledge that the country was charging along on the largest and most rapid military industrialization in history.

Certainly, George Marshall was a key figure in picking the right leaders for the fight and in overseeing the operations of the army's ground and air forces. Ernest King was second only to Marshall in providing this sort of total leadership for the navy's efforts, and from his first pronouncements in the Pacific, King's contributions as a true global strategist may have surpassed even Marshall's. But increasingly in the last year of Roosevelt's life, there is strong evidence that the man who picked up the presidential slack, the man who remained not only his number one military adviser but also became his unquestioned chief counselor and trusted confidant on *all* matters, was William D. Leahy.

Roosevelt's decline first attracted major attention when he failed to bounce back with his usual good humor and energy after the Teheran Conference of December 1943. He endured a tough winter of colds, stuffy sinuses, and bronchitis and showed little sign of recovering with the approach of spring. Nimitz met with him in Washington that March and came away convinced that the president was not well, recalling that "his face was ashen and his hands trembled." As Leahy discreetly put it, "The terrific burden of being in effect the Commander-in-Chief of the greatest global war yet recorded in history began to tell on Franklin Roosevelt in 1944."[4]

Even as the coming offensives at Normandy and in the Pacific demanded attention, Leahy found that "of great concern to all of us as the spring of 1944 approached was the failure of our Commander-in-Chief to regain his accustomed good health." Dr. Bruenn first diagnosed the real reason in an examination on March 28 that found the president to be suffering from hypertension and congestive heart failure. The solution was to pack FDR off to Bernard Baruch's Hobcaw estate in South Carolina for an uninterrupted rest. "The quiet of the place," Leahy remembered, "was almost oppressive."[5]

Pa Watson and Wilson Brown, the president's army and navy aides, respectively, accompanied the presidential party, as did Dr. Bruenn, but it was Leahy who served as the focal point for information flowing to and from FDR. In the morning, Leahy dealt with messages from Washington and London and dispatches that the Map Room in the White House otherwise sent to Leahy's office in the East Wing. Next came the mail and its required replies. While the president napped in the afternoon, Leahy caught up on other work before the president's requisite late afternoon outing that usually entailed a short drive or fishing excursion.

By the time Roosevelt was deemed well enough to return to Washington, a leisurely month had passed. For Leahy, who was so concerned about the sixty-two-year-old president, the visit ended on May 6, his own sixty-ninth birthday. It was not always a young man's war.

The president's absence from Washington that spring fueled speculation about whether he would be a candidate for reelection. In one unguarded moment, Roosevelt confessed to Leahy, "Bill, I just hate to run for election. Perhaps the war will by that time have pro-gressed to a point that will make it unnecessary for me to be a can-didate." But time was hardly on his side. Roosevelt nonetheless waited until July 11, just before the Democratic National Conven-tion convened, to announce his candidacy.[6]

But FDR never returned to his pre-1944 work schedule. Four-hour days became his norm, and frequently even those hours were abbreviated. Leahy inevitably picked up some of the slack, but then the workload — and the resultant power — centered all the more on the admiral when the president's other chief confidant, Harry Hop-kins, fell gravely ill.

Hopkins, who, Leahy said, "appeared to many of us to be living on borrowed time," was absent from the White House for much of 1944. Leahy generously claimed that the additional work left to him by Hopkins's absence "brought a new appreciation of the tremen-dous selfless contribution Hopkins had been making to his coun-try," but the end result was that the memo pad Leahy took each morning into the president's study "began to have more entries." In addition to the usual military matters, more and more foreign policy and political issues filled Leahy's docket.[7]

Next came the visit to Pearl Harbor, where Douglas MacArthur, who had not seen Roosevelt in person since 1937, added his own evaluation of the president's health. MacArthur professed to be "shocked" at the president's appearance and claimed, "He was just a shell of the man I had known." To his own physician, the general was even more blunt as he whispered, "Doc, the mark of death is on him! In six months he'll be in his grave."[8]

The Alaskan cruise and speech debacle at Bremerton followed, but before Roosevelt got into the fall campaign, another conference with Churchill at Quebec highlighted Leahy's ascendant role. Hop-kins was not present, and it was Churchill's wife, Clementine, who best put her finger on it. "[Hopkins] seems to have dropped out of the picture," she wrote their daughter Sarah. "We cannot quite make out whether Harry's old place in the President's confidence is vacant, or whether Admiral Leahy is gradually molding into it."[9]

There was no one moment or issue that cooled the relationship between FDR and Hopkins, but a combination of Harry's remarriage, his subsequent move out of the White House, and his ensuing illness robbed him of his status as the indispensable sidekick he had once been. Leahy, while never a "sidekick" in his relationship with FDR, nonetheless filled the void as counselor. And Hopkins's distancing from FDR did not necessarily mean that the administration was deprived of his advice. Hopkins and Leahy enjoyed a very close relationship and somewhat of a mutual admiration society for the work each knew the other was doing. Hopkins, for example, met with Leahy "on matters concerned with both domestic and international politics" just before Leahy left for Quebec with the president. This, of course, was a further broadening of Leahy's portfolio.[10]

But there was one other insight at Quebec into FDR's deteriorating condition. One evening, Roosevelt and assorted staff watched the new film *Wilson,* about the presidency of Woodrow Wilson and his ill-fated fight for the League of Nations. When the film reached the point where Wilson's health broke down and he suffered a stroke, Dr. Bruenn, who was sitting near the president, heard Roosevelt mutter, "By God, that's not going to happen to me!"[11]

What did happen, of course, was his reelection, with Harry Truman as his running mate. Leahy was among the close circle that gathered with the president at Hyde Park to monitor the returns. The dining room in the Springwood mansion was outfitted with two ticker tape recording devices and a radio speaker. As the election reports came in, the president and Leahy recorded them state by state. By the time northern New York, traditionally more Republican, was tallied, Roosevelt seemed confident of victory and sat down to a midnight supper. Leahy continued to tally results until 2:00 a.m., when the president's reelection was certain.

Leahy went to bed early that morning but had trouble sleeping, a fact he attributed to "coffee after dinner at midnight." Perhaps. He may also have been privately agonizing over how long the man who was clearly wasting away in front of him might live and what consequences it would have for the country.[12]

* * *

Ahead lay the Yalta Conference, but in the interim there would be increasing evidence of Leahy's growing role. Witness three otherwise unrelated episodes.

In mid-December, when Leahy received his appointment as the first five-star fleet admiral and undeniably the country's ranking military figure, among the congratulations that flowed in was a letter from Harry Hopkins. Far from resenting Leahy's ascendancy out of his own decline, Hopkins remained true in his friendship and advice to Leahy. "No one knows better than I," Hopkins concluded, "of your devoted service to the President and your country."[13] Coming from the consummate insider, that was high praise indeed.

Then there was a knock on Leahy's door at 5:00 p.m. on Christmas Eve. Even in wartime Washington, most were pausing, because it was also a Sunday night. Leahy's caller was Secretary of the Navy James Forrestal. The secretary wanted to discuss a major navy personnel issue — almost certain to be unpopular — about moving retired officers currently on active duty back to inactive duty as the war wound down. Forrestal was at Leahy's door that evening because the president, who had once immersed himself in navy minutia, had told Forrestal to resolve the matter with Leahy. Roosevelt was clearly comfortable giving Leahy wide latitude.[14]

Finally, there were the after-dinner remarks on the evening of Roosevelt's fourth inaugural. Given the wartime conditions, the inaugural ceremony itself, on January 20, 1945, was held on the south portico of the White House. At a small dinner that evening, FDR might well have made some appropriate remarks himself, but he asked Leahy to do it instead. In a speech of about six hundred words, lasting barely five minutes, Leahy put forth the Roosevelt Administration's overriding goal.

"I know no easy or happy words to say to you tonight," Leahy began. "I know only that as we sit here 8,000,000 of our sons and our daughters, too, are outside the continental limits of the United States, carrying the battle to the enemy. They are on every sea, in every sector of the globe from poles to tropics.... It is a global war without parallel in the history of the world."

Then Leahy got slightly disingenuous. "I know nothing of the intricacies of politics," he claimed. "It is not my job to know them, I am thankful for that." None of that was true, of course. Leahy was, in fact, almost as much of a master of politics as his boss. And the fact that he could be so self-deprecating in so important a setting was proof in itself that he had learned his lessons well.

The one mandate of the election, Leahy continued, was "to win the war...and I do not know any other person in the world who is so well qualified to execute the peoples' mandate as the talented and experienced statesman and patriot who was inaugurated today as president of the United States."[15] These final words were indeed a tribute to Roosevelt, but the fact that FDR had entrusted Leahy with the podium in the first place was a tribute to their relationship and the president's faith in his crusty sailor. Two days later, Roosevelt and Leahy left for Yalta.

Winston Churchill supposedly opined, "If we had spent ten years on research, we could not have found a worse place in the world than Yalta." It proved to be almost that bad. One wonders whether Churchill's initial wish to stage it close to Sevastopol to allow for accommodations on board ship might not have been better, but the retreating Germans had left that town in shambles, and the Russians were making the venue decision. They opted to have the British and American delegations fly into Saki and then motor ninety miles over winding mountain roads to Yalta. For his part, Leahy would later term the gathering "the most controversial of all of the nine Allied war councils."[16]

Roosevelt and Leahy left Washington by train for Newport News, Virginia, where they and their party embarked on the *Quincy,* the same class of heavy cruiser as the *Baltimore,* which had carried them around much of the North Pacific. Along with military aides Pa Watson and Wilson Brown, physician Ross McIntire, and the by now indispensable Dr. Bruenn, the presidential party included Roosevelt's only daughter, Anna Boettiger, who while always close to her father, had become his indefatigable champion and all-around protector in the last year of his life. Because Roosevelt, for whatever reason, preferred the starboard side of the ship, he was lodged in the captain's cabin, while Anna got the adjacent admiral's quarters on the port side. Leahy shared a cabin with James F. Byrnes, who was along as head of the Office of War Mobilization.[17]

The *Quincy* crossed the Atlantic without incident, including any repeat of the friendly torpedo attack that had occurred while crossing to the Teheran conference fifteen months before. The *Quincy* put into Malta, where the American Joint Chiefs had already assembled to meet with their British counterparts. After boarding the *Quincy* to pay their initial respects, King and Marshall came away gravely disturbed by the president's appearance. Unable to say anything in the presence of others, they nonetheless exchanged looks of consternation and nodded to each other in silence.[18]

There was still plenty of American-British bickering: the British preferred a single thrust by Montgomery into Germany, no matter how slow, to Eisenhower's strategy of a broad frontal advance; King was as adamant as ever that he wanted no help from the British fleet in the Pacific; and Churchill was *still* singing songs of the eastern Mediterranean. But a lot had changed militarily with their Russian allies since the Teheran Conference. In November 1943, the United States and Great Britain were still on the defensive with Stalin about a second front. Now, not only had Normandy been invaded, Paris liberated, and a drive across Europe begun in earnest, but American forces in the Pacific were preparing to invade Japan itself.

So, in a thunderous fleet of transport planes, the American and British delegations flew from Malta to the Crimea to meet Stalin. Leahy went with Roosevelt, of course. This was the first use of the presidential-purpose C-54 that came to be called the "Sacred Cow." The four-engine transport was equipped with a special elevator that could lift the wheelchair-bound president from tarmac to cabin in a few seconds. According to Leahy, Roosevelt, who tended to disregard his disability, "viewed these refinements as unnecessary." But Leahy, who endured rather than relished air travel, was not above appreciating the refinements that had been specially installed on the aircraft. "There was no gainsaying," he recalled, "that travel in the 'Sacred Cow' was luxurious in comparison with anything within my previous experience. However, I still continued to prefer to travel by ship, by railroad, or by foot if time were available!"[19]

Once in Yalta, the American delegation was housed in the fifty-room Livadia Palace, completed in 1911 by Tsar Nicholas II as a summer retreat. Leahy claimed that the Russians had done "an amazing job" of renovating the palace in just three weeks, but suitable bathrooms, let alone basic amenities, were sorely lacking. There was only one bathroom on the entire second floor and never enough clean towels. Leahy was quartered on the first floor adjacent to the president, who was the only one with a private bath. King and Marshall were housed in the tsar's bedroom chambers. Marshall drew the main bedroom, while King was consigned to the tsarina's boudoir. "Salty Admiral King," Leahy noted, "took a lot of kidding from the rest of us" because of it. Harry Hopkins, with a pallor of death over him at least as gray as that of Roosevelt, also had a room upstairs and spent most of his time in bed, except for the plenary sessions of the conference, which were also held at Livadia.[20]

Then FDR demonstrated his ultimate trust in Leahy by affirming his position at the pinnacle of his advisers. "Bill," the president said, "I wish you would attend all these political meetings in order that we may have someone in whom I have full confidence who will remember everything that we have done." This was a new role for Leahy. Now he would be the president's right hand in all matters, military and political. King and Marshall, for example, usually attended only the military sessions, and in fact King had so much time on his hands at Yalta that he made several side trips to inspect American coast guard cutters and the harbor at Sevastopol.[21]

Ever self-effacing, Leahy expressed surprise at FDR's request but quickly agreed to expand his role. Leahy surmised that this was perhaps evidence that Roosevelt's near-perfect memory was fading, but at least publicly—both at the time and afterward—Leahy, who saw the president every day, maintained that he saw "no sign of any serious weakness in the President's physical condition."[22]

Indeed, Leahy sometimes wondered whether Roosevelt wasn't testing *him*. Sometimes FDR would ask Leahy's opinion on a matter they had discussed months before and then, after Leahy offered his views, respond by saying, "Bill, that's not what you told me a year ago." The admiral would backpedal and manage an answer to the effect that: "Well, Mr. President, if I told you something different a year ago — that was wrong, because what I'm telling you now is right." According to Leahy, after this occurred several times, it became somewhat of a running personal joke between them.[23]

Still, it is hard to imagine that this banter occurred as late as Yalta or that Leahy was truly oblivious to the decline in his only client. For that is what FDR was to Leahy. On call around the clock, friendly but never a crony, totally loyal, and invariably discreet, Bill Leahy served but one master. But it would be a definite mistake to presume that he did so as a yes-man. Just the opposite was true. Leahy was not afraid to argue his personal views with FDR, but once the president made a decision, he could be confident that Leahy would carry it out to the letter no matter his prior position. Two examples of this occurred at Yalta.

In planning the United Nations, Roosevelt was under some pressure from the British and his own State Department to include France as one of the "great power" members. Leahy, who never had much use for the strutting Charles de Gaulle, was opposed, writing afterward about as snidely as he ever allowed himself to appear in print, "I felt that conferring that status on defeated France was an extravagant stretch of the English language." But Roosevelt deemed otherwise, and so Leahy supported the position.[24]

The other instance concerned Roosevelt's wish — "pet idea," Leahy called it — for a series of strategic military bases all over the world under the control of the United Nations. If that sounded vaguely Wilsonian, Leahy's opposition to it took on the aura of Senator Lodge and his conservative Republicans. Leahy "could never agree" with Roosevelt on that subject the many times they discussed it and "always felt that any bases considered essential for the security of our own country should be under the sovereignty of the United States." Roosevelt's support for the plan was based chiefly on his principle that the United States was not seeking to acquire any territory as a result of the war. Leahy thought that rather naive and repeatedly told Roosevelt he was wrong.[25]

George M. Elsey was a naval reserve officer who worked in the White House Map Room from 1941 to 1946 and as such was pretty much at Leahy's elbow on a daily basis. "Admiral Leahy was a pretty crusty and salty old fellow," Elsey recalled. "I don't think [he] ever really trusted *anybody* [emphasis in original] other than the United States, and had it been possible, he would have liked to have fought all wars without allies because he knew that you invariably had difficulties and difference of opinion with [them]."[26]

At Yalta, there were allies, and the long days and late night festivities were enough to tax even the healthiest of individuals. One Soviet dinner started at 9:00 p.m. and lasted until 1:00 a.m., complete with thirty-eight standing toasts. Leahy wryly noted, "The mosquitoes under the tables worked very successfully on my ankles [and] all the people who had any sense watered their liquor and managed to stay alert." Considering the important work to be accomplished, he considered such celebrations "an unwarranted waste of time."[27]

Leahy left Yalta with great feelings of foreboding. Soviet domination of Poland, France's admission to the big three, and the plan to demilitarize Germany totally — thus making the Soviet Union the dominant power in Europe — were all issues that weighed heavily on him and came to dominate postwar Europe. But those who blame the subsequent collapse of the wartime alliance with the Soviets on Roosevelt's declining health at Yalta do so without considering FDR's long-held desire for multilateralism and belief that he could genuinely elicit compromise from Stalin. Had Roosevelt at Yalta been the man he had been at Casablanca two-plus years before, the result may not have been any different. Conservative Leahy himself would have no doubt taken a harder line, but he served his more liberal master.[28]

Averell Harriman, who at the time of Yalta was the American ambassador to the Soviet Union, characterized Leahy as able to move easily into "almost anything that came into the White House, whether it be production matters or policy matters of almost any kind." But as several White House aides pointed out, "He was no empire builder. He simply wanted to get on with the war."[29]

Among those aides, assistant naval aide Lieutenant William M. Rigdon may have offered the clearest portrait. "Leahy was always close to the President," Rigdon recalled. "He was not only the President's chief planning officer, head of the Joint Chiefs of Staff, and the highest ranking American officer on military duty . . . but he was also the President's confidant and adviser on matters other than military. FDR trusted him completely." Noting that Leahy had had a reputation in navy circles before the war of being "extremely difficult to work for," Rigdon figured that Leahy had surely mellowed and "was one of the most thoughtful and appreciative men I have known."[30]

Perhaps most interesting about Leahy's accumulation of power is that it occurred with very little scrutiny from the press — certainly without any self-promotion. After his cover appearances on *Time* and *Life* in 1942, Leahy largely dropped out of sight of the mainstream press. In an era when *Time* was a meaty magazine of a hundred-plus pages, Leahy was mentioned only once in 1943 and not at all in the first six months of 1944. When his face appeared on the cover again in May 1945, it was largely to promote a war bond drive led by the five-star admirals and generals, of whom, *Time* readily acknowledged, "Leahy is the least known."[31]

A final point must be made about Leahy as presidential adviser. Given his long history of military service and de facto ranking as the country's senior soldier/sailor, it might be assumed that he supported the military position and emphasis to the exclusion of the political. In fact, particularly in this last year of FDR's life, Leahy seems to have done just the opposite.

As Roosevelt gathered more power into the White House and made military decisions that had increasingly political overtones, the State Department frequently took a backseat in U.S. policy, and "many decisions were made without foreign policy consideration having come into play." But this was not because of Leahy.

"Instead of being an anti–State Department man, as some people assumed that an old sailor automatically would be," Map Room aide George Elsey recalled, "Admiral Leahy was the *one* man around the White House who kept constantly saying, 'But the State Department ought to be consulted.' As the war went further and further along and as decisions began to be more and more political and less and less military, it was Leahy who *insisted* that there be a relationship with the State Department." Consequently, Leahy named Charles E. "Chip" Bohlen as his personal liaison and met with him daily to keep the State Department in the loop with the latest FDR-Churchill-Stalin messages and negotiations. "Admiral Leahy," Elsey maintained, "was perhaps the one *strong* man in the White House during the war who was *trying* [all emphasis in original] to keep political and foreign policy matters in some sort of perspective with President Roosevelt."[32]

Bill Leahy transferred this same degree of fidelity to Harry Truman. Returning to the United States after the strain of Yalta, Roosevelt's workday became even more compressed and less productive. All FDR wanted to do, it seemed to many observers, was sleep and sleep and sleep. The performer in Roosevelt rallied to give his last press conference on March 20 — the 997th of his presidency — but most who saw him found him listless, unengaged, and simply worn-out.[33]

On March 29, 1945, Leahy made a laconic, single-sentence entry in his diary: "The President departed for a vacation at Warm Springs, Georgia."[34] Save for a two-week trip to Warm Springs the previous December when Leahy remained in Washington, this would be the longest period they had been apart since Leahy became FDR's chief of staff. Simply put, Leahy had been at FDR's side everywhere, even through the monthlong stay at Hobcaw in the spring of 1944.

There is no clear reason why Leahy did not accompany Roosevelt to Warm Springs this last time, but the facts fuel much speculation. It is possible that Leahy did not go because he had so little substantive interaction with FDR anymore. Knowing full well the answers and directives he should give in the name of his boss, Leahy may well have figured that he could do his job far more readily from his office in the East Wing of the White House than from the backcountry of Georgia. Inconceivably, however, after Dr. Bruenn pronounced Roosevelt dead on April 12, Leahy learned the news from the radio while at home — not from a call from the White House. Leahy, as well as Marshall and King, met the president's train when it returned his body to Washington on Friday morning, April 14, and all three accompanied it to Hyde Park for burial the next day.

By then, Truman had already had his first meeting with the Joint Chiefs and a private conversation with Leahy. Truman asked the admiral to remain in his position, but Leahy was quick to note that he had spoken his own mind to Roosevelt and that if he remained chief of staff for Truman, "it will be impossible for me to change." Fine, Truman replied. "That is exactly what I want you to do." Leahy initially thought that this new engagement might last for a few months; instead, it lasted four years.[35]

Thus, Leahy and his staff prepared dozens of background papers for Truman as the new president oversaw the unconditional surrender of Germany on May 7 and prepared for the Potsdam Conference with Churchill and Stalin that July. All of these briefing papers were prepared under Leahy's direction or at his request, and he became the chief translator or interpreter of Roosevelt's policies for Truman. Significantly, by this time the major issues were increasingly political rather than military.[36]

Truman came to trust and value Leahy because the admiral was a thread of continuity running to Churchill, Stalin, and the Joint Chiefs. Leahy was also quite capable of being Truman's "enforcer," as in the case of James F. Byrnes. After Truman appointed Byrnes secretary of state in July 1945, Byrnes proceeded to conduct American foreign policy as if *he* had been Roosevelt's running mate instead of Truman.

The breaking point came when Byrnes returned from a trip to the Soviet Union in 1946 and called a press conference to report to the public without first reporting to Truman. The president's appointments secretary, Matthew J. Connelly, told Byrnes to cancel the press conference and hasten down to the presidential yacht, *Williamsburg,* for a heart-to-heart with Truman. But it was Leahy who "took [Byrnes] apart to a fare-the-well" and "never let him off the hook."[37] Byrnes resigned as secretary of state soon afterward.

Admiral Leahy's principal biographer would title his work *Witness to Power,* but particularly during the final year of FDR's life, Leahy wielded power as much as witnessed it. "Unseen Wielder of Power" might have been a more descriptive title. That Leahy did so in the name of his commander in chief, with no personal agenda of his own, is a testament to his long association with Roosevelt and his policies as well as his personal character.

CHAPTER TWENTY-FOUR

Toward Tokyo Bay

Having experienced some difficulties over the years with his own *American* allies in the Pacific—chief among them Douglas MacArthur—it came as no surprise that Ernest J. King was never enthusiastic about a role in the region for Great Britain's Royal Navy. But as the war in Europe showed signs of an Allied victory, this is exactly what Churchill sought to achieve. He had put the Americans on the spot at the Second Quebec Conference in September 1944 by grandly offering Roosevelt the British fleet for Pacific operations and then bluntly asking, right then and there, if his offer was accepted. There was little at the time that Roosevelt could say but yes, of course. One wry British observer noted that the official minutes should then have read, "At this point Admiral King was carried out."[1]

It wasn't quite that bad, but almost. King didn't want to take on the additional logistical burden of supplying British ships with stores and ammunition, or the operational headache of integrating them into Nimitz's command. The Pacific had been a decidedly American theater of operations since early 1942, and now, if it was not fully awash with American ships, there were certainly enough on station to complete the mission. In private, Roosevelt opined the obvious for Churchill's grand gesture: "All they want is Singapore back."[2]

But Roosevelt had accepted Churchill's grand gesture—no matter how politically motivated—and it was once again up to Leahy to see that the presidential directive was followed militarily. When King professed at a subsequent meeting of the Combined Chiefs of Staff that "the practicability of employing these forces would be a matter for discussion from time to time," Leahy interrupted to assert that "where they should be employed" was open to debate, but the question of "if" had been firmly answered by the president. If King had any further objections, he could take the matter up with FDR.[3]

It was December 1944 before the British Pacific Fleet, consisting of four carriers, two battleships, and fifteen destroyers—all told about the size of one of the task groups of Halsey's Third Fleet—arrived in Australia looking for a fight, presumably with the Japanese. Nimitz was hardly more keen on the British than King. "I do not need Paul Revere," Nimitz wrote King, "to tell me that the British are coming." Nimitz thought the Royal Navy's dispatches read like operations orders for an occupation. "Perhaps," he continued, "it is intended to be an occupation force."

But by the time Admiral Sir Bruce Fraser, the commander of the British fleet, arrived at Pearl Harbor just before Christmas 1944 to confer with the Americans, Nimitz was his usual gracious self. He and Fraser had met a decade before when Nimitz was commanding the *Augusta* on the Far East Station. Nimitz invited Fraser to be his houseguest and then set about sorting out the details of the British involvement.

A large part of the problem was that two centuries of "Rule, Britannia" aside, the British had no occasion or capacity during World War II to mount the type of sustained, oceangoing operations that the American navy routinely practiced. Fraser satisfied some of King's logistical concerns by assuring Nimitz that his fleet was equipped with its own oilers and supply ships, but the Royal Navy was simply not as proficient at underway refueling and provisioning as the Americans. When Fraser boasted to Nimitz that the British were able to remain at sea eight days out of the month, Nimitz shook his head in disbelief. That wouldn't do. "We compromised on twenty," Nimitz noted, and then turned Fraser over to Admiral Spruance with orders to work the British into the coming campaign against Okinawa.[4]

The other ally spoiling to get into the fight against Japan in the waning days was the Soviet Union. Stalin privately agreed with Churchill and Roosevelt at Yalta to do so ninety days after Germany surrendered. This was a highly guarded secret, but Leahy was among those who had misgivings about taking on another Pacific ally. While at the time Leahy never publicly voiced opposition to the Soviets entering the Pacific war—it would have been politically unrealistic to do so—his tendency was to hope privately that the war might end before they got involved. Marshall and King remained focused on purely military matters, but Leahy's growing concern about the Soviet Union and the state of the postwar alliance was just another example of his increasingly political role.[5]

As the war churned toward its inevitable conclusion, ingrained frictions also continued in the American high command. Despite his self-proclaimed triumphant return to the Philippines, Douglas MacArthur looked at a map of the Western Pacific and finally saw what King and Nimitz had been seeing for months. The direct route to Japan lay through Nimitz's provinces in the Central Pacific. Unless MacArthur quickly became engaged in that direction, his command would be left mopping up operations in the Philippines. The War Department, George Marshall, and, in the closing days of his life, Franklin Roosevelt, refused to let that happen. The army needed its heroes, too.

On April 3, 1945, the Joint Chiefs agreed to a plan for the final attack against Japan. MacArthur would command all army ground and air forces, while Nimitz would continue to command all naval forces. But it wasn't that simple and certainly not so quickly implemented. MacArthur's chief aides roared into Nimitz's forward headquarters on Guam and, with typical gusto reminiscent of the post-Tarawa conferences, began giving orders as if MacArthur was in charge of everything except ships at sea.

Once again, Nimitz politely but firmly stood his ground and salvaged the unity of command among the branches that he had worked so hard to nurture. MacArthur would eventually command the ground forces for the invasion, but in the interim Nimitz continued to command the flow of men, ships, and materiel, as well as the bases en route to Japan.[6]

The decision to invade the main islands of Japan was also not without controversy and debate. Two main alternatives presented themselves: a blockade coupled with a continuing bombing campaign that would eventually starve Japan into surrender, or a direct invasion that quite likely would make the casualties of Tarawa and Okinawa pale in comparison. Early in May 1945, the planners for the Joint Chiefs recommended the latter, arguing that the Japanese were unlikely to surrender without a direct invasion.

Leahy, and initially King, were highly skeptical of an invasion. Leahy had been lobbying against it for some time with Roosevelt and did not hesitate to do the same with Truman. Even if a blockade took longer, in Leahy's estimation it would cost fewer lives. Marshall, however, was inclined to keep up the momentum, fearing that any pause for a blockade would only give the Japanese time to organize homeland defenses, thus making the ultimate invasion that much more costly.

Leahy admitted that King "had never been as positively opposed to invasion as I had," and Marshall soon won King over to landings on Japan's southern island of Kyushu. Until then, King had not entirely given up his long-held interest in China as the best place from which to attack Japan proper. Marshall now instead convinced him that Kyushu was the most logical next step toward Tokyo Bay. Nimitz, who had also favored encirclement and continued bombing over a direct invasion, momentarily agreed with the rationale to seize Kyushu as a necessary staging area.

On the afternoon of June 18, the Joint Chiefs met with Truman and the secretaries of war and the navy at the White House to make a final decision. Marshall argued that regardless of the eventual strategy toward the other main islands, Kyushu was essential to tightening any blockade and increasing any bombing campaign.

King supported Marshall's views, Leahy acquiesced, and the decision was made for a direct assault on Japan. Ten days later, the Joint Chiefs set November 1, 1945, for the invasion of Kyushu, code-named Operation Olympic, and reaffirmed their earlier directive that MacArthur and Nimitz would be jointly responsible for the operation.[7]

The Marshall-King relationship, which had had its stormy moments, had matured and certainly become respectful — one might even say friendly. Far more than the requisite Christmas and birthday greetings praising the other's cooperation, Marshall and King seemed to look out for each other, even if only under the banner of harmony and a better image for their combined services.

When Marshall and King were asked to take part in pregame ceremonies for the Washington Senators' 1945 baseball season opener and march to the flagpole, Marshall worried about negative publicity from overseas if they formally participated in ball field ceremonies. "There is considerable difference," Marshall cautioned King, "between raising the flag at Griffith Park and raising it at Ehrenbreitstein or on Iwo Jima. I see no objection to possibly going to the game and sitting in a box but I don't like this idea at the present time of being sucked into the publicity formalities of the procedure. What is your reaction? Have you committed yourself?"

King's aide called Marshall's office two days later and said that the admiral agreed completely and would not attend the game, although he would ask that the box be held for members of his staff. It was a small example, perhaps, but lesser men might well have been content to see the other set up.[8]

In that same vein, King went out of his way to extend an invitation to Marshall to travel with him on his plane to the National Governors Conference on Mackinac Island in early July 1945. Both men were attending to brief the governors on the progress of the war, and King told Marshall that he would "like it very much if you will go with me." King described the schedule and noted that while he had to stop in Cleveland on the return trip, his plane would continue on to Washington with Marshall. Again, it was a small thing, but King didn't have to extend the invitation. Marshall accepted.[9]

King may well have been happy to cultivate his friendship with Marshall because his ties to both the White House and the secretary of the navy were now tenuous. King had never had much of a personal relationship with Roosevelt—in part because of personality and even more so because Leahy was FDR's top sailor—but the president was confident of King's abilities. After Roosevelt's death, King had almost no relationship with Truman, in large part because King had previously ignored Senator Truman's Special Committee to Investigate the National Defense Program as an intrusive waste of time.

Late in 1943, when Senator Truman had wanted information from the Joint Chiefs on the Canol pipeline project in western Canada, King had pled national security and denied his request. That didn't stop Truman, of course. As he told King in reply, "It seems to me the Senate is entitled to know the facts of the matter and we expect to know them." Truman eventually got what he wanted, on Canol and just about everything else, but he was not one to forget a snub.[10]

King's relationship with Secretary of the Navy James Forrestal wasn't much better. As navy undersecretary since 1940, Forrestal deserved high marks for his procurement role in getting the Atlantic and Pacific commands what they needed to fight the Axis. When Secretary of the Navy Frank Knox died in the spring of 1944, Forrestal was the hands-down favorite to replace him, and Roosevelt made the appointment. But whereas Knox had been a huge supporter of King and content to give him full rein—at least at the beginning of the war—Forrestal was adamant about civilian control of the military. This didn't stop King from carrying on as usual, but his brusque, make-a-decision manner conflicted with Forrestal's more cerebral, problem-solving approach and caused friction between the two.

King may well have been responsible for the beginnings of the rift when, late in 1943, he tried to implement one of his many reorganization plans. This one would have brought naval shipyards and some of Forrestal's procurement duties under King's command. King claimed — somewhat disingenuously if one looks at the turn-around times — that ship repairs were taking too long for fleet operations. Even Knox balked at this, as did Roosevelt, who sent Knox instructions to "tell Ernie *once more* [emphasis in original]: No reorganizing of the Navy Department's set-up during the war. Let's win it first."[11]

The Knox-Forrestal reaction was to promote a plan to separate once again the roles of chief of naval operations and commander in chief, United States Fleet, leaving King to tend to military operations only as COMINCH and not as CNO. King predictably opposed this, even though he always felt that the CNO should be "the top man in the Navy" — him, of course. (By contrast, the organization of the War Department made it quite clear that Marshall was the top soldier, responsible to the secretary of war and then the president.)

King continued in his dual roles but chafed under Forrestal's assertion of civilian control. He claimed that Forrestal "seemed bent on harassing [him] in some ways," but he hardly helped his own cause by occasionally berating the secretary as if he were a junior officer rather than his civilian superior. In the summer of 1945, the two came to verbal blows over the recommendations of the Flag Officer Selection Board. Rather than going to King, Forrestal summoned Marc Mitscher, the ranking member of the board then on permanent duty in Washington, and "took him to task for what he considered poor recommendations."

King exploded not only about Forrestal interfering in what had been an entirely proper selection process, but also about him summoning one member of the board to account for its total actions. Forrestal pulled rank on King by asking King to accompany him to the White House, implying that Truman would support Forrestal's list and not that of the selection board. It is difficult to see Roosevelt interfering in such a manner, but Truman approved the list as changed by Forrestal without asking King's views. King later summed up his relationship with Forrestal by observing, "I didn't like him and he didn't like me."[12]

But the rift certainly was not entirely King's fault. Chester Nimitz, who also could be bullheaded at times, was not immune from Forrestal's delving into matters Nimitz also considered solely within his own military purview. Forrestal once decided that CINCPAC should publish a daily newspaper, or at the very least, some sort of Pacific Fleet magazine. Nimitz had the public relations staff to do the job, but he felt the extra work of distribution was "just too much when we are trying to run a war." It appeared to be a huge waste of valuable time, particularly when overseas editions of *Time* and *Newsweek* were readily available.

Forrestal kept insisting that Nimitz take on this task until Nimitz stormed, "The publicity side of the war is getting so large, it almost overshadows the fighting side." Forrestal finally relented, but the incident earned Nimitz a spot on Forrestal's list as someone who could be almost as stubborn and recalcitrant as King, and it would play a role several months later when discussions turned to King's successor.[13]

Throughout July and early August, Halsey's Third Fleet made repeated carrier attacks against Tokyo and Japan's main islands. Halsey wondered why Nimitz placed several cities off-limits, but his planes struck the last remnants of the Japanese fleet at Kure and Kobe, sinking a battleship, two converted battleships, four cruisers, five destroyers, and three carriers, effectively eliminating any remaining vestiges of the Japanese navy. "If the enemy had not already heard the crack of doom," *Time* reported, "he heard it now."[14]

But there was more in the air than apparent doom for the Japanese empire. Throughout the summer, American intelligence had begun to show a massive buildup of Japanese forces on Kyushu, including kamikaze-style aircraft. Indeed, even before the Joint Chiefs' June decision on the invasion, Nimitz had reversed himself in a private memo to King. Given the lengthy and costly campaign on Okinawa, Nimitz now told King, "it would be unrealistic to expect that such obvious objectives as southern Kyushu and the Tokyo Plain will not be as well defended as Okinawa." Once again, to avoid staggering casualties, Nimitz became an advocate of blockade and bombing tactics.[15]

King kept Nimitz's views to himself, which set the stage for the war's final showdown between MacArthur and the navy. Earlier in the spring—before the Joint Chiefs' supposed "final" decision to invade Kyushu—King had adamantly told his fellow chiefs that while he was issuing orders to prepare the navy for an invasion of Kyushu, he expected to revisit the decision later in the summer. Now that time had come.

On the one hand, King had alarming intelligence reports of troop strength ashore, his top commander's opposition to a direct invasion, and fears of another round of deadly kamikaze attacks against his fleet. On the other hand, King had George Marshall and Douglas MacArthur. The former was still intent on occupying enemy territory but beginning to worry about Kyushu. The latter was busily giving his "personal estimate" that the forces said to be opposing Operation Olympic were "greatly exaggerated."[16]

MacArthur made a habit, his critics claimed, of underestimating his opposition's strength—as he had in invading Luzon—in order to carry out his personal strategic vision. In the case of Kyushu, MacArthur's goal may well have been his "personal interest in commanding the greatest amphibious assault in history." King, his own confidence in Olympic waning, decided to send Marshall's growing concerns and MacArthur's haughty reply to Nimitz for comment and instructed him to include MacArthur in his response. If Nimitz reiterated his summerlong opposition to invading Kyushu, as King assumed he would, it would drive a wedge deeper than ever into the interservice rivalry but give King the opportunity to have the Joint Chiefs rethink the entire invasion plan.[17]

Meanwhile, the reason for Nimitz withholding Hiroshima and Nagasaki from Halsey's target list became clear. King had learned about the atomic bomb program late in 1943 when Marshall had paid a quiet visit to his office and swore him to secrecy. Thereafter, Marshall kept King informed about developments at regular intervals. By February 1945, it was time to tell Nimitz, and King dispatched Commander Frederick L. Ashworth to Nimitz's headquarters on Guam to do so. Ashworth arrived hot and bedraggled by the Pacific climate, with the top secret dispatch crumpled in a sweaty money belt.

Nimitz seemed more focused on immediate operations than the promise of a superweapon, but it was his responsibility to provide logistics for the B-29s that would drop the bombs. Ashworth selected Tinian, between Saipan and Guam, as the forward base for the 509th Composite Group. Word of the new weapon was strictly on a need-to-know basis, and Nimitz did not inform Halsey until July 22.[18]

The reactions of the four fleet admirals to dropping the bomb mirrored their naval upbringing. They had come of age with the battleship and matured in leadership roles with the development of submarines and airpower. This new atomic power was something quite foreign and generally repulsive to them. It was a different kind of warfare, for which none of them had any enthusiasm.

Leahy had his doubts that the bomb would work, and even if it did, he wondered whether it should be used. He was with Truman when the new president was given "a scientist's version of the atomic bomb." According to Truman, Leahy called it "the biggest fool thing we have ever done" and claimed that it "will never go off, and I speak as an expert in explosives."[19]

Even after Truman received news at Potsdam of the first success-ful test in the New Mexico desert, Leahy remained skeptical. Meet-ing with King George VI in England en route home from Potsdam, Leahy told the king, "I do not think it will be as effective as is expected. It sounds like a professor's dream to me!" But a few days later, on August 6, reports of the destruction at Hiroshima reached the presidential party aboard the cruiser *Augusta* in the mid-Atlantic. Truman was excited and called it "the greatest thing in history." Leahy immediately thought of the future.[20]

"The lethal possibilities of such atomic action in the future is frightening," he wrote in his diary, "and while we are the first to have it in our possession, there is a certainty that it will in the future be developed by potential enemies and that it will probably be used against us."[21]

Leahy readily admitted that he had "misjudged the terrible effi-ciency" of the bomb, but that only hardened his resolve that it shouldn't have been used. Just as he had cautioned against an invasion of Japan, Leahy held the opinion that the bombing of Hiroshima and then Nagasaki three days later "was of no material assistance" to bringing about the Japanese surrender.

Leahy felt so strongly about this that he concluded his memoirs with a grim foreboding of what the atomic age meant. "My own feeling," he lamented, "was that in being the first to use it, we had adopted an ethical standard common to the barbarians of the Dark Ages. I was not taught to make war in that fashion." It was indeed a long way from those lusty cheers on the decks of the *Oregon* in 1898 after it had raced around Cape Horn. And significantly, Leahy wrote those words not as some decades-removed revisionism, but about 1949.[22]

King was of much the same mind. In his memoirs, he reverted to his opposition to an invasion of Japan and called the rationale that the bomb would save American lives misplaced because, had Truman been willing to wait, King thought, a blockade would have "starved the Japanese into submission" without its use. Privately, King declared that he "didn't like the atomic bomb or any part of it."[23]

Nimitz, too, was of an older school. He considered the bomb "somehow indecent, certainly not a legitimate form of warfare," and hoped it would not be used. Captain Edwin Layton, still the CINCPAC intelligence officer, offered the opinion that because it was such a radical change from conventional warfare, it might give the Japanese emperor an out to surrender and end the war without loss of face among his people. Nimitz was forced to agree, but that did not mean he had to like it. "Thank you very much," Nimitz said to Fred Ashworth after Ashworth delivered his sweaty communiqué about the bomb's existence. But as he left the room, Ashworth heard Nimitz mumble, half to himself, "You know, I guess I was just born a few years too soon."[24]

Only Halsey, his reasoning more military than humanitarian, disagreed slightly with the other three. "It was a mistake ever to drop it," he acknowledged. "Why reveal a weapon like that to the world when it wasn't necessary?" And Halsey believed that it wasn't necessary because Japan was "utterly defeated and knew it" before the Hiroshima blast. About all the bombs succeeded in doing, Halsey claimed with his usual bias, "was to leave less Japs to be fed."[25]

*   *   *

On August 10, with no immediate reaction from the Japanese to the two bombs, Nimitz pondered his reply to King, copy to MacArthur, on the Kyushu invasion plans. Even the normally diplomatic Nimitz might well have lit a powder keg, but other events were to intervene and void the necessity of his response.[26]

Early on August 11, King sent Nimitz another message. This time, it was a "peace warning." Indications were that Japan was about to surrender, and there was suddenly no rush on the Kyushu response. Truman and the Joint Chiefs wanted to keep up the pressure until a surrender was assured, so Halsey ordered another round of carrier attacks on Tokyo. Nimitz countermanded the order, but when no word of surrender came, he told Halsey to launch the strikes. On the morning of August 15, Halsey ordered a similar raid and told Nimitz he was doing so.

Nimitz concurred, but two hours later Ed Layton burst into Nimitz's office unannounced waving a sheet of paper. "This is the hottest thing we've had," Layton told the admiral. It was Japan's acceptance of unconditional surrender. CINCPAC flashed Halsey the order "Suspend air operations," then radioed all commands in the Pacific Ocean Area, "Cease offensive operations against Japanese forces... [but] beware of treachery or last moment attacks by enemy forces or individuals."[27]

Characteristically, Nimitz took the news calmly with a satisfied smile. Out on Halsey's flagship, it was another story. Four years earlier, Doug Moulton had rushed into Halsey's cabin on the *Enterprise* with word of the attack on Pearl Harbor. Now it was Moulton, still with the admiral as his air operations officer, who interrupted Halsey's breakfast on the *Missouri* with news of the surrender. Halsey whooped, hollered, and pounded the shoulders of everyone within reach. In Washington, King's reaction was more laconic: "I wonder what I am going to do tomorrow."[28]

V-J Day, as it came to be called, was especially poignant for Leahy. The man for whom he had worked so long and hard to bring this day about was no longer there to share the triumph. With

Truman's blessing, Leahy took to the airwaves to address the American public and those under arms in the field.

"My fellow Americans," Leahy began, "We, with our allies, have won what President Roosevelt called on December 8, 1941 the 'inevitable victory.' The terms we laid down at that time — unconditional surrender — have been met. . . . We must now turn to the binding up of our own and of the world's wounds."

Acknowledging the transformation in the nation's armed forces, Leahy declared, "Today we have the biggest and most powerful navy in the world, more powerful than any other two navies in existence. . . . But," he cautioned, "we must not depend on this strength and this power alone." America's true strength and the secret weapon that really won the war, he concluded, came "from our basic virtues as a freedom-loving nation."[29]

To that, FDR would have said amen. What Eleanor Roosevelt did say to Leahy was that her thoughts were with him and that "Franklin would want to clasp your hand and congratulate you for all you have done to make this victory possible."[30]

Later that day in the Pacific, Nimitz issued his own, more detailed instructions to his commands. "With the termination of hostilities against Japan," he cautioned, "it is incumbent on all officers to conduct themselves with dignity and decorum in their treatment of the Japanese and their public utterances in connection with the Japanese." These were the same people who had attacked Pearl Harbor, Nimitz continued, but "the use of insulting epithets in connection with the Japanese as a race or as individuals does not now become the officers of the United States Navy."[31]

Of course, one of the worst offenders was Halsey. Throughout the conflict, Halsey's exhortation to "kill more Jap bastards" was among the milder of his racially charged rants. Like Patton on land in the European Theater, Halsey made too many public relations gaffes simply by being himself. When asked earlier in the spring if the emperor's palace was a military objective, Halsey said no, but then in a moment of what even Halsey admitted was "thoughtless flippancy," he rushed on to say, "I'd hate to have them kill Hirohito's white horse, because I want to ride it."[32]

Innocuous as that may have sounded to some, the sanctity of the emperor to the Japanese people weighed heavily on Nimitz's mind. Riding a horse reserved only for the emperor was just the sort of degradation of the emperor's position that Nimitz hoped to avoid when he and MacArthur were relying on Japanese subservience to the emperor to effect a bloodless occupation.

Nimitz tried to downplay Halsey's boast, but newspapers seized on it, and soon a variety of equestrian gear—including a saddle complete with bridle, blanket, and lariat, from the Lions Club of Montrose, Colorado—began arriving in Halsey's mail. His cabin on the *Missouri* "began to look like a tack room." Even serious Raymond Spruance couldn't avoid the issue. Spruance was asked during a late August press conference aboard the *New Jersey* if he thought Halsey would ride the white horse through Tokyo. "I can't predict," Spruance deadpanned, adding "and I also don't know how long it has been since Halsey has ridden a white horse."[33]

On August 29, Nimitz and his staff flew into Tokyo Bay on two PB2Y Coronado seaplanes and taxied up to the battleship *South Dakota,* which was to serve as his flagship. Halsey's flagship, *Missouri,* was at anchor nearby. The next day, MacArthur landed at an airfield near Yokosuka. At the foot of the ramp to greet him was General Robert L. Eichelberger, whom MacArthur had once told in the dark days on New Guinea, "Go out there, Bob, and take Buna or don't come back alive." Now MacArthur grinned at him and said, "Bob, this is the payoff."[34]

Douglas MacArthur had every reason to be smug. On the evening of the Japanese surrender announcement, President Truman had appointed MacArthur supreme commander of the Allied powers and had directed him to receive Japan's formal surrender and oversee its occupation. To Nimitz and many of his naval brethren, this was a case of the army rushing to grab the glory after the sea-lanes had been secured by navy blood.

In truth, it had been a collaborative effort, and it was Secretary of the Navy Forrestal—always a navy champion, despite his infighting with King and Nimitz—who suggested that the ceremony take place on a ship and that if MacArthur was to sign as supreme Allied commander, Nimitz should sign for the United States. It helped to boost the navy's heroes when Forrestal recommended Halsey's *Missouri*—conveniently from Truman's home state—as the location.[35]

The world would watch MacArthur preside, but Nimitz never wavered in his assertions about the role sea power had played in the conflict. Meeting with correspondents in his cabin on the *South Dakota* on the evening of August 29, Nimitz reminded them that the surrender had come about before any invasion had been necessary primarily because of sea power, "spearheaded by carrier-borne aircraft and an excellent, efficient submarine force." And for all the awe of the atomic bomb, Nimitz maintained that sea power had made the bomb's use possible by providing bases from which planes could carry it. "Without seapower," the admiral concluded, "we could not have advanced at all."[36]

The next day, Nimitz and Halsey went ashore and toured the naval base at Yokosuka. It was a mess. Nimitz expressed scorn and surprise that the Japanese had taken no precautions to have "the station in a proper state of cleanliness for the occupation." During the tour, the Japanese automobile assigned for the occasion ran out of gas. Halsey never got to ride the emperor's white horse—Nimitz undoubtedly saw to that—but that didn't stop Halsey from venting his usual anger at his now vanquished foes. "Admiral Halsey's remarks," the *New York Times* reported, "were unprintable."[37]

None of this kept Nimitz from his usual letter writing to Catherine and his children. He remained prolific and, as always, evidenced his keen sense of humor. On September 1, after paying a visit to MacArthur in the latter's new headquarters in Yokohama, Nimitz wrote his daughter Kate, "In a few minutes I will go to call on Admiral Fraser, RN, on the *Duke of York,* anchored close by—partly on official business, partly because I like him, and mostly to get a Scotch and soda before dinner because our ships are dry."[38]

But the big day was to be Sunday, September 2. Nimitz arrived on board the *Missouri* with plenty of time for reminiscing with Halsey. The bad weather of the past several days was clearing. Nimitz, who had figuratively stood by Halsey through Leyte and two typhoons, was now literally standing beside him as Douglas MacArthur strode up the gangplank. Nimitz saluted; MacArthur returned the salute and shook hands with Nimitz and then Halsey.

Nimitz gestured MacArthur in the direction of the surrender ceremonies but immediately realized that he was on the right. Strict protocol gave MacArthur that spot as the ranking officer. With a gentle pat on MacArthur's left side, Nimitz steered the general to the right and deftly stepped to his left as they marched down the deck. Halsey followed. When they were assembled below a massive 16-inch turret with the representatives of the Allied powers and the cream of the American high command in the Pacific, a small launch pulled alongside bearing Japanese foreign minister Mamoru Shigemitsu and chief of the army general staff Yoshijiro Umezu.

MacArthur, who had so many times been theatrical in his actions, nonetheless always knew the power of understatement. His opening remarks were brief, powerful, and to the point. Having made them, he directed the representatives of Japan to sign the surrender documents. Then it was his turn. Using no less than six pens, MacArthur signed as supreme commander. It was arguably the pinnacle of his career, and—past arguments aside—he performed his duty with dignity and gratitude toward his navy comrades.

Nimitz chose only two pens for his signatures, one a gift from longtime friends and a reliable green Parker pen. Halsey and Rear Admiral Forrest Sherman, Nimitz's deputy chief of staff, stood behind Nimitz as he did so. Newsreel footage shows Halsey and MacArthur exchanging whispered remarks. According to Halsey, MacArthur instructed him to start a massive flyover of 450 carrier planes. After all the Allied representatives had signed, MacArthur made a few concluding remarks and then intoned, "These proceedings are closed."[39]

One obvious omission from the surrender ceremony was Raymond Spruance. MacArthur had invited him to attend, but Spruance had declined, saying that Nimitz had not ordered him to do so and that if Nimitz had wanted him aboard the *Missouri,* he would have ordered him to be there. Instead, Spruance spent September 2 on board his own flagship, *New Jersey,* off Okinawa. Since Nimitz and Spruance were and remained great friends, it is unreasonable to assign any personal snub or oversight to the absence of an order or invitation. It has been speculated that Nimitz may have been guarding against a worst-case scenario whereby some last-ditch Japanese attack decimated the Allied high command on the *Missouri*. The evidence is strong that there was no one Nimitz would have trusted more to lead renewed attacks against Japan than Spruance.[40]

Conversely, one of Nimitz's admirals summoned to attend the surrender was reluctant to do so. "Slew" McCain was still highly miffed over his reassignment to the Veterans Administration in the wake of the second typhoon and didn't want to linger, telling Halsey, "I want to get the hell out of here!" But Halsey would have none of it. "Maybe you do, but you're not going," he tartly replied. "You were commanding this task force when the war ended, and I'm making sure that history gets it straight."

So McCain lined up in the front row on the *Missouri* to watch the surrender. "Thank God you made me stay, Bill!" he exclaimed to Halsey afterward. "You had better sense than I did." Four days later, one day after his return to San Diego, McCain dropped dead of a heart attack.[41]

Nimitz wrote to Catherine on the afternoon of the surrender. "The big moment is over," he told her, "and the Japs have signed the formal terms of surrender. Everything clicked in a minute by minute schedule and the ceremony started at exactly 9 am Tokyo time."

But even in reporting this news of perhaps the greatest achievement of his life, Nimitz reverted to the personal between him and Catherine. He might well have said that their relationship was the greatest achievement of his life. "I was tremendously pleased (and surprised)," he now wrote her, "to receive your five letters of 23 and 24 Aug with enclosures—which were brought up from Guam by one of our officers who brought up important mail. This is rapid time—your 24 Aug letter written on my 25 Aug was only 7 days from Berkeley to Tokyo Bay."

He included a schematic of deck positions on the *Missouri* and confessed to a certain amount of "nervous excitement" when it was his turn to sign. "But I did sign in the correct places (one signer did not)," he assured her. "First copy signed with the Woo gift pen and second copy signed with my old green Parker pen."[42]

The next day, Nimitz boarded his Coronado and flew back to Guam. Among his passengers was a young marine lieutenant who had been captured on Bataan and released from a Tokyo prison only four days before. It was typical of Nimitz to provide the lift. World War II was over, the boys were coming home, and perhaps Nimitz summed up the feelings of almost every American serviceman and servicewoman when he told Catherine that the marine was "about the happiest young man I ever saw."[43]

CHAPTER TWENTY-FIVE

Measures of Men

In less than four years, the American navy had gone from the carnage of Battleship Row at Pearl Harbor to the largest and most powerful armada ever to sail the seas. It would have been difficult to forecast this day four years before, but in retrospect, three events in 1941 sealed the fate of the Axis powers: Germany's headlong rush to self-destruction by invading Russia; the American-British alliance affirmed by the Roosevelt-Churchill conference at Argentia; and the Japanese attack on Pearl Harbor, which unified American sentiment as few other events could have done.

None of these occurrences, however, was as remarkable as the speed with which the Axis powers were reduced to ruin once the United States entered the war. During the 1,366 days between December 7, 1941, and September 2, 1945, the tremendous outpouring of America's industrial might in ships, planes, tanks, and other armaments was matched only by the bravery and determination of the nation's men and women. In the navy alone, the fleet grew from 790 vessels to 6,768, and its complement of officers, sailors, and marines swelled from 383,150 to 3,405,525. New construction increased active ship levels, net of losses, by 6 battleships, 21 fleet carriers, 70 escort carriers, 35 cruisers, 206 destroyers, 361 destroyer escorts, 120 submarines, 451 minesweepers, 1,104 patrol boats, and 3,604 amphibious and auxiliary craft.[1]

Despite the Japanese surrender ceremony being held on the deck of a battleship, the war had been a final curtain call for battleship admirals and their revered gray behemoths. Stately and magnificent though they were, the battleships had been eclipsed by aircraft carriers and submarines as omnipotent offensive weapons. Never again would navies come at one another with 16-inch guns blazing.

Throughout most of their careers, King, Nimitz, and Halsey had been on the cutting edge of the developing innovations in naval aviation and undersea warfare. And while Leahy dragged his black shoes for years over the battleship's increased vulnerabilities, he came to embrace these newer weapons as essential to achieving the wartime goals he oversaw from the president's right hand. Naval aviation and America's submarine force would continue their ascension as both spear point and deterrent, but for the fleet admirals, September 2, 1945, was the apex of their careers.

America's five-star admirals met their postwar futures with varying outlooks. Citing "the capitulation of Japan and the cessation of hostilities throughout the world," Halsey asked for immediate retirement. "When you leave the Pacific, Bill," MacArthur supposedly told him, "it becomes just another damned ocean!" Nimitz approved Halsey's retirement request with an endorsement that asserted, "It will be difficult — if not impossible — to overestimate the value of Admiral Halsey's splendid service to our country."[2]

But that would have been too hasty an exit for one of America's most well-known heroes. In December 1945, within a week of his retirement, President Truman recalled Halsey to active duty and promoted him to the fourth set of fleet admiral stars so many felt he deserved. The following April, Congress made the ranks of all eight five-star generals and admirals permanent and assigned them to active duty for life, in part to provide continuing compensation greater than their pensions.

Halsey teamed up with Joseph Bryan III, who had served in the Southwest Pacific, to write the admiral's memoirs. These first appeared as an eight-part installment in the *Saturday Evening Post* and then in book form as *Admiral Halsey's Story*. Halsey proved his loyalty by continuing to stand by his friend Husband Kimmel over Pearl Harbor, but the battle that wouldn't die was Leyte Gulf. Halsey stood his ground and took on all comers, citing the divided commands between the Third and Seventh Fleets, Kinkaid's supposed lack of aggressiveness in guarding San Bernardino Strait, and Nimitz's grant of discretion in destroying the Japanese fleet. None of this, however, could erase the perception—no matter how successful the overall American results—that Halsey had been lured north by the Japanese, as postwar Japanese records made clear was indeed their intent.

On the personal side, Halsey quickly grew bored. A fund-raising post with the University of Virginia, which he had attended for one pre-Annapolis year, was unfulfilling. He served on the board of directors of the Carlisle Tire and Rubber Company, and later of ITT, but his duties were largely limited to those of a resident celebrity. Finally, there was Fan. The great love affair they had shared for years had crumbled during the war with Fan's increasingly manic-depressive condition. By 1950, Halsey had settled in New York, while Fan lived in California near their son, eventually entering a nursing home.

Halsey experienced what to varying degrees Nimitz, King, and Leahy all experienced—a severe letdown from the high-stress rush of complicated combat commands to a mundane life of occasional speeches and parades. Other than the continuing controversies over his actions off Leyte, there were few poignant moments in Halsey's last years. Once again assuming a fund-raising chairmanship, he tried in vain to save the vaunted *Enterprise* as a museum and memorial, but pleas for funds and designation as a national shrine came up short. In August 1958, the carrier was towed to the scrap yard.

About that same time, Robert Montgomery began production of a movie based on Halsey's role in the critical weeks of the Guadalcanal campaign. Eventually called *The Gallant Hours*, it starred

James Cagney, looking uncannily like the wartime Halsey. But Halsey did not live to see its release. In August 1959, he vacationed, as he had several times before, at the country club on Fishers Island offshore Mystic, Connecticut. Sun and the surf suited the admiral, but on the morning of August 16, he failed to appear for breakfast. The club manager found him alone in his room, dead at seventy-six from an apparent heart attack. Only weeks before, Halsey had taken yet another naval historian to task for second-guessing his actions at Leyte.

Halsey's body was flown by helicopter to Floyd Bennett Field in Brooklyn, New York, and then by plane to Washington, D.C. After lying in state in the National Cathedral's Bethlehem Chapel and a service on August 20, the state funeral procession of horse-drawn caisson and flag-draped casket made its way across the river to Arlington National Cemetery. Halsey was buried near his parents on the side of a knoll below the Custis-Lee Mansion, looking eastward to Washington. Chester Nimitz, representing President Eisenhower, stood at the head of the casket as it was lowered into the ground to a nineteen-gun salute, three rifle volleys, and taps.[3]

The only fleet admiral unhappier in retirement than Halsey was King. The autumn of 1945 passed, in King's words, "with the burdensome and somewhat tedious process of demobilization." King's turf battles with Forrestal also came to a head. The post of commander in chief, U.S. Fleet (COMINCH), was abolished, and as the newly defined CNO, King stepped into the role that was now legally the naval equivalent of what Marshall had been on the army side and King had already been de facto — the nation's top sailor.

High on the list of King's differences with Forrestal was King's wish that Nimitz succeed him as CNO. Nimitz was eager for the job, and King — though he still considered Nimitz somewhat of a "fixer" — nonetheless saw it as a way to reward Nimitz for his stalwart service. Marshall was doing the same by stepping down in favor of Eisenhower and King may also have privately thought that if the hero of Europe was filling Marshall's shoes, the hero of the Pacific should fill his. Forrestal's preferred candidate was Admiral

Richard S. Edwards, most recently King's deputy as both COMINCH and CNO. Edwards was clearly qualified, and Forrestal most likely preferred his easygoing manner and subservience to Nimitz's independent streak.

Finally, King forced Forrestal's hand by writing to Truman via Forrestal, asking the secretary within the letter to hand it to the president. King requested that Nimitz relieve him. Forrestal delivered the letter, and Truman agreed to the appointment. But Forrestal showed his authority by limiting Nimitz's tenure in office to two years instead of the traditional four and expediting the change of command.

King, conscious of history as he always was, had wanted to stay in office at least until December 17, the five-year anniversary of his return to sea duty with the Atlantic force, or December 30, the fourth anniversary of his appointment as COMINCH. King was also hoping to get Nimitz some well-deserved leave by making the change in January 1946. Instead, Forrestal picked a December 15 date, knowing full well the other considerations. In typical fashion, King did not ask the secretary to change the date because he "would not give [Forrestal] the opportunity to turn him down."[4]

Among the accolades that celebrated King's retirement and his service was a gold star in lieu of a third Distinguished Service Medal from President Truman; honorary degrees from Northwestern, Princeton, and Oxford; and an elaborate scroll befitting a king from the admiral's circle of regular newspaper correspondents. Even the British chiefs of staff, failing to mention the many turf battles and King's dogged devotion to the Pacific campaign, nevertheless went out of their way to praise his keen insight and "breadth of vision and unshakeable determination to secure the defeat of our enemies in the shortest possible time."[5]

By the following year, King was at work on what he hoped would be his account of the international conferences in which he had participated as a member of the Combined Chiefs of Staff. Walter Muir Whitehill, a Naval Reserve officer who had been instrumental in preparing King's wartime annual reports to the secretary of the navy, soon proposed a biography. King's conference memoirs and

Whitehill's planned biography merged, particularly after King suffered the first of a number of strokes in 1947. *Fleet Admiral King: A Naval Record* was published in 1952 in the third person with King and Whitehill as coauthors, but it is King's voice, transcribed by Whitehill from dozens of interviews, that resounds from its pages.

With his story in print, King was further plagued by declining health. There was not much more for him to do. As his principal biographer wrote, "King's life came to an end gradually, painfully, and pathetically." It was not the way he would have wanted it. With additional strokes, his mind was a prisoner in a body that became increasingly crippled and marked by slurred speech and an unsteady hand. He became a regular in a suite at the National Naval Medical Center in Bethesda, Maryland, journeying only to the naval hospital in Portsmouth, New Hampshire, for the summers.

But even as the inevitable appeared before him, King retained his sharp wit. When the navy dispatched George Russell, King's one-time flag secretary, to find out the admiral's wishes in keeping with the planned state funerals for five-star admirals and generals, King, when he learned the reason for the visit, gave a hearty laugh and remarked, "Well, Russell, I hope this isn't urgent."[6]

It wasn't, but eventually King died in Portsmouth on Monday afternoon, June 25, 1956, at the age of seventy-seven. His broken body was flown to Washington, D.C., and lay in state at the National Cathedral. King, who had approved or disapproved so much with a penciled "Yes, K," or "No, K," was responsible for the brevity of the service. Read from the Book of Common Prayer, it contained only one hymn: "Eternal Father, Strong to Save." Twenty minutes later, the procession formed for the drive to Fifteenth Street and Constitution Avenue and the march to the Capitol.

The day was sunny and pleasant in temperature — a rare touch of Washington at its best before the dog days of heat and humidity. Hymns that King had chosen, "Onward, Christian Soldiers" and "God of Our Fathers," with its stirring trumpet fanfares, accompanied the flag-draped casket on its way. But King's final destination was not to be Arlington. He wanted to be buried within sight of the grounds and the institution that had started him on his way and had always been part of who he was. He was going home to Annapolis. There, in the Naval Academy Cemetery on a tree-covered knoll above the Severn River, King was laid to rest. Mattie, who had suffered her own health problems and had been content to call Annapolis the family home over the years, would join him there in 1969.[7]

Nimitz, in part because of his personality but also because of Catherine and his abundant and supportive family, made the postwar transition far easier than King or Halsey. First came his two-year stint as CNO. He remained an ardent champion for the navy as he oversaw postwar demobilization and worked toward the structure of independent service branches within the unified Department of Defense that was finally instituted by the National Security Act of 1947. Perhaps most significantly, Nimitz advocated the navy sharing responsibility with the air force for delivering atomic weapons. In time, this resulted in submarines and aircraft carriers as key players in the nation's nuclear arsenal.

Nimitz steadfastly refused to write his own memoirs, but that did not stop him from writing articles supporting the navy and serving as coeditor of several books, including *Sea Power* with E. B. Potter, who at Catherine's request would eventually write the admiral's biography. Nimitz also steadfastly refused to linger in Washington once his tenure as CNO was complete, even though the navy offered to provide him with an office there as an active-duty fleet admiral. Instead, in December 1947 Chester and Catherine headed for California.

In San Diego, daughter Kate and James Lay's children, including a set of twins born in 1948, were key attractions for the doting grandparents. But it was in Berkeley, scene of their happy family days during Nimitz's NROTC tour at the University of California, that they found the perfect house. After years of navy bases and hotel rooms, Chester and Catherine settled into a Spanish-style home with a grand view of San Francisco Bay. Chet and Joan soon arrived in Berkeley with more grandchildren when Chet was assigned as executive officer of the campus NROTC unit. The senior Nimitz also became a regent of the university.

But by the end of 1948, Nimitz, too, was showing signs of an uneasy retirement. Even so patient a man as he could spend only so much time gardening—which he did with a vengeance—and attending occasional VIP events. With Catherine's blessing, he accepted a position with the United Nations as the plebiscite administrator for Kashmir, the area hotly contested between Pakistan and India as those countries split and became independent of Churchill's British Empire. When neither country could agree to a vote or Nimitz's subsequent attempts at arbitration, he returned to Berkeley in the spring of 1950, although he continued to serve as a roving ambassador for the United Nations for another two years.

Busy years in Berkeley followed. While Nimitz remained grimly indignant about the atrocities visited upon Allied personnel during World War II, he continued to respect the Japanese as a people and particularly appreciated their naval heritage. He encouraged the preservation of the Japanese battleship *Mikasa,* Admiral Togo's flagship at the Battle of Tsushima, and Togo's home, which Nimitz had visited in 1934.

By the summer of 1963, keeping up the house in Berkeley, which Chester and Catherine called Longview, had become a burden. The navy arranged for them to live in Quarters One on Yerba Buena Island in San Francisco Bay, where adequate staff could assist with their needs. Always a walker, who had led many a navy comrade uphill and down, Nimitz was finally slowed by a shattered kneecap and osteoarthritis of the spine. He insisted on risky back surgery in an attempt to relieve the pain but caught pneumonia in the process. Several small strokes followed, and there was evidence of congestive heart failure. In and out of the hospital, he wanted most to be home with Catherine, and there, with her at his side, he died on February 20, 1966, a few days short of his eighty-first birthday.

The obligatory state funeral in Washington, D.C., followed, but he came home a final time to California for burial under a simple regulation headstone adorned with five stars in Golden Gate National Cemetery. By agreement with his friends Raymond Spruance and Richmond Kelly Turner, they would all lie together with their wives along a treeless drive among rows and rows of the same headstones. "To me," said Catherine, "he has just gone to sea and, as I have done so many times in the past, some day I will follow him." She did in 1979.[8]

Leahy's postwar transition was perhaps the easiest of the four fleet admirals' because he remained as chief of staff to the president for another four years. In the wake of Roosevelt's death, Leahy had been blunt with Truman about his propensity to speak his own mind. Truman — himself no stranger to the blunt word — appreciated it and highly valued Leahy's independent advice, which continued to involve a wide range of foreign affairs as well as military issues.

Whatever else Leahy was, he was no yes-man. Among his disagreements with Truman was his adamant opposition to the creation of a Jewish state in Palestine. He felt that such an action would "needlessly alienate the Arabs and endanger American access to the oil of the Middle East."[9] Truman, of course, felt differently and prevailed. So, too, did the emerging Truman-Marshall line toward China after George Marshall became secretary of state in 1947. Leahy fully supported Chiang Kai-shek's Nationalist government. Instead, Truman and Marshall urged Chiang to work out some accommodation with Mao Tse-tung and eventually came to the conclusion that China was lost to the Communists. By contrast, Leahy's determination to aid Greece and Turkey against Soviet expansion contributed to the president's decision to issue the Truman Doctrine.

Events at home and abroad reached a boiling point in 1948 as Truman recognized the new state of Israel; the Soviets blockaded Berlin, resulting in the famous airlift; and Truman won a stunning come-from-behind election. Leahy wholeheartedly supported the airlift and Truman's election, but he remained skeptical of the politics of the Middle East. "The President's announcement [recognizing Israel]," Leahy wrote, "made with inadequate consideration leaves many questions unanswered" and could, he concluded, "drag the United States into a war between the two religious groups."[10]

During the heated 1948 campaign, some called for Leahy's dismissal as an aging — he was seventy-three — fossil of another age, a hard-line conservative bordering on reactionary. Leahy had already told Truman that he wished to retire after the election — no matter the outcome — but in September, in the face of such criticism, he offered to do so immediately. Truman would have none of it, telling Leahy in a letter handwritten from his whistle-stop campaign train, "You are my friend and I am yours come hell or high water."[11]

After the election, health problems called for Leahy's retirement as planned, but he stayed on active duty as a fleet admiral and regularly visited Truman at the White House and in Key West. In 1950, Leahy published his memoirs, *I Was There*, professing to be an eyewitness account of possibly the closest inside adviser ever to serve two presidents. The book was hardly a gripping saga, but rather a Leahy-esque recitation of the facts as he had seen them. Despite a foreword by Truman, it focused almost exclusively on Leahy's World War II service and not his years with Truman.

Perhaps the best measure of Leahy's worth to Truman — and Truman's acknowledgment of the admiral's stony discretion — was that the president confided to Leahy in November 1951 that he would not seek another term, a decision Truman did not announce publicly until late March 1952. And when Truman held his final farewell dinner in the State Dining Room of the White House for forty-two intimates in December 1952, it was Leahy, despite the fact that he had been out of the president's direct service for four years, who held the guest-of-honor's position at the president's right hand. Perhaps Truman realized that in those terrifying and hectic days following Roosevelt's death, the recent vice president of the United States, who had not even been told about the atomic bomb, owed his preparation for the world stage to Leahy's self-effacing loyalty to their country.[12]

Leahy's last major hurrah was his eightieth birthday party at the Carlton Hotel in Washington in 1955. "When I was a young officer," the current CNO, Admiral Robert B. "Mick" Carney, wrote in tribute, "the pronouncements of Admiral Leahy had all of the validity and authority of the Sinai tablets. Captain Leahy was my idea of what the Captain of the ship should be."[13]

Leahy was in and out of Bethesda naval hospital until the end came on July 20, 1959, with his son, William H. Leahy, himself a retired rear admiral, at his bedside. After seventeen years without his beloved Louise, Leahy was buried beside her in Arlington National Cemetery. "There never was a finer man or an abler public servant," Truman wrote Leahy's son. "I could always depend on him to tell me the truth, whether I liked it or not, a quality too seldom found in men of his position."[14]

Of the principal contemporaries of the fleet admirals, Raymond Spruance, always the cerebral scholar, got his wish and became president of the Naval War College. Retiring from the navy in 1948, he served a stint as ambassador to the Philippines and remained the exceedingly gracious gentleman he had always been until his death in 1969. He and Margaret are buried beside Chester and Catherine Nimitz in Golden Gate National Cemetery.

Douglas MacArthur remained in Japan throughout its occupation. America's only proconsul in the Roman tradition, he did not return to the United States until after his 1951 firing by President Truman over his demands to expand the Korean War into China. He died in 1964, after counseling both John F. Kennedy and Lyndon B. Johnson to avoid a military buildup in Vietnam.

Winston Churchill was unceremoniously voted out of office in July 1945 even as he attended the Potsdam Conference. But the bulldog returned as prime minister from 1951 to 1955. When he died in 1965, it marked the passing of the British Empire. Churchill had his quirks, but when it came to putting a determined face and a rallying rhetoric on the Allied cause, it is not unreasonable to call him, as *Time* did in its January 2, 1950, issue, "Man of the Half-Century."

The other contemporary of the four admirals who might well deserve a similar accolade—besides Franklin Roosevelt—was George Marshall. In his preparation for war, his unselfish leadership during the struggle, and his postwar service as secretary of defense and state, Marshall defined the Allied war effort and the free world's response to the postwar Cold War. Dwight D. Eisenhower went on to succeed Marshall as army chief of staff and later became a two-term president of the United States.

Many of the naval officers who served under King, Nimitz, and Halsey went on to lead the postwar navy. Nimitz's deputy Forrest Sherman; Halsey's chief of staff, Robert Carney; and Mitscher's chief of staff, Arleigh Burke, all became chief of naval operations. Others passed from the scene early, including Marc Mitscher, who died in 1947. Frank Jack Fletcher retired with the rank of full admiral that same year and did not help his reputation by refusing to be interviewed or to write his memoirs.

One of the most poignant appraisals of the four fleet admirals came from Roland N. Smoot after all were dead. Smoot was no outside observer. A 1923 graduate of the Naval Academy, he assumed command of the destroyer *Monssen* early in 1941. *Monssen* escorted *Hornet* on the Doolittle Raid, fought at Midway, and sank in Ironbottom Sound during the fury of the Guadalcanal campaign. Smoot later led a destroyer squadron at Surigao Strait and eventually retired as a vice admiral.

"I've tried to analyze the four five-star Admirals that we've had in this Navy," Smoot reminisced. "You have a man like King — a terrifically 'hew to the line' hard martinet, stony steely gentleman; the grandfather and really lovable old man Nimitz — the most beloved man I've ever known; the complete and utter clown Halsey — a clown but if he said, 'Let's go to hell together,' you'd go to hell with him; and then the diplomat Leahy — the open-handed, effluent diplomat Leahy. Four more different men never lived and they all got to be five-star admirals, and why?"[15]

Smoot answered his own question with one word: "leadership." Each of the fleet admirals, he said, had "the ability to make men admire them one way or another." But far more than instilling admiration alone, each in quite different ways possessed a commanding presence that engendered commitment and resolve toward a common purpose. King demonstrated it by bluster and verve; Nimitz by putting his hand on your shoulder and saying, Let's get this thing done; Halsey — still the fullback — by rushing though the line in such a way that everyone on the team wanted to go through with him; and Leahy by never letting his own personal feelings, or those

of others, interfere with the long-range objectives and best interests
of his country.

Of the four admirals, William D. Leahy is undoubtedly the most
overlooked. Yet given his roles as confidant, adviser, and enforcer
for two presidents, he was arguably the most influential—a fact little recognized at the time or in numerous accounts since. A 1950
review of *I Was There* captured the essence of Leahy's contribution.
Writing in the *New York Herald Tribune,* Walter Millis praised
Leahy's service to the nation, but then noted some uncertainty as to
what that service truly was. "Just what it was," Millis confessed, "a
service of loyalty, of temperament, of skill in persuasion or negotiation, or advice on men or policies—does not clearly appear from
this book."[16] It was, of course, a combination of all of those points,
and it is perhaps to Leahy's credit that his role remained publicly
undefined and unacknowledged.

In point of fact, Leahy was chief of staff to the president, chairman of the Joint Chiefs of Staff, and de facto national security advi-
sor all rolled into one. Leahy's "unique experience in the Navy and
diplomacy," the *Washington Post* observed on his eightieth birthday, "made his contribution in the war far more valuable than
appears in any public record."[17] That does not mean, however, that
Leahy was a man entirely devoid of vanity. Early on, Leahy kept
scrapbooks of newspaper clippings of his career and continued to
do so throughout World War II after Louise died.

The landmark study by Eric Larrabee, *Commander in Chief:
Franklin Delano Roosevelt, His Lieutenants and Their War,* accords
Leahy scant mention, while devoting chapters to the likes of Marshall, King, Nimitz, and Eisenhower. In so many accounts of World
War II, including Robert Sherwood's defining *Roosevelt and Hopkins,* "Hopkins's reputation as the President's principal assistant in
diplomacy and Marshall's image as Roosevelt's preeminent adviser
on military strategy . . . assume such heroic proportions that the contributions of other presidential advisers and assistants are virtually
eclipsed."[18] Truth be told, of course, Hopkins himself acknowledged
Leahy's central role in both diplomatic and military matters.

As for Marshall, Leahy came to disagree "sharply" with him on postwar foreign policy—Leahy's inherent conservatism versus Marshall's more liberal multilateralism, in addition to the specifics over China—but Leahy nonetheless said, "As a soldier, he was in my opinion one of the best, and his drive, courage, and imagination transformed America's great citizen army into the most magnificent fighting force ever assembled."[19]

Whatever his true opinions of his colleagues, Leahy characteristically kept them guarded and publicly polite. But his frankness nonetheless shone through when it came to the volatile King. "He was an exceptionally able sea commander," Leahy acknowledged, but "he also was explosive and at times it was just as well that the deliberations of the Joint Chiefs were a well-kept secret."[20]

And Leahy was certainly not afraid to take King to task when the situation warranted it. In February 1944, as Churchill pleaded for yet another summit, Leahy, Marshall, and King were not receptive, but King was unusually outspoken, saying that the British were "just playing games." As Leahy diplomatically put it, "The plain-spoken admiral did not hide his irritation at some of the tactics of our British ally....I got King in a corner...and asked him to be more polite."[21]

Whereas Leahy was stern, reserved, and even dour, King was nothing short of bombastic. Throughout his career, King's personality was routinely commented upon—and frequently feared—by his contemporaries and junior officers alike. His seniors usually found it merely annoying, although many— Forrestal was clearly an exception—tended to overlook his grating manner because there was no question that this demanding and strong-willed individual was also highly intelligent and capable of delivering results.

King simply had no tolerance for subordinates who failed to carry out his orders to his satisfaction. Considering that King's satisfaction was a very high bar, many failed to clear it. "On the job," wrote historian Robert Love in his history of the chiefs of naval operations, "[King] seemed always to be angry or annoyed."[22] But some of that anger or annoyance may well have been a mask that was best breached when one stood up to him or took the initiative in doing what King likely would have done had he been in the other's shoes.

When Captain Arleigh Burke was transferred to the Atlantic after his tenure with Mitscher in the fast carriers, he was immediately charged with routing certain ships as soon as possible. Alone in the Washington headquarters late one night, Burke issued a series of orders in King's name — as was custom but never done without King's or another admiral's approval. King called Burke into his office the next morning and proceeded to deliver a tongue-lashing about clearing such matters even though the exigency of the moment demanded action. Burke took the tirade without flinching, but as he was being dismissed, King almost winked at him and said quietly, "You did the right thing, son."[23]

If Leahy remains the most overlooked of the four fleet admirals, King may be the most overlooked strategist of the Allied planning counsels. It was King who pushed an offensive global strategy on Marshall as early as March 1942, issued absolute orders to Nimitz to hold the Pacific sea-lanes to Hawaii and Australia at all costs, and resolved to stop the Japanese advance in the Solomons no matter how grim the navy's toll became in the waters around Guadalcanal. And those who label King as a critic of Germany First need remember his early and continuing role in winning the Battle of the Atlantic against German U-boats and assembling the naval might to invade North Africa, Italy, and France. King articulated a global vision of victory, ran a two-ocean war, and finally reached the point in his career where he was able to delegate its execution to men like Nimitz and Halsey.

King frequently termed Nimitz a "fixer," a term King ascribed to most officers with experience in the Bureau of Navigation. But Nimitz's tenure at BuNav, as well as his own personality, gave him a broader view of leadership than King possessed. "Leadership," said Nimitz, "consists of picking good men and helping them do their best for you. The attributes of loyalty, discipline and devotion to duty on the part of subordinates must be matched by patience, tolerance and understanding on the part of superiors."[24]

In fact, Nimitz's years at BuNav gave him the keen insight into personnel that became so important to putting the right man in the right command. He possessed a shrewd ability to evaluate people and bring out their best. And if he was occasionally slow to find fault, it was due to the virtues of patience and loyalty, not indifference or neglect. Nimitz was "inspiring in his brilliance," recalled Roland Smoot, and "inspiring in his ability to let you feel that he has complete and utter confidence in you."[25]

Nimitz, and to an even greater extent Halsey, personified the American war effort in the Pacific. While songs, poems, and scuttlebutt about MacArthur tended toward the derogatory, those same ranks cheered Nimitz and Halsey. Nimitz himself was fond of a poem by Captain William Gordon Beecher, Jr., written from the perspective of a lowly enlisted man. Each verse started with "Me and Halsey and Nimitz" before concluding,

> *We're warnin' them never*
> *To start it again.*
> *For we've got a country*
> *With millions of men*
> *Like Nimitz and Halsey and me.*[26]

That Halsey enjoyed similar camaraderie with his men was evidenced by numerous comments and stories that circulated and made it seem as if "the old man" was half a step behind them all the way. Sometimes he was. Once, when two enlisted men were walking along a passageway shooting the breeze, one of them acknowledged, "I'd go to hell for that old son of a bitch." The sailor felt a poke in his back and turned around to find Halsey playfully wagging a finger. "Not so old, young man."[27] Later, when Halsey dispatched a shore party to rescue starving prisoners of war on the eve of the surrender ceremony in Tokyo Bay, one navy enlisted man, who had endured a long captivity, exclaimed, "I knew it! I told these Jap bastards that Admiral Halsey would be here after us."[28]

Yes, the fleet admirals were different, but each had an enduring sense of duty, mission, and love of country that had been honed years before on the banks of the Severn. Each of them first learned to be a follower. Then each unquestionably became a leader. All played pivotal roles in bringing the United States Navy to the pinnacle of naval power.

In 1953, after World War II was fought and won, a newspaper editor asked one of America's fleet admirals to participate in a series of articles by celebrated people on the turning point in their careers. "Looking back," the newsman queried, "what single act, incident, influence or encouragement set you in the direction of success instead of failure?"[29]

The seventy-eight-year-old admiral to whom this was addressed wrote in the first sentence of his reply that he was "unable to remember any acts, incidents or influence that were turning points in my naval career." But then he went on for almost four double-spaced, typewritten pages to reminisce about his time at the United States Naval Academy and the importance of those years and the relationships he had formed there — almost sixty years before — to the man he became. "Those of us who departed from the United States Naval Academy," Fleet Admiral William D. Leahy concluded, had acquired the requisite skills but, "without conscious effort," had also acquired something more.[30]

"You will," Leahy once told graduating midshipmen, "all have to a greater or lesser degree something else that is *intangible...* a combination of loyalty to ideals, tradition, courage, devotion, clean living, and clear thinking. It is more than 'esprit de corps' because it reaches far beyond the corps and comradeship."[31]

Just as this intangible element defined the navy's four fleet admirals, it characterizes all who pass through the gates of the United States Naval Academy and inexorably binds them to the navy, to one another, and to the steadfast service of their country.

Acknowledgments

Research for this book covered considerable ground and incurred many debts. The principal archive for three of the fleet admirals is the Library of Congress, Manuscript Division, in Washington, D.C. The primary Nimitz Collection is at the Naval History and Heritage Command at the Washington Navy Yard. I am indebted to the fine staff of both institutions, particularly John W. Greco at the latter.

I also greatly appreciate the assistance of David D'Onofrio at the Nimitz Library, United States Naval Academy; Dr. Evelyn Cherpak at the Naval Historical Collection of the Naval War College; and the staffs of the American Heritage Center, University of Wyoming; Joyner Library at East Carolina University; Hoover Institution at Stanford University; the National Archives and Records Administration at College Park, Maryland; the Franklin D. Roosevelt Library at Hyde Park, New York; the Submarine Force Museum at Groton, Connecticut; the Battleship New Jersey Museum and Memorial in Camden; the National World War II Museum in New Orleans; and the Smithsonian Institution's National Air and Space Museum. Shea Houlihan helped with research in Georgetown University's archives.

Having worked closely with museums for almost forty years, I am not inclined to rave unduly about them. The National Museum of the Pacific War (Nimitz Museum) at Fredericksburg, Texas, is, however, an exception. This is a wonderful facility that does a superb job of honoring the story of World War II in the Pacific.

I continue to appreciate those who have produced major secondary works in my areas of writing. Each of the fleet admirals has had a major biographer who either knew his subjects personally or had access to immediate family members and wartime associates. My debt here is to E. B. Potter, Thomas B. Buell, and Henry Adams.

Photographic assistance came from the National Archives and Records Administration; the Naval History and Heritage Command; the Harry S. Truman Presidential Library; the George C. Marshall Foundation, particularly Jeffrey Kozak; Gary Fabian of the UB88 project; the National Museum of the Pacific War, particularly Amy Bowman; the Library of Congress; and the American Heritage Center, University of Wyoming. Many thanks, as always, go to David Lambert for his crisp maps.

My greatest debt is to the historians who read all or portions of the manuscript and engaged in frequently lively discussions about these men: Dr. Paul Miles of Princeton University; John Lundstrom, "Mr. World War II in the Pacific"; and Dr. Jeffrey G. Barlow of the Naval History and Heritage Command. And where would I be without those breakfasts with my longtime friend and fellow historian Jerry Keenan?

This book and my career writing history would not have been possible without the consistent and unyielding support of my agent, Alexander C. Hoyt. At Little, Brown, I have found an engaged and insightful editor in John Parsley. I also greatly appreciate the enthusiasm shown by editor in chief Geoff Shandler and all the Little, Brown staff, particularly William Boggess, Theresa Giacopasi, Peggy Freudenthal, and Jayne Yaffe Kemp.

As for my usual time researching in the field, I sat on the veranda at Top Cottage above Hyde Park and considered Roosevelt meeting secretly there with King, walked the flag bridge on the *New Jersey* and pondered Halsey's dilemma at Leyte, and stood before the graves of all four men. My wife, Marlene, passed on winter research in Washington, but found a February trip to Pearl Harbor and an April visit to Fredericksburg — the bluebonnets were blooming — quite agreeable duty.

Appendixes

A. Comparative Ranks of Commissioned Officers in U.S. Military Services

Pay Grade	Navy Rank	Comparative Rank for Army, Air Force, and Marines
O-1	Ensign	Second Lieutenant
O-2	Lieutenant Junior Grade	First Lieutenant
O-3	Lieutenant	Captain
O-4	Lieutenant Commander	Major
O-5	Commander	Lieutenant Colonel
O-6	Captain	Colonel
O-7	Rear Admiral (lower half)	Brigadier General
O-8	Rear Admiral (upper half)	Major General
O-9	Vice Admiral	Lieutenant General
O-10	Admiral	General
O-11	Fleet Admiral	General of the Army/ Air Force

Note: The *rank* of commodore—one star and equivalent in grade to a brigadier general in the army—was abolished by the U.S. Navy in 1899, in part because it caused confusion with the *title* of commodore, the latter bestowed on the commanding officer of a squadron of ships no matter what his rank. Consequently, during the pre–World War II period, naval officers jumped from captain to rear admiral (two stars). The rank of commodore was temporarily reestablished during World War II, with similar resulting confusion, especially as to convoy commodores. In 1981, the U.S. Navy broke the rank of rear admiral into rear admiral lower half (one star) and rear admiral upper half (two stars).

B. World War II–Era General Protocols for Naming U.S. Navy Ships

Battleships (BB)	States of the Union
Aircraft carriers (CV, CVL)	Famous battles; famous predecessor ships
Escort carriers (CVE)	Sounds and bays; battles of World War II
Heavy cruisers (CA)	Cities and towns
Light cruisers (CL)	Cities and towns
Destroyers (DD)	U.S. Navy/Marine officers and enlisted men
Destroyer escorts (DE)	U.S. Navy/Marine officers and enlisted men
Submarines (SS)	Fish and marine creatures
Minelayers (CM, DM)	Historic monitors of the U.S. Navy
Minesweepers (AM)	Birds
Oilers (AO)	Rivers
Transports (AP)	Presidents; famous Americans; historic places
Hospital ships (AH)	Words of comfort
Ammunition ships (AE)	Volcanoes
Cargo ships (AK)	Stars; counties of the United States
Tugboats (ATA, ATF)	Indian tribes

C. Comparative Tonnages
and Armaments of Selected Ships

Ship Name	Commissioned	Length/Beam/Tons	Type	Decommissioned	Key Armaments
USS Cincinnati (C-7)	June 16, 1894	306 feet/42 feet/ 3,200 tons	Protected cruiser	April 20, 1919	1 × 6-inch guns; 10 × 5-inch guns
USS Oregon (BB-3)	July 15, 1896	348 feet/69 feet/ 10,288 tons	Battleship	October 4, 1919	4 × 13-inch guns
USS Decatur (DD-5)	May 19, 1902	250 feet/23.5 feet/ 420 tons	Destroyer	July 20, 1919	2 × 3-inch guns; 2 × 18-inch torpedo tubes
Mikasa (Japan)	March 1, 1902	432 feet/76 feet/ 15,000 tons	Battleship	September 20, 1923	4 × 12-inch guns
USS Plunger (SS-2)	September 19, 1903	64 feet/12 feet/ 109 tons	Submarine	November 3, 1905	1 × 18-inch torpedo tube
USS Shaw (DD-68)	April 9, 1917	315 feet/31 feet/ 1,100 tons	Destroyer	June 21, 1922	4 × 4-inch guns; 3 × 21-inch torpedo tubes
USS New Mexico (BB-40)	May 20, 1918	624 feet/97 feet/ 32,000 tons	Battleship	July 19, 1946	12 × 14-inch guns
USS Saratoga (CV-3)	November 16, 1927	880 feet/106 feet/ 33,000 tons	Aircraft carrier	August 15, 1946	91 aircraft

(continued)

Ship Name	Commissioned	Length/Beam/Tons	Type	Decommissioned	Key Armaments
USS *Augusta* (CA-31)	January 31, 1931	600 feet/66 feet/9,000 tons	Heavy cruiser	July 16, 1946	9 × 8-inch guns
HMS *Prince of Wales* (53)	January 19, 1941	745 feet/112.5 feet/44,000 tons	Battleship	December 10, 1941*	10 × 14-inch guns
USS *Arizona* (BB-39)	October 17, 1916	608 feet/97 feet/31,400 tons	Battleship	December 7, 1941*	12 × 14-inch guns
Bismarck (Germany)	August 24, 1940	823.5 feet/118 feet/46,000 tons	Battleship	May 27, 1941*	8 × 15-inch guns
Akagi (Japan)	March 25, 1927	855 feet/103 feet/42,000 tons	Aircraft carrier	June 5, 1942*	91 aircraft
USS *Haddo* (SS-255)	October 9, 1942	312 feet/27 feet/2,400 tons	Submarine	February 16, 1946	10 × 21-inch torpedo tubes (6 fore, 4 aft)
Yamato (Japan)	December 16, 1941	839 feet/128 feet/80,000 tons	Battleship	April 7, 1945*	9 × 18-inch guns
New Jersey (BB-62)	May 23, 1943	888 feet/108 feet/45,000 tons	Battleship	February 8, 1991**	9 × 16-inch guns

*Sunk

**Final Time

D. Chiefs of Naval Operations, 1915–1947

The position of chief of naval operations (CNO) was established at the urging of Secretary of the Navy Josephus Daniels in 1915. Initially, it was a coordinating and advisory role. Viewed as a "first among equals" of the bureau chiefs, he reported to the secretary of the navy. The CNO slowly evolved into a stronger position until Ernest J. King's appointment on March 26, 1942. Simultaneously CNO and commander in chief, U.S. Fleet, King was the operational head of all U.S. Navy and Marine forces.

Name	Dates of Service	U.S. Naval Academy Class
William S. Benson	May 11, 1915–September 25, 1919	1877
Robert E. Coontz	November 1, 1919–July 21, 1923	1885
Edward W. Eberle	July 21, 1923–November 14, 1927	1885
Charles F. Hughes	November 14, 1927–September 17, 1930	1888
William V. Pratt	September 17, 1930–June 30, 1933	1889
William H. Standley	July 1, 1933–January 1, 1937	1895
William D. Leahy	January 2, 1937–August 1, 1939	1897
Harold R. Stark	August 1, 1939–March 26, 1942	1903
Ernest J. King	March 26, 1942–December 15, 1945	1901
Chester W. Nimitz	December 15, 1945–December 15, 1947	1905

E. Commanders in Chief, U.S. Fleet, 1936–1945

The fleet structure of the United States Navy has changed many times throughout its history. General Order of December 6, 1922, combined the Atlantic and Pacific Fleets into one United States Fleet and delineated the main body of ships as the Battle Fleet, assigned to the Pacific, and a lesser complement termed the Scouting Fleet, assigned to the Atlantic. (These were subsequently called the Battle and Scouting Forces.) There were also independent commands for coastal forces (called for a time Base Force), ships deployed in the Far East (long called the Asiatic Fleet, although its numbers were very small by comparison), and submarines.

General Order 143, issued on February 1, 1941, abolished the United States Fleet; reinstated the Atlantic, Pacific, and Asiatic Fleets; and designated a commander in chief for each. Executive Order 8984 of December 18, 1941, reestablished the post of commander in chief, United States Fleet, and gave the position operational command of all naval forces: the Atlantic, Pacific, and Asiatic Fleets and all coastal forces. Roosevelt appointed King to this position. When King relinquished command on October 10, 1945, the position of commander in chief, United States Fleet, was abolished, and its responsibilities were assumed by the chief of naval operations.

Name	Dates of Service	U.S. Naval Academy Class
Arthur J. Hepburn	June 24, 1936–February 1, 1938	1897
Claude C. Bloch	February 1, 1938–January 6, 1940	1899
James O. Richardson	January 6, 1940–January 5, 1941	1902
Husband E. Kimmel	February 1, 1941–December 16, 1941 (Pacific Fleet)	1904
Ernest J. King	February 1, 1941–December 30, 1941 (Atlantic Fleet)	1901
Ernest J. King	December 30, 1941–October 10, 1945	1901

F. World War II–Era U.S. Battleships

More than just historical curiosity, this table clearly shows the World War I era of hasty battleship construction; the dramatic, almost-two-decade pause between the wars because of the Washington treaty restrictions; and then the pre–World War II rush of renewed construction. By the time the *Iowa*-class giants slid down the ways, the aircraft carrier had established its dominance as the navy's principal capital ship.

Ship Name (No.)	Commissioned–Decommissioned	Disposition
Utah (BB-31)	August 31, 1911–September 5, 1944	Sunk at Pearl Harbor
Wyoming (BB-32)	September 25, 1912–August 1, 1947	Scrapped
Arkansas (BB-33)	September 17, 1912–July 29, 1946	Sunk as postwar target
New York (BB-34)	April 15, 1914–August 29, 1946	Sunk as postwar target
Texas (BB-35)	March 12, 1914–April 21, 1948	Memorial, San Jacinto, TX
Nevada (BB-36)	March 11, 1916–April 21, 1948	Sunk as postwar target
Oklahoma (BB-37)	May 2, 1916–September 1, 1944	Sunk at Pearl Harbor*
Pennsylvania (BB-38)	June 12, 1916–August 29, 1946	Sunk as postwar target

Ship Name (No.)	Commissioned–Decommissioned	Disposition
Arizona (BB-39)	October 17, 1916–	Memorial, Pearl Harbor
New Mexico (BB-40)	May 20, 1918–July 19, 1946	Scrapped
Mississippi (BB-41)	December 18, 1917–December 17, 1956	Scrapped
Idaho (BB-42)	March 24, 1919–July 3, 1946	Scrapped
Tennessee (BB-43)	June 3, 1920–February 14, 1947	Scrapped
California (BB-44)	August 10, 1921–February 14, 1947	Scrapped
Colorado (BB-45)	August 30, 1923–January 7, 1947	Scrapped
Maryland (BB-46)	July 21, 1921–April 3, 1947	Scrapped
Washington (BB-47)	Never commissioned	Sunk as target, 1924
West Virginia (BB-48)	December 1, 1923–January 9, 1947	Scrapped
North Carolina (BB-55)	April 9, 1941–June 27, 1947	Memorial, Wilmington, NC
Washington (BB-56)	May 15, 1941–June 27, 1947	Scrapped
South Dakota (BB-57)	March 20, 1942–January 31, 1947	Scrapped
Indiana (BB-58)	April 30, 1942–September 11, 1947	Scrapped
Massachusetts (BB-59)	May 12, 1942–March 27, 1947	Memorial, Fall River, MA
Alabama (BB-60)	August 16, 1942–January 9, 1947	Memorial, Mobile, AL
Iowa (BB-61)	February 22, 1943–March 24, 1949**	Memorial, Los Angeles, CA
New Jersey (BB-62)	May 23, 1943–June 30, 1948**	Memorial, Camden, NJ

Ship Name (No.)	Commissioned– Decommissioned	Disposition
Missouri (BB-63)	June 11, 1944– February 26, 1955**	Memorial, Pearl Harbor
Wisconsin (BB-64)	April 16, 1944– July 1, 1948**	Memorial, Norfolk, VA

*Subsequently raised, stripped of guns and superstructure, and sold for scrap, but sank en route to San Francisco from Pearl Harbor, May 17, 1947.

**The four *Iowa*-class battleships were later variously recommissioned for action related to Korea and the Middle East.

Source: Adapted from "The Battleships" at www.navy.mil/navydata/ships/battleships/bb-list.asp

Note: Hull numbers BB-49 through BB-54 were assigned and hulls were laid down, but they were scrapped in 1923 under the terms of the Washington treaty.

G. World War II–Era U.S. Aircraft Carriers (CV1–CV21)

Early aircraft carrier construction was done on a ship-by-ship basis. *Langley* was a conversion from a collier; *Lexington* and *Saratoga* were initially laid down as battle cruiser hulls; *Ranger* was a transition from these to the four carriers that saved the Pacific — *Yorktown, Enterprise, Wasp,* and *Hornet*. Then came the *Essex*-class carriers. It might well be argued that these twenty-four carriers, quickly mass-produced with only minor modifications, were the determining factor in winning the war in the Pacific. Japanese industry simply could not match this outpouring of construction. *Note:* Do not confuse carriers bearing the same name. The first *Lexington* (CV-2), *Yorktown* (CV-5), *Wasp* (CV-7), and *Hornet* (CV-8) were sunk and replaced with *Essex*-class namesakes.

Ship Name (No.)	Commissioned–Decommissioned	Disposition
Langley (CV-1)	March 22, 1922–February 27, 1942	Sunk off Indonesia
Lexington (CV-2)	December 14, 1927–May 8, 1942	Sunk at Coral Sea
Saratoga (CV-3)	November 16, 1927–July 26, 1946	Sunk as postwar target
Ranger (CV-4)	June 4, 1934–October 18, 1946	Scrapped
Yorktown (CV-5)	September 30, 1937–June 7, 1942	Sunk at Midway
Enterprise (CV-6)	May 12, 1938–February 17, 1947	Scrapped
Wasp (CV-7)	April 25, 1940–September 15, 1942	Sunk at San Cristóbal Island
Hornet (CV-8)	October 20, 1941–October 26, 1942	Sunk at Santa Cruz Islands
Essex (CV-9)	December 31, 1942–June 20, 1969	Scrapped

Ship Name (No.)	Commissioned–Decommissioned	Disposition
Yorktown (CV-10)	April 15, 1943–June 27, 1970	Memorial, Charleston, SC
Intrepid (CV-11)	August 16, 1943–March 15, 1974	Memorial, New York, NY
Hornet (CV-12)	November 20, 1943–May 26, 1970	Memorial, Alameda, CA
Franklin (CV-13)	January 31, 1944–February 17, 1947	Scrapped
Ticonderoga (CV-14)	May 8, 1944–September 1, 1973	Scrapped
Randolph (CV-15)	October 9, 1944–February 13, 1969	Scrapped
Lexington (CV-16)	February 17, 1943–November 8, 1991	Memorial, Corpus Christi, TX
Bunker Hill (CV-17)	May 25, 1943–July 9, 1947	Scrapped
Wasp (CV-18)	November 24, 1943–July 1, 1972	Scrapped
Hancock (CV-19)	April 15, 1944–January 30, 1976	Scrapped
Bennington (CV-20)	August 6, 1944–January 15, 1970	Scrapped
Boxer (CV-21)	April 16, 1945–December 1, 1969	Scrapped

Note: CVL-22 through CVL-30 were classified as "light aircraft carriers" and designated CVL. *Bon Homme Richard* (CV-31), commissioned November 26, 1944, led the final eleven of the *Essex*-class CVs commissioned between 1945 and 1950. Despite the fine carriers now preserved as floating museums—*Yorktown* (CV-10), *Intrepid* (CV-11), *Hornet* (CV-12), *Lexington* (CV-16), and the postwar *Midway* (CV-B41)—it is a shame that the venerable *Saratoga* (CV-3) and *Enterprise* (CV-6) were not preserved. *Saratoga* met its end in a trial atomic blast in 1946, and *Enterprise*, despite many efforts to save the ship during the late 1940s and 1950s, was finally given up for scrap with the understanding that its proud name would live on in the navy's first nuclear-powered carrier, CVN-65.
Source: Adapted from "The Carriers" at www.navy.mil/navydata/ships/carriers/cv-list.asp

H. Ships Named for the Fleet Admirals

William D. Leahy

USS *Leahy* (CG-16, formerly DL-G16)
Lead ship in the *Leahy* class of guided missile cruisers
Bath Iron Works, Bath, Maine
535 feet long; 53 feet beam; 7,800 tons displaced
Launched: July 1, 1961
Sponsor: Mrs. Michael J. Mansfield
Commissioned: August 4, 1962
Decommissioned: October 1, 1993; sold for scrap

Ernest J. King

USS *King* (DDG-41, formerly DLG-10)
Fifth ship in the *Farragut* class of guided missile frigates (DLG), later
    reclassified as a guided missile destroyer (DDG)
Puget Sound Naval Shipyard, Bremerton, Washington
512.5 feet long; 52 feet beam; 5,800 tons displaced
Launched: December 6, 1958
Sponsor: Mrs. Oliver W. van den Berg (née Elizabeth King)
Commissioned: November 17, 1960
Decommissioned: March 28, 1991; sold for scrap

Chester W. Nimitz

USS *Nimitz* (CVN-68)
Lead ship in the *Nimitz* class of nuclear-powered aircraft carriers

Newport News Shipbuilding Company, Newport News, Virginia
1,092 feet long; 134 feet beam; 97,000 tons displaced
Launched: May 13, 1972
Sponsor: Mrs. James T. Lay (née Catherine Nimitz)
Commissioned: May 3, 1975
Active duty as of 2012

William F. Halsey, Jr.

USS *Halsey* (CG-23, formerly DLG-23)
Eighth ship in the *Leahy* class of guided missile cruisers
San Francisco Naval Shipyard, San Francisco, California
535 feet long; 53 feet beam; 7,800 tons displaced
Launched: January 15, 1962
Cosponsors: Miss Jane Frances Halsey and Mrs. Margaret Denham
Commissioned: July 20, 1963
Decommissioned: January 28, 1994; sold for scrap

USS *Halsey* (DDG-97)
Forty-seventh ship in the *Arleigh Burke* class of guided missile
    destroyers
Ingalls Shipbuilding, West Bank, Pascagoula, Mississippi
508.5 feet long; 67 feet beam; 9,200 tons displaced
Launched: January 9, 2004
Cosponsors: Mrs. Anne Halsey-Smith, Miss Heidi Cooke Halsey, and
    Mrs. Alice Spruance Talbot
Commissioned: July 30, 2005
Active duty as of 2012

I. Major World War II Conferences and Operations with Code Names

Major Strategic Conferences

Atlantic Charter Conference; August 1941; Placentia Bay, Newfoundland (Riviera)

First Washington Conference; December 1941; Washington, D.C. (Arcadia)

Second Washington Conference; June 1942; Washington, D.C. (Argonaut)

Casablanca Conference; January 1943; Casablanca, Morocco (Symbol)

Third Washington Conference; May 1943; Washington, D.C. (Trident)

First Quebec Conference; August 1943; Quebec, Canada (Quadrant)

Cairo Conference; November 1943; Cairo, Egypt (Sextant)

Teheran Conference; November 1943; Teheran, Iran (Eureka)

Second Quebec Conference; September 1944; Quebec, Canada (Octagon)

Yalta Conference; February 1945; Yalta, Soviet Union (Argonaut)

Potsdam Conference; July 1945; Potsdam, Germany (Terminal)

Major Military Operations

Bolero, preinvasion buildup of American troops in British Isles, 1942

Cartwheel, convergent South Pacific operations against Rabaul, 1943

Coronet, initial plans for invasion of Honshu and Tokyo Plain, 1946

Dragoon, invasion of southern France, August 1944

Flintlock, invasion of Marshall Islands, February 1944

Forager, invasion of Mariana Islands, June 1944

Galvanic, invasion of Gilbert Islands, November 1943

Gymnast, initial plans for invasion of North Africa, 1942
Husky, invasion of Sicily, July 1943
Iceberg, invasion of Okinawa, April 1945
King Two, invasion of Leyte, Philippines, October 1944
Olympic, plans for invasion of Kyushu, 1945
Overlord, invasion of France, June 1944
Roundup, initial plans for invasion of France, 1943
Sledgehammer, initial plans for small-scale attack on France, 1942
Torch, invasion of North Africa, November 1942
Watchtower, invasion of Guadalcanal and Tulagi, August 1942

Notes

Source Abbreviations for Frequently Used Manuscript Collections

CWN/NHHC   Admiral Chester W. Nimitz Collection, Operational Archives Branch, Naval History and Heritage Command, Washington, D.C.

CWN/USNA   Chester W. Nimitz Papers, MS 236, Special Collections and Archives Department, Nimitz Library, United States Naval Academy

EJK/LC   Ernest Joseph King Papers, Manuscript Division, Library of Congress, Washington, D.C.

EJK/NHC/ NWC   Ernest J. King Papers, Naval Historical Collection, Naval War College, Newport, Rhode Island. (Note: This Naval Historical *Collection* should not be confused with the Naval Historical *Center*, Washington, D.C., which since December 2008 has been designated the Naval History and Heritage Command.)

GCM/LC   Papers of George C. Marshall: Selected World War II Correspondence, Manuscript Division, Library of Congress, Washington, D.C.

RAS/NHHC   Papers of Raymond A. Spruance, Operational Archives Branch, Naval History and Heritage Command, Washington, D.C.

WDL/Diary   William D. Leahy Diary, William D. Leahy Papers, Manuscript Division, Library of Congress, Washington, D.C.

WDL/LC   William D. Leahy Papers, Manuscript Division, Library of Congress, Washington, D.C.

WDL/NHHC   Papers of William D. Leahy, Operational Archives Branch, Naval History and Heritage Command, Washington, D.C.

WFH/LC   William Frederick Halsey Papers, Manuscript Division, Library of Congress, Washington, D.C.

Chapter 1: Leahy

1. WDL/Diary, April 16, 1898; *Oregon* statistics from Patrick McSherry, "U.S.S. Oregon," Spanish-American War Centennial Website, http://www.spanamwar.com/oregon.htm accessed July 27, 2009.

2. Henry H. Adams, *Witness to Power: The Life of Fleet Admiral William D. Leahy* (Annapolis: Naval Institute Press, 1985), pp. 5–7; *Roster of Wisconsin Volunteers, War of the Rebellion, 1861–1865, Wisconsin Historical Society Library,* http://www.wisconsinhistory.org/roster/index.asp accessed July 27, 2009; "Delayed Certificate of Birth," front matter, WDL/Diary.

3. "You could no more" Lilian Handlin, *George Bancroft: The Intellectual as Democrat* (New York: Harper and Row, 1984), p. 208; "the temptations and distractions," "A Brief History of the United States Naval Academy," United States Naval Academy, http://www.usna.edu/VirtualTour/150years/, accessed June 27, 2010.

4. Congress recognized the existence of the school by voting $28,200 for repairs, improvements and instruction at Fort Severn in 1846. The system of congressional appointments was established in 1852.

5. "Pell mell, slipping," *Lucky Bag,* vol. 1, 1894, p. 35; Annapolis and West Point attendance figures from *Report of the Secretary of the Navy, 1893* (Washington, D.C., Government Printing Office, 1893), p. 197, and *Annual Report of the Superintendent of the United States Military Academy, 1893* (Washington, D.C., Government Printing Office, 1893), p. 4.

6. Adams, *Witness to Power,* pp. 9–10.

7. *Washington Post,* March 19, 1950.

8. Thomas C. Hart, *The Reminiscences of Thomas C. Hart* (New York: Columbia University Oral History Project, 1972), p. 44.

9. Adams, *Witness to Power,* p. 11; The Class of 1897 had the highest percentage of flag officers of any class to graduate from Annapolis: Leahy, four admirals, six rear admirals, and a major general in the Marine Corps.

10. Edmund Morris, *The Rise of Theodore Roosevelt* (New York: Coward, McCann & Geoghegan, 1979), pp. 154–55; "I hope [Roosevelt] has" and "too pugnacious," p. 555; "trouble with Cuba," p. 567.

11. Ibid., pp. 577–78; "To be prepared," p. 569. Great Britain captured Cuba in the last days of the Seven Years War, but the island was returned

under the terms of the 1763 Treaty of Paris.

12. Ibid., pp. 586–87.

13. The possibility of a coal bunker fire gains credibility when one considers that *Oregon* reportedly battled four simultaneous bunker fires on its voyage around South America. Given the difficulty stokers sometimes had in getting various grades of coal to burn in the fireboxes, one fireman wryly recorded in his diary, "It seemed as if there was one or more fires going all the time," and "it really seemed as if the only place that coal would burn was in the bunkers" (G[eorge] W. Robinson Diary, MS 344, Special Collections and Archives Department, Nimitz Library, United States Naval Academy, p. 8.

14. Morris, *The Rise of Theodore Roosevelt,* pp. 602–3.

15. WDL/Diary, ca. May 4, 1898; capture of Philadelphia and Boston rumor in Robinson Diary, p. 18.

16. "Dewey's Report of the Battle of Manila Bay," in *The Library of Historic Characters and Famous Events,* vol. 12 (Boston: J. B. Millet, 1907), p. 241.

17. "George Dewey," in ibid., p. 235.

18. David McCullough, *The Path Between the Seas: The Creation of the Panama Canal, 1870–1914* (New York: Simon & Schuster, 1977), pp. 254–255, 257.

19. WDL/Diary, July 3, 1898.

20. "Destruction of Cervera's Fleet," in *The Library of Historic Characters,* pp. 259–266; WDL/Diary, July 3, 1898.

21. Adams, *Witness to Power,* p. 17.

Chapter 2: King

1. Denis and Peggy Warner, *The Tide at Sunrise: A History of the Russo-Japanese War, 1904–1905* (New York: Charterhouse, 1974), pp. 15, 17–19. Two new, 7,000-ton cruisers, originally built in England for Argentina, subsequently refused by Russia and then secretly purchased by Japanese agents had arrived in Japanese hands only hours before the Port Arthur attack.

2. Ernest J. King and Walter Muir Whitehill, *Fleet Admiral King: A Naval Record* (New York: Norton, 1952), p. 51.

3. Thomas B. Buell, *Master of Sea Power: A Biography of Fleet Admiral Ernest J. King* (Boston: Little, Brown, 1980), pp. 3–8; "It's true" and "If I didn't," p. 4; King, *Fleet Admiral King,* pp. 9–15.

4. Buell, *Master of Sea Power,* pp. 8–9; King, *Fleet Admiral King,* pp. 18–21, "Don't you know," p. 21.

5. King, *Fleet Admiral King,* pp. 21–23; "action off Havana," p. 23; Buell, *Master of Sea Power,* pp. 11–12.

6. King, *Fleet Admiral King,* pp. 26–32; "the most beautiful," Buell, *Master of Sea Power,* p. 12; nicknames, "A man so various," "Hops," and "Temper?," *Lucky Bag,* vol. 8, 1901, p. 35 ("A man so various" is adapted from John Dryden's 1681 poem "Absalom and Achitophel," part 1, lines 545–46); as examples of nicknames continuing throughout one's naval career, see "Dear Dolly," Harry E. Yarnell to King, January 4, 1942, EJK/LC, Box 16 and an

exchange of "Dear Betty" and "Dear Rey" letters during World War II between Harold R. Stark and King, EJK/LC, Box 15.

7. King, *Fleet Admiral King*, pp. 35–38, 49–52; Buell, *Master of Sea Power*, pp. 20–24; "Ensign King is," p. 24.

8. Warner, *The Tide at Sunrise*, pp. 528–56; Mukden casualty figures, p. 513.

9. King, *Fleet Admiral King*, pp. 53–54, 61.

Chapter 3: Halsey

1. Theodore Roosevelt, *Theodore Roosevelt: An Autobiography* (New York: Scribner's, 1923), p. 558.

2. William F. Halsey and J. Bryan III, *Admiral Halsey's Story* (New York: McGraw-Hill, 1947); "bombarded her," p. 16; "We needed the stretches," p. 11.

3. Ibid., pp. 2–5; "big, violent men," p. 2; "I…have always" and "I didn't learn much," p. 4; "camped in McKinley's," p. 5; E. B. Potter, *Bull Halsey* (Annapolis: Naval Institute Press, 1985), pp. 19–27.

4. Halsey, *Admiral Halsey's Story*, pp. 5–8; "Sir, have you" and "Yes, sir," p. 6; "I wish you," p. 7; "But as usual," p. 8.

5. *Lucky Bag*, vol. 9 (1904), pp. 41, 149.

6. Halsey, *Admiral Halsey's Story*, p. 9.

7. Ibid., pp. 9–10.

8. "that the Pacific was," Roosevelt, *An Autobiography*, p. 548; "the two American achievements," pp. 549–50.

9. Halsey, *Admiral Halsey's Story*, pp. 11–14; Potter, *Halsey*, pp. 90–96.

Two battleships of the original Great White Fleet, *Maine* and *Alabama*, were relieved by *Nebraska* and *Wisconsin* on the West Coast for the remainder of the circumnavigation.

Chapter 4: Nimitz

1. E. B. Potter, *Nimitz* (Annapolis: Naval Institute Press, 1976), pp. 60–61.

2. Ibid., pp. 22–30; "Take English, son," Dede W. Casad and Frank A. Driscoll, *Chester W. Nimitz: Admiral of the Hills* (Austin, Tex.: Eakin Press, 1983), pp. 3–4. When Anna Nimitz lay dying in 1924, Chester rushed to her side from maneuvers in the Pacific and arrived in time to hear her last conscious words: "I knew my Valentine boy would come to see me" (Potter, *Nimitz*, p. 28).

3. Potter, *Nimitz*, pp. 49–50. Church went on to become a rear admiral and the uncle of U.S. senator Frank Church. Both his son and grandson were Annapolis graduates; the latter, Albert Thomas Church III, retired as a vice admiral in 2005.

4. *Lucky Bag*, vol. 12, 1905, pp. 76, 167, 183.

5. Potter, *Nimitz*, p. 52.

6. Edgar Stanton Maclay, *A History of the United States Navy from 1775 to 1901*, vol. 3 (New York: D. Appleton, 1901), p. 364.

7. Potter, *Nimitz*, p. 53.

8. "mixer of famous punches," *Lucky Bag*, vol. 12, 1905, p. 76; Nimitz recounted this story almost sixty years later in a letter to a midshipman collecting academy anecdotes for a term

paper (Nimitz to Williamson, January 23, 1962, CWN/NHHC, Series 13, Folder 120).

9. Potter, *Nimitz,* pp. 50n, 55–56.

10. Edmund Morris, *Theodore Rex* (New York: Random House, 2001), pp. 397–400.

11. Potter, *Nimitz,* pp. 56–57.

12. Ibid., pp. 58–59, 61; "I can practice," p. 58; "Your clothes will," p. 59; "On that black night," p. 61.

13. Ibid., pp. 61–62; "culpable inefficiency," p. 61; "made the trip" and "a cross between," p. 62.

Chapter 5: First Commands

1. "the most pleasant," WDL/Diary, undated, 1904; Adams, *Witness to Power,* pp. 21–23.

2. WDL/Diary, June 10, 1905.

3. Ibid., August 11, 1910.

4. Ibid., January 17, 1910.

5. Ibid., January 16, 1911.

6. Ibid., November 15, 1911.

7. Ibid., October 10, 1911.

8. King, *Fleet Admiral King,* pp. 63–64.

9. Buell, *Master of Sea Power,* pp. 26, 34–37.

10. Ernest J. King, "Some Ideas About Organization on Board Ship," *United States Naval Institute Proceedings* 35, no. 1 (March 1909), pp. 1–35; "clinging to things," p. 2.

11. Buell, *Master of Sea Power,* pp. 38–41; "would not lead," p. 38; King, *Fleet Admiral King,* pp. 76–83; "Young man, don't you," p. 83.

12. King, *Fleet Admiral King,* pp. 84–86.

13. Ibid., pp. 89–90.

14. "Do you realize," Potter, *Halsey,* p. 98; Halsey, *Admiral Halsey's Story,* pp. 15–16.

15. Halsey, *Admiral Halsey's Story,* pp. 17–18.

16. H. W. Brands, *Traitor to His Class: The Privileged Life and Radical Presidency of Franklin Delano Roosevelt* (New York: Doubleday, 2008), pp. 75–76.

17. "operated in the Atlantic," WDL/Diary, undated, 1915; "an appreciation of" and "there developed," William D. Leahy, *I Was There: The Personal Story of the Chief of Staff to Presidents Roosevelt and Truman Based on His Notes and Diaries Made at the Time* (New York: Whittlesey House, 1950), p. 3.

18. "Prohibition in the Navy: General Order 99, 1 June, 1914," Department of the Navy, Naval History and Heritage Command, http://www.history.navy.mil/faqs/faq59-11.htm, accessed August 22, 2009; *New York Times,* April 6, 1914. There is anecdotal evidence that the phrase "cup of joe" originated with Josephus Daniels's alcohol ban, which left coffee the most potent shipboard stimulant.

Chapter 6: Dress Rehearsal

1. Potter, *Nimitz,* p. 55; "a cross between," p. 62; "Pitt is the greatest," Clay Blair, Jr., *Silent Victory: The U.S. Submarine War Against Japan* (Philadelphia: Lippincott, 1975), p. 4. Pitt was intrigued by a design promoted by Robert Fulton, who soon turned his attention to steamboats.

2. Roosevelt to Charles Joseph Bonaparte, August 28, 1905, in *The Letters of Theodore Roosevelt*, vol. 4, ed. Elting E. Morison (Cambridge: Harvard University Press, 1951), pp. 1323–25.

3. Blair, *Silent Victory*, vol. 1, pp. 5, 9–10, 12, 14.

4. Potter, *Nimitz*, p. 116.

5. Ibid., p. 117.

6. C. W. Nimitz, "Military Value and Tactics of Modern Submarines," *United States Naval Institute Proceedings*, 38, no. 4 (December 1912), pp. 1193–1211, "The steady development," p. 1198; "the same cruising," p. 1196; "accompany a sea-keeping," p. 1198; "drop numerous poles," p. 1209; "taken down ready," p. 1194.

7. Potter, *Nimitz*, pp. 119, 124–126.

8. Ibid., pp. 126–127.

9. Blair, *Silent Victory*, vol. 1, pp. 15–22; "The submarine is" and "absolute and irremediable," p. 21; E. B. Potter, ed., *The United States and World Sea Power* (Englewood Cliffs, N.J.: Prentice-Hall, 1955), pp. 551–552; "If the present rate," Burton J. Hendrick, *The Life and Letters of Walter H. Page* (Garden City, N.Y.: Doubleday, Page, 1925), p. 396.

10. Potter, *Nimitz*, p. 129.

11. Halsey, *Admiral Halsey's Story*, pp. 24–33; "a hunch too strong," p. 24; "nursing midshipmen," p. 26; "makee-learn," p. 27; "First egg," p. 31; "had the time" and "proud as a dog," p. 33.

12. King, *Fleet Admiral King*, pp. 99, 101, 116–121. For the best account of the naval war between Great Britain and Germany, see Robert K. Massie, *Castles of Steel: Britain, Germany, and the Winning of the Great War at Sea* (New York: Ballantine, 2003).

13. King, *Fleet Admiral King*, pp. 144–145; "was more decisive," p. 145; "a proper realization" p. 144; "had an exceptionally" and "due performance," "Remarks Delivered December 3, 1936, to Los Angeles American Legion Post No. 8 in Honor of Admiral Mayo's 80th Birthday," EJK/LC, Box 4.

14. Blair, *Silent Victory*, vol. 1, pp. 22–24; Potter, *Nimitz*, pp. 129–131; Potter, *Sea Power*, p. 559.

Chapter 7: Battleships

1. Adams, *Witness to Power*, pp. 33–37.

2. Potter, *Sea Power*, pp. 561–562; Massie, *Castles of Steel*, pp. 786–788.

3. Franklin D. Roosevelt, "Shall We Trust Japan?" *Asia: The American Magazine on the Orient* 23, no. 7 (July 1923), p. 475; Potter, *Sea Power*, pp. 563–567.

4. Adams, *Witness to Power*, pp. 38, 40.

5. "the improbability" and "knew of no," *New York Times*, January 30, 1921.

6. Alfred F. Hurley, *Billy Mitchell: Crusader for Air Power* (Bloomington: Indiana University Press, 1975), pp. 60-61, 65-68; "Mitchell had sunk," p. 68.

7. WDL/Diary, June 1921.

8. Ibid., September 1921.

9. Adams, *Witness to Power*, pp. 45–47; "There was something," WDL/Diary, March 22, 1923.

10. Adams, *Witness to Power*, p. 48.

11. WDL/Diary, February 3, 1924. See chapter 23, note 11, for how Leahy's views of Wilson changed.

12. Halsey, *Admiral Halsey's Story,* p. 42.

13. Thomas B. Buell, *The Quiet Warrior: A Biography of Admiral Raymond A. Spruance* (Annapolis: Naval Institute Press, 1987), p. 46.

14. Halsey, *Admiral Halsey's Story,* p. 42.

15. "boozy picnics," Potter, *Halsey,* p. 118. A host of secondary sources refer to Spruance as "Ray Spruance," but there is little primary evidence to support the nickname. Indeed, Spruance signed letters even to his close associates as "Raymond A. Spruance." Nimitz, who arguably became as close to Spruance as anyone in the navy, addressed letters to "Dear Raymond" as late as 1946. See, for example, Nimitz to Spruance, June 24, 1944, and March 7, 1946, RAS/NHHC, Box 1, Folder S.

16. "What do you intend," Halsey, *Admiral Halsey's Story,* pp. 44–46; "In a minute," Potter, *Halsey,* p. 117.

Chapter 8: Submarines

1. Blair, *Silent Victory,* vol. 1, pp. 24, 26.

2. Nimitz to Anna Nimitz, November 18, 1919, in Potter, *Nimitz,* p. 132.

3. "Pearl Harbor: Its Origin and Administrative History Through World War II," Department of the Navy, Naval History and Heritage Command, http://www.history.navy.mil/docs/wwii/pearl/hawaii-2.htm; "Development of the Naval Establishment in Hawaii," Department of the Navy, Naval History and Heritage Command, http://www.history.navy.mil/docs/wwii/pearl/hawaii-3.htm, both accessed October 29, 2009.

4. Potter, *Nimitz,* pp. 133–34.

5. Stuart S. Murray, "Building the Submarine Base at Pearl Harbor," in *Submarine Stories: Recollections from the Diesel Boats,* ed. Paul Stillwell (Annapolis: Naval Institute Press, 2007), p. 41.

6. Buell, *Master of Sea Power,* p. 57.

7. Ernest J. King et al., "Report and Recommendations of a Board Appointed by the Bureau of Navigation Regarding the Instruction and Training of Line Officers," *United States Naval Institute Proceedings* 46, no. 210 (August 1920), pp. 1265–92.

8. King, *Fleet Admiral King,* pp. 152–53, 159.

9. Buell, *Master of Sea Power,* pp. 62–63. "a captain among" and "as usual, I had," p. 62; "Why are you underway," p. 63.

10. Ibid., p. 65.

11. King to Editor of *Waterbury Herald,* October 19, 1925, EJK/LC, Box 3.

12. Buell, *Master of Sea Power,* p. 71.

13. "Daddy, wasn't it," King, *Fleet Admiral King,* p. 171; "rookies," *New York Times,* September 29, 1925; "All hands here," King to C. S. Freeman, October 2, 1925, EJK/LC, Box 3; "Men cling," *New York Times,* October 1, 1925.

14. Buell, *Master of Sea Power,* p. 67.

15. King to Leahy, February 26, 1926, EJK/LC, Box 3.

16. King, *Fleet Admiral King,* pp. 173–185; Ernest J. King, "Salvaging U.S.S. *S-51,*" *United States Naval Institute Proceedings* 53, no. 2 (February 1927), pp. 137–152.

Chapter 9: Aircraft Carriers

1. Clément Ader, *Military Aviation,* ed. and trans. Lee Kennett (Maxwell Air Force Base, Ala.: Air University Press, 2003), p. 41.

2. "Eugene Ely's Flight from USS *Birmingham,* 14 November 1910," Department of the Navy, Naval History and Heritage Command, http://www .history.navy.mil/photos/events/ev-1910s/ev-1910/ely-birm.htm; "Eugene Ely's Flight to USS *Pennsylvania,* 18 January 1911," Department of the Navy, Naval History and Heritage Command, http://www.history.navy .mil/photos/events/ev-1910s/ev-1911/ ely-pa.htm, both accessed October 6, 2009. Tragically, Eugene Ely was killed nine months later while flying in an air show in Georgia.

3. Halsey, *Admiral Halsey's Story,* p. 49.

4. "USS Langley (CV 1)," United States Navy, http://www.navy.mil/ navydata/navy_legacy_hr.asp?id=10, accessed October 6, 2009.

5. "USS Lexington (CV 2)," http:// www.chinfo.navy.mil/navpalib/ships/ carriers/histories/cv02-lexington/ cv02-lexington.html; "USS Saratoga (CV 3)," http://www.chinfo.navy.mil/ navpalib/ships/carriers/histories/ cv03-saratoga/cv03-saratoga.html, both accessed October 6, 2009. These ships followed the U.S. Navy's custom of naming ships after predecessors, which in these cases had been initially named after Revolutionary War battles. This tendency toward multiple ships with the same name—albeit never at the same time—means that attention must be paid to the corresponding ship number so as not to confuse *Lexington* (CV-2) with the later *Lexington* (CV-16). As early as 1819, Congress gave the secretary of the navy the responsibility of assigning ship names. There was no rigid convention, although principal ships were generally named after states and lesser ships after rivers and towns. As new battleship construction surged after the Spanish-American War, nonbattleships with state names—such as the cruiser *Pennsylvania*—were renamed to make battleship names the exclusive province of the states.

With battleship names resolved, this led to a general convention that called for naming cruisers for cities (*Birmingham, Houston, Nashville*), destroyers for American naval heroes (*Yarnall, Aaron Ward*), and oilers for rivers (Nimitz's *Maumee*). Amateur ornithologist Franklin D. Roosevelt as assistant secretary of the navy even bestowed bird names on a class of minesweepers (*Falcon, Tanager*).

Submarines were somewhat of an exception, having first been named for fish, such as Nimitz's *Snapper* and *Skipjack,* then going through a long line of alphabet boats to delineate various classes, such as *S-51;* and finally reverting to fish names for the majority of the World War II boats. Starting with *Lexington* and *Saratoga,* early aircraft carriers were given the names of prior warships and, later, more recent battles. This methodology had a practical side: when a captain was ordered to join up with *Houston,* he immediately knew it was a cruiser.

These naming conventions survived World War II but since then have largely disintegrated, much to the chagrin of many old navy hands. Carriers began to be named after individuals, first with the *Midway*-class *Franklin D. Roosevelt* and then with the lead ship of the *Forrestal* class, named after Secretary of Defense James V. Forrestal. The *John F. Kennedy* inaugurated the presidents series of carrier names, although modern carriers also honor an admiral (*Nimitz*), a senator (*John C. Stennis*), and a congressman (*Carl Vinson*). With no more battleships to be commissioned, state names were assigned to submarines, although one submarine was named for a president (*Jimmy Carter*) and one president's name moved from a decommissioned sub to a carrier (*George Washington*). For more information on ship nomenclature, see "Ship Naming in the United States Navy," Department of the Navy, Naval History and Heritage Command, http://www.history.navy.mil/faqs/faq63-1.htm and "Naming Ships," Federation of American Scientists, Military Analysis Network, http://www.fas.org/man/dod-101/sys/ship/names.htm.

6. Potter, *Nimitz,* pp. 136–141; "one of the truly important," p. 136; "as laying the groundwork," p. 141.

7. William F. Trimble, *Admiral William A. Moffett: Architect of Naval Aviation* (Washington, D.C.: Smithsonian Institution Press, 1994), p. 18.

8. King to Kurtz, May 13, 1926, EJK/LC, Box 3.

9. Buell, *Master of Sea Power,* pp. 72–76; "It seemed to me," p. 72; "badgered the base commander" and "the damnedest party man," p. 74; King, *Fleet Admiral King,* pp. 186–90.

10. Buell, *Master of Sea Power,* pp. 76–78; King, *Fleet Admiral King,* pp. 195–204; Moffett to King, February 8, 1928, EJK/LC, Box 3; and "I hardly know" and "developments regarding," King to Moffett, February 13, 1928, ibid.

11. Bureau of Navigation to King, July 7, 1928, and Bureau of Navigation to King, August 4, 1928, confirming July 28, 1928, dispatch, EJK/LC, Box 1; King, *Fleet Admiral King,* pp. 206–7; "He learned to his disgust," p. 206; "annoying period," p. 207.

12. "love the job," King, *Fleet Admiral King,* p. 207; "It seems to me" and "Admiral, I request," Buell, *Master of Sea Power,* p. 79; turning down the *Saratoga,* King, *Fleet Admiral King,* pp. 213–14; "the finest ship," Buell, *Master of Sea Power,* p. 79.

13. Buell, *Master of Sea Power,* p. 81.

14. J. J. "Jocko" Clark with Clark G. Reynolds, *Carrier Admiral* (New York: David McKay, 1967), p. 45.

15. Buell, *Master of Sea Power,* pp. 80–89; "Where the hell," p. 84;

"Everyone was out," p. 84; "Ballentine, what is wrong," p. 86; "Under King," p. 92; "You ought to be," p. 89.

16. King, *Fleet Admiral King*, pp. 228–30.

17. Halsey, *Admiral Halsey's Story*, pp. 47–48.

18. Potter, *Halsey*, pp. 123–25; Halsey, *Admiral Halsey's Story*, pp. 50–55; "buying and abandoning," p. 54; "one of the most delightful," p. 50; "I jumped at," p. 52.

Chapter 10: First Stars

1. Adams, *Witness to Power*, pp. 52–53; "had an excellent chance," p. 58. Six proposed battleships, numbered BB-49 through BB-54, whose hulls had already been laid before the Washington treaty, were never completed and were sold for scrap in 1923; a seventh— *Washington* (BB-47)—was sunk as a target in 1924.

2. The publication was the *Roll Call*, with sketches reproduced in WDL/Diary, undated, 1928.

3. Adams, *Witness to Power*, p. 60.

4. WDL/Diary, October 14, 1927.

5. Ibid., undated, 1930; Adams, *Witness to Power*, pp. 60–65.

6. London Naval Treaty, April 22, 1930, part 4, article 22, in *Treaties and Other International Agreements of the United States of America, 1776–1949*, vol. 2, *Multilateral, 1918–1930* (Washington, D.C.: U.S. Department of State, 1968), p. 1070.

7. Adams, *Witness to Power*, p. 66.

8. "Japanese Invasion of Manchuria, September 1931," BlacksAcademy .net, http://www.blacksacademy.net/content/3112.html, accessed January 7, 2010.

9. WDL/Diary, October 19, 1931.

10. Ibid., January 29, 1932.

11. Ibid., July 1, 1932.

12. Ibid., July 16, 1932.

13. Ibid., September 8, 1932.

14. Ibid., November 12, 1932.

15. Ibid., January 26, 1933.

16. Ibid., March 7, 1933.

17. Adams, *Witness to Power*, pp. 71–72.

18. WDL/Diary, January 10, 1935.

19. Swanson to Vinson, June 21, 1935, WDL/LC, insert in WDL/Diary, June 1935.

20. WDL/Diary, March 27, 1935. The "Propaganda Book" was a handbook "who's who in the opposition" for Japanese naval officers, as well as a general puff piece for Japan's own navy.

21. Ibid., September 29, 1936.

22. Halsey, *Admiral Halsey's Story*, pp. 54–55.

23. Potter, *Bull Halsey*, pp. 127–29; orders of May 28, 1934, and August 21, 1934, WFH/LC, Box 1; "What do you think," *Admiral Halsey's Story*, p. 57.

24. Halsey, *Admiral Halsey's Story*, p. 62.

25. Ibid.

26. LaChance to King, April 29, 1933, and King to LaChance, May 18, 1933, EJK/LC, Box 4.

27. King to Spafford, May 19, 1933, EJK/LC, Box 4.

28. Buell, *Master of Sea Power*, p. 98.

29. Ibid., p. 101.

Chapter 11: Projecting Power

1. Potter, *Nimitz,* pp. 142–43, 147.
2. Ibid., p. 150.
3. Ibid., p. 152.
4. Ibid., pp. 156–57.
5. Ibid., pp. 158–60; "I think one can," p. 160.
6. Ibid., p. 1.
7. Adams, *Witness to Power,* p. 86.
8. WDL/Diary, November 10, 1936.
9. "Leahy: Would-Be West Pointer Climbs to Top of Navy Ladder," *Newsweek,* November 21, 1936, p. 12.
10. WDL/Diary, November 4, 1936.
11. Ibid., December 31, 1936.
12. FDR inaugural parade, ibid., January 20, 1937.
13. Harold L. Ickes, *The Secret Diary of Harold L. Ickes,* vol. 2, *The Inside Struggle, 1936–1939* (New York: Simon & Schuster, 1954), pp. 192–93.
14. WDL/Diary, September 21, 1937. The internal Chinese civil war between the Communists and Nationalists had been put on hold late in 1936 to counter this renewed Japanese threat. The infamous Rape of Nanking that followed the Japanese capture of Nanking continues to be controversial and a source of contention in Sino-Japanese relations.
15. Ibid., September 21, 1937.
16. Joseph C. Grew, *Ten Years in Japan* (New York: Simon & Schuster, 1944), p. 234; Samuel Eliot Morison, *History of United States Naval Operations in World War II,* vol. 3, *The Rising Sun in the Pacific* (Boston: Little, Brown, 1948), pp. 16–18.

17. WDL/Diary, December 12 and 13, 1937. Years later, *Time* published an apocryphal account of that meeting which had FDR asking, "Bill what will it take to lick Japan?" Leahy supposedly replied, "Fifty billion dollars a year—and I'd like the job." The president shook his head and replied, "It's too much. Send for Cordell Hull"—meaning a diplomatic rather than a military solution (*Time,* May 28, 1945, p. 15).
18. "ships of the Fleet," WDL/Diary, December 14, 1937; "we then blockaded," Leahy, *I Was There,* p. 64.
19. Morison, *Naval Operations,* vol. 3, p. 18.
20. Adams, *Witness to Power,* pp. 101–2; Brands, *Traitor to His Class,* pp. 495–96, 505; "subjected to a very severe," WDL/Diary, December 31, 1937; Norman Alley's footage, "China: Bombing of USS Panay Special Issue, 1937/12/12," at bliptv, http://blip.tv/file/898740, accessed November 11, 2009, including the narration phrase "war-crazed culprits."
21. Roosevelt to Leahy, December 30, 1937, WDL/Diary, December 30, 1937.
22. King to Standley, September 28, 1936, EJK/LC, Box 6. One of the books King probably took with him on this cruise was Edwin A. Falk's just-published *Togo and the Rise of Japanese Sea Power;* book order in King to Naval Institute Press, May 1, 1936, EJK/LC, Box 4.
23. King to McCain, September 12, 1936, EJK/LC, Box 6. McCain's philosophical response was, "It is an ill wind that blows no one any good"

(McCain to King, October 23, 1936, ibid.).

24. Buell, *Master of Sea Power,* p. 108.

25. King to Andrews, February 17, 1938, EJK/LC, Box 7.

26. Andrews declined King's proposal with a "My dear Rey" letter, Andrews to King, February 23, 1938, EJK/LC, Box 7.

27. Buell, *Master of Sea Power,* pp. 110–11.

28. King, *Fleet Admiral King,* p. 274.

29. Buell, *Master of Sea Power,* p. 113.

30. Halsey to King, November 15, 1938, EJK/LC, Box 7. Later, the *Essex*-class carriers of 1943 introduced deck-edge elevators that created more flight deck space and kept the shuttling of planes between the flight deck and hangar deck out of the way of most flight operations.

31. King to Halsey, November 18, 1938, EJK/LC, Box 7.

32. Halsey, *Admiral Halsey's Story,* p. 66.

33. King, *Fleet Admiral King,* p. 292.

34. Whitehill notes of conversation with King, undated, EJK/NHC/NWC, MS 37, Box 2, File Folder 1.

35. Buell, *Master of Sea Power,* p. 100.

36. Halsey to King, June 22, 1939, EJK/LC, Box 7.

37. Halsey, *Admiral Halsey's Story,* p. 68.

38. WDL/Diary, May 12, 1939.

39. Leahy to Bloch, May 17, 1939, Charles Claude Bloch Papers, Box 2, Naval Historical Foundation Collection, Manuscript Division, Library of Congress, Washington, D.C.

40. *Washington Post,* May 28, 1939.

41. *Washington Times-Herald,* June 2, 1939.

42. WDL/Diary, July 28, 1939; "The extraordinary qualities," Distinguished Service Medal citation, insert in ibid., August 1, 1939.

43. Roosevelt to Leahy, July 28, 1939, insert in ibid.

44. "This brings to an end," ibid.; "Bill, if we ever," *Life,* September 28, 1942, p. 102.

Chapter 12: At War All but in Name

1. Nimitz to Bloch, March 23, 1939, Bloch Papers, Box 2; "While the Navy," Bloch to Nimitz, April 14, 1939, ibid.

2. Hutchinson to Nimitz, June 16, 1939, CWN/NHHC, Series 2, Box 25.

3. Nimitz to Bloch, November 17, 1939, Bloch Papers, Box 2; "Whether this is important," Bloch to Nimitz, November 20, 1939, ibid.

4. Potter, *Nimitz,* p. 169.

5. Buell, *Master of Sea Power,* p. 123.

6. Ibid., p. 125; see note at p. 571 for Buell's analysis of FDR's role in King's assignment with Edison; temporary duty orders, March 23, 1940, EJK/LC, Box 1.

7. "peace-time psychology," Buell, *Master of Sea Power,* p. 125; "throw off a routine," p. 127; temporary duty orders, May 14, 1940, EJK/LC, Box 1.

8. Buell, *Master of Sea Power,* p. 127.

9. Ibid., pp. 127–28; orders, November 14, 1940, EJK/LC, Box 1.

10. Adams, *Witness to Power,* p. 131.

11. "simply would disappear" and "this streak," Harold L. Ickes, *The Secret Diary of Harold L. Ickes,* vol. 3, *The Lowering Clouds, 1939–1941* (New York: Simon & Schuster, 1954), p. 206; "Leahy thinks," p. 349. Certainly, no one ever questioned Leahy's personal courage. Getting into his car outside the El Cortez Hotel in San Diego in the fall of 1932, Leahy encountered a masked man in the rear seat who pointed a pistol at him and told him to get in quietly. Leahy slammed the door shut and dodged behind an adjacent car to enter the hotel and immediately call police. "This was my first close contact with a bandit and of course being in America I was unarmed" (WDL/Diary, October 1932).

12. "The senior officers," George C. Dyer, *On the Treadmill to Pearl Harbor: The Memoirs of Admiral James O. Richardson* (Washington, D.C.: Naval History Division, 1973), pp. 425, 435; WDL/Diary, October 8, 1940. Richardson later professed that his relief three months later came as "a real shock to me." In his memoirs more than thirty years later, he was still frank in his opinion of FDR: "I was deeply disappointed in my detachment, yet there was some feeling of prospective relief, for I had never liked to work with people whom I did not trust, and I did not trust Franklin D. Roosevelt" (Dyer, *On the Treadmill,* p. 420).

13. Naval message, FDR to Leahy, November 17, 1940, insert in WDL/Diary; "I can leave," Adams, *Witness to Power,* p. 5.

14. Buell, *Master of Sea Power,* p. 131.

15. CINCLANT Serial 053, January 21, 1941, in Buell, *Master of Sea Power,* pp. 521–23.

16. Buell, *Master of Sea Power,* p. 131.

17. Orders, February 12, 1941, EJK/LC, Box 1; Kimmel to Nimitz, January 12, 1941, CWN/NHHC, Series 13.

18. King to Knox, January 17, 1941, and Knox to King, January 27, 1941, EJK/LC, Box 12.

19. King to Nimitz, February 12, 1941, EJK/LC, Box 8; "I expect the officers," King, *Fleet Admiral King,* pp. 325–26.

20. Buell, *Master of Sea Power,* p. 150.

21. King, *Fleet Admiral King,* pp. 329–31.

22. Winston S. Churchill, *The Second World War,* vol. 3, *The Grand Alliance* (Boston: Houghton Mifflin, 1950), p. 307.

23. Buell, *Master of Sea Power,* p. 140.

24. Ibid., pp. 142–44; King, *Fleet Admiral King,* pp. 331–36; Churchill, *The Second World War,* vol. 3, pp. 431–32, 443–44; "formed a very good opinion," Robin Brodhurst, *Churchill's Anchor: The Biography of Admiral of the Fleet Sir Dudley Pound* (Barnsley, South Yorkshire: Leo Cooper, 2000), p. 186, quoting Pound to Cunningham, September 3, 1941.

25. Franklin D. Roosevelt, "Message to Congress on the Sinking of the *Robin Moor,* June 20, 1941," in *The Public Papers and Addresses of Franklin D. Roosevelt,* comp. Samuel I. Rosenman, vol. 10 (New York: Harper and Brothers, 1950), p. 230.

26. Buell, *Master of Sea Power,* p. 146.

27. Woody Guthrie, "Sinking of the Reuben James," 1941.

28. King to Nimitz, November 10, 1941, EJK/LC, Box 8. King, Halsey, and Leahy were all awarded the Navy Cross during World War I for similar routine service. At that time, the medal functioned as a form of distinguished service award. In 1942, the decoration was changed to a combat-only honor.

29. *Life,* November 24, 1941, pp. 92–108.

30. Halsey, *Admiral Halsey's Story,* pp. 69–71.

31. Stark to Bloch, July 14, 1941, Bloch Papers, Box 3.

32. Bloch to Nimitz, July 24, 1941, Bloch Papers, Box 2.

33. Bloch to Stark, November 14, 1941, Bloch Papers, Box 3.

34. "How far do you," Halsey, *Admiral Halsey's Story,* pp. 73–74.

Chapter 13: Searching for Scapegoats and Heroes

1. Albert A. Nofi, *To Train the Fleet for War: The U.S. Navy Fleet Problems, 1923–1940* (Newport, R.I.: Naval War College Press, 2010), p. 231.

2. Halsey, *Admiral Halsey's Story,* pp. 76–77.

3. Potter, *Nimitz,* p. 6.

4. Orders, December 10, 1941, EJK/LC, Box 1; King, *Fleet Admiral King,* p. 3.

5. WDL/Diary, December 8, 1941.

6. *Fleet Admiral King* draft notes, EJK/LC, Box 35.

7. Potter, *Nimitz,* p. 9.

8. Buell, *Master of Sea Power,* p. 153.

9. Exec. Order No. 8984, 41, Fed. Reg. 9587 (December 19, 1941).

10. King, *Fleet Admiral King,* p. 349.

11. Buell, *Master of Sea Power,* p. 154; King, *Fleet Admiral King,* p. 355.

12. Potter, *Nimitz,* p. 10.

13. Ibid., p. 172.

14. Potter, *Nimitz,* pp. 11–15; casualty reports, Gordon W. Prange, *At Dawn We Slept: The Untold Story of Pearl Harbor* (New York: Penguin, 1991), pp. 520, 539; Nimitz to Catherine Nimitz, December 20–24, 1941, CWN/NHHC, Section 14.

15. WDL/Diary, December 21, 1941.

16. Leahy to FDR, insert in WDL-Diary, December 22, 1941.

17. Knox to King, December 20, 1941, and Roosevelt to King, December 20, 1941), EJK/LC, Box 1; King, *Fleet Admiral King,* p. 352.

18. King, *Fleet Admiral King,* pp. 352–53.

19. "hoping that history," Buell, *Master of Sea Power,* p. 161; "Well, what are," Whitehill interview with King, August 14, 1949, EJK/NHC/ NWC, Box 7, File Folder 13.

20. "What news" and "When you get," Potter, *Nimitz,* p. 16; "must be very," Nimitz to Catherine Nimitz,

December 26–31, 1941, CWN/NHHC, Series 14.

21. For Nimitz's views of command ashore and the inadequacies of the Japanese attack, see Potter, *Nimitz,* p. 18. Japanese reactions to the attack, including Yamamoto's displeasure with Nagumo, are documented in Prange, *At Dawn We Slept,* p. 550.

22. Fred Borch and Daniel Martinez, *Kimmel, Short, and Pearl Harbor: The Final Report Revealed* (Annapolis: Naval Institute Press, 2005), pp. 40–41. The Roberts Commission report was released to the public on January 24, 1942. Short retired on February 28 and Kimmel on March 1. Borch and Martinez note that there is no evidence to support claims that they were "forced into retirement."

23. "because of one man," Halsey, *Admiral Halsey's Story,* p. 82; Husband E. Kimmel, *Admiral Kimmel's Story* (Chicago: Henry Regnery, 1955), pp. 168–69, quoting Halsey to Kimmel, July 20, 1953.

24. King to Kimmel, December 17, 1941, and February 27, 1942, Husband Edward Kimmel Papers, 1907–1999, Accession Number 3800, Box 3, File Folder J-F 1942, American Heritage Center, University of Wyoming, Laramie.

25. Borch and Martinez, *Kimmel, Short, and Pearl Harbor,* p. 42.

26. "Random Notes," EJK/LC, Box 35. King further wrote, "I again repeat that I have never been able to understand how or why F.D.R. could fire Admiral Stark without doing the same to General Marshall. In my opinion one could not possibly be more suspect than the other."

27. Jacobs to Kimmel, January 15, 1942, Kimmel Papers, Box 3, File Folder J-F 1942. This letter on Bureau of Navigation stationery is signed by Jacobs. A copy of the letter, with no underlying stationery but initialed "CWN" in Nimitz's hand in the signature block, can be found in CWN/NHHC, Series 13, causing some confusion as to the author.

28. William Manchester, *American Caesar, Douglas MacArthur, 1880–1964* (Boston: Little, Brown, 1978), pp. 205–12; Prange, *At Dawn We Slept,* p. 591; MacArthur recorded his own version: "Our bombers were slow in taking off and . . . our force was simply too small to smash the odds against them" (Douglas MacArthur, *Reminiscences* [New York: McGraw-Hill, 1964], p. 117).

29. Eisenhower, January 13, 1942, in *The Eisenhower Diaries,* ed. Robert H. Ferrell (New York: Norton, 1981), p. 43.

Chapter 14: Spread Thin

1. Edwin T. Layton, *"And I Was There": Pearl Harbor and Midway—Breaking the Secrets* (New York: William Morrow, 1985), pp. 74, 275; "certain key members," Potter, *Nimitz,* p. 21.

2. Halsey, *Admiral Halsey's Story,* pp. 84–85.

3. Ibid., pp. 88–89.

4. Ibid., pp. 90, 93.

5. Ibid., pp. 94, 96. Halsey was awarded the Distinguished Service

Medal for the Marshall operation. When Nimitz sent word to Halsey of the honor, he "quoted with pleasure" Secretary of the Navy Knox's message "to Vice Admiral William Henry [*sic*] Halsey Junior U S Navy...for his brilliant and audacious attack against Marshall and Gilbert Islands....," CINCPAC to Halsey, February 11, 1942, WFH/LC, Box 1). How Knox managed to get Halsey's middle name wrong is another matter. Later, the *Enterprise* and its crew were awarded a Presidential Unit Citation for their exploits in the first year of the war as the "galloping ghost of the Oahu coast."

6. Halsey, *Admiral Halsey's Story,* pp. 97–101.

7. Buell, *Master of Sea Power,* p. 178. Stark's role in wartime strategy, particularly with the British, has been traditionally downplayed. For a British perspective suggesting a greater importance of his role, see Brodhurst, *Churchill's Anchor: The Biography of Admiral of the Fleet Sir Dudley Pound.*

8. Exec. Order No. 9096, 42 Fed. Reg. 2195 (March 12, 1942).

9. Hopkins to King, March 13, 1942, EJK/LC, Box 12.

10. *Life,* March 23, 1942, p. 28; *Time,* March 16, 1942, p. 58.

11. Press release, March 26, 1942, EJK/LC, Box 23.

12. King, *Fleet Admiral King,* p. 321.

13. Marshall to King, August 15, 1941, GCM/LC, Reel 21.

14. Eisenhower, January 5, 1942, in *Eisenhower Diaries,* p. 40.

15. Ibid., February 23, 1942, p. 49.

16. Ibid., March 10, 1942, pp. 50, 403n.

17. Ibid., March 14, 1942, p. 51.

18. Dwight D. Eisenhower, *At Ease: Stories I Tell to Friends* (Garden City, N.Y.: Doubleday, 1967), p. 252.

19. Forrest C. Pogue, *George C. Marshall: Ordeal and Hope, 1939–1942* (New York: Viking, 1966), p. 372.

20. Eisenhower, January 19, 1942, in *Eisenhower Diaries,* p. 44.

21. Manchester, *American Caesar,* p. 152.

22. Pogue, *Marshall: Ordeal and Hope,* p. 234.

23. WDL/Diary, March 18, 1942. Leahy's opinion may have been colored by his esteem for the general's nephew, Douglas MacArthur II, who was serving under him in the Vichy embassy.

24. Eisenhower, February 23, 1942, in *Eisenhower Diaries,* p. 49.

25. Forrest C. Pogue, *George C. Marshall: Education of a General, 1880–1939* (New York: Viking, 1963), p. 282; Pogue, *Marshall: Ordeal and Hope,* p. 249.

26. Eisenhower, March 19, 1942, in *Eisenhower Diaries,* p. 51.

27. King to Reynolds, March 19, 1952, EJK/LC, Box 18.

28. Halsey, *Admiral Halsey's Story,* pp. 101–4; Potter, *Halsey,* pp. 58–62.

29. King, *Fleet Admiral King,* p. 376; King to Reynolds, March 25, 1952, EJK/LC, Box 18, "from our new secret base," Franklin D. Roosevelt, April 21, 1942, in *Complete Presidential Press Conferences of Franklin D.*

Roosevelt, vols. 19–20, 1942 (New York: Da Capo Press, 1972), p. 292.

30. John B. Lundstrom, *Black Shoe Carrier Admiral: Frank Jack Fletcher at Coral Sea, Midway, and Guadalcanal* (Annapolis: Naval Institute Press, 2006), p. 124.

31. Ibid., pp. 125–29.

32. Potter, *Nimitz,* pp. 69–70.

33. Lundstrom, *Black Shoe Carrier Admiral,* p. 168.

34. Ibid., p. 208.

35. Ibid., pp. 199–200. A great many congratulatory messages flew among the major military commanders. While many were sincere, most had underlying political or ego-stroking purposes as well. MacArthur, whose ego was the intended recipient of many such communications, was one of the few commanders who apparently took them to heart and quoted them at length in his autobiography.

36. Halsey, *Admiral Halsey's Story,* p. 105.

37. Potter, *Nimitz,* p. 78. One might well argue that the final flaw in the Japanese attack on Pearl Harbor had been not to capture Midway at the outset of the war as its main force retired westward from Hawaii.

38. Lundstrom, *Black Shoe Carrier Admiral,* pp. 211–12, 216–17. After the fact, King remembered the situation quite differently in his memoirs: "In King's view the important thing was Midway, for he felt that the Japanese could not do everything at once. Consequently, he directed Nimitz to bring his ships away from their stations in the South Pacific...and deploy them for the defense of Hawaii and Midway" (King, *Fleet Admiral King,* p. 379).

39. Buell, *Master of Sea Power,* pp. 201–2; "to employ," COMINCH to CINCPAC, May 17, 1942, no. 2220, Nimitz "Gray Book," p. 490, Naval History and Heritage Command, or online at http://www.ibiblio.org/anrs/docs/D/D7/nimitz_graybook5.pdf, accessed February 17, 2011. It helped their relationship, of course, that Nimitz was proved right at Midway.

40. Potter, *Halsey,* p. 77.

41. Lundstrom, *Black Shoe Carrier Admiral,* p. 228.

42. Ibid., p. 229.

43. Ibid., pp. 219–21, 237–39. See also Jonathan Parshall and Anthony Tully, *Shattered Sword: The Untold Story of the Battle of Midway* (Washington, D.C.: Potomac Books, 2005), pp. 43–45, for an analysis of Japanese plans to attack both Midway and Dutch Harbor simultaneously. When the Midway attack fell behind a day and didn't occur on June 3, Nimitz momentarily worried that his intelligence was wrong.

44. Parshall and Tully, *Shattered Sword,* pp. 417–20. Relying heavily on Japanese records, this is a revision of traditional casualty figures on the Japanese side.

45. Walter Lord, *Incredible Victory* (New York: Harper and Row, 1967), p. 286.

46. King, *Fleet Admiral King,* p. 380.

47. *Time,* June 15, 1942, p. 17.

48. Spruance to Nimitz, May 15, 1957, RAS/NHHC, Box 1.

49. Spruance to Nimitz, June 8, 1942, RAS/NHHC, Box 3. Spruance closed by telling Nimitz, "I appreciate more than I can tell you the fact that you had sufficient confidence in me to let me take this fine Task Force to sea during this critical period. It has been a pleasure to have such a well trained fighting force to throw against the enemy."

50. Lundstrom, *Black Shoe Carrier Admiral,* pp. 114, 293. See also p. 277 for the role Fletcher's relinquishment of overall command played in assessments of his career and pp. 508–12 for Spruance's continuing assertions of Fletcher's role.

51. Halsey, *Admiral Halsey's Story,* pp. 106–7.

Chapter 15: Deciding the Course

1. Buell, *Master of Sea Power,* pp. 188–89.

2. King to Roosevelt, memorandum, March 5, 1942, "Safe Files," Box 3, King Folder, Franklin D. Roosevelt Presidential Library and Museum, Hyde Park, N.Y.

3. Buell, *Master of Sea Power,* p. 189.

4. Pogue, *Marshall: Ordeal and Hope,* pp. 254–55.

5. Buell, *Master of Sea Power,* pp. 191–92.

6. Robert William Love, Jr., *The Chiefs of Naval Operations* (Annapolis: Naval Institute Press, 1980), p. 113.

7. Potter, *Nimitz,* p. 45; Buell, *Master of Sea Power,* p. 137. King, in fact, tried to use Ghormley's appointment as an excuse to put Fletcher ashore as temporary COMSOPAC prior to Ghormley arriving in the South Pacific. This would have removed Fletcher from an operational command — something Nimitz forcefully and successfully opposed at this point (Lundstrom, *Black Shoe Carrier Admiral,* p. 118). In a communication with the author, John Lundstrom speculated that part of King's insistence on Ghormley came from FDR, who reportedly abhorred Pye.

8. Buell, *Master of Sea Power,* pp. 197–98, 576.

9. *Time,* March 16, 1942, p. 59.

10. Buell, *Master of Sea Power,* p. 197.

11. King/Nimitz Pacific Conferences, minutes, April 25, 1942, NRS 1972-22, Department of the Navy, Naval History and Heritage Command.

12. WDL/Diary, January 1, 1942.

13. Leahy to FDR, insert in WDL/Diary, December 22, 1941.

14. Darlan to Leahy, March 8, 1942, in Leahy, *I Was There,* pp. 480–81.

15. Leahy to Darlan, March 9, 1942, in Leahy, *I Was There,* pp. 481–82.

16. Roosevelt to Leahy, April 3, 1942, in Leahy, *I Was There,* p. 482.

17. FDR to Leahy, insert in WDL/Diary, undated but ca. March 1, 1942. In this letter, FDR used the phrase "United Nations" in capital letters to refer to the Allies, one of its earliest uses.

18. WDL/Diary, April 6, April 7, and April 21, 1942.

19. FDR to Leahy, insert in WDL/Diary, April 21, 1942.

20. Leahy, *I Was There,* p. 96.

21. Pogue, *Marshall: Ordeal and Hope,* p. 299.

22. Ibid., pp. 298–99. Marshall's regard for Leahy was genuine. As Leahy departed for Vichy, Marshall wrote, "The sacrifice you make and the integrity of purpose you carry to your duties merit genuine public appreciation, and support. You have mine, in full measure," Marshall to Leahy, December 23, 1940, GCM/LC, Reel 22).

23. Leahy, *I Was There,* p. 96; "always liked Leahy," Whitehill interview with King, August 27, 1950, EJK/ NHC/NWC, Box 7, File Folder 19.

24. Roosevelt, July 21, 1942, in *Complete Presidential Press Conferences,* vol. 20, pp. 14–19. Newspapermen knew the term "legman" as one who did the digging and occasional dirty work for those getting their names in the bylines.

25. Leahy, *I Was There,* p. 97.

26. *New York Herald Tribune,* July 22, 1942, p. 1.

27. *Time,* August 3, 1942, p. 15.

28. Leahy, *I Was There,* p. 97; Paul L. Miles, Jr., "American Strategy in World War II: The Role of William D. Leahy," unpublished Ph.D. diss., Princeton University, 1999, p. 78n.

29. *New York Herald Tribune,* July 23, 1942.

30. *Washington Post,* July 23, 1942.

31. FDR to Leahy, June 26, 1941, in *F.D.R.: His Personal Letters, 1928–1945,* vol. 2, ed. Elliott Roosevelt (New York: Duell, Sloan and Pearce, 1950), p. 1177.

32. King to Roosevelt, memorandum, March 5, 1942.

33. Pogue, *Marshall: Ordeal and Hope,* p. 340, quoting Marshall and King to Roosevelt, July 10, 1942. In 1956, well after the fact, Marshall claimed it was a bluff, but there is ample evidence to suggest his strong displeasure regarding plans for Gymnast.

34. Roosevelt to Marshall, draft ca. July 14, 1942, in Miles, "American Strategy," p. 108.

35. Roosevelt to Hopkins, Marshall, and King, memorandum, July 16, 1942, "Safe Files," Box 4, Marshall Folder, Franklin Delano Roosevelt Presidential Library and Museum, Hyde Park, N.Y. (this appears to be the last version of at least one, possibly two, other drafts); Pogue, *Marshall: Ordeal and Hope,* pp. 341–42. Pogue notes a book then circulating among both British and American upper echelons, *Soldiers and Statesmen* by British field marshal Sir William Robertson, that was highly critical of politically inspired expeditions that shifted military emphasis away from the main front. Robertson gives as a prime example Churchill's role in the ill-fated Dardanelles campaign of World War I, when he was first lord of the Admiralty. Many whispered that the North African venture was another such scheme.

36. "It will be," Brooke, July 15, 1942, in Field Marshal Lord Alanbrooke, *War Diaries, 1939–1945,* ed. Alex Danchev and Daniel Todman (Berkeley: University of California Press, 2001), p. 280; "Marshall and King," Miles, "American Strategy," p. 89n.

37. Harry C. Butcher, *My Three Years with Eisenhower* (New York: Simon & Schuster, 1946), p. 29.

38. Pogue, *Marshall: Ordeal and Hope,* pp. 399–400. Leahy professed in his diary that he understood from the beginning that his duties included "presiding over the meetings of the Joint Chiefs of Staff and Combined Chiefs of Staff," while Marshall recalled Leahy's surprise at being asked to preside (Miles, "American Strategy," pp. 125–26).

39. Miles, "American Strategy," p. 54n; Winston S. Churchill, *The Second World War,* vol. 5, *Closing the Ring* (Boston: Houghton Mifflin, 1951), p. 6.

40. Buell, *Master of Sea Power,* p. 289.

41. Notes for *I Was There,* WDL/LC, Box 13, p. 331.

42. FDR to Eisenhower, November 14, 1942, in Roosevelt, *Public Papers and Addresses,* vol. 11, p. 472.

43. Eisenhower to King, November 2, 1942, in *The Papers of Dwight David Eisenhower: The War Years,* ed. Alfred D. Chandler, Jr., vol. 1 (Baltimore: Johns Hopkins University Press, 1970), p. 577.

44. Leahy, *I Was There,* p. 345.

45. Pogue, *Marshall: Ordeal and Hope,* p. 402.

46. "It has been," Leahy, *I Was There,* p. 111; Miles, "American Strategy," p. 120.

Chapter 16: Fighting the Japanese — and MacArthur

1. Manchester, *American Caesar,* p. 166.

2. MacArthur, *Reminiscences,* p. 121.

3. Theodore H. White, *In Search of History: A Personal Adventure* (New York: Harper and Row, 1978), p. 110. When White recounted this conversation decades later, he added that MacArthur "was completely wrong in this in the spring of 1942, for the U.S. Navy was about to prove it was the finest navy that ever cut the water; and Franklin D. Roosevelt and George C. Marshall were men greater than he."

4. *Washington Times-Herald,* June 7, 1942; "treat the operation," Marshall to King, June 6, 1942, GCM/LC, Reel 21; "the way to handle," Marshall to King, June 7, 1942, ibid.

5. Transcript of press conference, June 7, 1942, EJK/LC, Box 23.

6. King to Edson, September 29, 1949, EJK/LC, Box 17.

7. Ibid. Ghormley described the frustrations of supply from his perspective in a report he dictated on January 22, 1943; see Narrative, Vice Admiral R. L. Ghormley, U.S.N., South Pacific Command—April through October 1942, Robert L. Ghormley Papers, Collection No. 1153, Box 15, File Folder o, East Carolina Manuscript Collection, J. Y. Joyner Library, East Carolina University, Greenville, N.C.

8. King to Edson, September 29, 1949, EJK/LC, Box 17; "to 'educate' the Army," Buell, *Master of Sea Power,* pp. 216–17. For one example of Marshall turning to FDR to direct MacArthur, see Pogue, *Marshall: Ordeal and Hope,* p. 378.

9. Potter, *Nimitz,* pp. 110–11. The XPBS-1 (Experimental Patrol Bomber Seaplane) was the experimental version

of what became the Sikorsky VS-44. Only three were ever built: *Excalibur* (NC-41880) crashed off Newfoundland in 1942; *Excambian* (NC-41881) is restored at the Naval Aviation Museum in Pensacola, Florida; and *Exeter* (NC-41882) was apparently destroyed in South America.

10. COMINCH to CINCPAC et al., August 8, 1942, CWN/NHHC, Series 2, Box 25.

11. Pogue, *Marshall: Ordeal and Hope*, p. 382; "Narrative," p. 10, Ghormley Papers.

12. Lundstrom, *Black Shoe Carrier Admiral*, pp. 314, 385–86.

13. Potter, *Nimitz*, p. 181.

14. Buell, *Master of Sea Power*, pp. 221–22.

15. Potter, *Nimitz*, p. 183.

16. Lundstrom, *Black Shoe Carrier Admiral*, pp. 451, 477.

17. Nimitz photo, Frank Jack Fletcher Papers, Box 2, File Folder 41, American Heritage Center, University of Wyoming, Laramie; Fletcher to Nimitz, January 30, 1945, Fletcher Papers, Box 1, File Folder 25; King, *Fleet Admiral King*, pp. 377–78. Frank Jack Fletcher's reputation as a solid and steady, if not flashy, naval commander has undergone a reappraisal in recent years with the publication of Lundstrom's *Black Shoe Carrier Admiral: Frank Jack Fletcher at Coral Sea, Midway, and Guadalcanal* (Annapolis: Naval Institute Press, 2006).

18. Potter, *Halsey*, p. 150.

19. The quote is from Halsey, *Admiral Halsey's Story*, p. 108, which says that this occurred on *Saratoga* on September 12. Potter, *Nimitz*, p. 188, gives the date as September 12 on *Enterprise;* Potter, *Halsey*, p. 155, says *Saratoga* on September 22, with a footnote on p. 398 noting Halsey's date in *Admiral Halsey's Story* is wrong. Actually, this ceremony occurred on *Enterprise* on September 15 and was reported as being "aboard a fighting ship" — without mentioning the ship's name because of wartime censorship — by Robert Trumbull, who telephoned in the story for publication in the *New York Times* on September 16, 1942. The *Saratoga*, crippled from a second torpedo attack and with Frank Jack Fletcher on board, did not arrive in Pearl Harbor until September 21. Even without the evidence from the *Times*, it would have been totally out of character for Nimitz to introduce Halsey in such a manner in front of the returning Fletcher. Trumbull's account referred to Halsey as "Fighting Bill," with no mention of the nickname "Bull."

20. Potter, *Nimitz*, pp. 190–92; Lundstrom, *Black Shoe Carrier Admiral*, p. 485; H. Arthur Lamar, *I Saw Stars: Some Memories of Commander Hal Lamar, Fleet Admiral Nimitz' Flag Lieutenant, 1941–1945* (Fredericksburg, Tex.: Admiral Nimitz Foundation, 1985), p. 9.

21. Potter, *Nimitz*, pp. 193–94.

22. Halsey, *Admiral Halsey's Story*, p. 109.

23. Nimitz to R. L. Ghormley, Jr. [son], January 19, 1961, Ghormley Papers, Box 18, File Folder b.

24. Potter, *Halsey*, p. 159.

25. Potter, *Nimitz,* p. 197.

26. The omelet quote was attributed to Halsey in *Time,* November 30, 1942, p. 30; "saltier than" and "known throughout," *Time,* November 2, 1942, p. 31.

27. Potter, *Halsey,* p. 160.

28. Halsey, *Admiral Halsey's Story,* pp. 117, 139.

29. Gerald E. Wheeler, *Kinkaid of the Seventh Fleet* (Washington, D.C.: Naval Historical Center, 1995), pp. 273–86; see also John B. Lundstrom, *The First Team and the Guadalcanal Campaign: Naval Fighter Combat from August to November 1942* (Annapolis: Naval Institute Press, 1994), pp. 353, 356–459, arguably the best account of the Battle of the Santa Cruz Islands.

30. Halsey to Nimitz, October 31, 1942, CWN/NHHC, Series 13, "Fighting Bill" reference in *New York Times,* September 16, 1942.

31. Halsey was again critical of Kinkaid and felt that he should have arrived sooner. Afterward, Halsey relieved Kinkaid of command of Task Force 16. See Lundstrom, *Black Shoe Carrier Admiral,* pp. 493–95.

32. "US Navy and Marine Corps Personnel Casualties in World War II," Department of the Navy, Naval History and Heritage Command, www.history.navy.mil/faqs/faq11-1.htm, accessed January 19, 2011.

33. *Time,* November 30, 1942, p. 28.

34. Halsey, *Admiral Halsey's Story,* p. 132.

35. Halsey to Nimitz, November 6, 1942, CWN/NHHC, Series 13. "Cheerfully yours" and "Stay cheerful" were standard conversation and letter closings of the World War II era, not unlike "Have a nice day" and "Take care" would become to later generations.

36. Crosse to Halsey, November 18, 1942, WFH/LC, Box 38.

37. Crosse to Halsey, November 25, 1942, WFH/LC, Box 38.

38. South Pacific Force memo, pencil dated June 2, 1943, WFH/LC, Box 38.

39. Churchill Remarks at Lord Mayor's Luncheon, London, November 10, 1942.

40. "Battle of the Pacific," *Time,* December 7, 1942, pp. 30–34.

41. Potter, *Nimitz,* p. 175.

42. Nimitz, message, December 25, 1942, CWN/NHHC, Series 4, Speeches.

43. Marshall to King, December 22, 1942, and King to Marshall, December 23, 1942, EJK/LC, Box 13.

44. Halsey to Nimitz, November 6, 1942, CWN/NHHC, Series 13. To MacArthur's credit, by 1943 he was making inspection trips to the front lines, although they were heavily orchestrated for publicity purposes.

Chapter 17: From Casablanca to Teheran

1. King to Roosevelt, October 23, 1942, EJK/LC, Box 14; King, *Fleet Admiral King,* p. 412. FDR's present turned out to be a framed portrait of himself.

2. "a year of conferences," Leahy, *I Was There,* p. 142; Andrew Roberts, *Masters and Commanders: How Four*

Titans Won the War in the West, 1941–1945 (New York: Harper, 2009), p. 314.

3. WDL/Diary, January 9, 1943.

4. Whitehill Interview with King, August 26, 1950, EJK/NHC/NWC, Box 7, File Folder 28. Marshall's plane also carried British air marshal Sir Charles Portal, who technically outranked both Marshall and King.

5. H. H. Arnold, *Global Mission* (New York: Harper Brothers, 1949), p. 389.

6. Leahy, *I Was There,* p. 145.

7. Ibid., p. 144.

8. D. Clayton James, *The Years of MacArthur,* vol. 2, *1941–1945* (Boston: Houghton Mifflin, 1975), p. 242. Anecdotally, the story is told that MacArthur then raged to his corps commander in the area, Lieutenant General Robert L. Eichelberger, "Go out there, Bob, and take Buna or don't come back alive" (p. 244).

9. Halsey to Nimitz, February 13, 1943, WFH/LC, Box 15, File Folder, Special Correspondence, Nimitz, 1941–April 1943. For a time, Nimitz kept a photo of MacArthur on his desk. Some assumed this was in keeping with Nimitz's public demeanor of neither badmouthing MacArthur or the army nor allowing his subordinates to do the same. The true explanation, according to one report, was that Nimitz "kept the picture on his desk merely to remind himself not 'to make Jovian pronouncements complete with thunderbolts'" (Potter, *Nimitz,* p. 222).

10. Potter, *Nimitz,* p. 214. After sending a lengthy memo on strategy, MacArthur cabled Nimitz and Knox: "An exchange of views may preclude the necessity for an immediate conference that requires long journeys and prolonged absence of higher commanders" (ibid.).

11. Potter, *Halsey,* p. 215.

12. Halsey, *Admiral Halsey's Story,* pp. 154–55.

13. MacArthur, *Reminiscences,* pp. 173–74.

14. Nimitz to Halsey, May 14, 1943, CWN/NHHC, Series 13, Box 120.

15. Nimitz to Carpender, May 18, 1943, CWN/NHHC, Series 13, Box 120.

16. Potter, *Halsey,* pp. 219–20.

17. Potter, *Nimitz,* p. 233.

18. For Halsey's account of his involvement and subsequent leaks, see Halsey to Nimitz, May 26, 1943, WFH/LC, Box 15, File Folder, Special Correspondence, Nimitz, March–November 1943. Although written as a popular piece without footnotes, Burke Davis's *Get Yamamoto* (New York: Random House, 1969) may remain the best overall account of the decision making, as well as the flight itself. See also John T. Wible, *The Yamamoto Mission* (Fredericksburg, Tex.: Admiral Nimitz Foundation, 1988), and Donald A. Davis, *Lightning Strike: The Secret Mission to Kill Admiral Yamamoto and Avenge Pearl Harbor* (New York: St. Martin's Press, 2005). Leahy's diary makes no mention of this event or FDR's whereabouts. Adding to the lore of this mission is MacArthur's account in *Reminiscences,* pp. 174–75. With an almost "I was there" description, MacArthur manages to convey a sense that his command

was somehow involved in the mission and responsible for the results—even though he gave the intercept time as three in the afternoon instead of in the morning. After the Yamamoto mission, when the Americans returned to the Philippines, MacArthur's headquarters in the Price House was repeatedly attacked in a way that was almost certainly targeting him personally (Manchester, *American Caesar,* p. 397).

19. WDL/Diary, November 4, 1936.

20. Leahy, *I Was There,* pp. 150–51.

21. *Tucson Daily Citizen,* November 25, 1942.

22. *New York Times,* December 6, 1942. National profiles in *Life,* June 29, 1942, and the cover story in *Time,* November 30, 1942, did not mention the "Bull" nickname.

23. Crosse to Halsey, June 23, 1943, and Halsey to Crosse, July 3, 1943, WFH/LC, Box 35. A search of NewspaperARCHIVE.com on June 9, 2010, an admittedly small sample, nonetheless lists 13 results for "Bull Halsey" from 1940 to 1943, and 862 such results for 1944 to 1945.

24. Halsey to Belnap [*sic*], October 8, 1943, WDH/LC, Box 3. Halsey's secretary misspelled Charles Belknap's name.

25. Carpender to Nimitz, May 31, 1943, CWN/NHHC, Series 13.

26. Pogue, *Marshall: Ordeal and Hope,* p. 393.

27. Forrest C. Pogue, *Marshall: Organizer of Victory, 1943–1945* (New York: Viking, 1973), p. 200.

28. Roberts, *Masters and Commanders,* p. 358.

29. Leahy, *I Was There,* pp. 158–59.

30. "hours of argument," Alanbrooke, *War Diaries,* p. 401; "Hannibal and Napoleon," Buell, *Master of Sea Power,* p. 335.

31. Buell, *Master of Sea Power,* p. 332.

32. Ibid., pp. 332–33.

33. Alanbrooke, *War Diaries,* p. 405.

34. Roberts, *Masters and Commanders,* pp. 364–65.

35. Alanbrooke, *War Diaries,* p. 408.

36. For an overview of World War II in Alaska, see Walter R. Borneman, *Alaska: Saga of a Bold Land* (New York: HarperCollins, 2003).

37. Potter, *Nimitz,* pp. 241–42; Buell, *Master of Sea Power,* p. 356.

38. Larry I. Bland, ed., *George C. Marshall: Interviews and Reminiscences for Forrest C. Pogue* (Lexington, Va.: George C. Marshall Research Foundation, 1991), p. 622.

39. Alanbrooke, *War Diaries,* p. 442.

40. For one analysis and telling of this story, see Roberts, *Masters and Commanders,* pp. 405–6; King's account, saying the firing was by an aide and not Mountbatten himself, is in King, *Fleet Admiral King,* pp. 486–87. Arnold's account is in Arnold, *Global Mission,* pp. 443–44. Leahy mentions it in passing in *I Was There,* pp. 178–79.

41. Leahy, *I Was There,* p. 179.

42. WDL/Diary, November 12–13, 1943. For what it is worth, King's memoirs note the departure time as 12:06 a.m. (King, *Fleet Admiral King,* p. 499).

43. For versions of the torpedo incident, see Leahy, *I Was There,* p. 196; King, *Fleet Admiral King,* p. 501; and Buell, *Master of Sea Power,* pp. 419–20.

44. Buell, *Master of Sea Power,* pp. 420–21.

45. Whitehill interview with King, August 29, 1949, EJK/NHC/NWC, Box 7, File Folder 28. Eisenhower's corroboration of these events is in Dwight D. Eisenhower, *Crusade in Europe* (Garden City, N.Y.: Doubleday, 1949), p. 196.

46. Eisenhower, *Crusade in Europe,* p. 197.

47. Leahy, *I Was There,* p. 200.

48. Ibid., pp. 202–4, 208.

49. Ibid., pp. 214–15.

50. Eisenhower, *Crusade in Europe,* pp. 206–8.

Chapter 18: Take Care, My Boy

1. *Time,* May 18, 1942, p. 20.

2. Chester Nimitz, Jr., to Nimitz, February 7, 1944, CWN/NHHC, Series 2, Box 26; Blair, *Silent Victory,* pp. 589–92.

3. Blair, *Silent Victory,* pp. 692–94, 962–63.

4. Manning Kimmel to Husband E. Kimmel, December 18, 1941, Kimmel Papers, Box 2, File Folder "Correspondence, September–December, 1941."

5. Blair, *Silent Victory,* pp. 204, 309, 454, 599.

6. Ibid., pp. 660–61. See also Thomas Kimmel to Blair, January 10, 1973, Clay Blair, Jr., Papers, Box 68, File Folder 3, American Heritage Center, University of Wyoming, Laramie, in which Tom Kimmel answered a series of Blair's questions and said that he had never heard this story of his brother's fate. Kimmel hoped that it would not be published while his mother, Manning's widow, and their daughter were alive, but Blair published the story in *Silent Victory* in 1975. Blair also asked whether the Kimmel brothers were in any way "held back" or pushed forward because of their father's high rank. Tom responded, "As far as I could tell neither of us was actually 'held back' but we certainly were not pushed forward because of our father. As for causing us personal problems I do not know of any direct incidents. However during my career I was never offered any kind of a staff position and I had the underlying feeling that most Admirals would just as soon stay clear of the name—Kimmel." Tom retired from the navy as a captain in 1965.

7. Compiled from Pogue, *Marshall.*

8. WDL/Diary, June 26, 1927.

9. Rice to Buell, July 2, 1976, EJK/NHC/NWC, Box 7, File Folder 13.

10. Buell, *Master of Sea Power,* p. 512.

11. Potter, *Halsey,* pp. 126, 156, 234–35.

12. Halsey, *Admiral Halsey's Story,* p. 165.

13. Blair, *Silent Victory,* pp. 241–42, 412, 603–4; see also John McCain, *Faith of My Fathers* (New York: Random House, 1999).

14. Leahy to Wing, February 4, 1953, WDL/NHHC, Roll 1.

15. Nimitz to Catherine Nimitz, January 27, 1945, CWN/USNA, Box 1, File Folder 3.

16. The maternity care story is recounted in Cook to Buell, August 5, 1974, EJK/NHC/NWC, Box 1, File Folder 2.

17. This cursory opinion is based on Buell, *Master of Sea Power,* and the author's independent research.

18. See, for example, Halsey to King, May 16, 1938, WFH/LC, Box 14, acknowledging "Fan's illness," and Potter, *Halsey,* p. 262, about her inappropriate remarks.

19. *Time,* May 18, 1942, p. 20.

20. Halsey, *Admiral Halsey's Story,* p. 192.

Chapter 19: Driving It Home

1. Potter, *Nimitz,* p. 261.

2. Ibid., p. 264.

3. For Smith's continuing postwar criticism of Tarawa, see Holland M. Smith and Percy Finch, *Coral and Brass* (New York: Scribner's, 1949), pp. 111–12.

4. Spruance to Potter, December 1, 1964, RAS/NHHC, Box 3.

5. Potter, *Nimitz,* p. 247.

6. Ibid., p. 265.

7. Buell, *Quiet Warrior,* pp. 232–33.

8. Ibid., p. 239.

9. Ibid., p. 237.

10. Potter, *Nimitz,* pp. 267–68.

11. Buell, *Quiet Warrior,* p. 239.

12. Ibid., pp. 248–49.

13. *Washington Evening Star,* February 22, 1944.

14. Roosevelt, radio address, June 5, 1944, in *Public Papers and Addresses,* 1944–45 volume, pp. 147–52.

15. Leahy, *I Was There,* p. 240.

16. This account of the Normandy visit is taken from King, *Fleet Admiral King,* pp. 547–53; Arnold, *Global Mission,* pp. 503–9, specifically, "Admiral King," p. 505; Henry H. Arnold, *American Airpower Comes of Age: General Henry H. "Hap" Arnold's World War II Diaries,* ed. John W. Huston, vol. 2 (Maxwell Air Force Base, Ala.: Air University Press, 2002), pp. 154–55, specifically, "Our own Navy," p. 155; and Pogue, *Marshall: Organizer of Victory,* pp. 389–96. King's drinking is recounted in Buell, *Master of Sea Power,* p. 456.

17. Buell, *Master of Sea Power,* p. 448.

18. Leahy, *I Was There,* pp. 241–42.

19. Buell, *Master of Sea Power,* pp. 461–62.

20. Leahy, *I Was There,* p. 219.

21. Pogue, *Marshall: Organizer of Victory,* pp. 439–41.

22. Halsey, *Admiral Halsey's Story,* p. 186.

23. Potter, *Nimitz,* p. 283.

24. Ibid., pp. 283–84.

25. Halsey, *Admiral Halsey's Story,* pp. 189–90. Pronunciation of

Nimitz's name is from Potter, *Halsey,* p. 266.

26. Pogue, *Marshall: Organizer of Victory,* p. 441.

27. Ibid., p. 375.

28. Leahy, *I Was There,* p. 224.

29. Potter, *Nimitz,* p. 289. Another reason for MacArthur's change of face may have been the realization that his presidential prospects for 1944 were dimming. During this period, MacArthur was criticizing the navy and the Roosevelt administration, while at the same time denying any political ambitions. However, his penchant for grand and verbose statements got him into trouble when he corresponded with Congressman A. L. Miller of Nebraska. Miller made the letters public, and they painted MacArthur in an extremist light. See Manchester, *American Caesar,* pp. 362–63.

30. E. B. Potter, "The Command Personality," *United States Naval Institute Proceedings* 95, no. 791 (July 1969), p. 25.

31. Buell, *Quiet Warrior,* pp. 279–80.

32. Ibid., p. 285.

33. Ibid., p. 320. After the war, King reiterated this when he told his biographer, Walter Muir Whitehill, "When I got to Saipan, I said immediately, 'Spruance, what you decided was correct.' He had to remember the ships based on Japan itself" (Whitehill Interview with King, July 29, 1950, EJK/NHC/NWC, Box 7, File Folder 18).

34. Buell, *Quiet Warrior,* p. 303.

35. *Time,* June 26, 1944, cover.

36. King, *Fleet Admiral King,* p. 560.

Chapter 20: The Crippling Blow: Submarines or Airpower?

1. Halsey, *Admiral Halsey's Story,* p. 69.

2. Nimitz quote, U.S. Navy Submarine Museum, New London, Connecticut.

3. Charles A. Lockwood, *Sink 'Em All: Submarine Warfare in the Pacific* (New York: E. P. Dutton, 1951), p. 85.

4. Potter, *Sea Power,* p. 829.

5. Nimitz to Halsey, May 14, 1943, CWN/NHHC, Series 13, Box 120.

6. *United States Strategic Bombing Survey Summary Report (Pacific War)* (Washington, D.C.: Government Printing Office, 1946), pp. 12, 14.

7. The remaining losses were as follows: army land-based aircraft, 310 ships/0.7 million tons; navy surface craft, 123 ships/0.3 million tons; marine land-based aircraft, 99 ships/0.2 million tons; army and navy-marine aircraft in combination, 32 ships/0.2 million tons; mines laid by all services, 266 ships/0.6 million tons; other combinations and unknown causes, 64 ships/0.3 million tons. Reports of Japanese shipping losses vary slightly, mostly because some sources confuse *all* naval and merchant losses by *all* Allied countries and *all* causes with only those sunk by U.S. forces. These figures are from *Japanese Naval and Merchant Shipping Losses During World War II by All Causes,* "Joint Army-Navy Assessment Committee (JANAC), February 1947, http://www.history.navy .mil/library/online/japaneseshiploss

.htm, accessed December 28, 2010. Marshall and King formed this committee in January 1943 to evaluate enemy shipping losses. The other significant report of enemy naval losses is found in the *Strategic Bombing Survey Summary Report* of 1946.

8. Nimitz to Halsey, May 14, 1943, CWN/NHHC, Series 13, Box 120.

9. *Strategic Bombing Survey Summary Report*, p. 14.

10. Ibid., p. 25.

11. Ibid., p. 15.

12. For this and an economic analysis of the effectiveness of B-29s laying mines against shipping in the final year of the war versus submarine warfare, see Richard P. Hallion, "Decisive Air Power Prior to 1950," Air Force History and Museums Program, Headquarters, USAF, Bolling AFB, http://www.airforcehistory.hq.af.mil/EARS/Hallionpapers/decisiveairpower1950.htm, accessed December 22, 2010.

13. Ibid. In truth, the number of bombs dropped on the home islands of Japan was but a small fraction of the number dropped in the European Theater: 160,800 tons versus 2.7 million tons, half of which was dropped within Germany's own borders (*Strategic Bombing Survey Summary Report*, p. 16).

14. Arnold, *American Airpower Comes of Age*, vol. 2, p. 318.

15. King, *Fleet Admiral King*, pp. 602–3.

Chapter 21: Halsey's Luck

1. Halsey, *Admiral Halsey's Story*, p. 197.

2. James M. Merrill, *A Sailor's Admiral: A Biography of William F. Halsey* (New York: Crowell, 1976), p. 120.

3. MacArthur to Halsey, undated, WFH/LC, Box 15.

4. MacArthur, *Reminiscences*, p. 192.

5. Leahy, *I Was There*, p. 247.

6. Roosevelt, July 11, 1944, in *Complete Presidential Press Conferences*, vol. 24, pp. 24–25.

7. Leahy, *I Was There*, pp. 247–48.

8. WDL/Diary, July 22, 1944. On July 21, with almost maddening brevity and lack of any political feeling, Leahy wrote, "The Democratic Party today nominated Senator Truman, of Missouri, as candidate for Vice President."

9. James, *Years of MacArthur*, vol. 2, pp. 527–28; Leahy, *I Was There*, pp. 249–50. Others, including Samuel Rosenman, have quoted FDR as saying a version of the Leahy quote about MacArthur's attire.

10. James, *Years of MacArthur*, vol. 2, p. 529.

11. Newspaper clippings, 1944, CWN/NHHC, Series 8.

12. Manchester, *American Caesar*, p. 368.

13. King, *Fleet Admiral King*, pp. 566–67.

14. Manchester, *American Caesar*, p. 369.

15. Miles, "American Strategy," pp. 117–18. For King's feelings about Nimitz, see Buell, *Master of Sea Power*, p. 469.

16. Leahy, *I Was There*, p. 250. After reporting the results of the con-

ference to the Joint Chiefs upon his return to Washington, Leahy noted, "They may have been somewhat surprised to learn that Nimitz and MacArthur said they had no disagreements at the moment and that they could work out their joint plans in harmony" (Leahy, *I Was There*, p. 255).

17. Roosevelt, July 29, 1944, in *Complete Presidential Press Conferences*, vol. 24, pp. 26–37; WDL/Diary, July 29, 1944.

18. Schoeffel to Buell, September 9, 1974, EJK/NHC/NWC, Box 2, File Folder 19.

19. Nimitz to Halsey, May 14, 1943, CWN/NHHC, Series 13, Box 120.

20. Halsey, *Admiral Halsey's Story*, p. 197.

21. Ibid., pp. 199–200.

22. Pogue, *Marshall: Organizer of Victory*, pp. 453–54. Significantly, the decision was made without consulting the British chiefs of staff. Here was just one more indication that the Americans considered the Pacific largely their own domain. During the Quebec Conference, King got into quite a row with the British over their plans for the Royal Navy to join Pacific operations and belatedly share in the final victory. For more information, see chapter 24.

23. Halsey, *Admiral Halsey's Story*, pp. 205–8. Ulithi, with its fine anchorage, was occupied by a regimental combat team without opposition on September 23, a week after the Peleliu invasion.

24. C. Vann Woodward, *The Battle for Leyte Gulf: The Incredible Story of World War II's Largest Naval Battle* (New York: Skyhorse Publishing, 2007), pp. 19–20. Halsey recounts the burning Japanese planes in *Admiral Halsey's Story*, pp. 206–7.

25. Woodward, *Leyte Gulf*, pp. 42, 90, 159.

26. Halsey to King via Nimitz, November 13, 1944, Action Report Third Fleet, p. 2, WFH/LC, Box 35.

27. Halsey, *Admiral Halsey's Story*, p. 214.

28. Action Report, pp. 4–5.

29. For information about the timing of this turnaround message and Halsey's knowledge of it, see Evan Thomas, *Sea of Thunder: Four Commanders and the Last Great Naval Campaign, 1941–1945* (New York: Simon & Schuster, 2006), pp. 226–27.

30. Potter, *Halsey*, p. 297. For a slightly different version, see Theodore Taylor, *The Magnificent Mitscher* (New York: Norton, 1954), pp. 260–62.

31. Woodward, *Leyte Gulf*, pp. 118–19.

32. Action Report, Enclosure A, pp. 28, 31.

33. Ibid., p. 34.

34. Thomas, *Sea of Thunder*, p. 300.

35. Halsey, *Admiral Halsey's Story*, p. 220.

36. Action Report, Enclosure A, p. 33.

37. This battle of CVEs off Samar is an epic that is well told in Evan Thomas's *Sea of Thunder* and other books. The pilots who flew off these escort carriers to provide air cover and

close-in support over the beachheads were a hardy lot. A few verses of one carousing song said it all:

> *Navy fliers fly off the big carriers,*
> *Army fliers aren't seen oe'r the sea;*
> *But we're in the lousy Marine*
> *   Corps,*
> *So we get these dang CVEs!*
> *O Midway has thousand-foot*
> *   runways,*
> *And Leyte, eight hundred and ten.*
> *We'd still not have much of a carrier*
> *With two of ours laid end to end.*
> *We envy the boys on the big ones.*
> *And we'd trade in a minute or two,*
> *'Cause we'd like to see those poor*
> *   bastards*
> *Try doing the things we do!*

From "Cuts and Guts," http://www.ibiblio.org/hyperwar/USN/ships/ships-cv.html, accessed June 23, 2010.

38. *Strategic Bombing Survey Summary Report,* p. 8.

39. Woodward, *Leyte Gulf,* p. 216.

40. Halsey to Nimitz, MacArthur, Kinkaid, and King, radio message, October 25, 1944, date-time group 251317 at pp. 2392–93 of "Nimitz Gray Book," Naval History and Heritage Command, or online at http://www.ibiblio.org/anrs/docs/D/D7/nimitz_graybook5.pdf, accessed February 19, 2011.

41. Potter, *Nimitz,* p. 344.

42. Ibid., p. 344.

43. King, *Fleet Admiral King,* p. 580; example of cartoons in King to Halsey, August 26, 1949, WFH/LC, Box 14.

44. Halsey, *Admiral Halsey's Story,* pp. 226–27. Jocko Clark recalled being in King's office the morning of the uncertainty over Task Force 34. King was "pacing up and down in a towering rage," certain that the Japanese were about to annihilate the Leyte beachhead (Clark, *Carrier Admiral,* p. 201).

45. Schoeffel to Buell, September 9, 1974, EJK/NHC/NWC, Box 2, File Folder 19. Malcolm Shoeffel, then King's assistant chief of staff for operations, also noted, however, "I should add that if any of us, including King suspected at that time the Japanese had deliberately lured Halsey away, none of us voiced the thought" (p. 6).

46. Thomas, *Sea of Thunder,* p. 325, quoting Sutherland papers.

47. James, *Years of MacArthur,* vol. 2, p. 565.

48. Potter, *Nimitz,* pp. 342–43.

49. Whitehill interview with King, July 29, 1950, EJK/NHC/NWC, Box 7, File Folder 18.

Chapter 22: Two Typhoons and Five Stars

1. Merrill, *A Sailor's Admiral,* pp. 187–88; Buckner F. Melton, Jr., *Sea Cobra: Admiral Halsey's Task Force and the Great Pacific Typhoon* (Guilford, Conn.: Lyons Press, 2007), p. 100.

2. Merrill, *A Sailor's Admiral,* p. 189.

3. Ibid., pp. 191–92.

4. "Record of Proceedings of a Court of Inquiry Convened Onboard the

USS *Cascade* by order of the Commander in Chief, U.S. Pacific Fleet, United States Fleet, December 26, 1944," p. 160, Naval History and Heritage Command, microfilm NRS 1978-43, Court of Inquiry, Typhoon of 18 December 1944 (hereafter cited as "1944 Court of Inquiry"). Later, the court of inquiry determined that this late run to the northeast contributed to the disaster, "since this maneuver held the fleet in or near the path of the storm center, and was an error in judgment on the part of Commander Task Force 38 [McCain] who directed it and of Commander THIRD fleet [Halsey] who permitted it."

5. Halsey, *Admiral Halsey's Story,* p. 239.

6. Halsey to MacArthur, radio message, date-time group 172318, and Halsey to Nimitz, date-time group 172333, December 17, 1944, at pp. 2461–62 of "Nimitz Gray Book," Naval History and Heritage Command, or online at http://www.ibiblio.org/anrs/docs/D/D7/nimitz_graybook5.pdf, accessed February 19, 2011.

7. "1944 Court of Inquiry," pp. 70, 75–76.

8. Ibid., p. 77.

9. Ibid., p. 160.

10. Ibid., pp. 166–67.

11. Ibid., Nimitz Endorsement of Findings to Judge Advocate General, January 22, 1945.

12. Ibid., appendixes, CINCPAC to Pacific Fleet and Naval Shore Activities, Pacific Ocean Area, February 13, 1945, p. 3.

13. Ibid., King Endorsement of Findings to Secretary of the Navy, February 21, 1945, p. 1.

14. Buell, *Master of Sea Power,* p. 384.

15. Leahy, *I Was There,* p. 221.

16. Public Law 482, 78th Congress, December 14, 1944.

17. At least anecdotal proof of Halsey's enduring fame comes from the author's experiences in writing this book. When he would mention that he was writing about America's four fleet admirals and then pause expectantly, Halsey, with Nimitz a very close second, was the first name that was inevitably offered up. King was occasionally named, Leahy almost never.

18. King to Spruance, June 21, 1948, EJK/LC, Box 18.

19. Spruance to King, June 24, 1948, EJK/LC, Box 18.

20. Spruance to Nimitz, May 15, 1957, RAS/NHHC, Box 1.

21. Spruance to Potter, August 18, 1968, RAS/NHHC, Box 4. Among those interested in belatedly getting Spruance five stars was NBC anchorman Chet Huntley. Although Spruance's contributions were well known, Leahy's close association with Roosevelt was not fully appreciated, as is evidenced by what retired rear admiral Richard W. Bates told Huntley in 1961: "I think that had the President not given five stars to Admiral Leahy, they would definitely have been given to Admiral Spruance" (Bates to Huntley, May 17, 1961, Richard W. Bates Papers, Box 3, File Folder 21, Naval War College, Newport, R.I.). Regardless

of how deserving Spruance was, there had never been any question that Roosevelt would accord the first five-star set to his closest and most trusted sea dog.

22. Potter, *Halsey*, pp. 324–27.

23. Alton Keith Gilbert, *A Leader Born: The Life of Admiral John Sidney McCain, Pacific Carrier Commander* (Philadelphia: Castmate, 2006), p. 186. General background for the second typhoon story is from Merrill, *A Sailor's Admiral*, pp. 216–29, and Potter, *Halsey*, pp. 336–40.

24. Clark, *Carrier Admiral*, pp. 234–38.

25. Merrill, *A Sailor's Admiral*, p. 227.

26. Ibid., p. 227.

27. Ibid.

28. Clark, *Carrier Admiral*, p. 240.

29. Merrill, *A Sailor's Admiral*, p. 228.

30. Whitehill interview with King, July 29, 1950, EJK/NHC/NWC, Box 7, File Folder 18.

Chapter 23: Interim President

1. WDL/Diary, July 29, 1944.

2. Leahy, *I Was There*, p. 254; Robert H. Ferrell, *The Dying President: Franklin D. Roosevelt, 1944–1945* (Columbia: University of Missouri Press, 1998), pp. 82–83; Geoffrey C. Ward, ed., *Closest Companion: The Unknown Story of the Intimate Relationship Between Franklin Roosevelt and Margaret Suckley* (New York: Simon & Schuster, 1995), p. 321; William M. Rigdon, *White House Sailor* (New York: Doubleday, 1962), pp. 129–31. An FDR letter to Suckley, dated March 23, 1936, and published in *Closest Companion* suggests that Roosevelt stayed at least one night on board the destroyer *Dale* while in Florida.

3. Roosevelt, address to Teamsters, September 23, 1944, in *Public Papers and Addresses*, 1944–45 volume, p. 290.

4. "his face was ashen," Potter, *Nimitz*, p. 288; "The terrific burden" Leahy, *I Was There*, p. 220.

5. Leahy, *I Was There*, pp. 234–35; Ferrell, *Dying President*, p. 37.

6. Leahy, *I Was There*, pp. 239, 245. Leahy acknowledged, "While I have long been sure that the President would like to retire from his present office, this is the first time he has expressed himself to me clearly in regard to his attitude toward renomination." For a detailed look at FDR's work schedule and health situation while at Hobcaw, see Ferrell, *Dying President*, pp. 68–74.

7. Leahy, *I Was There*, p. 220.

8. MacArthur, *Reminiscenses*, p. 199; Manchester, *American Caesar*, p. 368. Perhaps no one had more reason to be concerned about Roosevelt's health than his new vice presidential candidate. Harry Truman had long professed no interest in the vice presidency, but once on the ticket, he expressed grave worry about Roosevelt's appearance after he met with the president for a photo op on the White House lawn shortly after FDR's return from Alaska. Afterward, Truman confessed to his

executive assistant, Matthew J. Connelly, that he was worried about Roosevelt's health. Noting that he had been assigned Secret Service protection, Truman told Connelly, "I hope nothing happens to the President" (Matthew J. Connelly, Oral History Interview, Harry S. Truman Library and Museum, Independence, Mo., November 28, 1967, pp. 111–12; for Truman disclaiming interest in the vice presidency, see p. 90).

9. Doris Kearns Goodwin, *No Ordinary Time: Franklin and Eleanor Roosevelt—The Home Front in World War II* (New York: Simon & Schuster, 1994), p. 545.

10. WDL/Diary, September 9, 1944.

11. Ferrell, *Dying President*, p. 85. Leahy had seen the movie the week before in Washington with his granddaughter and sat in front of Wilson's widow, Edith Bolling Galt Wilson. Despite his strident comments on Wilson's death in 1923, the movie left Leahy "with a more sympathetic attitude, at least for the time being, toward Mr. Wilson," although he continued to acknowledge Wilson's complete failure at the Paris Peace Conference (WDL/Diary, September 7, 1944). Alexander Knox, who portrayed Wilson, was nominated for best actor for his performance.

12. WDL/Diary, November 7–8, 1944.

13. Adams, *Witness to Power*, p. 266, quoting Hopkins to Leahy, December 21, 1944. See also Leahy's "Dear Harry" response of the same date, say-

ing, "You may be sure I have never had any doubt whatever in regard to your attitude toward me," Leahy to Hopkins, December 21, 1944, Harry L. Hopkins Papers, Series 1, Box 12, File Folder 19, Special Collections, Georgetown University Library, Washington, D.C.

14. WDL/Diary, December 24–25, 1944. Leahy was able to spend Christmas Day uninterrupted with his two grandchildren. It was probably the last Christmas, he noted rather wistfully, that eight-year-old Robert would "believe in Santa Claus."

15. Leahy, FDR inaugural dinner remarks, January 20, 1945, WDL/NHHC, Reel 8.

16. "If we had spent," Buell, *Master of Sea Power*, p. 483; "the most controversial," Leahy, *I Was There*, p. 291. King reported afterward that the harbor at Sevastopol was in fact in "good shape" and that five major units of the Soviet Black Sea Fleet were present there (King, *Fleet Admiral King*, p. 592).

17. Leahy, *I Was There*, pp. 291–92.

18. King, *Fleet Admiral King*, p. 586.

19. Leahy, *I Was There*, pp. 295–96.

20. King, *Fleet Admiral King*, p. 588; Leahy, *I Was There*, p. 297.

21. Leahy, *I Was There*, p. 297; King, *Fleet Admiral King*, p. 592.

22. Leahy, *I Was There*, p. 290.

23. Ibid., p. 298.

24. Ibid.

25. Ibid., p. 314.

26. George M. Elsey, Oral History Interview, Harry S. Truman Library

and Museum, Independence, Mo., July 7, 1970, pp. 334–35.

27. Leahy, *I Was There*, p. 311.

28. Ibid., p. 323. For the impact of Roosevelt's health on policy at Yalta, see, for example, Warren F. Kimball, *Forged in War: Roosevelt, Churchill, and the Second World War* (New York: William Morrow, 1997), pp. 339–41.

29. Adams, *Witness to Power*, pp. 236–37.

30. Rigdon, *White House Sailor*, p. 100.

31. *Time*, May 28, 1945, p. 14.

32. Elsey interview, April 9, 1970, pp. 320–21. Examples of military decisions with political overtones include invading the Philippines instead of Formosa, thus bringing less aid to Chiang Kai-shek's government, and not racing the Soviets to a meeting point farther east in Europe. Elsey's view of Leahy's receptiveness to State Department advice is seconded by Bohlen, who reported to the White House as State Department liaison after Secretary of State Cordell Hull—who insisted on managing his own communications with the White House—left office for health reasons in November 1944. Bohlen did, however, acknowledge Leahy's "snapping-turtle manner" (Charles E. Bohlen, *Witness to History, 1929–1969* [New York: Norton, 1973], pp. 165–67, 206).

33. Ferrell, *Dying President*, pp. 110–13. For an insider's view of Roosevelt's failing health, see Margaret Suckley's comments of him looking "terribly badly—so tired that every word seems to be an effort" (Ward, *Closest Companion*, pp. 400–1).

34. WDL/Diary, March 29, 1945.

35. Leahy, *I Was There*, pp. 347–48. Within a week of FDR's death, Leahy's references to "the President" in his diary would mean Truman.

36. Elsey interview, April 9, 1970, pp. 252–53.

37. Connelly interview, pp. 99–100. Bohlen recalled that Leahy "was incensed—at Byrnes's failure to report fully" to the president (Bohlen, *Witness to History*, p. 251).

Chapter 24: Toward Tokyo Bay

1. Roberts, *Masters and Commanders*, pp. 519–20; "At this point," Pogue, *Marshall: Organizer of Victory*, p. 453.

2. Kimball, *Forged in War*, p. 273. During 1943, after early losses decimated American carrier ranks and before the arrival of the *Essex*-class fast carriers, the British loaned the Americans their prewar carrier HMS *Victorious* to bolster naval air operations in the Pacific.

3. Miles, "American Strategy," pp. 183–84.

4. Potter, *Nimitz*, pp. 347–48. As late as the Potsdam Conference, King had to remind his British allies that the Americans were still calling the shots in the Pacific. British operational participation under Nimitz's command did not give them equal say in strategy (Buell, *Master of Sea Power*, p. 494).

5. See, for example, Elsey interview, July 7, 1970, pp. 333–35. The

Soviet Union declared war on Japan on August 8, 1945.

6. Potter, *Nimitz,* pp. 378–80.

7. Leahy, *I Was There,* pp. 384–85; King, *Fleet Admiral King,* pp. 605–6; Buell, *Master of Sea Power,* p. 491; Pogue, *Marshall: Organizer of Victory,* p. 528; Richard B. Frank, *Downfall: The End of the Imperial Japanese Empire* (New York: Random House, 1999), p. 34.

8. Marshall to King, March 15, 1945, and staff memo to Marshall, March 17, 1945, GCM/LC, Reel 21.

9. King to Marshall, June 29, 1945, GCM/LC, Reel 21.

10. King to Truman, December 16, 1943, and Truman to King, December 29, 1943, EJK/LC, Box 22.

11. Townsend Hoopes and Douglas Brinkley, *Driven Patriot: The Life and Times of James Forrestal* (New York: Knopf, 1992), p. 175.

12. King, *Fleet Admiral King,* pp. 631, 634–35; Buell, *Master of Sea Power,* p. 501; "I didn't like," Hoopes and Brinkley, *Driven Patriot,* p. 180. One area where King cooperated with Forrestal was Forrestal's strong push for more than token racial integration of the navy. Lester Granger, who later became Forrestal's special representative on racial matters and was long associated with the National Urban League, recounted this story: Forrestal went to King and expressed his frustration, saying, "I want to do something about it, but I can't do anything about it unless the officers are behind me. I want your help. What do you say?" According to Granger, King sat quiet for a moment, looked out the window, and then replied, "You know, we say that we are a democracy and a democracy ought to have a democratic Navy. I don't think you can do it, but if you want to try, I'm behind you all the way" (Morris J. McGregor, Jr., *Integration of the Armed Forces, 1940–1965* [Washington, D.C.: United States Army, Center of Military History, 1981], pp. 88-89).

13. Potter, *Nimitz,* p. 382.

14. Potter, *Halsey,* pp. 343–45; "If the enemy," *Time,* July 23, 1945, p. 27. *Time* also called Halsey "the tough, stubby seadog whom the Japanese mortally hate & fear."

15. Frank, *Downfall,* pp. 147, 212–13.

16. Ibid., pp. 274–75.

17. Ibid., p. 276.

18. King, *Fleet Admiral King,* pp. 620–21; Potter, *Nimitz,* pp. 381–82; Halsey, *Admiral Halsey's Story,* p. 266.

19. Harry S. Truman, *Memoirs,* vol. 1, *1945: Year of Decisions* (Garden City, N.Y.: Doubleday, 1955), p. 11.

20. Leahy, *I Was There,* pp. 430–31.

21. WDL/Diary, August 8, 1945.

22. Leahy, *I Was There,* pp. 440–41.

23. "starved the Japanese," King, *Fleet Admiral King,* p. 621; "didn't like," Buell, *Master of Sea Power,* p. 497.

24. Potter, *Nimitz,* pp. 382, 386; Layton, *"And I Was There,"* p. 492.

25. Merrill, *A Sailor's Admiral,* p. 233.

26. Frank, *Downfall,* pp. 276, 419–20n.

27. Potter, *Nimitz,* pp. 388–89.

28. Ibid., p. 389; Potter, *Halsey,* pp. 347–48; "I wonder," Buell, *Master of Sea Power,* p. 498.

29. Leahy, radio address, August 15, 1945, WDL/NHHC, Reel 8.

30. Leahy, *I Was There,* p. 365.

31. Potter, *Nimitz,* p. 390.

32. Halsey, *Admiral Halsey's Story,* p. 290.

33. Ibid.; *New York Times,* August 26, 1945.

34. Potter, *Nimitz,* p. 391.

35. Ibid., p. 390.

36. *New York Times,* August 30, 1945.

37. *New York Times,* August 31, 1945. Later, Halsey was photographed, cigarette in hand and looking haggard, in the saddle on a horse white washed for the occasion as a spoof by Major General William C. Chase of the First Cavalry Division.

38. Potter, *Nimitz,* p. 393.

39. "Japanese Sign Final Surrender!," United News newsreel, 1945, http://www.youtube.com/watch_popup?v=vcnH_kF1zXc&feature=player_embedded, accessed March 28, 2011; Halsey, *Admiral Halsey's Story,* p. 283.

40. Buell, *Quiet Warrior,* p. 399; E. P. Forrestel, *Admiral Raymond A. Spruance, USN: A Study in Command* (Washington, D.C.: Government Printing Office, 1966), p. 223.

41. Halsey, *Admiral Halsey's Story,* p. 284.

42. Nimitz to Catherine Nimitz, September 2, 1945, CWN/USNA.

43. Nimitz to Catherine Nimitz, September 3, 1945, CWN/USNA.

Chapter 25: Measures of Men

1. "Personnel Strength of the U.S. Navy: 1775 to Present," Department of the Navy, Naval History and Heritage Command, www.history.navy.mil/faqs/faq65-1.htm, accessed February 6, 2011 (personnel figures include officers, nurses, enlisted, and officer candidates); "U.S. Navy Active Ship Force Levels, 1917–," www.history.navy.mil/branches/org9-4.htm#1938, accessed February 6, 2011.

2. Merrill, *A Sailor's Admiral,* p. 245.

3. For Halsey's postwar activities, see chapter 22 of Potter, *Halsey.* Halsey continued to receive full active-duty pay even though he was moved to the retired list in 1947 for reasons of physical disability. Frances "Fan" Grandy Halsey died in 1968. The Leyte argument just before Halsey's death was with E. B. Potter over a chapter in *Sea Power,* a textbook slated for use at the Naval Academy. Potter's associate editor, Chester Nimitz, urged Potter to remove his editorial remarks second-guessing Halsey, which he did.

4. King, *Fleet Admiral King,* p. 636.

5. Ibid., p. 637.

6. Buell, *Master of Sea Power,* p. 508.

7. Ibid., pp. 509, 511–12.

8. For Nimitz's role as CNO, see Steven T. Ross, "Chester William

Nimitz," in Love, *Chiefs of Naval Operations,* and Jeffrey G. Barlow, *From Hot War to Cold: The U.S. Navy and National Security Affairs, 1945–1955* (Stanford, Calif.: Stanford University Press, 2009). In *Nimitz,* Potter gives an anecdote-filled portrayal of the admiral's retirement years based on interviews with Catherine Nimitz and family members, including "To me, he has" (p. 472).

9. Adams, *Witness to Power,* p. 307. Leahy repeatedly expressed his concerns over the Middle East; see, for example, WDL/Diary, October 10, November 5, and November 29, 1947, and the list of concerns in May 1948.

10. WDL/Diary, May 14, 1948.

11. WDL/Diary, inserts: Leahy to Truman, September 20, 1948, offering to resign immediately; Truman to Leahy, September 23, 1948, handwritten letter; Truman to Leahy, September 27, 1948, reiterating the sentiments of his handwritten letter ("My position and my feeling toward you has never changed and it never will"). When Leahy finally stepped down as chief of staff, the *Washington Post* called the move "a victory for civilian supremacy" and noted, "There is no need for the post in peacetime. That Mr. Truman kept Admiral Leahy at his side after he had exhausted Leahy's rich store of information was merely a testament to Leahy's companionability and to Mr. Truman's loyalty" (*Washington Post,* March 29, 1949).

12. WDL/Diary, November 19, 1951, and December 18, 1952.

13. Adams, *Witness to Power,* p. 344.

14. Ibid., p. 346.

15. Roland N. Smoot, *The Reminiscences of Vice Admiral Roland N. Smoot, U.S. Navy (Ret.)* (Annapolis: Naval Institute Press, 1972), p. 18.

16. *New York Herald Tribune Book Review,* March 19, 1950, p. 5. In his review of *I Was There,* Ferdinand Kuhn wrote, "Admiral Leahy was always something of a puzzle to the public in his White House days" (*Washington Post,* March 19, 1950).

17. *Washington Post,* May 7, 1955.

18. Miles, "American Strategy," p. 9.

19. Leahy, *I Was There,* p. 104.

20. Ibid., p. 104.

21. Ibid., p. 224.

22. Love, "Ernest Joseph King," in *Chiefs of Naval Operations,* p. 140.

23. E. B. Potter, *Admiral Arleigh Burke: A Biography* (New York: Random House, 1990), p. 260.

24. This Nimitz quote appears in many places, but it may have been first published in *Boys' Life,* the magazine of the Boy Scouts, the month before his death (Chester W. Nimitz, "My Way of Life: The Navy," as told to Andrew Hamilton, *Boys' Life,* January 1966, p. 56).

25. Smoot, *Reminiscences,* p. 88.

26. William Gordon Beecher rose to vice admiral but was also a published songwriter of some note. This version of "Nimitz and Halsey and Me" is from

Time, October 22, 1945, after Nimitz recited it at a welcome-home dinner at New York's Waldorf-Astoria.

27. Potter, *Halsey,* p. 234.

28. Halsey, *Admiral Halsey's Story,* pp. 278–79.

29. Wing to Leahy, January 27, 1953, WDL/NHHC, Reel 1.

30. Leahy to Wing, February 4, 1953, WDL/NHHC, Reel 1.

31. Leahy, Annapolis speech, March 18, 1934, WDL/NHHC, Reel 8.

Bibliography

BOOKS

Adams, Henry H. *Witness to Power: The Life of Fleet Admiral William D. Leahy* (Annapolis: Naval Institute Press, 1985).

Adams, John A. *If Mahan Ran the Great Pacific War: An Analysis of World War II Naval Strategy* (Bloomington: Indiana University Press, 2008).

Ader, Clément. *'L'Aviation Militar: é* (Paris: Berger-Levrault et Cie, 1909).

Alanbrooke, Field Marshal Lord (Alex Danchev and Daniel Todman, eds.), *War Diaries, 1939–1945* (Berkeley: University of California Press, 2001).

Arnold, H. H. *Global Mission* (New York: Harper Brothers, 1949).

Barlow, Jeffrey G. *From Hot War to Cold: The U.S. Navy and National Security Affairs, 1945–1955* (Stanford, Calif.: Stanford University Press, 2009).

Beach, Edward L. *Scapegoats: A Defense of Kimmel and Short at Pearl Harbor* (Annapolis: Naval Institute Press, 1995).

Blair, Clay, Jr. *Silent Victory: The U.S. Submarine War Against Japan* (Philadelphia: Lippincott, 1975).

Bland, Larry I., ed. *George C. Marshall: Interviews and Reminiscences for Forrest C. Pogue* (Lexington, Va.: George C. Marshall Research Foundation, 1991).

———. *The Papers of George Catlett Marshall,* vol. 3, "The Right Man for the Job, December 7, 1941–May 31, 1943" (Baltimore: Johns Hopkins University Press, 1991).

Bohlen, Charles E. *Witness to History 1929–1969* (New York: W. W. Norton, 1973).

Borch, Fred, and Daniel Martinez. *Kimmel, Short, and Pearl Harbor: The Final Report Revealed* (Annapolis: Naval Institute Press, 2005).

Bradford, James C. *Admirals of the New Steel Navy: Makers of American Naval Tradition, 1880–1930* (Annapolis: Naval Institute Press, 1990).

Brands, H. W. *Traitor to His Class: The Privileged Life and Radical Presidency of Franklin Delano Roosevelt* (New York: Doubleday, 2008).

Brodhurst, Robin. *Churchill's Anchor: The Biography of Admiral of the Fleet Sir Dudley Pound* (Barnsley, South Yorkshire, U.K.: Leo Cooper, 2000).

Buell, Thomas B. *Master of Sea Power: A Biography of Fleet Admiral Ernest J. King* (Boston: Little, Brown, 1980).

———. *The Quiet Warrior: A Biography of Admiral Raymond A. Spruance* (Annapolis: Naval Institute Press, 1987).

Butcher, Harry C. *My Three Years with Eisenhower* (New York: Simon and Schuster, 1946).

Casad, Dede W., and Frank A. Driscoll. *Chester W. Nimitz: Admiral of the Hills* (Austin, Tex.: Eakin Press, 1983).

Chandler, Alfred D. Jr., ed. *The Papers of Dwight David Eisenhower: The War Years,* vol. I (Baltimore: Johns Hopkins University Press, 1970).

Churchill, Winston S. *The Second World War*, vol. 3, "The Grand Alliance" (Boston: Houghton Mifflin, 1950).

———. *The Second World War*, vol. 5, "Closing the Ring" (Boston: Houghton Mifflin, 1951).

Clark, J. J., with Clark G. Reynolds, *Carrier Admiral* (New York: David McKay, 1967).

Daniels, Jonathan. *White House Witness, 1942–1945* (New York: Doubleday, 1975).

Davis, Burke. *Get Yamamoto* (New York: Random House, 1969).

Davis, Donald A. *Lightning Strike: The Secret Mission to Kill Admiral Yamamoto and Avenge Pearl Harbor* (New York: St. Martin's, 2005).

Driscoll, Joseph. *Pacific Victory, 1945* (Philadelphia: Lippincott, 1944).

Dyer, George C. *On the Treadmill to Pearl Harbor: The Memoirs of Admiral James O. Richardson* (Washington, D.C.: Naval History Division, 1973).

Eisenhower, David. *Eisenhower at War: 1943–1945* (New York: Random House, 1986).

Eisenhower, Dwight D. *At Ease: Stories I Tell to Friends* (Garden City, N.Y.: Doubleday, 1967).

———. *Crusade in Europe* (Garden City, N.Y.: Doubleday, 1949).

Ellsberg, Edward. *On the Bottom* (New York: Literary Guild, 1929).

Ferrell, Robert H. *The Dying President: Franklin D. Roosevelt, 1944–1945* (Columbia: University of Missouri Press, 1998).

Ferrell, Robert H., ed. *The Eisenhower Diaries* (New York: W. W. Norton, 1981).

Forrestel, E. P. *Admiral Raymond A. Spruance, USN: A Study in Command* (Washington, D.C.: Government Printing Office, 1966).

Frank, Richard B. *Downfall: The End of the Imperial Japanese Empire* (New York: Random House, 1999).

———. *MacArthur* (New York: Palgrave MacMillan, 2007).

Gilbert, Alton Keith. *A Leader Born: The Life of Admiral John Sidney McCain, Pacific Carrier Commander* (Philadelphia: Castmate, 2006).

Goodwin, Doris Kearns. *No Ordinary Time: Franklin and Eleanor Roosevelt: The Home Front in World War II* (New York: Simon and Schuster, 1994).

Grew, Joseph C. *Ten Years in Japan* (New York: Simon and Schuster, 1944).

Halsey, William F., and J. Bryan III. *Admiral Halsey's Story* (New York: McGraw-Hill, 1947).

Handlin, Lilian. *George Bancroft: The Intellectual as Democrat* (New York: Harper and Row, 1984).

Hart, Thomas C. *The Reminiscences of Thomas C. Hart* (New York: Columbia University Oral History Project, 1972).

Hayes, Grace Person. *The History of the Joint Chiefs of Staff in World War II: The War Against Japan* (Annapolis: Naval Institute Press, 1982).

Hendrick, Burton J. *The Life and Letters of Walter H. Page* (Garden City, N.Y.: Doubleday, Page, 1925).

Hoopes, Townsend, and Douglas Brinkley. *Driven Patriot: The Life and Times of James Forrestal* (New York: Knopf, 1992).

Hopkins, William B. *The Pacific War: The Strategy, Politics, and Players That Won the War* (Minneapolis: Zenith Press, 2008).

Hornsfischer, James D. *Neptune's Inferno: The U.S. Navy at Guadalcanal* (New York: Bantam, 2011).

———. *Ship of Ghosts: The Story of the* USS Houston, *FDR's Legendary Lost Cruiser, and the Epic Saga of Her Survivors* (New York: Bantam, 2006).

Hoyt, Edwin P. *Nimitz and His Admirals: How They Won the War in the Pacific* (Guilford, Conn.: Lyons Press, 2002).

Hurley, Alfred F. *Billy Mitchell: Crusader for Air Power* (Bloomington: Indiana University Press, 1975).

Huston, John W., ed. *American Airpower Comes of Age: General Henry H. "Hap" Arnold's World War II Diaries* (Maxwell Air Force Base, Ala.: Air University Press, 2002).

Ickes, Harold L. *The Secret Diary of Harold L. Ickes,* vol. II, "The Inside Struggle, 1936–1939" (New York: Simon and Schuster, 1954).

———. *The Secret Diary of Harold L. Ickes,* vol. III, "The Lowering Clouds, 1939–1941" (New York: Simon and Schuster, 1954).

James, D. Clayton. *The Years of MacArthur,* vol. I, "1880–1941" (Boston: Houghton Mifflin, 1970).

————. *The Years of MacArthur,* vol. II, "1941–1945" (Boston: Houghton Mifflin, 1975).

————. *The Years of MacArthur,* vol. III, "1945–1964" (Boston: Houghton Mifflin, 1985).

Kennett, Lee, ed. *Clément Ader, Military Aviation* (Maxwell Air Force Base, Ala.: Air University Press, 2003).

Kimball, Warren F. *Forged in War: Roosevelt, Churchill, and the Second World War* (New York: William Morrow, 1997).

Kimmel, Husband E. *Admiral Kimmel's Story* (Chicago: Henry Regnery, 1955).

King, Ernest J., and Walter Muir Whitehill. *Fleet Admiral King: A Naval Record* (New York: W. W. Norton, 1952).

Lamar, H. Arthur. *I Saw Stars: Some Memories of Commander Hal Lamar, Fleet Admiral Nimitz' Flag Lieutenant, 1941–1945* (Fredericksburg, Tex.: Admiral Nimitz Foundation, 1985).

Larrabee, Eric. *Commander in Chief: Franklin Delano Roosevelt, His Lieutenants and Their War* (New York: Harper and Row, 1987).

Layton, Edwin T. *"And I Was There": Pearl Harbor and Midway—Breaking the Secrets* (New York: William Morrow, 1985).

Leahy, William D. *I Was There: The Personal Story of the Chief of Staff to Presidents Roosevelt and Truman Based on His Notes and Diaries Made at the Time* (New York: Whittlesey House, 1950).

Leutze, James. *A Different Kind of Victory: A Biography of Admiral Thomas C. Hart* (Annapolis: Naval Institute Press, 1981).

Lockwood, Charles A. *Sink 'Em All: Submarine Warfare in the Pacific* (New York: Dutton, 1951).

Lord, Walter. *Incredible Victory* (New York: Harper and Row, 1967).

Love, Robert William, Jr., ed. *The Chiefs of Naval Operations* (Annapolis: Naval Institute Press, 1980).

Lundstrom, John B. *Black Shoe Carrier Admiral: Frank Jack Fletcher at Coral Sea, Midway, and Guadalcanal* (Annapolis: Naval Institute Press, 2006).

————. *The First Team and the Guadalcanal Campaign: Naval Fighter Combat from August to November 1942* (Annapolis: Naval Institute Press, 1994).

————. *The First Team: Pacific Naval Air Combat from Pearl Harbor to Midway* (Annapolis: Naval Institute Press, 1984).

MacArthur, Douglas. *Reminiscences* (New York: McGraw-Hill, 1964).

Maclay, Edgar Stanton. *A History of the United States Navy from 1775 to 1901* (New York: Appleton, 1901).

Mahan, A. T. *The Influence of Sea Power upon History, 1660–1783* (New York: Dover, 1987); originally published in 1890.

Manchester, William. *American Caesar, Douglas MacArthur, 1880–1964* (Boston, Little, Brown, 1978).

Massie, Robert K. *Castles of Steel: Britain, Germany, and the Winning of the Great War at Sea* (New York: Ballantine, 2003).

McCain, John, with Mark Salter. *Faith of My Fathers: A Family Memoir* (New York: Random House, 1999).

McCullough, David. *The Path Between the Seas: The Creation of the Panama Canal, 1870–1914* (New York: Simon and Schuster, 1977).

McGregor, Morris J., Jr. *Integration of the Armed Forces, 1940–1965* (Washington, D.C.: Center of Military History, United States Army, 1981).

Melton, Buckner F., Jr. *Sea Cobra: Admiral Halsey's Task Force and the Great Pacific Typhoon* (Guilford, Conn.: Lyons Press, 2007).

Merrill, James M. *A Sailor's Admiral: A Biography of William F. Halsey* (New York: Thomas Y. Crowell, 1976).

Morison, Elting E., ed. *The Letters of Theodore Roosevelt* (Cambridge, Mass.: Harvard University Press, 1951).

Morison, Samuel Eliot. *History of United States Naval Operations in World War II*, vol. 3, "The Rising Sun in the Pacific" (Boston: Little, Brown, 1948).

———. *The Two-Ocean War: A Short History of the United States Navy in the Second World War* (Boston: Little, Brown, 1963).

Morris, Edmund. *The Rise of Theodore Roosevelt* (New York: Coward, McCann and Geoghegan, 1979).

———. *Theodore Rex* (New York: Random House, 2001).

Mullins, Wayne, ed. *1942: "Issue in Doubt"* (Austin, Tex.: Eakin Press, 1994).

Murray, Williamson, and Allan R. Millett. *A War to Be Won: Fighting the Second World War* (Cambridge, Mass.: Belknap Press of Harvard University Press, 2000).

Nofi, Albert A. *To Train the Fleet for War: The U.S. Navy Fleet Problems, 1923–1940* (Newport, R.I.: Naval War College Press, 2010).

Parshall, Jonathan, and Anthony Tully. *Shattered Sword: The Untold Story of the Battle of Midway* (Washington, D.C.: Potomac Books, 2005).

Pogue, Forrest C. *George C. Marshall: Education of a General, 1880–1939* (New York: Viking, 1963).

———. *George C. Marshall: Ordeal and Hope, 1939–1942* (New York: Viking, 1966).

———. *George C. Marshall: Organizer of Victory, 1943–1945* (New York: Viking, 1973).

———. *George C. Marshall: Statesman, 1945–1959* (New York: Viking, 1987).

Potter, E. B. *Admiral Arleigh Burke: A Biography* (New York: Random House, 1990).

———. *Bull Halsey: A Biography* (Annapolis: Naval Institute Press, 1985).

———. *Nimitz* (Annapolis: Naval Institute Press, 1976).

Potter, E. B., ed. *The United States and World Sea Power* (Englewood Cliffs, N.J.: Prentice-Hall, 1955).

Prange, Gordon W. *At Dawn We Slept: The Untold Story of Pearl Harbor* (New York: Penguin, 1991).

Reynolds, Clark G. *Admiral John H. Towers: The Struggle for Naval Air Supremacy* (Annapolis: Naval Institute Press, 1991).

———. *The Fast Carriers: The Forging of an Air Navy* (New York: McGraw Hill, 1968).

Rigdon, William M. *White House Sailor* (New York: Doubleday, 1962).

Roberts, Andrew. *Masters and Commanders: How Four Titans Won the War in the West, 1941–1945* (New York: Harper, 2009).

Roosevelt, Elliott, ed. *F.D.R. His Personal Letters, 1928–1945,* vol. II (New York: Duell, Sloan and Pearce, 1950).

Roosevelt, Franklin D. *Complete Presidential Press Conferences of Franklin D. Roosevelt* (New York: Da Capo Press, 1972).

———. *The Public Papers and Addresses of Franklin D. Roosevelt,* compiled by Samuel I. Rosenman (New York: Harper and Brothers, 1950).

Roosevelt, Theodore. *The Naval War of 1812* (Annapolis: Naval Institute Press, 1987; originally published in 1882 by G. P. Putnam's Sons).

———. *Theodore Roosevelt: An Autobiography* (New York: Charles Scribner's Sons, 1923).

Simpson, B. Mitchell, III. *Admiral Harold R. Stark: Architect of Victory, 1939–1945* (Columbia: University of South Carolina Press, 1989).

Smith, Holland M., and Percy Finch. *Coral and Brass* (New York: Charles Scribner's Sons, 1949).

Solberg, Carl. *Decision and Dissent: With Halsey at Leyte Gulf* (Annapolis: Naval Institute Press, 1995).

Sprantakes, Nicholas Evan. *Allies Against the Rising Sun* (Lawrence: University Press of Kansas, 2009).

Stanton, Doug. *In Harm's Way: The Sinking of the* USS Indianapolis *and the Extraordinary Story of Its Survivors* (New York: Henry Holt, 2001).

Stillwell, Paul, ed. *Submarine Stories: Recollections from the Diesel Boats* (Annapolis: Naval Institute Press, 2007).

Taylor, Theodore. *The Magnificent Mitscher* (New York: W. W. Norton, 1954).

Thomas, Evan. *Sea of Thunder: Four Commanders and the Last Great Naval Campaign, 1941–1945* (New York: Simon and Schuster, 2006).

Trimble, William F. *Admiral William A. Moffett: Architect of Naval Aviation* (Washington, D.C.: Smithsonian Institution Press, 1994).

Truman, Harry S. *Memoirs,* vol. 1, "Year of Decisions" (Garden City, N.Y.: Doubleday, 1955).

———. *Memoirs,* vol. 2, "Years of Trial and Hope" (Garden City, N.Y.: Doubleday, 1956).

Ward, Geoffrey C., ed., *Closest Companion: The Unknown Story of the Intimate Relationship Between Franklin Roosevelt and Margaret Suckley* (New York: Simon and Schuster, 1995).

Warner, Denis and Peggy. *The Tide at Sunrise: A History of the Russo-Japanese War, 1904–1905* (New York: Charterhouse, 1974).

Weintraub, Stanley. *Long Day's Journey into War, December 7, 1941* (New York: Dutton, 1991).

Wheeler, Gerald E. *Kinkaid of the Seventh Fleet* (Washington, D.C.: Naval Historical Center, 1995).

White, Theodore H. *In Search of History: A Personal Adventure* (New York: Harper and Row, 1978).

Wible, John T. *The Yamamoto Mission* (Fredericksburg, Tex.: Admiral Nimitz Foundation, 1988).

Wildenberg, Thomas. *All the Factors of Victory: Adm. Joseph Mason Reeves and the Origins of Carrier Airpower* (Washington, D.C.: Potomac, 2003).

Woodward, C. Vann. *The Battle for Leyte Gulf: The Incredible Story of World War II's Largest Naval Battle* (New York: Skyhorse Publishing, 2007).

Wukovits, John. *Admiral "Bull" Halsey: The Life and Wars of the Navy's Most Controversial Commander* (New York: Palgrave MacMillan, 2010)

ARTICLES

"Destruction of Cervera's Fleet," *The Library of Historic Characters and Famous Events,* vol. 12 (Boston: J. B. Millet, 1907).

"Dewey's Report of the Battle of Manila Bay," *The Library of Historic Characters and Famous Events,* vol. 12 (Boston: J. B. Millet, 1907).

Frank, Richard B. "Picking Winners?" *Naval History Magazine,* vol. 25, no. 3 (June 2011), accessed May 12, 2011 at www.usni.org/print/7701.

"George Dewey," *The Library of Historic Characters and Famous Events,* vol. 12 (Boston: J. B. Millet, 1907).

Hallion, Richard P., "Decisive Air Power Prior to 1950," Air Force History and Museums Program, Headquarters, USAF, Bolling AFB, accessed December 22, 2010 at www.airforcehistory.hq.af.mil/EARS/Hallionpapers/decisiveairpower1950.htm.

King, Ernest J. "Salvaging U.S.S. *S-51*," *United States Naval Institute Proceedings,* vol. 53, no. 2 (February 1927), pp. 137–52.

King, E. J. "Some Ideas about the Effects of Increasing the Size of Battleships," *United States Naval Proceedings,* vol. 45, no. 193 (March 1919), pp. 387–406.

King, Ernest J., "Some Ideas about Organization on Board Ship," *United States Naval Institute Proceedings,* vol. 35, no. 1 (March 1909), pp. 1–35.

———. "A 'Wrinkle or Two' in Handling Men," *United States Naval Institute Proceedings,* vol. 49, no. 241 (March 1923), pp. 427–31.

King, Ernest J., et al. "Report and Recommendations of a Board Appointed by the Bureau of Navigation Regarding the Instruction and Training of Line Officers," *United States Naval Institute Proceedings,* vol. 46, no. 210 (August 1920), pp. 1265–92.

"Leahy: Would-be West Pointer Climbs to Top of Navy Ladder," *Newsweek,* November 21, 1936, p. 12.

Nimitz, C. W. "Military Value and Tactics of Modern Submarines," *United States Naval Institute Proceedings,* vol. 38, no. 4 (December 1912), pp. 1193–1211.

Nimitz, Fleet Admiral Chester W., as told to Andrew Hamilton, "My Way of Life: The Navy," *Boys' Life,* January 1966, p. 56.

Potter, E. B. "The Command Personality," *United States Naval Institute Proceedings,* vol. 95, no. 791 (July 1969), pp. 18–25.

Roosevelt, Franklin D. "Shall We Trust Japan?" *Asia: The American Magazine on the Orient,* vol. 23, no. 7 (July 1923), pp. 475–78.

Stoler, Mark A. "The 'Pacific-First' Alternative in American World War II Strategy," *International History Review,* vol. 2, no. 3 (July 1980), pp. 432–52.

PERSONAL PAPERS AND MANUSCRIPT COLLECTIONS

Henry Harley Arnold Papers, Manuscript Division, Library of Congress, Washington, D.C.

John J. Ballentine Papers, Naval Historical Foundation Collection, Manuscript Division, Library of Congress, Washington, D.C.

Richard W. Bates Papers, Naval Historical Collection, Naval War College, Newport, Rhode Island.

Clay Blair, Jr., Papers, American Heritage Center, University of Wyoming, Laramie, Wyoming.

Charles Claude Bloch Papers, Naval Historical Foundation Collection, Manuscript Division, Library of Congress, Washington, D.C.

Frank Jack Fletcher Papers, American Heritage Center, University of Wyoming, Laramie, Wyoming.

Robert L. Ghormley Papers, Special Collections Department, J. Y. Joyner Library, East Carolina University, Greenville, North Carolina.

William Frederick Halsey Papers, Manuscript Division, Library of Congress, Washington, D.C. (cited as WFH/LC).

Harry L. Hopkins Papers, Special Collections, Georgetown University Library, Washington, D.C.

Husband Edward Kimmel Papers, 1907–1999, American Heritage Center, University of Wyoming, Laramie, Wyoming.

Ernest Joseph King Papers, Manuscript Division, Library of Congress, Washington, D.C. (cited as EJK/LC).

Ernest J. King Papers, Naval Historical Collection, Naval War College, Newport, Rhode Island (cited as EJK/NHC/NWC).

William D. Leahy Diary, William D. Leahy Papers, Manuscript Division, Library of Congress, Washington, D.C. (cited as WDL/Diary).

William D. Leahy Papers, Manuscript Division, Library of Congress, Washington, D.C. (cited as WDL/LC).

Papers of William D. Leahy, Operational Archives Branch, Naval History and Heritage Command, Washington, D.C. (cited as WDL/NHHC).

Papers of George C. Marshall: Selected World War II Correspondence, Manuscript Division, Library of Congress, Washington, D.C. (cited as GCM/LC).

Henry T. Mayo Papers, Naval Historical Foundation Collection, Manuscript Division, Library of Congress, Washington, D.C.

John L. McCrea Papers, Naval Historical Foundation Collection, Manuscript Division, Library of Congress, Washington, D.C.

Admiral Chester W. Nimitz Collection, Operational Archives Branch, Naval History and Heritage Command, Washington, D.C. (cited as CWN/NHHC).

Chester W. Nimitz Papers, MS 236, Special Collections & Archives Department, Nimitz Library, United States Naval Academy, Annapolis, Maryland (cited as CWN/USNA).

G[eorge] W. Robinson Diary, MS 344, Special Collections & Archives Department, Nimitz Library, United States Naval Academy, Annapolis, Maryland.

Franklin D. Roosevelt "Safe Files," Franklin D. Roosevelt Presidential Library and Museum, Hyde Park, New York.

Raymond A. Spruance Papers, Naval Historical Collection, Naval War College, Newport, Rhode Island.

Papers of Raymond A. Spruance, Operational Archives Branch, Naval History and Heritage Command, Washington, D.C. (cited as RAS/NHHC).

John H. Towers Papers, Naval Historical Foundation Collection, Manuscript Division, Library of Congress, Washington, D.C.

Harry E. Yarnell Papers, Naval Historical Foundation Collection, Manuscript Division, Library of Congress, Washington, D.C.

ORAL HISTORY

Matthew J. Connelly, Oral History Interview, Harry S. Truman Library and Museum, November 28, 1967.

George M. Elsey, Oral History Interview, Harry S. Truman Library and Museum, April 9 and July 7, 1970.

Roland N. Smoot, *The Reminiscences of Vice Admiral Roland N. Smoot, U.S. Navy, Ret.* (Annapolis: U.S. Naval Institute, 1972).

UNPUBLISHED DISSERTATION

Miles, Paul L., Jr. "American Strategy in World War II: The Role of William D. Leahy," unpublished Ph.D. dissertation, Princeton University, 1999.

GOVERNMENT DOCUMENTS AND PUBLICATIONS

Annual Report of the Superintendent of the United States Military Academy, 1893 (Washington, D.C.: Government Printing Office, 1893).

Executive Order 8984, F.R. Doc. 41-9587, December 19, 1941.

Executive Order 9096, F.R. Doc. 42-2195, March 12, 1942.

General Order 99, June 1, 1914.

King/Nimitz Pacific Conferences Minutes, 1942–45, NRS 1972-22, Naval History and Heritage Command.

Lucky Bag, 1894, 1901, 1904, 1905 (yearbook of the United States Naval Academy).

"Nimitz Gray Book," Naval History and Heritage Command, or online at www.ibiblio.org/anrs/docs/D/D7/nimitz_graybook5.pdf.

Public Law 482, Seventy-eighth Congress, December 14, 1944.

"Record of Proceedings of a Court of Inquiry Convened onboard the USS *Cascade* by order of the Commander in Chief, U.S. Pacific Fleet, United States Fleet, December 26, 1944" (at NHHC as microfilm NRS 1978-43, Court of Inquiry, Typhoon of 18 Dec. 1944).

Report of the Secretary of the Navy, 1893 (Washington, D.C.: Government Printing Office, 1893).

Treaties and Other International Agreements of the United States of America, 1776–1949, vol. 2, "Multilateral," 1918–1930 (Washington, D.C.:

Department of State, 1968), p. 1070 (London Naval Treaty, April 22, 1930, Part IV, Article 22).

"United States Strategic Bombing Survey Summary Report (Pacific War)," (Washington: United States Government Printing Office, 1946).

ONLINE RESOURCES

"A Brief History of the United States Naval Academy," www.usna.edu/ VirtualTour/150years, accessed June 27, 2010.

"China: Bombing of USS Panay Special Issue, 1037/12/12," blip.tv/file/ 898740, accessed November 11, 2009.

"Cuts and Guts," www.ibiblio.org/hyperwar/USN/ships/ships-cv.html, accessed June 23, 2010.

"Development of the Naval Establishment in Hawaii," www.history.navy .mil/docs/wwii/pearl/hawaii-3.htm, accessed October 29, 2009.

"Eugene Ely's Flight from USS *Birmingham,* 14 November 1910," Department of the Navy, Naval Historical Center, www.history.navy.mil/photos/ events/ev-1910s/ev-1910/ely-birm.htm, accessed October 6, 2009.

"Eugene Ely's Flight to USS *Pennsylvania,* 18 January 1911," Department of the Navy, Naval Historical Center, www.history.navy.mil/photos/events/ ev-1910s/ev-1911/ely-pa.htm, accessed October 6, 2009.

"Japanese invasion of Manchuria, September 1931," www.blacksacademy .net/content/3112.html, accessed January 7, 2010.

"Japanese Sign Final Surrender," United News newsreel, www.youtube .com/watch_popup?v=vcnH_kF1zXc&feature=player_embedded, accessed March 28, 2011.

"Joint Army-Navy Assessment Committee (JANAC) report of 1947," www .history.navy.mil/library/online/japaneseshiploss.htm, accessed December 28, 2010.

"Naming Ships," www.fas.org/man/dod-101/sys/ship/names.htm, accessed October 6, 2009.

"Nimitz Gray Book," www.ibiblio.org/anrs/docs/D/D7/nimitz_graybook5 .pdf multiple accesses.

"Pearl Harbor: Its Origin and Administrative History Through World War II," www.history.navy.mil/docs/wwii/pearl/hawaii-2.htm, accessed October 29, 2009.

"Personnel Strength of the U.S. Navy: 1775 to present," www.history.navy .mil/faqs/faq65-1.htm, accessed February 6, 2011.

"Prohibition in the Navy," General Order 99, June 1, 1914, www.history.navy .mil/faqs/faq59-11.htm, accessed August 22, 2009.

Roster of Wisconsin Volunteers, War of the Rebellion, 1861–1865, An Online Digital Book from the Wisconsin Historical Society Library, www .wisconsinhistory.org/roster/index.asp, accessed July 27, 2009.

"Ship Naming in the United States Navy," www.history.navy.mil/faqs/ faq63-1.htm, accessed October 6, 2009.

"U.S. Navy Active Ship Force Levels, 1917–," www.history.navy.mil/ branches/org9-4.htm, accessed February 6, 2011.

"U.S. Navy and Marine Corps Personnel Casualties in World War II," www .history.navy.mil/faqs/faq11-1.htm, accessed January 19, 2011.

"USS *Langley* (CV-1)," www.navy.mil/navydata/navy_legacy_hr.asp?id=10, accessed October 6, 2009.

"USS *Lexington* (CV-2)," www.chinfo.navy.mil/navpalib/ships/carriers/ histories/cv02-lexington/cv02-lexington.html, accessed October 6, 2009.

"USS *Oregon,*" www.spanamwar.com/oregon.htm, accessed July 27, 2009.

"USS *Saratoga* (CV-3)," www.chinfo.navy.mil/navpalib/ships/carriers/ histories/cv03-saratoga/cv03-saratoga.html, accessed October 6, 2009.

NEWSPAPERS AND NEWSMAGAZINES

Life
Newsweek
New York Herald Tribune
New York Times
Time
Tucson Daily Citizen
Washington Evening Star
Washington Post
Washington Times-Herald

Index

Page numbers in italic refer to maps.

About the Author

Walter R. Borneman is the author of seven works of nonfiction, including *1812, The French and Indian War,* and *Polk*. He holds both a master's degree in history and a law degree. He lives in Colorado.

Reading Group Guide

THE
ADMIRALS

NIMITZ, HALSEY, LEAHY, and KING—
The Five-Star Admirals
Who Won the War at Sea

WALTER R. BORNEMAN

History's Lesson:
Sea Power Defines a Nation

Seventy-one years ago, the battles of Coral Sea and Midway set the United States firmly on course to become the world's undisputed naval power. How long it will remain so and whether it matters are questions central to any debate about U.S. military spending. These questions should not be answered lightly. Few lessons from history have remained as incontestable as the importance of sea power to a nation's political and economic standing.

Sea power has been the ultimate measure of global reach and influence since the Greeks stemmed Persia's land conquests with a naval victory at Salamis Bay in 480 BC. Despite having the largest and best-trained army in Europe in the mid-1700s, France lost its overseas empire, including Canada, to Great Britain because France could not support its colonies via the seas. Great Britain held on to a worldwide empire where the "sun never set" throughout the nineteenth century only because of the superiority of the Royal Navy.

By 1898, the United States was flexing its muscles on two oceans. New innovations in iron and steel battleships produced an arms race in dreadnoughts that were capable of ever-increasing speed, range, and firepower. Great Britain fought to maintain its dominance, while Germany, in particular, challenged its naval strength. Ironically, during World War I, Germany poured huge resources into creating a powerful fleet but then used it tentatively before sequestering it in safe ports for the duration. But recognizing how close Germany had come to mastering the seas, Great Britain and its allies, including the United States, made certain that Germany's fleet was confiscated at the war's end.

After this war to end all wars, idealists from the major powers convened in Washington, DC, in November 1921 for the Washington Conference. The results were limits on naval tonnage and capital ship construction. If navies were kept small, the argument ran, there could be no great clash of arms. Japan, a nominal member of the World War I victors, was only too glad to accept levels below those of Great Britain and the United States, because while these latter countries respected the limits for the better part of fifteen years, Japan ignored them and surged toward parity in naval might.

Only Franklin D. Roosevelt's slow buildup of the American navy during the late 1930s kept Japan from surpassing American naval strength. As devastating as the surprise attack on Pearl Harbor was, the American navy had already begun to embrace aircraft carriers and naval aviation—instead of battleships—as the new weapons of naval superiority. Japan's attacks throughout the Pacific in December 1941 were evidence of the effectiveness of these weapons, but the Americans would soon prove it in spades.

In May 1942, just five months after Pearl Harbor, Allied naval forces led by the American carriers *Lexington* and *Yorktown* engaged in the first sea battle fought exclusively between aircraft and blunted the Japanese advance at the battle of Coral Sea. The action protected the critical West Coast–to–Australia lifelines and arguably saved Australia from invasion. Less than a month later, American pilots from three carriers near Midway sank four Japanese carriers that Japanese shipyards could not readily replace. The United States, on the other hand, not only replaced the *Lexington,* sunk at Coral Sea, and *Yorktown*'s loss at Midway, but also launched twenty-one other fast carriers over the next three years.

By the time Fleet Admiral Chester W. Nimitz signed the Japanese surrender for the United States aboard the battleship *Missouri* in Tokyo Bay in 1945, the United States was the undisputed naval power in the world. Its opponents had been crushed and its allies weakened by the demands of victory. Only the United States had been able to flex its industrial muscle and float new ship construction, after total battle losses, to include the fast carriers, 70 escort carriers, 35 cruisers, 206 destroyers, 361 destroyer escorts, and 120 submarines—most built during a three-year period. Today, the entire American fleet has only 286 ships, about half the number of the Reagan Administration's buildup of the late 1980s.

After World War II, land-based air power became both an essential Cold War capability and a deterrent. Yet it has consistently been sea power, frequently delivered by aircraft carriers, that has maintained America's political and economic leadership. The United States Navy quarantined Cuba during the missile crisis and kept the Strait of Hormuz and other vital waterways open, and has dispatched American aid around the globe in response to military crises and for humanitarian efforts.

How long American naval superiority will last is uncertain, but as to whether or not it matters, history shows the answer to be a resounding yes. China holds approximately $1.2 trillion of United States debt. In a global economy of friendly competition, many view this as a matter of course. But what if China used $12 billion of this debt — 1 percent — to deploy an aircraft carrier operating off each coast of the United States? The dynamics suddenly change. Whether the threat comes from another country or from machine-gun-toting pirates or suicide terrorists, an international economy requires naval power.

Those who say that threats have diminished do not understand history. With 70 percent of the globe covered by water, the country that wields naval power most effectively has always maintained a position of political and economic leadership. The dominance of the United States Navy must be maintained if America is serious about continuing its role as a global leader in the twenty-first century. There is no substitute for sea power, and history has proven that if the United States doesn't exercise it, some other nation will.

"History's Lesson: Sea Power Defines a Nation" by Walter R. Borneman originally appeared on Time.com.

One Veteran's Story

One afternoon six months after I turned in the manuscript for this book, I was at the post office in my little mountain town and I noticed an elderly gentleman behind me in line. He wore a battered green cap with the words "*Lexington,* CV-2" emblazoned on the front. It didn't seem possible, but I had to ask: "Were you on the original *Lexington*?"

"Yes," he answered proudly, "but it was sunk."

"I know," I replied, "at Coral Sea in 1942."

That exchange made eighty-nine-year-old Bill Dye and me quick friends. Dye had enlisted in the navy right out of high school. After basic training and electrician school, he reported aboard the *Lexington* at San Diego in October 1941. After Pearl Harbor, Dye was promoted to Electrician's Mate, Third Class, the inside joke being that he was now qualified to screw in a light bulb without stripping the threads.

May 8, 1942, proved the fatal day. From his station in E Division, Bill Dye felt the *Lexington* shudder as two torpedoes slammed into the carrier's portside. These were followed by three bomb hits along the flight deck. The ship listed to port with its engineering spaces partially flooded and fires raging. The crew fought back, counterflooded some compartments, and soon had the ship making twenty-five knots. Then vapors from spilled aviation gas ignited. Dye and his shipmates scrambled topside as the order was given to abandon ship.

Afterward, it was the little things Dye remembered the best: The neat line of shoes along the edge of the flight deck as sailors took them off and went over the side. The ice cream—usually a rationed treat—that appeared as if by magic and was devoured by greasy hands. The twenty-six dollars Dye left in his wallet in his locker below.

Out of a complement of 2,951 on board *Lexington* that morning, only 137 were killed. That was due, Dye says, to the fact that "not one man on that ship got out of line." Dye was put on a transport and shipped back to San Diego. From there he served on the submarine chaser PC-626 off North Africa and in the invasions of Sicily and Italy. By the time he finally got to New York City on leave, Dye remembers, "there wasn't a bad-looking woman in the world."

Bill Dye is one of the few remaining members of the greatest generation who sailed into harm's way as fresh-faced teenagers. He once admitted to me that he couldn't remember what he had for breakfast, but his memories of the *Lexington,* he said, were crystal clear.

In-the-Field Research

I have always appreciated and tried to emphasize the strong link between history and geography. It is difficult for me to write about events without having experienced their physical locations. Admittedly, with this book the vast stage of the seas played a large role, but that did not stop me from visiting the shore locations central to this story. Among them were the United States Naval Academy; Pearl Harbor; the Washington Navy Yard and Arlington National Cemetery; Hyde Park, New York; Newport, Rhode Island; and the Nimitz family home in Fredericksburg, Texas. Standing before the graves of my subjects always provokes a slight shiver.

As far as physical visits to the sea locations, the best alternative is to visit the ships on which these men sailed. All four *Iowa*-class battleships have been preserved and are open as museums in Los Angeles (*Iowa*), Camden (*New Jersey*), Pearl Harbor (*Missouri*), and Norfolk (*Wisconsin*). King's old flagship from the Atlantic squadron, the battleship *Texas,* is a memorial at San Jacinto, Texas. Sadly, the aircraft carriers that Halsey commanded and that stemmed the Japanese tide in 1942 were all sunk or later scrapped, including the venerable *Enterprise.* But the second *Yorktown* and the *Intrepid* are memorials at Charleston, South Carolina, and New York City, respectively.

A Conversation with Walter Borneman

How did you get interested in history?

I was in third grade and it was the beginning of the centennial of the Civil War. That was more than fifty years ago, but I found the stories of generals and battles quite exciting. I think that it helped my interest that as a child I got to visit places like Gettysburg and Yorktown. Later, it was mountains, railroads, and mining towns that intrigued me in Colorado. This country is a wonderful mosaic of the experiences of many different people, and it is fascinating to watch the development of the American nation through those collective experiences.

Why did you decide to write about these admirals and the United States Navy?

Navies and sea power are major themes in two of my earlier books. It was the power of the Royal Navy that controlled the seas and won Great Britain a global empire during the French and Indian War. The War of 1812 is filled with stories of ship-to-ship battles on the high seas and, far more important to the outcome of the war, naval battles on the Great Lakes and Lake Champlain. In some respects, *The Admirals* is a continuation of those themes of national expansion and sea power. As Nimitz, Halsey, Leahy, and King were graduating from Annapolis, the United States was stepping onto the world stage as a global power. Forty years later at the end of World War II, it had become the most dominant sea power in the history of the world.

Who are some of your heroes in this book?

Actually, since its publication, the men and women who have written me about their experiences in World War II have become my heroes.

All were very young at the time, but they went where they were ordered and served our country an ocean or two away from home. For many, their service became the defining period of their lives. I recall in particular Richard E. Bennink, who was a 1938 NROTC graduate of Harvard. Bennink commanded three waves of Higgins boats landing a battalion of marines on the tiny island of Gavutu just north of Guadalcanal in early August 1942. He repeatedly went ashore under heavy fire to make certain that his disembarked troops could hold their positions and to evacuate their wounded.

What is the most important contribution that The Admirals *makes to the history of World War II?*

To my thinking, it is the largely overlooked role of William D. Leahy. I have stopped short of calling him "acting president" in the final year of Franklin Roosevelt's life, but he was very close to it. And because of Leahy's self-effacing personality, most of the country knew almost nothing about him. It goes beyond the scope of this book, but the equally amazing thing about Leahy is that he went on to give the same service to Harry Truman for the first four years of Truman's presidency. I challenge you to name another person who performed so close and important an adviser role, not to just one but to two presidents.

What are you working on next?

Up next is *American Spring,* a book on the first six months of the American Revolution. It fills a void between my earlier work on the French and Indian War, which in many respects created the climate that fostered revolution, and the War of 1812, which is the defining moment that proves the United States will not only survive as an independent nation but also expand across the continent. Those early months of 1775 are a tense tangle of emotions on all sides and they ignite a powder keg that burns for another six years, until the British surrender at Yorktown.

Questions and Topics for Discussion

1. What role did the United States Naval Academy play in the careers of these four men?

2. How was the career of each man entwined with new developments in submarines and carrier aviation?

3. Contrast the differing leadership styles of Nimitz, Halsey, Leahy, and King.

4. Why didn't King initially succeed Leahy as Chief of Naval Operations, and what series of events gave him a second chance at the job?

5. Why was the relationship between the U.S. Navy and General Douglas MacArthur so confrontational? Were there times when the relationship was less fraught?

6. Discuss King and Nimitz's relationship, particularly King's role in crafting global strategy and the extent to which Nimitz was given rein to implement it in the Pacific.

7. How did King interact with Army Chief of Staff George Marshall and with their counterparts on the British General Staff?

8. Did Halsey's prior operational commands prepare him to command the Third Fleet? How did that experience, or lack of it,

affect his decisions at the Battle of Leyte Gulf and in the subsequent typhoons?

9. Who was more deserving of the final set of five stars — William Halsey or Raymond Spruance?

10. Why has Leahy's role in FDR's White House been overlooked? Did FDR plan such a role, or did it evolve with the circumstances?

Suggested Reading

The individual biographies of these four admirals and their contemporaries are listed in the bibliography. I particularly recommend Thomas B. Buell, *The Quiet Warrior: A Biography of Admiral Raymond A. Spruance* (Boston: Little, Brown, 1987), and John B. Lundstrom, *Black Shoe Carrier Admiral: Frank Jack Fletcher at Coral Sea, Midway, and Guadalcanal* (Annapolis: Naval Institute Press, 2006).

More recent titles of note include James D. Hornfischer, *Neptune's Inferno: The U.S. Navy at Guadalcanal* (New York: Bantam, 2011), a gripping saga of the full Guadalcanal campaign; Craig L. Symonds, *The Battle of Midway* (New York: Oxford University Press, 2011), which is a powerful narrative of the first six months of the war; and Barrett Tillman, *Enterprise: America's Fightingest Ship and the Men Who Helped Win World War II* (New York: Simon & Schuster, 2012), a gritty tale of the "Big E."

Other classics include Andrew Roberts, *Masters and Commanders: How Four Titans Won the War in the West, 1941–1945* (New York: Harper, 2009); Evan Thomas, *Sea of Thunder: Four Commanders and the Last Great Naval Campaign, 1941–1945* (New York: Simon & Schuster, 2006); and Gordon W. Prange, *At Dawn We Slept: The Untold Story of Pearl Harbor* (New York: Penguin, 1991).